Part I:

An Overview: Critical Thinking and Argumentation

Chapter 1: *Reading Arguments* 3

Chapter 2: *Writing Arguments* 42

Chapter 3: *Patterns of Argument* 81

Part II:

Writing Research Papers

Chapter 4: *Writing from Research* 135

Chapter 5: *Finding a Topic* 144

Chapter 6: *Finding and Filtering Internet Sources* 166

Chapter 7: *Gathering Data in the Library* 190

Chapter 8: *Conducting Research Outside the Library* 211

Chapter 9: *Understanding and Avoiding Plagiarism* 222

Chapter 10: *Reading and Evaluating the Best Sources* 237

Chapter 11: *Organizing Ideas and Setting Goals* 262

Chapter 12: *Writing Notes* 279

Chapter 13: *Drafting the Paper in an Academic Style* 292

Chapter 14: *Blending Reference Material into Your Writing by Using MLA Style* 311

Chapter 15: *Writing the Introduction, Body, and Conclusion* 336

Chapter 16: *Revising, Proofreading, and Formatting the Rough Draft* 354

Chapter 17: *Works Cited: MLA Style* 384

Chapter 18: *Writing in APA Style* 436

Chapter 19: *The Footnote System: CMS Style* 473

Chapter 20: *CSE Style for the Natural and Applied Sciences* 502

The following section shows you how to conduct research, to find and cite multiple sources, and to evaluate sources. This section also shows you how to organize, format, and write your paper.

Part III:

Perspectives on Contemporary Issues

Chapter 21: *Rap Culture: Is It Too Negative?* 525

Chapter 22: *College Sports* 537

Chapter 23: *Animal Rights: Should They Compromise Human Needs?* 551

Chapter 24: *Immigration: Should We Limit It?* 562

Chapter 25: *Affirmative Action* 573

Chapter 26: *Capital Punishment: Should We Take a Human Life?* 595

Chapter 27: *The Internet: What Are the Prospects for Cyberspace?* 612

Chapter 28: *Work, Money, and Class: Who Benefits?* 633

Chapter 29: *The Media: Do We Control It, or Does It Control Us?* 658

Chapter 30: *Education: How Do We Teach and Learn?* 681

Chapter 31: *The Environment: How Can We Preserve It?* 707

Chapter 32: *Human Rights: Why Does Society Need Them?* 734

Chapter 33: *Terrorism: How Should We Meet the Challenge?* 760

The following section contains essays clustered around particular contemporary issues. Each chapter presents an overview of an issue followed by a selection of essays representing different points of view about the issue as well as different rhetorical styles.

Part I:

An Overview: Critical Thinking and Argumentation

Chapter 1: *Reading Arguments* *3*

Chapter 2: *Writing Arguments* *42*

Chapter 3: *Patterns of Argument* *81*

RESEARCH *and* WRITING

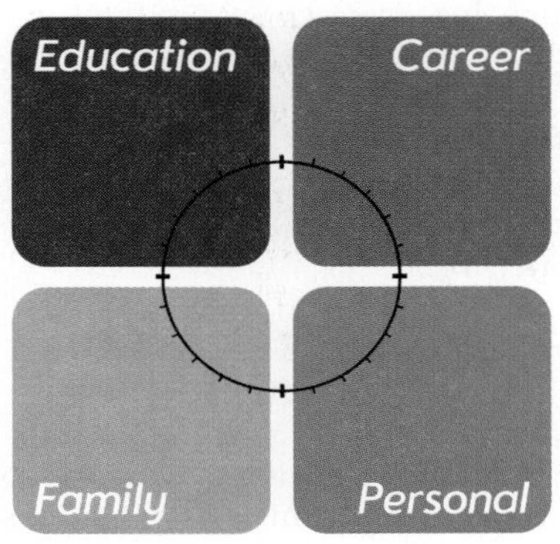

CUSTOM EDITION

Taken from:
Writing Research Papers: A Complete Guide, Eleventh Edition
by James D. Lester and James D. Lester, Jr.

To the Point: Reading and Writing Short Arguments
by Gilbert H. Muller and Harvey S. Wiener

Taken from:

Writing Research Papers: A Complete Guide, Eleventh Edition
by James D. Lester and James D. Lester, Jr.

Published by Pearson Longman, Inc.
New York, New York 10036

To the Point: Reading and Writing Short Arguments
by Gilbert H. Muller and Harvey S. Wiener

Published by Pearson Longman, Inc.

Printed in the United States of America

11

ISBN 0-536-97722-4

2005240359

AP

Please visit our web site at *www.pearsoncustom.com*

PEARSON CUSTOM PUBLISHING
75 Arlington Street, Suite 300, Boston, MA 02116
A Pearson Education Company

Contents

Introduction *vii*

PART I An Overview: Critical Thinking and Argumentation 1

CHAPTER 1 Reading Arguments 3

CHAPTER 2 Writing Arguments 42

CHAPTER 3 Patterns of Argument 81

PART II Writing Research Papers 133

CHAPTER 4 Writing from Research 135

CHAPTER 5 Finding a Topic 144

CHAPTER 6 Finding and Filtering Internet Sources 166

CHAPTER 7 Gathering Data in the Library 190

CHAPTER 8 Conducting Research Outside the Library 211

CHAPTER 9 Understanding and Avoiding Plagiarism 222

CHAPTER 10 Reading and Evaluating the Best Sources 237

CHAPTER 11 Organizing Ideas and Setting Goals 262

CHAPTER 12 Writing Notes 279

CHAPTER 13 Drafting the Paper in an Academic Style 292

CHAPTER 14 Blending Reference Material into Your Writing by Using MLA Style 311

CHAPTER 15 Writing the Introduction, Body, and Conclusion 336

CHAPTER 16 Revising, Proofreading, and Formatting the Rough Draft 354

CHAPTER 17 Works Cited: MLA Style 384

CHAPTER 18 Writing in APA Style 436

CHAPTER 19 The Footnote System: CMS Style 473

CHAPTER 20 CSE Style for the Natural and Applied Sciences 502

PART III Perspectives on Contemporary Issues 523

CHAPTER 21 Rap Culture: Is It Too Negative? 525

CHAPTER 22 College Sports 537

CHAPTER 23 Animal Rights: Should They Compromise Human Needs? 551

CHAPTER 24 Immigration: Should We Limit It? 562

CHAPTER 25 Affirmative Action 573

CHAPTER 26 Capital Punishment: Should We Take a Human Life? 595

CHAPTER 27 The Internet: What Are the Prospects for Cyberspace? 612

CHAPTER 28 Work, Money, and Class: Who Benefits? 633

CHAPTER 29 The Media: Do We Control It, or Does It Control Us? 658

CHAPTER 30 Education: How Do We Teach and Learn? 681

CHAPTER 31 The Environment: How Can We Preserve It? 707

CHAPTER 32 Human Rights: Why Does Society Need Them? 734

CHAPTER 33 Terrorism: How Should We Meet the Challenge? 760

APPENDICES A and B A-1

APPENDIX A Glossary: Rules and Techniques for Preparing the Manuscript in MLA Style A-3

APPENDIX B Finding Reference Works for Your General Topic B-27

Credits C-1

Index I-1

Introduction

Welcome to Research and Writing. This course is designed to develop the fundamental research and documentation skills necessary for academic research and writing. It will also develop skills in critical thinking and argumentation.

This text is divided into four parts. Part I "An Overview of Critical Thinking and Argumentation," discusses the reasons why we argue, the patterns of arguments and the vocabulary of arguments. Part II, "Writing Research Papers," shows you to conduct research, find and cite multiple sources, and to evaluate sources. This section also shows you how to organize, format and write your paper. Part III, "Perspectives on Contemporary Issues," contains several essays that eloquently argue a point of view on a current topic. Exercises and discussion questions at the end on the essays develop both your writing and critical thinking skills. The last part of the book contains two appendices. Appendix A contains rules and techniques for preparing your manuscripts in MLA Style. Appendix B contains databases and helpful Internet sites that will help you in your research.

1 Reading Arguments

Contemporary American culture often seems dominated by argument. Television talk show hosts and radio shock jocks battle over countless issues. Hip-hop artists contrive elaborate "beefs" to get under the skin of their rivals. Politicians are in constant attack mode. Advertisements and commercials seduce us into crazed consumption. Internet chat rooms flame with aggressive language. Deborah Tannen, in *The Argument Culture* (1998), terms this phenomenon the "ethic of aggression." Indeed, the world is awash in what passes for argument, but frequently in its most irritating, insulting, ill-conceived, and illogical forms.

Forget about argument as a quarrel or a beef. Instead, think of argument as *any text—in written, spoken, or visual form—that presents a debatable point of view*. Closely related to argument (and in practice often indistinguishable from it) is *persuasion*, the attempt to get others to act in a way that will advance a cause or position. The kind of argument we deal with in this text involves a carefully reasoned attempt to get people to believe or act according to our own beliefs or points of view. Typically this type of argument requires you to deal with significant issues about which individuals might justifiably disagree. It also requires you to respectfully consider the positions and perspectives of others in an effort to promote civil discourse.

Why Argue?

You argue in order to influence others to think or believe as you do about an idea or issue, or to act as you would act. Stated differently, you argue to *convince* an audience about your point of view or to *persuade* this audience to adopt a desired course of action or behavior. When you read and write arguments, you enter into a dialogue with this audience. This dialogue or conversation is typically dramatic because your point of view must be defended and usually is open to dispute or debate. Admittedly, much argument—and courtroom dramas in real life or on television provide excellent examples—results in winners and losers.

Argumentation, however, is not always about winning and losing. You can argue for other reasons as well. Sometimes you argue *to explore* why you think or act in a certain way. Exploration enables you *to make decisions*: Should you vote for one candidate or another, attend a private or public college, date a certain person, support abortion, oppose the death penalty, believe in God? You engage constantly in these forms of argument, either on your own or with others, in matters both large and small. You develop options and make decisions through a complex process of internal thinking and even meditation. To be able to arrive at a valid conclusion about an issue or course of action is a powerful aspect of argumentation that involves critical thinking and self-discovery.

Even as you use argument to clarify opinions and beliefs, you can employ argument *to form a consensus* with others about ideas that otherwise might divide or polarize individuals. Rather than constantly battling people and groups, you can advance an argument in order to engage others in a conversation that might produce common ground concerning ideas, policies, and programs. With this approach to argument, you seek a win/win outcome. Looked at this way, argument is integral to free speech and open inquiry and is vital to civil society. Honest and truthful argument (which admittedly is difficult to achieve) is essential to the health of democracy and of nations around the world.

Argument, as you will see, is as old as Aristotle and as new as questions on a standardized writing test that you might have taken when applying for college. Valid argument can produce toleration, consensus, and understanding among people holding diverse points of view. It can be subtle and liberating, encouraging you to examine and perhaps even change what you think or believe about critical ideas and issues.

The Vocabulary of Argument

Before reading or writing arguments, you need to know the basic vocabulary of the argumentative process. Think of the vocabulary of argument as the rules that create the outlines of a special type of game. Just as in any game—whether basketball or chess or poker—the vocabulary of argumentation establishes and governs the playing field. This vocabulary helps you to understand both the uniqueness and the utility of argumentation as a form of discourse.

At the outset, it is important to understand that argument relies on *logic*—on an appeal to reason—more than other kinds of writing. This does not mean that arguments lack emotion. In fact, as you will see later in this chapter, a carefully constructed argument often blends rational, emotional, and ethical elements. Moreover, other forms of writing—narration, description, and varieties of exposition like analysis and definition—often are used to advance arguments, as we illustrate in Chapter 3. Some teachers maintain that all writing, to the extent that it tries to make a point, is inherently argumentative. Nevertheless, the starting point of any effective argument is the application of certain standards of reason—a logical train of thought—to a topic that normally can be debated. Argumentation creates a "court of standards" in which the rules of reason and evidence apply.

Here, then, are some of the critical terms that will help you to read and ultimately write arguments effectively:

1. *Argument* is a process of reasoning that presents reasons or proofs to support a position, belief, or conclusion.
2. A *claim* is the main idea or conclusion in an argument. It is the statement that needs to be justified or proved. A claim is like a *thesis* or main idea that can be debated, argued, or proved.
3. A *proposition* is another term for a claim. The *major proposition* is the main point of the argument. It is what you are trying to prove based on what there is in common in a certain number of acts of knowing, asserting, believing, or doubting. *Minor propositions* are the reasons offered to support the major proposition.
4. *Grounds* are like minor propositions. They are the reasons, support, and evidence offered to support a claim. Grounds are any material that serves to prove a claim.
5. *Evidence* supports the claim and the minor propositions of an argument. Evidence can be facts, statistics, accepted opinions, expert testimony, examples, or personal experience. Valid evidence will be accurate and true.
6. A *fact* is information that can be taken as verifiable. Stated differently, a fact is something believed to have objective reality. Facts differ from *opinions*, which are judgments based on the facts and, if valid, careful reasoning.
7. A *warrant* is the connection, typically assumed and unstated, between a claim and the supporting reasons. It is the rule, belief, or principle underlying the argument, the assumption that makes the claim appear to be acceptable. A *backing* is an even larger principle that serves as the foundation for a warrant.
8. *Deduction* is a process of reasoning that seeks valid conclusions. Deduction establishes that a conclusion must be true because the *premises*, or statements on which it is based, are also true. As a way of reasoning, deduction proceeds from the general to the particular. By contrast, *induction* is a way of reasoning in which a general statement is reached on the basis of specific examples. As such, induction moves from the particular to the general.
9. A *fallacy* is an error of reasoning based on faulty use of evidence or incorrect reasoning from premises or assumptions.
10. *Refutation* is the attempt to rebut, weaken, or invalidate the viewpoints of the opposition.

Justifying an Argument

Argument involves a complex pattern of thought that does not appear in every statement. It is inaccurate to claim that "everything is an argument" because, when thought about carefully, every statement is *not* an argument.

You need to determine through a basic *test of justification* whether or not a statement qualifies as an argument.

Imagine what you were thinking about when you woke up this morning. Here are some possibilities:

1. *What a beautiful day—so clear and sunny!*
2. *Did I complete my homework assignment for English composition?*
3. *I'm looking forward to seeing that good-looking classmate in my first-period class.*
4. *I'll wear something light because it is warm outside.*
5. *I need to change my major and get another advisor because I'm not satisfied with either.*

All of these sentences involve varieties of thinking, but not all of them express an argument. Sentence 1 is a simple statement of fact: if indeed the day *is* clear and sunny, who would want to argue with you about its beauty? Sentence 2 is an effort at recall, framed as a question, and generally interrogative and imperative (involving commands or prayers) statements do not express claims or propositions. Sentence 3 suggests a bit of pleasant daydreaming; it does not rise to the level of argumentation. Sentence 4 reflects a mental activity that could qualify as an argument if stated differently, but in this form it simply reflects a decision—not essentially debatable—deriving from an observation. The first four sentences suggest a range of thinking largely devoid of argumentation.

Now read again sentence 5, which contains an argument and therefore passes the test of justification. To begin, you see clearly that there is an "argumentative edge" to this statement. Sentence 5 reflects a traditional approach to argument in which a combative or debatable point of view appears. (Greek theorists called this the "agonistic" theory of argument.) This statement, reflecting dissatisfaction with both a major and an advisor, actually has several argumentative and persuasive purposes embedded in it. Reading this statement critically, you sense that the speaker will have to *explore options, inform, convince*, and *make decisions*—four common goals in the construction of an argument. Sentence 5 reflects a process of reasoning and the implicit need to advance reasons or proofs in order *to justify* how an individual thinks and acts, which form the core of argument.

Aristotle and the Appeal to Reason

Arguments must be read critically, based in part on your understanding of concepts, methods, and conventions that follow a long tradition starting with Aristotle (384–322 B.C.). According to Aristotle in his *Rhetoric*, the best arguments contain logical, emotional, and ethical appeals. In other words, reason (which classical commentators termed *logos*), emotion (*pathos*), and moral authority (*ethos*) appear in varying degrees in arguments, working together to change opinions and prompt action. When you read argumentative essays, you see that these three appeals can support a point of view, change attitudes, elicit desired responses, and meet various needs. For now, we will focus on logical appeals—the process of reasoning—and the ways they appear when you read texts.

The ancients emphasized that an argument presupposes a topic, what the Greeks called *topos*. The essays you will read in this book contain a central topic that you should be able to identify. Aristotle claimed that every argument contains this statement of a central topic and proof to support it. For example, Martin Luther King Jr.'s famous speech, "I Have a Dream," takes as its topic the need for an American society reflecting equality for everyone. His speech contains echoes of many classic documents, among them the Declaration of Independence, which appears in Chapter 3. It is useful to examine the key idea—or topic—that is the essence of the classic document written by Thomas Jefferson and his collaborators and that influenced King as he prepared his speech.

> We hold these truths to be self-evident, that all men are created equal: that they are endowed by their Creator with certain inalienable rights; and that among these rights are life, liberty, and the pursuit of happiness.

You will have the opportunity to read, discuss critically, and respond in writing to the texts by Jefferson and King, but for now it is only necessary to understand that the topic at the center of these texts is controversial and open to challenge. For example, do you believe that everyone is created equal? Do you think that a Creator endows us with inalienable rights? Do you anticipate, as Martin Luther King Jr. does, that some day all God's children will be free at last? Where is the *proof*? The topics you will be reading about in this book require judgment, evaluation, and confirmation. In essence, you have to test the *assumptions*, or underlying beliefs governing certain statements. Your critical response to these essays will benefit from your understanding of the reasoning or logic supporting the assumptions that are made.

A stated assumption is called a *premise*, and premises are the first elements you must uncover when reading an argumentative essay. You probably have heard about syllogistic reasoning, that type of logic in which a major premise, followed by a minor premise, produces a conclusion. This is the method of *deduction*, the process of reasoning where a conclusion is taken to be true because the statements on which it is based are true. The most famous syllogism, of course, is the one using Socrates as an example.

> *Major premise*: All human beings are mortal.
> *Minor premise*: Socrates is a human being.
> *Conclusion*: Therefore, Socrates is mortal.

This example demonstrates that the validity of any syllogism rests on the "truth" of the premises. In other words, if you accept the truth of the major and minor premises, then you must accept the conclusion.

Of course, there can be false and misleading applications of syllogistic reasoning. For the purposes of this book, we need not go into these errors in syllogistic reasoning in depth, but instead we illustrate the problem with two examples. Here is the first:

Major premise: All cats die.
Minor premise: Socrates died.
Conclusion: Socrates was a cat.

Here the premises are true but the conclusion clearly is false, and thus the argument is not valid.

Consider a second, more subtle (some might say devious) example of syllogistic reasoning:

Major premise: Unwantedness leads to high crime.
Minor premise: Abortion leads to less unwantedness.
Conclusion: Abortion leads to less crime.

Two noted scholars—an economist at the University of Chicago and a professor of law at Stanford—have provoked debate by publishing a paper that can be reduced to this syllogism. They maintain that because of *Roe* v. *Wade*, precisely those women—poor, single, black, or teenage—who might have given birth to unwanted children opted for abortions instead. Thus, the unwanted children who would have committed crimes were never born, and consequently overall crime has declined in the United States. Do you think that the two premises are true? If so, then you must accept the conclusion. If not, you can reject the conclusion because it does not follow from the premises.

The two contemporary professors who base their paper on the relationship between abortion and crime used deduction—what Aristotle termed *artistic appeal*—to construct their argument. In practice, however, as Aristotle asserts, few individuals rigorously apply "artistic" or deductive reasoning to the development of their compositions. More often than not, they use what Aristotle labeled *inartistic appeals*—varieties of *inductive* logic where evidence (in the form of facts, statistics, reports, testimonies, interviews, and other evidentiary modes) support a claim or proposition. When inductive thinking appears in an argumentative essay, the writer gathers and applies evidence in order to make *empirical* (based on observation and experiment) claims. Inductive thinking appears most rigorously in scientific and technical reports, where claims require unassailable evidence or, in Aristotle's words, where statements require proof. But inductive logic is also at the heart of most personal, expository, and argumentative writing. In fact, most of the writing you do in response to the essays in this book will require you to martial evidence to support the propositions or claims that you establish.

You can best appreciate the importance of inductive logic by considering Aristotle's observation that every argument can be reduced to two basic parts:

Statement + Proof. To use contemporary terms, we would say that an argument requires a claim that is supported by evidence. If you become familiar with this approach to argumentation, you will find it much easier to read and write arguments with a critical eye. Remember that any debatable thesis, claim, or proposition (to get you comfortable with these interchangeable terms) requires evidence to back it up. The varieties of evidence will be considered later in this chapter. For now, examine the way in which evidence supports the claim in the following paragraph by Marian Wright Edelman, a noted attorney, activist, and founding president of the Children's Defense Fund:

> The legacies that parents and church and teachers left to my generation of Black children were priceless and not material: a living faith reflected in daily service, the discipline of hard work and stick-to-itness, and a capacity to struggle in the face of adversity. Giving up and "burnout" were not part of the language of my elders—you got up every morning and you did what you had to do and you got up every time you fell down and tried as many times as you had to get it done right. They had grit. They valued family life, family rituals, and tried to be and to expose us to good role models. Role models were of two kinds: those who achieved in the outside world (like Marian Anderson, my namesake) and those who didn't have a whole lot of education or fancy clothes but who taught us by the special grace of their lives the message of Christ and Tolstoy and Gandhi and Heschel and Dorothy Day and Romero and King that the Kingdom of God was within—in what you are, not what you have. I still hope I can be half as good as Black church and community elders like Miz Lucy McQueen, Miz Tee Kelly, and Miz Kate Winston, extraordinary women who were kind and patient and loving with children and others and who, when I went to Spellman College, sent me shoeboxes with chicken and biscuits and greasy dollar bills.
>
> —*The Measure of Our Success: A Letter to My Children and Yours*

Edelman shapes her message (which is another way to say that she presents a claim or proposition) around evidence drawn from personal experience. She supports her claim—that she grew up in a community where children were valued and where beliefs were transmitted from one generation to the next—with references to numerous role models that molded her values and beliefs. Here we have clear "proof" of the validity of the basic Aristotelian equation: **Argument = Statement + Proof.** Essays based on personal experience offer real intellectual pleasure as well as an accessible way of understanding the arguments they can frame. When you examine the paragraph by Edelman, for example, you see that it is not about "winning" but rather about the strengths of individuals and communities, as well as Edelman's desire to enter into a dialogue with you—the reader—about her complex but nurturing world.

Emotional and Ethical Appeals

An argumentative essay has to be rational, reflecting a process of logical thinking. When reading an argumentative essay for its logical or rational appeal, we have to ask these questions:

- *Is the claim or proposition presented in a logical way?*
- *Is the claim presented accurately and fairly?*
- *What reasons or minor propositions support the claim?*
- *What evidence supports the minor proposition?*
- *Is the entire argument logically convincing?*

However, we do not read arguments purely for their logical content. The rational basis of an argument typically contains other essential qualities, appealing also to emotion and ethics. Remember that the best arguments, as Aristotle maintained, contain these emotional and ethical appeals.

Many issues—race and ethnicity, sexuality and gender, crime and punishment, to name just three—are complex, emotional, and touch on personal sensitivities. Consequently, it is not surprising that writers would approach such topics not from a strictly logical perspective but also from perspectives touching on emotion and ethics. For example, topics relating to race—as you saw in the paragraph by Marian Wright Edelman—provoke complex meanings, emotions, and beliefs. Reread Edelman's paragraph to see how emotional and ethical appeals support her argument. Use the following questions, which can be applied to all essays you read, to determine the nature of her emotional appeal.

- Does the writer appeal to basic human emotions such as love, caring, sympathy, rejection, pity, fear?
- Does the writer appeal to the basic senses of sight, smell, hearing, taste, and touch?
- Does the writer appeal to essential physical needs or desires?
- Does the writer appeal to such "higher" emotions or universal truths as patriotism, loyalty, belief in various gods, freedom, and democracy?

Although using claims and evidence to arrive at certain truths is the primary goal of argumentative writing, the appeal to emotion is complementary and perhaps even more powerful than logic in its effect on an audience. Logicians often warn us against the use of emotion in argument, and in fact certain false emotional appeals will be considered in the next chapter. Nevertheless, emotional appeals—especially when they involve the use of humor, satire, and irony—can work effectively in the effort to persuade a reader to accept the writer's point of view.

Consider the emotional impact of these representative paragraphs from an essay titled "Women Are Just Better" by the columnist Anna Quindlen:

> The inherent superiority of women came to mind just the other day when I was reading about sanitation workers. New York City has finally hired women to pick up the garbage, which makes sense to

> me, since, as I discovered, a good bit of being a woman consists of picking up garbage. There was a story about the hiring of these female sanitation workers, and I was struck by the fact that I could have written that story without ever leaving my living room—a reflection not on the quality of the reporting but the predictability of the male sanitation worker's response. . . .
>
> As a woman who has done dishes, yard work, and tossed a fair number of Hefty bags, I was peeved—more so because I would fight for the right of any laid-off sanitation man to work, for example, at the gift-wrap counter at Macy's, even though any woman knows that men are hormonally incapable of wrapping packages and tying bows.

The emotional *tone* (the writer's attitude toward the topic, self, and audience) of these two paragraphs is evident. The writer, a woman, is angry, provocative, and downright savage in her humor. But the emotional edge is part of the writer's effort to persuade. Of course, her emotional tone might provoke readers—especially those men who know how to wrap packages and tie bows, and even those who don't but believe that those skills have nothing to do with superiority of gender. Nevertheless, Quindlen does have a point or claim that is suggested by the very title of the essay, and she attempts to stir the reader's feelings as well as opinions through the evocation of emotion. Here, emotion sustains what the writer presents as a debatable proposition: that women are better than men.

Another paragraph, this time by Lorenzo Albacete, a Roman Catholic priest and theologian writing in "The Struggle with Celibacy," raises the role of ethical appeals when considering the overall effectiveness of an argument.

> In the future, the church may decide that particular pastoral situations require a change in the requirement of priestly celibacy. Still, I believe that even if priests marry, they are called to be witnesses of that "celibacy of the heart" that human love requires—namely, the absolute respect for the loved one's freedom. It's time for those of us who treasure priestly celibacy to live in accordance with its intended message or else give it up as an obstacle to what we wish to say.

This paragraph shows the quality of *ethos* that Aristotle mentioned—the presence of the writer offering himself to the reader or audience as an ethical authority worthy of trust and acceptance. Good sense, goodwill, high moral character—these are the three qualities of the writer discussed by Aristotle and the ancients that make the rhetorical situation of any argument complete. Albacete *claims authority* about his subject based on his personal knowledge and experience of the subject, as well as his background, position, and reputation as a scholar. You thus have to pay attention to this writer, even as his bold and provocative argument in the essay—that celibacy should not be a casualty of the recent scandals involving the priesthood—might raise objections or rebuttals. In fact, when a topic is controversial, readers might understandably be skeptical about the writer's claim to authority. Nevertheless, the sort of thoughtfulness and candor shown in Albacete's remarks is an excellent way to establish *ethos*, which involves a willingness by the audience to trust the writer's viewpoint. When you read the entire essay in Chapter 3, you will see that Albacete also adds logical and emotional appeals to his ethical stance.

When considering the impact of ethical appeal in an argumentative essay, pose the following questions:

- What is the tone or *voice* of the writer, and does this tone enhance the logic of the argument?
- What is the writer's training or expertise, and how does this knowledge establish credibility?
- Does the writer have the goodwill of the audience in mind? Why or why not?
- Does the writer have a strong sense of right and wrong in approaching the subject? How strong is this moral sense?
- Does the writer seem honest and trustworthy? How are these qualities revealed?

Building credibility—creating a relationship of trust—is essential to good argument. A writer speaks to readers in many voices, and it is up to you as an active reader to determine if the voice selected is appropriate for the argument the writer presents.

Toulmin Arguments

A currently popular way of reading arguments derives from the ideas of British philosopher Steven Toulmin, who in *The Uses of Argument* (1958) offers a method that updates the argumentative systems of the ancients. According to Toulmin and teachers of writing who have modified his ideas, you do not read or write argumentative essays that follow the demands of formal logic. Instead, writers compose arguments according to the ways they actually think carefully and critically through an issue or debate. As such, Toulmin offers an easy way to understand the dynamics of argumentative and persuasive prose.

Toulmin asserts that all arguments begin with a *claim*—a word that you already are familiar with. Claims, you will recall, are statements of belief or truth that involve positions that others might find controversial or debatable. In other words, a writer's audience must perceive that a statement is open to controversy. There is no sense in arguing that it is not a beautiful day if indeed the sun is out, the temperature is perfect, and the sky is clear. No one would declare that this statement about the weather conditions is ripe for argument.

An essay that contains a claim tends to address readers by taking a stand or arguing a case. Here are some statements that clearly contain claims:

The September 11, 2001, terrorist attacks could have been prevented.
The SATs should be abolished.
There is no such thing as global warming.
Eminem is the greatest rap artist today.

These are debatable points. In themselves, however, they prove nothing. They assuredly do not prove a case. According to Toulmin, a claim is just the first logical and necessary step in a process of reasoning designed to make or prove a case.

Any claim needs *reasons* to support it. Again, you already have learned about the need for reasons drawn from personal experience, facts, authorities, and other sources to create the framework for an argument. Writers often provide readers with *arguments in brief*—a claim appearing early in an essay, perhaps in an introductory or concluding paragraph, and followed by a few reasons. Aristotle called these compressed arguments *enthymemes*. Here is an enthymeme drawn from one of the previous examples:

> The SATs should be abolished because they place undue emphasis on certain learning styles, create false impressions of a student's real talents and abilities, and are culturally biased.

Here you see how both the terms and the framework for an argument develop from the enthymeme. Toulmin, however, would say that these reasons are assumptions that need to be tested and supported further. The need for *connections* between the claim and the reasons takes us to the next step in Toulmin argument.

Toulmin calls the connection between the claim and the supporting reasons in an argument the *warrant*. (This word appears in the "Vocabulary of Argument" section presented earlier in this chapter, but it requires further explanation.) Often unstated or implied, a warrant establishes the authority underlying a particular claim and its supporting reasons. If the warrant is sound, the evidence assembled to support the claim appears to be justified. On the other hand, if the warrant itself can be challenged or is debatable, then you would expect the writer to defend it.

Based on Toulmin's method, we can diagram the connections among claim, reason(s), and warrant.

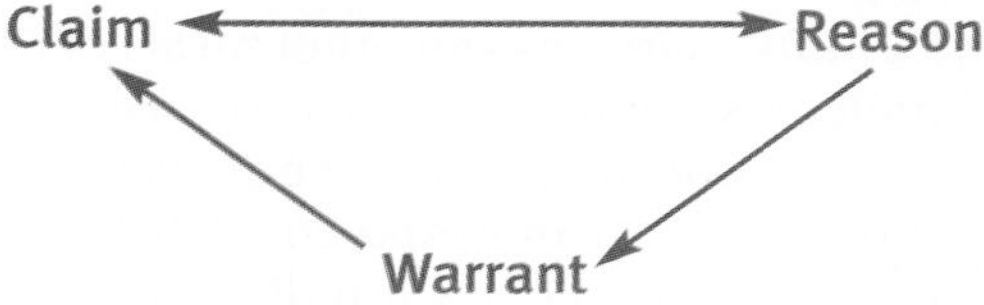

This diagram suggests that a warrant is the glue that holds a claim and the reasons supporting the claim together. It is the general principle or underlying assumption that makes the claim plausible or fundamentally acceptable.

Look now at a simple application of the Toulmin diagram to a common situation.

> Don't go swimming—there is a strong undertow.

The reason ("there is a strong undertow") is connected to the claim ("Don't go swimming") by the following warrant:

> If there is a strong undertow, it is dangerous to go swimming.

Do you see how the warrant is the principle underlying the entire statement consisting of the claim and the reason? Although we could state it in different ways, the warrant for this statement is obvious: you do not want to go swimming in dangerous waters. Diagrammed, the example would look like this:

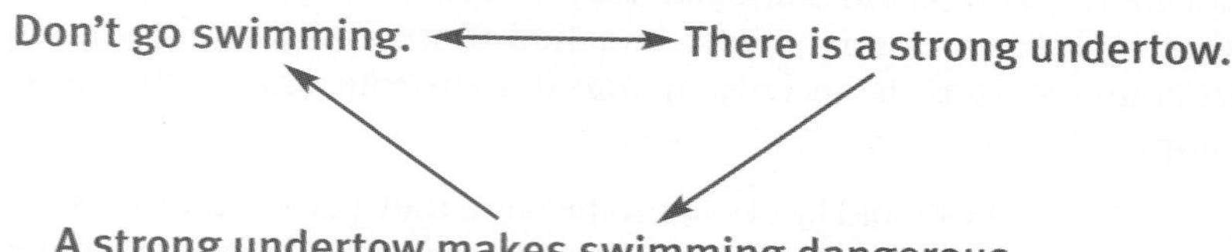
Don't go swimming.
There is a strong undertow.
A strong undertow makes swimming dangerous.

A warrant implying we should avoid a specific dangerous—indeed, life-threatening—situation when deciding whether or not to swim is commonsensical. Such a plausible warrant makes the claim and reason supporting it seem reasonable.

The Use of Evidence

Claims, warrants, and reasons are the framework of a Toulmin argument, or any argument for that matter, but *evidence* is what makes the case. Evidence—various items of information that support a claim as well as the reasons supporting a claim—is what you look for in any pattern of argument. Toulmin reduces this need for evidence to a question: "What have you got to go on?" Only evidence, carefully selected and clearly presented, permits a writer to present an argument fully and convincingly. If the evidence in an argument is too sparse, it will not convince an audience. If it is too flimsy—based on mere opinion, hearsay, or colorful comparisons or analogies—it will not support an otherwise valid claim or generalization.

You already know that evidence can consist of facts and examples, specific cases and events, statistics and other forms of data, expert opinion, and, if used judiciously and in a representative rather than idiosyncratic way, personal experience. Evidence also can derive from scientific observation, field research, and controlled experimentation—forms of evidence common to technical writing and often appearing in tables, graphs, and other visual documents. In all instances, the most distinctive feature of evidence is that it supports a relevant generalization.

An example from an essay by Ronald Takaki, "The Harmful Myth of Asian Superiority," which appears in Chapter 3 of this book, illustrates the way in which evidence provides a degree of authority for any proposition or generalization:

> The "model minority" image homogenizes Asian Americans and hides their differences. For example, while thousands of Vietnamese American young people attend universities, others are on the streets.

> They live in motels and hang out in pool halls in places like East Los Angeles; some join gangs.
>
> Twenty-five percent of the people in New York City's Chinatown lived below the poverty level in 1980, compared with 17 percent of the city's population. Some 60 percent of the workers in the Chinatowns of Los Angeles and San Francisco are crowded into low-paying jobs in garment factories and restaurants.
>
> "Most immigrants coming into Chinatown with a language barrier cannot go outside the confined area into the mainstream of American industry," a Chinese immigrant said. "Before, I was a painter in Hong Kong, but I can't do it here. I got no license, no education. I want a living; so it's dishwasher, janitor, or cook."

Takaki, who is an authority on ethnicity in American life, makes his case by fleshing out the claim or generalization that appears in the first sentence with examples, statistics, and interviews. Evidence supports his claim.

The chain of argument is never complete without authoritative and compelling evidence. When you read an essay, ask the following questions about the nature of the evidence that a writer presents:

- Are the examples relevant and convincing? Are they sufficient to make the case?
- Is the evidence presented clearly?
- Is the evidence used to support a warrant (we call such evidence *backing*), a claim, or minor propositions, and in each case is it sufficient?
- If statistics appear, are they relevant, accurate, current, complete, and from a reliable source?
- If the writer offers quotations or expert testimony, is it from a knowledgeable, trustworthy, and authoritative source?

Not all evidence is of the same quality or validity. When reading an argumentative essay, you have to be prepared to think critically about the evidence and even enter into a conversation with the writer in which you ask if the factual information is convincing.

Reading Visual Arguments

Visual images are as old as the cave paintings of your Neolithic ancestors and as new as the latest streaming advertisements on your computer screen. In fact, some commentators argue that we are in the process of moving from a print-oriented society toward new forms of literacy in which visual images predominate over written texts. It is probably more useful to appreciate the ways in which visual materials—photographs, cartoons, posters, computer graphics, tables and graphs, various forms of type and other design elements, and more—contribute to written texts. If, as Marshall McLuhan declared more than forty years ago, "the medium is the message," then you should pay attention to the ways in which visual texts mold your response to ideas, information, and arguments.

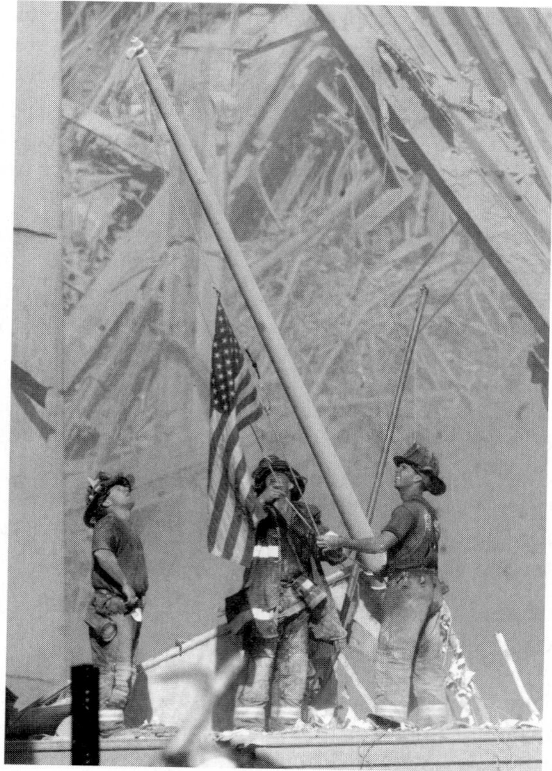

FIGURE 1.1 Firefighters at the World Trade Center.

Visual texts can convey powerful cultural messages and arguments. Figure 1.1 shows firefighters at the site of the World Trade Center erecting an American flag over the rubble that was once the Twin Towers. How do you "read" this photograph? What does the symbolism of the heap of twisted metal and of the flag convey? In what way does a similar image (see Figure 1.2) of soldiers raising the American flag at Iwo Jima during World War II deepen your interpretation of the message? A photograph is a representation of reality, and here we sense that the photographer has framed a scene in order to convey both the horror of the attack against the heart of America and the heroic resilience of its citizens to respond.

When reading and interpreting visual texts that contain explicit or implicit arguments, you have to be aware of the ways in which the creators or designers "massage" their message in order to influence (and sometimes control) your response. When, for instance, you see a 30-second television commercial for a particular brand of beer in which attractive young people are having a great time, you readily sense the massage and the message. When the blurred, decidedly unappealing image of a political candidate appears in a negative campaign ad, you also know the creators' purpose. Or when great

FIGURE 1.2 Iwo Jima.

graphics pop up on your screen extolling the virtues of a new snowboard, you know you have been targeted. (How did they know you were a boarder?)

Of course, not all visual arguments sell a product or a person. Ideas—as you see in the photographs from Iwo Jima and the Twin Towers—also can be presented; or complex data can be made manageable while advancing a writer's technical or scientific argument. Again, you might use a Power Point presentation to highlight the outlines of a speech you have to give to the class advocating free downloading of music on the Internet. In all of these cases, you see that visual texts present a dialogue or conversation, a struggle of sorts, for your time, money, allegiance, attention, or action.

Visual literacy involves an ability to analyze simple and complex images in terms of their design and content. Here are the key questions that you should consider when attempting to decipher a visual argument:

- What specific images or details draw your attention immediately? What sorts of design elements (print, media, photographs, video clips, etc.) come into play? How are color and light used? If there is printed text, what does the visual contribute to it?
- What is the argumentative purpose of the visual? What is the claim or message? What is its intended effect? Do you respond positively or negatively to the visual, and why?
- What is the overall design of the visual? From what perspective (for example, left to right, top to bottom, foreground to background) do various elements appear? What emphases and relationships do you see among these details? What is the effect of this design on the argumentative message?

- Who is the audience for this visual, and what cultural assumptions about this audience's values does it suggest?
- What is the nature of the evidence presented in the visual, and how can it be verified?

As with written arguments, you should take nothing for granted when considering visual texts containing arguments, especially when they promote products, personalities, and ideas. When examining visual texts, think critically about their validity and whether or not they are grounded in sound logical, emotional, and ethical appeals.

In the final analysis, reading argumentative texts cannot be reduced to any single system, whether it is Aristotelian, Toulmin, or any other. But you know a good argument when you see that claims are clear, support is good, and evidence is solid. (A sound argumentative essay also typically deals with the opposition and anticipates the possible objections of readers—what Toulmin calls "the conditions of rebuttal.") As you read the five essays appearing next in this chapter, begin to develop a critical perspective on the terms and conditions of argumentation and the various rhetorical and stylistic strategies writers use to bring you around to their point of view.

Reading and Writing About Five Current Issues

BARBARA EHRENREICH
From Stone Age to Phone Age

Biologist Barbara Ehrenreich (she got her Ph.D. from Rockefeller University in 1968) became involved in political activism during the Vietnam War and began writing on topics such as feminism, class in America, and health care. Her books include The American Health Empire: Power, Profits, and Politics *(1970) and* The Hearts of Men: American Dreams and the Flight from Commitment *(1983). She has written for the* Progressive, In These Times, *the* Nation, Time, *and many other magazines. Her book* Nickel and Dimed: On (Not) Getting by in America *(2001), recounting her experience working in low-class jobs, was a bestseller. In this selection, which appeared in 1999, Ehrenreich takes a whimsical look at the ubiquitous phenomenon of cell phones.*

Prereading: Thinking About the Essay in Advance

If you use a cell phone, how is it useful? Why did you want one in the first place? Could you live without it? Why or why not? If you don't own a cell phone, do you want one? Explain.

Words to Watch

primal (par. 1) old, instinctive
savanna (par. 2) area of tropical grasslands
hordes (par. 3) large groups
eons (par. 4) millions of years
convivial (par. 12) friendly, social
atomized (par. 12) broken up into small units

I was struck by the primal force of my craving for a cell phone. Obviously, others must have felt this, too, since there are now an estimated 100 million people worldwide running around and talking into the air, with only a small black object nestling against one ear to distinguish them from the deinstitutionalized psychotics. It had become impossible to go anywhere—out on the street, to a shopping mall, or to an airport—without noticing that every other person in earshot was engaged in a vast and urgent ongoing conversation which excluded only myself. 1

For a stylish explanation of primal urges and even ordinary whims, we turn to evolutionary psychology, which claims that we do what we do because our apelike ancestors once did the same thing. It doesn't matter that our ape-like ancestors did not possess cell phones; they no doubt had cell-phone-related urges. Like most of our primate cousins, humans are social animals. Paleo-anthropologists think we got this way when we left the safety of the forests for the wide open savanna, where we had to band together for defense against a slew of nasty predators. Hence, we are hardwired for wireless telecommunications, or at least for the need to be verbally connected to others of our kind—in case a leopard is lurking nearby. The explosion of cell phone use is simply a reflection of the genetically scripted human inclination to huddle in groups. 2

There is another interpretation of the evolutionary psychology of cell phones, according to which the cell phone users are seeking not fellowship but isolation from the hordes of fellow humans around them. To a non-cell-phone user, the cell phoners marching through supermarkets and malls project an aura of total inaccessibility. Maybe they are really having meaningful and satisfying conversations. And maybe they are simply trying to repel the advances of any phone-less fellow humans who happen to be physically present. 3

In their 1992 book, *The Social Cage: Human Nature and the Evolution of Society* (Stanford University Press), Alexandra Maryanski and Jonathan H. Turner argue that for eons before our ancestors were forced to band together in the savanna, they lived contented solitary lives in the trees, much like orangutans today. Our arboreal ancestors were probably pleased to run into others of their own kind only at mating time; otherwise, they regarded each other as competitors for the nicest berries and comfiest nesting spots. If these orangutan-type pre-humans had cell phones, they would have used them to signal each other: "Bug off. Can't you see I have an important call right now?" 4

5 Yet another evolutionary-psychological factor probably contributed to cell phone mania. Since the advent of agriculture about 10,000 years ago, and possibly well before then, humans have lived in hierarchical societies where we have been eager to signal our status with accessories such as feather-tufted spears and shrunken-head pendants.

6 Cell phones serve much the same function, and will continue to do so until they become as common as Walkmen. Thus, the point is not to communicate with distant kin and colleagues, but with all the anonymous others who are around at the moment.

7 If you doubt this, consider when you last heard someone say into a cell phone: "Yes, I am a worthless turd, and if I screw up again, please hasten to fire me." What the person is saying, instead, is invariably, "God damn it, Craig, I told you we need that order by Thursday and no later," or something very similar. It was the opportunity to speak commandingly in public places that tempted me, for several years, to find a fake cell phone designed for playpen use so that I, too, could stride along the sidewalk barking at imaginary brokers and underlings.

8 As soon as I got my own cell phone, I was disappointed to find that, although we may have evolved to be psychologically cell-phone-dependent, our anatomy is still stuck in the era when technology consisted of a sharpened stone.

9 For one thing, our fingertips are too fat for the keypad, so that it takes several tries to dial even "911" with any degree of accuracy.

10 Then there's the tiny size of the phones themselves—more appropriate to a lemur or some other remote primate ancestor than to full-grown Homo sapiens. My own phone's total length is about four-and-a-half inches, so that if I wish to speak and listen at the same time, I have to reduce the distance between mouth and ear by screwing my mouth way over into my right cheek, as if suffering an attack of extreme insecurity. The only hope is that the process of natural selection will soon lead to humans with antenna-like fingers and mouths situated at temple level.

11 Another problem is that my relationships with other humans have not yet evolved to the point that would be truly helpful in the cell phone era. I have the usual quota of friends, relatives, and so-called business associates, but none of them is so underemployed that I can call and ask: "Hey there, you got a few minutes to walk me over to the bank so that I don't look like I, uh, don't have anyone to talk to?" Sometimes there is no alternative but to dial up 1-900-WEATHER and pretend to converse with it, and I suspect that many other cell phone users are doing the same.

12 So here's what I conclude about the evolutionary psychology of cell phones: We are social animals, no question about it, better suited to traveling in convivial bands, hooting and chattering, than to wandering alone in crowds. But few such convivial bands exist within our famously atomized and individualistic capitalist society, where most human relationships now take the sinister form of "deals." So we have regressed to a modified orang-

utan state: Despairing of true sociality, we settle for faking it. The satisfaction, such as it is, lies in making our equally lonely fellow humans feel jealous.

I do have one new friend, though. Everywhere I go now, it comes along, tucked neatly in my pocket or purse. At night I plug it into the wall to recharge, and hear its happy little beep as the nurturing current flows in. Sometimes I take it out during the day, play with its keypad, and confide into its mouthpiece for a moment. Pathetic? Perhaps, but it's not easy striding out into that savanna alone. 13

Building Vocabulary

Define the following terms from the professional vocabulary of the social sciences:

1. psychotics (par. 1)
2. evolutionary psychology (par. 2)
3. primate cousins (par. 2)
4. paleo-anthropologists (par. 2)
5. hierarchical societies (par. 5)
6. Homo sapiens (par. 10)
7. natural selection (par. 10)
8. capitalist (par. 12)

Thinking Critically About the Argument

Understanding the Writer's Argument

1. What does the writer mean by the "primal force" of her "craving for a cell phone"? (par. 1)
2. What scientific discipline does the writer use to explain her urge for a cell phone? Why does she choose that discipline?
3. What is the paleo-anthropologists' explanation for why humans are "social animals"?
4. What are two other interpretations, from the world of evolutionary psychology, for why people like to talk on cell phones?
5. Why, according to the writer, would people pretend to be on a cell phone?

Understanding the Writer's Techniques

1. Why does the writer admit at the start of her essay that she craved a cell phone? What argumentative purpose does that serve?
2. What are Ehrenreich's implied warrant or warrants in this essay?
3. How does she move from discussing herself and her personal relation to cell phones to discussing humanity as a whole? Why does she do this?
4. Where is the writer's central claim? Write the sentence that best expresses it.

5. Ehrenreich offers several variations on the theme of her claim. List those variations and paraphrase each one.
6. What is the writer's tone? How do you know? Use quotes from the essay to demonstrate your answer.
7. How does the writer's argument change after she says, in paragraph 8, that she got her own cell phone?
8. Near the end of her essay, the writer attempts to reconcile the variations on the theme of her claim and make one central argument. What is that argument, and is her closing effective?

Exploring the Writer's Argument

1. There are two types of arguments here: serious attempts at a critique of cell phone use and flip, jokey attempts at humor. Give an example of each, and analyze the writer's use of humor.
2. After answering question 1, discuss whether you think the jokey quality of the essay is effective or not, and explain your answer.
3. One of the points is that cell phones are status symbols. Explain why you think that is either true or not true.

Ideas for Writing Arguments

Prewriting

Jot down recollections of incidents when you have seen and heard someone talk on a cell phone in an inappropriate place or in an inappropriate way.

Writing a Guided Argument

Write an essay in which you argue that there are some places where cell phones should not be allowed. Before writing, make sure that you build evidence, coming up with good examples to back up your minor propositions.

1. Begin by establishing rapport with the reader by making it clear that you too use a cell phone or that you are not against cell phones as a rule.
2. Explain the fact that people can often be rude.
3. Make your claim in a clear, declarative sentence.
4. Offer several examples for cell-phone-free zones, using examples to back up your claims.
5. Anticipate one objection for each of your points.
6. It is important to conclude with a statement of solidarity with cell phone users, except for the rude ones.

Thinking, Arguing, and Writing Collaboratively

Form into groups of three or four. In these groups, discuss modern technological devices other than cell phones that are used widely or becoming increasingly popular. Each group should choose one device and apply Ehrenreich's method to that device. Come up with at least two or three explanations based in paleo-anthropology. Then each student should write a paragraph on the topic chosen by the group. Exchange paragraphs and peer-critique them.

Writing About the Text

Ehrenreich published this article in 1999, when cell phones were just starting to become popular. Cell phones are much more common now. How is Ehrenreich's essay out of date? How could you update it and still keep her central claim? Is it possible to write an essay such as this without the risk of being out of date several years later? Write an essay responding to one or more of these questions.

More Writing Ideas

1. Many states are passing laws that ban drivers from talking on handheld cell phones. Many drivers disagree with these laws. In your journal, come up with reasons for both sides of the argument.
2. Write a paragraph or two about the benefits cell phones have brought to humankind.
3. Find a magazine ad for cell phone service or for a kind of cell phone with special features and analyze the images and text in the advertisement. Write an essay comparing the promises the ad makes to the consumer—both stated and implied—with the realities of owning and using a cell phone.

Woody Hochswender

Did My Car Join Al Qaeda?

A former reporter and fashion columnist for The New York Times, *Woody Hochswender has also edited for* Esquire *magazine. He is the coauthor of* The Buddha in Your Mirror, *a book that attempts to apply the lessons of Buddhism to everyday life. In this selection Hochswender, who lives in Connecticut, defends his use of the small truck known as the SUV, or sport utility vehicle.*

Prereading: Thinking About the Essay in Advance

The SUV famously gets very low gas mileage, and thus conservationists accuse drivers of SUVs of being wasteful. What do you think about drivers of SUVs? If a friend or someone in your family has an SUV, do you agree with the purchase? Why or why not?

Words to Watch

petrodollars (par. 2) money from oil and gasoline
transmigrate (par. 2) move
implicate (par. 3) accuse of guilt

insidious (par. 4) sinister, dangerous
propensity (par. 6) tendency
harrowing (par. 6) terrifying
voracious (par. 8) hungry

1 I drive a large, four-wheel-drive vehicle. Does that mean I'm a bad person?

2 You might think so, from all the sturm und drang we've heard lately from the Virtuous Ones who insist that America's fuel consumption—indeed, our very style of life—is somehow responsible for the enmity toward us in the Middle East, not to mention the rest of the world. A series of TV commercials put together by the columnist Arianna Huffington and Lawrence Bender, the Hollywood producer behind "Pulp Fiction," have even linked S.U.V.'s with Mideast terrorism. The idea is that the petrodollars transmigrate from the Gas 'n' Go to the oil sheiks to the hands of maniacs wielding AK-47's.

3 Leaving aside for the moment that this is trendy, illogical thinking—and leaving aside also the odd sensation of being lectured on socially responsible behavior by the producer of "Pulp Fiction"—isn't this really a backdoor way of blaming America for Sept. 11 and other crimes like it? Those who implicate Americans—particularly our adventurous habits, offbeat choices and breathtaking freedoms, including the freedom to drive to a poetry reading followed by dinner at a French restaurant in the midst of a raging snowstorm—validate the terrorists as essentially right.

4 Where I live, about 100 miles north of New York City, at least half of all the vehicles you see on the road are S.U.V.'s or other light trucks. They make a great deal of sense. This is not just because we have plenty of long steep driveways and miles and miles of dirt roads. We also have had more than 70 inches of snow this winter. When the sun goes down and the melted snow re-freezes, the roads are covered with insidious stretches of black ice.

5 Four-wheel-drive vehicles allow workers to get to and from their jobs, and parents to transport their children safely to school, sporting events, ballet classes and the rest. Yes, there is something vaguely obscene about driving solo to the supermarket in Beverly Hills to pick up a carton of milk in your two-ton Navigator. But not so much in Portland or Green Bay or Chicago.

6 The well-publicized notion that S.U.V.'s are actually unsafe, based on their propensity to roll over, does not take into account personal responsibility. Rollover accidents tend to be something the driver has a substantial degree of control over. I choose not to whip around corners or to follow others so closely and at such high speeds that I have to make harrowing emergency stops. I drive so as not to roll over.

7 However, if some drunken driver veers across the center divider—a situation I have no control over—I would prefer that my 9-year-old and I not be inside a Corolla. From the standpoint of a reasoned individualism, S.U.V.'s are safer in many situations than cars. I think a lot of intelligent people realize that.

Of course, S.U.V.'s use a lot of gas. This goes for my wife's all-wheel-drive Volvo as well as for my voracious mistress, my 1989 GMC. But a car's miles-per-gallon rating is only one measure of fuel efficiency. Miles driven is another. People who drive light trucks quickly learn not to drive around aimlessly. We tend to combine trips and to keep engines finely tuned and tires properly inflated. It all comes down to home economics. 8

What are we supposed to do now, turn our S.U.V.'s in? En masse? Only the independently wealthy can treat their cars purely as fashion items. 9

The S.U.V.-bashers' argument also falls apart on macro-economic grounds. Were we to somehow cut our national fuel consumption by 20 percent, would that deprive the terrorism sponsors of cash? Unfortunately, the world oil market is, well, a market. Even if America were energy independent, there is no guarantee that Exxon, Texaco, and Getty—or, for that matter, France, the Netherlands, and Japan—would cease buying oil from Middle Eastern states. 10

My guess is that this campaign has less to do with politics and economics than with an American tendency to mind everybody else's business. So busybodies, let me ask you a question. How big is your house? Ms. Huffington's is reported to be 9,000 square feet. We all know what it costs to heat and air-condition a joint like that. A couple of years ago I replaced the aging oil furnace in my 3,000-square-foot house with a new fuel-injected system. It saves me about 800 gallons of oil a year. Hey, that's almost precisely the yearly fuel consumption of my GMC. I think of that as progress for me, as a world citizen. Maybe I'm not such a bad person after all. 11

Building Vocabulary

Hochswender uses some common phrases and idioms to enrich his essay. Below are some that he uses. Explain what each phrase or idiom means, and use each in a sentence:

1. sturm und drang (par. 2)
2. whip around corners (par. 6)
3. home economics (par. 8)
4. en masse (par. 9)
5. macro-economic (par. 10)
6. energy independent (par. 10)
7. busybodies (par. 11)
8. a joint (par. 11)

Thinking Critically About the Argument

Understanding the Writer's Argument

1. What is the major objection against driving SUVs, according to the writer? What is he being accused of?
2. What does the writer mean when he says, "Those who implicate Americans . . . validate the terrorists as essentially right"? (par. 3)

3. How does the SUV make life easier for the writer?
4. Why is the SUV safer than a smaller car?
5. The writer admits in paragraph 8 that the SUV uses a great deal of gasoline. How does he defend himself against the accusation of being wasteful?
6. The writer says that "the SUV-bashers' argument also falls apart on macro-economic grounds." (par. 10) What does he mean by this? How does the argument fall apart, according to him?

Understanding the Writer's Techniques

1. What do you think about the opening? Is it effective?
2. Who is the audience? How does that affect the tone of this essay?
3. Where does the writer express his major proposition most clearly and fully?
4. Hochswender has several minor propositions, and they are essentially of two kinds: propositions that are positive reasons to own SUVs and propositions that are rebuttals to perceived oppositions. Make an outline of the propositions offered in the body of his essay.
5. In paragraph 7, the writer mentions his 9-year-old child. Why does he do that? What is the effect of bringing a child into the argument?
6. In paragraph 7, the writer states, "I think a lot of intelligent people realize that." To what is he referring, and what argumentative purpose does this serve?
7. Which minor proposition do you find most effective? Why?
8. What do you think of the conclusion?
9. Why does the writer echo his statement from the beginning of the essay?

Exploring the Writer's Argument

1. One of the writer's arguments is that he drives "so as not to roll over." (par. 6) Why is this proposition weak? Could you strengthen his argument in this section?
2. One objection that some people have to SUVs that the writer doesn't mention is that although they might be safer for those driving them, they can be dangerous to those in smaller cars in the event of an accident. What might the author say to defend against this charge?
3. Paragraph 9 is short, but it includes an interesting idea. Paraphrase the idea, and think of a rebuttal to the point.

Ideas for Writing Arguments

Prewriting

Make a list of lifestyle choices that you have made, actions that you perform often, or decisions that still have an impact on your life now (smoking, piercing), that people might have objections to, and try to come up with answers to objections.

Writing a Guided Argument

Woody Hochswender saw an aspect of his lifestyle that the media and people around him were attacking, and he wrote an essay defending himself. Write an essay in which you identify an aspect of *your* lifestyle that someone conceivably could object to on moral grounds, and defend yourself against the charges. For example, you might smoke cigarettes or cigars; you might consume alcohol; you might like loud music.

1. Begin by explaining your lifestyle choice to your reader, appealing to the reader's compassion.
2. Continue by describing the person or people who accuse you of acting poorly because of your lifestyle choice.
3. Next, offer a minor proposition that explains a positive side of your choice.
4. Then explain one of the objections to your choice, and give your rebuttal.
5. Repeat the process in order, alternating a positive idea with a rebuttal.
6. Emphasize an emotional appeal to the reader.
7. Conclude the essay with a reiteration of the beginning appeal.

Thinking, Arguing, and Writing Collaboratively

In small groups, compare the lists you made for the Prewriting exercise. Allow your fellow students to help you choose a lifestyle choice that would be best for the Guided Argument assignment, and then ask them for objections to your choice. Collect their answers and use them in your rebuttals.

Writing About the Text

In an essay, answer Hochswender's question to his audience in the negative—that no, he is not a bad person, but argue that he has a bad argument. Analyze his argument for him, focusing on how successful his individual points are. Address each minor proposition in his essay, and offer some suggestions for revisions.

More Writing Ideas

1. In your journal, freewrite about this topic: freedoms you enjoy that might hurt other people. Write for 15 minutes without editing your writing. Then exchange your writing with a partner and discuss your ideas as a possible basis for an essay.
2. Write a paragraph in which you critique the argumentative basis for this statement: "Everyone does it, so I should be allowed to also." Is there anything valid about that reasoning? Explain your answer fully.
3. Terrorism, of course, is the reason Hochswender wrote this essay in the first place. He was upset that people accused him and other SUV drivers of supporting terrorism. Write an essay about other day-to-day activities that you think unintentionally might support terrorism.

James Traub
All Go Down Together

James Traub is a freelance writer and the author of Too Good to Be True *(1990), a book about a corporate corruption and fraud case in New York in the 1980s, and* City on a Hill *(1994), a history of City College of New York, a public institution in Harlem. He has also written a book about Times Square in New York,* The Devil's Playground *(2004). In this selection, Traub addresses the pitfalls of the country's all-volunteer military and a possible alternative.*

Prereading: Thinking About the Essay in Advance

France and Israel, among other countries, require all citizens of a certain age to serve in the military for a fixed term. Do you think this is a good idea? Why or why not?

Words to Watch

beneficiaries (par. 1) those benefiting
deferment (par. 1) putting off until later
conscription (par. 2) military draft
equitable (par. 2) fair
imperative (par. 5) necessity
calculus (par. 6) method of figuring out

1 When Richard Nixon abolished the draft in 1973, I was one of the beneficiaries. I had just become eligible, and in the normal course of things I would have been assigned a lottery number. Of course, it's unlikely that I would have donned a uniform even if I had come up No. 1; there was always a way out if you had access to the right lawyers and doctors. At the time, I knew literally no one who served—no one. Thanks to college deferment, during the Vietnam War, college students served at only half the rate of high-school graduates, and the higher up you went in the socioeconomic scale, the likelier it was that you would keep out of harm's way.

2 But what if conscription were equitable and were used to fill a military that was widely respected rather than scorned? This was the case, after all, in the period between the Korean and Vietnam Wars, when military service was widely accepted as the price of citizenship. Why wouldn't that be true today? Why wouldn't it be just the kind of sacrifice young Americans would agree to make at a time of heightened patriotism? The idea has been in the air since earlier this year, when Representative Charles Rangel of New York introduced a bill to restore conscription. Since Rangel got a grand total of 11 co-sponsors, it is safe to say that conscription is an idea whose time has not come, but it's still one worth thinking seriously about.

3 The most obvious objection to a restoration of the draft is that the all-volunteer force, as it is known, is one of the most successful institutions in the

country. The A.V. F. is both the world's most powerful fighting force and a shining example of harmonious race relations and affirmative action. When asked about the draft, Secretary of Defense Donald H. Rumsfeld has essentially said, Why fix what isn't broken? There are several answers to this question. First of all, the war on terrorism is already straining the military and imposing terrible burdens on reservists. Second, we may soon be redefining such civilian tasks as border patrol and airport security as military ones, thus requiring a much larger uniformed force. Charles Moskos, a professor of sociology at Northwestern and an expert on military affairs, has proposed a three-tier draft involving a military, a homeland defense and a civilian component, the last essentially a form of "national service." So a draft would satisfy manpower needs that an all-volunteer force might not. It would also almost certainly be cheaper.

But the ultimate justification for conscription must be moral. Both Rangel and Moskos argue that the A.V. F. recruits working-class young men and women with bleak job prospects and pays them to put their lives on the line. "These people should not have to die merely because they were born to a class of people that lacked the advantages of other people," as Rangel says. There is also an important issue of political philosophy. Conscription assumes a relationship between citizen and state that makes most conservatives, and many liberals, uncomfortable. Libertarian conservatives like Milton Friedman object vehemently to any form of compulsion on the part of the state that's not absolutely unavoidable. Liberals have traditionally feared the use to which the state puts its soldiers. In 1970, at the height of the Vietnam War, the political philosopher Michael Walzer wrote that since many citizens are bound to find almost any use of military power unjust, conscription may be justified only when the state's very existence is threatened. We owe the state no more than that. 4

But is that so? In the age of terrorism, doesn't the imperative of self-defense go well beyond acts of direct territorial threat? What's more, is the draft really a form of tyranny? We live in a culture in which everyone has rights and no one has obligations; the social contract has never been so wan. Perhaps now that our collective safety is jeopardized, the time has come to rethink that contract. Moskos says that in the Princeton class of 1956, from which he graduated, 450 of 750 men served in the military. Last year, Moskos says, 3 of Princeton's approximately 1,000 graduates served. That can't be a good thing for the country. 5

Of course, the country was at peace in 1956. A young man or woman drafted today might very well face combat—and might even have to serve in a war, like Iraq, that he or she considered wrongheaded—the Walzer problem. Perhaps draftees could be permitted to elect other forms of national service. But a truly democratic draft might also, as Rangel suggests, alter the strategic calculus: if the children of journalists, legislators and policy experts were called to military service, we might do a more thorough, and a more honest, job of deciding exactly what it is that's worth fighting for. 6

7 I have a 12-year-old son. The idea that in six or seven years Alex might be drafted is a little bit comical, but mostly appalling. My wife thinks I'm crazy even to suggest the idea. Nevertheless, it's true that we live in a genuinely threatening world; that is, alas, the very reason that military service, or at least some kind of service, should be mandatory, rather than a matter of individual conscience or marketplace choice.

Building Vocabulary

1. Traub uses some words that refer to political ideologies and situations. Identify the following and offer examples from history or the present day:
   - **a.** conservatives (par. 4)
   - **b.** liberals (par. 4)
   - **c.** libertarian (par. 4)
   - **d.** tyranny (par. 5)
2. A number of words in this essay refer to social service concepts. Identify the following and use them in a sentence of your own:
   - **a.** socioeconomic scale (par. 1)
   - **b.** bill (par. 2)
   - **c.** co-sponsors (par. 2)
   - **d.** affirmative action (par. 3)
   - **e.** social contract (par. 5)

Thinking Critically About the Argument

Understanding the Writer's Argument

1. Why does the writer start his essay with his experience?
2. Why did Richard Nixon abolish the draft in 1973?
3. During the Vietnam War, why were wealthier young men able to "keep out of harm's way"? (par. 1)
4. Why do Charlie Rangel and other members of Congress want to restore conscription?
5. What is the writer's answer to the objection that the all-volunteer military is working well as it is?
6. The writer gives statistics in paragraph 5 for the number of students in two classes at Princeton who served in the military. Why does he do this?
7. Why does the writer mention his son at the end of his essay?

Understanding the Writer's Techniques

1. What is the tone in this essay? Who is the audience, and how does this affect the tone?
2. Where does his claim appear most clearly? If you don't see the claim, how does the essay succeed without it?
3. What is the argumentative effect of opening this essay with a personal recollection?
4. What, according to the writer, is the main ground for his claim? Where does he express it most clearly?

5. In paragraphs 3 and 5, the writer asks rhetorical questions. Why does he do this, and how effective are they? In the conclusion, what is the rhetorical effect of the writer's mentioning his son and his wife? How effective is the technique?
6. In addition to responding to arguments by the opposition, the writer puts forward his own arguments. What are these, and why are they presented in the order in which they are presented?
7. What is the meaning of the title? How does it reflect Traub's claim?

Exploring the Writer's Argument

1. Traub says in paragraph 2 that the lack of congressional support for the Rangel bill shows that "conscription is an idea whose time has not come, but it's still one worth thinking seriously about." Does this admission weaken the argument or strengthen it? Why?
2. In this essay, the writer is never absolutely specific about what a draft would entail. Is this a problem with the argument? Why or why not? What do you think would be the writer's answer if you asked him what form he preferred the draft came in?
3. Paraphrase the writer's argument in paragraph 6. What is "the Walzer problem"? Are you convinced by the argument in this paragraph? Explain your answer fully.

Ideas for Writing Arguments

Prewriting

Do a focused 10 to 15 minute freewrite about what you think your reaction would be if you were drafted to be in the United States military right now.

Writing a Guided Argument

Pretend that the United States has reinstated the draft, and both men and women are eligible. Write a letter to the draft board either telling them that you will appear as requested, or that you refuse to serve, knowing that the former decision could put you in harm's way and that the latter decision could mean jail time. For either choice, explain yourself fully.

1. Begin, "Dear Draft Board:"
2. Indicate your own particular socioeconomic level, and explain why this has influenced your choice and why it is relevant to your argument.
3. Give at least two grounds for your choice, referring at least once to the arguments over the obligation of the citizen to the state as introduced in paragraph 4 of Traub's essay.
4. Write a rebuttal to a perceived objection to your choice.
5. Include evidence in the form of examples or cause-and-effect analysis for each of your points.

6. Conclude your letter by saying that your choice is one that all young people should make, and reiterate the grounds for your decision.
7. Sign your name (don't worry—it's not official).

Thinking, Arguing, and Writing Collaboratively

Exchange a draft of your Guided Argument assignment with a classmate. Review your partner's essay for its success in following the steps. Is the major proposition expressed as a choice? Is the major proposition reflected in the minor propositions? Is there sufficient evidence to back up the minor propositions? Write a paragraph evaluating the essay and suggesting revisions.

Writing About the Text

Traub writes several statements in this selection that point to the political spectrum, from conservative to liberal, but he never identifies his own politics. In fact, he seems to avoid the subject explicitly. Try to identify Traub's political bent or ideology and write an argumentative essay to defend your claim.

More Writing Ideas

1. What does a citizen owe his or her country? What is "the price of citizenship"? Write about this in your journal.
2. Write a paragraph in which you argue in favor of or against Charles Moskos's proposed three-tier draft.
3. In an essay, argue that the situation in the United States today falls under Michael Walzer's criterion for conscription, that "the state's very existence is threatened."

PAUL KRUGMAN
A Failed Mission

Paul Krugman went to college at Yale University and received his doctorate from MIT in 1977. Since then he has taught at Yale, Stanford, and MIT, and he now holds a position at Princeton University. Krugman's work on economics, especially in the field of international trade, has been significant; he received the prestigious John Bates Clark medal for economics in 1991. Krugman has written extensively on many topics. In this article he presents an unpopular argument about the space shuttle. The piece appeared in The New York Times *soon after the* Columbia *shuttle exploded in the atmosphere in early 2003.*

Prereading: Thinking About the Essay in Advance

Do you remember the space shuttle *Columbia* disaster? What were your feelings at the time, or now, reflecting on it? More specifically, what does the accident say about humanity's desire to explore space? Why is the endeavor important?

Words to Watch

boon (par. 3) benefit
prohibitively (par. 6) not allowing
epiphany (par. 8) sudden realization
dubious (par. 9) questionable

Some commentators have suggested that the Columbia disaster is more than a setback—that it marks the end of the whole space shuttle program. Let's hope they're right. 1

I say this with regret. Like millions of other Americans, I dream of a day when humanity expands beyond Earth, and I'm still a sucker for well-told space travel stories—I was furious when Fox canceled "Firefly." I also understand that many people feel we shouldn't retreat in the face of adversity. But the shuttle program didn't suddenly go wrong last weekend; in terms of its original mission, it was a failure from the get-go. Indeed, manned space flight in general has turned out to be a bust. 2

The key word here is "manned." Space flight has been a huge boon to mankind. It has advanced the cause of science: for example, cosmology, and with it our understanding of basic physics, has made huge strides through space-based observation. Space flight has also done a lot to improve life here on Earth, as space-based systems help us track storms, communicate with one another, even find out where we are. This column traveled 45,000 miles on its way to *The New York Times:* I access the Internet via satellite. 3

Yet almost all the payoff from space travel, scientific and practical, has come from unmanned vehicles and satellites. Yes, astronauts fitted the Hubble telescope with new eye glasses; but that aside, we have basically sent people into space to show that we can. In the 1960's, manned space travel was an extension of the cold war. After the Soviet Union dropped out of the space race, we stopped visiting the moon. But why do we still send people into orbit? 4

In space, you see, people are a nuisance. They're heavy; they need to breathe; trickiest of all, as we have so tragically learned, they need to get back to Earth. 5

One result is that manned space travel is extremely expensive. The space shuttle was supposed to bring those costs down, by making the vehicles reusable—hence the deliberately unglamorous name, suggesting a utilitarian bus that takes astronauts back and forth. But the shuttle never delivered significant cost savings—nor could it really have been expected to. Manned space travel will remain prohibitively expensive until there is a breakthrough in propulsion—until chemical rockets are replaced with something better. 6

And even then, will there be any reason to send people, rather than our ever more sophisticated machines, into space? 7

I had an epiphany a few months ago while reading George Dyson's "Project Orion," which tells the true story of America's efforts to build a nuclear-powered spacecraft. The project was eventually canceled, in part because the proposed propulsion system—a series of small nuclear 8 explosions—would have run afoul of the test-ban treaty. But if the project had proceeded, manned spacecraft might have visited much of the solar system by now.

9 Faced with the thought that manned space travel—the real thing, not the show NASA puts on to keep the public entertained—could already have happened if history had played out a bit differently. I was forced to confront my youthful dreams of space flight with the question, So what? I found myself trying to think of wonderful things people might have done in space these past 30 years—and came up blank. Scientific observation? Machines can do that. Mining the asteroids? A dubious idea—but even if it makes sense, machines can do that too. (A parallel: Remember all those predictions of undersea cities? Sure enough, we now extract lots of valuable resources from the ocean floor—but nobody wants to live there, or even visit in person.)

10 The sad truth is that for many years NASA has struggled to invent reasons to put people into space—sort of the way the Bush administration struggles to invent reasons to . . . but let's not get into that today. It's an open secret that the only real purpose of the International Space Station is to give us a reason to keep flying space shuttles.

11 Does that mean people should never again go into space? Of course not. Technology marches on: someday we will have a cost-effective way to get people into orbit and back again. At that point it will be worth rethinking the uses of space. I'm not giving up on the dream of space colonization. But our current approach—using hugely expensive rockets to launch a handful of people into space, where they have nothing much to do—is a dead end.

Building Vocabulary

The following are concepts and terms of which the author of this selection assumes knowledge. Identify and define:

1. cosmology (par. 3)
2. Hubble telescope (par. 4)
3. cold war (par. 4)
4. space race (par. 4)
5. NASA (par. 9)
6. asteroids (par. 9)
7. International Space Station (par. 10)

Thinking Critically About the Argument

Understanding the Writer's Argument

1. Why has space flight been a "huge boon to mankind"? (par. 3)
2. Why, according to the writer, did we pursue manned space travel starting in the 1950s?
3. Why is manned space flight a "nuisance"?
4. How has the space shuttle not fulfilled its promise?

5. What is the writer's reaction to his realization that manned space travel to the entire solar system is possible?
6. How does the writer compare the ocean floor to space?
7. In paragraph 10, the author writes that "NASA has struggled to invent reasons to put people into space—sort of the way the Bush administration struggles to invent reasons to . . . but let's not get into that today." To what is he referring, and why does he include this reference?

Understanding the Writer's Techniques

1. What is the writer's claim in this essay? Where does he best express it?
2. Why does he start out by saying that he hopes the *Columbia* disaster would spell the end of the space shuttle program? What rhetorical effect is he going for? Is it effective? Explain your answer.
3. What is the writer's tone in this essay? Is the chosen tone effective? Why or why not? Rewrite paragraph 5 to make the tone more serious.
4. Why does Krugman place the word *manned* in quotation marks?
5. What is the rhetorical effect of the writer's question in paragraph 7?
6. How many minor propositions does the writer have? List them.
7. Is the closing effective? Why or why not?

Exploring the Writer's Argument

1. Why does Krugman argue that we should end the space shuttle program without suggesting an alternative? Do you think he has an alternative in mind? What might that be?
2. Has space flight been, as Krugman says, a "boon for mankind," or have there been negative effects in our forays into space? Explain your answer.
3. At the end of his essay, the writer uses the phrase "dead end." Remember that this was written a short time after the *Columbia* exploded. Do you think the writer's language is insensitive or inappropriate? Why or why not? Where else could his language be considered insensitive?

Ideas for Writing Arguments

Prewriting

Think about how popular culture images of space have influenced our desire to explore the solar system and beyond. Freewrite for at least 10 minutes about which TV shows, movies, or images you think have influenced space travel.

Writing a Guided Argument

Pretend you are an official at NASA, and you have read Paul Krugman's column. Form a rebuttal to his arguments and write your own argument in an essay, explaining why the space shuttle program must go on. Do some research online, if necessary, to build evidence. Examine NASA's Web site for information about the shuttle.

1. Begin with a reference to Krugman's essay and an explanation that he is not the only one who feels this way.
2. Gain sympathy for NASA and the space shuttle program by casting the agency as having the minority opinion.
3. State your major proposition clearly.
4. Offer your central ground for the survival of the space shuttle program clearly, with evidence to support your idea.
5. Rebut at least one of Krugman's points, quoting from his essay and critiquing the quote.
6. Link paragraphs between rebuttals with appropriate transitions.
7. In your conclusion, appeal once more to the reader's emotions and sense of hope.

Thinking, Arguing, and Writing Collaboratively

In small groups, discuss the freewriting you did for the Prewriting exercise. Attempt to develop a claim about how popular culture about space and the real-life space program affect each other. In your group, work together to make an outline for an essay on the topic.

Writing About the Text

Write an essay on Krugman's style. Examine his use of idiom and vocabulary. What does the fact that Krugman wrote this as a newspaper column suggest about why he chose his style? Does it make a difference that the column appeared in *The New York Times*?

More Writing Ideas

1. In your journal, make a list of everything that comes to mind about the phrase "space shuttle." Share your list with your fellow students. Are their lists similar? Different? How so?
2. In a paragraph, speculate on how the history of the space shuttle could have been a success. What would have made it a success, especially in Krugman's eyes?
3. Some experts think that the future of manned space travel is not astronauts doing science experiments but rather commercial travel—tourism. Write an essay arguing either that space tourism is a good idea or that it is a bad one.

ANNA QUINDLEN
One Nation, Indivisible? Wanna Bet?

Anna Quindlen has written extensively, but most visibly as a columnist for The New York Times *from 1981 to 1994. In 1992 she won a Pulitzer Prize for her commentary. A collection of columns,* Thinking Out Loud, *was published in 1993. She is also a novelist.* One True Thing *(1994) was adapted into a movie in 1998. She is now a columnist for* Newsweek *magazine's "Last Word" back-page feature. Her position as an observer of American life serves her well in this selection from* Newsweek, *which examines the controversy over the words "under God" in the Pledge of Allegiance.*

Prereading: Thinking About the Essay in Advance

The Constitution of the United States calls for a separation of religion and government, more commonly known as "church and state." Do you think this is a good idea? Why or why not? When have you seen a blending of church and state in the United States?

Words to Watch

impermissible (par. 2) not allowed
jingoism (par. 2) excessive patriotism
deplorable (par. 4) morally wrong
machinations (par. 4) workings
spate (par. 6) outburst
eschew (par. 6) avoid

Every year somebody or other finds a way to show that American kids are ignorant of history. The complaint isn't that they don't know the broad strokes, the rationale the South gave for keeping slaves, the ideas behind the New Deal. It's always dates and names, the game-show questions that ask what year the Civil War began and who ordered the bombing of Hiroshima, the stuff of the stand-up history bee. But if American adults want to give American kids a hard time about their dim knowledge of the past and how it's reflected in the present, they might first become reasonable role models on the subject. And the modeling could begin with the members of Congress, who with few exceptions went a little nuts when an appeals court in California ruled that the phrase "under God" in the Pledge of Allegiance was unconstitutional. 1

I don't really know whether that is an impermissible breach of the firewall between church and state. The proper boundaries 'twixt secular and sacred have been argued long and hard by legal minds more steeped in the specific intricacies than my own. But I do know this: attempts to make the pledge sound like a cross between the Ten Commandments and the Constitution are laughable, foolish and evidence of the basest sort of political jingoism. 2

So let's go to the history books, as citizens of this country so seldom do. The Pledge of Allegiance started in 1892 as a set piece in a magazine, nothing more, nothing less. It was written by a man named Francis Bellamy in honor of Columbus Day, a holiday that scarcely exists anymore except in terms of department-store sales and parades. The words "under God" were nowhere in it, hardly surprising since Bellamy had been squeezed out of his 3 own church the year before because of his socialist leanings. His granddaughter said he would have hated the addition of the words "under God" to a statement he envisioned uniting a country divided by race, class and, of course, religion.

4 Those two words went into the pledge nearly 50 years ago, and for the most deplorable reason. It was the height of the Red scare in America, when the lives of those aligned or merely flirting with the Communist Party were destroyed by paranoia, a twisted strain of uber-patriotism and the machinations of Sen. Joseph McCarthy, after whom an entire vein of baseless persecution is now named. Contrary to the current political argument that "under God" is not specifically devout, the push to put it in the pledge was mounted by the Knights of Columbus, a Roman Catholic men's organization, as an attempt to counter "godless communism." President Dwight D. Eisenhower signed a bill making this law, saying that the words would help us to "remain humble."

5 Humility had nothing to do with it. Americans are not a humble people. Instead the pledge had become yet another cold-war litmus test. The words "under God" were a way to indicate that America was better than other nations—we were, after all, under the direct protection of the deity—and adding them to the pledge was another way of excluding, of saying that believers were real Americans and skeptics were not. Would any member of Congress have been brave enough at that moment to say that a Pledge of Allegiance that had been good enough for decades was good enough as it stood?

6 Would any member of Congress, in the face of the current spate of unquestioning flag-waving, have been strong enough to eschew leaping to his feet and pressing his hand over his heart, especially knowing that the percentage of atheist voters is in the low single digits? Well, there were a few, a few who said the decision was likely to be overturned anyhow, a few who said there were surely more pressing matters before the nation, a few who were even willing to agree with the appeals court that "under God" probably did not belong in the pledge in a country founded on a righteous division between government and religion.

7 But most of the rest went wild. Even Sen. Hillary Clinton invoked "divine providence," even Sen. Dianne Feinstein called the court decision "embarrassing." What was embarrassing was watching all those people—Republicans, Democrats, liberals, conservatives—shout "under God" on the Senate floor, as though government were a pep rally and they were on the sanctified squad. Sen. Bob Smith of New Hampshire had this to say: "If you don't believe there's a God, that's your privilege, but it is still a nation under God." Huh?

8 I have a warm personal relationship with God; I often picture her smiling wryly and saying, in the words of Shakespeare's Puck, "Lord, what fools these mortals be!" Or perhaps something less fond. Now, as almost 50 years ago, a nation besieged by ideological enemies requires nuanced and judicious statecraft and instead settles for sloganeering, demonizing and politicking. One senator

said after the court decision was handed down that the Founding Fathers must be spinning in their graves. The person who must be spinning is poor Francis Bellamy, who wanted to believe in an inclusive utopia and instead became in our time the father of convenient rhetoric.

Building Vocabulary

This selection requires knowledge of some concepts, issues, and people relating to U.S. politics. Check with a dictionary or other reference work and define, identify, and explain the relevance of the following:

1. the New Deal (par. 1)
2. the Red scare (par. 4)
3. Joseph McCarthy (par. 4)
4. cold war (par. 5)
5. litmus test (par. 5)
6. Sen. Hillary Clinton (par. 7)
7. Sen. Dianne Feinstein (par. 7)
8. Sen. Bob Smith (par. 7)

Understanding the Writer's Argument

1. Why does Quindlen compare the members of Congress to ignorant schoolchildren? What point is she making?
2. What is the "firewall" between church and state? To what is she referring?
3. What are the origins of the Pledge of Allegiance?
4. What would the writer of the Pledge have thought of the addition of the words "under God" inserted in his work? How do you know?
5. Why were the words "under God" finally inserted into the Pledge?
6. Why were members of Congress so against taking out those words? Did any think taking them out was a good idea?

Understanding the Writer's Techniques

1. What tone is set by the title of the essay?
2. The body of the essay includes some strong and combative language that sets a certain tone reflecting how Quindlen feels about the issue. How would you describe that tone, and why? Do you think it is consistent with the title? Why?
3. Where does the major proposition appear most clearly and fully?
4. What argumentative function does the opening serve?
5. Paraphrase the minor proposition in paragraph 2.
6. The writer uses the facts of history to help argue her case. Where in the essay does she do this? Explain why the technique is effective.
7. How do paragraphs 6 and 7 support her position?
8. What is your view of the conclusion? Do you think it is effective? Why or why not?

Exploring the Writer's Argument

1. Quindlen accuses members of Congress of being extreme in their politics. Do you think she is being extreme as well? Why or why not?
2. To help make her case, the author writes in paragraph 5 that "Americans are not a humble people." Do you think this is true? Why or why not?
3. The author says that the Pledge didn't have the words "under God" in it for more than 50 years, so why shouldn't we change it back to how it was? But now the phrase has been in there for almost 50 years. Which tradition should take precedence? Explain your answer fully.

Ideas for Writing Arguments

Prewriting

Read the words to "America the Beautiful," a song that is now sung during the seventh-inning stretch at baseball games in place of "Take Me Out to the Ballgame." What is your reaction to the lyrics of "America the Beautiful" in light of this essay? Why is this a different case?

Writing a Guided Argument

Write an essay arguing that we don't need a Pledge of Allegiance at all.

1. Open your essay with a recollection of reciting or learning the Pledge and of the first time you thought about the words.
2. Refer to the controversy that Quindlen discusses, using a quote from her essay and commenting on it.
3. Use a tone similar to Quindlen's.
4. Clearly state your position and the main ground for your position.
5. Anticipate the main objection to dropping the Pledge in one paragraph, and in a separate paragraph, using proper transitions, rebut the objection.
6. Close the body of your essay with an appeal to the true meaning of America.
7. Conclude by restating your position in light of your supporting points and your rebuttal.

Thinking, Arguing, and Writing Collaboratively

In small groups, examine the concept of jingoism. Where do you see jingoism in your neighborhood? In the media? Write individually on this topic for 10 minutes, and then come together and share your thoughts with your group. Then, as a class, discuss the dangers of jingoism and why it is so tempting.

Writing About the Text

Quindlen uses a sarcastic tone in this selection. Write an essay in which you argue that this tone and use of language is effective here, and explain why. In your essay, be sure to explain exactly which passages you find sarcastic, and explore why you think she uses that language.

More Writing Ideas

1. Do some research on the history of the division between church and state. Quindlen writes that the United States was "founded on a righteous division between government and religion." In which founding document is this division guaranteed, and where? What exactly does the document say? Write a journal entry exploring the quote you find.
2. Use your work on question 1 to add to Quindlen's argument. Write a paragraph in which you develop a minor proposition using the evidence you have gathered.
3. What other rights, privileges, or guarantees from the Constitution do you think are eroding in our times? Write an essay on this question, explaining your answer fully.

2 Writing Arguments

As you attend the various courses in your college program, you probably have already noticed that your instructors across the spectrum of study are asking you to take a stand on a topic and support it with thoughtful, well-reasoned detail. In the previous chapter we suggested that the world of academic writing has its roots in argumentation. In history, biology, psychology, sociology, computer applications, education, in midterms and finals and research papers, you have to state a position on an issue, propose (or imply) that position in a thesis, and defend that position logically. An important part of argumentation in the disciplines is *persuasion,* that is, effecting some action on the part of your reader—from doing something tangible like buying a battery-driven car or joining a political action group to adopting a point of view, such as acknowledging that global warming is a serious threat to the world. As a writer, you need to persuade readers as a result of your appeals to their intelligence, emotions, and beliefs.

You've already seen that it's important to distinguish written arguments from the heated verbal interchange you have with roommates, friends, or family members. In such an exchange, your position on an issue can stimulate strong emotions on either side of a topic and arouse passionate feelings (and loud voices). We rarely plan our verbal arguments; mostly they just burst open in the course of conversation, and we just as rarely have the luxury to think them out clearly or to marshal convincing support in our own behalf.

Strong written argument, on the other hand, prides itself on its cool logic and substantive details to back up a position. Its purpose is clear. It takes into account its audience. It follows a lucid plan based on careful organization. It builds on appropriate rhetorical strategies—description, narration, comparison and contrast, classification, and definition, to name a few. It draws on reflective research. And through drafting and revision, it develops its thesis through suitable language and style.

The Writing Process

As you saw in Chapter 1, we can identify the qualities of well-written arguments when an end product is at hand. As a writer, you need to know how to get to such a place yourself—the production of an effective argumentative paper that is to the point and fulfills the requirements of your assignment. You have to think of writing your argument as the culmination of a process, not simply a one-shot effort but a series of interrelated activities that can help you construct a successful paper.

Within the writing process, most writers identify various stages and activities in creating a piece of writing. Although we can name, more or less, the major elements in this process and encourage you to rely on them as you write, we don't want you to think of them as lock-step procedures where all efforts follow sequentially and require mindless adherence. Many of the steps overlap, some you can take simultaneously, and you may have good reason to skip some steps along the way.

The strategies that follow are essential elements in the writing process. We'll have more to say about many of them later in this chapter as we explore the writing of an argumentative paper.

Stages in the Writing Pro'cess

- Discuss your ideas with reliable people who can provide an initial reaction to your proposal.
- Do preliminary research online and in your library.
- Do *prewriting*—warmup activities before you start to draft your paper.
- Limit your topic.
- Identify your purpose and audience.
- State your claim in a thesis.
- Identify supporting details and evidence.
- Organize your ideas.
- Prepare a first draft.
- Share your draft.
- Revise your draft based on readers' comments and suggestions.
- Produce and edit your final copy.
- Proofread your final draft.

First Steps

After initial thought and preliminary research, the stages of the writing process usually begin with *prewriting*, a convenient term to identify the limbering-up activities writers produce on paper *before* they start creating a draft. (You know that the prefix *pre* means "prior to" or "before.") This is a very important stage in writing your paper: prewriting helps you thrash out ideas and circle your topic until you can identify clearly what you want to write about. If you begin a draft too soon, you may find that you have to start over and over again, wasting your valuable time and increasing your frustrations as a writer.

Prewriting Options

- *Make a list of ideas that your topic stimulates in your mind.* You can use this list to expand ideas and eliminate others.
- *Keep a journal of thoughts and ideas.* Jot down anything that comes to mind about any topic in an informal notebook that you can return

to regularly to help identify a subject that you could develop into an argumentative paper.

- *Freewrite.* Write nonstop for 15 minutes or so. Do not stop to edit or revise. Just let your thoughts fill the page, no matter how disjointed or even silly they seem to you as you write. Free association gets words on the page; if you suffer from writer's block, you know how important it is simply to have something concrete to look at. You can use these words and sentences to zero in on a topic or to eliminate those topics that don't fit your intended task.
- *Use a visual aid.* With a subject map or subject tree, you can write a key word on a blank page and, using lines to indicate roads or branches, follow different elements of the topic by connecting them to lines or shapes that help you track different possibilities.
- *Brainstorm.* Raise unedited questions about the topic. Questions can dislodge answers that might set you on the right track to a strong essay. On a sheet of paper, write the reporter's essential questions, the five *W*'s—*who, what, where, when, why*—and also *how.* Use these to start your own list of questions about your topic.
- *Make a scratch outline.* As ideas take shape in your mind, they can suggest linkages and interrelations, and you can capture them in a scratch outline. Write down an aspect of your topic, and underneath it list the various subtopics that come to mind. A scratch outline is an informal first step in organizing your ideas and can help you later on as you aim for a coherent, unified paper.

Of course, you'll need to pick and choose among these steps. Nobody takes all of them all the time. But if you're attentive to prewriting efforts, you'll discover many possibilities for developing a fruitful topic. As we point out later, once you have a topic, you can proceed to writing a thesis around a debatable issue, finding supporting detail to back up your assertions, organizing your information into a coherent entity, and writing an initial draft and any subsequent drafts that advanced thinking on your topic might require. Editing your manuscript and submitting it for review are important culminating acts in the writing process.

Identifying Issues

A manageable topic is the best way to assure that your essay won't derail as you move through the various stages of the writing process. Where do you begin your efforts to find a topic that you can develop into a thoughtful argument?

If your instructor has made an assignment—the extinction of the dinosaurs, let's say, or the causes of the Boer War, or the psychological manifestations of Alzheimer's disease—some of your work is done for you. (You'll still have to limit the topic, no doubt, in ways that we explain later on.) With an open-ended topic, however, you should let your interests and concerns lead you. Are you worried about global warming? Does the death penalty trouble you? Do the potentials of cyberspace stimulate your thoughts? *(To the*

"We're not certain why they disappeared, but archeologists speculate that it may have had something to do with their size."

Point presents controversial essays on these topics; if you've read and discussed a selection in class, one of the ideas emerging from the essay may generate a good topic starting point.) The best papers always emerge from a writer's lively interests, and you want to honor your own curiosity and awareness of the world around you. Some global issue may pique your interest—the American military, taxes, famine in Africa—and you'll be able to form an opinion about them. Because of their complexity, you'd have to provide convincing reasons and evidence to support your claim. But topics of more personal and immediate concern also have rich potential as argumentative papers, and you should consider them. Should a strip mall open adjacent to the campus? Is the ban of religious symbols in the town square appropriate? Is the nutritional content of Burger King meals open to serious criticism? Should parents of very young girls allow them to participate in beauty contests?

On reflection, you may find that a topic that interests you is just not arguable or is not worth arguing about. If you believe that children should never be allowed to sample alcohol, for example, who would disagree with you? Almost everyone concurs that alcohol and children are a dangerous mix, and you'd be shouting in the wind—who would listen?—no matter how strongly you made your case.

Limiting Your Topic

When you have the germ of a topic in mind, you have to limit it. The best way to begin to limit your topic is, as we've suggested, thinking carefully in advance about it through some of the prewriting strategies presented in the previous section, including, of course, browsing on the Web and in the library. You want to narrow down your topic so that you can accomplish your assigned writing task in a reasonable time. Often, you can narrow your topic in stages so that you can reach a desired level of specificity.

In the following table, look at the way writers have limited the broad topics in the first column into more productive argumentative essay topics. Items in the last column stand the best chance of developing into powerful argumentative essays.

Broad Topic	Limited Topic	Even More Limited
Cell phones	Dangers in using cell phones	The dangers of using cell phones while driving automobiles
Home instruction for children	Teaching children basic skills at home	Teaching reading skills to preschoolers in a home setting
Terrorists	Home-grown terrorists	Conditions in homes and schools that can create terrorists among American teenagers

Writers using the limited topics will have an easier time than those approaching the issues with too broad a scope. For the topic on cell phones, for instance, the writer can rule out any ideas about their use in public places like restaurants and movie theaters. The writer can rule out skyrocketing costs for cell phones and for required monthly service. Though these topics also might make effective papers, for this writer the issue is the dangers of cell phone use while driving automobiles. Any research efforts would concentrate on that dimension of the topic.

Knowing Your Purpose and Audience

Once you have limited your topic, you have to consider your *purpose* and *audience.* Purpose relates to what you hope to accomplish in your essay. Will your argument about the dangers of cell phones center on a narrative of some dangerous uses you witnessed or read about? Will you explain how to avoid the dangers? Will you show the causes and effects of dangerous use? Will you compare and contrast safe and hazardous cell phone uses? Your argumentative essay will allow you great latitude in addressing your topic through proven rhetorical strategies, and you have to determine which will enhance your topic development. In writing your argument, your purpose might be to propose that some belief or activity is good or bad, moral or immoral, harmful or beneficial. You might wish to push your readers to take some course of action that you deem essential or merely to have them consider a familiar issue in a new light. Being certain of your purpose will help you state your claim forcefully as you continue to think about your essay.

When your purpose is clearly in mind, you need to focus on your intended audience. Just what kind of reader are you aiming for? The glib response here, of course, is "I'm writing for my teacher so I can get a good grade." That's true, certainly, but not to the exclusion of other possible audiences: your classmates, perhaps, or the editor of the school newspaper, or the CEO of some company that treated you badly. When writing, it's always best to imagine specific audiences other than your English professor. In general, your teacher can adapt easily and can assume the personality and characteristics of varied reader audiences. Define a reader, and approach that reader with strategies targeted to her interests.

To take one example, with your cell phone topic, just think about how your approach would differ if your were writing your essay for teachers of driver education in urban high schools or for applicants for drivers' licenses at the Department of Motor Vehicles or for high-level executives at AT&T, whose corporate growth over the past several years hinged on increased sales of cellular telephones. Similarly, if you wrote about home teaching, your methods would vary significantly if you wrote for future mothers as opposed to booksellers at a national convention or teachers in your local elementary school. Vocabulary, style, sentence structure, and diction—audience and purpose markedly influence these fundamental elements of writing.

Making a Claim in Your Thesis

Among the many important steps in the writing process, creating a thesis is high on the ladder of developing an argument. In an argumentative essay, you have to take a position on—that is, make a claim about—a topic. Your thesis must present an arguable topic. So even with a limited subject, you need to restrict your paper's concerns even further: you need to take a position on the topic, and the position on the topic must be debatable.

Note how writers have developed theses from the limited topics you looked at before.

Limited Topic	Possible Thesis
The dangers in using a cell phone while driving an automobile	The dangers to people who use cell phones while operating an automobile are serious, and current laws requiring "hands-free" technology do not adequately address the problems.
Teaching reading skills to preschoolers in a home setting	Teaching reading to preschoolers at home subverts the teacher's role, and parents should avoid the trap of becoming their children's teachers.
Conditions in homes and schools that can create terrorists among American teenagers	Home environments with remote, self-absorbed parents and ready access to weaponry—no matter what the social and financial conditions of the household or the psychological makeup of the child—contribute more than any other factor to developing teenage school terrorists.

Note how one could argue easily *against* any of these claims, which is the best assurance that each has the potential for becoming a successful paper. The topics are arguable; people stand on both sides of the issues. Many writers will produce an antithesis—that is, a thesis sentence opposite to the one they propose—to assure that their own position is arguable.

Possible Thesis	Antithesis
The dangers to people who use cell phones while operating an automobile are serious, and current laws requiring "hands-free" technology do not adequately address the problems.	"Hands-free" technology has reduced dramatically the dangers of cell-phone use by drivers on the road.

Once again, we put in a few words about flexibility here. Your thesis must be flexible. As you write your first and subsequent drafts, you may have to change your thesis as your topic takes shape and your claim undergoes refinement. Don't adhere blindly to the thesis you first developed, no matter how good it seems to you. As you marshal evidence, change your thinking, and delve deeply into evidence from many sources, your thesis may change considerably, usually for the good. Just be sure that you state your topic clearly, that you have identified your position on the topic, and that you make a claim that is debatable.

Supporting Your Claim

After you have decided on your position and stated it as your claim in a thesis sentence, you have some important work ahead. Because your objective is to convince readers that your claim is valid and worth considering, only strong supporting detail drawn from personal experience or reliable sources will help you win over your audience. As you'll see later on, refutation—that is, acknowledging (and also challenging) viewpoints that oppose your own—is a key element in successful argumentation; not only must you discover information that supports your position, but you must also seek information that tells you what the other side is arguing. As you sift through the potential sources of supporting details, pay close attention to what those who disagree with you say. You'll need to give them due consideration when you write. (We'll say more about refutation later in this chapter.)

If you want to convince readers to accept your claim based on your own observations, you'll need to draw on concrete sensory detail to evoke the moment you are highlighting. Color, sound, and images of smell and touch all can set your reader in the scene as you see it and help make your points. Drawing on personal experience to support an argument doesn't *prove* anything easily, but it can convince readers if the illustration is apt. If you choose to draw on testimony from others—providing proof or evidence—you need to seek out the best possible information to back up your claim about the topic.

For example, arguing that global warming is a serious threat based only on days of high heat and humidity in your hometown during a winter season would not easily convince your readers. Similarly, arguing that your state should lower the driving age to 15 based on your own excellent (if illegal) tractor driving on your aunt's farm would not *prove* anything really, other than that in a single instance a teenager showed responsibility and skill in manipulating a gas-driven vehicle. You'd need to supplement these moments in your personal life with other convincing examples drawn from personal experience or with expert testimony from reliable sources in books and articles and on Web sites.

To prod readers to accept your claim, you often must draw on material that is solid and plentiful, evidence that is plausible, and reasoning that is not faulty. Here, the Internet and library catalogs can point you in the right direction. The World Wide Web has evolved into an invaluable research tool for writers, and you can find list serves and links from which to download abstracts, chapters, articles, and even full books. You already know, no doubt, that amid its many riches, the Web also can lead you on a path to disaster. Misinformation abounds; unreliable sources making wild claims may appear as regular popup windows on your computer or as unsolicited spam e-mail messages. Many chat rooms are notorious hotbeds of hysterical proclamations and assertions that defy logic even on superficial inspection. Also, some assessments on the Web are not current or reliable, or the site may not be open about its biases and objectives.

Therefore, we recommend some serious work at your college or local library, where research librarians can help you appraise Web sites and refer you to appropriate electronic sources. Your librarians, of course, also can put you on the trail to books and periodicals that will supplement your cyberspace ventures with solid resources on the library shelves or on microfilm or microfiche.

Your initial browsing in the library and on the Web helped you find a topic; now, as we have indicated, you need to amass supporting details to back up the topic you've chosen. Read as widely as you can; visit valid Web sites; watch television programs and films; talk with anyone who will listen. Take notes on what you've read and seen and be prepared to present some of your materials as evidence to your argument. Use the three *C*'s as you evaluate your evidence: *currency*, *completeness*, and *credibility*.

Don't be surprised if you find yourself changing the terms of your argument dramatically. The more deeply you explore the topic, the more potential information you have to solidify your position or to alter it dramatically or subtly. With a great deal of resources at hand, you can select those details that seem best to bolster your position.

Organizing Your Argument

The supporting details—the reasons and evidence you garner—make up the *grounds* of your argument, the key elements that establish the validity of your claim. Your claim, stated in your thesis, establishes your general point of view; the grounds provide the reasons and evidence. As you gather information, you should be thinking of how to organize your materials once you're ready to begin. You need to keep in mind the way your grounds will devolve to minor propositions and how you actually will use your evidence to support your claim or to refute an opposing claim.

You might find it helpful even at this stage to consider using one of the following patterns as a guide when writing your essay.

Pattern 1: Refutation First	**Pattern 2: Refutation Last**	**Pattern 3: Refutation Point by Point**
Introduce your claim.	Introduce your claim.	Introduce your claim.
State opposing arguments and refute them.	State first minor proposition and supporting information.	State first minor proposition and supporting information and refute opposing arguments.
State first minor proposition and supporting information.	State second minor proposition and supporting information.	State second minor proposition and supporting information and refute opposing arguments.
State second minor proposition and supporting information.	State third minor proposition and supporting information.	State third minor proposition and supporting information and refute opposing arguments.
State third minor proposition and supporting information.	State opposing arguments and refute them.	Conclude the essay.
Conclude the essay.	Conclude the essay.	

We don't propose these patterns as absolutes, and it's probably a bit too early in the writing process for you to map out the full approach your essay will take. Nevertheless, keeping in mind the possibilities for organizing your information and conveying it logically will help you over the hurdles when it comes to drafting your paper.

Checking Your Assumptions (or Warrants)

As you learned in Chapter 1, a warrant is the essential underpinning for your assertion. It establishes the certainty underlying a particular claim and its supporting reasons. A firm warrant justifies the supporting information that you assemble to support your contention. However, if your readers can challenge your warrant, you'll have to defend it.

Why do you have to think about warrants when you write your essays? In many of your argumentative assignments, you can assume that your readers—generally your instructor, other students, family members, or the particular readers that you have defined—are friendly and won't question the warrants supporting your claim. Yet warrants based on certain cultural assumptions, systems of belief, or core values often require their own defense because they too are debatable. When your warrant is controversial, you need to explain or qualify it.

Consider the ongoing debate over abortion rights. Some would use as a warrant the belief that all life from conception is sacred and would build a case from there against all forms of abortion. Others would establish as a warrant that idea that freedom of choice is the principle upon which a woman makes a decision involving abortion. There are numerous additional warrants underlying the abortion debate that often serve as "universal" values that in themselves are controversial. Defending the warrant is as important as providing points to support your assertion. Differing warrants or assumptions underlying debates over abortion, gun control, the death penalty, and other hot-button issues require writers to subject these warrants to the same scrutiny that they bring to their claims and supporting evidence.

Refutation: Meeting the Opposition

Particularly with assertions that you know many people would disagree with, effective arguments always consider the opposition's point of view. As we pointed out briefly before, you have to be aware of what contrasting arguments suggest, and you have to treat them fairly in your essay.

You have some options here. One strategy is to indicate the views that run counter to your own and simply to admit that some parts of these arguments are legitimate—but that your point is more substantial and worthy of greater support. Conceding arguments is an attractive option: this tactic shows your lack of prejudice and your ethical approach to the issue. Essentially, you are saying here "I know that others disagree with me—and here are some of their reasons, which have some validity. Nevertheless, the points I will make are much more convincing."

Another strategy is to identify opposing arguments and then refute them as part of your own presentation. How can you refute an opposing argument?

- Question the evidence proposed by the opposing camp. Is it valid? Up to date? Sufficient? Accurate?
- Probe the warrants of an opposing argument. What are the underlying assumptions and beliefs for the writer's claim? Has the writer offered a substantive rationale for the warrants on which he builds his argument?
- Identify evidence that challenges the specific elements in the opposing arguments. Thus, you can extract fundamental points and rebut them one at a time rather than making a sweeping refutation.

With either strategy, concession or refutation, you must treat the opposing arguments justly and respectfully. True, satirists and ironists often mock opposing views, but in your papers you want to aim for fairness that will establish your credibility and lack of bias as a writer and win over your readers.

Avoiding Traps in Appeals and Logic

Argumentative essays often deal with heated topics, but as a fair and thoughtful writer, you want to be aware of excessive appeals to emotion and to a wide range of logic traps that can show fault lines in your thinking. Be alert to these logic traps and wrongheaded emotional appeals as you write your papers.

- *Ad hominem ("to the man") arguments*. These discredit the person rather than the argument: "Gloria Lee never married. How can she talk about the sacredness of marriage between men and women?" Here, the attack is against the person, not the issue. Avoid *ad hominem* arguments—but do not shrink from challenging someone if the person lacks appropriate credentials to make the claim. You would be right to contest the author of a pro-death penalty Web site put up by a dentist who has no authority in the debate other than his passionate commitment to the issue.
- *Arguments based on longevity*. Avoid proving a point by stating that people always believed it, so why should we change it now? "Women have never competed in professional football in the past, and there's no need to alter common practice." We'd still be talking about an earth-centered universe if we adhered to beliefs based only on their standing through time.
- *Arguments based on transfer*. Here the argument connects the point to a famous person in order to win support. This is an example of *positive* transfer: "President Bill Clinton is a brilliant scholar and his recent support of the newly nominated federal judge should not be questioned." This is an example of *negative* transfer (or name calling): "President Bill Clinton's personal behavior challenged family values. Why should we consider as relevant his defense of the family support bill?" Neither example makes any logical connection between the person and the issue and, in fact, the transfer distracts the reader from the point to the person.
- *Hasty generalizations*. In this logic trap, you leap to false conclusions based on insufficient, untrue, or unrepresentative evidence. "Cats are disloyal pets. Our cat Phoebe, whom we had for five years, ran off one day and never returned." One example cannot support the generalization. Hasty generalizations at their most pernicious lead to stereotyping, when you use reductive generalizations to characterize an individual or group. "Our South American gardener is sluggish and has no resolve. Newly arrived immigrants in our country are lazy and unambitious."

- *Broad generalizations.* By using words like *never*, *always*, and *all* in an argument, you leave yourself open to accusations of overstatement. "George Washington always knew how to lead a battle"; "All Germans supported the Nazi purge of Jews during World War II"—sweeping statements like these are open easily to challenge. It's best to qualify them: "George Washington almost always knew how to lead a battle"; "Large numbers of Germans supported the Nazi purge of Jews during World War II."
- *Post hoc, ergo propter hoc ("after this, therefore because of this").* This is a logical fallacy built on false cause-and-effect relationships. "The boys ran out of the department store quickly. They must have stolen the woman's purse." Just because their departure was hasty and might seem suspicious, there is no necessary cause and effect relationship between the boys' rapid disappearance and the purse snatching. Our most ingrained superstitions—bad luck following a black cat's crossing our path, for example—assume that one event in time causes another soon after. Be sure that any cause-and-effect relationships that you establish are valid.
- *Argumentum ad populum ("to the people").* Arguments that draw on highly charged language can manipulate readers' responses by arousing strong emotions. Words that appeal to virtuous elements, such as patriotism, motherhood, and America, can produce "glittering generalities" that distort meaning so that readers must accept a premise through illogical association. Negative words similarly can make illogical connections: "The dictatorial president of the Student Association has made another bad choice."
- *Bandwagon arguments.* In these arguments the writer falsely generalizes that the voice of the people is always right. "The citizens of this city are voting to renew Proposition 13, and you should too." Just because everyone's doing it doesn't make it desirable.
- *Begging the question.* Here, the writer takes a conclusion for granted before she proves it. "Teenagers are by nature reckless and will benefit greatly from required counseling prior to any voluntary abortion." The writer can go on to indicate the benefits of this counseling; but she has not offered any proof for her conclusion that teenagers are irresponsible. Another dimension of begging the question is assuming in your premise what your conclusion should prove. Thus, if you argue that elected officials' greed is unavoidable because they put personal gain above service to constituents, you are not proving your premise and hence are begging the question.
- *Oversimplified arguments.* Oversimplification is a major impediment to logical argumentation and can take many forms.
  - *One solution.* Complicated issues usually have more than one resolution, and you don't want to argue for just one solution to a sticky problem. "Censoring violence on television will reduce violence in our communities." Surely other possible solutions warrant consideration in the serious issue of violent behavior.

- *Either-or reasoning*. You shouldn't assume that only two sides exist on an issue—yes or no, good or bad, right or wrong. "He failed so many courses because he works after school and on weekends. Either you work or go to school; you can't do both."
- *No cost or harm*. If you project a benefit for some course of action, don't assume automatically that no problems, costs, or penalties will follow. "Prohibit all pagers and cell phone use in public places." The benefits are clear: no interruptions, annoying rings or music, or loud talking in indoor spaces. But what about consequences: preventable emergencies, parents needing to be in touch with children, doctors on call. No-harm generalizations often overlook precarious repercussions.

- *Non sequitur ("It does not follow")*. This logical fallacy draws conclusions when no logical connection exists between ideas. "Arnold Schwarzenegger will be a good governor for California because he is a very popular actor." He may be popular, and people might have voted for him because he's popular, but that doesn't guarantee that he will be a good governor. The argument's conclusions do not stem from its premise. The writer might see a logical connection between popularity and leadership, but he should make it explicit. Otherwise, he has generated a non sequitur—that is, disconnected ideas.
- *Weak or untrue analogies*. A familiar tool of argument is the analogy, a type of comparison that relates one object or idea to a basically dissimilar idea so that readers can see the point in a new light. Alfred Posamentier, a professor of education, made this comment about the anxiety at the start of a new school year awash with new policies and procedures: "It's akin to an engineering firm that develops this new machine and doesn't know if all the parts are going to behave the way they are supposed to behave when they flip the switch on a certain day." Analogies enliven writing and help illustrate a point but never serve as evidence. Posamentier, after all, hasn't proved that the system is untested and risks uncoordination. But his analogy helps us see how he views the problem.
- *The straw man*. An argument sets up a straw man when it asserts a weak or invented argument attributed to an opponent for the exclusive purpose of disproving it. "The television commentator would no doubt approve of music that glorifies drugs and indifferent sex. Only an extremist libertine who doesn't believe in family values would question the censorship of any material aimed at teenagers." The statement asserts that the commentator would endorse music that praises drugs and sex—but the operative words here are "no doubt." The phrase suggests an invented argument, one that the writer can attack along with the person who made the argument.

Strong written arguments reflect logical thinking, and we've tried to point out ways in which you can produce thoughtful topics; carefully stated assertions; well-defined claims, grounds, and evidence; and objective data and testimony. These elements in your writing will mark you as a fair analyst with a lively, inquiring mind, and they will help you to produce strong argumentative papers.

Perspectives on Love and Marriage: Reading and Writing About a Critical Issue

JUDY BRADY
I Want a Wife

Judy Brady was born in 1937 and went to college at the University of Iowa. A breast cancer survivor, she is an activist with the Women's Cancer Resource Center and a cofounder of the Toxic Links Coalition, which works to prevent cancer by reducing pollution. In this funny but bitter satire, which appeared in Ms. *magazine in 1971, Brady, a wife and mother, argues that she, too, would like someone to take care of her.*

Prereading: Thinking About the Essay in Advance

Think about the traditional roles that men and women have played in their relationships. What is expected of a husband? Of a wife? Do you think things are the same now as in 1971 when Brady wrote the piece? Why or why not?

Words to Watch

nurturant (par. 3) giving attention and affection
hors d'oeuvres (par. 6) appetizers
adherence (par. 8) faithful attachment

I belong to that classification of people known as wives. I am A Wife. And, not altogether incidentally, I am a mother. 1

Not too long ago a male friend of mine appeared on the scene fresh from a recent divorce. He had one child, who is, of course, with his ex-wife. He is obviously looking for another wife. As I thought about him while I was ironing one evening, it suddenly occurred to me that I, too, would like to have a wife. Why do I want a wife? 2

I would like to go back to school so that I can become economically independent, support myself, and, if need be, support those dependent upon me. I want a wife who will work and send me to school. And while I am going to school, I want a wife to keep track of the children's doctor and dentist appointments. And to keep track of mine, too. I want a wife to make sure my children eat properly and are kept clean. I want a wife who will wash the children's clothes and keep them mended. I want a wife who is a good nurturant attendant to my children, who arranges for their schooling, makes sure that they have an adequate social life with their peers, takes 3

Surfing Couples (© Peter M. Fisher/CORBIS)

them to the park, the zoo, etc. I want a wife who takes care of the children when they are sick, a wife who arranges to be around when the children need special care, because, of course, I cannot miss classes at school. My wife must arrange to lose time at work and not lose the job. It may mean a small cut in my wife's income from time to time, but I guess I can tolerate that. Needless to say, my wife will arrange and pay for the care of the children while my wife is working.

4 I want a wife who will take care of *my* physical needs. I want a wife who will keep my house clean. A wife who will pick up after me. I want a wife who will keep my clothes clean, ironed, mended, replaced when need be, and who will see to it that my personal things are kept in their proper place so that I can find what I need the minute I need it. I want a wife who cooks the meals, a wife who is a *good* cook. I want a wife who will plan the menus, do the necessary grocery shopping, prepare the meals, serve them pleasantly, and then do the cleaning up while I do my studying. I want a wife who will care for me when I am sick and sympathize with my pain and loss of time from school. I want a wife to go along when our family takes a vacation so that someone can continue to care for me and my children when I need a rest and change of scene.

5 I want a wife who will not bother me with rambling complaints about a wife's duties. But I want a wife who will listen to me when I feel the need to explain a rather difficult point I have come across in my course of studies. And I want a wife who will type my papers for me when I have written them.

I want a wife who will take care of the details of my social life. When my wife and I are invited out by my friends, I want a wife who will take care of the babysitting arrangements. When I meet people at school that I like and want to entertain, I want a wife who will have the house clean, will prepare a special meal, serve it to me and my friends, and not interrupt when I talk about the things that interest me and my friends. I want a wife who will have arranged that the children are fed and ready for bed before my guests arrive so that the children do not bother us. I want a wife who takes care of the needs of my guests so that they feel comfortable, who makes sure that they have an ashtray, that they are passed the hors d'oeuvres, that they are offered a second helping of the food, that their wine glasses are replenished when necessary, that their coffee is served to them as they like it. 6

And I want a wife who knows that sometimes I need a night out by myself. 7

I want a wife who is sensitive to my sexual needs, a wife who makes love passionately and eagerly when I feel like it, a wife who makes sure that I am satisfied. And, of course, I want a wife who will not demand sexual attention when I am not in the mood for it. I want a wife who assumes the complete responsibility for birth control, because I do not want more children. I want a wife who will remain sexually faithful to me so that I do not have to clutter up my intellectual life with jealousies. And I want a wife who understands that *my* sexual needs may entail more than strict adherence to monogamy. I must, after all, be able to relate to people as fully as possible. 8

If, by chance. I find another person more suitable as a wife than the wife I already have, I want the liberty to replace my present wife with another one. Naturally, I will expect a fresh, new life; my wife will take the children and be solely-responsible for them so that I am left free. 9

When I am through with school and have a job, I want my wife to quit working and remain at home so that my wife can more fully and completely take care of a wife's duties. 10

My God, who *wouldn't* want a wife? 11

Building Vocabulary

1. After checking a dictionary for Brady's specific use of each of the following words, write out their definitions:
   a. attendant (par. 3)
   b. adequate (par. 3)
   c. peers (par. 3)
   d. tolerate (par. 3)
   e. rambling (par. 5)
   f. replenished (par. 6)
   g. monogamy (par. 8)

2. Write an original sentence for each word.

Thinking Critically About the Argument

Understanding the Writer's Argument

1. What made Brady think about wanting a wife for herself?
2. How would a wife help the writer continue her education?
3. In what way would a wife help the writer around the house?
4. Why does the writer want someone to help her take care of the children?
5. How would a wife change the writer's sex life?
6. What kind of freedom does the writer want, finally?

Understanding the Writer's Techniques

1. What is Brady's major claim in this essay? Consider the ironic meaning of her essay, and decide if she ever truly expresses her claim. Explain your answer.
2. What are the implied warrants in this essay? How do you know?
3. What minor propositions does Brady give to show that she wants a wife?
4. Do you detect a pattern of coherence among the minor propositions? Why does she include them in the order she does? Would you change the order at all?
5. What is the effect of Brady's use of the word "I"? Do you find it effective? Why or why not?
6. What is Brady's tone in this essay? Explain your answer.
7. Why does the writer separate the idea that "sometimes I need a night out by myself" in paragraph 7? What rhetorical purpose does this serve?
8. What is the effect of the rhetorical question at the end of the essay and of the use of the phrase "My God" and the word "wouldn't" in italics?

Exploring the Writer's Argument

1. Brady wrote this essay two years before she and her husband separated. How does this knowledge change your opinion of the essay?
2. This essay was published in 1971. Do you think that this essay could be published in a major magazine today? Why or why not? Do husbands still expect their wives to perform all of these duties without help? Explain what has changed.
3. Brady lists many domestic duties traditionally assigned to the homemaker. What "wifely responsibilities" exist today that she doesn't mention?
4. In what ways are Brady's arguments old fashioned? In what ways are they relevant to today's men and women?

Ideas for Writing Arguments

Prewriting

What kind of help do you need in life? What kind of person would you need? If you are living at home, would it be helpful to have a student of your own?

Writing a Guided Argument

Write an essay titled "I Want a Student."

1. Begin your essay by identifying yourself as a student. You will argue that you want a student to help you with your life as a student.
2. Offer a brief personal story (as Brady does in par. 2) to explain why you decided you wanted your own student.
3. Using Brady as a guide, support your main idea with supporting points, explaining the various activities your very own student could help you with in your life as a student.
4. Organize your points in an effective order, using transition words and phrases to improve the flow from paragraph to paragraph.
5. Use repetition in your language for rhetorical effect.
6. End your essay with a question, making that question as effective and dramatic as possible.

Thinking, Arguing, and Writing Collaboratively

Help to divide the class into two groups: one consisting of all the men in the class and the other consisting of all the women. Working in these groups, have the men come up with reasons why husbands (and boyfriends) need extra help, and have the women list reasons why wives (and girlfriends) need help. Each group should assign a representative to put the reasons on the board. The class should discuss the effectiveness of each reason.

Writing About the Text

Write an essay about the use of irony in this essay. What is the effect of writing such an emotional essay in such a straightforward style? Discuss Brady's use of humor.

More Writing Ideas

1. In your journal, explain which of Brady's complaints you find most effective and which you find most whiny or weak.
2. In a paragraph, argue for or against this statement: "Men should stay home while women go out and earn a living."
3. Write an essay arguing that it is more difficult to be a man in today's society than it is to be a woman.

Nicolas Kristof
Love and Race

Born in 1959, Nicolas Kristof was raised in Oregon, educated at Harvard, and won a Rhodes scholarship to Oxford University in England. He and his wife, also a journalist, won a Pulitzer Prize for their work in China during the Tiananmen Square uprising. In this selection, Kristof sings the praises of the current rise in marriage between the races.

Prereading: Thinking About the Essay in Advance

Do you know any interracial couples? If so, what problems do they face, if any, and why? If you do not know any, what problems do you think they might face in society today?

Words to Watch

genome (par. 6) entire code for DNA in a cell
superficial (par. 7) unimportant, only on the surface
miscegenation (par. 10) mixing of races
guru (par. 13) leader and guide
surge (par. 14) sharp rise

1 In a world brimming with bad news, here's one of the happiest trends: Instead of preying on people of different races, young Americans are falling in love with them.

2 Whites and blacks can be found strolling together as couples even at the University of Mississippi, once the symbol of racial confrontation.

3 "I will say that they are always given a second glance," acknowledges C. J. Rhodes, a black student at Ole Miss. He adds that there are still misgivings about interracial dating, particularly among black women and a formidable number of "white Southerners who view this race-mixing as abnormal, frozen by fear to see Sara Beth bring home a brotha."

4 Mixed-race marriages in the U.S. now number 1.5 million and are roughly doubling each decade. About 40 percent of Asian-Americans and 6 percent of blacks have married whites in recent years.

5 Still more striking, one survey found that 40 percent of Americans had dated someone of another race.

6 In a country where racial divisions remain deep, all this love is an enormously hopeful sign of progress in bridging barriers. Scientists who study the human genome say that race is mostly a bogus distinction reflecting very little genetic difference, perhaps one-hundredth of 1 percent of our DNA.

7 Skin color differences are recent, arising over only the last 100,000 years or so, a twinkling of an evolutionary eye. That's too short a period for substantial genetic differences to emerge, and so there is perhaps 10 times more genetic difference within a race than there is between races. Thus we should welcome any trend that makes a superficial issue like color less central to how we categorize each other.

The rise in interracial marriage reflects a revolution in attitudes. As recently as 1958 a white mother in Monroe, N.C., called the police after her little girl kissed a black playmate on the cheek; the boy, Hanover Thompson, 9, was then sentenced to 14 years in prison for attempted rape. (His appeals failed, but he was released later after an outcry.) 8

In 1963, 59 percent of Americans believed that marriage between blacks and whites should be illegal. At one time or another 42 states banned intermarriage, although the Supreme Court finally invalidated these laws in 1967. 9

Typically, the miscegenation laws voided any interracial marriages, making the children illegitimate, and some states included penalties such as enslavement, life imprisonment, and whippings. My wife is Chinese-American, and our relationship would once have been felonious. 10

At every juncture from the 19th century on, the segregationists warned that granting rights to blacks would mean the start of a slippery slope, ending up with black men marrying white women. The racists were prophetic. 11

"They were absolutely right," notes Randall Kennedy, the Harvard Law School professor and author of a dazzling new book, "Interracial Intimacies," to be published next month. "I do think [interracial marriage] is a good thing. It's a welcome sign of thoroughgoing desegregation. We talk about desegregation in the public sphere; here's desegregation in the most intimate sphere." 12

These days, interracial romance can be seen on the big screen, on TV shows, and in the lives of some prominent Americans. Former Defense Secretary William Cohen has a black wife, as does Peter Norton, the software guru. The Supreme Court justice Clarence Thomas has a white wife. 13

I find the surge in intermarriage to be one of the most positive fronts in American race relations today, building bridges and empathy. But it's still in its infancy. 14

I was excited to track down interracial couples at Ole Miss, thinking they would be perfect to make my point about this hopeful trend. But none were willing to talk about the issue on the record. 15

"Even if people wanted to marry [interracially], I think they'd keep it kind of quiet," explained a minister on campus. 16

For centuries, racists warned that racial equality would lead to the "mongrelization" of America. Perhaps they were right in a sense, for we're increasingly going to see a blurring of racial distinctions. But these distinctions acquired enormous social resonance without ever having much basis in biology. 17

Building Vocabulary

Explain the meaning of the following examples of figurative language. Rewrite the sentences by putting the figure of speech in your own words:

1. "all this love is an enormously hopeful sign of progress in *bridging barriers.*" (par. 6)
2. "Skin color differences are recent, arising over only the last 100,000 years or so, a *twinkling of an evolutionary eye.*" (par. 7)
3. "the segregationists warned that granting rights to blacks would mean the start of a *slippery slope.*" (par. 11)
4. "these distinctions acquired enormous social *resonance.*" (par. 17)

Thinking Critically About the Argument

Understanding the Writer's Argument

1. Why is it significant that interracial couples exist at the University of Mississippi?
2. What lessons do the writer suggest we learn from the statistic that skin color differences are a relatively recent development evolutionarily?
3. What were segregationists afraid of in the 19th century?
4. Explain Randall Kennedy's quote, "We talk about desegregation in the public sphere; here's desegregation in the most intimate sphere." Paraphrase his quote.
5. What evidence does the writer give that interracial marriages are becoming more mainstream?
6. Why wouldn't students at Ole Miss discuss intermarriage with Kristof?

Understanding the Writer's Techniques

1. What is the writer's major proposition? Where is it best stated?
2. What minor propositions does the writer use to support his major proposition?
3. What evidence does the writer use to support his minor propositions? Make a rough outline of the essay's argument.
4. How effective is Kristof's use of statistics in paragraphs 4 through 7?
5. Does the writer only rely on rational arguments? What other kinds of appeals can you find? Explain your answer.
6. What is the persuasive effect of the writer explaining in paragraph 10 that he is in an interracial marriage?
7. How effective is the last paragraph?

Exploring the Writer's Argument

1. Do you find paragraphs 2 and 3 in Kristof's essay contradictory? Why or why not?
2. If racial differences are not that important and have little basis in biology, why does Kristof repeat his argument about racial distinctions in paragraph 17? Does he have a rhetorical reason? Could you strengthen his point here?
3. Do you think the structure of Kristof's essay is effective? Why or why not? Could you suggest a better structure? How would you structure the essay if you were assigned to write a column on the same issue?
4. Why does Kristof use the example of Hanover Thompson in paragraph 8? Why that example? He could have found a much more tragic example from the early part of the 20th century. There were many lynchings of African Americans who merely looked at a white woman in a way she didn't like. Why, then, does he offer an example from 1958?

Ideas for Writing Arguments

Prewriting

How common is interracial marriage where you live? Why do you think that is? Write about whether you think it is getting more common, and explain why it is or why it is not.

Writing a Guided Argument

Write an essay about a lifestyle that still is not accepted fully in society (for example, openly gay couples or unmarried couples living together). Argue that you see an improvement in the level of tolerance toward that lifestyle.

1. Begin your essay with a declaration that things are getting better.
2. Continue by offering examples or statistics to bolster your claim. Do some research, if you must, to gather evidence and, preferably, quotes. Save at least two pieces of evidence for later in your essay, under step 6.
3. While keeping an impartial distance to your writing, establish an optimistic tone.
4. In the next section, discuss the history of your chosen subject.
5. Develop and discuss the idea of opposing views to your subject.
6. Provide evidence to show how tolerance is increasing by offering evidence.
7. Link your ideas with well-developed transitions.
8. In your conclusion, link the fears opponents have about your subject with the reality or the coming reality in society.

Thinking, Arguing, and Writing Collaboratively

In small groups, share your papers that grew out of the Writing a Guided Argument assignment. Discuss suggestions for improvements in tone and word choice. Also, help your classmates to develop evidence for their essays by paying close attention to any pieces of evidence that are irrelevant and by helping with any awkward phrasing.

Writing About the Text

Write an essay in which you evaluate Kristof's use of statistics in this essay. Which do you find most impressive or effective for helping his claim? Which are less effective? What other statistics would you have liked to see?

More Writing Ideas

1. Are there any negative effects of interracial relationships on the children of those unions? Write in your journal about this topic.
2. Write a paragraph about why you think someone would be opposed to interracial marriage. What are people afraid of? Is there anything you could say to alleviate their fears?
3. In an essay, write about Kristof's statement in his conclusion that "we're increasingly going to see a blurring of racial distinctions." How would life in the United States change if he is correct? How is it already heading in that direction?

ANN PATCHETT
Kissing Cousins

Ann Patchett was born in Los Angeles in 1963 and moved to Nashville, Tennessee, with her family at the age of six. She was educated at Sarah Lawrence College and at the prestigious Writer's Workshop at the University of Iowa. She is the author of four novels: The Patron Saint of Liars *(1992),* Taft *(1994),* The Magician's Assistant *(1997), and* Bel Canto *(2001), which won the PEN/Faulkner award for fiction. She also has written for many publications, including the* Chicago Tribune, The Village Voice, GQ, Elle, Gourmet, Vogue, *and* The New York Times Magazine. *This selection appeared in 2002.*

Prereading: Thinking About the Essay in Advance

What do you think of first cousins becoming romantically involved? Can you imagine falling in love with your first cousin? Why do you think there is a stigma on first cousins marrying?

Words to Watch

star-crossed (par. 1) ill-fated
nominal (par. 3) almost nothing
lethal (par. 3) deadly
stigma (par. 5) part of someone's identity that causes shame
taboos (par. 5) things banned because of morality or social custom
pyromaniac (par. 8) one who enjoys lighting fires

1 Thanks to 12 years of Catholic single-sex education, a lack of brothers, and an over developed interest in reading as a child, I grew up in a world almost completely devoid of boys. Except, of course, for those boys I was related to. I had 25 first cousins, and I remember many summer family reunions eating sand-infused slices of sheet cake on the beaches of Southern California, so lost in the cousin crush of the moment that I could hardly swallow. These feelings were for the most part unexpressed and interchangeable (I liked cousin Lenny as much as his brother Greg). One crush, however, started when I was 8 and proved hearty enough to follow me into adulthood. Whenever this cousin and I were on the same side of the country there were dinners, hand-holding, and a certain amount of sighing. Alas, we would be perfect for each other if only we weren't cousins. But we were, and so, feeling genetically star-crossed we always said good night and went our separate ways.

2 It turns out we didn't have to.

3 Popular mythology often takes the place of science. Lemmings do not, in fact, hurl themselves into the sea by the thousands to drown, and the country folk in the film "Deliverance" were not the product of parents who failed to take the initiative to go any farther than their aunt and uncles' houses to look for a spouse. An article published recently in *The Journal of Genetic Counsel-*

ing says that the increased risk of birth defects to children born of first cousins is nominal. This isn't exactly breaking news, either; research has been in for some time. Could it be that we are so unnerved by the idea of the union of cousins that we didn't even want to hear about it? The fact that marriage between first cousins is illegal in 24 states will probably go the way of laws that banned interracial marriage. The norm is capable of change. After all, my grandmother was forbidden to serve apple pie with cheddar cheese when she was a young waitress in Kansas. (The combination was once believed to be as lethal as cousin love.)

Certainly in just about every other place in the world, marrying your 4
first cousin is an unremarkable event. For centuries royalty has had to look in the bank of immediate relatives to find suitable mates. Who would be good enough for a Hapsburg but another Hapsburg? The notion that there was something genetically weakening, if not downright creepy, about intermarriage is one that is distinctly American. Perhaps it is born from a distaste of what our ancestors left behind when they boarded their ships to the New World. What is thought of as essential in the highest social classes of other countries is seen as a mark of the most backward and impoverished factions of our own. Now we find out that all of those jokes about Appalachian families are utterly baseless.

Still, to think that the laws against close family marriages are entirely 5
based in a concern over the medical well-being for the child that might come of that union seems to miss a large part of the point: marrying a cousin at 60 carries almost the same burden of stigma as marrying a cousin at 16. It's one of those things we're not supposed to do, and these days sexually active Americans have precious few limitations. For better or worse, we cling to the few taboos we have left. If the *Journal of Genetic Counseling* told us that there would be no major medical repercussions from reproduction with your brother or aunt, I don't think we would heave a national sigh of relief and say, well, as long as there are no medical issues. . . . Remember Oedipus and Jocasta? The story didn't turn out too well for them.

If you had to mark out the boundaries of incest, some of us are going 6
to put first cousins on one side of the line and some are going to put them on the other. A friend of mine from Los Angeles recently met a first cousin once removed from Israel who she never knew existed. They fell madly in love at a family reunion in Spain. While they are working through cultural differences, a language barrier, and a long commute, the only thing that gives her a moment's pause is the blood tie, even though they have no plans to have children. Yet it seems impossible that a little thing like a common relative should ruin her chances for happiness.

Other cousins, the ones who were more like the pseudo-siblings of your 7
entire youth, may take more consideration. But true love is a rare and wonderful thing, and if you happen to find it with a first cousin in one of the 24 states of the union that will still put you in jail for your marriage, the wisest choice may simply be moving. There are enough of those couples in America now to merit an extensive and thoughtful Web site, cousincouples.com.

They supply not only support and inspirational stories but also a very helpful map to show you just what your state thinks of your love life.

8 I, for one, am glad to have grown up in an era that made me feel that following through on any of my earlier crushes would have been akin to my being pyromaniac. For me, cousin love was like a set of romantic training wheels: safe, steady little things that screwed onto the real wheels of the bike I wasn't actually big enough to ride. Watching the boys swim out into the ocean at those sunburned family reunions, I got to have all the fun without the chance of actually getting hurt. As for the cousin I thought I was in love with, after a few years we turned out not to get along at all. That had nothing to do with our being related but I thank my lucky gene pool that it kept me from marrying him.

Building Vocabulary

This selection requires knowledge of some history and art. Identify the following terms and explain their significance for this article:

1. the film "Deliverance" (par. 3)
2. Hapsburg (par. 4)
3. Appalachian (par. 4)
4. Oedipus and Jocasta (par. 5)

Thinking Critically About the Argument

Understanding the Writer's Argument

1. What does Patchett mean when she writes that she was "so lost in the cousin crush of the moment that I could hardly swallow"? (par. 1)
2. What are some myths about cousin marriage?
3. How does the writer describe these myths?
4. What does Patchett mean when she says that "the notion that there was something genetically weakening, if not downright creepy, about intermarriage is one that is distinctly American"? (par. 4)
5. Why is the first cousin relationship on the borderline between acceptability and disgust, according to the writer?
6. How many states in the United States allow first cousins to marry?
7. What was the most positive thing for the writer about having crushes on her cousins?

Understanding the Writer's Techniques

1. What is the writer's major proposition? Where is it best expressed? If you can't find it, why do you think that is? If you can't find it, put her claim into your own words.
2. Why does the writer begin her essay with a recollection of her experiences with her many cousins? What argumentative purpose does this serve?
3. Outline the essay to highlight the minor propositions.

4. What evidence or support does the writer present for her minor propositions?
5. Which evidence in the essay do you think is the most effective? Why?
6. How effective is the writer's insistence in paragraph 7 that "true love" is the most important thing here?
7. In her closing, the writer moves away from saying that "cousin love" is a positive thing and says that it was only a good thing as "romantic training wheels." Why does she shy away from completely endorsing cousin love?

Exploring the Writer's Argument

1. Does Patchett's last sentence contradict the rest of her essay and its message of tolerance? Why or why not? Explain.
2. Many anthropologists believe that the taboo against incest is ingrained in humans as a survival instinct; the species would get stronger, evolutionarily, if people ventured out to other families rather than taking mates from their own families. They say the taboo exists for good reason. Do you agree or not, and why? What would Patchett say to that?
3. Do you think that Patchett's conclusion helps or hurts her argument? Explain your answer. Refer to question 7 in the "Understanding the Writer's Techniques" assignment.

Ideas for Writing Arguments

Prewriting

What were some beliefs you had when you were a child that you now know were false, were myths? Where did those myths come from? How did they come to be dispelled? Did you learn the truth from books? From friends? From parents? From siblings? How did you feel when you learned the truth?

Writing a Guided Argument

Write an essay in which you examine a popular myth you grew up with (for example, that your father was the strongest man in the world or that there was a tooth fairy or Santa Claus). Argue that those mythologies were wrong, and dispel them for your reader.

1. Begin your essay with a recollection of growing up with a myth, and explain the myth's origins.
2. Write about your good or bad memories of the myth.
3. Note how the myth from your childhood affects your life today.
4. Write your major proposition, dispelling the myth.
5. In the next few paragraphs, write minor propositions in which you support the idea in your major proposition.
6. Offer specific examples or anecdotes to support each of your minor propositions.

7. Attempt to use a poetic or nostalgic tone.
8. Close by discussing whether or not you are glad that you believed the myth when you were younger.

Thinking, Arguing, and Writing Collaboratively

Assist in dividing the class into three parts. Each group should prepare for a debate on "cousin love," doing research on the Web (you may visit the Web site Patchett suggests, cousincouples.com) and in the library. Each group should develop some familiarity with the history and practice of cousin marriage around the world. The aim of the debate is to win based on persuasive illustration. Stage the debate, with one group arguing in favor of cousin marriage and the other arguing against it. The third group will act as a jury. The jury should deliberate, vote on the winner, and make a presentation explaining in a written statement the results of the vote.

Writing About the Text

Patchett is a novelist and is known for her prose style. Write an essay in which you examine how Patchett adapts techniques from writing fiction to the essay form. Look especially at how she sets a scene. Does she have any characters? How is her word choice and tone affected?

More Writing Ideas

1. Visit the Web site cousincouples.com, which Patchett mentions in paragraph 7. Record your impressions of the Web site's content in your journal.
2. Research one of the terms in the "Building Vocabulary" exercise, and write a paragraph explaining how it relates to the idea of incest.
3. In paragraph 5, Patchett writes, "For better or worse, we cling to the few taboos we have left." Besides incest, what other taboos do we have? Write an essay in which you answer this question, offering an explanation of each one as well as a judgment about whether we should still hold on to that taboo.

ANDREW SULLIVAN

Let Gays Marry

Andrew Sullivan was born in 1963 in a small town in England. He went to Oxford University and Harvard University, where he earned his Ph.D. in 1989. He was editor at The New Republic *magazine at the age of 27. Sullivan, who is openly homosexual, wrote* Virtually Normal: An Argument About Homosexuality *(1995), a book about gay rights. He resigned from* The New Republic *in 1996 and continues to write widely for many publications. In this selection, Sullivan makes the case for allowing homosexual couples to marry in civil ceremonies.*

Prereading: Thinking About the Essay in Advance

Do you agree with the title of this essay? Should homosexuals be able to marry? Why or why not? If you agree that gays should marry, what do you think would be some common arguments against it?

Words to Watch

subvert (par. 2) overturn
sanction (par. 6) officially approve of
fidelity (par. 7) faithfulness

"A state cannot deem a class of persons a stranger to its laws," declared the Supreme Court last week. It was a monumental statement. Gay men and lesbians, the conservative court said, are no longer strangers in America. They are citizens, entitled, like everyone else, to equal protection—no special rights, but simple equality. 1

For the first time in Supreme Court history, gay men and women were seen not as some powerful lobby trying to subvert America, but as the people we truly are—the sons and daughters of countless mothers and fathers, with all the weaknesses and strengths and hopes of everybody else. And what we seek is not some special place in America but merely to be a full and equal part of America, to give back to our society without being forced to lie or hide or live as second-class citizens. 2

That is why marriage is so central to our hopes. People ask us why we want the right to marry, but the answer is obvious. It's the same reason anyone wants the right to marry. At some point in our lives, some of us are lucky enough to meet the person we truly love. And we want to commit to that person in front of our family and country for the rest of our lives. It's the most simple, the most natural, the most human instinct in the world. How could anyone seek to oppose that? 3

Yes, at first blush, it seems like a radical proposal, but, when you think about it some more, it's actually the opposite. Throughout American history, to be sure, marriage has been between a man and a woman, and in many ways our society is built upon that institution. But none of that need change in the slightest. After all, no one is seeking to take away anybody's right to marry, and no one is seeking to force any church to change any doctrine in any way. Particular religious arguments against same-sex marriage are rightly debated within the churches and faiths themselves. That is not the issue here: there is a separation between church and state in this country. We are only asking that when the government gives out *civil* marriage licenses, those of us who are gay should be treated like anybody else. 4

Of course, some argue that marriage is *by definition* between a man and a woman. But for centuries, marriage was *by definition* a contract in which the wife was her husband's legal property. And we changed that. For centuries, marriage was *by definition* between two people of the same race. 5

And we changed that. We changed these things because we recognized that human dignity is the same whether you are a man or a woman, black or white. And no one has any more of a choice to be gay than to be black or white or male or female.

Some say that marriage is only about raising children, but we let childless heterosexual couples be married (Bob and Elizabeth Dole, Pat and
6 Shelley Buchanan, for instance). Why should gay couples be treated differently? Others fear that there is no logical difference between allowing same-sex marriage and sanctioning polygamy and other horrors. But the issue of whether to sanction multiple spouses (gay or straight) is completely separate from whether, in the existing institution between two unrelated adults, the government should discriminate between its citizens.

This is, in fact, if only Bill Bennett could see it, a deeply conservative cause. It seeks to change no one else's rights or marriages in any way. It
7 seeks merely to promote monogamy, fidelity, and the disciplines of family life among people who have long been cast to the margins of society. And what could be a more conservative project than that? Why indeed would any conservative seek to oppose those very family values for gay people that he or she supports for everybody else? Except, of course, to make gay men and lesbians strangers in their own country, to forbid them ever to come home.

Building Vocabulary

This essay is making a strong point, and thus it is trying to undermine the opposition's position. List five words or phrases in this essay that aim to strengthen the writer's position and weaken the opposition's. Explain how each word does this.

Thinking Critically About the Argument

Understanding the Writer's Argument

1. Explain in your own words what the Supreme Court means by "A state cannot deem a class of persons a stranger to its laws."
2. Why is marriage so important to gays and lesbians, according to Sullivan?
3. According to Sullivan, what is the difference in the debate between the civil and religious worlds?
4. What is Sullivan's answer to those who say that marriage is by definition between a man and a woman?
5. How does he respond to those who say marriage is only for procreation?
6. Why is gay marriage actually a "conservative project"? Explain what this means.

Understanding the Writer's Techniques

1. Is the writer's major proposition the same as the title? If so, show where it appears in the essay. If not, what is the major proposition?

2. Analyze paragraph 2 and explain why it is effective.
3. What are the writers' minor propositions? Outline the body of the essay.
4. For what argumentative purpose does the writer make the distinction between marriage within a religion and civil marriage?
5. How would you characterize the writer's tone? Why do you think he wrote the essay in this tone? Do you think the fact that this appeared in *Newsweek*, a magazine read by a wide audience, made a difference? Why or why not?
6. Paraphrase the writer's argument in paragraph 5. Is it effective? Why or why not?
7. What minor proposition do you think is the writer's most effective?
8. Analyze the writer's use of the word "home" in paragraph 7.

Exploring the Writer's Argument

1. Sullivan is both openly gay and openly conservative. What is conservatism? How might Sullivan's two identities clash? Do you see evidence of the clash in his essay? Does he reconcile them persuasively?
2. Answer Sullivan's question in paragraph 3.
3. Sullivan says in paragraph 4 that "there is a separation of church and state in this country." Do you think that is absolutely true? How does the religious faith of our leaders affect policy, more specifically, policy toward homosexuality and gay marriage? Examine recent statements made by the president of the United States and members of Congress about the issue and compare them to Sullivan's assertions. Do you think he might persuade them? Explain your answer.

Ideas for Writing Arguments

Prewriting

Will gay marriage inevitably be legalized? Write down some of your thoughts about how that might come about or why it would not come about.

Writing a Guided Argument

Many people think that the legalization of gay marriage is only a matter of time. What does that mean? Argue in an essay that gay marriage will or will not be legal nationally within the next 10 years.

1. Begin your essay with a quote from Sullivan's essay that asserts the moral right of gays to marry.
2. Continue with an analysis of how other social progress has been made.
3. Compare that progress with the advent of gay marriage and make your claim in the form of a prediction.
4. Give at least two minor propositions for why you think gay marriage will or will not soon be legal nationally.

5. Support your ideas with further evidence from other areas of civil rights.
6. Imagine a point the opposition might make; rebut the opposition's point.
7. Conclude your essay with an appeal to the reader's emotions and sense of morality.

Thinking, Arguing, and Writing Collaboratively

Exchange papers from your Writing a Guided Argument assignment with a classmate. Read the student's paper for the success of the argument. Outline the student's essay, listing his or her major proposition and minor propositions, with an indication of the support the student gives. Write a couple of paragraphs to the student, one praising the positive aspects of the paper and the other explaining what is weak and could be improved. Return the paper and your outline and notes.

Writing About the Text

In an essay, compare Sullivan's argument about gay marriage with Ann Patchett's argument about marriage between first cousins in "Kissing Cousins." How are their arguments similar, and how are they different?

More Writing Ideas

1. Gay marriage issues have filled the news recently with officials in some cities and states issuing marriage licenses and performing ceremonies for gay couples. Check newspaper and magazine articles and write a journal entry about your reactions to these official acts.
2. In 2003 the Supreme Court handed down a landmark decision in *Lawrence v. Texas* that has a bearing on gay marriage. The Court struck down sodomy laws in Texas and other states that made homosexual sex a crime. Write a paragraph summarizing either the Court's majority opinion (striking down the sodomy laws), or the dissent (which was written by the justices who wanted to uphold them). What were their claims?
3. In an essay, defend either the majority decision or the dissenting opinion. Use evidence from the texts to make your case.

Barbara Kantrowitz
Unmarried, with Children

Barbara Kantrowitz was educated at Cornell University and Columbia University. She is married with two children and lives in New York City. She has written for many magazines and newspapers, including The New York Times, The Philadelphia Inquirer, Newsday, Martha Stewart

Living, *and* Newsweek, *where this article appeared in 2001 and where she is now senior editor. In this essay, Kantrowitz discusses the ever-shifting face of the American family, especially the mainstream acceptance of single-parent families.*

Prereading: Thinking About the Essay in Advance

How has the American family changed in the past 20 years? 10 years? 5 years? What was a "traditional" family years ago, and what is a "traditional" family today?

Words to Watch

negotiating (par. 1) dealing with
postmodern (par. 2) contemporary
demographers (par. 3) scientists who study patterns of human populations
stigma (par. 4) part of one's identity that seems shameful
watershed (par. 4) significant
serendipitous (par. 9) chance
futile (par. 14) without effect

Just imagine what would happen if June and Ward Cleaver were negotiating family life these days. The scenario might go something like this: they meet at the office (she's in marketing; he's in sales) and move in together after dating for a couple of months. A year later June gets pregnant. What to do? Neither feels quite ready to make it legal and there's no pressure from their parents, all of whom are divorced and remarried themselves. So little Wally is welcomed into the world with June's last name on the birth certificate. A few years later June gets pregnant again with the Beav. Ward's ambivalent about second-time fatherhood and moves out, but June decides to go ahead on her own. In her neighborhood, after all, single motherhood is no big deal; the lesbians down the street adopted kids from South America, and the soccer mom next door is divorced with a live-in boyfriend. 1

Figures released last week from the 2000 Census show that this postmodern June would be almost as mainstream as the 1950s version. The number of families headed by single mothers has increased 25 percent since 1990, to more than 7.5 million households. Contributing to the numbers are a high rate of divorce and out-of-wedlock births. For most of the past decade, about a third of all babies were born to unmarried women, compared with 3.8 percent in 1940. Demographers now predict that more than half of the youngsters born in the 1990s will spend at least part of their childhood in a single-parent home. The number of single fathers raising kids on their own is also up; they now head just over 2 million families. In contrast, married couples raising children—the "Leave It to Beaver" models—account for less than a quarter of all households. 2

3 Demographers and politicians will likely spend years arguing about all this and whether the shifts are real or just numerical flukes. But one thing everyone does agree on is that single mothers are now a permanent and significant page in America's diverse family album. "We can encourage, pressure, preach, and give incentives to get people to marry," says Stephanie Coontz, author of "The Way We Never Were" and a family historian at the Evergreen State College in Olympia, Wash. "But we still have to deal with the reality that kids are going to be raised in a variety of ways, and we have to support all kinds of families with kids."

4 This new breed of single mother doesn't fit the old stereotype of an unwed teen on welfare. She's still likely to be financially insecure, but she could be any age and any race. The median age for unmarried mothers is the late 20s, and the fastest-growing category is white women. She may be divorced or never-married. Forty percent are living with men who may be the fathers of one or more of their children; as the Census numbers also showed, there's been nearly a 72 percent increase in the number of cohabiting couples, many of whom bring along children from previous relationships. She may also be a single mother by choice. Unwed motherhood has lost much of its stigma and has even been glamorized by celebrity role models like Rosie O'Donnell and Calista Flockhart. "Twenty years ago middle-class women believed it took a man to have a child, but that's no longer true," says Rosanna Hertz, chair of the women's studies department at Wellesley College. "We've reached a watershed moment."

5 More women are better educated and better able to support themselves—so a husband is no longer a financial prerequisite to motherhood. That's a huge social change from the past few decades. Carolyn Feuer, 30, a registered nurse from New York, decided not to marry her boyfriend when she became pregnant with Ryan, now 6. "It wouldn't have been a good marriage," she says. "It's better for both of us this way, especially my son." Her steady salary meant she had choices. "I had an apartment," she says. "I had a car. I felt there was no reason why I shouldn't have the baby. I felt I could give it whatever it needed as far as love and support and I haven't regretted it for even a minute since."

6 For many women, the barrier to marriage may be that they care too much about it, not too little, and they want to get it right. If they can't find the perfect soulmate of their dreams, they'd rather stay single. So they're postponing that walk down the aisle until after college, grad school, or starting a career and putting a little money in the bank. "Paradoxically, more people today value marriage," says Frank Furstenberg, professor of sociology at the University of Pennsylvania. "They take it seriously. That's why they're more likely to cohabit. They want to be sure before they take the ultimate step." The average age of first marriage is now 25 for women and 27 for men—up from 20 and 23 in 1960. That's the highest ever, which leaves plenty of time for a live-in relationship to test a potential partner's compatibility. "Today it's unusual if you don't live with someone before you marry

them," says Andrew Cherlin, a sociologist at Johns Hopkins University. "Before 1970, it wasn't respectable among anyone but the poor."

Some of these women are adult children of divorce who don't want to make their own offspring suffer the pain of watching a parent leave. They see living together as a kind of trial marriage without the legal entanglements that make breaking up so hard to do—although research indicates that cohabiting couples don't have a much better track record. "They're trying to give their marriages a better chance," says Diane Sollee, founder of the Coalition for Marriage, Family, and Couples Education. "They're not trying to be immoral and get away with something." 7

And if the first (or the second) relationship doesn't work out, many women think there's no reason to forgo motherhood. Wellesley researcher Hertz has been studying middle-class single mothers older than 35. Most of the 60 women she has interviewed in-depth became pregnant "accidentally." While their babies may have been unplanned, they were not unwanted. Hertz says that for many of these women, the decision to become a mother was all about the modern version of "settling." In the old days a woman did that by marrying Mr. Almost Right. Now settling means having the baby even if you can't get the husband. "When I started this project in the mid-'90s," Hertz says, "these women were tough to find. Now they're all over—next door, at the playground, in your kid's classroom. They've become a normal part of the terrain." 8

Not all single mothers by choice wait for a serendipitous pregnancy. There are so many options: sperm banks, adoption. New Yorker Gail Janowitz, a market researcher in her mid-40s, decided to adopt two years ago. She always wanted to be a mother, but never married. "As I got older," she says, "I didn't know if the timing of meeting a man was going to work out. I thought, well, I'll do the child part first." A year ago she adopted Rose, now 18 months old, in Kazakhstan. Although there have been difficult moments, Janowitz says she has no regrets. "I've never stopped knowing it was the right thing to do," she says. "I think I will still have the opportunity or the option, hopefully, to get married. But right now, I have a family." 9

Even under the very best of conditions, single motherhood is a long, hard journey for both mother and children. No one really knows the long-term consequences for youngsters who grow up in these new varieties of single-parent and cohabiting homes. Much of the research in the past on alternative living arrangements has concentrated on children of divorce, who face very different issues than youngsters whose mothers have chosen to be single from the start or are cohabiting with their children's fathers or other partners. "We need to start paying attention to how these kids" living in cohabiting homes are doing, says Susan Brown, a sociologist at Bowling Green State University in Ohio. "All the evidence we have suggests that they are not doing too well." 10

Single mothers in general have less time for each individual child than two parents, and cohabiting relationships are less stable than marriages. 11

That means that children living in these families are more likely to grow up with a revolving set of adults in their lives. And the offspring of single parents are more likely to skip the altar themselves, thus perpetuating the pattern of their childhood. "Children living outside marriage are seven times more likely to experience poverty and are 17 times more likely to end up on welfare and to have a propensity for emotional problems, discipline problems, early pregnancy, and abuse," says Robert Rector, a senior research fellow at the Heritage Foundation, a conservative think tank. "It can be a recipe for disaster."

12 The average kid in a single-parent family looks much the same emotionally as children who grow up in the most conflicted two-parent homes, says Larry Bumpass, a sociologist at the University of Wisconsin. But, he adds, "the average is not the script written for every child. The outcomes are not all negative; it's just a matter of relative probability . . . the majority will do just fine." Lyn Freundlich, who is raising two boys in Boston with their father, Billy Brittingham, says her home is as stable as any on the block. Freundlich and Brittingham have no plans to marry even though they've been living together for 13 years. "It's not important to me," says Freundlich, 36, who works for the Boston AIDS Action Committee. "Marriage feels like a really unfair institution where the government validates some relationships and not others. I can't think of any reason compelling enough to become part of an institution I'm uncomfortable with." When she was pregnant with their first son, Jordan, now 6, Brittingham's parents "waged a campaign for us to get married," she says. His father was relieved when they decided to draft a will and sign a medical proxy. These days, the possibility of marriage hardly crosses her mind. "I'm so busy juggling all the details of having a two-career family, taking care of my kids, seeing my friends, and having a role in the community that it's just not something I think about," she says.

13 If Freundlich isn't thinking about marriage, a lot of politicians are—from the White House on down. In a commencement address at Notre Dame on Sunday, President George W. Bush planned to stress the need to strengthen families and assert that "poverty has more to do with troubled lives than a troubled economy," according to an aide. Bush believes funding religious initiatives is one way Washington can foster family stability. Policies to encourage marriage are either in place or under discussion around the country. Some states, such as Arizona and Louisiana, have established "covenant" marriages in which engaged couples are required to get premarital counseling. It's harder to get divorced in these marriages. Utah allows counties to require counseling before issuing marriage licenses to minors and people who have been divorced. Florida now requires high-school students to take marriage-education classes that stress that married people are statistically healthier and wealthier.

Some researchers who study the history of marriage say that such efforts may be futile or even destructive. "Giving incentives or creating pressures for unstable couples to wed can be a huge mistake," says family historian Coontz. "It may create families with high conflict and instability—the worst-case scenario for kids." Other scientists say that lifelong marriage may be an unrealistic goal when humans have life expectancies of 80 or older. In their new book, "The Myth of Monogamy," David Barash and Judith Lipton say that in the natural world, monogamy is rare. And even among humans, it was probably the exception throughout much of human history. In "Georgiana: Duchess of Devonshire," biographer Amanda Foreman details bed-hopping among the 18th-century British aristocracy that would make even a randy Hollywood icon blush. 14

If a long and happy marriage is an elusive goal for couples in any century, most women—even those scarred by divorce—say it's still worth pursuing. When Roberta Lanning, 37, of Woodland Hills, Calif., became pregnant with her fifth child after a bitter divorce, she decided not to marry her boyfriend and raise Christian, now 9, on her own. As a child of divorce herself, she never wanted to raise a family on her own. "Single motherhood is not a good thing," she says. "It's definitely one hurdle after another." And despite everything, she hasn't given up. "It's been my heart's desire to have a father and mother in a structured home situation" for Christian, she says. "It just hasn't happened for me. Believe me, I've certainly been looking." If she finds the right man, chances are he'll probably have a couple of kids of his own by now, too. 15

Building Vocabulary

Explain in your own words the meanings of the following phrases and words. Use clues from the surrounding text to help you understand or use reference texts:

1. soccer mom (par. 1)
2. out-of-wedlock births (par. 2)
3. median age (par. 4)
4. cohabitating couples (par. 4)
5. legal entanglements (par. 7)
6. Mr. Almost Right (par. 8)
7. think tank (par. 11)
8. religious initiatives (par. 13)
9. bed-hopping (par. 14)
10. aristocracy (par. 14)

Thinking Critically About the Argument

Understanding the Writer's Argument

1. June and Ward Cleaver were the parents in the TV series *Leave It to Beaver*, which showed an extremely traditional family in the 1950s. Why would the writer's hypothetical June Cleaver in paragraph 1 be mainstream today?
2. Why are so many families today headed by single moms?
3. Why does Stephanie Coontz say that people need to accept all kinds of families?
4. Who is today's single mother, and how has the profile changed?
5. Why are more and more women choosing to adopt or get artificially inseminated?
6. What are the different opinions the writer presents about the effect of single parenthood on children?
7. Why would conservatives' religious initiatives to foster traditional marriages "be futile or even destructive"? (par. 14)

Understanding the Writer's Techniques

1. What is the writer's claim? Does she place it effectively? If so, explain. If not, where would you put it?
2. What is the argumentative effect of the scenario outlined in paragraph 1?
3. In paragraph 5, the argument shifts. How would you characterize this shift?
4. Outline the minor propositions the writer gives for her claim. Which proposition is most interesting? Is that also the most effective? What is the weakest? What kind of evidence does the writer use to support her minor propositions?
5. What is the effect of the sentences at the beginning of paragraphs 13, 14, and 15 that act as transitions?
6. How effective is the writer's discussion in paragraphs 10 through 12 about how single-parent families affect the lives of children?
7. How does the writer rebut Robert Rector's quote in paragraph 11? Is her technique effective? Explain the effect the final example of Roberta Lanning has on the writer's argument.

Exploring the Writer's Argument

1. The writer of this essay has obviously done a great deal of reporting. She uses several single mothers as examples. Do you find this excessive? Are some of the examples more persuasive than others, and, more important, are they *meant* to be persuasive? If not, what is their purpose? If so, how are they persuasive?
2. Do you find this essay completely coherent? The concept of single motherhood is a wide topic, and the writer does a lot of work to tie everything together, exploring all the different reasons why women

would be single parents or would choose that lifestyle. Where in the essay do you think the discussion becomes too broad?

3. The writer uses many quotes and opinions of other writers and thinkers, but rarely comes out and expresses her own opinions. Examine where in the essay the writer's own ideas stand out. Does she hide behind her research? Explain your answer.

Ideas for Writing Arguments

Prewriting

Are there any examples in your life, or in the lives of your family members or friends, that show that children suffer from divorce? Write a few notes about some of the negative effects of divorce on children.

Writing a Guided Argument

Kantrowitz seems to think that "a long and happy marriage is an elusive goal," but she also says that divorce is usually difficult for everyone involved. Write an essay about how people give up on marriages too readily and why they should seek counseling if they are considering divorce.

1. Open with an example of how divorce can be harmful to everyone involved in a marriage.
2. Indicate that perhaps married couples need to be less hasty in getting divorces.
3. Give at least two grounds for your claim.
4. Use a tone of concerned detachment in your essay.
5. Support your ideas with statistics from Kantrowitz's essay.
6. Give an example of a success story by describing a couple at risk of divorce who sought counseling.
7. Conclude your essay by referring to the divorce rate and explaining why the rate is alarming.

Thinking, Arguing, and Writing Collaboratively

In small groups of three or four, choose two different quotes from single mothers in Kantrowitz's essay. Compare couples the women's approaches to the situation and discuss which you think is the more positive attitude. Present your opinions to the class.

Writing About the Text

Andrew Sullivan's "Let Gays Marry" states that most gay people want the opportunity to marry. Many observers think that gay marriage will soon be a reality: it already is in Canada, and some American cities have provided marriage licenses to gay couples. Write an essay explaining what lessons homosexuals could learn about marriage from Kantrowitz's essay. Argue that gays should still want to get married or that they should avoid the institution.

More Writing Ideas

1. In your journal, freewrite about the topic of adoption. Do not edit your writing. Write nonstop for at least 15 minutes. When you finish, exchange your journal with another student. Do you see any potential major propositions in your classmate's freewriting?
2. Do you think men—or women—are to blame for the high rate of divorce in this country? Write a paragraph defending your position.
3. Write an essay in the form of a letter to one of the experts quoted in Kantrowitz's essay, arguing against their position. Do research on the Web or in the library if necessary to build evidence for your claim.

3 Patterns of Argument

Why do we write essays? We might write to amuse, to excite, to educate, to clarify, to direct, and, of course, we might write to persuade or defend a reasoned position. We might even write because our teachers told us to. No matter what the reason, we write for an audience. Because we will always write for an audience, we have to understand which of these reasons motivate our writing. Once you understand your goals, you can understand how to achieve them.

Each piece of writing requires a different approach, and luckily you have many tools at your disposal. In the Socratic dialogue *Gorgias* by Plato, philosophers debate the meaning of the art of rhetoric—the art of using language effectively. One of the definitions that they uncover is that rhetoric is the art of "manufacturing persuasion." This is an important definition, because it underlines the fact that no matter what kind of writing you do, you are, in some way, making a point. There will always be an aspect of argumentation in every essay you write.

Since Plato's time, writing teachers have studied rhetoric extensively and discovered that there are a number of techniques that all writers of essays use to make their points. These techniques are called rhetorical modes. A writer might recount an experience, explore the meaning of a term or concept, or compare two ideas to underline their similarities or differences. Each of these goals can advance an idea and make a point. These are, again, tools, means for supporting a claim, and not ends in themselves. This chapter shows how various rhetorical modes can help you advance a major proposition and make it persuasive to a reader.

One of the most vivid of the rhetorical modes is narration, or telling a story. The advantages of using narration are fairly obvious: The reader is interested and drawn into the events that are narrated. Also, we usually tell stories in chronological order, so that they are easy to follow. Remember that narration, as with all the rhetorical modes, is not an end in itself. It must support a claim. If you want to persuade your mother that you should go on a trip to Europe, you might tell her the story of a friend who recently went to Europe. In your story, you would highlight the positive aspects about his trip and leave out the fact that he really only partied or that he was mugged in Amsterdam. You are in control of the story, so the details you choose can be persuasive.

Fae Myenne Ng, in her narrative essay "False Gold," tells the story of her father's emigration from China to the United States. She fills her essay with vivid details of her father's miserable experience, making her point about the unearned reputation of America as a promised land for Chinese immigrants. She uses her anecdotes to make a powerful point.

Another useful rhetorical mode is description. Think about how you experience the world. The human body takes in sensations through the eyes, nose, ears, skin, and tongue. Because writing is a way to communicate ideas and feelings to a reader, and because you as a writer want to influence your reader as much as possible, you want to make your reader experience what you want her to experience. (Writers frequently use description when writing narrative. As we will see, the rhetorical modes often are used together.) Joan Didion, in her essay "Marrying Absurd," uses the five senses to comment on the kitchy world of Las Vegas nuptials. The well-placed sensory detail can say more than much abstract writing.

Imagine a friend is telling you about a recent movie that she hated. She is arguing for the poor quality of the film. If she told you simply that the movie was terrible, you would not be convinced. You would demand specific examples of why she didn't like the movie: the lighting was bad, or the acting was weak, or—better yet and more specifically—the lead actor's performance lacked energy. When you are making your case, offering examples—detailed, specific examples—can often mean the difference between a successful argument and an unsuccessful one. Illustration—that is, providing examples—can help bring abstract ideas to life. For instance, Manning Marable offers many examples of injustice against African Americans to make his argument for reparations for slavery stronger. Once again, you will notice some overlapping here: narrative, examples, and description all can interweave to hold the reader's attention.

Comparing or contrasting two points of view or two subjects in an essay can also help support your claim. You can strengthen an argument about proper behavior by standing an exemplar of properness next to someone poorly behaved. In "And Rarely the Twain Shall Meet," Deborah Tannen writes about the differences between how girls and boys approach competition in sports and playtime, and how that difference continues into adulthood. Her juxtaposing of examples and anecdotes of each sex (girls negotiate, boys fight) help make her powerful point.

A writer might choose to make a point by exploring the various facets of a term or phrase. An extended definition of marriage as, say, a prison, can be the basis for examples of henpecked husbands or dissatisfied housewives. As the writer of an essay, it is up to you to define your terms and lead your reader down the path you have set out, especially when readers might misconstrue your chosen concept or if you think it has been misinterpreted. Lorenzo Albacete, in "The Struggle with Celibacy," attempts to clarify the concept of priestly celibacy in the Catholic Church by limning its boundaries. His essay adds up to an extended definition of celibacy that is in service of his central point about the usefulness and significance of the practice.

Process, or writing instructions for an activity, carries with it an implicit argument as well. In "How to Duck Out of Teaching," Douglas Stalker's amusing instructions to professors on how to waste time in the classroom has a pointed message and a claim: Classroom time is something to be wasted, if possible. Stalker's essay, of course, aims for humor, but writers can make serious claims using process. For example, a writer might offer simple instructions on how to keep a bicycle in a city in order to support a proposition that more people in cities *should* travel by bicycle instead of by car.

If a writer explains to her readers the various reasons that she arrived at her point, she is using causal analysis to influence her readers. A writer arguing against the death penalty might explain the events or reasoning that led to her position. In perhaps the most famous causal argument in American history, Thomas Jefferson wrote in the Declaration of Independence the many reasons why the colonies were breaking off from Great Britain. The best feature of causal analysis is that we do it all the time instinctively. Why didn't you do your homework? "The dog ate it" is a causal analysis in service of your claim that your lack of homework wasn't your fault. We live in a causal world, and analyzing the world from that point of view can enrich your arguments.

Readers of essays don't appreciate confusion. They want clear transitions, clear divisions between ideas. Classification, or breaking down an issue or subject into its constituent parts, can help your readers orient themselves conceptually, and therefore classification is a powerful tool rhetorically. An argument that only movie comedies made before 1940 are any good would benefit from a classification of the different types of comedies made before and since, so that your reader understands the topic. Amartya Sen argues in "A World Not Neatly Divided" that we should not classify people and societies. Categories diminish them, he believes. But he has a difficult task in his argument because classification helps people understand their world. It can help them understand your argument better, as well.

Of course, as suggested earlier, these rhetorical modes are not mutually exclusive. Writers often use them in conjunction to make a strong case. Ronald Takaki, in "The Harmful Myth of Asian Superiority," uses illustration to make his point against seeing Asians as a model minority. He breaks down the large group, Asians, into various nationalities, thus using classification. He also engages causal analysis and extended definition. In your reading and in your writing, pay attention to the use of these various tools and how they can work together effectively.

In truth, in almost every essay you write you are making an argument, whether you want to or not. If you are mindful of the techniques available to you, your arguments will be stronger and your language more effective. You will be, as Plato says, "manufacturing persuasion."

Argument Through Narrative

FAE MYENNE NG
False Gold

Fae Myenne Ng, a first-generation Chinese-American, was born in 1957 and grew up in San Francisco's Chinatown. Her father was a cook for a University of California at Berkeley fraternity house, her mother a seamstress. After graduating from Berkeley, Ng went East and received a Master's degree from Columbia University in 1984. Not long after, she moved to Brooklyn, where she continued to work on her first novel, Bone. *The book is the story of a first-generation Chinese-American family and their trials and tribulations.* Bone *earned Ng many awards and honors. Much of Ng's work is autobiographical, and she uses narrative techniques to advance her main ideas and claims. She says that her primary goal is to "write about true life."*

Prereading: Thinking About the Essay in Advance

Where were your ancestors born? Have you heard their stories, either directly or through stories others have told? What lessons can you learn from their experiences? Think about whether the people who told you their stories were trying to teach you a lesson.

Words to Watch

ancestor (par. 1) forefather
duped (par. 1) fooled
communal (par. 4) shared
brothel (par. 7) where prostitutes work
indentured (par. 8) forced to work

1 It's that same old, same old story. We all have an immigrant ancestor, one who believed in America; one who, daring or duped, took sail. The Golden Venture emigrants have begun the American journey, suffering and sacrificing, searching for the richer, easier life. I know them; I could be one of their daughters. Like them, my father took the sacrificial role of being the first to venture. Now, at the end of his life, he calls it a bitter, no-luck life. I have always lived with his question, Was it worth it? As a child, I saw the bill-by-bill payback and I felt my own unpayable emotional debt. Obedience and Obligation: the Confucian curse.

2 For $4,000 my father became the fourth son of a legal Chinese immigrant living in San Francisco. His paper-father sent him a coaching book, detailing complicated family history. It was 1940; my father paid ninety more dollars for passage on the SS *Coolidge*. He had little hand luggage, a change of clothes, herbs and seeds and a powder for soup. To soothe his pounding

heart during the fifteen-day voyage he recited the coaching book over and over again. It was not a floating hell. "The food was Chinese. We traveled third-class. A bunk was good enough space." He was prepared for worse. He'd heard about the Peruvian ships that transported Chinese coolies for plantation labor in the 1850s. (Every generation has its model.) One hundred and twenty days. Two feet by six for each man. Were these the first ships to be called floating hells?

Gold Mountain was the name of my father's America. In February, when 3 the Golden Venture immigrants sailed from Bangkok, they were shouting, Mei Guo! Mei Guo! "Beautiful Country" was the translation they preferred. America is the land of light and hope. But landing here is only the beginning of a long tale. When I saw the photos of the shipwrecked Chinese on the beach, I was reminded of the men kept on Angel Island, the detention center in the middle of San Francisco Bay. A sea of hats on the deck of the ship. Triple-decked bunkers. Men in loose pants playing volleyball. "Was volleyball fun?" I wanted to know. My father shrugged, "Nothing else to do. It helped pass the day." Our fathers spent months detained on Angel Island. Their name for it was Wooden House. What, I wonder, are the Chinese calling the detention center in Bethlehem, Pennsylvania?

After his release from Angel Island, my father lived at a bachelor hotel 4 on Waverly Place with a dozen other bachelors in one room, communal toilets, no kitchen. He had breakfast at Uncle's Cafe, dinners at the Jackson Cafe, midnight noodles at Sam Wo's. Drinks at the Li Po Bar or Red's Place, where fat burlesque queens sat on his lap. Marriage for duty. Sons for tradition. My father left the hotel but kept the habits. He still eats like a mouse, in the middle of the night, cooking on a hot plate in his room. (I do my version of the same.) He keeps his money under the floorboard. When I have it, I like to have a grip, bill by bill. Like everyone, too little money upsets me; but more money than I can hold upsets me too. I feel obliged to give it away. Is it a wonder that money has a dirty feel? Get it and get it fast. Then get rid of it.

I remember this Angel Island photograph. Thirty bare-chested Chinese 5 men are waiting for a medical examination. The doctor, a hunching man with a scraping stare, sits at a small desk, elbows and thick hands over a black book. At his side, a guard in knee-high boots measures a boy's forehead. Arranged by height, baby-eyed boys stand stoop-shouldered on the outer edge. The men, at least a head taller, stand toward the center of the room, staring at the examiner. Those eyes scare me. Bold and angry and revengeful. Eyes that owe. Eyes that will make you pay. Humiliation with a vengeance.

As boldly, the Golden Venture men have looked into American cameras. 6 (If they believed a foot on soil would make them legal, a photo in an American newspaper would be as good as a passport.) There was a "See me!" bounce in their faces. They'd arrived, and now they wanted to send their news back home. And back home, a grateful father jumped when he picked out his son as one of the survivors, "He's alive! My son made it."

7 Another photo. A Golden Venture man looks out from a locked door, his face framed by a tight window. He has a jail-view of the Beautiful Country. How would he describe his new world? I imagine he'd use his own body as a measure. "Window, two head high. Sun on both ears." Can we forget the other "face" photograph taken earlier this century? The sold and smuggled prostitute, demoted from brothel to a crib, a wooden shack with barred windows that barely fits a cot. Looking out from her fenced window, she has the same downcast eyes, the same bitter-strange lips that seem to be smiling as well as trembling. The caption quotes her price: "Lookee two bits, feelee floor bits, doee six bits."

8 Life was and still is weighed in gold. People buy people. Sons and wives and slaves. There was the imperial edict that forbade Chinese to leave China; there was China's contribution to France during World War I, in which tens of thousands of Chinese lived horrible lives as indentured slaves. I've heard parents threaten to sell children who misbehave. (Mine threatened to throw me into the garbage can where they claimed they found me.) There's the story of Old Man Jeong, the one on Beckett Alley. Lonely after his wife died, fearful no one would care for him in his senile retirement, he went back to his home village and bought himself a wife. A woman born in 1956.

9 Listen to the animal names. Snakes sneak into America. The Golden Venture was a snake ship. The emigrants are snake cargo; the middleman, a snakehead. In my father's time, a pig was sold to America. A pig gets caught, a pig gets cheated. My father feels cheated, sold, on an easy story.

10 On a recent visit to my father's house in Guangzhou, I found his original coaching book. I knew it had been untouched since he last held it. In my hand, the loosely bound papers felt like ashes. I thought about how when he committed everything to memory, he became another man's son. There's an elaborate map of the family compound; each page is lined with questions and answers, some marked with red circles. Tedious questions and absurd details. How much money did Second Brother send to Mother? How much farmland did Mother have and what vegetables were harvested? Third Brother's wife's feet, were they big or bound? The book has a musty smell that reaches into my throat.

11 One out of every four relations let me know they wanted to come to America. At the end of my visit, a distant relation and her 13-year-old daughter followed me into the rice paddies. "I'm selling her," the mother told me.

12 "What did you say? Say again?" I replied.

13 She held a palm over her (golden) lower teeth, and said it again, "Don't know what I'm saying? Sell. We sell her."

14 I stared at her. She laughed some more and then just walked away, back toward the village. The girl followed me, quiet till we got to the river, where she posed for some pictures and then asked for my address. I wrote it on the back of a business card. (I considered giving her my post office box.) I hope never to be surprised. I hope never to see this child at my door holding the card like a legal document.

"Don't add and don't take away" was the advice of an uncle who heard that I wrote things. Stay safe. Keep us safe. How right that "China" is written with the character "middle." Obedience is a safe position. The Golden Venture men trusted the stories they heard. Their clansmen entrusted their dreams to them. The question is not how bad it is in China. The question is how good it can be in America. My father believes the Golden Venturers have only passed through the first hell. In coming to America, he laments (there is no other word) that he trusted too much. Ironic that in Chinese he bought a name that reads, To Have Trust. 15

Building Vocabulary

Ng's essay contains words about the Asian immigrant experience you might not be familiar with. Identify the following, consulting reference works if necessary:

1. Confucian (par. 1)
2. coolies (par. 2)
3. Bangkok (par. 3)
4. burlesque (par. 4)
5. Guangzhou (par. 10)
6. rice paddies (par. 11)

Thinking Critically About the Argument

Understanding the Writer's Argument

1. Why does Ng call the selection "False Gold"?
2. Why did Ng's father leave China? Why did he come to the United States?
3. In paragraph 1, what is the "bill-by-bill payback" Ng refers to? What does she mean by an "unpayable emotional debt"?
4. How is "Obedience and Obligation" the "Confucian curse"? What does that phrase mean?
5. What is the Golden Venture? What prompts Ng's trip back to China? Why would she make the opposite trip her father made years before?
6. In paragraph 2, what is the "coaching book" her father received?
7. Why does Ng give the 13-year-old girl her address on the back of a business card if she hopes she is never surprised by her presence?
8. What did Ng's father mean that "he trusted too much"? (par. 15)

Understanding the Writer's Techniques

1. What is the essay's claim? If there isn't one, what paragraph tells the reader what Ng's main idea is most clearly? Which sentence in that paragraph best states the main proposition?
2. Ng begins her essay by claiming that the story of her father's experience is typical, that it is "that same old, same old story." Why does she do this, and do you think she is right?

3. A narrative essay uses description to bring to life certain events. What images in Ng's essay do you find most effective?
4. Why does Ng include, in paragraphs 5 and 7, descriptions of photographs that she has seen?
5. What is your opinion of the conclusion of Ng's essay? What does it say about Ng as a writer? As a daughter? As an Asian American? As an American?

Exploring the Writer's Argument

1. Ng never tells us the conditions of the Golden Venture immigrants back in China. She writes, "The question is not how bad it is in China. The question is how good it can be in America." Why doesn't she explore the problems back in China?
2. Ng seems to suggest that the promises given to her father and other Golden Venture immigrants like him were wrong. Do you think they were? Why or why not?
3. Do you find Ng's essay too bitter about her father's experience? Do you think her bitterness is warranted? Why or why not?
4. In paragraph 15, Ng writes that "the Golden Venture men trusted the stories they heard." She seems to suggest that they believed in those stories because they were Chinese. What do you think it is about your ethnic background that made your ancestors come to the United States?

Ideas for Writing Arguments

Prewriting

What prompts people to leave their country? What would force you to leave your country and go elsewhere? How would you choose where to go?

Writing a Guided Argument

Write a narrative essay in which you imagine the experience of your ancestors or family members who came to the United States. What prompted them to come, and what was their experience? Make sure that you, like Ng, have a claim, positive or negative, about the United States.

1. Begin your essay by giving some background about your ancestors. Who were they, and where did they come from? Why did they want to leave? Write your thesis statement at the end of the first paragraph.
2. First, tell the story of your ancestor's trip to this country.
3. Try to use vivid description to bring the story to life, even if it means inventing details to make it more dramatic.
4. Then write a narrative about how your ancestor came to the decision to leave.
5. Finally, write about the ancestor's experience in this country.
6. End your essay by commenting on the stories you presented. What is your opinion? Restate the claim in new words, and then bring the discussion around to you and your experience of the United States.

Thinking, Arguing, and Writing Collaboratively

Exchange drafts of your Writing a Guided Argument essay with another student in the class. Analyze your fellow student's essay for effective use of detail and description. Does the narrative serve the purpose of a main idea or proposition, or is it there merely as a narrative? If there is no claim, suggest one, and work together to come up with an acceptable one. If there is a claim, try to improve it together. Also, take out unnecessary details and events that do not serve the main idea.

Writing About the Text

Ng's style in this essay is distinctive. How would you characterize her style of writing? How does she use language to express the main idea of the essay? Write an essay about Ng's use of language, including her use of fragments and choppy sentences.

More Writing Ideas

1. We are not today immigrating to the United States, but all of us have a dream that can count as "false gold." Write a journal entry about what your personal "false gold" is.
2. In a paragraph, analyze a photograph of older family members. What does the photograph tell you about the people in it. Only say what you can figure out from what you see.
3. Ng is writing about a phenomenon that many others have written about: the United States being perceived as the promised land by immigrants. Write an essay in which you argue that the United States does or does not live up to these expectations.

Argument Through Description

JOAN DIDION
Marrying Absurd

Joan Didion was born in 1934 in Sacramento, California. Her family has been in California for five generations, and she often writes about the state. She began her writing career when she won an essay contest sponsored by Vogue *magazine, which then hired her. Her first book, a novel called* Run River, *was published in 1963. She has written a number of other novels, but she is best known for her books of collected essays including* Slouching Toward Bethlehem *(1968) and* The White Album *(1979). Her writing is distinguished by her vividness of description and accurate dialogue.*

Prereading: Thinking About the Essay in Advance

What does "absurd" mean? Under what circumstances might marrying be considered "absurd"? This essay is about marriage in Las Vegas. How does that change your answer?

Words to Watch

moonscape (par. 1) a landscape marked by terrain that looks like the surface of the moon
mesquite (par. 1) a tree that grows in the desert
en masse (par. 1) as a whole, all together
allegorical (par. 2) symbolical
implausibility (par. 2) unbelievability
nosegay (par. 4) bouquet of flowers
Panglossian (par. 5) excessively optimistic

1 To be married in Las Vegas, Clark County, Nevada, a bride must swear that she is eighteen or has parental permission and a bridegroom that he is twenty-one or has parental permission. Someone must put up five dollars for the license. (On Sundays and holidays, fifteen dollars. The Clark County Courthouse issues marriage licenses at any time of the day or night except between noon and one in the afternoon, between eight and nine in the evening, and between four and five in the morning.) Nothing else is required. The State of Nevada, alone among these United States, demands neither a premarital blood test nor a waiting period before or after the issuance of a marriage license. Driving in across the Mojave from Los Angeles, one sees the signs way out on the desert, looming up from that moonscape of rattle-snakes and mesquite, even before the Las Vegas lights appear like a mirage on the horizon: "GETTING MARRIED? Free License Information First Strip Exit." Perhaps the Las Vegas wedding industry achieved its peak operational efficiency between 9:00 p.m. and midnight of August 26, 1965, an otherwise unremarkable Thursday which happened to be, by Presidential order, the last day on which anyone could improve his draft status merely by getting married. One hundred and seventy-one couples were pronounced man and wife in the name of Clark County and the State of Nevada that night, sixty-seven of them by a single justice of the peace, Mr. James A. Brennan. Mr. Brennan did one wedding at the Dunes and the other sixty-six in his office, and charged each couple eight dollars. One bride lent her veil to six others. "I got it down from five to three minutes," Mr. Brennan said later of his feat. "I could've married them *en masse*, but they're people, not cattle. People expect more when they get married."

2 What people who get married in Las Vegas actually do expect—what, in the largest sense, their "expectations" are—strikes one as a curious and self-contradictory business. Las Vegas is the most extreme and allegorical of American settlements, bizarre and beautiful in its venality and in its devotion to immediate gratification, a place the tone of which is set by mobsters and call girls and ladies' room attendants with amyl nitrate poppers in their uni-

form pockets. Almost everyone notes that there is no "time" in Las Vegas, no night and no day and no past and no future (no Las Vegas casino, however, has taken the obliteration of the ordinary time sense quite so far as Harold's Club in Reno, which for a while issued, at odd intervals in the day and night, mimeographed "bulletins" carrying news from the world outside); neither is there any logical sense of where one is. One is standing on a highway in the middle of a vast hostile desert looking at an eighty-foot sign which blinks "STARDUST" or "CAESAR'S PALACE." Yes, but what does that explain? This geographical implausibility reinforces the sense that what happens there has no connection with "real" life; Nevada cities like Reno and Carson are ranch towns, Western towns, places behind which there is some historical imperative. But Las Vegas seems to exist only in the eye of the beholder. All of which makes it an extraordinarily stimulating and interesting place, but an odd one in which to want to wear a candlelight satin Priscilla of Boston wedding dress with Chantilly lace insets, tapered sleeves and a detachable modified train.

And yet the Las Vegas wedding business seems to appeal to precisely that impulse. "Sincere and Dignified Since 1954," one wedding chapel advertises. There are nineteen such wedding chapels in Las Vegas, intensely competitive, each offering better, faster, and, by implication, more sincere services than the next: Our Photos Best Anywhere, Your Wedding on A Phonograph Record, Candlelight with Your Ceremony, Honeymoon Accommodations, Free Transportation from Your Motel to Courthouse to Chapel and Return to Motel, Religious or Civil Ceremonies, Dressing Rooms, Flowers, Rings, Announcements, Witnesses Available, and Ample Parking. All of these services, like most others in Las Vegas (sauna baths, payroll-check cashing, chinchilla coats for sale or rent) are offered twenty-four hours a day, seven days a week, presumably on the premise that marriage, like craps, is a game to be played when the table seems hot. 3

But what strikes one most about the Strip chapels, with their wishing wells and stained-glass paper windows and their artificial bouvardia, is that so much of their business is by no means a matter of simple convenience, of late-night liaisons between show girls and baby Crosbys. Of course there is some of that. (One night about eleven o'clock in Las Vegas I watched a bride in an orange minidress and masses of flame-colored hair stumble from a Strip chapel on the arm of her bridegroom, who looked the part of the expendable nephew in movies like *Miami Syndicate*. "I gotta get the kids," the bride whimpered. "I gotta pick up the sitter, I gotta get to the midnight show." "What you gotta get," the bridegroom said, opening the door of a Cadillac Coupe de Ville and watching her crumple on the seat, "is sober.") But Las Vegas seems to offer something other than "convenience"; it is merchandising "niceness," the facsimile of proper ritual, to children who do not know how else to find it, how to make the arrangements, how to do it "right." All day and evening long on the Strip, one sees actual wedding parties, waiting under the harsh lights at a crosswalk, standing uneasily in the parking lot of the Frontier while the photographer hired by The Little 4

Church of the West ("Wedding Place of the Stars") certifies the occasion, takes the picture: the bride in a veil and white satin pumps, the bridegroom usually in a white dinner jacket, and even an attendant or two, a sister or a best friend in hot-pink *peau de soie*, a flirtation veil, a carnation nosegay. "When I Fall in Love It Will Be Forever," the organist plays, and then a few bars of Lohengrin. The mother cries; the stepfather, awkward in his role, invites the chapel hostess to join them for a drink at the Sands. The hostess declines with a professional smile; she has already transferred her interest to the group waiting outside. One bride out, another in, and again the sign goes up on the chapel door: "One moment please—Wedding."

5 I sat next to one such wedding party in a Strip restaurant the last time I was in Las Vegas. The marriage had just taken place; the bride still wore her dress, the mother her corsage. A bored waiter poured out a few swallows of pink champagne ("on the house") for everyone but the bride, who was too young to be served. "You'll need something with more kick than that," the bride's father said with heavy jocularity to his new son-in-law; the ritual jokes about the wedding night had a certain Panglossian character, since the bride was clearly several months pregnant. Another round of pink champagne, this time not on the house, and the bride began to cry. "It was just as nice," she sobbed, "as I hoped and dreamed it would be."

Building Vocabulary

1. Define the following words and use each in a sentence of your own:
   a. mirage (par. 1)
   b. liaisons (par. 4)
   c. expendable (par. 4)
   d. crumple (par. 4)
   e. corsage (par. 5)
2. Didion makes several references that might be unfamiliar, some because they are obsolete. Identify the following:
   a. justice of the peace (par. 1)
   b. amyl nitrate poppers (par. 2)
   c. mimeographed (par. 2)
   d. phonograph (par. 3)
   e. chinchilla coats (par. 3)
   f. craps (par. 3)
   g. dinner jacket (par. 4)

Thinking Critically About the Argument

Understanding the Writer's Argument

1. Nevada doesn't require a blood test for marriage. Why would other states require one?
2. In paragraph 1, Didion refers to a draft and states that 171 couples were married the last day that marriage would improve one's draft status. What draft is she referring to, and why does she include this information?

3. What is Didion's characterization of Las Vegas? What words does she use that help build that image?
4. How is Las Vegas different from other places, according to Didion?
5. Why are people who want to get married attracted to Las Vegas, besides the lack of a blood-test requirement?
6. What kinds of people typically get married in Las Vegas, according to Didion?
7. In what ways is Las Vegas "odd" (par. 2)? What examples does she give?

Understanding the Writer's Techniques

1. Didion places her claim, or main proposition, about halfway through the essay. What is the claim, and is the entire meaning of the essay expressed in only one sentence?
2. Why does Didion begin her essay with a rundown of the rules for getting married in Las Vegas?
3. What warrants are implied here? How does the reader "learn" to read this essay as he or she moves through it?
4. What points does Didion make to support her central proposition?
5. Who is Didion's ideal audience? What is Didion's tone, and how does she tailor it for her audience?
6. Didion relies on vivid description to help make her points. Why, for example, does she include the description of the bride in the "orange minidress" in paragraph 4? What effect does the description have on the reader?
7. What other images or descriptions are most effective in Didion's argument?
8. Why does Didion end the essay with the pregnant bride crying for joy?

Exploring the Writer's Argument

1. Didion's writing is often considered ironic. Do you think there is too much irony here? Why or why not?
2. Didion's extensive use of description can be quite effective, but sometimes it is possible to push her point too far. Are there any moments where you think Didion's description goes too far?
3. Are there moments when Didion does not use enough description? What would you add?
4. Didion has an argument here, but she only overtly judges her subject in the title by calling the things she is describing "absurd." Where in the essay does Didion stray from subtlety into open judgment?

Ideas for Writing Arguments

Prewriting

Take a good look at the place where you live. What is it about your town or city that might seem odd to an outsider? Do a guided freewrite on the topic, traveling in your mind through your city as a tourist.

Writing a Guided Argument

Write an essay called " . . . Absurd" and choose some aspect about where you live that seems strange when you look at it too closely, such as commuting, exercising, or living in small apartments or in large mansions.

1. Begin your essay by describing people in the process of performing your subject, and show—don't tell—how it is absurd.
2. Finish your introduction by explaining to your reader what your major proposition is.
3. Explain and then describe what people expect from performing your subject.
4. Describe what it is about your town that makes people do your subject.
5. Explain one aspect of your subject that is absurd.
6. Describe the first aspect by giving details based on images, sounds, smells, and your other senses.
7. Explain another aspect of your subject that is absurd, and bring the explanation to life with a strong description.
8. Finish your essay by highlighting the most absurd quality of your subject, and describe people in the process of going about their lives doing that action without realizing that they are being absurd.

Thinking, Arguing, and Writing Collaboratively

In groups of four or five, discuss ways to defend the subjects of Didion's essay from her charges of absurdity. How are the people she describes and quotes just being themselves and enjoying themselves? Come up with a rebuttal to Didion's strong argument.

Writing About the Text

Didion seems to be intensely dissatisfied and judgmental about how people come together in Las Vegas. She allows people like the justice of the peace, James Brennan, to say things she obviously thinks are silly, as in paragraph 1, when she quotes him as saying, "I could've married them *en masse*, but they're people, not cattle." She is obviously speaking ironically. How could you satisfy Didion? What does she want? What would she like to see change in Las Vegas? Write an essay in which you explore ways of reforming the marriage industry in Las Vegas, explaining what you think Didion's objections are and addressing them one by one.

More Writing Ideas

1. Write a journal entry about a place you've been that has seemed absurd to you. Why did it seem so absurd?
2. Write a paragraph describing a wedding or other ceremony you have been to. Describe the food, the sights, the sounds.
3. Some people now question the notion of marriage as an antiquated idea. Almost half of all marriages end in divorce. Write an essay in which you argue for or against marriage. Use strong descriptive passages to show marital bliss or discord.

Argument Through Illustration

MANNING MARABLE
An Idea Whose Time Has Come

Manning Marable is a professor of history and political science at Columbia University, where he is also the director of both the Institute for Research in African-American Studies and the Center for Contemporary Black History. Among his works are The Crisis of Color and Democracy *(1992),* Beyond Black and White *(1995), and* Black Leadership *(1998). He is also the editor of the anthology* Freedom on My Mind *(2003). This essay was published in* Newsweek *in 2001.*

Prereading: Thinking About the Essay in Advance

What is your responsibility for the crimes committed by or against your ancestors? Do you have any responsibility? If so, what is that responsibility, and if not, why not?

Words to Watch

fundamental (par. 2) basic
coded (par. 2) deeply ingrained
paradoxically (par. 4) in a way that is self-contradictory
disproportionate (par. 5) vastly unequal
reparations (par. 6) payments for damages

In 1854 my great-grandfather, Morris Marable, was sold on an auction block in Georgia for $500. For his white slave master, the sale was just "business as usual." But to Morris Marable and his heirs, slavery was a crime against our humanity. This pattern of human-rights violations against enslaved African-Americans continued under Jim Crow segregation for nearly another century. 1

The fundamental problem of American democracy in the 21st century is the problem of "structural racism": the deep patterns of socioeconomic inequality and accumulated disadvantage that are coded by race, and constantly justified in public discourse by both racist stereotypes and white indifference. Do Americans have the capacity and vision to dismantle these structural barriers that deny democratic rights and opportunities to millions of their fellow citizens? 2

This country has previously witnessed two great struggles to achieve a truly multicultural democracy. The First Reconstruction (1865–1877) ended slavery and briefly gave black men voting rights, but gave no meaningful compensation for two centuries of unpaid labor. The promise of "40 acres and a mule" was for most blacks a dream deferred. 3

The Second Reconstruction (1954–1968), or the modern civil-rights movement, outlawed legal segregation in public accommodations and gave 4 blacks voting rights. But these successes paradoxically obscure the tremendous human costs of historically accumulated disadvantage that remain central to black Americans' lives.

5 The disproportionate wealth that most whites enjoy today was first constructed from centuries of unpaid black labor. Many white institutions, including Ivy League universities, insurance companies, and banks, profited from slavery. This pattern of white privilege and black inequality continues today.

6 Demanding reparations is not just about compensation for slavery and segregation. It is, more important, an educational campaign to highlight the contemporary reality of "racial deficits" of all kinds, the unequal conditions that impact blacks regardless of class. Structural racism's barriers include "equity inequity," the absence of black capital formation that is a direct consequence of America's history. One third of all black households actually have negative net wealth. In 1998 the typical black family's net wealth was $16,400, less than one fifth that of white families. Black families are denied home loans at twice the rate of whites.

7 Blacks remain the last hired and first fired during recessions. During the 1990–1991 recession, African-Americans suffered disproportionately. At Coca-Cola, 42 percent of employees who lost their jobs were black. At Sears, 54 percent were black. Blacks have significantly shorter life expectancies, in part due to racism in the health establishment. Blacks are statistically less likely than whites to be referred for kidney transplants or early-stage cancer surgery.

8 In criminal justice, African-Americans constitute only one seventh of all drug users. Yet we account for 35 percent of all drug arrests, 55 percent of drug convictions and 75 percent of prison admissions for drug offenses.

9 White Americans today aren't guilty of carrying out slavery and segregation. But whites have a moral and political responsibility to acknowledge the continuing burden of history's structural racism.

10 A reparations trust fund could be established, with the goal of closing the socioeconomic gaps between blacks and whites. Funds would be targeted specifically toward poor, disadvantaged communities with the greatest need, not to individuals.

11 Let's eliminate the racial unfairness in capital markets that perpetuates black poverty. A national commitment to expand black homeownership, full employment, and quality health care would benefit all Americans, regardless of race.

12 Reparations could begin America's Third Reconstruction, the final chapter in the 400-year struggle to abolish slavery and its destructive consequences. As Malcolm X said in 1961, hundreds of years of racism and labor exploitation are "worth more than a cup of coffee at a white cafe. We are here to collect back wages."

Building Vocabulary

Identify the following terms and references related to the history of slavery in America. (*Hint:* Item 4 comes from a famous poem):

1. auction block (par. 1)
2. Jim Crow (par. 1)
3. 40 acres and a mule (par. 3)
4. a dream deferred (par. 3)
5. voting rights (par. 4)
6. Malcolm X (par. 12)

Thinking Critically About the Argument

Understanding the Writer's Argument

1. Why does Marable begin with his great-grandfather being sold as a slave?
2. Marable says in paragraphs 1 and 2 that the sale of his great-grandfather was part of a pattern. What does this pattern consist of?
3. What, in your own words, is "structural racism"? (par. 2)
4. According to Marable, what did the first reconstruction achieve? What did the second achieve?
5. What did both reconstructions fail to achieve?
6. Why, according to Marable, do white people have more wealth than black people, on average?
7. In what form does Marable expect reparations to come?
8. What are the major problems in the black community?
9. Why does Marable quote Malcolm X at the end of his essay?

Understanding the Writer's Techniques

1. What is the main proposition in this essay? Is it in an effective place? Explain.
2. Who is Marable's audience? How would you characterize his tone?
3. Why does Marable include the history lesson in the first part of his essay? Is it effective? Why or why not?
4. How does Marable support his argument?
5. What examples does Marable use to support his claim?
6. What kinds of support does he use? Is it effective? Why or why not?
7. How does Marable develop his conclusion?

Exploring the Writer's Argument

1. Why, according to Marable, has progress been so slow toward getting rid of "equity inequality"? Is his explanation satisfying? Why or why not?
2. Does Marable do a good job of connecting the statistics in paragraphs 6 through 8 to the history of "structural racism"? Why or why not?

3. In paragraph 9, Marable writes that "whites have a moral and political responsibility to acknowledge the continuing burden of history's structural racism." Do you agree? Why or why not?
4. If, as Marable says, "white Americans today aren't guilty of carrying out slavery and segregation," why are whites responsible for granting reparations?
5. Marable calls for funds "targeted specifically toward poor, disadvantaged communities with the greatest need, not to individuals." Does the United States have anything like this today? Why doesn't Marable talk about existing programs?
6. Marable writes in paragraph 11 that "a national commitment to expand black homeownership, full employment, and quality health care would benefit all Americans, regardless of race." What does he mean? How do you think that could happen?

Ideas for Writing Arguments

Prewriting

Black slavery was a terrible crime and a monumental event of the early history of our country. There's a museum for the Holocaust in Washington, D.C., and memorials for the Vietnam, Korean, and World Wars, but there is neither a museum nor a memorial to the victims of slavery. Why do you think this is so?

Writing a Guided Argument

Write an essay arguing for a museum, in Washington, D.C., or some other city in the United States, which focuses on the history of slavery. Refer to Marable's essay at least twice in your essay.

1. Begin by illustrating the horror of American slavery with a striking story or fact.
2. Make your central claim in your introduction.
3. Offer examples of how tragedies and events have their own museums and question why slavery does not.
4. Give examples of what those museums do to educate the public.
5. Point out at least three things a museum could accomplish for the history of slavery and offer vivid examples of how you envision that happening.
6. Use at least one statistic in your essay.
7. Explain how a museum might accomplish some of what Marable wants to accomplish with reparations.

Thinking, Arguing, and Writing Collaboratively

Break into small groups and exchange drafts of your Writing a Guided Argument essay. Write comments on each other's papers, focusing specifically on the success of the use of examples in the essays. How can the writer's examples be more effective?

Writing About the Text

Often, for effect, a writer will use phrases and words that he or she knows the reader will recognize. Marable uses allusions or references to a number of people and phrases important in black history. Research these allusions and write an essay explaining them.

More Writing Ideas

1. If you were responsible for distributing reparations, how would you go about it? Write a journal entry addressing this problem.
2. At the end of his essay, Marable quotes Malcolm X on the subject of reparations. Malcolm X often differed with Martin Luther King Jr. on issues of civil rights. Do some research and write a paragraph or two on what Dr. King said or would say about reparations.
3. Write an essay exploring Marable's idea in paragraph 6 that a reparations program could be an "educational campaign." What does he mean? Explore how you think this might work or not work.

Argument Through Comparison and Contrast

DEBORAH TANNEN
And Rarely the Twain Shall Meet

Deborah Tannen is a professor of linguistics at Georgetown University. She has also taught at Princeton University. Her work specializes in linguistic differences between genders. She has written many books on the subject, including You Just Don't Understand: Women and Men in Conversation *(1991) and* Gender and Discourse *(1994). She has also published poetry, short stories, and essays, and has written plays. In this selection, Tannen displays her expertise in analyzing the differences between how boys and girls play sports and how those differences extend into adulthood.*

Prereading: Thinking About the Essay in Advance

What do you think are the differences between how men and women approach competition? Do they approach work differently? How?

Words to Watch

authoritarian (par. 6) overbearing
linguist (par. 6) one who studies language
compromising (par. 15) giving up something for something else
beseeching (par. 16) pleading
adamant (par. 18) firm, unmoving
trump card (par. 23) winning hand in many card games
perspective (par. 24) point of view

1 Bob Hoover of the Pittsburgh Post-Gazette was interviewing me when he remarked that after years of coaching boys' softball teams, he was now coaching girls and they were very different. I immediately whipped out my yellow pad and began interviewing him—and discovered that his observations about how girls and boys play softball parallel mine about how women and men talk at work.

2 Hoover told me that boys' teams always had one or two stars whom the other boys treated with deference. So when he started coaching a girl's team, he began by looking for the leader. He couldn't find one. "The girls who are better athletes don't lord it over the others," he says. "You get the feeling that everyone's the same." When a girl gets the ball, she doesn't try to throw it all the way home as a strong-armed boy would; instead, she throws it to another team member, so they all become better catchers and throwers. He goes on, "If a girl makes an error, she's not in the doghouse for a long time, as a boy would be."

3 "But wait," I interrupt. "I've heard that when girls make a mistake at sports, they often say 'I'm sorry,' whereas boys don't."

4 That's true, he says, but then the girl forgets it—and so do her teammates. "For boys, sports is a performance art. They're concerned with how they look." When they make an error, they sulk because they've let their teammates down. Girls want to win, but if they lose, they're still all in it together—so the mistake isn't as dreadful for the individual or the team.

5 What Hoover describes in these youngsters are the seeds of behavior I have observed among women and men at work.

6 The girls who are the best athletes don't "lord it over" the others—just the ethic I have found among women in positions of authority. Women managers frequently tell me they are good managers because they do not act in an authoritarian manner. They say they do not flaunt their power, or behave as though they are better than their subordinates. Similarly, linguist Elisabeth Kuhn has found that women professors in her study inform students of course requirements as if they had magically appeared on the syllabus ("There are two papers. The first paper, ah, let's see, is due . . . It's back here [referring to the syllabus] at the beginning"), whereas the men professors make it clear that they set the requirements ("I have two midterms and a final"). A woman manager might say to her secretary, "Could you do me a favor and type this letter right away?" knowing that her secretary is going to type the letter. But her male boss, on hearing this, might conclude she doesn't feel she deserves the authority she has, just as a boys' coach might think the star athlete doesn't realize how good he is if he doesn't expect his teammates to treat him with deference.

7 I was especially delighted by Hoover's observation that, although girls are more likely to say, "I'm sorry," they are actually far less sorry when they make a mistake than boys who don't say it, but are "in the doghouse" for a long time. This dramatizes the ritual nature of many women's apologies. How often is a woman who is "always apologizing" seen as weak and lacking in confidence? In fact, for many women, saying "I'm sorry" often doesn't

mean "I apologize." It means "I'm sorry that happened." Like many of the rituals common among women, it's a way of speaking that takes into account the other person's point of view. It can even be an automatic conversational smoother. For example, you leave your pad in someone's office; you knock on the door and say, "Excuse me, I left my pad on your desk," and the person whose office it is might reply, "Oh, I'm sorry. Here it is." She knows it is not her fault that you left your pad on her desk; she's just letting you know it's okay.

Finally, I was intrigued by Hoover's remark that boys regard sports as "a performance art" and worry about "how they look." There, perhaps, is the rub, the key to why so many women feel they don't get credit for what they do. From childhood, many boys learn something that is very adaptive to the workplace: Raises and promotions are based on "performance" evaluations and these depend, in large measure, on how you appear in other people's eyes. In other words, you have to worry not only about getting your job done but also about getting credit for what you do. 8

Getting credit often depends on the way you talk. For example, a woman tells me she has been given a poor evaluation because her supervisor feels she knows less than her male peers. Her boss, it turns out, reached this conclusion because the woman asks more questions: She is seeking information without regard to how her queries will make her look. 9

The same principle applies to apologizing. Whereas some women seem to be taking undeserved blame by saying "I'm sorry," some men seem to evade deserved blame. I observed this when a man disconnected a conference call by accidentally elbowing the speaker-phone. When his secretary reconnects the call, I expect him to say, "I'm sorry; I knocked the phone by mistake." Instead he says, "Hey, what happened?! One minute you were there, the next minute you were gone!" Annoying as this may be, there are certainly instances in which people improve their fortunes by covering up mistakes. 10

If Hoover's observations about girls' and boys' athletic styles are fascinating, it is even more revealing to see actual transcripts of children at play and how they mirror the adult workplace. Amy Sheldon, a linguist at the University of Minnesota who studies children talking at play in a day care center, has compared the conflicts of pre-school girls and boys. She finds that boys who fight with one another tend to pursue their own goals. Girls tend to balance their own interests with those of the other girls through complex verbal negotiations. 11

Look at how different the negotiations are: 12

Two boys fight over a toy telephone: Tony has it; Charlie wants it. Tony is sitting on a foam chair with the base of the phone in his lap and the receiver lying beside him. Charlie picks up the receiver, and Tony protests, "No, that's my phone!" He grabs the telephone cord and tries to pull the receiver away from Charlie, saying, "No, that—uh, it's on MY couch. It's on MY couch. Charlie. It's on MY couch. It's on MY couch." It seems he has only one point to make, so he makes it repeatedly as he uses physical force to get the phone back. 13

14 Charlie ignores Tony and holds onto the receiver. Tony then gets off the couch, sets the phone base on the floor and tries to keep possession of it by overturning the chair on top of it. Charlie manages to push the chair off, gets the telephone, and wins the fight.

15 This might seem like a typical kids' fight until you compare it with a fight Sheldon videotaped among girls. Here the contested objects are toy medical instruments: Elaine has them; Arlene wants them. But she doesn't just grab for them; she argues her case. Elaine, in turn, balances her own desire to keep them with Arlene's desire to get them. Elaine loses ground gradually by compromising.

16 Arlene begins not by grabbing but by asking and giving a reason: "Can I have that, that thing? I'm going to take my baby's temperature." Elaine is agreeable, but cautious: "You can use it—you can use my temperature. Just make sure you can't use anything else unless you can ask." Arlene does just that; she asks for the toy syringe: "May I?" Elaine at first resists, but gives a reason: "No. I'm gonna need to use the shot in a couple of minutes." Arlene reaches for the syringe anyway, explaining in a "beseeching" tone, "But I—I need this though."

17 Elaine capitulates, but again tries to set limits: "Okay, just use it once." She even gives Arlene permission to give "just a couple of shots." Arlene then presses her advantage, and became possessive of her property: "Now don't touch the baby until I get back, because it IS MY BABY! I'll check her ears, okay?" (Even when being demanding, she asks for agreement: "okay?")

18 Elaine tries to regain some rights through compromise: "Well, let's pretend it's another day, that we have to look in her ears together." Elaine also tries another approach that will give Arlene something she wants: "I'll have to shot her after, after, after you listen—after you look in her ears," suggests Elaine. Arlene, however, is adamant: "Now don't shot her at all!"

19 What happens next will sound familiar to anyone who has ever been a little girl or overheard one. Elaine can no longer abide Arlene's selfish behavior and applies the ultimate sanction: "Well, then, you can't come to my birthday!" Arlene utters the predictable retort: "I don't want to come to your birthday!"

20 The boys and girls have followed different rituals for fighting. Each boy goes after what he wants; they slug it out; one wins. But the girls enact a complex negotiation, trying to get what they want while taking into account what the other wants.

21 Here is an example of how women and men at work use comparable strategies.

22 Maureen and Harold, two managers at a medium-size company, are assigned to hire a human-resources coordinator for their division. Each favors a different candidate, and both feel strongly about their preferences. They trade arguments for some time, neither convincing the other. Then Harold says that hiring the candidate Maureen wants would make him so uncomfortable that he would have to consider resigning. Maureen respects Harold. What's more, she likes him and considers him a friend. So she says what

seems to her the only thing she can say under the circumstances: "Well, I certainly don't want you to feel uncomfortable here. You're one of the pillars of the place." Harold's choice is hired.

What is crucial is not Maureen's and Harold's individual styles in isolation but how they play in concert with each other's style. Harold's threat to quit ensures his triumph—when used with someone for whom it is a trump card. If he had been arguing with someone who regards his threat as simply another move in the negotiation rather than a nonnegotiable expression of deep feelings, the result might have been different. For example, had she said, "That's ridiculous; of course you're not going to quit!" or matched it ("Well, I'd be tempted to quit if we hired your guy"), the decision might well have gone the other way. 23

Like the girls at play, Maureen balances her perspective with those of her colleague and expects him to do the same. Harold is simply going for what he wants and trusts Maureen to do likewise. 24

This is not to say that all women and all men, or all boys and girls, behave any one way. Many factors influence our styles, including regional and ethnic backgrounds, family experience, and individual personality. But gender is a key factor, and understanding its influence can help clarify what happens when we talk. 25

Building Vocabulary

For each of the following words, write a definition and a sentence of your own making:

1. flaunt (par. 6)
2. deference (par. 6)
3. agreeable (par. 16)
4. syringe (par. 16)
5. capitulates (par. 17)
6. abide (par. 19)
7. sanction (par. 19)
8. retort (par. 19)

Thinking Critically About the Argument

Understanding the Writer's Argument

1. When Bob Hoover tells Tannen that he is coaching girls and they are different from boys, she immediately stops his interview of her and starts interviewing him. Why do you think she reacts like this?
2. According to Hoover, what are the differences between boys' teams and girls' teams, in your own words?
3. According to Tannen, what is the difference between how men and women view getting credit in the workplace?

4. What do the University of Minnesota studies show about how girls negotiate?
5. What do they reveal about how boys negotiate?
6. The last two paragraphs are set apart after a line break. Why?

Understanding the Writer's Techniques

1. Why does Tannen describe the difference between boys and girls in sports at the start of her essay?
2. What is Tannen's main proposition? Where does she express it most clearly?
3. Where does Tannen contrast the behaviors of boys/men and girls/women? Write an outline of the essay, showing the various areas of contrast.
4. Which technique does Tannen use to contrast, ABAB or AABB? Why, do you think?
5. Choose one area of contrast that Tannen uses. What examples does she use to illustrate that area?
6. Who is Tannen's audience? How does that affect the tone of her essay?
7. Which of Tannen's illustrations most effectively supports her main idea?

Exploring the Writer's Argument

1. Which gender is Tannen most interested in? Why? How do you know that?
2. Why does Tannen point out that there are gender differences? Isn't that obvious? What do you think is her unstated reason for writing this essay?
3. What other conclusions can you draw from the University of Minnesota studies?
4. Why is it so important to understand the differences in how the genders behave?
5. Tannen seems to assume that the differences between girls and boys are always played out between women and men. Do you agree? Why or why not?

Ideas for Writing Arguments

Prewriting

Make two columns, one labeled "Men" and the other labeled "Women." Think of a different area of contrast than the one Tannen focuses on—attitudes toward love or sex, for example—and list points of contrast between the two columns.

Writing a Guided Argument

Write an essay that contrasts the ways in which men and women approach some aspect of life besides the one Tannen explores.

1. Begin your essay with an anecdote in which you are watching a man and woman or boy and girl interact. Explain why this experience led you to think about the differences between the sexes in the area you are exploring.

2. Make sure your claim reflects the comparison your essay will make between men and women.
3. Give a few examples of how women demonstrate how they react to your subject.
4. Wrap up your discussion of women with a conclusion about them.
5. Give a few examples of how men demonstrate how they react to your subject.
6. Wrap up your discussion of men with a conclusion about them.
7. End your essay by evaluating which you think is the proper attitude to the subject you chose. Attempt to choose the opposite sex's attitude.

Thinking, Arguing, and Writing Collaboratively

Exchange drafts of your Writing a Guided Argument essay with another student in the class. After making some general comments on the essay, write a paragraph or two on how successfully your partner achieved the goal of contrasting. Does the essay maintain coherence? Discuss your comments with your partner.

Writing About the Text

Write an essay based on questions 2 or 4 in Exploring the Writer's Argument.

More Writing Ideas

1. In your journal, write an entry about an experience you had that highlighted a difference between the sexes.
2. Write a paragraph comparing how you act at home with how you act at work.
3. Which method of negotiating—a man's or a woman's—is more effective? Write an essay explaining your choice.

Argument Through Definition

Lorenzo Albacete
The Struggle with Celibacy

Lorenzo Albacete is a Catholic priest and writer. He is a professor of theology at St. Joseph's Seminary in New York and previously served as an associate professor of theology at the John Paul II Institute for Studies in Marriage and Family. In this selection, which appeared in The New York Times Magazine *on March 31, 2002, Albacete comments on the effect the priest molestation scandals have on an age-old priestly tradition—celibacy.*

Prereading: Thinking About the Essay in Advance

In this article, Albacete attempts a definition of the Catholic priestly vow of celibacy. Why might celibacy need to be defined? In what ways could it be misinterpreted?

Words to Watch

pedophilia (par. 5) sexual attraction toward children
implicated (par. 5) guilty by association
garb (par. 5) clothes
scandalized (par. 7) shocked
caste (par. 8) rank or class in a hierarchy
trepidation (par. 9) hesitation

1 When I was in fifth grade and was invited to become an altar boy, my father would not allow it. He had made a promise to safeguard my faith, he explained, and if I got too close to priests, I might lose that faith, or—what seemed worse for him—I might become one of them. My father was born in Spain, and Spanish anticlericalism flowed through his veins.

2 His main objection was to priestly celibacy. He thought it divided priests into three kinds: saints who lived by it, rascals who took advantage of it to hide sexual desires of which they were ashamed, like homosexuality, and those who cheated. Since I gave no evidence of being saintly, I think he feared I might end up in one of the other categories.

3 I was angry and hurt by this response. I felt accused of something, though I wasn't sure exactly of what.

4 Eventually my father relented, and I became an altar boy. I tried hard to prove him wrong, and I resisted every indication of a priestly vocation. Many years later, though, having already begun my life as a secular adult, and on the verge of choosing a wedding date with my girlfriend, I found I could not resist anymore. My second Mass after ordination was at my father's grave. I hoped he would understand.

5 Now, with each new revelation of priestly pedophilia, in addition to shock and anger, I feel accused again. I worry that my altar boys and girls—not to mention their parents—are looking at me as a dirty old man, as a possible threat. When a case of abuse is exposed involving a married man, I doubt that most other married men feel implicated, embarrassed in front of their friends and relatives. They don't worry that the parents of their children's friends suspect them of horrible crimes. But because of my vow, even wearing my priestly garb has made me want to scream, "I'm not one of those!"

6 Like my father back then, an increasing number of people today think that celibacy must be blamed for this shameful situation. With none of the usual outlets, the theory goes, sexual energy inevitably explodes in manipulative forms based on the abuse of power.

7 This has not been my experience of celibacy. Still, I cannot help believing that there is some truth in the suspicion that celibacy is somehow re-

lated to the present crisis. There are those who use priestly celibacy to hide sexual desires. But I know a good many priests—in line, I believe, with the vast majority—who struggle to be faithful to a vow they hold dear and are appalled to see it abused by others. They wonder how the requirement can be maintained without facing these issues. We priests owe an answer to our scandalized people.

My opinion is that the problem lies not with celibacy as such, but with the way it is understood and lived. One standard defense of celibacy is that it frees priests from the obligations of marriage and thereby allows them to respond to the needs of the faithful without reservations. I believe this to be completely false. I think it is an insult to the countless married doctors, social activists, non-Catholic clergy and counselors whose dedication to others is second to none. In fact, there is the danger that celibacy will give priests a feeling of being separated from others, forming a caste removed from ordinary men and women. I think it is precisely because priests evoke this mysterious world of the sacred that pedophilia among them seems more despicable—and more compelling—than the same behavior among nonclerical men. 8

When I decided to go into the seminary at the age of 28, I broke up with my girlfriend—not because I was suddenly opposed to marriage, but because church law requires it. Asked whether I would have chosen a life of celibacy had it not been required, I have to admit that I would not have. But I experienced a profound call to follow without reservations or conditions, and in that spirit, I accepted the celibacy requirement with trepidation, but with the faith that I would be sustained in doing whatever it took to conform to it. Throughout the years, though, I have come to value the vow of celibacy highly. 9

I began to understand the meaning of celibacy, oddly, during a time when I was seriously questioning it. A dear friend of mine in Europe had sent his only son to study in the United States and asked me to watch over him. This friend told me how much he was suffering from this separation. I told him that at least he had a son, whereas I would never experience being a father. This aspect of celibacy, I said to him, was much more difficult than the lack of a sexual companion. 10

"But you have many sons and daughters," he said. "Look at the way young people follow you. You are a true father to them." 11

"Yes," I replied, "but let's be honest. They are not really my sons and daughters. Each one of them would have existed even if I had not. They are not mine as J. is *your* son." 12

"But Lorenzo," he said, "that is the point. J. is not *my* son. I do not own him. I must respect his freedom. And I thought that's why priests took a vow of celibacy, to help spouses and parents understand that to love is not to own, but to affirm, to help, to let go. I need this help now that J. has left home." 13

I understood then that celibacy has more to do with poverty than with sex. It is the radical, outward expression of the poverty of the human heart, the poverty that makes true love possible by preventing it from corrupting 14 into possession or manipulation. That is why child abuse by priests is so shocking, so horrible, so destructive. It places celibacy at the service of power and lust, not of love.

15 In the future, the church may decide that particular pastoral situations require a change in the requirement of priestly celibacy. Still, I believe that even if priests marry, they are called to be witnesses of that "celibacy in the heart" that human love requires—namely, the absolute respect for the loved one's freedom. It's time for those of us who treasure priestly celibacy to live it in accordance with its intended message or else give it up as an obstacle to what we wish to say.

Building Vocabulary

Albacete uses several terms used in religion in general and the Catholic Church in particular. Identify the following terms, and explain how each is used in Catholicism:

1. faith (par. 1)
2. anticlericalism (par. 1)
3. vocation (par. 4)
4. Mass (par. 4)
5. ordination (par. 4)
6. pastoral (par. 15)

Thinking Critically About the Argument

Understanding the Writer's Argument

1. What is Albacete's father's main reason for not wanting his son to get "too close" to priests? Albacete's father divided priests into three kinds. What are they, and what effect did this division have on Albacete?
2. What does Albacete mean by his "priestly vocation," and why did he resist it?
3. Albacete mentions recent scandals in the Catholic Church over pedophilia. To what is he referring? What effect have the scandals had on Albacete and his fellow priests? Does Albacete think that priestly celibacy is related to the pedophilia scandals? Why or why not?
4. What is one of the ways to defend celibacy against its critics? In his own life, did Albacete choose celibacy enthusiastically? Why or why not?
5. Why would pedophilia among priests seem "more despicable"? (paragraph 8)
6. How does Albacete's experience with his friend, described in paragraphs 10 to 13, change his view of celibacy?
7. What does Albacete think is the future of the Catholic Church's views of celibacy?
8. Does Albacete think there should be priestly celibacy or does he give another answer? If the latter, what is that answer?

Understanding the Writer's Techniques

1. What is the major proposition in Albacete's essay? How do you know?
2. Why does Albacete begin his essay with a discussion of his father's opinion of priests?
3. How does Albacete's title work? Who is struggling with celibacy?
4. For whom has Albacete written this essay? How do you know? What is his tone? Give examples that led to your answer.
5. Albacete is writing as a priest and a man. What gives his essay authority? Why is he a good person to define celibacy? How, precisely, does he develop his extended definition?
6. What examples of transition words and phrases can you find in this essay? Why are they effective?
7. The essay shifts tone at the beginning of paragraph 8. How does it shift, and why?
8. After paragraph 8, Albacete makes a number of claims about celibacy. What are they, and what examples does he give to prove those claims?
9. Why does Albacete move away from explication and tell the story of his friend in paragraphs 10 to 13? How does this help his thesis?
10. The end of Albacete's essay is a little ambiguous in its conclusions. Why do you think that is, and is it an effective closing?

Exploring the Writer's Argument

1. Do you think Albacete's father was right to argue with his son against priests? Why or why not? What does Albacete think?
2. Do you think all priests should feel "implicated," as Albacete says in paragraph 5, for the crimes of their fellow priests who are caught molesting children? Why?
3. Albacete says that "priests owe an answer to our scandalized people." Do you think he's right? Why or why not?
4. One of Albacete's points about celibacy is that it gives "priests a feeling of being separated from others, forming a caste removed from ordinary men and women." Do you think this feeling of separation, of forming an exclusive club, is positive or negative? Justify your position.
5. Do you agree with Albacete's friend that priests are more like parents than one's biological parents? Explain.

Ideas for Writing Arguments

Prewriting

Freewrite about a lifestyle choice that you have made, such as getting married, living alone, or living with a dog or other pet. Consider any criticisms of your lifestyle and your answer to those critics.

Writing a Guided Argument

Write an extended definition of a lifestyle choice that you have made. What does that choice mean to you? Defend your choice against any criticisms that you might imagine someone making. Address how important to your identity your choice has become.

1. Begin with an anecdote that introduces to the reader your subject, and end with a definition of your lifestyle choice.
2. Write a paragraph about the way the wider population has also made your choice.
3. Mention at least two objections someone might have to your lifestyle choice, and for each objection, defend your choice.
4. Give an example for each defense showing that your choice has been right for you.
5. Explain how you came to make your lifestyle choice.
6. Give an example or write a short narrative that shows a time in your life when your conception of your choice changed and you had a deeper understanding of it.
7. Explain what your altered definition of your choice is.
8. Conclude with a projection of the future of your lifestyle choice.

Thinking, Arguing, and Writing Collaboratively

In groups of three, read each other's Writing a Guided Argument essays and write a critique of each of the two essays you have read. Focus on how effective and convincing the writer's definition is. Are the examples detailed enough? Then read the critiques of your essay and think about how you can revise it to make it more accurate and convincing.

Writing About the Text

Focusing on Albacete's assertion that "celibacy has more to do with poverty than with sex," write an essay that disagrees with him and argues that celibacy is only about sex. Fully explain in your essay what Albacete's opinion is and why he thinks that.

More Writing Ideas

1. In your journal, write about an experience you have had with a priest, imam, rabbi, or other clerical figure who changed your mind about their religion.
2. In a paragraph, attempt a definition of pedophilia. Is pedophilia the act or is it thinking about the act? Be accurate.
3. Write an essay about some aspect of your religion or the religion that you grew up with that you either disagree with or have disagreed with in the past. Attempt an accurate definition of that aspect.

Argument Through Process Analysis

DOUGLAS STALKER
How to Duck Out of Teaching

Douglas Stalker is a professor of philosophy at the University of Delaware. He writes on medical, aesthetic, and logic topics, and is the editor of Grue! A New Riddle of Induction *(1994) and coeditor of* Examining Holistic Medicine *(1986). In this selection from* The Chronicle of Higher Education, *Stalker advises teachers (including yours) about how to reduce their work burdens.*

Prereading: Thinking About the Essay in Advance

What do you think your professors consider to be their most unpleasant duties? Put yourself in their shoes. What would you like to avoid?

Words to Watch

tenured (par. 1) protected from dismissal
isometric (par. 7) with muscular contraction
mea culpa (par. 8) Latin for "it's my fault"
cognitive (par. 13) relating to thought
paradigms (par. 16) models
hermeneuticist (par. 22) one who studies theories of interpretation
ergo (par. 23) Latin for "therefore"

What's new on campus? Duping! It's all the rage with professors who are tired of giving lectures to the drifting youth of America. Duping is, quite simply, not doing. It is avoiding, evading, eluding, abstaining, dodging, and good old ducking. And it is now on display on almost every campus in the United States. Here are eight duping techniques that will work for any professor, tenured or untenured, in the time it takes to erase a moderate-size blackboard: 1

The Title Trick

Give the students honorary titles to make them feel special—and willing to take on new duties. It is easy to think of titles that sound great. For example, call everyone in class a peer editor. Then you can have the students pair up and take turns going over each other's term papers. Tell the students that you are going to selflessly give up some of your professorial power in order to empower them. When all is said and done, you won't have to raise your red pen even once. 2

You can also get students to record all the grades and sign the grade roster for you. Have a drawing (that is the democratic way, of course) to see 3 who gets to have the title of peer executive officer for the day. Tell the students that this is an exercise in leadership and management ability. Remember to make a solemn display of handing over the official pen, grade book, and grade roster to the peer executive officer.

The Computer Razzle-Dazzle

4 If something is done with a computer, it must be educationally great. So set up a computer dupe: a computer-based course in which students have to send e-mail messages to each other a minimum of 10 times per day. To get them going, tell them psychological research has shown that first thoughts are always best thoughts, and that contact with your peers is essential to building and maintaining academic self-esteem. They will spend so much time on e-mail that they won't notice you haven't logged on for days.

5 You can add a personal touch by sending randomly generated e-mail messages to each student. Any high-school kid who likes computers can set the system up for you. You can easily create the messages by modifying the horoscopes in your daily newspaper. For example, one message might say: "You are doing well but have doubts about future endeavors like reading the next chapter. I know you have what it takes to overcome obstacles! Turn the pages of the textbook for yourself! Take responsibility for sharpening your own pencils! Your last fill-in-the-blank test showed great promise of things to come. Do not be surprised if I repeat this message to reinforce its meaning for you."

The Great Group Dupe

6 Tell the students that yours is a problem-based course with group learning, and have them divide up into groups. It doesn't matter whether any group actually solves the problems, what the problems are, or even if there are any problems at all. Everyone will be happy about working in a group because they will believe that things are getting done—even if nothing really happens. Like most people who can program a VCR, today's students are perfectly happy to confuse the process with the product.

7 It might be good to walk among them every few weeks, reminding everyone that the whole is greater than the sum of its parts, to discourage individual effort. You might want to walk around the room saying "Cohesion, think cohesion!" as you do some isometric push-pull exercises with your hands to make the point more vivid.

The Mea-Culpa Escape

8 Stand in front of your students and confess everything. Tell them that higher education has become an institutionalized fraud because it keeps the students passive, subjects them to lectures, coerces them to take notes, and makes them endure tests. All that is miles away from real, multidimensional learning that lasts a lifetime. You need to pull out all the stops as you wail

about the sins of academic America. Draw a circle on the board and keep pointing to it—try pounding your fist on the board—as you mention the cycle of passivity and the economic consequences associated with stunted growth and sheltered lives.

Then, with a selfless gesture toward the exits, send the students out into the world to do experiential projects of their own devising, like running a lawn-care business for the semester. Make sure that they do your lawn on their rounds so that you can turn in some grades, and tell them not to come by too early in the morning. Word that instruction in terms of their being sensitive to the needs of others. 9

The Ticktock of Pointless Talk

You have about 2,000 minutes to fill during a 14-week semester. Why not fill them with chitchat? Anyone who watches daytime TV simply loves pointless talk and, sooner or later, comes to believe that it has a point. If you have 2.5 hours of class time to fill per week and a class of 30 students, you have to get each student to speak for only five minutes a week. Following the three principles of chat satisfaction can make that relatively simple task a breeze. 10

Principle 1 is essential: There is no topic like no particular topic. Your students can have a good chat bouncing from the last episode of *Friends* to anything else they care to discuss—the popularity of sport-utility vehicles, the history of pizza, the price of body piercing, you name it. 11

Principle 2 follows directly from Principle 1: Sticking to the topic is for dorks. Coherence is irrelevant; indeed, relevance is irrelevant. Mental drift is in fashion, and it is fine to have a remark like "Burping should be a collegiate sport" followed by the statement "Cancún could be the 51st state." 12

Principle 3 is the basis of cognitive democracy: No one has to know what he or she is talking about. In the true marketplace of ideas, a marginal student can speak at length on everything from Sumerian poetry to soggy French fries. 13

The Yo-Yo Presentation

Why do professors have to stand in the front of the classroom—like truly alienated workers—trying to explain things? Why do they have to carry the load, day after day? You can redress that injustice with the best role reversal around: class presentations. You go from active to passive; your students go from passive to active. 14

The best topics, you should emphasize, are those with personal meaning to the presenter. Remind your students, in addition, that information is not learning. That is code for: No time in the library is required. Then just hand the students the formula: what ______________ means to me. In class, they can say their talk is titled "A Personal Perspective on ______________." Anything can go in the blank—the Yalta conference, the supply curve, Kant's categorical imperative, angular momentum. 15

16 Recitations are a dandy variation. They have another benefit: You can dispense with assigned readings because you have students read the books out loud in class. Plays are the paradigms here. You can have someone be Hamlet, someone else be Claudius, and so on. The students stand in front of the room and read their parts out loud to the rest of the class—no need for them to memorize anything beforehand. Other natural subjects for recitations are Plato's dialogues, Blake's poetry, and Faulkner's novels. Heck, it can work with anything that has sentences.

17 When reading paragraphs gets old, you might want to suggest that your students act out a page or two of text. Suppose, for instance, you are teaching an introductory biology course. Think about the improvisational possibilities inherent in the parts of the cell. Some students can play the cell wall; others can be structures in the cytoplasm. If they are honors students, they might even put together a little dance of cell division. (As for grading presentations, see my article titled "A Classroom Application of the Radio Shack Digital Sound-Level Meter.")

The Furniture Flimflam

18 Some of the best ideas are right under your nose—or your posterior. Rearrange the classroom each day. Have the students put the chairs in a different configuration—a circle, a triangle, a trapezoid. Any polygon or closed curve will do, but the best arrangements are those that take up to 10 minutes to complete. If you spend 10 minutes per class moving chairs, in two and a half years you will duck out of teaching the equivalent of an entire three-credit course. Over a 30-year career, that becomes a dozen courses. The furniture flimflam is actually a course-reduction measure.

19 Today's students are used to putting chairs in a circle, so most of them won't ask any dumb questions about why they are moving the furniture. If a few of them cop an attitude, just mumble something about the difference between confronting and communicating, or how a classroom should facilitate their transformation into a community of learners.

20 You can get students really motivated by mentioning scientific studies. Tell them about the research comparing people in hospital rooms with and without a view of the outside, which showed that the people with a view were discharged earlier and used fewer pain pills during their hospitalization. Who, then, would hesitate to arrange the chairs so that they face the windows? If you don't know of any relevant research, make some up.

21 Or you could go metaphysical and download for your class some New Age hooey from the Web, or material from the dozen or more sites devoted to feng shui. With a few Chinese terms, you can energize students to lay out the chairs in a hexagon contiguous with a rhomboid.

The Heavenly Remote

22 Any hermeneuticist knows that the medium is the message. And what is the medium for today's professor? Every plugged-in classroom in America

has it: a VCR. Bring in a video for class, dim the lights, push the play button on the remote, and you've done your academic work for the day.

You can use any video in any course. For openers, you have the presumption of relevance on your side: Everything that happens during class has something to do with the course. You can also rely on the dominant mental activity in higher-education circles, free association. With a little free association, your students will begin to believe that any video has something to do with the course. That is a logical point—everything freely associates with everything else; *ergo,* you're home free. 23

If rewinding and returning videos gets to be too much, start taping TV programs. You can spend class after class watching your homemade tapes of, say, daytime talk shows, reruns of sitcoms, detective shows, even the Weather Channel from time to time. For example, if you teach logic, tape Regis and that Kathie Lee impostor. When you show the tape in class, tell the students that you want them to spot the fallacious arguments that Regis tries to foist off on surrogate Kathie. If you teach ethics, tape Jerry Springer. For aesthetics, tape music videos from MTV. Marketing? Those Budweiser frogs are worth two or three upper-level courses. Physics? Professional beach volleyball on ESPN2. Criminal justice? Reruns of *Hawaii Five-O*. 24

It's a great time for a professor to be alive, isn't it? Unfortunately, it still takes some effort to record TV shows at home and bring the tapes to your campus. Why can't each classroom be hooked up to cable TV? Surely your college or university can get group rates from a cable company and find a TV manufacturer to donate the sets. Very few administrators seem to realize how much that could mean to the educational process, especially insofar as it would allow them to say things like "We've got cable in all the classrooms, but Harvard and Yale don't." Perhaps faculty members will have to get the ball rolling by contacting their AAUP representatives so that cable service can get on the table at the next contract negotiation, right there alongside the dental plan and the early-retirement options. 25

Building Vocabulary

1. In his essay, Stalker makes many cultural references that might seem obscure to you. Choose at least ten and identify them.
2. Define the following and write a sentence for each:
   a. empower (par. 2)
   b. solemn (par. 3)
   c. passivity (par. 8)
   d. stunted (par. 8)
   e. marginal (par. 13)
   f. alienated (par. 14)
   g. paradigms (par. 16)
   h. surrogate (par. 24)

Thinking Critically About the Argument

Understanding the Writer's Argument

1. What is "duping," and why, according to Stalker, do teachers do it?
2. What is the advantage, according to Stalker, of working with a computer in the classroom?
3. What does Stalker mean by a "mea-culpa escape"? (paragraph 8)
4. Why are the best topics "those with personal meaning to the presenter"?
5. What is the "presumption of relevance"? (paragraph 23)
6. What does Stalker say are the benefits of showing movies in class?
7. What suggestions does Stalker make at the end of his essay for further reducing the workload for teachers?

Understanding the Writer's Techniques

1. What is the writer's claim?
2. Why does Stalker put his eight duping techniques in this order?
3. Explain Stalker's use of process analysis to make his argument.
4. Why does Stalker offer detailed examples, such as in paragraph 24, in which he suggests that showing Budweiser commercials could work in a marketing class?
5. Explain how Stalker moves from reasonable suggestions to over-the-top ideas. Where does he do this, and why?

Exploring the Writer's Argument

1. What is Stalker's unstated purpose for writing this essay? Can you determine a subtext?
2. This essay is obviously humorous, but can any of his suggestions be considered serious? Which ones, and why?
3. How has reading this essay changed your view of your professors?
4. Do you think that Stalker imagined his students reading this essay? What might be the downside to students like you reading it?
5. Stalker's essay is funny, but are there any times when the humor fails him? Does he ever try too hard? Where, and why do you say that?

Ideas for Writing Arguments

Prewriting

Freewrite on ways that students can fill word requirements in paper assignments without really saying anything.

Writing a Guided Argument

Write an essay called "How to Fake Your Way Through Writing an Essay." Come up with a number of suggestions for your fellow students for how to complete a particularly odious writing assignment with a minimum of ideas.

1. Write an opening in the spirit of Stalker's essay, explaining the purpose of your essay and how many suggestions you will give.
2. Offer your reader at least four ideas for how they can pad their essays with the least amount of work.
3. Give the benefits of each idea.
4. Explain to your reader how versatile your ideas will be, not only in college but after college as well.
5. Write a conclusion that outlines the success you have had with your ideas.

Thinking, Arguing, and Writing Collaboratively

Working with your fellow students in small groups, figure out how many minutes of class time are left in your semester. Write a list of suggestions of ways you as students can dupe your professor by wasting class time. Fill up the total number of minutes left, offering specific suggestions for how to fill the time. Share your plan with the rest of the class.

Writing About the Text

Stalker is a professor at a university, and this essay appeared in a journal of university affairs, yet the language he uses is not always formal. How does he use a combination of formal words and slang? Write an essay explaining why he uses the words he does, focusing particularly on his use of slang. Give examples, and show how the use of slang helps to achieve his thesis.

More Writing Ideas

1. In your journal, write an entry about times when your teachers have done what Stalker suggests.
2. Write a paragraph or two about which duping technique you wish your teachers would take most advantage of.
3. Write an essay in which you argue that Stalker's techniques, if altered slightly, can be extended to any profession.

Argument Through Causal Analysis

THOMAS JEFFERSON
The Declaration of Independence

Thomas Jefferson (1743–1826) was the first secretary of state and the third president of the United States of America. During the Revolutionary War, he was the governor of Virginia. He was one of the members of the Continental Congress in Philadelphia in 1775. In addition to being a politician, Jefferson was an architect (he designed, among other things, his estate, Monticello) and an educator (he founded the University of Virginia). Jefferson was one of only a few men who designed the political and legal basis for the colonies' break from Great Britain, but he was the main author of the Declaration of Independence, which laid out, in forceful phrases, the colonies' case against the king, George III.

Prereading: Thinking About the Essay in Advance

What do you know about the reasons the United States seceded from Great Britain? Make a list of the reasons.

Words to Watch

dissolve (par. 1) break apart
unalienable (par. 2) not able to be denied
usurpations (par. 2) takeovers of power
despotism (par. 2) tyranny
sufferance (par. 2) suffering
inestimable (par. 5) valuable
abdicated (par. 16) given up
magnanimity (par. 22) generosity

1 When in the Course of human events it becomes necessary for one people to dissolve the political bands which have connected them with another, and to assume among the powers of the earth, the separate and equal station to which the Laws of Nature and of Nature's God entitle them, a decent respect to the opinions of mankind requires that they should declare the causes which impel them to the separation.

2 We hold these truths to be self-evident, that all men are created equal, that they are endowed by their Creator with certain unalienable Rights, that among these are Life, Liberty and the pursuit of Happiness.—That to secure these rights, Governments are instituted among Men, deriving their just powers from the consent of the governed.—That whenever any Form of Government becomes destructive of these ends, it is the Right of the People to alter or to abolish it, and to institute new Government, laying its foundation on such principles and organizing its powers in such form, as to them

shall seem most likely to effect their Safety and Happiness. Prudence, indeed, will dictate that Governments long established should not be changed for light and transient causes; and accordingly all experience hath shewn that mankind are more disposed to suffer, while evils are sufferable, than to right themselves by abolishing the forms to which they are accustomed. But when a long train of abuses and usurpations, pursuing invariably the same Object evinces a design to reduce them under absolute Despotism, it is their right, it is their duty, to throw off such Government, and to provide new Guards for their future security.—Such has been the patient sufferance of these Colonies; and such is now the necessity which constrains them to alter their former Systems of Government. The history of the present King of Great Britain is a history of repeated injuries and usurpations, all having in direct object the establishment of an absolute Tyranny over these States. To prove this, let Facts be submitted to a candid world.

He has refused his Assent to Laws, the most wholesome and necessary for the public good. 3

He has forbidden his Governors to pass Laws of immediate and pressing importance, unless suspended in their operation till his Assent should be obtained; and when so suspended, he has utterly neglected to attend to them. 4

He has refused to pass other Laws for the accommodation of large districts of people, unless those people would relinquish the right of Representation in the Legislature, a right inestimable to them and formidable to tyrants only. 5

He has called together legislative bodies at places unusual, uncomfortable, and distant from the depository of their public Records, for the sole purpose of fatiguing them into compliance with his measures. 6

He has dissolved Representative Houses repeatedly, for opposing with manly firmness his invasions on the rights of the people. 7

He has refused for a long time, after such dissolutions, to cause others to be elected; whereby the Legislative powers, incapable of Annihilation, have returned to the People at large for their exercise; the State remaining in the mean time exposed to all the dangers of invasion from without, and convulsions within. 8

He has endeavoured to prevent the population of these States; for that purpose obstructing the Laws for Naturalization of Foreigners; refusing to pass others to encourage their migrations hither, and raising the conditions of new Appropriations of Lands. 9

He has obstructed the Administration of Justice, by refusing his Assent to Laws for establishing Judiciary powers. 10

He has made Judges dependent on his Will alone, for the tenure of their offices, and the amount and payment of their salaries. 11

He has erected a multitude of New Offices, and sent hither swarms of Officers to harass our people, and eat out their substance. 12

He has kept among us, in times of peace, Standing Armies without the Consent of our legislatures. 13

14 He has affected to render the Military independent of and superior to the Civil power.

15 He has combined with others to subject us to a jurisdiction foreign to our constitution, and unacknowledged by our laws; giving his Assent to their Acts of pretended Legislation:

For quartering large bodies of armed troops among us:
For protecting them, by a mock Trial, from punishment for any Murders which they should commit on the Inhabitants of these States:
For cutting off our Trade with all parts of the world:
For imposing Taxes on us without our Consent:
For depriving us in many cases, of the benefits of Trial by jury:
For transporting us beyond Seas to be tried for pretended offences:
For abolishing the free System of English Laws in a neighboring Province, establishing therein an Arbitrary government, and enlarging its Boundaries so as to render it at once an example and fit instrument for introducing the same absolute rule into these Colonies:
For taking away our Charters, abolishing our most valuable Laws and altering fundamentally the Forms of our Governments:
For suspending our own Legislatures, and declaring themselves invested with power to legislate for us in all cases whatsoever.

16 He has abdicated Government here, by declaring us out of his Protection and waging War against us.

17 He has plundered our seas, ravaged our Coasts, burnt our towns, and destroyed the lives of our people.

18 He is at this time transporting large Armies of foreign Mercenaries to complete the works of death, desolation and tyranny, already begun with circumstances of Cruelty & Perfidy scarcely paralleled in the most barbarous ages, and totally unworthy the Head of a civilized nation.

19 He has constrained our fellow Citizens taken Captive on the high Seas to bear Arms against their Country, to become the executioners of their friends and Brethren, or to fall themselves by their Hands.

20 He has excited domestic insurrections amongst us, and has endeavoured to bring on the inhabitants of our frontiers, the merciless Indian Savages, whose known rule of warfare, is an undistinguished destruction of all ages, sexes and conditions.

21 In every stage of these Oppressions We have Petitioned for Redress in the most humble terms: Our repeated Petitions have been answered only by repeated injury. A Prince, whose character is thus marked by every act which may define a Tyrant, is unfit to be the ruler of a free people.

22 Nor have We been wanting in attentions to our British brethren. We have warned them from time to time of attempts by their legislature to extend an unwarrantable jurisdiction over us. We have reminded them of the circumstances of our emigration and settlement here. We have appealed to their native justice and magnanimity, and we have conjured them by the ties of our common kindred to disavow these usurpations, which would inevitably in-

terrupt our connections and correspondence. They too have been deaf to the voice of justice and of consanguinity. We must, therefore, acquiesce in the necessity, which denounces our Separation, and hold them, as we hold the rest of mankind, Enemies in War, in Peace Friends.

We, therefore, the Representatives of the United States of America, in General Congress, Assembled, appealing to the Supreme Judge of the world for the rectitude of our intentions, do, in the Name, and by Authority of the good People of these Colonies, solemnly publish and declare, That these United Colonies are, and of Right ought to be Free and Independent States; that they are Absolved from all Allegiance to the British Crown, and that all political connection between them and the State of Great Britain, is and ought to be totally dissolved; and that as Free and Independent States, they have full Power to levy War, conclude Peace, contract Alliances, establish Commerce, and to do all other Acts and Things which Independent States may of right do. And for the support of this Declaration, with a firm reliance on the protection of divine Providence, we mutually pledge to each other our Lives, our Fortunes and our sacred Honor. 23

Building Vocabulary

Connotation refers to the shades of meaning or emotional associations a word or phrase provokes in readers. Explain the connotations raised by the following and why you think Jefferson selected them.

1. Nature's God (par. 1)
2. unalienable rights (par. 2)
3. Life, Liberty, and the pursuit of Happiness (par. 2)
4. absolute Tyranny (par. 2)
5. plundered . . . ravaged . . . burnt . . . destroyed (par. 17)
6. our British brethren (par. 22)

Thinking Critically About the Argument

Understanding the Writer's Argument

1. Paraphrase Jefferson's first paragraph.
2. Why, according to Jefferson, are governments formed?
3. Why, in a few words, are the colonies determined to "throw off" the British government?
4. Why is Jefferson's objection in paragraph 13 important?
5. According to Jefferson, what actions did the colonies take before writing this declaration?
6. What, in the last paragraph, does Jefferson list as the powers of the United States?

Understanding the Writer's Techniques

1. What is the main proposition of the Declaration of Independence? Where does Jefferson most forcefully express it?
2. Why does Jefferson place the claim where he does?

3. What is Jefferson's central reason for his main proposition?
4. What are Jefferson's best three supports for his reason? Are there other reasons? What are they?
5. In paragraph 2, Jefferson sets up his warrant. Paraphrase the warrant.
6. What effects does Jefferson predict will come as a result of the declaration?
7. What purpose does the conclusion serve? What does Jefferson hope to accomplish with this conclusion?

Exploring the Writer's Argument

1. What information would you like to have to understand the declaration better?
2. Why in paragraph 2, does Jefferson explain that "Governments long established should not be changed for light and transient causes"?
3. Jefferson's warrants, as listed in paragraph 2, are described as self-evident. Why does he find them to be self-evident?
4. Why does Jefferson describe the world as "candid" in paragraph 2?
5. Unconsented taxes were a large part of why the colonies went to war. Why does Jefferson place that as a reason in paragraph 15?
6. This is a political document, but it is also a call to arms. Is it effective in this way? If so, how?

Ideas for Writing Arguments

Prewriting

Freewrite for 10 minutes, making a list of grievances you have against your boss, a parent, or a teacher.

Writing a Guided Argument

Write a declaration of independence of your own that shows the causes for your dissatisfaction with a figure in authority—a parent, an elder, a boss, a teacher—giving examples throughout. What are the worst offenses? In what order will you list them? What form of satisfaction do you demand? Do not write directly to the person but rather to a third person to whom you are making your case.

1. Start with an opening that uses ceremonial speech, in much the same way the Declaration of Independence does. Write in such a way that your reader knows that you are being serious.
2. Begin laying out your list of grievances, your causes for desiring your independence, by offering examples for each cause. Make sure you have at least three and that your examples are detailed.
3. Explain that you have attempted to express your unhappiness but that your pleas have not been answered.
4. Conclude by declaring your independence again, in formal language.

Thinking, Arguing, and Writing Collaboratively

In small groups, exchange your Writing a Guided Argument papers with members of your class. Circle any grievances that you think are not backed up with enough evidence. Try to strengthen your classmates' cases against their chosen authority figure.

Writing About the Text

Jefferson wrote a document that was meant to incite the population of the colonies to rise up against the King of England. Examine his language and choice of words. How does he choose carefully in order to raise the emotional level of this very legalistic essay? Write an essay of your own that explores Jefferson's word and phrase choices, and explain how he achieves his goals in this way.

More Writing Ideas

1. Pretend that you are George III. Write a journal entry in the form of a letter to Thomas Jefferson and the colonists arguing why the colonies are the property of Great Britain and should not be independent.
2. Write a paragraph about the power of the opening of the Declaration of Independence. Those words have been quoted often. What makes them so powerful?
3. For many Americans who are not familiar with the founding documents of the United States, reading the Declaration of Independence for the first time, or for the first time in a while, can be an interesting experience and full of surprises. Write an essay outlining the reasons you were surprised upon this reading of the declaration.

Argument Through Classification

AMARTYA SEN
A World Not Neatly Divided

Amartya Sen was born in Santiniketan, India, in 1933 and received a B.A. in economics from Presidency College in Calcutta, India, in 1953. He went on to earn a second B.A. from Trinity College in Cambridge, England, in 1955, and his Ph.D. from that school in 1959. Sen has taught at Harvard University, the London School of Economics, and Oxford, and he is currently a professor at Trinity College in Cambridge. His books Collective Choice and Social Welfare *(1970),* On Economic Inequality *(1973), and* Commodities and Capabilities *(1985) examine the role of poverty in the world. Sen won the Nobel Prize for economics in 1998. At the time, the Nobel committee wrote that Dr. Sen's work has "enhanced our understanding of the economic mechanisms underlying famines."*

Prereading: Thinking About the Essay in Advance

How can the world be "neatly divided"? How does the world resist division? What kinds of division exist?

Words to Watch

befuddling (par. 2) confusing
impoverished (par. 2) not detailed enough
futile (par. 2) useless
pluralist (par. 3) consisting of many
homogeneous (par. 4) containing parts that are the same
excommunicating (par. 4) expelling from a group
heresy (par. 4) unorthodox ideas about religion
imperious (par. 5) overbearing
flammable (par. 7) dangerous

1 When people talk about clashing civilizations, as so many politicians and academics do now, they can sometimes miss the central issue. The inadequacy of this thesis begins well before we get to the question of whether civilizations must clash. The basic weakness of the theory lies in its program of categorizing people of the world according to a unique, allegedly commanding system of classification. This is problematic because civilizational categories are crude and inconsistent and also because there are other ways of seeing people (linked to politics, language, literature, class, occupation, or other affiliations).

2 The befuddling influence of a singular classification also traps those who dispute the thesis of a clash: To talk about "the Islamic world" or "the Western world" is already to adopt an impoverished vision of humanity as unalterably divided. In fact, civilizations are hard to partition in this way, given the diversities within each society as well as the linkages among different countries and cultures. For example, describing India as a "Hindu civilization" misses the fact that India has more Muslims than any other country except Indonesia and possibly Pakistan. It is futile to try to understand Indian art, literature, music, food, or politics without seeing the extensive interactions across barriers of religious communities. These include Hindus and Muslims, Buddhists, Jains, Sikhs, Parsees, Christians (who have been in India since at least the fourth century, well before England's conversion to Christianity), Jews (present since the fall of Jerusalem), and even atheists and agnostics. Sanskrit has a larger atheistic literature than exists in any other classical language. Speaking of India as a Hindu civilization may be comforting to the Hindu fundamentalist, but it is an odd reading of India.

3 A similar coarseness can be seen in the other categories invoked, like "the Islamic world." Consider Akbar and Aurangzeb, two Muslim emperors of the Mogul dynasty in India. Aurangzeb tried hard to convert Hindus into Muslims and instituted various policies in that direction, of which taxing the non-Muslims was only one example. In contrast, Akbar reveled in his multi-

ethnic court and pluralist laws, and issued official proclamations insisting that no one "should be interfered with on account of religion" and that "anyone is to be allowed to go over to a religion that pleases him."

If a homogeneous view of Islam were to be taken, then only one of these emperors could count as a true Muslim. The Islamic fundamentalist would have no time for Akbar; Prime Minister Tony Blair, given his insistence that tolerance is a defining characteristic of Islam, would have to consider excommunicating Aurangzeb. I expect both Akbar and Aurangzeb would protest, and so would I. A similar crudity is present in the characterization of what is called "Western civilization." Tolerance and individual freedom have certainly been present in European history. But there is no dearth of diversity here, either. When Akbar was making his pronouncements on religious tolerance in Agra, in the 1590's, the Inquisitions were still going on; in 1600, Giordano Bruno was burned at the stake, for heresy, in Campo dei Fiori in Rome. 4

Dividing the world into discrete civilizations is not just crude. It propels us into the absurd belief that this partitioning is natural and necessary and must overwhelm all other ways of identifying people. That imperious view goes not only against the sentiment that "we human beings are all much the same," but also against the more plausible understanding that we are diversely different. For example, Bangladesh's split from Pakistan was not connected with religion, but with language and politics. 5

Each of us has many features in our self-conception. Our religion, important as it may be, cannot be an all-engulfing identity. Even a shared poverty can be a source of solidarity across the borders. The kind of division highlighted by, say, the so-called "antiglobalization" protesters—whose movement is, incidentally, one of the most globalized in the world—tries to unite the underdogs of the world economy and goes firmly against religious, national, or "civilizational" lines of division. 6

The main hope of harmony lies not in any imagined uniformity, but in the plurality of our identities, which cut across each other and work against sharp divisions into impenetrable civilizational camps. Political leaders who think and act in terms of sectioning off humanity into various "worlds" stand to make the world more flammable—even when their intentions are very different. They also end up, in the case of civilizations defined by religion, lending authority to religious leaders seen as spokesmen for their "worlds." In the process, other voices are muffled and other concerns silenced. The robbing of our plural identities not only reduces us; it impoverishes the world. 7

Building Vocabulary

The writer lists several religions in paragraph 2. Provide definitions for these words:

1. Hindus
2. Muslims

3. Buddhists
4. Jains
5. Sikhs
6. Parsees
7. Christians

Thinking Critically About the Argument

Understanding the Writer's Argument

1. What, in Sen's opinion, is the "basic weakness" of the thesis of clashing civilizations?
2. Why is classifying people in terms of their civilization "crude and inconsistent"?
3. What is the weakness in the argument that India is a "Hindu civilization"?
4. What does "singular classification" mean?
5. How does Sen demonstrate that a "homogeneous view of Islam" is wrong?
6. Paraphrase Sen's argument in paragraph 5.
7. Where does the "main hope for harmony" lie, according to Sen?

Understanding the Writer's Techniques

1. What technique does Sen use in his introduction?
2. In this classification essay, Sen argues against classification, yet he does have a structure. What is that structure? How does he classify?
3. Sen relies on many examples to make his point. Mention two examples he gives, and explain what purpose they serve in the essay.
4. Much of this essay is used to work against a popular viewpoint. How does Sen work to refute this idea?
5. Near the end of the essay, Sen stops giving examples. Why does he do this, and is this effective?
6. Paraphrase Sen's argument in his conclusion. Is the closing effective? Why?

Exploring the Writer's Argument

1. Do singular classifications always have a negative effect on public discourse? Can you think of any examples of how they can have a positive effect? What are they?
2. Sometimes, it seems, classifying a group of people by a single concept is unavoidable. What would Sen say to this objection, in your opinion?
3. Sen is particularly worried about the use of singular classification by political leaders. Are they the people we need to worry about? Argue for or against this idea.

Ideas for Writing Arguments

Prewriting

Make a list of singular classifications that you come across every day—for example, New Yorkers, bald people, dog lovers. How are those classifications useful? Why do we persist in employing them in everyday speech? Are they harmless, beneficial, or neutral?

Writing a Guided Argument

Many singular classifications not related to charged topics such as religion or race do not have the same emotion attached to them, and they cannot be seen as quite as dangerous. Nevertheless, these singular classifications can have their harmful effects on both the subject and the speaker of the terms. Write a humorous essay in which you choose three classifications and offer examples of how "harmful" they can be.

1. Begin with a declaration of mock alarm, explaining that there is a serious problem.
2. Discuss the "dangers" of speaking in generalizations about groups of people.
3. Offer your first example, and show how people might "suffer" from being classified. For example, New Yorkers might begin to see themselves as rude if defined that way, and begin to act rudely.
4. Give examples of how the negative effects take hold.
5. Repeat the process for the other two classifications.
6. Conclude by proposing alternate ways of referring to people. Instead of Californians, for example, people from San Francisco. Explain why this would help.

Thinking, Arguing, and Writing Collaboratively

In small groups, discuss the stereotypes associated with your ethnic groups, and offer examples of why that stereotype is often not true. One person in the group should create a list of the group's members' ethnic groups and the debunking examples. Offer the evidence to the rest of the class.

Writing About the Text

Sen mentions a number of different religions in paragraph 2, including Hindi, Islam, Judaism, Christianity, Buddhism, and the Jain and Sikh religions. Choose one of these religions, and write an essay of classification. Look up the traditional divisions within the religion you choose, and explain the differences and similarities. Explain which form of the religion has been most tolerant over history.

More Writing Ideas

1. Do some research to find an example of a political leader who thought in terms of singular classification even though, as Sen mentions in his conclusion, his or her "intentions [were] very different." Write in your journal about what happened.
2. In a paragraph, define what is meant by "globalization" and why someone would be against it.
3. What particular prejudices are present in your community? Write an essay about the problems of singular classification in your neighborhood. Offer examples of intolerance, and propose a solution at the end.

Mixing Patterns

RONALD TAKAKI
The Harmful Myth of Asian Superiority

Ronald Takaki is Professor of Ethnic Studies at the University of California, Berkeley, from which he received his Ph.D. in 1967. His books include Pau Hana: Plantation Life and Labor in Hawaii *(1983),* Strangers from a Different Shore: A History of Asian Americans *(1989), and* Hiroshima *(2001). In this selection, Takaki writes about the way even positive stereotypes can have unexpected negative effects.*

Prereading: Thinking About the Essay in Advance

What are the positive stereotypes of various immigrant groups? Why might those stereotypes be "harmful"?

Words to Watch

provocatively (par. 2) designed to get a reaction
ubiquity (par. 2) state of being everywhere
entrepreneurial (par. 2) individually business-minded
plight (par. 3) serious problem
homogenizes (par. 7) makes the same
median (par. 12) a kind of statistical average
paragons (par. 12) perfect examples
exacerbates (par. 15) makes worse

1 Asian Americans have increasingly come to be viewed as a "model minority." But are they as successful as claimed? And for whom are they supposed to be a model?

2 Asian Americans have been described in the media as "excessively, even provocatively" successful in gaining admission to universities. Asian Ameri-

can shopkeepers have been congratulated as well as criticized, for their ubiquity and entrepreneurial effectiveness.

If Asian Americans can make it, many politicians and pundits ask why can't African Americans? Such comparisons pit minorites against each other and generate African American resentment toward Asian Americans. The victims are blamed for their plight, rather than racism and an economy that has made many young African American workers superfluous. 3

The celebration of Asian Americans has obscured reality. For example, figures on the high earnings of Asian Americans relative to Caucasians are misleading. Most Asian Americans live in California, Hawaii, and New York—states with higher incomes and higher costs of living than the national average. 4

Even Japanese Americans, often touted for their upward mobility, have not reached equality. While Japanese American men in California earned an average income comparable to Caucasian men in 1980, they did so only by acquiring more education and working more hours. 5

Comparing family incomes is even more deceptive. Some Asian American groups do have higher family incomes than Caucasians. But they have more workers per family. 6

The "model minority" image homogenizes Asian Americans and hides their differences. For example, while thousands of Vietnamese American young people attend universities, others are on the streets. They live in motels and hang out in pool halls in places like East Los Angeles; some join gangs. 7

Twenty-five percent of the people in New York City's Chinatown lived below the poverty level in 1980, compared with 17 percent of the city's population. Some 60 percent of the workers in the Chinatowns of Los Angeles and San Francisco are crowded into low-paying jobs in garment factories and restaurants. 8

"Most immigrants coming into Chinatown with a language barrier cannot go outside this confined area into the mainstream of American industry," a Chinese immigrant said, "Before, I was a painter in Hong Kong, but I can't do it here. I got no license, no education. I want a living; so it's dishwasher, janitor, or cook." 9

Hmong and Mien refugees from Laos have unemployment rates that reach as high as 80 percent. A 1987 California study showed that three out of ten Southeast Asian refugee families had been on welfare for four to ten years. 10

Although college-educated Asian Americans are entering the professions and earning good salaries, many hit the "glass ceiling"—the barrier through which high management positions can be seen but not reached. In 1988, only 8 percent of Asian Americans were "officials" and "managers," compared with 12 percent for all groups. 11

Finally, the triumph of Korean immigrants has been exaggerated. In 1988, Koreans in the New York metropolitan area earned only 68 percent of the median income of non-Asians. More than three-quarters of Korean greengrocers, those so-called paragons of bootstrap entrepreneurialism came to America with a college education. Engineers, teachers, or administrators while in Korea, they became shopkeepers after their arrival. For 12 many of them, the greengrocery represents dashed dreams, a step downward in status.

13 For all their hard work and long hours, most Korean shopkeepers do not actually earn very much: $17,000 to $35,000 a year, usually representing the income from the labor of an entire family.

14 But most Korean immigrants do not become shopkeepers. Instead, many find themselves trapped as clerks in grocery stores, service workers in restaurants, seamstresses in garment factories, and janitors in hotels.

15 Most Asian Americans know their "success" is largely a myth. They also see how the celebration of Asian Americans as a "model minority" perpetuates their inequality and exacerbates relations between them and African Americans.

Building Vocabulary

Takaki uses terms and concepts drawn from the social sciences, especially sociology and economics. Define the following terms:

1. "model minority" (par. 1)
2. racism (par. 3)
3. upward mobility (par. 5)
4. poverty level (par. 8)
5. "glass ceiling" (par. 11)
6. median income (par. 12)

Thinking Critically About the Argument

Understanding the Writer's Argument

1. Why are Asian Americans considered a "model minority"?
2. How is the supposed business success of Asian Americans misinterpreted?
3. How does the image of Asian Americans as a "model minority" affect African Americans, according to Takaki?
4. How does the idea of the model minority "homogenize" Asian Americans?
5. What problems do college-educated Asian Americans face?
6. Why is the success of Korean shopkeepers not considered a success for many of the shopkeepers themselves?

Understanding the Writer's Techniques

1. What is Takaki's claim?
2. The writer uses a number of different rhetorical modes in this essay. What are they? Give examples.
3. Takaki writes two questions in the first paragraph. Why does he do that? Does he answer his own questions? Where, and if not, why not?

4. Takaki makes a number of points to back up his claim. What are the arguments he outlines?
5. There are a number of examples in this essay. Make a list of the examples and the point each one makes.

Exploring the Writer's Argument

1. If the term "Asian American" is too broad, what do you think Takaki would say about the term "Chinese" or "Korean"? Are those terms too broad? Why or why not?
2. Takaki mentions many ways in which the idea of the Asian American as a model minority can be a negative thing, but can it be positive? Can it work for Asian Americans?
3. Takaki states that many Korean immigrants consider their position as shopkeepers to be a step down. If this is true, why did they come to the United States? Does your answer change your view of Takaki's argument?

Ideas for Writing Arguments

Prewriting

Do you know someone who people consider successful but who does not consider himself or herself successful? What are the reasons for the difference of opinion? Write down examples of the person's self-perception and those of his or her friends and neighbors.

Writing a Guided Argument

Write an essay called "The Myth of Success" about an acquaintance, family member, friend, or yourself. Make the myth an idea that people have about the success of that person, and explore the difference between the person's public persona and how the person feels about himself or herself. Perhaps the person is a successful teacher who feels like a failure or a good mother who thinks she could do better.

1. Begin by stating the myth. Question the myth's truth, or raise the idea of it being an idea or point of view.
2. Explain the difference between the myth and the person's perception of himself or herself.
3. Use at least three examples of how the external view of the person and the person's view of himself or herself differs.
4. Use techniques of comparison and contrast, illustration, definition, and narration to advance the claim of what you think is the proper view of the person.
5. Conclude by restating your belief about the success of the person, and give an example of why you think this is so.

Thinking, Arguing, and Writing Collaboratively

Exchange Writing a Guided Argument essays with another member of the class. Has your partner written an effective paper? Is the myth well defined? Is the difference between points of view clear? Is there a thesis, and is it backed up by good examples? Write a note to your partner explaining how his or her paper can be improved.

Writing About the Text

In an essay, compare Takaki's argument with Amartya Sen's. Can you find any differences? What are the similarities? What is your personal opinion about stereotypes, both positive and negative?

More Writing Ideas

1. Write a journal entry about the struggles of your ancestors who were immigrants. How do you think society perceived them?
2. What myths are attached to your ethnic group? Write a paragraph in which you outline the harmful myths attached to your ethnic group.
3. Many immigrant groups struggle when they come to the United States. Read "False Gold" by Fae Myenne Ng and write an essay about the harmful myth of American success to Asian immigrants, offering examples from both Ng's and Takaki's essays.

4 Writing from Research

This text builds on the assumption that you will write, at some point, a fully developed research paper that incorporates multiple sources. Thus, it gives complete coverage of the writing process and the mechanics of documentation. However, it also serves another purpose: It will make you confident in your ability to find information and present it effectively in all kinds of ways and for all sorts of projects:

- A theme in freshman English on the value of comedy
- A paper in history on President Franklin D. Roosevelt's New Deal
- A report in a physics class on the moon's effects on ocean tides
- An archeological field report on Indian burial mounds
- A brief biographical study of a famous person, such as Alexander Hamilton

All of these papers require some type of researched writing. Papers similar to these will appear on your schedule during your first two years of college and increase in frequency in upper-division courses. This text relieves the pressure—it shows you how to research comedy or the New Deal, and it demonstrates the correct methods for documenting your sources.

We conduct informal research all the time. We examine various models and their options before buying a car, and we check out another person informally before proposing or accepting a first date. We sometimes search the classified ads to find a summer job, or we roam the mall to find a new tennis racket, the right pair of sports shoes, or the latest CD. Research, then, is not foreign to us. It has become commonplace to use a search engine to explore the Internet for information on any subject—from personal concerns, such as the likely side effects of a prescribed drug, to complex issues, such as robotics or acupuncture.

In the classroom, we begin thinking about a serious and systematic activity, one that involves the library, the Internet, or field research. A research paper, like a personal essay, requires you to choose a topic you care about and are willing to invest many hours in thinking about. However, unlike a personal essay or short report, you will develop your ideas by gathering an array of information, reading sources critically, and collecting notes. As you pull your project together, you will continue to express personal ideas, but now they are supported by and based on the collective evidence and the opinions of experts on the topic.

Some instructors prefer the description *researched writing,* for this type of writing grows from investigation, and the research is used in different ways, in different amounts, and for different purposes. Each classroom and each instructor will make different demands on your talents. The guidelines here are general; your instructors will provide the specifics.

This text therefore introduces research as an engaging, sometimes exciting pursuit on several fronts—your personal knowledge, ideas gleaned from printed and electronic sources, and research in the field.

Why Do Research?

Instructors ask you to write a research paper for several reasons:

Research teaches methods of discovery. It asks you to discover what you know on a topic and what others can teach you. Beyond reading, it often expects you to venture into the field for interviews, observation, and experimentation. The process tests your curiosity as you probe a complex subject. You may not arrive at any final answers or solutions, but you will come to understand the different views on a subject. In your final paper, you will synthesize your ideas and discoveries with the knowledge and opinions of others.

Research teaches investigative skills. A research project requires you to investigate a subject, gain a grasp of its essentials, and disclose your findings. The exercise teaches important methods for gaining knowledge on a complex topic. Your success will depend on your negotiating the various sources of information, from reference books in the library to computer databases and from special archival collections to the most recent articles in printed periodicals. The Internet, with its vast quantity of information, will challenge you to find reliable sources. If you conduct research by observation, interviews, surveys, and laboratory experiments, you will discover additional methods of investigation.

Finding material on the Internet: Chapter 6.

Research teaches critical thinking. As you wade through the evidence on your subject, you will learn to discriminate between useful information and unfounded or ill-conceived comments. Some sources, such as the Internet, will provide timely, reliable material but may also entice you with worthless and undocumented opinions.

Research teaches logic. Like a judge in the courtroom, you must make perceptive judgments about the issues surrounding a specific topic. Your decisions, in effect, will be based on the wisdom gained from research of the subject. Your paper and your readers will rely on your logical response to your reading, observation, interviews, and testing.

Research teaches the basic ingredients of argument. In most cases, a research paper requires you to make a claim and support it with reasons and evidence. For example, if you argue that "urban sprawl has invited wild animals into our backyards," you will learn to anticipate challenges to your theory and to defend your assertion with evidence.

Learning Format Variations

Scholarly writing in each discipline follows certain conventions—that is, special forms are required for citing the sources and for designing the pages. These rules make uniform the numerous articles written internationally by millions of scholars. The society of language and literature scholars, the Modern Language Association, has a set of guidelines generally known as MLA style. Similarly, the American Psychological Association has its own APA style. Other groups of scholars prefer a footnote system, while still others use a numbering system. These variations are not meant to confuse; they have evolved within disciplines as the preferred style.

What is important for you, right now, is to determine which format to use. Many composition instructors will ask you to use MLA style, as explained in Chapters 14–17, but they are just as likely to ask for APA style (Chapter 18) if your topic concerns one of the social sciences. In a like manner, your art appreciation instructor might expect the footnote style but could just as easily request the APA style. Ask your instructor early which style to use and organize accordingly.

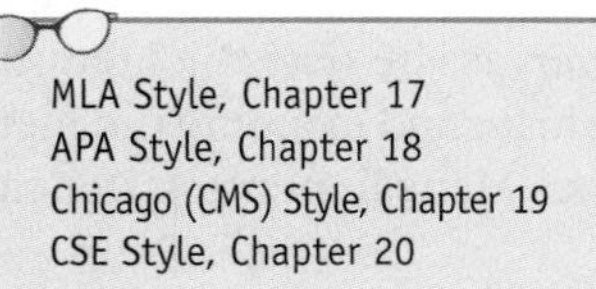

MLA Style, Chapter 17
APA Style, Chapter 18
Chicago (CMS) Style, Chapter 19
CSE Style, Chapter 20

Understanding a Research Assignment

Beyond selecting an effective subject, you need a reason for writing the paper. Literature instructors might expect you to make judgments about the structure of a story or poem. Education instructors might ask you to examine the merits of a testing program. History instructors might want you to explore an event—perhaps the causes and consequences of the 2003 U.S. war on Iraq.

Your inquiry can be a response to a question, such as "What about Hamlet and his long-winded speeches?" Prompted by her own question, Melinda Mosier developed a paper on Hamlet's soliloquies, which is reproduced in Chapter 16. Another student, Valerie Nesbitt-Hall, noticed a cartoon on the Internet that tickled her fancy and caused her to wonder about and then investigate online matchmaking services and chat rooms. Her research helped her develop a paper entitled "Arranged Marriages: The Revival Is Online" (see Chapter 18). Thus, different kinds of topics and questions can motivate you to explore your own thoughts and discover what others are saying.

Understanding the Terminology

Assignments in literature, history, and the fine arts will often require you to *interpret, evaluate,* and *perform causal analysis*. Assignments in education, psychology, political science, and other social science disciplines will usually require *analysis, definition, comparison,* or a search for *precedents* leading to a *proposal*. In the sciences, your experiments and testing will usually require a discussion of the *implications* of your findings. The next few pages explain these assignments.

Evaluation

To evaluate, you first need to establish clear criteria of judgment and then explain how the subject meets these criteria. For example, student evaluations of faculty members are based on a set of expressed criteria—an interest in student progress, a thorough knowledge of the subject, and so forth. Similarly, you may be asked to judge the merits of a poem, an art show, or new computer software. Your first step should be to create your criteria. What makes a good movie? How important is a poem's form and structure? Is space a special factor in architecture? You can't expect the sources to provide the final answers; you need to experience the work and make your final judgments on it.

Let's see how evaluation develops with one student, Sarah Bemis, who was asked to examine diabetes. At first, Sarah worked to define the disease and its basic attack on the human system. However, as she read the literature she shifted her focus from a basic definition to evaluate and examine the methods for controlling diabetes. Her paper, "Diabetes Management: A Delicate Balance," appears in Chapter 20.

The same evaluative process applies to other subjects. For example, student Jamie Johnston conducted his inquiry on how prehistoric tribes were not the noble savages that some historians thought them to be. His study evaluated recent sources to learn that, in truth, war has long been a part of human history. His paper, "Prehistoric War: We Have Always Hated Each Other," is located in Chapter 19.

In many ways, every research paper is an evaluation.

Interpretation

To interpret, you must usually answer, "What does it mean?" You may be asked to explain the symbolism in a piece of literature, examine a point of law, or make sense of test results. Questions often point toward interpretation:

What does this passage mean?
What are the implications of these results?
What does this data tell us?
Can you explain your reading of the problem to others?

For example, your instructor might ask you to interpret the Supreme Court's ruling in *Roe* v. *Wade,* interpret test results on pond water at site A and site B, or interpret a scene from Shakespeare's *A Midsummer Night's Dream*.

In her paper on Internet dating, Nesbitt-Hall found herself asking two interpretive questions: What are the social implications of computer dating? and What are the psychological implications?

Definition

Sometimes you will need to provide an extended definition to show that your subject fits into a selected and well-defined category. Note these examples:

1. Slapping a child on the face is child abuse.
   You will need to define child abuse and then show that an act of slapping fits the definition.
2. Title IX is a law, not an option, for athletic programs.
   You will need to define the law in detail.
3. Plagiarism should be considered a criminal misdemeanor.
   You will need to define a criminal misdemeanor and prove that plagiarism fits the definition.
4. Cheerleaders are athletes who deserve scholarships.
   You will need to define "athletes who deserve scholarships" and find a way to place cheerleaders within that category.

These examples demonstrate how vague and elusive our language can be. We know what an athlete is in general, but the argument needs a careful analysis of the term *scholarship athlete*. The writer will need to work carefully to reach agreement with the reader about the terminology. What's more, the writer will need to define in some detail the term *cheerleader*.

A good definition usually includes three elements: the subject (cheerleaders); the class to which the subject belongs (athlete); and the difference from others in this class (gymnast). The assumption is that a gymnast is a scholarship athlete. If the writer can associate the cheerleader with the gymnast, then the argument might have merit.

Definition will almost always become a part of your work when some of the terminology is subjective. If you argue, for example, that medical experiments on animals are cruel and inhumane, you may need to define what you mean by *cruel* and explain why *humane* standards should be applied to animals that are not human. Thus, definition might serve as your major thesis.

Definition is also necessary with technical and scientific terminology, as shown by Sarah Bemis in her paper on diabetes. The paper needed a careful, detailed definition of the medical disorder in addition to the methods for managing it. By her inquiry, she reached her conclusion that medication in harmony with diet and exercise were necessary for victims of the disease.

Thus, most writers build their paper on an issue that gives them a reason for inquiry and investigation of their own attitudes and beliefs as well as ideas from written sources, interviews, observation, and other research methods.

Proposal

This type of argument says to the reader, "We should do something." It often has practical applications, as shown by these examples:

1. We should change the annual yearbook into a semiannual magazine because student interest and participation in and response to the yearbook are extremely poor.
2. We should cancel all drug testing of athletes because it presumes guilt and demeans the innocent.
3. A chipping mill should not be allowed in this area because its insatiable demand for timber will strip our local forests.

As shown by these examples, the proposal argument calls for action—a change in policy, a change in the law, and, sometimes, an alteration of accepted procedures. Again, the writer must advance the thesis and support it with reasons and evidence.

In addition, a proposal demands special considerations. First, writers should convince readers that a problem exists and is serious enough to merit action. In the example above about chipping mills, the writer will need to establish that, indeed, chipping mills have been proposed and perhaps even approved for the area. Then the writer will need to argue that they endanger the environment: They grind vast amounts of timber of any size and shave it into chips that are reprocessed in various ways. As a result, lumberjacks cut even the immature trees, stripping forests into barren wastelands. The writer presumes that clear-cutting damages the land.

Second, the writer must explain the consequences to convince the reader that the proposal has validity. The paper must defend the principle that clear-cutting damages the land, and it should show, if possible, how chipping mills in other parts of the country have damaged the environment.

Third, the writer will need to address any opposing positions, competing proposals, and alternative solutions. For example, chipping mills produce chip board for decking the floors of houses, thus saving trees that might be required for making expensive plywood boards. Without chipping mills, we might run short on paper and homebuilding products. The writer will need to note opposing views and consider them in the paper.

In its own way, Sarah Bemis's paper on diabetes offers a proposal, one that people with this disorder might use to manage it—a balance of medication, exercise, and diet.

Causal Argument

Unlike proposals, which predict consequences, causal arguments show that a condition exists because of specific circumstances—that is, something has caused or created this situation, and we need to know why. For example, a student's investigation uncovered reasons why schools in one state benefit greatly from a lottery but do not in another.

Let's look at another student who asked the question, "Why do numerous students, like me, who otherwise score well on the ACT test, score poorly in the math section of the test and, consequently, enroll in developmental courses that offer no college credit?" This question merited his investigation, so he gathered evidence from his personal experience as well as data drawn from interviews, surveys, critical reading, and accumulated test results. Ultimately, he explored and wrote on a combination of related issues—students' poor study skills, bias in the testing program, and inadequate instruction in grade school and high school. He discovered something about himself and many things about the testing program.

Student Norman Berkowitz uses causal analysis to build his paper, "The World's Water Supply: The Ethics of Distribution" (see Chapter 16). He traces the causes of water shortages, identifies key areas approaching a desert status, and discusses the consequences, saying that people with water must be willing to help those without.

In addition, Valerie Nesbitt-Hall (see Chapter 18) uses causal argument in her essay about online romance, showing that availability, privacy, and low cost are forces that drive this new type of dating. Sarah Bemis (see Chapter 20) uses a similar kind of causal argument in her essay on diabetes management; she traces the causes for the disease and then examines the methods for controlling it: medication, diet, and exercise.

Comparison, Including Analogy

An argument often compares and likens a subject to something else. You might be asked to compare a pair of poems or to compare stock markets—Nasdaq with the New York Stock Exchange. Comparison is seldom the focus of an entire paper, but it can be useful in a paragraph about the banking policy of Andrew Jackson and that of his congressional opponents.

An analogy is a figurative comparison that allows the writer to draw several parallels of similarity. For example, the human circulatory system is like a transportation system with a hub, a highway system, and a fleet of trucks to carry the cargo.

Valerie Nesbitt-Hall uses comparison in her essay. She describes online matchmaking as similar to the practice of prearranged marriages. When families arrange a marriage, they cautiously seek a good match in matters of nationality, economics, political alliances, and so forth. In comparison, says Nesbitt-Hall, couples on the Internet can seek a good match on similar grounds.

Precedence

Precedence refers to conventions or customs, usually well established. In judicial decisions, it is a standard set by previous cases, a *legal precedent*. Therefore, a thesis statement built on precedence requires a past event that establishes a rule of law or a point of procedure. As an example, let's return to the argument against the chipping mill. If the researcher can prove that another mill in another part of the country ruined the environment, then the researcher has a precedent for how damaging such an operation can be.

Norman Berkowitz, in his study of the world's water supply, examines the role of a commodity, such as timber and oil resources, and its precedence in the case of water. If water is a commodity, nations can buy and sell. The courts in Canada are currently resolving that issue.

Implications

If you conduct any kind of test or observation, you will probably make field notes in a research journal and tabulate your results at regular intervals. At some point, however, you will be expected to explain your findings, arrive at conclusions, and discuss the implications of your scientific inquiry. Lab reports are elementary forms of this task. What did you discover, and what does it mean?

For example, one student explored the world of drug testing before companies place the products on the market. His discussions had chilling implications for consumers. Another student examined the role of mice as carriers of Lyme disease. This work required reading as well as field research and testing to arrive at final judgments. In literature, a student examined the recurring images of birds in the poetry of Thomas Hardy to discuss the implications of the birds in terms of his basic themes.

In review, fit one or more of these argument types to the context of your project:

- Evaluation
- Interpretation
- Definition
- Proposal
- Causal argument
- Analogy
- Precedence
- Implications

Establishing a Schedule

The steps for producing a research paper have remained fundamental for many years. You will do well to follow them, even to the point of setting deadlines on the calendar for each step. In the spaces below, write dates to remind yourself when deadlines should be met.

_____ *Topic approved by the instructor*. The topic must have a built-in question or argument so you can interpret an issue and cite the opinions found in the source materials.

_____ *Reading and creating a working bibliography*. Preliminary reading establishes the basis for your research, helping you discover the quantity and quality of available sources. If you can't find much, your topic is too narrow. If you find far too many sources, your topic is too broad and needs narrowing. Chapters 6 and 7 explain the processes of finding reliable, expert sources online and in the library.

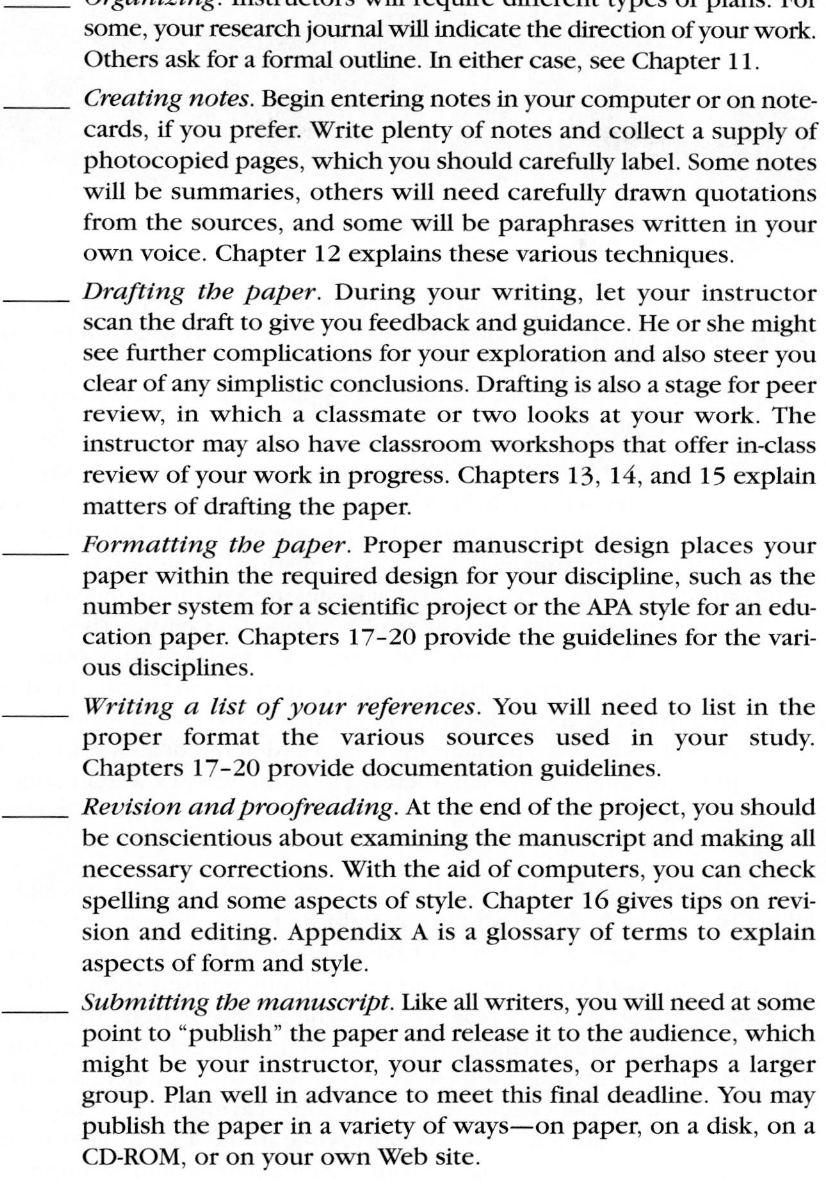

_____ *Organizing.* Instructors will require different types of plans. For some, your research journal will indicate the direction of your work. Others ask for a formal outline. In either case, see Chapter 11.

_____ *Creating notes.* Begin entering notes in your computer or on notecards, if you prefer. Write plenty of notes and collect a supply of photocopied pages, which you should carefully label. Some notes will be summaries, others will need carefully drawn quotations from the sources, and some will be paraphrases written in your own voice. Chapter 12 explains these various techniques.

_____ *Drafting the paper.* During your writing, let your instructor scan the draft to give you feedback and guidance. He or she might see further complications for your exploration and also steer you clear of any simplistic conclusions. Drafting is also a stage for peer review, in which a classmate or two looks at your work. The instructor may also have classroom workshops that offer in-class review of your work in progress. Chapters 13, 14, and 15 explain matters of drafting the paper.

_____ *Formatting the paper.* Proper manuscript design places your paper within the required design for your discipline, such as the number system for a scientific project or the APA style for an education paper. Chapters 17–20 provide the guidelines for the various disciplines.

_____ *Writing a list of your references.* You will need to list in the proper format the various sources used in your study. Chapters 17–20 provide documentation guidelines.

_____ *Revision and proofreading.* At the end of the project, you should be conscientious about examining the manuscript and making all necessary corrections. With the aid of computers, you can check spelling and some aspects of style. Chapter 16 gives tips on revision and editing. Appendix A is a glossary of terms to explain aspects of form and style.

_____ *Submitting the manuscript.* Like all writers, you will need at some point to "publish" the paper and release it to the audience, which might be your instructor, your classmates, or perhaps a larger group. Plan well in advance to meet this final deadline. You may publish the paper in a variety of ways—on paper, on a disk, on a CD-ROM, or on your own Web site.

5 Finding a Topic

Instructors usually allow students to find their own topics for a major writing assignment; thus, choose something of interest so you won't get bored after a few days. At the same time, your chosen topic will need a scholarly perspective. To clarify what we mean, let's take a look at how two students launched their projects.

- Valerie Nesbitt-Hall saw a cartoon about a young woman saying to a man, "Sorry—I only have relationships over the Internet. I'm cybersexual." Although laughing, Valerie knew she had discovered her topic—online romance. Upon investigation, she found her scholarly angle: Matching services and chat rooms are like the arranged marriages from years gone by. You can read her paper in Chapter 18.
- Norman Berkowitz, while watching news reports of the Iraqi War of 2003, noticed dry and barren land, yet history had taught him that this land between the Tigris and the Euphrates rivers was formerly a land of fruit and honey, perhaps even the Garden of Eden. What happened to it? His interest focused, thereafter, on the world's water supply, and his scholarly focus centered on the ethics of distribution of water. You can read his paper in Chapter 16.

As these examples show, an informed choice of subject is crucial for fulfilling the research assignment. You might be tempted to write from a personal interest, such as "Fishing at Lake Cumberland"; however, the content and the context of your course and the assignment itself should drive you toward a serious, scholarly perspective: "The Effects of Toxic Chemicals on the Fish of Lake Cumberland." This topic would probably send you into the field for hands-on investigation (see Chapter 8 for more on field research).

Look for a special edge or angle. The topic "Symbolism in Hawthorne's Fiction" has no originality, but "Hester Prynne in the Twenty-First Century" does. Similarly, "The Sufferings of Native Americans" could be improved to "Urban Sprawl in Morton County: The Bulldozing of Indian Burial Grounds." Melina Mosier, in Chapter 16, entitles her paper "Listening to Hamlet: The Soliloquies," but her special focus is the setting within which Hamlet performs—that is, the events prior to, during, and after each of his speeches.

In another example, you might be tempted by the topic "Computer Games," but the research assignment requires an evaluation of issues, not a description. It also requires detailed definition. A better topic might be "Learned Dexterity with Video and Computer Games," which requires the definition of learned dexterity and how some video games promote it. Even in a first-year composition class, your instructor may expect discipline-specific topics, such as:

Education	The Visually Impaired: Options for Classroom Participation
Political Science	Conservative Republicans and the Religious Right
Literature	Kate Chopin's *The Awakening* and the Women's Movement
Health	The Effects of Smoking during Pregnancy
Sociology	Parents Who Lie to Their Children

A scholarly topic requires inquiry, like those above, and it sometimes requires problem solving. For example, Sarah Bemis has a problem—she has diabetes—and she went in search of ways to manage it. Her solution—a balance of medication, monitoring, diet, and exercise—gave her the heart and soul of a good research paper.

Thus, your inquiry into the issues or your effort to solve a problem will empower the research and the paper you produce. When your topic addresses such issues, you have a reason to:

- Examine with intellectual curiosity the evidence found in the library, on the Internet, and in the field.
- Share your investigation of the issues with readers, bringing them special perspectives and enlightening details.
- Write a meaningful conclusion that discusses the implications of your study rather than merely presenting a summary of what you said in the body.

This chapter will help you mold a general subject into a workable topic. It explains how to:

- Relate your personal ideas to a scholarly problem.
- Search computer sources for issues worthy of investigation.
- Participate in online discussion groups to see what others consider important.
- Examine the library's printed sources for confirmation that your topic has been discussed in the academic literature.

CHECKLIST

Narrowing a General Subject into a Scholarly Topic

Unlike a general subject, a scholarly topic should:

- Examine one narrowed issue, not a broad subject.
- Address knowledgeable readers and carry them to another plateau of knowledge.
- Have a serious purpose—one that demands analysis of the issues, argues from a position, and explains complex details.
- Meet the expectations of the instructor and conform to the course requirements.

Relating Your Personal Ideas to a Scholarly Problem

Try to make a connection between your interests and the inherent issues of the subject. For instance, a student whose mother became seriously addicted to the Internet developed a paper from the personal experiences of her dysfunctional family. She worked within the sociology discipline and consulted journals of that field. Another student, who worked at Wal-Mart, developed a research project on discount pricing and its effect on small-town shop owners. She worked within the discipline of marketing and business management, reading appropriate literature in those areas. Begin with two activities:

1. Relate your experiences to scholarly problems and academic disciplines.
2. Speculate about the subject by listing issues, asking questions, engaging in free writing, and using other idea-generating techniques.

Connecting Personal Experience to Scholarly Topics

You can't write a personal essay and call it a research paper, yet you can choose topics close to your life. Use one of the techniques described below:

1. Combine personal interests with an aspect of academic studies:

Personal interest:	Skiing
Academic subject:	Sports medicine
Possible topics:	"Protecting the Knees"
	"Therapy for Strained Muscles"
	"Skin Treatments"

2. Consider social issues that affect you and your family:

Personal interest:	The education of my child
Social issue:	The behavior of my child in school
Possible topics:	"Children Who Are Hyperactive"
	"Should Schoolchildren Take Medicine to Calm Their Hyperactivity?"

3. Consider scientific subjects, if appropriate:

Personal interest:	The ponds and well water on the family farm
Scientific subject:	Chemical toxins in the water
Possible topic:	"The Poisoning of Underground Water Tables"

4. Let your cultural background prompt you toward detailed research into your roots, your culture, and the mythology and history of your ethnic background:

Ethnic background:	Native American
Personal interest:	History of the Apache tribes
Possible topic:	"The Indian Wars from the Native American's Point of View"

Ethnic background:	Hispanic
Personal interest:	Struggles of the Mexican child in an American classroom
Possible topic:	"Bicultural Experiences of Hispanic Students: The Failures and Triumphs"

HINT: Learn the special language of the academic discipline and use it. Every field of study, whether sociology, geology, or literature, has words to describe its analytical approach to topics, such as the *demographics* of a target audience (marketing), the *function* of loops and arrays (computer science), the *symbolism* of Maya Angelou's poetry (literature), and *observation* of human subjects (psychology). Part of your task is learning the terminology and using it appropriately.

Speculating about Your Subject to Discover Ideas and to Focus on the Issues

At some point you may need to sit back, relax, and use your imagination to contemplate the issues and problems worthy of investigation. Ideas can be generated in the following ways:

Free Writing

To free write, merely focus on a topic and write whatever comes to mind. Do not worry about grammar, style, or penmanship, but keep writing nonstop for a page or so to develop valuable phrases, comparisons, personal anecdotes, and specific thoughts that help focus issues of concern. Below, Jamie Johnston comments on violence and, perhaps, finds his topic.

> The savagery of the recent hazing incident at Glenbrook North High School demonstrates that humans, men and women, love a good fight. People want power over others, even in infancy. Just look at how siblings fight. And I read one time that twins inside the womb actually fight for supremacy, and one fetus might even devour or absorb the other one. Weird, but I guess it's true. And we fight vicariously, too, watching boxing and wrestling, cheering at fights during a hockey game, and on and on. So personally, I think human beings have always been blood thirsty and power hungry. The French philosopher Rousseau might claim a "noble savage" once existed, but personally I think we've always hated others.

This free writing set the path for this writer's investigation into the role of war in human history. Johnston found a topic for exploration. (The complete paper, Prehistoric Wars: We've Always Hated Each Other, is located in Chapter 19.)

Listing Keywords

Keep a list of words, the fundamental terms, that you see in the literature. These can help focus the direction of your research. Jamie Johnston built this list of terms:

prehistoric wars	early weapons	noble savages
remains of early victims	early massacres	slaves
sacrificial victims	human nature	power
limited resources	religious sacrifices	honor

These key words can help in writing the rough outline, as explained below.

Arranging Keywords into a Preliminary Outline

Writing a rough outline early in the project might help you see if the topic has substance so you can sustain it for the length required. At this point, the researcher needs to recognize the hierarchy of major and minor issues.

```
Prehistoric wars
    Evidence of early brutality
        Mutilated skeletons
```

Evidence of early weapons

Clubs, bows, slings, maces, etc.

Walled fortresses for defense

Speculations on reasons for war

Resources

Slaves

Revenge

Religion

Human nature and war

Quest for power

Biological urge to conquer

This initial ranking of ideas would grow in length and mature in depth during Johnston's research (see Chapter 19 for his paper).

Clustering

Another method for discovering the hierarchy of your primary topics and subtopics is to cluster ideas around a central subject. The cluster of related topics can generate a multitude of interconnected ideas. Here's an example by Jamie Johnston:

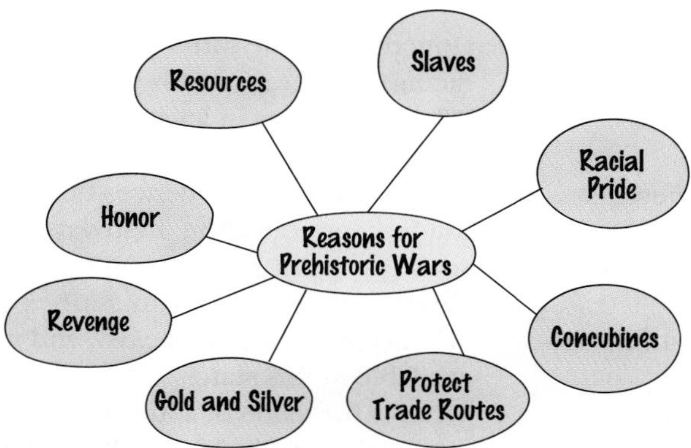

Narrowing by Comparison

Comparison limits a discussion to specific differences. Any two works, any two persons, any two groups may serve as the basis for a comparative study. Historians compare Robert E. Lee and Ulysses S. Grant. Political scientists compare conservatives and liberals. Literary scholars compare the merits of free verse and those of formal verse. Jamie Johnston discovered a comparative study in his work, as expressed in this way:

Ultimately, the key questions about the cause of war, whether ancient or current, centers on one's choice between biology and

> culture. One the one side, society as a whole wants to preserve its culture, in peace if possible. Yet the biological history of men and women suggests that we love a good fight.

That comparative choice became the capstone of Johnston's conclusion (see Chapter 19).

Asking Questions

Stretch your imagination with questions.

1. General questions examine terminology, issues, causes, etc. For example, having read Henry Thoreau's essay "Civil Disobedience," one writer asked:

   What is civil disobedience?
   Is dissent legal? Is it moral? Is it patriotic?
   Is dissent a liberal activity? Conservative?
   Should the government encourage or stifle dissent?
   Is passive resistance effective?

   Answering the questions can lead the writer to a central issue or argument, such as "Civil Disobedience: Shaping Our Nation by Confronting Unjust Laws."
2. Rhetorical questions use the modes of writing as a basis. One student framed these questions:

Comparison:	How does a state lottery compare with horse racing?
Definition:	What is a lottery in legal terms? in religious terms?
Cause/Effect:	What are the consequences of a state lottery on funding for education, highways, prisons, and social programs?
Process:	How are winnings distributed?
Classification:	What types of lotteries exist, and which are available in this state?
Evaluation:	What is the value of a lottery to the average citizen? What are the disadvantages?

3. Academic disciplines across the curriculum provide questions, as framed by one student on the topic of sports gambling.

Economics:	Does sports gambling benefit a college's athletic budget? Does it benefit the national economy?
Psychology:	What is the effect of gambling on the mental attitude of the college athlete who knows huge sums hang in the balance on his or her performance?

History:	Does gambling on sporting events have an identifiable tradition?
Sociology:	What compulsion in human nature prompts people to gamble on the prowess of an athlete or team?

4. Journalism questions explore the basic elements of a subject: Who? What? Where? When? Why? and How? For example:

Who?	Athletes
What?	Illegal drugs
When?	During off-season training and also on game day
Where?	Training rooms and elsewhere
Why?	To enhance performance
How?	By pills and injections

The journalist's questions direct you toward the issues, such as "win at all costs" or "damaging the body for immediate gratification."

5. Kenneth Burke's *pentad* questions five aspects of a topic: act, agent, scene, agency, purpose.

What happened (the act)?	Crucifixion scene in *The Old Man and the Sea*.
Who did it (agent)?	Santiago, the old fisherman.
Where and when (scene)?	At the novel's end.
How did it occur (the agency)?	Santiago carries the mast of his boat up the hill.
What is a possible motive for this event (purpose)?	Hemingway wanted to make a martyr of the old man.

Example from a journal entry as based on these questions and answers:

> The crucifixion scene in Hemingway's *The Old Man and the Sea* shows Santiago hoisting the mast of his boat on his shoulder and struggling up the Cuban hillside. Hemingway suggests Christian connotations with this scene, so I wonder if, perhaps, he has used other Christian images in the novel.

This researcher can now search the novel with a purpose—to find other Christian images, rank and classify them, and determine if, indeed, the study has merit.

Talking with Others to Refine the Topic

Personal Interviews

Like some researchers, you may need to consult formally with an expert on the topic or explore a subject informally while having coffee or a soda with

CHECKLIST

Exploring Ideas with Others

- Consult with your instructor.
- Discuss your topic with three or four classmates.
- Listen to the concerns of others.
- Conduct a formal interview (see Chapter 8).
- Join a computer discussion group.
- Take careful notes.
- Adjust your research accordingly.

a colleague, relative, or work associate. Ask people in your community for ideas and for their reactions to your general subject. For example, Valerie Nesbitt-Hall knew about a couple who married after having met initially in a chat room on the Internet. She requested an interview and got it.

Nesbitt-Hall's interview, Chapter 8; the interview in the finished paper, Chapter 18.

Casual conversations that contribute to your understanding of the subject need not be documented. However, the conscientious writer will credit a formal interview if the person approves. The interviewed subjects on pages 212–213 preferred anonymity.

Internet Discussion Groups

What are other people saying about your subject? You might use the computer to share ideas and messages with other scholars interested in your subject. Somebody may answer a question or point to an interesting aspect that has not occurred to you. With discussion groups, you have a choice:

- Classroom e-mail groups that participate in online discussions of various issues
- Online courses that feature a discussion room
- MUD and MOO discussion groups on the Internet
- Real-time chatting with participants online—even with audio and video, in some cases

For example, your instructor may set up an informal classroom discussion list and expect you to participate online with her and your fellow students. In other cases, the instructor might suggest that you investigate a specific site, such as

alt.religion

for a religious subject or

alt.current-events.usa

for a paper on gun control laws. You can find many discussion groups, but the manner in which you use them is vital to your academic success. Rather than chat, solicit ideas and get responses to your questions about your research.

Using the World Wide Web to Refine Your Topic

The Internet provides a quick and easy way to find a topic and refine it to academic standards. Chapter 6 discusses these matters in greater detail. For now, use the subject directories and keyword searches.

Internet searches, Chapter 6.

Using an Internet Subject Directory

Many search engines have a directory of subjects on the home page that can link you quickly to specific topics. With each mouse click, the topic narrows. For example, one student studying Thomas Jefferson consulted AltaVista's subject categories and clicked on Reference where she found Archives, then Early American Archives, and eventually *Early American Review,* a journal that featured an article entitled "Jefferson and His Daughters." The search occurs quickly—in seconds, not minutes.

However, the Internet has made it difficult to apply traditional evaluations to an electronic article: Is it accurate, authoritative, objective, current, timely, and thorough in coverage? Some Internet sites are advocates to special interests, some sites market products or sprinkle the site with banners to commercial sites and sales items, some sites are personal home pages, and then many sites offer objective news and scholarly information. The answers:

1. Go to the reliable databases available through your library, such as InfoTrac, PsychInfo, UMI ProQuest, Electric Library, and EBSCOhost. These are monitored sites that give information filtered by editorial boards and peer review. You can reach them from remote locations at home or the dorm by connecting electronically to your library.
2. Look for articles on the Internet that first appeared in a printed version. These will have been, in most cases, examined by an editorial board.
3. Look for a reputable sponsor, especially a university, museum, or professional organization.
4. Go to Chapter 6, which discusses the pros and cons of Internet searching, and also look at the Web site accompanying this book for additional tips on methods for evaluating Internet sources, with examples, at <**http://longman.awl.com/lester/**>.

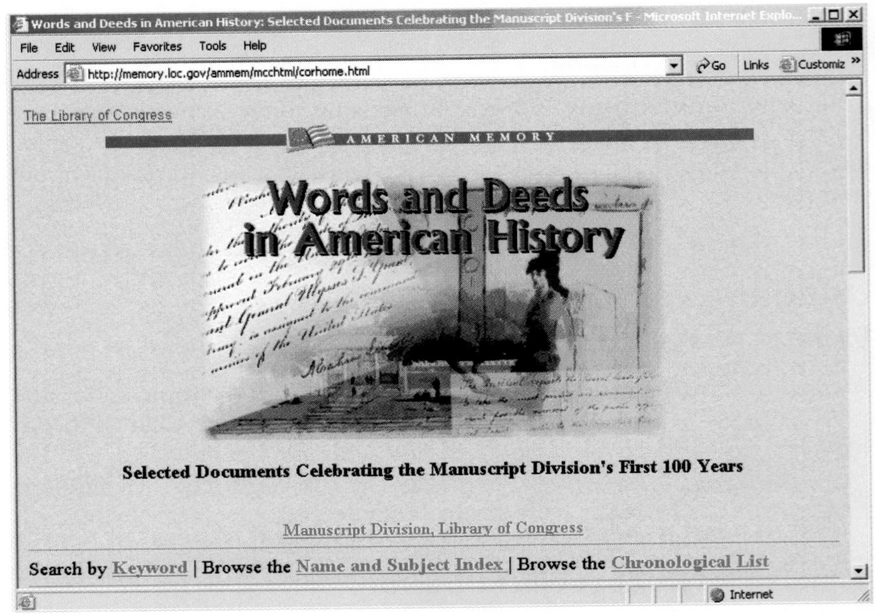

FIGURE 5.1 A Library of Congress site "Words and Deeds in American History," found by using a keyword search for American history manuscripts.

Using an Internet Keyword Search

To find sites quickly, enter the keywords for a topic you wish to explore. For example, entering "American history manuscripts" at one of the browsers such as Google will produce a page like that shown in *Figure 5.1*. It has links to search the files by keyword, name, subject, and chronological list. From there you can search for comments on the Puritans, the Jeffersonian years, the Andrew Jackson administration, and so forth.

Internet search engines will force you to narrow your general subject. For example, one student entered "Internet + addiction," and the computer brought up thousands of sources. By tightening the request to the phrase "Internet addiction," enclosed within quotation marks, she cut the list considerably and discovered other keywords: cyber-wellness, weboholics, and netaddiction. She realized she had a workable topic.

Help with keyword searches, Chapter 6.

Using the Library's Electronic Databases to Find and Narrow a Subject

College libraries have academic databases not found on general search engines, such as InfoTrac, Silverplatter, and UMI-ProQuest. These database

Evaluating Internet Sources, Chapter 6, and also this book's Web site at <http://www.longman.awl/lester>.

files are reliable because they refer you to thousands of articles that have been peer reviewed by experts or filtered through editorial processes. For now, examine various titles as you search for your own topic. If you see one of interest, click on it for more information. Follow these steps:

1. **Select a database.** Some databases, such as InfoTrac and UMI-ProQuest, are general; use them to find a subject. Other databases focus on one discipline; for example, PsycINFO searches psychological sources, ERIC indexes educational sources, and Health & Wellness describes itself. These databases will move you quickly to a list of articles on your topic.
2. **List keywords or a phrase to describe your topic, enclosed within quotation marks.** Avoid using just one general word. For example, the word *food* on the EBSCOhost database produced 10,000 possible sites. The two-word phrase "healing foods" produced a manageable 22 sites. Here is one of 22 entries: "Healing Foods." *Psychology Today* 32.4 (July-Aug. 1999): 24.
3. **Examine the various entries for possible topics.** Look for relevant articles, browse the descriptions, read the abstracts, and—when you find something valuable—print the full text, if it's available.

Using the Library's Electronic Book Catalog to Find a Topic

Instructors expect you to cite information from a few books, and the library's book index will suggest topics and confirm that your subject has been treated with in-depth studies in book form, not just on the Internet or in magazines. Called by different names at each library (e.g., Acorn, Felix, Access), the electronic index lists all books housed in the library, plus film strips, videotapes, and similar items. It does not index articles in magazines and journals, but it will tell you which periodicals are housed in the library and whether they are in printed form or on microforms. Like the electronic databases, the index will help you find a workable topic by guiding you quickly from general subjects to subtopics and, finally, to specific books.

Chapter 7 describes the process in great detail with examples. For now, enter your subject, such as *food, nutrition, allergies,* to see what titles are available in the library. The titles, such as *Children and Food Allergies, Environmental Poisons in Our Food,* or *Living with Something in the Air,* will suggest a possible topic, perhaps "Special Diets to Control Allergic Reactions to Food." If you go into the stacks to find a book, take the time to examine nearby books on the same shelf, for they will likely treat the same subject.

With your working topic in hand, do some exploratory reading in books to enhance your understanding of the topic. Look to see how your subject is discussed in the literature. Carefully read the **titles** of books and chapter titles, noting any key terms:

The Lessons of the French Revolution
Napoleon's Ambition and the Quest for Domination
"Perspectives: Napoleon's Relations with the Catholic Church"

These titles provide several keywords and possible topics for a research paper: *Napoleon's ambition, Napoleon and the church, the French Revolution.*

Inspect a book's **table of contents** to find topics of interest. A typical history book might display these headings in the table of contents:

The French Revolution
The Era of Napoleon
Reaction to Napoleon and More Revolutions
The Second Empire of France

If any of these headings look interesting, go to the book's **index** for additional headings, such as this sample:

Napoleon
    becomes Emperor, 174–176
    becomes First Consul, 173
    becomes Life Consul, 174
    and the Catholic Church, 176–178
    character of, 168–176
    and codes of law, 178–179
    defeated by enemies, 192–197
    defeats Austrians, 170
    encounters opposition, 190–191
    extends empire in Europe, 180–189
    seizes power for "One Hundred Days" 198
    sent to Elba, 197
    sent to St. Helena, 199

If you see something that looks interesting, read the designated pages to consider the topic further. For example, you might read about Napoleon's return from Elba to his beloved France for a few additional days of glory before the darkness of confinement at St. Helena.

HINT: Topic selection goes beyond choosing a general category (e.g., "single mothers"). It includes finding a research-provoking issue or question, such as "The foster parent program seems to have replaced the orphanage system. Has it been effective?" That is, you need to take a stand, adopt a belief, or begin asking questions.

Expressing a Thesis Sentence, Enthymeme, or Hypothesis

One central statement will usually control an essay's direction and content, so as early as possible, begin thinking in terms of a controlling idea. Each has a separate mission:

- A **thesis sentence** advances a conclusion the writer will defend: *Contrary to what some philosophers have advanced, human beings have always participated in wars.*
- An **enthymeme** uses a *because* clause to make a claim the writer will defend: *There has never been a "noble savage," as such, because even prehistoric human beings fought frequent wars for numerous reasons.*
- A **hypothesis** is a theory that must be tested in the lab, in the literature, and/or by field research to prove its validity: *Human beings are motivated by biological instincts toward the physical overthrow of perceived enemies.*

Let us look at each type in more detail.

Thesis

A thesis sentence expands your topic into a scholarly proposal, one that you will try to prove and defend in your paper. It does not state the obvious, such as "Langston Hughes was a great poet from Harlem." That sentence will not provoke an academic discussion because your readers know that any published poet has talent. The writer must narrow and isolate one issue by finding a critical focus, such as this one that a student considered for her essay:

> Langston Hughes used a controversial vernacular language that paved the way for later artists, even today's rap musicians.

This sentence advances an idea the writer can develop fully and defend with evidence. The writer has made a connection between the subject, *Langston Hughes,* and the focusing agent, *vernacular language*. Look at two other writers' preliminary thesis statements:

THESIS: Chat rooms and online matching services enable people to meet only after a prearranged engagement by email.

THESIS: Hamlet's character is shaped, in part, by Shakespeare's manipulation of the stage setting for Hamlet's soliloquies.

In the first, the writer will defend online romance as similar to prearranged marriages of the past. In the second, the writer will discuss how various shifts in dramatic setting can affect the message of the primary character.

Depending on the critical approach, one topic might produce several issues from which the writer might pick:

Biological approach: Functional foods may be a promising addition to the diet of those who wish to avoid certain diseases.

Economic approach: Functional foods can become an economic weapon in the battle against rising health care costs.

Historic approach: Other civilizations, including primitive tribes, have known about food's healing properties for centuries. Why did we let modern chemistry blind us to its benefits?

Each statement above will provoke a response from the reader, who will demand a carefully structured defense in the body of the paper.

Your thesis anticipates your conclusion by setting in motion the examination of facts and pointing the reader toward the special idea of your paper. Note below how three writers developed different thesis sentences even though they had the same topic, "Santiago in Hemingway's *The Old Man and the Sea*." (This novel narrates the toils of an old Cuban fisherman named Santiago, who desperately needs the money to be gained by returning with a good catch of fish. On this day he catches a marlin. After a long struggle, Santiago ties the huge marlin to the side of his small boat. However, during the return in the darkness, sharks attack the marlin so that he arrives home with only a skeleton of the fish. He removes his mast and carries it, like a cross, up the hill to his home.)

Thesis: Poverty forced Santiago to venture too far and struggle beyond reason in his attempt to land the marlin.

This writer will examine the economic conditions of Santiago's trade.

Thesis: The giant marlin is a symbol for all of life's obstacles and hurdles, and Santiago is a symbol for all suffering humans.

This writer will examine the religious and social symbolism of the novel.

Thesis: Hemingway's portrayal of Santiago demonstrates the author's deep respect for Cuba and its stoic heroes.

This writer takes a social approach in order to examine the Cuban culture and its influence on Hemingway.

Enthymeme

Your instructor might want the research paper to develop an argument expressed as an enthymeme, which is a claim supported with a *because* clause. Examples:

Enthymeme: Hyperactive children need medication because ADHD is a medical disorder, not a behavioral problem.

The claim that children need medication is supported by the stated reason that the condition is a medical problem, not one of behavior. This writer will need to address any unstated assumptions—for example, that medication alone will solve the problem.

ENTHYMEME: Because people are dying all around the globe from water shortages, the countries with an abundance of water have an ethical obligation to share it.

The claim that countries with water have an ethical obligation to share is, of course, the point of contention.

Hypothesis

As a theory, the hypothesis requires careful examination to prove its validity, and sometimes that doesn't happen. The proof isn't there, so the writer must present negative results—and that's okay. Disproving a theory is just as valid as proving it. Here are the various types of hypotheses.

The Theoretical Hypothesis:

Discrimination against young women in the classroom, known as "shortchanging," harms the women academically, socially, and psychologically.

Here the student will produce a theoretical study by citing literature on "shortchanging."

The Conditional Hypothesis:

Diabetes can be controlled by medication, monitoring, diet, and exercise.

Certain conditions must be met. The control will depend on the patient's ability to perform the four tasks adequately to prove the hypothesis valid.

The Relational Hypothesis:

Class size affects the number of written assignments by writing instructors.

This type of hypothesis claims that as one variable changes, so does another, or it claims that something is more or less than another. It could be tested by examining and correlating class size and assignments, a type of field research (see pages 218–220).

The Causal Hypothesis:

A child's toy is determined by television commercials.

This causal hypothesis assumes the mutual occurrence of two factors and asserts that one factor is responsible for the other. The student who is a parent could conduct research to prove or disprove the supposition. A review of the literature might also serve the writer.

In effect, your work as based on a hypothesis might be a theoretical examination of the literature, but it might also be an actual visit to an Indian burial ground or a field test of one species of hybrid corn. Everything is subject to examination, even the number of times you blink while reading this text.

Drafting a Research Proposal

A research proposal is presented in one of two forms: (1) a short paragraph to identify the project for yourself and your instructor, or (2) a formal, multipage report that provides background information, your rationale for conducting the study, a review of the literature, your methods, and the conclusions you hope to prove.

The Short Proposal

A short proposal identifies five essential ingredients of your work:

- The specific topic
- The purpose of the paper (explain, analyze, argue)
- The intended audience (general or specialized)
- Your voice as the writer (informer or advocate)
- The preliminary thesis sentence or opening hypothesis

For example, here is the proposal of Norman Berkowitz (see his paper in Chapter 16):

> The world is running out of fresh water while we sip our Evian. However, the bottled water craze signals something—we don't trust our fresh tap water. We have an emerging crisis on our hands, and some authorities forecast world wars over water rights. The issue of water touches almost every facet of our lives, from religious rituals and food supply to disease and political instability. We might frame this hypothesis: Water will soon replace oil as the economic resource most treasured by nations of the world. However, that assertion would prove difficult to defend and may not be true at all. Rather, we need to look elsewhere, at human behavior, and at human responsibility for preserving the environment for our children. Accordingly, this paper will examine (1) the issues with regard to supply and demand, (2) the political power struggles that may emerge, and (3) the ethical implications for those who control the world's scattered supply of fresh water.

This writer has identified the basic nature of his project and can now go in search of evidence that will defend the argument.

The Long Proposal

Some instructors may assign the long proposal, which includes some or all of the following elements:

1. A *cover page* with the title of the project, your name, and the person or agency to whom you are submitting the proposal:

   Arranged Marriages: The Revival Is Online

   By Valerie Nesbitt-Hall

   Submitted to

   Dr. Lee Ling and

   The University Committee on Computers

2. An *abstract* that summarizes your project in 50 to 100 words (see Chapter 16 for additional information).

   Arranged marriages are considered old-fashioned or a product of some foreign cultures, but the Internet, especially its online dating services and chat rooms, has brought arranged marriages into the twenty-first century. The Internet provides an opportunity for people to meet, chat, reveal themselves at their own pace, and find, perhaps, a friend, lover, and even a spouse. Thus, computer matchmaking has social and psychological implications that have been explored by psychologists and sociologists. The social implications affect the roles of both men and women in the workplace and in marital relations. The psychological implications involve online infidelity, cybersexual addiction, and damage to self-esteem; yet those dangers are balanced against success stories. Those persons who maintain an anonymous distance until a true romance blossoms are anticipating, in essence, a carefully arranged date that might become a marriage.

3. A *purpose statement* with your *rationale* for the project. In essence, this is your thesis sentence or hypothesis, along with your identification of the audience that your work will address and the role you will play as investigator and advocate.

   This project was suggested by Dr. Lee Ling to fulfill the writing project for English 2100 and also to serve the University Committee on

CHECKLIST

Addressing the Reader

Identify your audience. Have you visualized your audience, its expertise, and its expectations? Your perception of the reader will affect your voice, style, and choice of words.

Identify your discipline. Readers in each discipline will bring differing expectations to your paper with regard to content, language, design, and documentation format.

Meet the needs of your readers. Are you saying something worthwhile? something new? Do not bore the reader with known facts from an encyclopedia. (This latter danger is the reason many instructors discourage the use of an encyclopedia as a source.)

Engage and even challenge your readers. Find an interesting or different point of view. For example, a report on farm life can become a challenging examination of chemical contamination because of industrial sprawl into rural areas, and an interpretation of a novel can become an examination of the prison system rather than a routine discourse on theme or characterization.

Computers, which has launched a project on Student Internet Awareness. This paper, if approved, would become part of the committee's *Student Booklet on Internet Protocol*.

4. A *statement of qualification* that explains your experience and, perhaps, the special qualities you bring to the project. Nesbitt-Hall included this comment in her proposal:

    I bring first-hand experience to this study. I have explored the Internet like many other students. I joined a service, entered my profile, and began looking at photographs and profiles. It was exciting at first, but then I became bored; it seemed that everything and everybody blended into a fog of indifference. Then when some jerk sent a vulgar message I withdrew my profile and user name. I'll just remain old-fashioned and start my dates with a soda at the student center.

    If you have no experience with the subject, you can omit the statement of qualification.

5. A *review of the literature*, which surveys the articles and books that you have examined in your preliminary work.

Limited research is being done in the area of online romance. My search of the literature produced a surprisingly short list of journal articles. Maheu (1999) has discussed methods of helping clients, even to the point of counseling in cyberspace itself, which would establish professional relationships online. Schneider and Weiss (2001) describe it but offer little psychoanalysis. Cooper (2002) has an excellent collection of articles in his guidebook for clinicians, and he has argued that online dating has the potential to lower the nation's divorce rate. Kass (2003) has identified the "distanced nearness" of a chat room that encourages "self-revelation while maintaining personal boundaries" (cited in Rasdan, 2003, p. 71). Epstein (2003) has argued that many arranged marriages, by parents or by cyberspace, have produced enduring love because of rational deliberation performed before moments of passionate impulse. In addition, Schneider and Weiss (2001) have listed some of the advantages to online romance: It links people miles apart; impressions are made by words, not looks; there is time to contemplate a message; there is time to compose a well-written response; and messages can be reviewed and revised before transmission (p. 66).

6. A *description of your research methods,* which is the design of the *materials* you will need, your *timetable,* and, where applicable, your *budget.* These elements are often a part of a scientific study, so see Chapters 18 and 20 for work in the social, physical, and biological sciences. Here is Nesbitt-Hall's description:

This paper will examine online dating as a forum for arranging dates and even marriages. The Method section will explore the role of Match.com and other dating services as a testing board for people with similar interests to form communication lines that might last one minute or one year. The Subjects section will examine the people who participate, from the modest person to one who is aggressive, and from high-profile people like Rush Limbaugh to those with low profiles and quiet lifestyles. The Procedures section examines the process so common to the services: to bring two compatible people together on the Web. There they can e-mail each other, participate in IM chats, send attachments of favorite songs or personal photographs, and

CHECKLIST

Explaining Your Purpose in the Research Proposal

Research papers accomplish several tasks:

- They explain and define the topic.
- They analyze the specific issues.
- They persuade the reader with the weight of the evidence.

1. Use *explanation* to review and itemize factual data. Sarah Bemis explains how diabetes can be managed (see Chapter 20), and Jamie Johnston explains the nature of prehistoric wars (see Chapter 19).
2. Use *analysis* to classify various parts of the subject and to investigate each one in depth. Melinda Mosier examines Hamlet's soliloquies (Chapter 16) and Valerie Nesbitt-Hall analyzes Internet romance (Chapter 18).
3. Use *persuasion* to question the general attitudes about a problem and then to affirm new theories, advance a solution, recommend a course of action, or—in the least—invite the reader into an intellectual dialog. Norman Berkowitz argues for ethical distribution of the world's water supply (Chapter 16).

eventually exchange real names, phone numbers, and addresses. The various services provide not only lists of available people but also personality tests, detailed profiles of subjects, and even nightclubs with calling cards for patrons to share with others whom they find interesting. The Results section explains the obvious—that online romance can prove productive for some people, interesting for the lurking voyeur, and an absolute disaster for the gullible and careless. The Case Study provides a success story for online dating. The Discussion section explores the social and psychological implications for men and women, especially for those captured by cybersexual addiction.

YOUR RESEARCH PROJECT

1. Make a list of your personal interests and items that affect your mental and physical activities, such as homework, hiking, or relations with your family. Examine each item on the list to see if you can find an academic angle that will make the topic fit the context of your research assignment. See Relating Your Personal Ideas to a Scholarly Problem, earlier in this chapter for more help.
2. Ask questions about a possible subject, using the list in this chapter.
3. Look around your campus or community for subjects. Talk with your classmates and even your instructor about campus issues. Focus on your hometown community in search of a problem, such as the demise of the Main Street merchants. Investigate any environmental concerns in your area, from urban sprawl to beach erosion to waste disposal. Think seriously about a piece of literature you have read, perhaps Fitzgerald's *The Great Gatsby*. If you are a parent, consider issues related to children, such as finding adequate child care. Once you have a subject of interest, apply to it some of the narrowing techniques, such as clustering, free writing, or listing keywords.
4. To determine if sufficient sources will be available and to narrow the subject even further, visit the Internet, investigate the library's databases (e.g., InfoTrac), and dip into the electronic book catalog at your library. Keep printouts of any interesting articles or book titles.

6 Finding and Filtering Internet Sources

The **Internet** is now a major source of research information, and we know that many students start their research on the World Wide Web. That's okay. You may start your research on the Web, but don't you dare stop there! Let's address immediately the good, the bad, and the ugly on matters of Internet sources. First, the ugly: You can buy a canned research paper and submit it as your own. However, just because you buy a research paper does not mean you own it and can put your name on it. You always have the obligation of identifying the source, and the author or publisher retains rights to the content, whether in printed form or an electronic format. Also ugly, and also considered **plagiarism,** is downloading Internet material into your paper without citation and documentation, thereby making it appear to be your own work.

More about plagiarism, Chapter 9.

Second, the bad: You will find articles that are not worthy of citation in your research paper. You must filter personal opinion pieces that are unsubstantiated in any way. These will pop up on your browser list and may be nothing more than a home page. You must also filter commercial sites that disguise their sales pitch with informative articles. In other cases, you will encounter advocacy pages with a predetermined bias that dismisses objective analysis of an issue in favor of the group's position on the environment, gun control, abortion, and so forth. This chapter will help you identify the bad.

Third, the good: The Internet, if you know where to look, is loaded with absolutely marvelous material that was unattainable just a few years ago. It offers instant access to millions of computer files relating to almost every subject, including articles, illustrations, sound and video clips, and raw data. Much of it meets basic academic standards, yet you should keep in mind that the best academic material is available only through databases at your college library, such as InfoTrac and PsycINFO. That is, you can rest assured that scholarly articles found through the library's Web are far more reliable than those you might find by general access through Google or Yahoo!

Therefore, this chapter will help you with two tasks: (1) to become an efficient searcher for academic information on the Web, and (2) to become accomplished at evaluating and filtering the complex web of Internet sites.

CHECKLIST

Using Online Rather Than Print Versions

Online versions of articles offer advantages, but they also present problems. On the plus side, you can view them almost instantly on the monitor rather than searching, threading, and viewing microfilm or microfiche. You can save or print an abstract or article without the hassle of photocopying, and you can even download material to your disk and, where appropriate, insert it into your paper. However, keep these issues in mind:

- The text may differ from the original printed version and may even be a digest. Therefore, cite the Internet source to avoid giving the appearance of citing from the printed version. There are often major differences between the same article in *USA Today* and in *USA Today DeskTopNews*. Cite the correct one in your Works Cited.
- Online abstracts may not accurately represent the full article. In fact, some abstracts are not written by the author at all but by an editorial staff. Therefore, resist the desire to quote from the abstract and, instead, write a paraphrase of it—or, better, find the full text and cite from it (see also Chapter 7).
- You may need to subscribe (at a modest cost) to some sites. A company has the right to make demands before giving you access.

Beginning an Internet Search

To trace the good and the bad, let's follow the trail of one student, Sherri James, who has decided, because she is a competitive swimmer, to investigate the use of drugs for enhancing one's performance in the pool—not that she wants to try drugs but rather to educate herself and produce a research paper at the same time. Remember, we said to find topics that affect you personally.

Probably the first thing most of you do, like Sherri James, is visit your favorite browser, such as one of these:

About.com	**http://home.about.com/index.htm**
AltaVista	**http://altavista.digital.com/**
AOL Netfind	**http://www.aol.com/netfind**
Excite	**http://www.excite.com**
Google	**http://www.google.com/**
Hotbot	**http://www.hotbot.com**
Infoseek	**http://infoseek.com**
InferenceFind	**http://www.inference.com/**

Lycos	**http://www.lycos.com**
Magellan	**http://www.magellan.com**
Webcrawler	**http://webcrawler.com**
Yahoo!	**http://www.yahoo.com**

At the search window, Sherri James typed "fitness and drugs." Immediately, she was directed to Beachbody.com, healthandfitness.com, and truly huge.com. Notice that all three sites are commercial sites (*.com*). Also, they each want to sell something—Power 90 supplements, a carb-electrolyte drink, and cybergenics nutritional products and instructional videos. One site advertised steroids for sale, such as Epogen and Erythropoietin. For Sherri James, these Internet locations offered no information, except to suggest this note that she jotted into her research journal:

> With supplements, drugs, and even steroids readily available on Web sites, it's no wonder so many athletes get caught in the "quick-fix" bodybuilding trap.

Next, Sherri James found two articles about swimming: "Three Steps to Swimming Success" and "Beat Fatigue in Long Meets." These were written by Rick Curl, a noted swim coach who has trained Olympic champions. Curl advocates three elements in training: in-pool workouts, out-of-pool training, and nutrition. For nutrition, the article encourages swimmers to "refuel their muscles with a sports drink containing plenty of carbohydrates." And guess what? The articles are promoting and selling two sports drinks. Sherri James noticed that the site, Powering Muscles, is sponsored by PacificHealth Laboratories, the makers of ACCELERADE sports drink and Eudurox Recovery drink. This site, too, was a *.com* site. Thus, Sherri James wrote a note to position the good instruction from the swim coach within the context of the site:

> Despite promoting two commercial supplements for swimmers, successful swim coach Rick Curl goes beyond pitching the nutritional products to offer valuable advice on in-pool techniques as well as out-of-pool aerobic training, stretching, and calisthenics.

At this point, Sherri James decided to try the browser's directory. In Yahoo! she found hyperlinks to:

Business and Economy
Computer and Internet
News and Media
Entertainment
Recreation and Sports

She clicked on the last one and found another list, which contained what she was looking for: a hyperlink to **Drugs in Sports**. At this site she found 13 links, among them:

Doping and Sports—collective expert assessment on doping by bicyclists

Drugs in Sport—provides information on performance-enhancing drugs in sport, the latest articles on the subject, reports, resources, and useful Web sites

Findlaw: Drug Use in Sports—includes a story archive and background information on testing, prevention, policies, and commonly used drugs.

NCAA Drug Testing—information on the association's drug testing policy

PlayClean—promotes anti-doping policies and preventing youth drug use through sports; from the Office of National Drug Control Policy

Sherri had now found site domains other than commercial ones, such as *.org*, *.gov*, *.net*, and *.edu*. At NCAA.org she was able to print out the NCAA (National Collegiate Athletic Association) Drug-Testing Program and use portions of the rules in her paper. Here is one of her notes:

> The NCAA clearly forbids blood doping. It says, "The practice of blood doping (the intravenous injection of whole blood, packed red blood cells or blood substitutes) is prohibited and any evidence confirming use will be cause for action consistent with that taken for a positive drug test" (Bylaw 31.1.3.1.1).

At Playclean, Sherri found a link to **www.whitehousedrugpolicy.gov** and an article entitled "Women and Drugs" by the Office of National Drug Control Policy. She was now finding material worthy of notetaking:

> A study by scientists at Columbia University has found the signals and situations of risk are different for girls and that "girls and young women are more vulnerable to abuse and addiction: they get hooked faster and suffer the consequences sooner than boys and young men" ("Women and Drugs").

Sherri James has begun to find her way to better sources on the Internet, but she will still need to examine the academic databases by logging on at her college library (see Chapter 7, where we will again watch Sherri search for sources). She will also need to consider doing field research, such as interviewing fellow athletes or developing a questionnaire (see Chapter 8).

CHECKLIST

Evaluating Internet Sources

The Internet supplies huge amounts of material, some of it excellent and some not so good. You must make judgments about the validity and veracity of these materials. In addition to your commonsense judgment, here are a few guidelines:

1. Prefer the *.edu* and *.org* sites. Usually, these are domains developed by an educational institution, such as Ohio State University, or by a

(continued on page 170)

(continued from page 169)

professional organization, such as the American Psychological Association. Of course, *.edu* sites also include many student papers, which can include unreliable information.

2. The *.gov* (government) and *.mil* (military) sites usually have reliable materials. The *.com* (commercial) sites are suspect for several reasons: (1) they are selling advertising space, (2) they often charge for access to their files, (3) they can be Internet service provider (ISP) sites, which people pay to use and to post their material. Although some ISP sites have good information, they are usually no more reliable than vanity presses or want ads.
3. Look for the *professional* affiliation of the writer, which you will find in the opening credits or an e-mail address. Go in search of the writer's home page. Type in the writer's name at a search engine to see how many results are listed. Also, type in the writer's name at **Amazon.com** for a list of his or her published books. If you find no information on the writer at these various sources, abandon the writer's words and search elsewhere.
4. Look for a bibliography that accompanies the article, which will indicate the scholarly nature of this writer's work.
5. Usenet discussion groups offer valuable information at times, but some articles lack sound, fundamental reasoning or evidence to support the opinions.
6. Treat e-mail messages as *mail,* not scholarly articles. A similar rule applies to chat.
7. Check whether the site gives you hypertext links to professional sites or to commercial sites. Links to other educational sites serve as a modern bibliography to more reliable sources. Links to commercial sites are often attempts to sell you something.
8. Learn to distinguish among the different types of Web sites, such as advocacy pages, personal home pages, informational pages, and business and marketing pages. This site provides evaluation techniques: **http://www2.widener.edu/Wolfgram-Memorial-Library/webevaluation/webeval.htm**
9. Your skills in critical thinking can usually determine the validity of a site. For more help in critical thinking, visit Robert Harris's site: **http://www.virtualsalt.com/evalu8it.htm**

Reading an Internet Address

For most of you, this basic information is unnecessary, but a few might need it. In the library, you must employ a book's call number to find it. On the Internet, you employ a Uniform Resource Locator (URL), like this one: http://www.georgetown.edu/library_catalogues.html

- The *protocol* (http://) transmits data.
- The *server* (www, for World Wide Web) is the global Internet service that connects the multitude of computers and the Internet files.
- The *domain* (georgetown.edu) names the organization feeding information into the server with a *suffix* to label the type of organization: *.com* (commercial), *.edu* (educational), *.gov* (government), *.mil* (military), *.net* (network organization), and *.org* (organization).
- The *directory/file* (library_catalogues) finds one of the server's directories and then a specific file.
- The *hypertext markup language* (html) names the computer language used to write the file.

Often, knowing just the protocol and the server.domain will get you to a home site from which you can search deeper for files. The URL http://lcweb.loc.gov/homepage will take you to the Library of Congress (see Figure 6.1), where you can examine a specific directory, such as Thomas: Congress at Work (see Figure 6.2). In Thomas, you have access to legislation of both the House and Senate, with links to many other sites and a search engine for finding specific information.

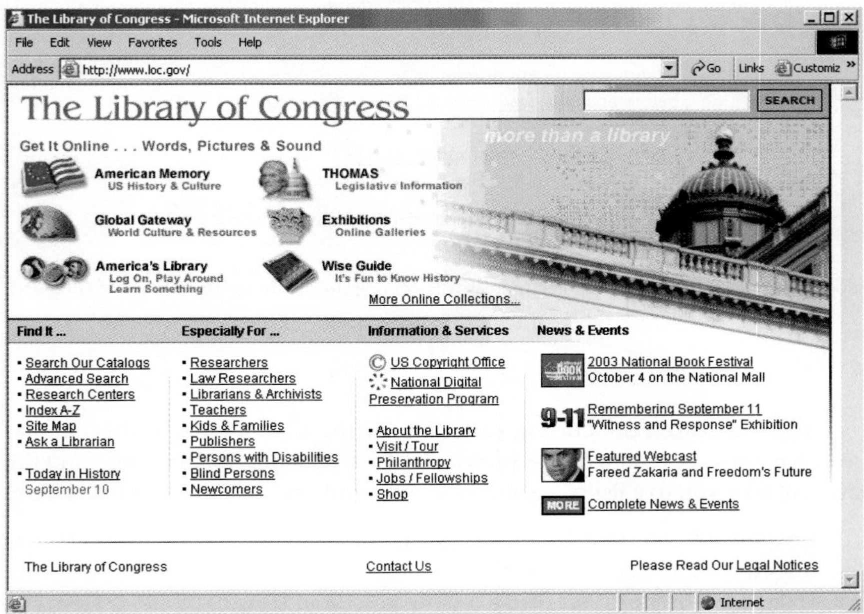

FIGURE 6.1 The home page for the Library of Congress.

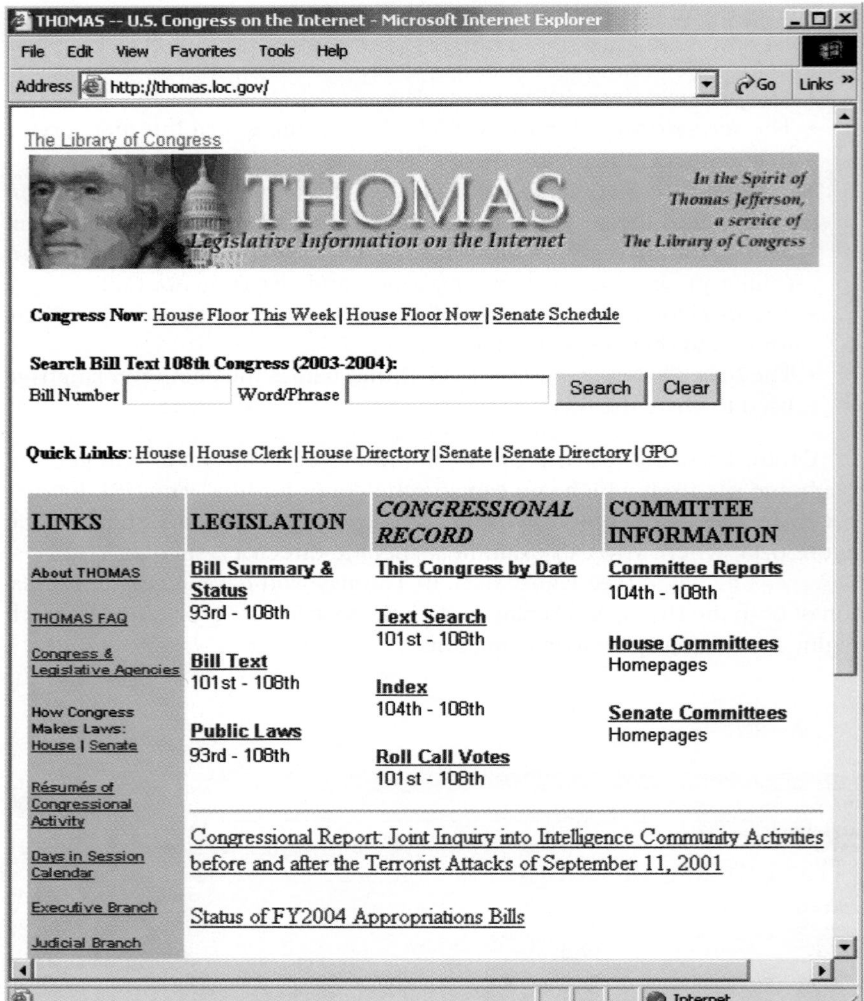

FIGURE 6.2 The home page for Thomas, the congressional site for the Library of Congress.

You can search the current Congress for the text of bills. At the Thomas search engine, enter a word or phrase, such as "student financial aid," and the site will take you to a list of resolutions, bills, and acts, like the five listed here:

1. Responsible Student Financial Assistance Assurance Act of 2003 (Introduced in House) [H.R.696.IH]
2. Hazing Prohibition Act of 2003 (Introduced in House) [H.R.1207.IH]

3. To express the support and commitment of the U.S. House of Representatives for the troops serving to protect and defend the United States of America by encouraging actions to extend . . . (Introduced in House) [H.RES.158.IH]
4. To express the sense of the House of Representatives that the maximum Pell Grant should be increased to $5,800. (Introduced in House) [HRES.144.I]
5. Educational Excellence for All Learners Act of 2003 (Introduced in Senate) [S.8.IS]

At this point, you have the option of reading the House bills, the resolution, or the Senate bill by clicking on the colored links. The House bill on hazing and loss of financial aid is shown in Figure 6.3. In effect, you will have moved rather quickly from the home page of the Library of Congress to a specific piece of legislation you might wish to use in your paper.

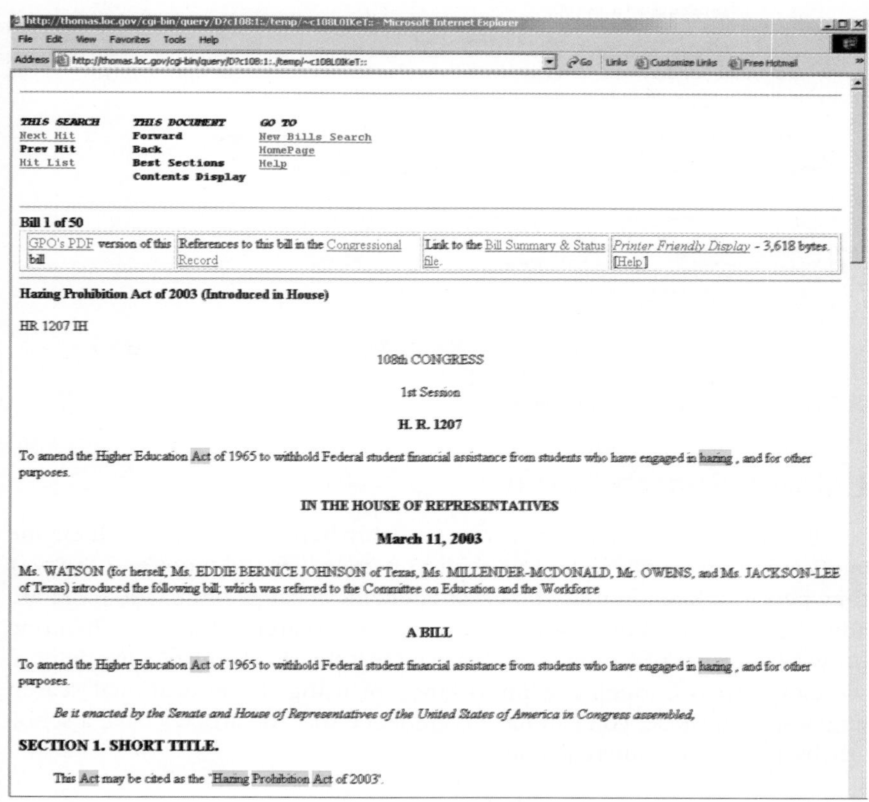

http://thomas.loc.gov/cgi-bin/query/D?c108:1:./temp/~c108L0IKeT:: - Microsoft Internet Explorer

File Edit View Favorites Tools Help

Address http://thomas.loc.gov/cgi-bin/query/D?c108:1:./temp/~c108L0IKeT::

THIS SEARCH	THIS DOCUMENT	GO TO
Next Hit	Forward	New Bills Search
Prev Hit	Back	HomePage
Hit List	Best Sections	Help
	Contents Display	

Bill 1 of 50

GPO's PDF version of this bill	References to this bill in the Congressional Record	Link to the Bill Summary & Status file.	Printer Friendly Display - 3,618 bytes. [Help]

Hazing Prohibition Act of 2003 (Introduced in House)

HR 1207 IH

108th CONGRESS

1st Session

H. R. 1207

To amend the Higher Education Act of 1965 to withhold Federal student financial assistance from students who have engaged in hazing, and for other purposes.

IN THE HOUSE OF REPRESENTATIVES

March 11, 2003

Ms. WATSON (for herself, Ms. EDDIE BERNICE JOHNSON of Texas, Ms. MILLENDER-MCDONALD, Mr. OWENS, and Ms. JACKSON-LEE of Texas) introduced the following bill; which was referred to the Committee on Education and the Workforce

A BILL

To amend the Higher Education Act of 1965 to withhold Federal student financial assistance from students who have engaged in hazing, and for other purposes.

Be it enacted by the Senate and House of Representatives of the United States of America in Congress assembled,

SECTION 1. SHORT TITLE.

This Act may be cited as the 'Hazing Prohibition Act of 2003'.

FIGURE 6.3 H.R.1207.I, a bill in the House of Representatives on hazing. (*Continued on page 174*)

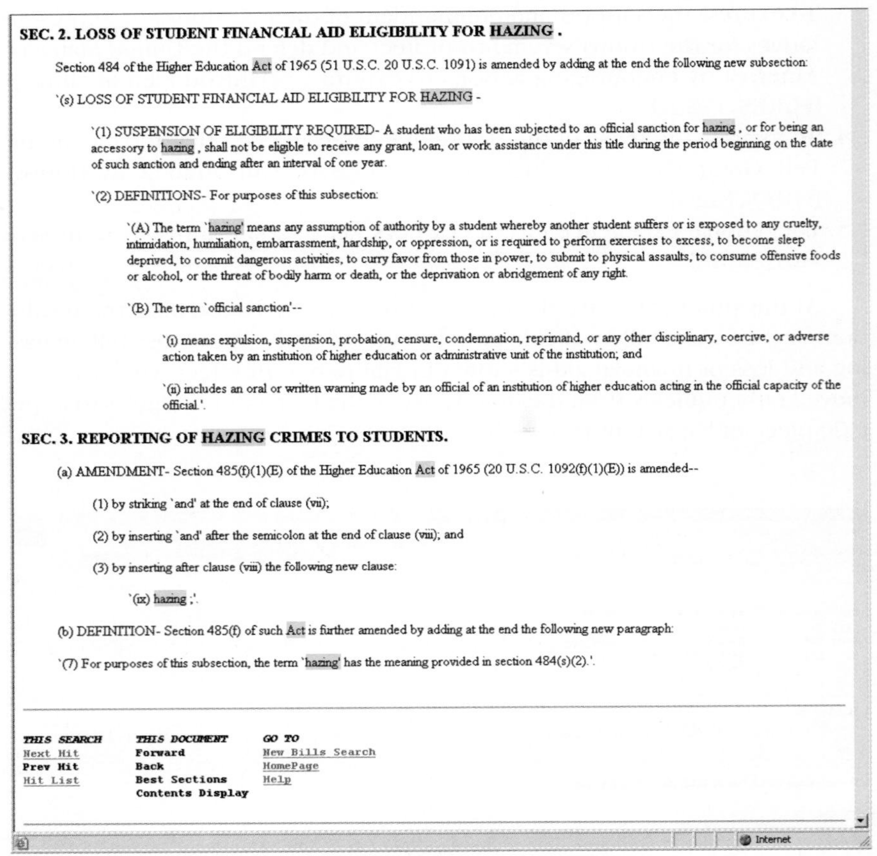

SEC. 2. LOSS OF STUDENT FINANCIAL AID ELIGIBILITY FOR HAZING .

Section 484 of the Higher Education Act of 1965 (51 U.S.C. 20 U.S.C. 1091) is amended by adding at the end the following new subsection:

`(s) LOSS OF STUDENT FINANCIAL AID ELIGIBILITY FOR HAZING -

`(1) SUSPENSION OF ELIGIBILITY REQUIRED- A student who has been subjected to an official sanction for hazing , or for being an accessory to hazing , shall not be eligible to receive any grant, loan, or work assistance under this title during the period beginning on the date of such sanction and ending after an interval of one year.

`(2) DEFINITIONS- For purposes of this subsection:

`(A) The term `hazing' means any assumption of authority by a student whereby another student suffers or is exposed to any cruelty, intimidation, humiliation, embarrassment, hardship, or oppression, or is required to perform exercises to excess, to become sleep deprived, to commit dangerous activities, to curry favor from those in power, to submit to physical assaults, to consume offensive foods or alcohol, or the threat of bodily harm or death, or the deprivation or abridgement of any right.

`(B) The term `official sanction'--

`(i) means expulsion, suspension, probation, censure, condemnation, reprimand, or any other disciplinary, coercive, or adverse action taken by an institution of higher education or administrative unit of the institution; and

`(ii) includes an oral or written warning made by an official of an institution of higher education acting in the official capacity of the official.'.

SEC. 3. REPORTING OF HAZING CRIMES TO STUDENTS.

(a) AMENDMENT- Section 485(f)(1)(E) of the Higher Education Act of 1965 (20 U.S.C. 1092(f)(1)(E)) is amended--

(1) by striking `and' at the end of clause (vii);

(2) by inserting `and' after the semicolon at the end of clause (viii); and

(3) by inserting after clause (viii) the following new clause:

`(ix) hazing ;'.

(b) DEFINITION- Section 485(f) of such Act is further amended by adding at the end the following new paragraph:

`(7) For purposes of this subsection, the term `hazing' has the meaning provided in section 484(s)(2).'.

THIS SEARCH	THIS DOCUMENT	GO TO
Next Hit	Forward	New Bills Search
Prev Hit	Back	HomePage
Hit List	Best Sections	Help
	Contents Display	

FIGURE 6.3 *(Continued from page 173)*

Using a Search Engine

By this point in your career, you probably have a favorite search engine and know how to use it. So this section merely lists the types and the way they perform. Keep in mind that search engines change often, and more are added each year while others disappear. Also, search with more than one browser, because one cannot catalog even half the sites available. In addition, we can't stress enough the importance of using the educational search engines; with those, you can have confidence that the articles have a scholarly basis, not a commercial one.

Subject Directory Search Engines

These search engines are human compiled and indexed to guide you to general areas that are then subdivided to specific categories. Your choices control the list.

About.com	http://home.about.com/index.htm
Go.network	http://go.com
Lycos	http://www.lycos.com
Yahoo!	http://www.yahoo.com

Yahoo! is an edited site with plenty of directories and subdirectories. Figure 6.4 shows the opening page from Yahoo! with circled numbers to its features keyed to the numbered comments below the screen shot. You can make a keyword search or click on one of the categories, such as Health, to go deeper into the Web directories and, eventually, the articles.

FIGURE 6.4 Opening home page of the search engine Yahoo!

1. Type a keyword into the Search field.
2. Use Advanced Search to refine date, language, or number of results.
3. Click on hyperlinks for specific types of information—auctions, maps, movies, and so forth.
4. Use the subject directory to move quickly from a general subject to specific categories and specific articles.
5. For current events, click on hyperlinks to news, sports, and events.

Robot-Driven Search Engines

Another set of engines responds to a keyword by electronically scanning millions of Web pages. Your keywords will control the size of the list.

AltaVista	**http://altavista.digital.com**
AOL Netfind	**http://www.aol.com/netfind**
AskJeeves	**http://www.askjeeves.com**
Excite	**http://www.excite.com**
Google	**http://www.google.com**
Hotbot	**http://www.hotbot.com**
Infoseek	**http://infoseek.com**
InferenceFind	**http://www.inference.com**
Magellan	**http://www.magellan.com**
NorthernLight	**http://www.northernlight.com**
Webcrawler	**http://webcrawler.com**

Metasearch Engines

A metasearch examines your topic in several of the search engines listed above. Thus, you need not search each engine separately. For example, when you enter a query at the Mamma.com Web site, the engine simultaneously queries about ten of the major search engines, such as Yahoo!, Webcrawler, and Magellan. It then provides you with a short, relevant set of results. You will get fewer results than might appear at one of the major search engines. For example, the request for "chocolate + children" produced 342,718 results on AltaVista but only fifty on Mamma.com. The claim is that a metasearch engine gives you the more relevant sites. This claim is based on the fact that the metasearch engine selects the first few listings from each of the other engines under the theory that each engine puts the most relevant sites at the top of its list; however, some commercial sites are able to buy their way to the top of various lists. Here are four metasearch engines:

Dogpile	**http://dogpile.com**
Mamma.com	**http://mamma.com**
Metacrawler.com	**http://metacrawler.com**
Metafind.com	**http://metafind.com**

Specialized Search Engines

Other search engines specialize in one area, such as WWWomen (women's studies), TribalVoice (Native American Studies), and Bizweb (business studies). In addition, many Web sites, such as the Library of Congress and New York Times Online, have search engines just for themselves. Even the sites for local newspapers have search engines to their own archives.

To discover any specialized search engine, go to one of the major sites, such as AltaVista, and ask, "Where can I find a search engine on journalism?" or "Where can I find a search engine on the environment?" The computer will name specialized search engines, such as these two:

www.journalism.net
www.gis.org (Geographical Information System)

Educational Search Engines

Educational search engines provide subject indexes to the various disciplines (humanities, sciences) and to subtopics under those headings (history, literature, biochemistry, etc.). Try several, because they will take you to academic material, not commercial sites with advertising banners popping up all over the screen.

Argus Clearinghouse	http://www.clearinghouse.net
English Server	http://eserver.org.
Internet Public Library	http://ipl.sils.umich.edu/
Knowledge Source (SIRS)	http://www.sirs.com
Library of Congress Subject	http://lcweb.loc.gov/global/
Planet Earth	http://www.nosc.mil/planetearth/info.html
SavvySearch	http:/www.cs.colostate.edu/~dreiling/smartform.html
SearchEDU	http://www.searchedu.com
SearchGOV	http://www.searchgov.com
SearcheBOOKS	http://www.searchebooks.com
SearchMIL	http://www.searchmil.com
Voice of the Shuttle	http://humanitas.ucsb.edu/

Returning once again to Sherri James and her investigations, we find her entering the phrase "blood doping" at the SearchEDU engine, which directed her to the United States Olympic Committee at http://www.usoc.org/. There she is linked to an article on Drug Education, sponsored by the United States Anti-Doping Agency.

Drug Education

As a result of the recommendations by the U.S. Olympic Committee's Select Task Force a group called the U.S. Anti-Doping Agency (USADA) was created to eliminate the practice of doping in sports. USADA was given the responsibility to test and educate Olympic, Pan American and Paralympic athletes along with developing a national anti-doping program for the Olympic Movement in the United States.

New USOC Anti-Doping Policy (Oct. 5)
Mission

The mission of this group is to eliminate the practice of doping among athletes competing in the Olympic, Pan American and Paralympic Games. This group is responsible for managing the testing process for the athletes. They are dedicated to preserving the well-being of sport's integrity and competition and ensuring the health of athletes through research initiatives and education programs.

Vision

USADA works with all athletes, while giving special emphasis to U.S. Olympic, Pan American and Paralympic athletes, in its efforts to eliminate doping in sport.

- Manage a fair and impartial testing process to identify athletes who use performance enhancing compounds
- Develop a fair adjudication program that will be fair if an athlete is found to be in violation of anti-doping rules
- Support educational programs in areas of performance substances
- Participate both nationally and internationally with other anti-doping organizations

Sherri James can draw several ideas from this source.

Educational Search Engines Maintained by Libraries

Here's a list of excellent sites that provide valuable academic information. Each one features a directory of hyperlinks to academic subjects and a search engine to the archives.

BUBL Link	**http://bubl.ac.uk/link**
Internet Public Library	**http://www.ipl.org/ref**
Librarians Index to the Internet	**http://lii.org**
Scout Select	**http://www.ilrt.bris.ac.uk/mirrors/scout/toolkit/bookmarks/index.html**

HINT: Most Web programs include a Bookmark or Favorites tool to save addresses for quick access. When you find a file you want to access later, create a bookmark so you can revisit it with just a click of the mouse. For example, in Netscape, simply click on Bookmarks, then click on Add Bookmark. This will automatically add the URL to the list of bookmarks. In Microsoft Internet Explorer, use the button bar marked Favorites to make your bookmarks. *Note:* If you are working at a university computer laboratory, do not add bookmarks to the hard drive. Instead, save the bookmarks to your disk by using Save As in the File menu.

Searching for Articles in Journals and Magazines

The Internet helps you find articles in online journals and magazines. *Note:* The ***best*** source for academic journals is your library's database collection.

Online Journals

You can find online journals in one of three ways:

- First, access your favorite search engine and use a keyword search for "journals" plus the name of your subject. For example, one student accessed AltaVista and used a keyword search for "journals + fitness." The search produced links to 20 online journals devoted to fitness, such as *Health Page, Excite Health*, and *Physical Education*. Another student's search for "women's studies + journals" produced a list of relevant journals, such as *Feminist Collections, Resources for Feminist Research,* and *Differences*. By accessing one of these links, the student can examine abstracts and articles.
- Second, access a search engine's subject directory. In Yahoo!, for example, one student selected Social Science from the key directory, clicked on Sociology, clicked on Journals, and accessed links to several online journals, such as *Edge: The E-Journal of Intercultural Relations* and *Sociological Research Online*.
- Third, if you already know the name of a journal, go to your favorite search engine to make a keyword query, such as "Psycholoquy," which will link you to the social science journal of that name.

Many of the online periodicals offer keyword searches to their articles. In addition, they often provide full-text articles that you may download; however, some online journals charge a fee or require you to join an association before they permit you access.

Online Magazines

Several directories exist for discovering articles in magazines

NewsDirectory.Com **http://www.newsdirectory.com/new/**

This search engine directs you to magazine home pages where you can begin your free search in that magazine's archives. Under "current events," for example, it will send you to *Atlantic Monthly* at <theatlantic.com>, *Harper's* at <Harpers.org>, and *Newsweek* at <Newsweek.com>.

Electric Library **http://www3.elibrary.com/**

This site has a good search engine, but it requires membership (which is free for one month).

Remember to cancel your membership after you finish research, or charges will accrue.

Pathfinder http://pathfinder.com/

This site gives you free access to *Time* magazine; it has a good search engine with links to thousands of archival articles.

ZD Net http://www.zdnet.com/

This search engine provides excellent access to industry-oriented articles in banking, electronics, computers, management, and so on. It offers two weeks of free access before charges begin to accrue.

Another way to access online magazines is through a search engine's directory. For example, one student accessed AltaVista, clicked on Health and Fitness in the directory on the home page, clicked on Publications, then Magazines. The result was a list of 40 magazines devoted to various aspects of health and fitness, such as *Healthology* and *The Black Health Net*.

Searching for Articles in Newspapers and Media Sources

First, to find almost any newspaper in the United States, even the local weeklies, consult:

www.newspapers.com

This site takes you to the *Aspen Times* or the *Carbondale Valley Journal* or one of 800-plus newspapers. In most cases, the online newspaper has its own internal search engine that enables you to examine articles from its archives. Figure 6.5 shows the opening page of the online site for a local newspaper in Los Angeles, California. Notice especially the hyperlink at the upper left, **Archives,** a feature that enables you to find articles from past issues.

Most major news organizations maintain Internet sites. Consult one of these:

The Chronicle of Higher Education http://www.chronicle.com

This site requires a paid subscription, so access it through your library at no cost.

CNN Interactive http://www.cnn.com

CNN maintains a good search engine that takes you quickly, without cost, to transcripts of its broadcasts. It's a good source for research in current events.

The CQ Weekly http://library.cq.com

This magazine, formerly named *The Congressional Quarterly Weekly*, keeps tabs on congressional activities in Washington.

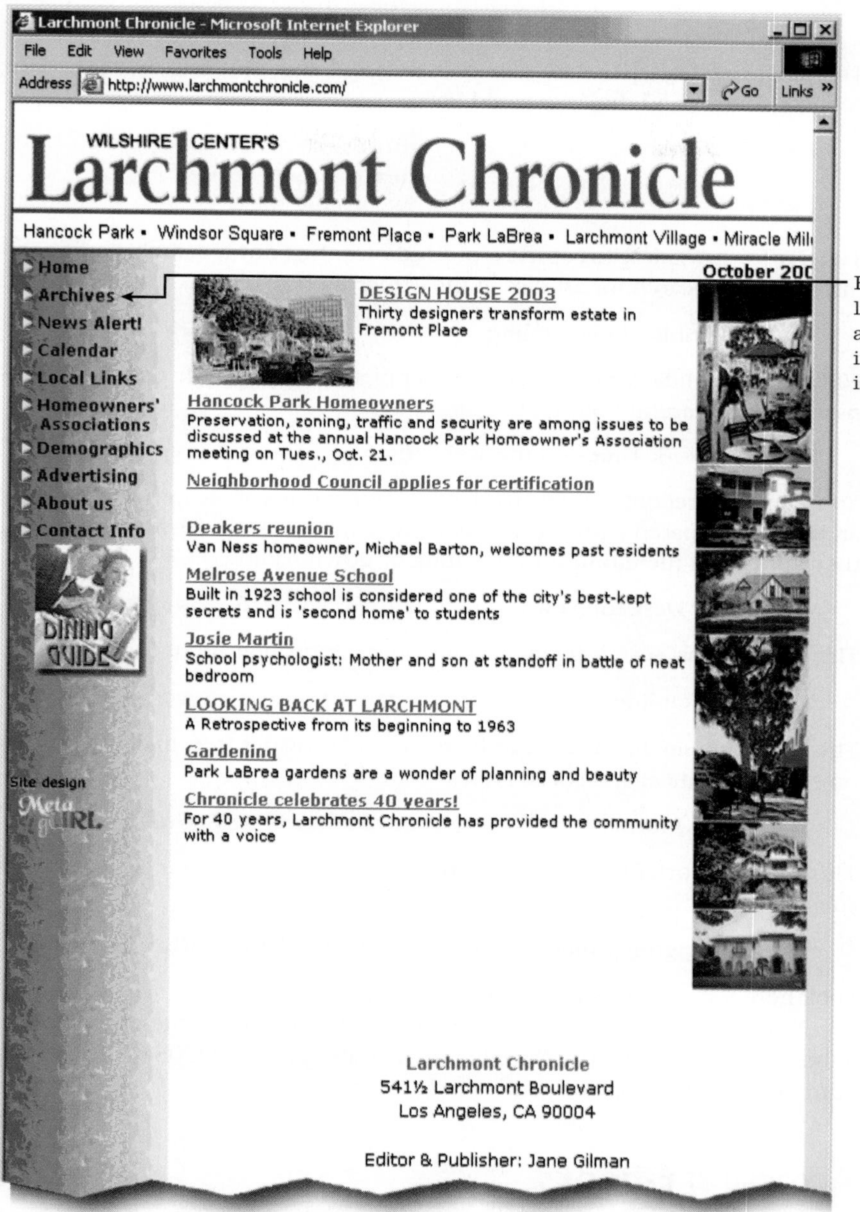

FIGURE 6.5 Los Angeles's *Larchmont Chronicle*.

C-SPAN Online http://www.c-span.org

This site focuses on public affairs and offers both a directory and a search engine for research in public affairs, government, and political science.

Fox News http://www.foxnews.com

This site provides articles from its own network and also from news services such as Reuters and the Associated Press.

London Times http://www.thetimes.co.uk/news/pages/Times/frontpage.html

The *Times* provides directories and indexes, but not a search engine, so improve your search for articles in the *Times* with searchuk.com.

National Public Radio Online http://www.npr.org

NPR provides audio articles via RealPlayer or some other audio engine. Be prepared to take careful notes.

The New York Times on the Web http://www.nytimes.com

You can read recent articles for free. However, if you search the 365-day archive, be prepared with your credit card. Articles cost $2.50. After purchase, they appear on the monitor for printing or downloading.

USA Today DeskTopNews http://www.usatoday.com

This site has a fast search engine that provides information about current events.

U.S. News Online http://www.usnews.com

This magazine site has a fast search engine and provides free, in-depth articles on current political and social issues.

Wall Street Journal http://www.wsj.com

This business-oriented site has excellent information, but it requires a subscription.

The Washington Times http://www.washingtontimes.com/

Look here for up-to-the-minute political news.

To find other newspapers and online media, search for "newspapers" on Yahoo! or AltaVista. Your college library may also provide LEXIS-NEXIS, which searches news sources for you.

Accessing E-books

One of the best sources of full-text online books is the Online Books Page at the University of Pennsylvania: http://digital.library.upenn.edu/books/. This site indexes books by author, title, and subject. It has a search engine that will take you quickly, for example, to the full text of Thomas Hardy's *A Pair of Blue Eyes* or to Linnea Hendrickson's *Children's Literature: A Guide to the Criticism*. This site adds new textual material almost every day, so consult it first. Understand, however, that contemporary books, still under copyright protection, are not included. That is, you can freely download an Oscar Wilde novel but not one by John Updike. JSTOR is another site for accessing books in a photocopied format. *Caution*: Other sites offer e-books, but they are commercial and require a subscription.

Using Listserv, Usenet, and Chat Groups

E-mail discussion groups have legitimacy for the exchange of academic ideas when everybody in the group has the same purpose, project, or course of study. Chat rooms seldom have academic value. Let's look at each briefly.

E-mail News Groups

The word ***listserv*** is used to describe discussion groups that correspond via e-mail about a specific educational or technical subject. For example, your literature professor might ask everybody in the class to join a *listserv* group on Victorian literature. To participate, you must have an e-mail address and subscribe to the list as arranged by your instructor.

In like manner, online courses, which have grown in popularity, usually have a discussion area where students are expected to participate by responding to general questions for the group or corresponding with each other about assignments, issues, and other topics. On the Blackboard system, for example, online students have a Discussion Board with any number of Forums where they may participate or where they are required to participate.

Liszt **http://www.liszt.com**
Search Liszt's main directory of more than 90,000 mailing lists. Also, you may click on a topic, such as Computers (250 lists), Health (271 lists), Humanities (254 lists), and many others.

Tile.Net **http://www.tile.net/**
This site provides access to lists, usenet newsgroups, and other sites.

At some point you may wish to join a list, and each site will explain the procedure for subscribing and participating via e-mail in a discussion. However, you are advised to use extreme caution if you visit the usenet groups via the commercial search engines. Student Sherri James visited the Yahoo! site for listserv groups in swimming, but she abandoned the search because the groups, by their very titles, seemed obscene (e.g., "See Girls in Their Speedos").

A few additional aspects of *listserv* and *usenet* are FAQ, lurking, and moderated and unmoderated lists.

- *FAQs* (frequently asked questions) provide answers to questions by new members.
- *Lurking* is to watch messages on the list without participating.
- A *moderated list* has an editor who screens messages before they are posted to the list.
- *Unmoderated lists* have an automatic process that distributes any message that comes through.

Real-Time Chatting

Usenet and chat groups use Internet sites with immediate messaging rather than e-mail. To access usenet, go to <dogpile.com> or <metacrawler.com> and click the People & Chat button before launching the search. Typing "fitness" might take you, under a fictional name, to a reasonable discussion, but probably not. Another way to find discussion groups is through a keyword search for "List of online chat groups" at one of the search engines. If you want a commercial site that requires a monthly fee, try Usenet.com. However, *you cannot cite from these anonymous sources*, so they are best avoided for your academic work.

Examining Library Holdings via Internet Access

Most public libraries now offer access to their library catalog via the Web. This allows you to search their collections for books, videos, dissertations, audio tapes, special collections, and other items. However, you must open an account and use your identification to log in, just as you do with your college library. You may sometimes order books online through interlibrary loan. Additionally, some libraries now post full-text documents, downloadable bibliographies, databases, and links to other sites.

If you need identification of all books on a topic, as copyrighted and housed in Washington, DC, consult:

Library of Congress **http://www.loc.gov**

This site allows you to search by word, phrase, name, title, series, and number. It provides special features, such as an American Memory Home Page, full-text legislative information, and exhibitions, such as the various drafts of Lincoln's "Gettysburg Address."

For an Internet overview of online libraries, their holdings, and addresses, consult:

LIBCAT **http://www.metronet.lib.mn.us/lc/lc1.html**

This site gives you easy access to almost 3,000 online library catalogs.

LIBWEB **http://sunsite.berkeley.edu/libweb**

This site takes you to home pages of academic, public, and state libraries. You will be prompted for a public-access login name, so follow the directions for entering and exiting the programs.

Another kind of online library is:

Carl UnCover **http://www.carl.org.uncover/**

This site provides a keyword search of 17,000 journals by author, title, or subject. Copies of the articles can be faxed to you, usually within the hour, for a small fee.

Finding an Internet Bibliography

You can quickly build a bibliography on the Internet in two ways: by using a search engine or by visiting an online book store.

Search Engine

At a search engine on the Internet, such as AltaVista, enter a descriptive phrase, such as "Child Abuse Bibliographies." You will get a list of bibliographies, and you can click the mouse on one of them, such as:

> **Child Abuse**
> Child Abuse. Child Abuse Articles. Child Abuse Reports.
> **http://www.childwelfare.com**

Clicking with the mouse on the hypertext address will carry you to a list:

> **Child Abuse Articles**
> **Child Abuse Reports**
> **Child Sexual Abuse**
> **Substance Abuse**

Clicking on the first item will produce a set of hypertext links to articles you might find helpful, such as this one:

> "Suffer the children: How government fails its most vulnerable citizens—abused and neglected kids," by David Stoesz and Howard Jacob Karger (*The Washington Monthly*, 1996).

Online Bookstore

Use the search engines of Amazon.com and BarnesandNoble.com to gain a list of books currently available. In most cases, the books on the list will be available in your library. For example, one student searched BarnesandNoble.com for books on "fad dieting." She received the list as shown in Figure 6.6, which gave her the beginnings of a complete bibliography.

Conducting Archival Research on the Internet

The Internet has made possible all kinds of research in library and museum archives. You may have an interest in this type of work. If so, consider several ways to approach the study.

Go to the Library

Go physically into a library and ask about the archival material housed there, or use the library's electronic catalog. Most libraries have special

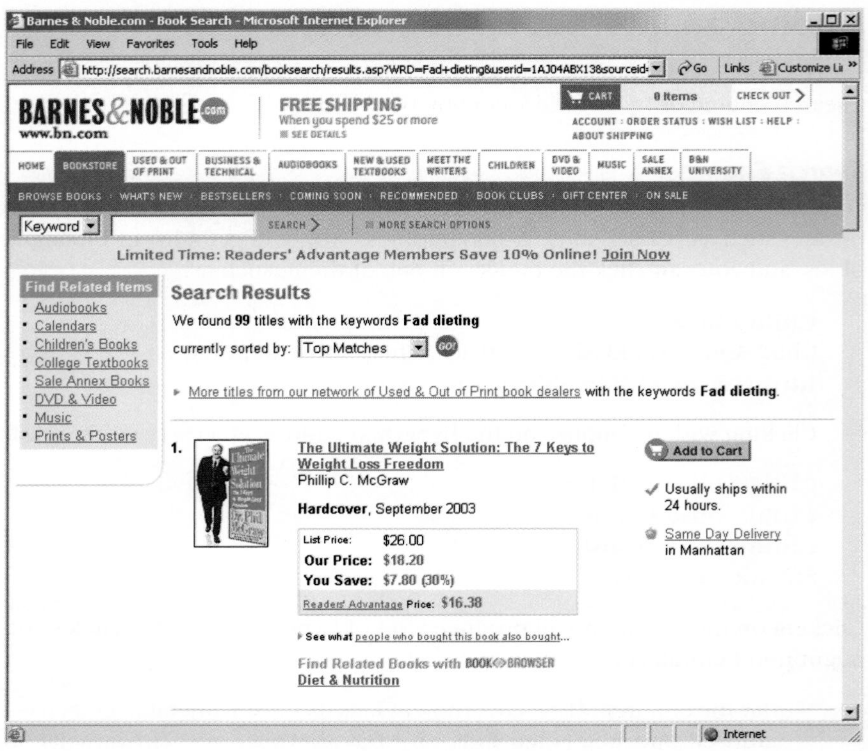

FIGURE 6.6 A page from the Barnes & Noble Internet site listing books on the topic "fad dieting."

collections. The Stanford University Library, for example, offers links to antiquarian books, old manuscripts, and other archives. It also provides ways to find material by subject, by title, and by collection number. It carries the researcher to a link, such as the London (Jack) Papers, 1897–1916 at the Online Archive of California. These can be accessed by Internet if the researcher has the proper credentials for entering and using the Stanford collection.

Go to an Edited Search Engine

An edited search engine, such as Yahoo!, may give you results quickly. For example, requesting "Native American literature + archives" produced such links as:

American Native Press Archives
Native American History Archive
Native Americans and the Environment

Indigenous Peoples' Literature
Sayings of Chief Joseph

One or more of these collections might open the door to an interesting topic and enlightening research.

Go to a Metasearch Engine

A metasearch engine such as dogpile.com offers a way to reach archival material. Make a keyword request, such as "Native American literature + archives." Dogpile will list such sites as Reference Works and Research Material for Native American Studies, which is located at www.stanford.edu. There, the Native American Studies Collections offers several valuable lists:

Native American Studies Encyclopedias and Handbooks
Native American Studies Bibliographies
Native American Studies Periodical Indexes
Native American Biography Resources
Native American Studies Statistical Resources
Links to other Native American sites on the Internet
Links to usenet discussion groups related to Native Americans

Thus, the researcher would have a wealth of archival information to examine.

Use Search Engine Directories

Use the directory and subdirectories of a search engine and let them take you deeper and deeper into the files. Remember, this tracing goes quickly. Here are examples of links at several engines:

Excite Guide	Lifestyle: Cultures and Groups: Native Americans: Literature
Lycos	Entertainment: Books: Literature: Native American Literature
AltaVista	Society: History: Indigenous People: Native Americans: Art

The latter site, for example, carried one researcher to the Red Earth Museum in Oklahoma City (see Figure 6.7).

Go to a Listserv or Usenet Group

Using a search engine, simply join your topic with the word listserv: "Native American literature + listserv." The search engine will produce such links as Native-L: Native Literature listserv and archives. By following the proper procedures, you can log on and begin corresponding. Participants might quickly point you in the direction of good topics and sources for developing the paper.

FIGURE 6.7 The home page to the Red Earth Museum, where a student might find archival information on Native Americans.

Go to Newspaper Archives

Use www.newspapers.com to locate a newspaper of interest, and then use the newspaper's search engine to explore its archives of articles.

YOUR RESEARCH PROJECT

1. To look for an Internet discussion group on your topic, go to a metasearch engine; however, before entering your subject, select the button for searching newsgroups rather than the Web. Explore the choices. You may also search the lists described earlier in this chapter.
2. Voice of the Shuttle is a large and powerful search engine for educational information. Enter this URL, http://humanitas.ucsb.edu/, and search for your topic. If unsuccessful, try one of the other educational search engines.
3. When you have found an Internet article directly devoted to your subject, apply to it an evaluation. Ask yourself, "Does this site have merit?" Apply that same test to other Internet articles as you find them.

4. Practice using the Bookmark feature of your browser. That is, rather than print an article from the Internet, bookmark it instead for future reference.
5. As you would with library sources, begin making bibliography entries and writing notes about promising Internet sources. Begin building a computer file of promising sources, develop a folder of printouts from the Internet, and save pertinent information you will need for your bibliography entries later on (see Chapter 7 for more information on a working bibliography, and see Chapter 17 for examples of the bibliography for Internet sources).

7 Gathering Data in the Library

The library should be the center of your research, whether you access it electronically from your dorm room or go there in person. As the repository of the best books and periodicals, you cannot ignore it.

Why is the library a better source than the Internet? Scholarship, that's why! The articles you access through the library are, in the main, written by scholars and published in journals only after careful review by a board of like-minded scholars.

Also, in today's modern electronic libraries, the material can be accessed just as easily as the Internet. In fact, many of the library's databases are part of the Web. Logged in at the library, you can download articles to your computer, print files, and read some books online. But you also need to visit the library in person to soak up the atmosphere of academia as well as consult books in the reference room and visit the stacks to find and check out books.

Launching the Search

Your research strategy in the library should include four steps, with adjustments for your individual needs.

1. **Conduct a preliminary search for relevant sources.** Scan the reference section of your library for its electronic sources as well as the abundance of printed indexes, abstracts, bibliographies, and reference books. Search the library's electronic book catalog and dip into the electronic networks, such as InfoTrac's Academic Index. This preliminary work will serve several purposes:
   - It shows the availability of source materials with diverse opinions.
   - It provides a beginning set of reference citations, abstracts, and full-text articles.
   - It defines and restricts your subject.
   - It gives you an overview of the subject by showing how others have researched it.

   Your preliminary search should include a survey of the entire library if orientation classes have not given you an overview.
2. **Refine the topic and evaluate the sources.** On this first trip to the library or on later visits, narrow your topic to something you believe will

be manageable. As soon as you refine the topic, you can spend valuable time reading abstracts, articles, and pertinent sections of books. Most instructors will expect you to cite from the library's scholarly sources, so a mix of journal articles and books should accompany your Internet articles and field research.

3. **Take shortcuts.** First, consult Appendix B of this book, "Finding Reference Works for Your General Topic," which lists appropriate electronic and printed sources. It sends you to key sources in psychology, art, literature, and most other disciplines. For example, if your work is on an education topic, it sends you to ERIC (online), *Current Index to Journals in Education,* and Edweb (online), but it sends computer science students to INSPEC (online) or to *Computer Literature Index.*

   In addition, you will need to access a variety of computer sources in the library, such as the electronic book catalog and the electronic services like InfoTrac and Silverplatter. Without leaving the computer workstation in the reference room of the library, you can develop a working bibliography, read a few abstracts and full-text articles, and, in general, make substantive advances before you ever enter the library stacks.

   Note: As you probably know, many of these sources can be accessed from your dorm room or home computer.

4. **Read and take notes.** Examine books, articles, essays, reviews, computer printouts, and government documents. Whenever possible, write complete notes as you read so you can transcribe them or paste them into your text. Don't delay the writing task until you face a huge, imposing pile of data.

HINT: Just as we learn proper Internet behavior, we learn basic library etiquette, such as talking softly out of respect for others and not bringing in food or drinks. Also, the best researchers do *not* reshelve books and periodicals; they leave them at the reshelving bins so librarians can return them to the correct place. They rewind microfilm and leave it in the reshelving bin. They avoid breaking down the spines of books in attempts to copy the pages. At the computer station, they analyze sources and then print; they do not randomly print everything. (See Chapter 6 for methods of analyzing a source.)

Developing a Working Bibliography

Because the research paper is a major project involving many papers and notes, organization is crucial. That means keeping a copy of every abstract, article, and downloaded file with full publication information and the URLs of Internet materials.

More examples of bibliography format, Chapters 17–20.

Your final manuscript will require a bibliography page listing all your sources, so now is the time to start accumulating the data.

If you want to be fully organized—and your instructor may require this—write as an ongoing project a working bibliography. This list of the sources may be kept on cards or, more efficiently, on a computer file. Either way, producing a set of bibliography entries has three purposes:

1. It locates articles and books for notetaking purposes.
2. It provides information for the in-text citations, as in this example in MLA style:

   The healing properties of certain foods have been noted by Milner (682-88) and Hasler (6-10).

3. It provides information for the final reference page (see Chapters 17-20). If you keep your entries current in a computer file, you can easily insert them into your Works Cited page at the end of your manuscript.

Whether you keyboard your sources or make handwritten cards for easy shuffling, each working bibliography entry should contain the following information—with variations, of course, for books, periodicals, and government documents:

1. Author's name
2. Title of the work
3. Publication information
4. Library call number
5. (Optional) A personal note about the location or contents of the source
6. The URL for Internet sources

Bibliography Entry for a Book (MLA style):

E185.625 .T38 2003

Tatum, Beverly Daniel. "Why Are All the Black Kids Sitting Together in the Cafeteria?": And Other Conversations about Race. New York: BasicBooks, 2003.

Books, Level 3

Bibliography Entry for a Journal Article (MLA style):

McLeod, Christopher. "Sacred Land Film Project." Earth Island Journal 18 (2003): 16-17.

Bibliography Entry for a Magazine Article (MLA style):

Casey, Kathy. "Riding the Currents of History in Maryland." American Heritage May 2003: 37-41.

Bibliography Entry for an Article Found on an Academic Database (MLA style):

Davis, Sandra K. "The Politics of Water Scarcity in the Western States." The Social Science Journal 38 (2002): 527- . Expanded Academic ASAP. InfoTrac. Vanderbilt U, Heard Lib. 9 Apr. 2003 <http://www.galegroup.com/>.

Bibliography Entry for an Internet Article (MLA style):

O'Malley, Martin, and John Bowman. "Selling Canada's Water." CBC News Online. June 2001. 9 Apr. 2003 <http://www.cbc.ca/news/indepth/water/>.

Finding Books on Your Topic

The library is no longer a repository of printed materials only. It has gone high-tech like the business world. Thus, much of your research will be conducted on the library's electronic network with call numbers to its own books and with links to sources around the world.

Using Your Library's Electronic Book Catalog

Your library's computerized catalog to its holdings probably has a special name, such as LIBNET, FELIX, ACORN, UTSEARCH, and so forth. In theory, it includes every book in the library filed by subject, author, and title. Begin your research at the catalog by using a *keyword search* to a subject, such as "Fitness." You will get a list of books on the monitor, and you can click the mouse on each one to gather more information. The list will look something like this:

Search Results

Getting Fit, Staying Healthy. Hearings before the Committee on Health, Education, Labor, and Pensions, U.S. Senate. 2003.

Resistance to Exercise: A Social Analysis of Inactivity. Mary McElroy. 2002.

Introduction to Physical Education, Fitness, and Sport. Daryl Siedentop. 2001.

Sports Nutrition. Judy A. Driskell. 2002.

The electronic card catalog, in effect, has provided a bibliography that lists a variety of available books on a particular subject. The next procedure is to click on one, such as *Sports Nutrition,* to get the full details with call number and availability, as shown in the example below. You can print the information and use it to find the book in the stacks and to write your working bibliography. The entry at your library will be similar to the following example.

Sports Nutrition / Judy A. Driskell.
By Driskell, Judy A. (Judy Anne)
Boca Raton, FL: CRC Press, 2000
Subjects: Athletes—Nutrition—Physical fitness—Nutritional aspects
Description: 280 p.; ill.; 26 cm.
Series: Nutrition in exercise and sport
COPY / HOLDING INFORMATION

Location	**Collection**	**Call No.**	**Status**
Woodward Library	General Book Collection, Level 3	TX361.A8 D75 2000	Available

The card catalog will also help you find subject-specific bibliographies. For instance, one student entered "bibliographies + women's studies." The catalog provided a large list of sites, each appearing as a hypertext link to full data on the source. Here's an example of four items from a list of 30 or more:

- **Bibliographies on Native American Women's Theatre (2000)**
- **Bibliography: Gender and Technology (1994)**
- **Bibliography of Ecofeminist Resources (2000)**
- **Bibliography on Women and the Internet (1997)**

HINT: Many college libraries as well as public libraries are now part of library networks. The network expands the holdings of every library because one library will loan books to another. Therefore, if a book you need is unavailable in your library, ask a librarian about an interlibrary loan. Understand, however, that you may have to wait several days for its delivery. Periodical articles usually come quickly by fax.

Using the Library's Printed Bibliographies

You may need to supplement your computer printouts with old-fashioned searching of printed reference guides, bibliographies, and indexes.

Searching the General Bibliographies

When ordering its research databases, the library subscribes to electronic versions or print versions. You will need to determine which are available. Three general works provide page numbers to many books and journals that contain bibliographies on numerous subjects.

Bibliographic Index: A Cumulative Bibliography of Bibliographies. New York: Wilson, 1938–date. Available both in print and online within your library's network.

Hillard, James, and Bethany J. Easter. *Where to Find What: A Handbook to Reference Service.* 4th ed. Metuchen, NJ: Scarecrow, 1999.

Balay, Robert, et al. *Guide to Reference Books.* 11th ed. Chicago: ALA, 1996.

Prehistoric War

LeBlanc, Steven A. *Constant Battles: The Myth of the Peaceful, Noble Savage.* New York: St. Martins, 2003 p 247–64

FIGURE 7.1 Example from *Bibliographic Index,* 2003.

These guides will also give you a list of books relating to your subject. Figure 7.1 shows how *Bibliographic Index* will send you to bibliographic lists that are hidden inside books; these are sources you might not find otherwise. Entries will look something like this to show that a bibliography will be found in LeBlanc's book on pages 247–64. Such a list could be a valuable resource in the early stages of research.

If the book fits your research, you will probably want to write a bibliography entry for this source. Then you can examine the text as well as the bibliography on pages 247–64 of LeBlanc's book, where you might find additional articles on this topic. Here is a student's bibliography notation:

LeBlanc, Steven A. Constant Battles: The Myth of the Peaceful, Noble Savage. New York: St. Martins, 2003. Bibliography on pages 247–64.

Using the Trade Bibliographies

Trade bibliographies, intended primarily for use by booksellers and librarians, can help you in three ways:

1. Discover sources not listed in other bibliographies or in the card catalog.
2. Locate facts of publication, such as place and date.
3. Determine if a book is in print.

Search this work for your topic:

Subject Guide to Books in Print (New York: Bowker, 1957–date).

Note: Online, this source may appear as **Books in Print.**

Use this work for its subject classifications, any one of which will provide a ready-made bibliography to books. Figure 7.2 shows a sample found with the keyword "diet."

The following trade bibliographies may also lead you to valuable sources available online or in printed versions:

Books in Print lists by author and title all books currently in print.

Publishers' Weekly offers the current publication data on new books and new editions.

Paperbound Books in Print locates all paperback books on one topic; these are usually books available at local bookstores.

Cumulative Book Index provides complete publication data on one book but will also locate *all* material in English on a particular subject.

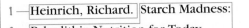

1 — Heinrich, Richard. Starch Madness:
2 — Paleolithic Nutrition for Today.
3 — LC 98-33637. (Illus.) xviii, 155p. 1998. — 4, 5
6 — 12.95 *(157733-027-7)* B. Dolphin Pub. — 7, 8

FIGURE 7.2

1. Author
2. Title
3. Library of Congress number
4. Number of pages
5. Date of publication
6. Price
7. International Standard Book Number (used when ordering)
8. Publisher

From *Subject Guide to Books in Print,* 2000.

Library of Congress Catalog: Books, Subject provides a ready-made bibliography to books on hundreds of subjects.

Ulrich's International Periodicals Directory helps you locate current periodicals, both domestic and foreign, and to order photocopies of articles.

Using the Bibliographies in Appendix B

Go to Appendix B of this book. It furnishes a guide to important reference works—some in print at the library, some online in the library's electronic network, and others available on the World Wide Web. Reference sources are listed for nine major categories. Here are three examples of titles to reference works that you will find under the heading "Issues in the Arts, Literature, Music, and Language." The first is a printed source in the library, the second is available on the library's electronic network, and the third is available on the World Wide Web.

Literary Research Guide. Ed. James L. Harner. 4th ed. New York: MLA, 2002. This work provides a step-by-step program for discovering the fascinating world of research and research writing.

MLA International Bibliography of Books and Articles on the Modern Languages and Literatures. New York: MLA, 1921–date. This reference work indexes major literary figures, literary issues, and language topics; may be listed on the library's network as *MLA Bibliography.*

Netlibrary **http://www.netlibrary.com**. This site provides a vast collection of full-text stories, poems, novels, and dramas; search by title or author and then read the text online or print it out; must create a membership account.

Searching for Bibliographies in Encyclopedias

Search for specialized encyclopedias in your field at the electronic book catalog. Entering "encyclopedia of psychology" might give you a list that looks like this:

BF31.E52 2000
Encyclopedia of psychology

BF31. E52 2001
The Corsini encyclopedia of psychology and behavioral science

BF 31 .B25 1999
Baker encyclopedia of psychology and counseling

Click on one, scan an article, and look especially at the end of the article for a bibliography. It might point you to additional sources, like the one shown in Figure 7.3 at the bottom of the page.

Examining the Bibliography at the End of a Book

When you get into the stacks, look for bibliographies at the end of books. Jot down titles on cards or photocopy the list for further reference. An example is shown in Figure 7.4 on the next page.

Searching for Bibliographies at the End of Journal Articles

Look for bibliographies at the end of articles in scholarly journals. For example, students of history depend on the bibliographies in various issues of *English Historical Review,* and students of literature find bibliographies in *Studies in Short Fiction.* In addition, the journals themselves provide subject indexes to their own contents. If your subject is "Adoption," you will discover that a majority of your sources are located in a few key journals. In that instance, going straight to the annual index of one of those journals will be a shortcut.

See also "Citation Searching," Chapter 10.

FURTHER REFERENCES

Clarke, E., & Dewhurst, K. *An illustrated history of brain function.*
Clarke, E., & O'Malley, C.D. *The human brain and spinal cord.*
Ferrier, D. *The functions of the brain.*
Finger, S., & Stein, D.G. *Brain damage and recovery: Research and clinical perspectives.*
McHenry, L.C., Jr. *Garrison's history of neurology.*

FIGURE 7.3 Sample bibliography from the end of an article in *Encyclopedia of Psychology.*

SECONDARY SOURCES

Abbott, Edith. "The Civil War and the Crime Wave of 1865–70." *Social Service Review,* 1977.
Amis, Moses N. *Historical Raleigh,* 1913.
Andrews, Marietta M. *Scraps of Paper.* 1929.
Badeau, Adam. *Military History of U. S. Grant.* 1885.
Bailey, Mrs. Hugh. "Mobile's Tragedy: The Great Magazine Explosion of 1865." *Alabama Review,* 1968.
Bakeless, John. "The Mystery of Appomattox." *Civil War Times Illustrated,* 1970.

FIGURE 7.4 A portion of a bibliography list at the end of N. A. Trudeau's book, *Out of the Storm.*

Finding Articles in Magazines and Journals

An index furnishes the exact page number(s) of specific sections of books and of individual articles in magazines, journals, and newspapers. The library's online index of databases not only directs you to articles in magazines, it also often gives you an abstract of the article, and more and more often, it provides the full text. Thus, at the library's computer terminals, you might download several articles without going into the stacks at all.

Searching the General Indexes to Periodicals

The library network gives you access to electronic databases. Here are just a few of the many that will be available to you:

AGRICOLA	Agriculture, animal and plant sciences
America: History and Life	U.S. history
American Chemical Society Publications	Chemistry
BioOne	Biological, ecological, and environmental sciences
CINAHL	Nursing, public health, and allied health fields
ERIC	Education and mass communication
GPO	Government publications on all subjects
HighWire	Science, technology, and medicine
InfoTrac	All subjects
JSTOR	Social sciences
Lexis-Nexis Academic	News, business, law, medicine, reference
MLA Bibliography	Literature, linguistics, and folklore

Music Index	Music
ProjectMUSE	Social sciences, arts, humanities
PsycINFO	Psychology, medicine, education, social work
Westlaw	Legal subjects, including laws and cases

One of these databases will usually guide you to several sources, provide an abstract, and often provide a full-text version of the article, as shown in Figure 7.5 at the bottom of this page.

Finding Indexes by Topic in Appendix B

Appendix B in this textbook, lists many indexes to periodical articles. The list is organized by topic, so you can find the best references for your field. Shown below are a few of the entries for Music:

Bibliographic Guide to Music. Boston: Hall, 1976–present. Annually. This reference work provides an excellent subject index to almost every topic in the field of music. It will give you the bibliographic data to several articles on most topics in the field.

Music Article Guide. Philadelphia: Information Services, 1966–present. This reference work indexes music education and instrumentation in such journals as *Brass and Wind News, Keyboard, Flute Journal,* and *Piano Quarterly.*

Business Week, Oct 14, 2002 i3803 p124

CLOSING THE SCHOOL GAP: If no child is to be left behind, we must overhaul funding.

Full Text: COPYRIGHT 2002 The McGraw-Hill Companies, Inc.

Byline: William C. Symonds.

Half a century after the U.S. Supreme Court struck down racial segregation in education, it's now economic segregation that plagues the nation's public schools. From Chicago to Baltimore and beyond, children in leafy suburbs benefit from better teachers, nicer facilities, and more resources than do kids in poor city neighborhoods. Spending discrepancies are one reason that, by the eighth grade, poor students are three years behind middle-class children in reading and math, according to the Education Trust, a nonprofit group in Washington, D.C. No wonder well-heeled students are seven times as likely to earn a college degree. Disparities among the states are even greater: Connecticut and Wisconsin spend 50% more per student than California and Mississippi, even after adjusting for regional cost differences.

FIGURE 7.5 InfoTrac printout with abstract.

Music Index. Warren, MI: Information Coordinators, 1949–date. This reference work indexes music journals such as *American Music Teacher, Choral Journal, Journal of Band Research, Journal of Music Therapy.*

Popular American Music of the Twentieth Century. **http://www.pratt.lib.md.us/slrc/far/musiclinks.html**. This site features links to music libraries, orchestra sites, music societies, and music programs.

Musicals in the Ithaca College Library. **http://www.ithaca.edu/library/music_bibliographies.html**. This site provides an excellent site with links to bibliographies on scores and librettos, and other sites.

Using the H.W. Wilson Indexes

For many years, the Wilson Company in Minneapolis has provided excellent indexes to periodical literature. The tradition continues, and the indexing firm has kept its lists current by making its indexes available online as well as in printed versions. The index topics will send you to articles in a wide variety of periodicals in many disciplines.

Readers' Guide to Periodical Literature

The *Readers' Guide to Periodical Literature* (online and in print) indexes important reading for the early stages of research in magazines such as:

Aging
American Scholar
Astronomy
Bioscience
Business Week
Earth Science
Foreign Affairs
Foreign Policy
Health
Negro History
Oceans
Physics Today
Psychology Today
Scientific Review
Science Digest
Science
SciQuest
Technology Review

An entry from *Readers' Guide to Periodical Literature* will look something like this:

Salute to fathers. (Ebony Bookshelf).
Ebony June 2003 v58 i8 p18(3) (1028 words)
Text with graphics / Library holdings

This entry identifies the title, the magazine, and the publication information, and it provides a hyperlink to the full text and to any library holdings of *Ebony.* Make a bibliography entry to the source if it looks promising:

"Salute to Fathers." Ebony June 2003: 18+.

Note: Writing the pages as "18+ " means page 18 and discontinuous pages thereafter.

Social Sciences Index

The *Social Sciences Index* (online and in print) indexes journal articles for 263 periodicals in these fields:

anthropology	geography	political science
economics	law and criminology	psychology
environmental science	medical science	sociology

Humanities Index

The *Humanities Index* (online and in print) catalogs 260 publications in several fields:

archeology	folklore	performing arts
classical studies	history	philosophy
language and literature	literary	religion
area studies	political criticism	theology

Other Indexes

Other indexes of importance include:

Applied Science and Technology Index for articles in chemistry, engineering, computer science, electronics, geology, mathematics, photography, physics, and related fields.

Biological and Agricultural Index for articles in biology, zoology, botany, agriculture, and related fields.

Education Index for articles in education, physical education, and related fields.

Business Periodicals Index for articles in business, marketing, accounting, advertising, and related fields.

Recently Published Articles for articles in history and related fields.

In addition to these major indexes, you should examine the reference work for your topic as listed in Appendix B of this book.

Searching for an Index to Abstracts

An abstract is a brief description of an article, usually written by the author. An index to abstracts can accelerate your work by allowing you to read the abstract before you assume the task of locating and reading the entire work. You may find them at the electronic book catalog by entering the keyword "abstracts," which will produce a list with great variety. It will look something like this:

Show detail	Abstracts of current studies
Show detail	Dissertation abstracts international
Show detail	Social work abstracts
Show detail	Women studies abstracts

A more specific keyword search will include your discipline, such as "psychology abstracts." This will produce a reference, most likely, to PyscINFO, the searchable database produced by the American Psychological Association. It will give you the type of entry shown in Figure 7.6, on the next page.

Record 1 of 34 in PsycINFO 1999-2001/01

1 AN: 2000-15373-006

2 DT: Journal-Article

3 TI: Evaluating an electronic monitoring system for people who wander.

4 AU: Altus,-Deborah-E; **Mathews,-R.-Mark**; Xaverius,-Pamela-K; Engelman,-Kimberely-K; Nolan,-Beth-A-D

5 SO: American-Journal-of-Alzheimer's Disease. 2000 Mar-Apr; Vol 15(2): 121-125

6 PB: US: Prime National Publishing Corp.

7 IS: 0182-5207

8 PY: 2000

9 AB: Wandering away from home, or elopement, is a behavior that places persons with dementia at risk of serious injury and may lead family caregivers to place their loved ones in institutions or to severely restrict their independence. This study evaluated the Mobile Locator, an electronic device designed to help caregivers quickly locate a person who has eloped. This 6 month pilot study included case studies of 7 users and an opinion survey of family caregivers, professional caregivers, and search and rescue workers. The survey results showed that respondents were positively impressed by the device, only identifying cost as a potential drawback. Case studies revealed that the equipment was easy to use, effective, and helpful to caregivers' peace of mind. These results suggest that the Mobile Locator is a valuable tool deserving of further study. (PsycINFO Database Record © 2000 APA, all rights reserved)

FIGURE 7.6 Sample entry from PsycINFO.
(1) AN = accession number; (2) DT = document type; (3) TI = title of the article; (4) AU = author; (5) SO = source; (6) PB = publisher; (7) IS = ISSN number; (8) PY = publication year; (9) AB = abstract of the article.

Searching for Abstracts of Dissertations

You may also wish to examine the abstracts to the dissertations of graduate students in *Dissertation Abstracts International,* which you can access online at the electronic book catalog under *ProQuest Digital Dissertation* or find in a printed version in the library's reference room. In the printed versions, you will need to look for issue no. 12, Part 11, of each volume, for it contains the cumulated subject and author indexes for Issues 1–12 of the volume's two sections—A: *Humanities and Social Sciences,* and B: *Sciences and Engineering.* For example, the index of *Dissertation Abstracts International* of June 1999, lists the following entries under the heading "Novels":

Novels

1 — Constructions of power in Thomas Hardy's major novels.
2 — *Johansen, Kristen.*, p.4436A — 3
Modern novels: The disruption of form, the incorporation of space. *De Weille, Karin Gerry,* p.4424A
The limits of doubt: A critique of representational scepticism in the late novels of Henry James. *Kohan, Keven Michael,* p.4427A

FIGURE 7.7
From the Index to vol. 59, *Dissertation Abstracts International,* 1999, showing (1) title of dissertation, (2) author, (3) page number where abstract can be found.

The abstract of Kristen Johansen's dissertation is shown in Figure 7.8.

You may cite the abstract in your paper, but inform your readers you are citing from the abstract, not the actual dissertation. If you need the full dissertation and have time, order a copy of the complete work from Bell & Howell Information and Learning Company. Address your request to Bell & Howell Information and Learning Company, 300 North Zeeb Road, Ann Arbor, MI 48106-1346 USA. Telephone (734) 761-7400; **info@bellhowell.infolearning.com**; **http://www.bellhowell,infolearning.com**.

Searching for a Biography

When you wish to examine the life of a person, you will find biographies in both books and articles and in print versions as well electronic versions. The electronic card catalog will usually provide multiple sources if you enter the keywords "biography + index."

Show detail	Black biography, 1790–1950
Show detail	Index to literary biography
Show detail	Index to artistic biography
Show detail	Biography index

Several electronic indexes, like InfoTrac and ProQuest, will provide you with abstracts to some biographies and even full-text biographies, such as these:

Biography Reference Bank
Current Biography: 1940–Present
Current Biography Illustrated
Marquis Who's Who Online
Wilson Biographies Plus Illustrated

Other indexes, in print and online, also have value for finding biographies.

1 — **Constructions of power in Thomas Hardy's major novels.**
2 — Johansen, Kristen., *Ph.D. Bowling Green State University, 1998.*
3 — 171pp. Advisor: Khani Begum — 4
5 — **Order Number DA9913585**

6 — Thomas Hardy's fiction works to unravel and expose the many facets surrounding the productions of power. In short, who has power, why, and how can it be resisted? The answers to these questions are as varied as his five major novels; common to all the constructions of power, however, is that power is composed and maintained at multiple levels, in multiple points and in multiple intersections. Specifically, power in Hardy's novels tends to function in the realms of gender and class, and the ways these two categories are inscribed in sexuality and on the body. And because encompassing power constructions such as knowledge, discourse, gender, sexuality, and class are constituted by the reiteration of small acts, gestures, and speech acts, power functions differently in different contexts. Hardy's work, when illuminated by theorists such as Michel Foucault and Judith Butler, details how these factors work together and against one another to aid or oppose the individual, generally, and the independent woman, more specifically. Ultimately, Hardy's fiction serves as an alternative layer of historical sedimentation, an example of how gender regimes are maintained or changed in a particular historical moment.

FIGURE 7.8
From *Dissertation Abstracts International,* 1999, showing (1) title of dissertation, (2) author, degree earned, school, and date, (3) total number of pages of the dissertation, (4) faculty chairman of the dissertation committee, (5) order number if you desire to order a copy of the complete work, (6) the abstract.

Biography Index

The *Biography Index,* in its printed form, has long been a starting point for studies of famous persons. It will lead you to biographical information for people of all lands. See Figure 7.9 on the next page for the type of information it provides.

Current Biography Yearbook

Current Biography Yearbook provides a biographical sketch of important people. Most articles are three to four pages in length, and they include references to other sources at the end. It is current, thorough, and has international scope.

Contemporary Authors

Contemporary Authors provides a biographical guide for current writers in fiction, nonfiction, poetry, journalism, drama, motion pictures, television,

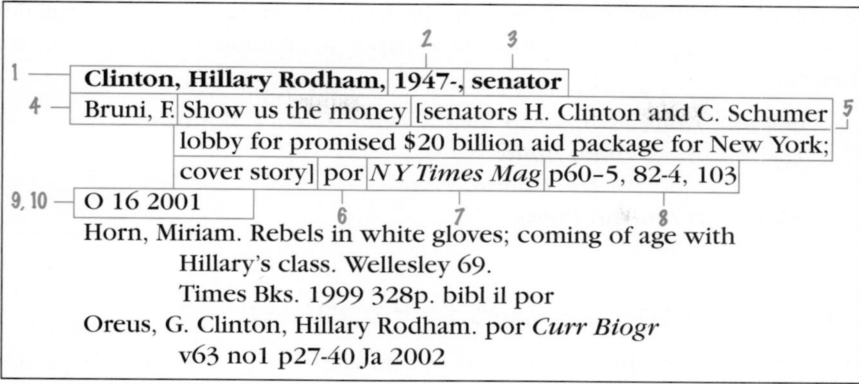

Clinton, Hillary Rodham, 1947-, senator
Bruni, F. Show us the money [senators H. Clinton and C. Schumer lobby for promised $20 billion aid package for New York; cover story] por *N Y Times Mag* p60–5, 82-4, 103 O 16 2001
Horn, Miriam. Rebels in white gloves; coming of age with Hillary's class. Wellesley 69. Times Bks. 1999 328p. bibl il por
Oreus, G. Clinton, Hillary Rodham. por *Curr Biogr* v63 no1 p27-40 Ja 2002

FIGURE 7.9
From *Biography Index,* 2000, showing (1) subject, (2) dates of subject's birth and death, (3) subject's profession, (4) author of the biography, (5) title of the biography, (6) contains portraits, (7) publisher, (8) specific pages, (9) publication date, (10) publication data for a periodical.

and a few other fields. It provides a thorough overview of most contemporary writers, giving a list of writings, biographical facts (including a current address and agent), a list of writings, sidelights, and, in many cases, an interview by the editors of the guide with the author. Most entries include a bibliography of additional sources about the writer. It has good coverage of major writers and stays current with updates on the important authors.

Dictionary of Literary Biography

Dictionary of Literary Biography provides profiles of thousands of writers in over 100 volumes under such titles as these:

American Humorists, 1800–1950
Victorian Novelists after 1885
American Newspaper Journalists, 1926–1950

Searching for Articles in the Newspaper Indexes

For many years, searching for newspaper articles was difficult, if not impossible. There were no indexes capable of doing the task. Now the electronic networks enable you to find newspaper articles from across the nation. Your library may have a newspaper search engine on its network, or you may need to go to the World Wide Web and access newspapers.com. It will take you quickly to over 800 newspapers, from the *Aspen Times* to the *Carbondale Valley Journal.* In most cases, online newspapers have their own internal search engine that

More on newspapers on the Internet, Chapter 6.

enables you to examine articles from the archives. See Chapter 6 for a full discussion and image of a hometown newspaper. In addition, several indexes are helpful:

Bell and Howell's Index to the Christian Science Monitor
The New York Times Index
Official Index [to *The London Times*]
Wall Street Journal Index

Searching the Indexes to Pamphlet Files

Librarians routinely clip items of interest from newspapers, bulletins, pamphlets, and miscellaneous materials and file them alphabetically by subject in loose-leaf folders.

Vertical File Index

Make the pamphlet file a regular stop during preliminary investigation. Sometimes called the *vertical file,* it will have clippings on many topics, such as:

"Asbestos in the Home"
"Carpel Tunnel Syndrome"
"Everything Doesn't Cause Cancer"
"Medicare and Coordinated Care Plans"

The *Vertical File Index* gives a description of each entry, the price, and how to order the pamphlet. Check at your library's electronic card catalog to see if your librarians have created an online index to local pamphlets.

Social Issues Resources Series *(SIRS)*

Also important to you are published pamphlets that feature articles on a common topic. *Social Issues Resources Series (SIRS),* online and in print, collects articles on special topics and reprints them as one unit on a special subject, such as abortion, AIDS, prayer in schools, or pollution. With *SIRS,* you will have 10 or 12 articles readily available in one booklet.

The CQ Researcher

Like *SIRS, The CQ Researcher,* online and in print, devotes pamphlets to one topic, such as "Energy and the Environment." The pamphlet will examine central issues on the topic, give background information, show a chronology of important events or processes, express an outlook, and provide an annotated bibliography. In one place, you have material worthy of quotation and paraphrase as well as a list of additional sources. Figure 7.10 on the next page shows one of numerous sources on this topic as listed in *The CQ Researcher*'s bibliography:

Gelbspan, Ross. *The Heat Is On: The High-Stakes Battle over Earth's Threatened Climate,* Addison-Wesley Publishing Co., 1997.

As scientific data increasingly support the theory that global warming is already well under way, environmental advocates, countries that are at risk of flooding from rising sea levels, and global insurance companies are joining hands in a campaign to support international efforts to slow climatic change.

FIGURE 7.10 An annotated bibliography from *The CQ Researcher.*

HINT: For the correct citation forms to articles found in *SIRS* or *The CQ Researcher,* see Chapter 17.

Searching for Government Documents

All branches of the government publish massive amounts of material. Many of these documents have great value for researchers, so investigate the following source if your topic is one that government agencies might have investigated.

GPO on Silverplatter on your library's network or
GPOAccess on the Internet

Either of these sites will take you to the files of the Government Printing Office. The database list includes *Congressional Bills, Congressional Record, Economic Indicators, Public Laws,* the *U.S. Constitution,* and much more. A keyword search will provide an entry similar to that shown in Figure 7.11 on the next page.

A working bibliography entry to the source shown in Figure 7.11, a Senate hearing, should look like this:

United States. Senate. Special Committee on Aging. Forum on "Nursing Home Residents: Short-Changed by Staff Shortages." *Hearings.* 106th Cong., 1st sess. S. Hearing 106-444. Washington: GPO, 1999.

Other works that provide valuable information on matters of the government are:

Monthly Catalog of the United States Government Publications. The printed version of GPO.

Public Affairs Information Service Bulletin (PAIS), online and in print. This work indexes articles and documents published by miscellaneous organizations. It's a good place to start because of its excellent index.

Congressional Record, online and in print. This daily publication features Senate and House bills, documents, and committee reports.

Record 5 of 366 in GPO on SilverPlatter 1976-2000/10
1 — AN: 99053103
2 — SU: Y 4.AG 4:S.HRG.106-444
3 — CA: United States. Congress. Senate. Special Committee on Aging.
4 — TI: Nursing home residents: short-changed by staff shortages : forum before the Special Committee on Aging, United States Senate, One Hundred Sixth Congress, first session, Washington, DC, November 3,1999.
5 — SO: Washington: U.S. G.P.O.: For sale by the U.S. G.P.O., Supt. of Docs. Congressional Sales Office, 1999 [i.e. 2000].
6 — SE: United States. Congress. Senate. S. hrg.; 106-444.
7 — IT: 1009-B-01 1009-C-01 (MF)

FIGURE 7.11 From GPO on Silverplatter.
(1) AN = accession number, (2) SU = document number, (3) CA = corporate author, (4) TI = title, (5) SO = source, (6) SE = series, (7) IT = GPO item number.

Public Papers of the Presidents of the United States, online and in print. This work is a publication of the Executive Branch, which includes not only the president but also all members of the cabinet and various agencies.

The U.S. Code, online and in print. The Supreme Court regularly publishes decisions, codes, and other rulings, as do appellate and district courts. State courts also publish rulings and court results on a regular basis.

Bibliography citations for government documents, Chapter 17.

Searching for Essays within Books

Some essays get lost in collections and anthologies. You can find essays listed by subject on this database at your library:

Essay and General Literature Index on Silverplatter

The print version is:

Essay and General Literature Index, 1900–1933. New York: H. W. Wilson, 1934. Supplements, 1934–date.

This reference work helps you find essays hidden in anthologies. It indexes material of both a biographical and a critical nature. The essay listed in the example on the next page might easily have been overlooked by any researcher.

King, Martin Luther, 1929–1968

Raboteau, A.J. Martin Luther King and the tradition of black religious protest. (*In* Religion and the life of the nation; ed. by R.A. Sherrill, p. 46-65.)

Using the Microforms

Online sources are gradually replacing microforms, but your library may have magazines and newspapers converted to a small, single sheet of film called *microfiche* (flat sheet of film) or *microfilm* (roll). Your library will specify in the cardex files (the list of periodicals) how journals and magazines are housed—whether they are in bound printed volumes or microforms.

Your library may also house guides to special microform holdings with titles such as *American Culture 1493–1806: A Guide to the Microfilm Collection.* Every library has its own peculiar holdings of microfilm and microfiche materials; if you need assistance, the librarian can help you.

YOUR RESEARCH PROJECT

1. If you have not already done so with an orientation group, take the time to stroll through your library. Identify its various sections and the types of information available there. Especially learn about the reference room, the stacks, and the printed periodical articles. Pick up a bound volume of a journal, open it, and notice how it contains 12 issues (or 6) of one year's publications.
2. At the library, sit down at one of the computer terminals and investigate its options. Make up a topic for the moment and search for books or articles at the terminal. Try to find an abstract or a full-text article and then print it.
3. Go to the reference desk and ask the librarian for a specialized bibliography on your topic—that is, say something like this: "Do you have a specialized bibliography on global warming?"
4. Locate the library's holdings of *The CQ Researcher* and *Social Issues Resources Series.* Page through the various booklets to note how they provide several penetrating articles on a common topic. In the indexes, search to see if your favorite topic has been treated in a special issue.
5. To test the resources of the library, go in search of information about the day you were born. Don't limit yourself to major events of the day; go also in search of hometown news. Look at the advertisements to see what people were wearing and what things cost back then.

CHECKLIST

The Library Search

When you start your research on a topic, you will need to switch between the computer terminals, the library stacks of books and periodicals, and the printed bibliographies and indexes, according to the resources in your library. Start, perhaps, with the sources on this list.

To find books:
- electronic book catalog with keyword
- online with keywords "bibliographies + [your discipline]"

To find periodical articles:
- an electronic database with a keyword
- online with keywords "indexes + [your discipline]"
- the Wilson indexes

To find an abstract:
- online with keywords "abstracts + [your discipline]"

To find biographies in books and periodicals:
- online with keywords "biography + indexes"
- *Biography Index,* online or in print

To find newspaper articles:
- Internet at **http://www.newspapers.com**
- electronic database under keyword "newspapers"

To find pamphlet files:
- online with the library's network to *SIRS* and *The CQ Researcher*
- Ask your librarian for local files

To find government documents:
- online with the library network to **GPO on Silverplatter**
- Internet access to **GPOAccess**

To find essays within books:
- *Essay and General Literature Index,* online or in print

To find microforms:
- online with the library network to **ERIC**

8 Conducting Research Outside the Library

Field research refers, in general, to any studies conducted outside the library, such as digging at an archeology site, measuring a sinkhole fault, observing student behavior at a parking lot, or surveying a selected group with a questionnaire. This type of work is not beyond the realm of first-year students, and you should consider it an important ingredient in your research plans. Therefore, converse with people by letter or e-mail, and if time permits it, conduct personal one-on-one interviews or use a questionnaire. Watch television specials, visit the courthouse archives, and conduct research by observation under the guidance of an instructor.

Set up your field research in an objective manner in order to control subjective feelings. Student Gena Messersmith (see her letter on pages 213–214) had strong personal feelings about her own daughter's condition as she researched attention deficit hyperactivity disorder, so she had to force herself to look objectively for viable evidence. Questionnaires and observations that are slanted to get a desired report should be avoided. Allow your instructor to review your methods and apparatus before launching the study. All writers get deeply involved in their subject, but they must couple that involvement with the skill of detachment. What are the facts? What conclusions do they support? Conduct the test, get results, and then discuss their implications.

Build a table, graph, or chart with the evidence collected and make it part of your study. Your instructor may ask you to place evidence of your research—field notes, interview transcripts, survey data—in an appendix at the end of your paper. You may also be asked to design your finished paper with the scientific paradigm, in which you establish a hypothesis, discuss your design and method, reveal the results of your study, and then discuss their implications.

Investigating Local Sources

Interviewing Knowledgeable People

Talk to people who have experience with your subject. Personal interviews can elicit valuable in-depth information. Interviews provide information that few others will have. Look to organizations for knowledgeable experts. For example, if writing on folklore, you might contact the county historian, a senior citizens' organization, or the local historical society. If necessary, post a notice soliciting help: "I am writing a study of local folklore. Wanted: People who have a knowledge of regional tales." Another way to accomplish this task is to join an e-mail discussion group to invite commentary from a group interested in the same topic (see pages 152–153 for more details). Try using the discussion board if yours is an online class. For accuracy, save files or record the interview with a tape recorder (with permission of the person interviewed, of course). When finished, make a bibliography entry just as you would for a book:

Thornbright, Mattie Sue. E-mail interview. 15 Jan. 2003.

Note: For a paper written in APA style, you should document an e-mail interview in the text only, not in the references. To maintain the anonymity of the source, write this in-text citation: (Anonymous interview, April 6, 2003). The APA style requires that you omit from the References items that are not retrievable, such as e-mail messages, interviews, personal letters, memos, or private papers.

In addition to the checklist of guidelines listed in this chapter you need to remember several vital matters. First, be prepared for interviews, which means that you know your interviewee's professional background and that you have a set of pertinent questions, with followups. Second, keep your focus on the principal issue. Subjects may wish to wander toward tangential ideas, so you need to bring them back to the central subject with an appropriate question. Third, maintain an ethical demeanor that honors with accuracy the statements of the subject.

Student Valerie Nesbitt-Hall researched the role of matching services and chat rooms in promoting online romance. Because she was acquainted with a couple that had met online and eventually married, she decided to request an interview—online, of course. These were her questions and, in brief form, the responses of the subjects, Stephen of Scotland and Jennifer of the United States. (See Nesbitt-Hall's paper in Chapter 18):

To see how this interview was used in the final paper, see Chapter 18.

1. When did you first meet online? Answer: *September of 1996*
2. What prompted you to try an online matching service? Answer: *We didn't really try online matching services. We chatted in a chat room, became friends there, and met in person later.*
3. Who initiated the first contact? Answer: *Stephen initiated the first online chat.*
4. How long into the relationship did you correspond by e-mail before one of you gave an address and/or phone number? Who did it first, Steve or Jennifer? Answer: *We chatted and corresponded by e-mail for nine months before Jennifer shared her phone number.*
5. How long into the relationship did you go before sharing photographs? Answer: *At nine months we began to share written correspondence and photographs.*

6. Who initiated the first meeting in person? Where did you meet? How long were you into the relationship before you met in person? Answer: *Stephen first requested the meeting, and Jennifer flew from the States to Glasgow, Scotland. This was about a year into the relationship.*
7. How much time elapsed between your first online meeting and your marriage? Answer: *One and a half years after our first chat, we were married.*
8. Did you feel that online romance enabled you to prearrange things and protect your privacy before meeting in person? Answer: *Yes. We were cautious and at times reluctant to continue, but we kept coming back to each other, online, until we knew the other well enough to trust in the relationship. Once we got offline into what we might call real-time dating, the love blossomed quickly.*
9. Did you feel, when you finally met in person, that you really knew the other person—Spiritually? Emotionally? Intellectually? Answer: *Yes.*
10. Not to put you on the spot, but do you feel as a couple that the relationship has been excellent to this point? Answer: *Yes, super.*
11. Has the difference in nationalities been a problem? Answer: *Yes, but only in relation to sorting out immigration matters. Also, Jennifer's parents were concerned that she was going to another country to see someone she had never met.*
12. Finally, would you recommend online matching services or chat rooms to others who are seeking mates? Answer: *Yes, in the right circumstances. We were lucky; others might not be.*

Writing Letters and Corresponding by E-mail

Correspondence provides a written record of research. As you would in an interview, ask pointed questions so correspondents respond directly to your central issues. Tell the person who you are, what you are attempting to do, and why you have chosen to write to this particular person or set of persons. If germane, explain why you have chosen this topic and what qualifies you to write about it.

Gena Messersmith
12 Morningside Road
Clarksville, TN

Ms. Rachel G. Warren, Principal
Glenview Elementary School
Clarksville, TN

Dear Ms. Warren:

I am a college student conducting research into methods for handling hyperactive children in the public school setting. I am surveying each elementary school principal in Montgomery County. I have contacted the central office also, but I wished to have perspectives from those of you on the front lines. I have a child with ADHD, so I have a personal as well as a scholarly reason for this research. I could ask specific questions on policy, but I have gotten that from the central office. What I would like from you is a brief paragraph that describes your policy and procedure when one of your teachers reports a hyperactive child. In particular, do you endorse the use of medication for calming the child? May I quote you in my report? I will honor your request to withhold your name. I have enclosed a self-addressed, stamped envelope for your convenience. You may e-mail me at messersmithg@apsu.edu.

Sincerely,

Gena Messersmith

> If Messersmith decided to build a table or graph from the nine replies of the various principals, she would need to document the survey in a Works Cited entry as shown later in this chapter on page 218.

This letter makes a fairly specific request for a minimum amount of information. It does not require an expansive reply. Should Messersmith use a quotation from the reply, she should provide a bibliography entry on her Works Cited page.

Warren, Rachel G. Principal of Glenview Elementary School, Clarksville, TN. E-mail to the author. 5 Apr. 2003.

Reading Personal Papers

Search out letters, diaries, manuscripts, family histories, and other personal materials that might contribute to your study. The city library may house private collections, and the city librarian can usually help you contact the county historian and other private citizens who have important documents. Obviously, handling private papers must be done with the utmost decorum and care. Again, make a bibliography entry for such materials:

Joplin, Lester. "Notes on my visits to the Robert Penn Warren family home and museum in Guthrie, Kentucky." Unpublished paper. Nashville, 2003.

Attending Lectures and Public Addresses

Watch bulletin boards and the newspaper for featured speakers who might visit your campus. When you attend a lecture, take careful notes and, if it is available, request a copy of the lecture or speech. Remember, too, that many lectures, reproduced on video, will be available in the library or in departmental files. Always make a bibliography entry for any words or ideas you use.

Petty-Rathbone, Virginia. "Edgar Allan Poe and the Image of Ulalume." Lecture. Heard Library, Vanderbilt U., 2000.

Investigating Government Documents

Documents are available at four levels of government—city, county, state, and federal. As a constituent, you are entitled to examine many kinds of records on file at various agencies. If your topic demands it, you may contact the mayor's office, attend and take notes at a city council assembly, or search out printed documents.

Local Government

Visit the courthouse or county clerk's office, where you can find facts on elections, censuses, marriages, births, and deaths. These archives include wills, tax rolls, military assignments, deeds to property, and much more. Therefore, a trip to the local courthouse can be rewarding, helping you trace the history of the land and its people.

State Government

Contact by phone a state office that relates to your research, such as Consumer Affairs (general information), Public Service Commission (which regulates public utilities such as the telephone company), and the Department of Human Services (which administers social and welfare services). The agencies may vary by name in your state. Remember, too, that the state will have an archival storehouse whose records are available for public review. Figure 8.1 shows the type of information readily available to a student conducting research on a city's population and demographics.

Federal Government

Your United States senator or representative can send you booklets printed by the Government Printing Office (GPO). A list of these materials, many of which are free, appears in a monthly catalog issued by the Superintendent of Documents: *Monthly Catalog of United States Government Publications,* Washington, DC 20402. This list is also available with an excellent search engine at www.access.gpo.gov/. In addition, you can gain access to the National Archives Building in Washington, DC, or to one of the regional branches in Atlanta, Boston, Chicago, Denver, Fort Worth, Kansas City, Los Angeles, New York, Philadelphia, and Seattle. Their archives contain court records and government documents, which you can review in two books: *Guide to the National Archives of the United States* and *Select List of Publications of the National Archives and Record Service* (see http://www.archives.gov.) You can borrow some documents on microfilm if you consult the *Catalog of National Archives Microfilm Publications*. One researcher, for example, found the table shown in Figure 8.1 while looking for information on shifts in population:

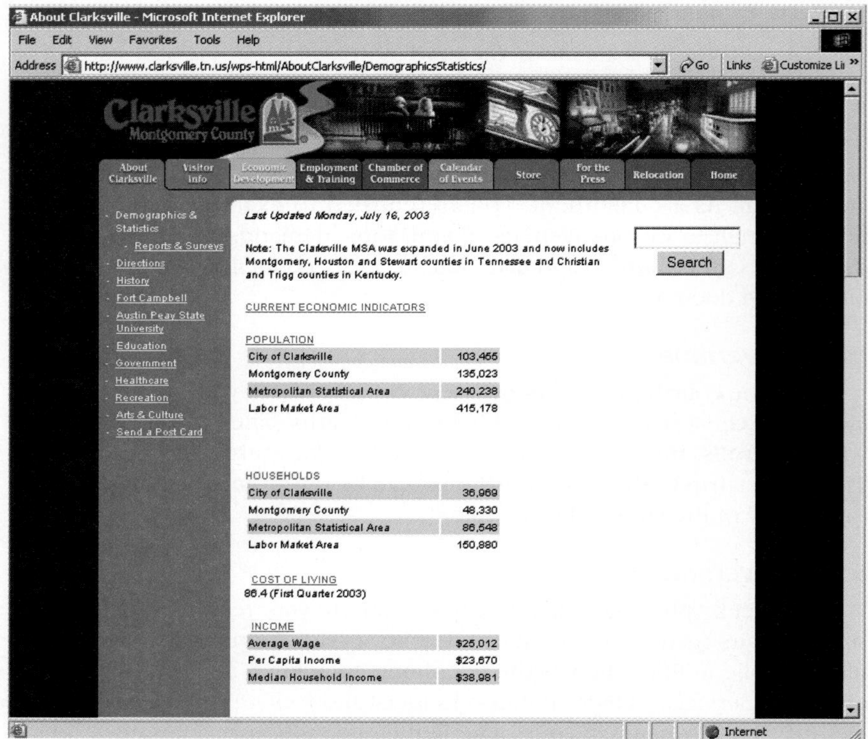

FIGURE 8.1 Population and demographics: Clarksville, Montgomery County, Tennessee.

The researcher also made a bibliography entry to record the source of this table.

> Clarksville-Montgomery County Economic Development Council. "Population and Demographics: Clarksville / Montgomery County Tennessee." 2 June 2003 <www.clarksville.tn.us>.

Examining Audiovisual Materials, Television, and Radio

Important data can be found in audiovisual materials: films, filmstrips, music, CDs, slides, audio cassettes, video cassettes, and DVDs. You will find these sources both on and off campus. Consult such guides as *Educators Guide* (film, filmstrips, and tapes), *Media Review Digest* (nonprint materials), *Video Source Book* (video catalog), *The Film File,* and *International Index*

CHECKLIST

Interviews, Letters, Private Papers, Courthouse Documents

- Set up appointments in advance.
- Consult with experienced persons. If possible, talk to several people in order to weigh their different opinions. Telephone and e-mail interviews are acceptable.
- Be courteous and on time for interviews.
- Be prepared in advance with a set of focused, pertinent questions for initiating and conducting the interview.
- Handle private and public papers with great care.
- For accuracy, record the interview with a tape recorder (with permission of the person interviewed, of course).
- Double-check direct quotations with the interviewee or the tape.
- Get permission before citing a person by name or quoting his or her exact words.
- Send helpful people a copy of your report, along with a thank-you note.

to Recorded Poetry. Television, with its many educational channels, such as *The History Channel,* offers invaluable data. With a VCR, you can record a program for detailed examination. Again, write bibliography entries for any materials that contribute to your paper.

Fleischer, Ari. "Taking on the Press." Interview. CNN. 1 June 2003.

Conducting a Survey with a Questionnaire

Questionnaires can produce current, firsthand data you can tabulate and analyze. Of course, to achieve meaningful results, you must survey a random sample—that is, each one must represent the whole population in terms of age, sex, race, education, income, residence, and other factors. Various degrees of bias can creep into the questionnaire unless you remain objective. Thus, use the formal survey only when you are experienced with tests and measurements as well as with statistical analysis or when you have an instructor who will help you with the instrument. Be advised that most schools have a Human Subjects Committee that sets guidelines, draws up consent forms, and requires anonymity of participants for information gathering that might

CHECKLIST

Using Media Sources

- Watch closely the opening and closing credits to capture the necessary data for your bibliography entry. The format is explained in Chapter 20.
- Your citations may refer to a performer, director, or narrator, depending on the focus of your study.
- As with live interviews, be scrupulously accurate in taking notes. Try to write with direct quotations because paraphrases of television commentary can unintentionally be distorted and colored by bias.
- Plan carefully the review of a media presentation, even to the point of preparing a list of questions or a set of criteria to help with your judgment.

be intrusive. An informal survey gathered in the hallways of campus buildings lacks credibility in the research paper. If you build a table or graph from the results, see Appendix A, for examples and instructions. Label your survey in the bibliography entry:

```
Mason, Valerie, and Sarah Mossman. "Child Care Arrangements
     of Parents Who Attend College." Questionnaire. Knoxville:
     U of Tennessee, 2003.
```

Unlike interview questions, which are meant to elicit a response from one person or a couple, questionnaires are designed for multiple responses from many people, from 25 or 30 up to several thousand. Design them for ease of tabulation with results you can arrange in graphs and charts.

Conducting Experiments, Tests, and Observation

Empirical research, usually performed in a laboratory, can determine why and how things exist, function, or interact. Your paper will explain your methods and findings in pursuit of a hypothesis (your thesis). An experiment thereby becomes primary evidence for your paper.

Observation is field research that occurs outside the lab—"in the field"—which might be a child care center, a movie theater, a parking lot, or the counter of a fast-food restaurant. The field is anywhere you can observe,

CHECKLIST

Conducting a Survey

- Keep the questionnaire short, clear, and focused on your topic.
- Write unbiased questions. Let your professor review the instrument before using it.
- Design a quick response to a scale (Choose A, B, or C), to a ranking (first choice, second choice, and so on), or to fill the blanks.
- Arrange for an easy return of the questionnaire, even to the point of providing a self-addressed, stamped envelope.
- Retain e-mail responses until the project is complete.
- Provide a sample questionnaire and your tabulations in an appendix.
- Tabulate the results objectively. Even negative results that deny your hypothesis have value.

count, and record behavior, patterns, or systems. It might also include observing and testing the water in a stream, the growth of certain wildflowers, or the nesting patterns of deer. We seldom notice the careful study conducted by retail merchandisers who want to know our buying habits or the analysis by a basketball coach on the shot selections by members of his team. Gathering data is a way of life—by television networks, politicians, and thousands of marketing firms.

Most experiments and observations begin with a *hypothesis*, which is similar to a thesis sentence (see Chapter 5). The hypothesis is a statement assumed to be true for the purpose of investigation. *Hummingbirds live as extended families governed by a patriarch* is a hypothesis needing data to prove its validity. *The majority of people will not correct the poor grammar of a speaker* is a hypothesis that needs testing and observation to prove its validity.

However, you can begin observation without a hypothesis and let the results lead you to conclusions. Assignment 1, of this chapter, asks you to conduct a double-entry observation for one week and to write a short reflection about what you learned by keeping the field notes. This could be your introduction to field research.

Generally, a report on an experiment or observation follows an expected format featuring four distinct parts: introduction, method, results, discussion. Understanding these elements will help you design your survey:

Introduction to explain the design of your experiment:

- Present the point of the study.
- State the hypothesis and how it relates to the problem.

- Provide the theoretical implications of the study.
- Explain the manner in which this study relates to previously published work.

Method to describe what you did and how you conducted the study:

- Describe the subjects who participated, whether human or animal.
- Describe the apparatus to explain your equipment and how you used it.
- Summarize the procedure in execution of each stage of your work.

Results to report your findings:

- Summarize the data you collected.
- Provide the necessary statistical treatment of the findings with tables, graphs, and charts.
- Include findings that conflict with your hypothesis.

Discussion that explains the implications of your work:

- Evaluate the data and its relevance to the hypothesis.
- Interpret the findings as necessary.
- Discuss the implications of the findings.
- Qualify the results and limit them to your specific study.
- Make inferences from the results.

Your experiment and the writing of the report will require the attention of your instructor. Seek his or her advice often. *Note*: This paradigm can also be used for a fully developed proposal. In fact, instructors often ask for proposals that will never be implemented as research toward a completed report.

Consult the Lester Web site **http://www.longman.awl/lester** for additional information, examples, and links to sites that discuss in greater detail the matters of experiment and observation.

CHECKLIST

Conducting an Experiment or Observation

- Express a clear hypothesis.
- Select the proper design for the study—lab experiment, observation, or the collection of raw data in the field.
- Include a review of the literature, if appropriate.
- Keep careful records and accurate data.
- Don't let your expectations influence the results.
- Maintain respect for human and animal subjects. In that regard, you may find it necessary to get approval for your research from a governing board. Read your college's rules and regulations on research that requires the use of humans and animals.

YOUR RESEARCH PROJECT

1. Select an event or object from nature to observe daily for one week. Record field notes in a double-entry format by using the left side of the page to record and the right side of the page to comment and reflect on what you have observed. Afterwards, write a brief paragraph discussing your findings.

Record:	***Response:***
Day 1	
10-minute session at window, three hummingbirds fighting over the feeder	Is the male chasing away the female, or is the female the aggressor?
Day 2	
10-minute session at window, saw eight single hummingbirds and one guarding feeder by chasing others away	I did some research, and the red-throated male is the one that's aggressive.

2. Look carefully at your subject to determine if research outside the library will be helpful for your project. If so, what kind of research: correspondence? local records? the news media? a questionnaire? an observation or experiment?
3. Work closely with your instructor to design an instrument that will affect your research and your findings. In fact, most instructors will want to examine any questionnaire that you will submit to others and will want to approve the design of your experiment or observation.
4. Follow university guidelines on testing with humans and animals.

9 Understanding and Avoiding Plagiarism

You probably know that turning in someone else's research paper as your own work is plagiarism of the worst kind. But do you really understand what is plagiarism and what isn't? Are you comfortable that you understand when to document (cite) sources and when it's okay not to? Do you know what criteria to use? Most problems related to plagiarism arise in college writing because students lack clear and confident answers to these questions—and not because students want to cheat the system. In this chapter, we'll define plagiarism, explore the ethical and community standards for writing in an academic environment, and provide examples of the worst and best of citations.

Plus, here's the newest problem: The Internet makes it easy to copy and download material and paste it into a paper—which in itself is not a problem *unless* the writer fails to acknowledge the source with an in-text citation of some sort and a bibliography entry at the back of the paper.

Let's look at it this way: Intellectual property has value just like the cash drawer at the local McDonald's. Yet words are not hard currency, and they can't be confined to somebody's cash box. In fact, ideas and theories must be shared if they are to multiply and grow. What's more, the law gives students limited rights to copy from sources. Nevertheless, the word *plagiarism* raises red flags and frightens some students to the point of stifling their research. The purpose of this chapter is to make you comfortable with and knowledgeable about the ethics of research, especially about these matters:

- Using sources to enhance your credibility
- Using sources to place your work in its proper context
- Honoring property rights
- Avoiding plagiarism
- Sharing credit and honoring it in collaborative projects
- Honoring and crediting sources in online classrooms
- Seeking permission to publish material on your Web site

Using Sources to Enhance Your Credibility

What some students fail to realize is that citing a source in their papers, even the short ones, signals something special and positive to your readers—

that you have researched the topic, explored the literature about it, and have the talent to share it. Research is something you need to share, not hide. Research writing exercises your critical thinking and your ability to collect ideas. You will discuss not only the subject matter, such as water pollution in the Delaware River, but also the *literature* of the topic, such as articles from the Internet and current periodicals found at your library's databases. By announcing clearly the name of a source, you reveal the scope of your reading and thus your credibility, as in this student's notes:

> Americans consume an average of 300 plus liters of water per day per capita while the average person needs only 20 to 40 liters, according to O'Malley and Bowman.
>
> Sandra Postel says water is "a living system that drives the workings of a natural world we depend on" (19).
>
> Postel declares: "A new water era has begun" (24). She indicates that the great prairies of the world will dry up, including America's. Hey, when folks in America notice the drought, then maybe something will happen.

These notes, if transferred into the paper, will enable readers to identify the sources used. The notes give clear evidence of the writer's investigation into the subject, and they enhance the student's image as a researcher. You will get credit for displaying the sources properly. The opposite, plagiarism, presents the information as though it were your own:

> The great prairies of the world will soon dry up, and that includes America's, so a new water era has begun.

That sentence borrows too much. If in doubt, cite the source and place it within its proper context.

Placing Your Work in Its Proper Context

Your sources will reflect all kinds of special interests, even biases, so you need to position them within your paper as reliable sources. If you must use a biased or questionable source, tell your readers up front. For example, if you are writing about the dangers of cigarette smoke, you will find different opinions in a farmer's magazine, a health and fitness magazine, and a trade journal sponsored by R.J. Reynolds. You owe it to your readers to scrutinize Internet sites closely and examine printed articles for:

- Special interests that might color the report
- Lack of credentials
- An unsponsored Web site
- Opinionated speculation, especially that found in chat rooms
- Trade magazines that promote special interests
- Extremely liberal or extremely conservative positions

Here's an example: Norman Berkowitz, in researching articles on the world's water supply, found an article of interest but positioned it with a description of the source, as shown in this note.

> Earth First, which describes itself as a radical environmental journal, features articles by an editorial staff that uses pseudonyms, such as Sky, Jade, Wedge, and Sprig. In his article "The End of Lake Powell," Sprig says, "The Colorado River may soon be unable to provide for the 25 million people plumbed into its system" (25). The danger, however, is not limited to Lake Powell. Sprig adds, "This overconsumption of water, compounded with a regional drought cycle of 25 years, could mean that Lake Powell and every other reservoir in the upper Colorado River area will be without water" (24-25).

Not only does Berkowitz recognize the source with name, quotations marks, and page numbers, he identifies the nature of the magazine for his readers.

Honoring Property Rights

If you invent a new piece of equipment or a child's toy, you can get a patent that protects your invention. You now own it. If you own a company, you can register a symbol that serves as a trademark for the products produced. You own the trademark. In like manner, if you write a set of poems and publish them in a chapbook, you own the poems. Others must seek your permission before they can reproduce the poems, just as others must buy your trademark or pay to produce your toy.

The principle behind the copyright law is relatively simple. Copyright begins at the time a creative work is recorded in some tangible form—a written document, a drawing, a tape recording. It does not depend on a legal registration with the copyright office in Washington, DC, although published works *are* usually registered. Thus, the moment you express yourself creatively on paper, in song, on a canvas, that expression is your intellectual property. You have a vested interest in any profits made from the distribution of the work. For that reason, songwriters, cartoonists, fiction writers, and other artists guard their work and do not want it disseminated without compensation. Recent attempts to prevent the downloading of music onto private computers is a demonstration of this concern.

Scholarly writing is not a profitmaking profession, but the writers certainly deserve recognition. We can give that recognition by providing in-text citations and bibliography entries. As a student, you may use copyrighted material in your research paper under a doctrine of *fair use* as described in the U.S. Code, which says:

> The fair use of a copyrighted work . . . for purposes such as criticism, comment, news reporting, teaching (including multiple copies for classroom use), scholarship, or research is not an infringement of copyright.

Thus, as long as you borrow for educational purposes, such as a paper to be read by your instructor, you should not be concerned. Just give the source the proper recognition and documentation, as explained next in Avoiding Plagiarism. However, if you decide to *publish* your research paper on a Web site, then new considerations come into play (see "Seeking Permission to Publish Material on Your Web Site").

Avoiding Plagiarism

First, develop personal notes full of your own ideas on a topic. Discover how you feel about the issue. Then, rather than copy sources one after another onto your pages of text, try to express your own ideas while synthesizing the ideas of the authorities by using summary, paraphrase, or direct quotation, which are explained fully in Chapter 12. Rethink and reconsider ideas gathered during your reading, make meaningful connections, and, when you refer to the ideas or exact words of a source—as you inevitably will—give the other writer full credit.

To repeat, plagiarism is offering the words or ideas of another person as one's own. Major violations, which can bring failure in the course or expulsion from school, are:

- The use of another student's work
- The purchase of a canned research paper
- Copying whole passages into a paper without documentation
- Copying a key, well-worded phrase into a paper without documentation
- Putting specific ideas of others into your own words without documentation

These instances reflect a deliberate attempt on the part of the writer to deceive.

Closely related, but not technically plagiarism, is to fabricate information knowingly—that is, just make it up off the top of your head. Some news reporters have lost their jobs because of fabrication.

In addition, a gray area of plagiarism exists: errors caused by carelessness. For example:

- The writer fails to enclose quoted material within quotation marks, yet he or she provides an in-text citation with name and page number.
- The writer's paraphrase never quite becomes paraphrase—too much of the original is left intact—but he or she provides a full citation to name and page.

In these situations, instructors must step in and help the beginning researcher, for although these cases are not flagrant instances of plagiarism, they can mar an otherwise fine piece of research.

What's more, double standards exist. Magazine writers and newspaper reporters offer citations to quotations and paraphrases that seldom show academic documentation. For example, the magazine might say:

> Randall Hicks, in his essay "A Lesson for the Future," says "young people's ability to think about the future is not very well developed and their images tend to be pessimistic."

That's it—no page number and no bibliography at the end of the magazine article. The magazine citation gives minimal information, but usually enough that a reader could go in search of the full essay by Hicks.

However, as an academic writer, you must document fully any borrowed ideas and words. The academic citation—author, page number, and bibliography entry—establishes two things beyond your reliability and credibility:

1. A clear trail for other researchers to follow if they also want to consult the source
2. Information for other researchers who might need to replicate (reproduce) the project

When you provide an academic citation, you've made it clear *who* you've read, *how* you used it in your paper, and *where* others can find it.

Even then, scholarly documentation differs from field to field—that is, literary papers are written in a different style from a scientific paper. In the social sciences, a paraphrase does not require a page number. In the applied sciences, a number replaces the authority's name, the year, and even the page number. So you will find that standards shift considerably as you move from class to class and from discipline to discipline. The good writer learns to adapt to the changes in the academic standards. Thus, this book devotes separate chapters to MLA, APA, CSE, and CMS styles.

Common Knowledge Exceptions

Common knowledge exceptions exist under several circumstances:

1. **Local knowledge.** You and your reader might share local or regional knowledge on a subject. For example, if you attend Northern Illinois University, you need not cite the fact that Illinois is known as the Land of Lincoln, that Chicago is its largest city, or that Springfield is the capital city. Information of this sort requires *no* in-text citation, as shown in the following example.

> The flat rolling hills of Illinois form part of the great Midwestern Corn Belt. It stretches from its border with Wisconsin in the north to the Kentucky border in the south. Its political center is Springfield in the center of the state, but its industrial and commercial center is Chicago, that great boisterous city camped on the shores of Lake Michigan.

CHECKLIST

Documenting Your Sources

- Let the reader know when you begin borrowing from a source by introducing the quotation or paraphrase with the name of the authority.
- Enclose within quotation marks all quoted materials—both key phrases and sentences.
- Use an indented block for quotations of four lines or more.
- Make certain that paraphrased material has been rewritten in your own style and language. The simple rearrangement of sentence patterns is unacceptable.
- Provide specific in-text documentation for each borrowed item, but keep in mind that styles differ for MLA, APA, CSE, and CMS standards.
- Provide a bibliography entry in the Works Cited for every source cited in the paper, including sources that appear only in content footnotes or an appendix.

However, a writer in another place and time might need to cite the source of this information. Most writers would probably want to document this next passage.

> Early Indian tribes on the plains called themselves *Illiniwek* (which meant strong men), and French settlers pronounced the name *Illinois* (Angle 44).

2. **Shared experiences.** Coursework and lectures will give you and members of your class a similar perspective on the subject. For example, students in a literary class studying African American writers would share common information, so the student might write, without documentation, something like this:

> Langston Hughes, an important poet in the 1920s and 1930s, became a leader of the Harlem Renaissance, and like so many writers, he took great pride in his African American heritage. He was not afraid to use the vernacular black dialect, and I would say that he is one of the fathers of today's rap music.

If the student shifts to nongeneral information, then a citation is in order:

> Hughes has been described by Gerald Early as the major artistic link between the revolutionary poet Paul Lawrence Dunbar and the radical poet Amiri Baraka (246).

3. **Common facts.** Common factual information that one might find in an almanac, fact book, or dictionary need not be cited. Here is an example:

> President George Herbert Walker Bush launched the Desert Storm attack in 1991 against Iraq and its leader, Saddam Hussein, with the support of allies and their troops from several nations. His son, President George W. Bush, launched a similar attack in 2003 against the same dictator and his army.

The passage needs no documentation, but the farther we move in history from that time and place, the more likely will be the need for documentation. Of course, provide a citation for analysis that goes beyond common facts.

> The elder Bush demonstrated great mastery in his diplomatic unification of a politically diverse group of allies (Wolford 37).

Correctly Borrowing from a Source

The next examples in MLA style demonstrate the differences between the accurate use of a source and plagiarism. First is the original reference material that discusses methods for solving the world's water shortage; it is followed by the student versions that use the passage, along with discussions of their failures and merits.

Original Material:

> We know how to solve these problems, without a doubt. To begin with, I believe we must restore a sense of individual

CHECKLIST

Common Knowledge Exceptions

- Do not document the source if an intelligent person would and should know the information, given the context of both writer and audience.
- Do not document terminology and information from a classroom environment that has become common knowledge to all members of the class.
- Do not document the source if you knew the information without reading it in an article or book.
- Do not document almanac-type information, such as date, place of birth, occupation, and so on.
- Do not document information that has become general knowledge by being reported repeatedly in many different sources (i.e., Michael Jordan holds several National Basketball Association [NBA] scoring records).

> responsibility and involvement, and get away from the idea that conservation is the responsibility of somebody else—the federal government, the state, the corporations, the rich. We must each face up to the need to develop an ecologically sustainable way of living; we need to look at our patterns of consumption and behavior, and shed those practices that contribute to the continuing destruction of nature. Ray Dasmann, "The Tide Is Rising and the World Is Coming to Your Front Door," *Earth Island Journal* 18 (2003): 48.

STUDENT VERSION A (a case of blatant plagiarism that is ethically and morally wrong)

> The ethical implications of the water shortage raise a question: What responsibilities do the rich nations, especially the United States, have to assure the fair and equitable distribution of water resources? Some might say that the economic forces will solve the problem, but that probably means the rich will capitalize. Meanwhile, the poor mothers in Basra or New Delhi will still walk for miles in hopes of filling a jug to carry home for their children. We know how to solve these problems, without a doubt. To begin with, we must restore a sense of individual responsibility and involvement, and get away from the idea that conservation is the responsibility of somebody else—the federal government, the state, the corporations, the rich. We must each face up to the need to develop an ecologically sustainable way of living; we need to look at our patterns of consumption and behavior, and shed those practices that contribute to the continuing destruction of nature.

This passage reads well, and the unsuspecting reader will probably think so also. However, the writer has borrowed the entire passage of Dasmann, so it's plagiarism of the first order. The writer implies to the reader that these sentences are an original creation when, actually, sentences 4, 5, and 6 are stolen.

STUDENT VERSION B (plagiarism that steals the ideas of another)

> The ethical implications of the water shortage raise a question: What responsibilities do the rich nations, especially the United States, have to assure the fair and equitable distribution of water resources? Some might say that the economic forces will solve the problem, but that probably means the rich will

capitalize. Meanwhile, the poor mothers in Basra or New Delhi will still walk for miles in hopes of filling a jug to carry home for their children. The truth is, we can solve these problems; we know how. The first step is to stop expecting somebody else to manage the problem, whether it's the local corporations, the state, or the federal government. Each person must accept responsibility and find ways to conserve water at home and in the neighborhood. We have to stop wasting water and destroying nature.

This version borrows extensively from the original with paraphrasing. The writer has stolen the keys ideas of the original without credit of any sort. The *words* might belong to the student writer, but the *ideas* belong to Dasmann.

The next version provides a citation, but it too has errors.

STUDENT VERSION C (plagiarism that paraphrases improperly and offers a vague citation)

The ethical implications of the water shortage raise a question: What responsibilities do the rich nations, especially the United States, have to assure the fair and equitable distribution of water resources? Some might say that the economic forces will solve the problem, but that probably means the rich will capitalize. Meanwhile, the poor mothers in Basra or New Delhi will still walk for miles in hopes of filling a jug to carry home for their children. However, we know how to solve these problems, and we can do so by restoring individual responsibility to the conservation effort. We cannot wait for the state, the federal government, or corporations to solve the problem. Each of us must face up to our responsibility, which is to sustain the environment and cast off habits that contribute to the destruction of nature (Dasmann 48).

This version is somewhat better. It provides a reference to Dasmann, but readers cannot know that the paraphrase contains far too much of Dasmann's language—words that should be enclosed within quotation marks. Also, the citation to Dasmann is ambiguous; when does the borrowing begin? The next version handles these matters in a better fashion.

STUDENT VERSION D (an acceptable version with a proper citation to a block quotation)

The ethical implications of the water shortage raise a question: What responsibilities do the rich nations, especially the United States, have to assure the fair and equitable distribution of water resources? Some might say that the economic forces will solve the problem, but that probably means the rich will capitalize. Meanwhile, the poor mothers in Basra or New Delhi will still walk for miles in hopes of filling a jug to carry home for their children. Environmentalist Ray Dasmann puts it like this:

> We know how to solve these problems, without a doubt. To begin with, I believe we must restore a sense of individual responsibility and involvement, and get away from the idea that conservation is the responsibility of somebody else—the federal government, the state, the corporations, the rich. We must each face up to the need to develop an ecologically sustainable way of living; we need to look at our patterns of consumption and behavior, and shed those practices that contribute to the continuing destruction of nature. (48)

This version represents a satisfactory handling of the source material. The source is acknowledged at the outset of the borrowing, the passage has been quoted as a block, and a page citation closes the material. Let's suppose, however, that the writer does not wish to quote the entire passage. The following example shows a paraphrased version.

STUDENT VERSION E (an acceptable version with several citations to a set of paraphrases)

The ethical implications of the water shortage raise a question: What responsibilities do the rich nations, especially the United States, have to assure the fair and equitable distribution of water resources? Some might say that the economic forces will solve the problem, but that probably means the rich will capitalize. Meanwhile, the poor mother in Basra or New Delhi will still walk for miles in hopes of filling a jug to carry home for her children. Environmentalist Ray Dasmann has addressed the question by putting the responsibility on each person, you and me, who must get involved (48). He says we cannot wait for others—the government and big business—to solve the problems. We have behaviors, he argues, that destroy nature, not sustain it, so we each need a personal plan to protect our personal environment (48). That plan, would, if implemented nationwide, go a long way toward solving this shortage of water that looms ever nearer.

This version also represents a satisfactory handling of the source material. In this case, no direct quotation is employed, the author and the authority are acknowledged and credited, and the essence of Dasmann's ideas are paraphrased in the student's own language. Let's look now at a version that uses both direct quotation of the source and paraphrase.

STUDENT VERSION F (an acceptable version with a series of citations to both direct quotations and paraphrased passages)

The ethical implications of the water shortage raise a question: What responsibilities do the rich nations, especially the United States, have to assure the fair and equitable distribution of water resources? Some might say that the economic forces will solve the problem, but that probably means the rich will capitalize. Meanwhile, the poor mothers in Basra or New Delhi will still walk for miles in hopes of filling a jug to carry home for their children. Environmentalist Ray Dasmann has a suggestion: "I believe we must restore a sense of individual responsibility and involvement, and get away from the idea that conservation is the responsibility of somebody else—the federal government, the state, the corporations, the rich" (48). We have behaviors, he argues, that destroy nature, not sustain it, so we each need a personal plan to protect our personal environment. He wants us to "develop an ecologically sustainable way of living" and "shed those practices that contribute to the continuing destruction of nature" (48). In short, we need to make drastic changes in our consumption of water.

In this version, the student writer uses a combination of direct quotation and paraphrase yet makes clear when and how he borrows from the source.

CHECKLIST

Required Instances for Citing a Source

1. An original idea derived from a source, whether quoted or paraphrased. This next sentence requires an in-text citation and quotation marks around a key phrase

    Genetic engineering, by which a child's body shape and intellectual ability is predetermined, raises for one source "memories of Nazi attempts in eugenics" (Riddell 19).

2. Your summary of original ideas by a source

    Genetic engineering has been described as the rearrangement of the genetic structure in animals or in plants, which is a technique that takes a section of DNA and reattaches it to another section (Rosenthal 19–20).

3. Factual information that is not common knowledge within the context of the course

    Genetic engineering has its risks: a nonpathogenic organism might be converted into a pathogenic one or an undesirable trait might develop as a result of a mistake (Madigan 51).

4. Any exact wording copied from a source

    Kenneth Woodward asserts that genetic engineering is "a high-stakes moral rumble that involves billions of dollars and affects the future" (68).

Sharing Credit in Collaborative Projects

Joint authorship is seldom a problem in collaborative writing, especially if each member of the project understands his or her role. Normally, all members of the team receive equal billing and credit. However, it might serve you well to predetermine certain issues with your peer group and the instructor:

- How will the project be judged and grades awarded?
- Will all members receive the same grade?
- Can a nonperformer be dismissed from the group?
- Should each member write a section of the work and everybody edit the whole?

- Should certain members write the draft and other members edit and load it onto a CD or onto the Web?
- Can the group work together via e-mail rather than meeting frequently for group sessions?

Resolving such issues at the beginning of a project can go a long way toward eliminating entanglements and disagreements later on. *Note*: Electronic publishing of your collaborative project on the Web raises other legal and ethical questions.

Honoring and Crediting Sources in Online Classrooms

A rapidly growing trend in education is the Web-based course or online course via e-mail. In general, you should follow the fair use doctrine of printed sources (see above)—that is, give proper credit and reproduce only limited portions of the original.

The rules are still emerging, and even faculty members are often in a quandary about how to transmit information. For educational purposes, the rules are pretty slack, and most publishers have made their texts or portions thereof available on the Web. Plus, the copyrights of many works have expired, are now in the public domain, and are therefore free. In addition, many magazines and newspapers have made online versions of their articles available for free.

What you send back and forth with classmates and the instructor(s) has little privacy and even less protection. Rules are gradually emerging for electronic communication. In the meantime, abide by a few commonsense principles:

1. Credit sources in your online communications just as you would in a printed research paper, with some variations:
   - The author, creator, or Webmaster of the site
   - The title of the electronic article
   - The title of the Web site
   - The date of publication on the Web
   - The date you accessed the site
   - The address (URL)
2. Download to your file only graphic images and text from sites that have specifically offered users the right to download them.
3. Non-free graphic images and text, especially an entire Web site, should be mentioned in your text, even paraphrased and quoted in a limited manner, but not downloaded into your file. Instead, link to them or point to them with URL addresses. In that way, your reader can go find the material and count it as a supplement to your text.
4. Seek permission if you download substantive blocks of material. See Seeking Permission to Publish Material on Your Web Site on the next page if you wish to publish your work on the Web.
5. If in doubt, consult by e-mail with your instructor, the moderator of a listserv, or the author of an Internet site.

Seeking Permission to Publish Material on Your Web Site

If you have your own home page and Web site, you might wish to publish your papers on the Web. However, the moment you do so, you are *publishing* the work and putting it into the public domain. That act carries responsibilities. In particular, the *fair use* doctrine of the U.S. Code refers to the personal educational purposes of your usage. When you load onto the Internet borrowed images, text, music, or artwork, you are making that intellectual property available to everybody all over the world.

Short quotations, a few graphics, and a small quantity of illustrations to support your argument are examples of fair use. Permission is needed, however, if the amount you borrow is substantial. The borrowing cannot affect the market for the original work, and you cannot misrepresent it in any way. The courts are still refining the law. For example, would your use of three Doonesbury comic strips be substantial? Yes, if you reproduce them in full. Would it affect the market for the comic strip? Perhaps. Follow these guidelines:

> More on fair use laws: **http://longman.awl.com/lester**.

- Seek permission for copyrighted material you publish within your Web article. Most authors will grant you free permission. The problem is tracking down the copyright holder.
- If you make the attempt to get permission and if your motive for using the material is *not for profit,* it's unlikely you will have any problem with the copyright owner. The owner would have to prove that your use of the image or text caused him or her financial harm.
- You may publish without permission works that are in the public domain, such as a section of Hawthorne's *The Scarlet Letter* or a speech by the president from the White House.
- Document any and all sources that you feature on your Web site.
- If you provide hypertext links to other sites, you may need permission to do so. Some sites do not want their address clogged by inquiring students. However, right now the Internet rules on access are being freely interpreted.
- Be prepared for people to visit your Web site and even borrow from it. Decide beforehand how you will handle requests for use of your work, especially if it includes your creative efforts in poetry, art, music, or graphic design.

YOUR RESEARCH PROJECT

1. Begin now to maintain a systematic scrutiny of what you borrow from your sources. Remember that direct quotation reflects the voice of your

source and that paraphrase reflects your voice. Just be certain, with paraphrase, that you don't borrow the exact wording of the original.

2. Look at your college bulletin and the student handbook. Do they say anything about plagiarism? Do they address the matter of copyright protection?
3. Consult your writing instructor whenever you have a question about your use of a source. Writing instructors at the freshman level are there to serve you and help you avoid plagiarising (among other responsibilities).
4. If you think you might publish your paper on the Web and if it contains substantial borrowing from a source, such as five or six cartoons from the *New Yorker* magazine, begin now to seek permission for reproducing the material. In your letter or e-mail, give your name, school, the subject of your research paper, the material you want to borrow, and how you will use it. You might copy or attach the page(s) of your paper in which the material appears.

10 Reading and Evaluating the Best Sources

The research paper assignment requires you to bring outside sources into your paper, so it only makes good sense to choose the most reliable and well-written sources you can find. We discussed this matter in Chapters 6 and 7, but further review is certainly in order.

With your research and writing, you will enter the intellectual discussions found in numerous places, but questions will arise quickly during your reading:

- How do I find the best, most appropriate sources?
- Should I read all or just part of a source?
- How do I respond to it?

One answer to all three questions is this: Be skeptical and cautious. Don't accept every printed word as the truth. Constantly review and verify to your own satisfaction the words of your sources, especially in this age of electronic publication. It is wise to consider every article on the Internet as suspect until you verify its sponsoring organization and scholarly intent (see especially Chapter 6 for guidelines on judging the value of Internet articles).

Your task is twofold: (1) You must read and personally evaluate the sources for your own benefit as a writer, and (2) you must present them to your reader in your text as validated and authentic sources. This chapter offers a few tips on those two responsibilities.

HINT: Some student researchers photocopy entire journal articles and carry an armload of books from the library. Such diligence is misplaced. The quality of your citations and the way you position them far outweigh the quantity of your source materials.

Finding the Best Source Materials

Several resources are readily at hand to point you in the right direction.

Your instructors. Do not hesitate to ask your instructor for help in finding sources. Instructors know the field, know the best writers, and can provide a brief list to get you started. Sometimes instructors will even pull books from their office shelves to give you a starting point.

Librarians. Nobody knows the resources of the library like the professionals. They are evaluated on how well they address your needs. If you appeal for help, they will often walk into the stacks with you to find the appropriate reference books or relevant journal articles.

The library. The college library provides the scholarly sources—the best books, certainly, but also the appropriate databases and the important journals—in your field of study. As we discussed in Chapter 6, the library databases are grounded in scholarship and, in general, they are not available to the general public on the Web. Your access is by your student identification. A public library may have, but seldom does have, the scholarly merit of an academic library.

The date. Try to use recent sources. A book may appear germane to your work, but if its copyright date is 1955, the content has probably been replaced by recent research and current developments. Scientific and technical topics *always* require up-to-date research. Learn to depend on monthly and quarterly journals as well as books.

Choices. An inverted pyramid shows you a progression from excellent sources to less reliable sources. The pyramid chart does not ask you to dismiss items at the bottom, but it endorses a sponsored Web site over an individual home page and favors an encyclopedia over a chat group.

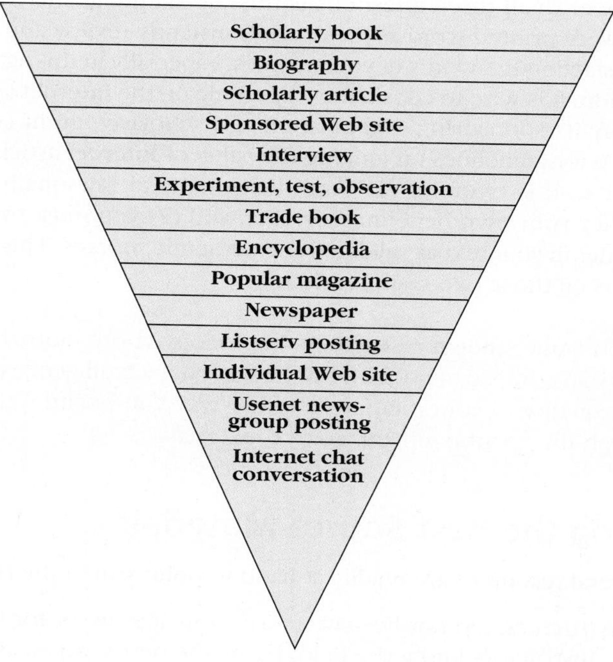

Scholarly Book

A college library is a repository for scholarly books—technical and scientific works, doctoral dissertations, publications of university presses, and textbooks. These sources offer in-depth discussions and careful documentation of the evidence. Two works will help you evaluate a book:

Book Review Digest provides an evaluation of several thousand books each year. Arranged alphabetically, it features summaries and brief quotations from the reviews to uncover the critical reception of the work.

The Booklist, a monthly magazine that reviews new books for librarians, includes brief summaries and recommendations.

Book reviews hidden within magazines and journals can be found by using these sources:

Book Review Index will send you to reviews in 225 magazines and journals.

Index to Book Reviews in the Humanities indexes book reviews in history, philosophy, literature, art, and similar fields.

Index to Book Reviews in the Social Sciences indexes book reviews in education, psychology, political science, and similar fields.

Current Book Review Citations gives an author-title index to book reviews in more than 1,000 periodicals.

Another quick source of the review is the computer. One student in Caribbean Studies used her library to access Project Muse to find a review on the writer Jamaica Kincaid. Using the site's search mechanism, she found this listing:

Reviews
Forbes, Curdella.
Writing the Autobiography of My Father (review) [Access article in HTML] [Access article in PDF] *Subjects:*
Kincaid, Jamaica. Mr. Potter.
Chauffeurs—Fiction.

Clicking on the access link took the student to the book review by Curdell Forbes on Jamaica Kincaid's book *Mr. Potter.* A portion of the review is reproduced below to show you that book reviews can provide penetration into the essence of a text.

Writing the Autobiography of My Father
Curdella Forbes
***Mr. Potter*, Jamaica Kincaid.** New York: Farrar, Strauss and Giroux, 2002. ISBN: 0374214948

A man, hungry, unable to read or write, curses God. He dies violently, still cursing, howling at history. His offspring, unacknowledged, perpetuate their father's bequest of material and mental poverty. Out of this erasure of history emerges one son who, not being able to read or write or (therefore) reflect on his own being, "has a line drawn through him." He nevertheless produces a daughter,

(continued on page 240)

(continued from page 239)

who writes his story. By shaping him in terms of the written word, she grants him recognition, names him with a name, invites us to "Hear Mr. Potter! Touch Mr. Potter! See Mr. Potter"—reference to whom now begins every sentence of his own (unknown to him) redacted memoir.

Rendered in stunningly compelling prose, Jamaica Kincaid's *Mr. Potter* recalls music and song—fugue, religious litany, (parodic) biblical enunciation of genealogies, Nordic lament, children's nursery rhyme, the *Weltanschauung* of T. S. Eliot's *Wasteland. Mr. Potter* is also elegy and revenge code; history (auto/biography) and myth; a project of identification and the deliberate negation of identity; a discourse about writing and the erasure of sentences.

The hologrammatic "portrait" that this matrix of discursive possibilities overlays is Kincaid's father, who "has been the central figure in [her] life without either of [them] knowing it." The book is the latest in the cycle of autobiographical and putatively fictional writings about Kincaid's relations with her family, writings through which Kincaid has sought to work through the problematics of a personal, literary, and historical (West Indian) identity. These texts represent a series of journeys that paradoxically end where they begin: with the conviction that a radical form of self-empowerment is necessary and capable of achievement only through the rejection of antecedents—that is to say, through the credo of a new self in imperative disjunction from the histories from which it was produced. With *My Brother,* the motif of the mother as the point of severance began to be mediated; with *Mr. Potter,* which might well have been subtitled *The Autobiography of My Father,* the paternal connection is examined.

Biography

The librarian can help you find an appropriate printed biography from among the thousands available. Short biographies appear in such works as *Contemporary Authors, Dictionary of American Negro Biography,* and *Who's Who in Philosophy*. Longer critical biographies are devoted to the life of one person, such as Richard Ellmann's *Oscar Wilde,* a study of the British poet and playwright, and Alf Mapp's *Thomas Jefferson: A Strange Case of Mistaken Identity,* which interprets the life and times of the former president. To find a critical biography, use the electronic card catalog at the library. You can also find biographies on the Internet. Most notable figures have several Web sites devoted to them that include articles by and about them.

Reference works by topics and issues, Appendix B.

Refer to biography for these reasons:

1. To verify the standing and reputation of somebody you want to paraphrase or quote in your paper.
2. To provide biographical details in your introduction. For example, the primary topic may be Carl Jung's psychological theories of the unconscious, but information about Jung's career might be appropriate in the paper.
3. To discuss a creative writer's life in relation to his or her work. That is, Jamaica Kincaid's personal life may shed some light on your reading of her stories or novels.

Scholarly Article

A scholarly article usually appears in a journal you access through the library's databases. With a journal article, you may feel confident in its authenticity because the authors of journal articles write for academic honor, they document all sources, and they publish through university presses and academic organizations that use a jury to judge an article before its publication. Thus, a journal article about child abuse found in *Child Development* or in *Journal of Marriage and the Family* should be reliable, but an article about child abuse in a popular magazine may be less reliable in its facts and opinions. Usually, but not in every case, you can identify a journal in these ways:

1. The journal does not have a colorful cover; in fact, the table of contents is often displayed on the cover.
2. No colorful drawings or photography introduce each journal article, just a title and the name of the author(s).
3. The word *journal* often appears in the title (e.g., *The Journal of Sociology*).
4. The yearly issues of a journal are bound into a book.
5. Usually, the pages of a journal are numbered continuously through all issues for a year (unlike magazines, which are paged anew with each issue).

Yet some magazines are noted for their quality—*Atlantic Monthly, Scientific Review, Psychology Today,* and many others. The major newspapers—*New York Times, Atlanta Constitution, Wall Street Journal,* and others—hire the best writers and columnists, so quality articles can be found in both printed newspapers and newspapers online.

Sometimes you may face a bewildering array of articles, and you will wonder which are the best. One way to evaluate a set of articles is with *citation searching,* which will search for authors who have been cited repeatedly in the literature. For example, Norman Berkowitz, while researching for sources on the world's water supply, saw repeated references to Sandra Postel and S. Postel, in these four citations:

Postel, S. 1992. *Last Oasis: Facing Water Scarcity*. New York: W. W. Norton.

Postel, Sandra. *Dividing the Waters: Food Security, Ecosystem Health, and the New Politics of Scarcity*. Washington (DC): Worldwatch Institute.

Postel, S., Carpenter S. 1997. Freshwater ecosystem services. Pages 195–214 in Daily, G. C., ed. *Nature's Services: Societal Dependence on Natural Ecosystems*. Washington (DC): Island Press.

Postel, S., Daily, G. C., Ehrlich, P. R. 1996. Human appropriation of renewable freshwater. *Science* 271: 785–788.

Common sense told Berkowitz to search out something by Postel; that she is respected in this field was evident in these numerous citations in the literature. As a result, he cited from two works by Postel in his paper (see Chapter 16).

Three reference books provide citation indexes:

Arts and Humanities Citation Index (AHCI) 1977–date
Science Citation Index (SCI) 1961–date
Social Sciences Citation Index (SSCI) 1966–date

Sponsored Web Site

Online article, annotated by a student, page 250.

The Internet supplies both excellent information and some that is questionable in value. You must make judgments about the validity of these materials. On that note, see Evaluating Internet Sources on pages 169–170. Ask yourself a few questions about any article from a Web site:

Is it appropriate to my work?
Is it reliable and authoritative?
Is it sponsored by an institution or organization?

Usually, just the name of a Web site offers clues about its validity. For example, how would you rank the following sites as most reliable for information?

Spank! Youth Culture Online: An Ezine for Youth and Teens
Project Muse: Scholarly Journals Online
www.factmonster.com
CBC News: Canada's Online Information Service
Thomas: Legislative Information on the Internet, sponsored by the Library of Congress

Probably you picked Project Muse and Thomas first, with CBC News third—all good choices.

Interview

Interviews with knowledgeable people provide excellent information for a research paper. Whether conducted in person, by telephone, or by e-mail, the interview brings a personal, expert perspective to your work. The key element, of course, is the expertise of the person. For full details about conducting an interview, see Interviewing Knowledgeable People in Chapter 8. For one student's use of an interview, see Valerie Nesbitt-Hall's research paper, Chapter 18.

Experiment, Test, or Observation

Gathering your own data for research is a staple in many fields, especially the sciences. An experiment will bring primary evidence to your paper as you explain your hypothesis, give the test results, and discuss the implications of your findings. For a full discussion on conducting scientific investigation, with guidelines and details on format, see Conducting Experiments, Tests, and Observation, pages 218–220.

Trade Book

How to Launch a Small Business and *Landscaping with Rocks* are typical titles of nonfiction trade books to be found in bookstores and some public libraries, but not usually in a college library. Designed for commercial consumption, trade books seldom treat with depth a scholarly subject. Trade books have specific targets—the cook, the gardener, the antique dealer. In addition, trade books, in general, receive no rigorous prepublication scrutiny like that of scholarly books and textbooks. For example, if your topic is "dieting" with a focus on "fad diets," you will find plenty of diet books at the local bookstore and on commercial Web sites. However, pass them by in favor of serious discussions backed by careful research that you will find by searching your library's databases.

Encyclopedia

By design, encyclopedias contain brief surveys of well-known persons, events, places, and accomplishments. They will serve you well during preliminary investigation, but most instructors prefer that you go beyond encyclopedias in order to cite from scholarly books and journal articles. Encyclopedias seldom have the critical perspective you can gain from books and journal articles. There are some exceptions, of course, because specialized encyclopedias (see page 197) often have in-depth articles by noted scholars.

Popular Magazine

Like trade books, magazines have a targeted audience—young women, wrestling fans, computer connoisseurs, travelers. The articles are written rather quickly and seldom face critical review by a panel of experts. Therefore, exercise caution when reading a popular commercial magazine. However, some magazines target an intellectual audience and thereby have a superior quality with academic merit; these include *Atlantic Monthly, Scientific Review, Astronomy, Smithsonian, Discover, Harper's,* and the *New Yorker.* In general, college libraries house the intellectual magazines, but they can also be found at most chain bookstores, such as Borders and Barnes & Noble.

Newspaper

In the main, newspaper reporters write under the pressure of deadlines. Seldom do they have the time for careful research, and many articles receive no copyediting or peer review. On occasion, a feature reporter will build a series of articles on a complex topic, and these often have merit. Thus, newspaper articles must be used only after cautionary and critical evaluation.

Listserv

E-mail information via listserv deserves consideration when it focuses on an academic issue, such as British Romantic literature or, more specifically, Shelley's poetry. In many cases, listservs originate from a college or scholarly organization. In fact, many instructors establish their own listserv sites for individual classes. Online courses usually feature a listserv site for exchange of ideas and peer review. These listservs can be a great way to seek out possible topics and learn what literature teachers or sociologists are talking about these days. Caution: Use the listserv to generate ideas, not as a source for facts to use in quotations.

Individual Web Site

A person's home page provides a publication medium for anybody who presumes to a knowledge they do or do not possess. You can't avoid home pages because they pop up on search engines, but you *can* approach them with caution. For example, one student, investigating the topic "fad diets," searched the Web, only to find mostly commercial sites that were blatant in their commercial attempts to sell something and home pages that described personal battles with weight loss. Caution is vital. On this point see pages 169–170.

Usenet

Usenet newsgroups post information on a site. Like call-in radio shows, they invite opinions from a vast cross section of people, some reliable and some not. In most cases, participants employ a fake pseudonymous username, rendering their ideas useless for a documented paper.

Internet Chat Conversations

Chat rooms have almost no value for academic research. In most cases, you don't even know who you are chatting with, and the conversations are seldom about scholarly issues.

Selecting a Mix of Primary and Secondary Sources

Primary sources include novels, speeches, eyewitness accounts, interviews, letters, autobiographies, and the results of original research. Feel free to quote often from a primary source if it has direct relevance to your discussion. If you examine a poem by Dylan Thomas, you must quote the poem. If you examine President George W. Bush's domestic policies on healthcare, you must quote from White House documents.

Secondary sources are writings *about* the primary sources, *about* an author, or *about* somebody's accomplishments. Examples of secondary sources are a report on a presidential speech, a review of new scientific findings, and an analysis of a poem. A biography provides a secondhand view of the life of a notable person. A history book interprets events. These evaluations, analyses, or interpretations provide ways of looking at primary works, events, and lives.

Do not quote liberally from secondary sources. Be selective. Use a well-worded sentence, not the entire paragraph. Incorporate a key phrase into your text, not eight or nine lines.

The subject area of a research paper determines in part the nature of the source materials. Use the following chart as a guide:

Citing from Primary and Secondary Sources

	Primary Sources	***Secondary Sources***
Literature	Novels, poems, plays, short stories, letters, diaries, manuscripts, autobiographies, films, videos of live performances	Journal articles, reviews, biographies, critical books about writers and their works
Government, Political Science, History	Speeches, writings by presidents and others, the *Congressional Record,* reports of agencies and departments, documents written by historic figures	Newspaper reports, news magazines, political journals and newsletters, journal articles, history books
Social Sciences	Case studies, findings from surveys and questionnaires, reports of social workers, psychiatrists, and lab technicians	Commentary and evaluations in reports, documents, journal articles, and books
Sciences	Tools and methods, experiments, findings from tests and experiments, observations, discoveries, and test patterns	Interpretations and discussions of test data as found in journals and books (scientific books, which are quickly dated, are less valuable than up-to-date journals)
Fine Arts	Films, paintings, music, sculptures, as well as reproductions and synopses of these designed for research purposes	Evaluations in journal articles, critical reviews, biographies, and critical books about the authors and their works

	Primary Sources	*Secondary Sources*
Business	Market research and testing, technical studies and investigations, drawings, designs, models, memorandums and letters, computer data	Discussion of the business world in newspapers, business magazines, journals, government documents, and books
Education	Pilot studies, term projects, sampling results, tests and test data, surveys, interviews, observations, statistics, and computer data	Analysis and evaluation of educational experimentation in journals, pamplets, books, and reports

Reading All or Part of a Source

Confronted by several books and articles, many writers have trouble determining the value of material and the contribution it will make to the research paper. To save time, you must be selective in your reading. To serve your reader, cite only carefully selected material that is pertinent to the argument. To avoid the loss of your own voice, do not dump large blocks of quotation into the paper.

Reading the Key Parts of an Article

Look closely at these parts of any article that look promising.

1. The **title.** Look for the words that have relevance to your topic before you start reading the article. For example, "Children and Parents" may look ideal for child abuse research until you read the subtitle: "Children and Parents: Growing Up in New Guinea."
2. An **abstract.** Reading an abstract is the best way to ascertain if an essay or a book will serve your specific needs. Some are available at the beginning of printed articles; others are provided by abstracting services (e.g., *Psychological Abstracts*). Most articles found through the library's databases will feature an abstract that you should read before printing or downloading the entire article. Save a tree, read before printing.
3. The **opening paragraphs.** If the opening of an article shows no relevance to your study, abandon it.
4. The **topic** sentence of each paragraph of the body. These first sentences, even if you scan them hastily, will give you a digest of the author's main points.
5. The **closing paragraph(s).** If the opening of an article seems promising, skim the closing for relevance.
6. **Author credits.** Learn something about the credentials of the writer. Magazine articles often provide brief biographical profiles of authors.

Journal articles and Internet home pages generally include the author's academic affiliation and credentials.

Read an entire article only if a quick survey encourages you to further investigation. Student Norman Berkowitz scanned an article for his paper on the world's water supply. Figure 10.1 shows how he highlighted key phrases with

Voice: The Tide Is Rising and the World Is Coming to Your Front Door

Ray Dasmann as Interviewed by David Kupfer

When an environment has become unbalanced, polluted, or devastated to the point where it is no longer healthy or able to sustain life, restoration becomes necessary. Then you must ask, what is it you are trying to restore?

This writer and the magazine are environmentally sensitive and conservative.

Ecosystems are always changing, whether you are doing anything or not: What direction are they going in, and why? These basic questions have to be kept in mind from the start. Most restoration aims to regain the condition existing when the Indians inhabited this land prior to the Euro-Caucasians. The question is, is that what you want? Native Americans also deliberately managed the environment.

Nature changes all the time. So what do we want from it?

We are at the point where we have to think globally. There is no option. The tide is rising and the world is coming to your front door. It used to seem rather simple: just create a national Park. But that is only the beginning. You must get people involved—not just local people, but all people interested in the place. Here in California, I see an opportunity for restoring the land to the condition in which the Euro-Americans "inherited" it from the Native Americans. But we must consider how we want to restore the land.

We must think globally about conditions elsewhere that will affect us in time.

I believe the biggest challenge will be restoring nearshore marine ecosystems. This is one area that is receiving considerable damage. If you're looking for biodiversity, that is where you will find it. Marine systems are far more diverse than terrestrial ones in that there is a tremendous amount of life we are affecting, a lot of which we cannot even see. And of course climate change is hitting the oceans particularly hard. So we can sit around and watch Manhattan gradually sink into the water or we can do something about it. If you're living on a Pacific island, that's no joke.

We must restore the marine ecosystems.

He uses scare tactics to excite anybody living on one of the coasts or an island.

We know how to solve these problems, without a doubt. To begin with, I believe we must restore a sense of individual responsibility and involvement, and get away from the idea that conservation is the responsibility of somebody else—the federal government, the state, the corporations, the rich. We must each face up to the need to develop an ecologically sustainable way of living; we need to look at our patterns of

We need to restore individual responsibility and involvement.

(continued)

FIGURE 10.1

Article with highlighting and marginal comments on items that the student considered important to his thesis.

Source: Earth Island Journal 18 (2003): 48.

consumption and behavior, and shed those practices that contribute to the continuing destruction of nature.

An essential individual change is the need to stop thinking of living beings as things to be exploited or manipulated and recognize that they are partners in a community of fellow beings. We must start to develop that reverence for life that Albert Schweitzer called for long ago. We need to lose some of our much-vaunted objectivity, which is useful only for certain purposes, and develop a greater subjectivity, empathy, feeling. This does not mean we stop using plants or animals for food, but it begins to prevent gross excess.

We must realize that we are partners with the animals and all elements of nature.

A third step for those who are in a position to do it—and not everybody is—is finding like-minded people and developing ecologically sustainable communities that can unhook themselves from the waste- and pollution-producing systems that prevail in the society at large.

Somehow, we must develop ecologically sustainable communities that avoid any systems that cause pollution.

These are only beginnings, but they are essential beginnings. Other things must happen also. The government, corporations, industries, and consumer society are still there. They have to be influenced. Throughout the nation what is needed is an increasing degree of local and regional self-sufficiency, leading to self-sufficiency for the nation as a whole. There is no need to give up trade and commerce, or to cease consumption of things that are produced elsewhere, but there *is* a need to get out of a state of dependence on the exploitation of other people, places, and communities.

We need self-sufficiency of the nation as a whole.

Somehow, we must stop the exploitation of people, places, and communities locally and worldwide.

FIGURE 10.1 ***(continued)***

marginal comments that were germane to his study. Note that he recognizes the bias expressed throughout the environmental magazine *Earth Island Journal.*

Reading the Key Parts of a Book

A **book** requires you to survey several items beyond those listed on above articles:

1. The **table of contents.** A book's table of contents may reveal chapters that pertain to your topic. Often, only one chapter is useful. For example, Richard Ellmann's book *Oscar Wilde* devotes one chapter, "The Age of Dorian," to Wilde's *The Picture of Dorian Gray*. If your research focuses on this novel, then the chapter, not the entire book, will demand your attention.
2. The **book jacket,** if one is available. For example, the jacket to Richard Ellmann's *Oscar Wilde* says:

> Ellmann's *Oscar Wilde* has been almost twenty years in the work, and it will stand, like his universally admired *James Joyce,* as the definitive life. The book's emotional resonance, its riches of authentic color and conversation, and the subtlety of its critical illuminations give dazzling

> life to this portrait of the complex man, the charmer, the great playwright, the daring champion of the primacy of art.

Such information can stimulate the reading and notetaking from this important book.

3. The **foreword, preface,** or **introduction.** An author's *preface* or *introduction* serves as a critical overview of the book, pinpointing the primary subject of the text and the particular approach taken. For example, Ellmann opens his book *Oscar Wilde* by saying:

   > Oscar Wilde: we have only to hear the great name to anticipate that what will be quoted as his will surprise and delight us. Among the writers identified with the 1890s, Wilde is the only one whom everyone still reads. The various labels that have been applied to the age—Aestheticism, Decadence, the Beardsley period—ought not to conceal that fact that our first association with it is Wilde, refulgent, majestic, ready to fall.

   This introduction describes the nature of the book: Ellmann will portray Wilde as the dominating literary figure of the 1890s. A *foreword* is often written by somebody other than the author. It is often insightful and worthy of quotation.
4. The **index.** A book's index lists names and terms with the page on which they are mentioned within the text. For example, the index to *Oscar Wilde* lists about eighty items under *The Picture of Dorian Gray,* among them:

   homosexuality and, 312, 318
   literature and painting in, 312–313
   magazine publication of, 312, 319, 320
   possible sources for, 311
   underlying legend of, 314–315
   W's Preface to, 311, 315, 322, 335
   W's self-image in, 312, 319
   writing of, 310–314

   An index, by its detailed listing, can determine the relevance of the book to your research.

Guidelines for evaluating Internet sources, Chapter 6.

Reading the Key Parts of an Internet Article

The techniques listed above for evaluating periodical articles apply also to Internet articles. In addition, examine:

1. The **home page,** if there is one. Prefer sites sponsored by universities and professional organizations. You may have to truncate the URL to find the home page where such information is featured. For example, this URL: www.theatlantic.com/unbound/wordpolice/three/ can be truncated to www.theatlantic.com/, which is the magazine's home page.
2. The **hypertext links** to other sites whose quality can again be determined by the domain tags *.edu*, *.org*, *.gov*. Be wary of sites that have the tag *.com.*

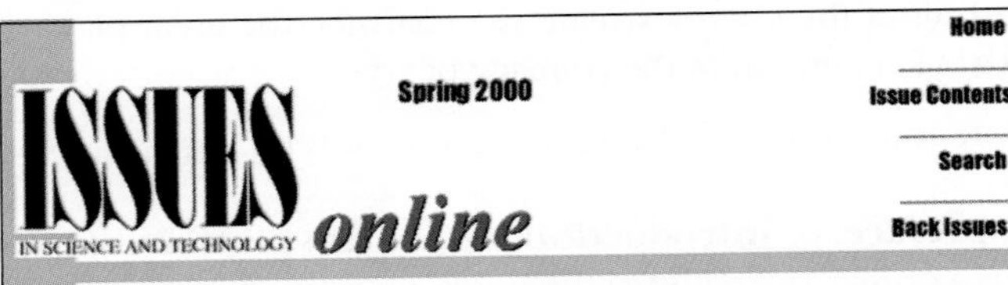

The Delicate Balance: Environment, Economics, Development

DAVID WESTERN

Conservation in a Human-Dominated World

Forging a tangible connection among environment, development, and welfare is a formidable challenge, given the complex global interactions and slow response times involved. The task is made all the harder by quickening change, including new ideas about conservation and how it can best be done. Present policies and practices, vested in government and rooted in a philosophy that regards humanity and nature as largely separate realms, do little to encourage public participation or to reinforce conservation through individual incentives and civil responsibility. The challenge will be to make conservation into a household want and duty. This will mean moving the focus of conservation away from central regulation and enforcement and toward greater emphasis on local collaboration based on fairness, opportunity, and responsibility. Given encouragement, such initiatives will help reduce extinction levels and the isolation of parks by expanding biodiversity conservation in human-dominated landscapes.

Western addresses the problems of effective conservation.

Instead of expecting the government to handle conservation, people must do it on their own as a civic responsibility.

The problems that beset current conservation efforts are daunting. Three factors in particular threaten steady economic and social progress as well as conservation: poverty, lack of access rights linked to conservation responsibilities, and environmental deterioration. Poverty and lack of access rights, especially in Africa, will keep populations growing and will fuel Rwandan-like emigration and political unrest. With short-term survival as its creed, poverty accelerates environmental degradation and habitat fragmentation. The peasant lacking fuel and food will clear the forest to plant crops or will poach an elephant if there is no alternative. So, for example, tropical forests–home to half the world's species–are being lumbered, burned, grazed, and settled. Forest destruction precipitates local wrangles between indigenous and immigrant communities over land and squabbles between North and South over carbon sinks and global warming.

Poverty must be controlled.

We cannot rely on the trickle-down effect of economic development and liberalism to eradicate poverty, solve access problems, or curb environmental losses–at least not soon. It was, after all, unfettered consumerism in the West that killed off countless animal species, stripped the forests, and polluted the air and water. And the same consumer behavior and commercial excesses are still evident, depleting old-growth forests and fighting pollution legislation every step of the way.

He says consumer behavior has destroyed the environment, and it's human behavior that must change.

FIGURE 10.2 Internet article from Issues in Science and Technology Online.

Figure 10.2 on the next page displays a sponsored Web site Norman Berkowitz discovered in his search for sources about conservation and the world's water supply. It shows an online article by David Western accompanied by the student's marginal notes to key ideas. Examine your Internet articles in like manner.

Outlining a Source

You can frame an outline to capture an author's primary themes by listing statements that reveal the major issues and any supporting ideas. A quick outline of the Dasmann article, might look like this:

Restoration becomes necessary when the environment becomes polluted.

We must think globally because the entire earth has become unbalanced.

The land needs restoration.

Marine ecosystems need immediate attention.

Three steps are necessary for reviving the environment.

Restore individual responsibility and involvement.

Stop manipulating and exploiting natural resources.

Develop communities that sustain the ecology.

Develop local and regional self-sufficiency to end exploitation of our natural resources.

This quickly drawn outline by Norman Berkowitz provides an overview of the article with the issues clearly labeled. Now Berkowitz can go in search of other sources that address these issues.

Summarizing a Source

A summary condenses into a brief note the general nature of a source. Writing a summary forces you to grasp the essence of the material. You might even use the summary in your paper, and it could serve as the heart of an annotated bibliography, which is a citation with a summary attached. Here is Norman Berkowitz's summary of the Dasmann article.

Ray Dasmann offers his views on environmental damage and what each of us can do to correct it. He says we must think in terms of the entire earth, not just our little neighborhood, and three events must occur. We must each accept individual responsibility for the environment and get involved in protecting it. We must change our attitude about exploiting the natural resources and develop communities that will sustain the ecological balance. And we must have local self-sufficiency that will lead to national awareness for the

CHECKLIST

Responding to a Source

- Read and make marginal notes on your sources. See previous pages for details and an example.
- Search out scholarly materials—books and journals—by accessing your college library's resources. Don't depend entirely on the Internet.
- If appropriate, use a mix of quotations from primary sources, such as a novel, as well as paraphrases and quotations from secondary sources on page 260.
- Assess the nature of the source for any bias it might contain. See Chapter 13 for details.
- Read and highlight the key parts of the source, whether it be an article, book, or Internet site. See pages 246–250 for further details.
- Outline key ideas to identify the issues.
- Write a summary that captures the essence of the article.

Preparing an Annotated Bibliography

An *annotation* is a summary of the contents of a book or article. A *bibliography* is a list of sources on a selected topic. Thus, an annotated bibliography does two important things: (1) it gives a bibliographic list of a selection of sources, and (2) it summarizes the contents of each book or article. Writing an annotated bibliography may at first appear to be busywork, but it will help you evaluate the strength of your sources.

The annotated bibliography that follows summarizes a few sources on the issue of tanning, tanning beds, lotions, and the dangers of skin cancer.

Levenson 1

Norman Levenson

Professor Davidson

English 1020

24 July 2003

Annotated Bibliography

Brown, Edwin W. "Tanning Beds and the 'Safe Tan' Myth." Medical Update 21 (1998): 6. Brown makes the point that there is "no such thing as a 'safe' or 'healthy' tan. He explains that tanning is the skin's reaction to radiation damage, and "tanned skin is damaged skin." He cautions that tans from tanning beds are no different than those produced by the sun. Like others, he encourages the use of SPF 15 or higher.

Cohen, Russell. "Tanning Trouble: Teens Are Using Tanning Beds in Record Numbers." Scholastic Choices 18 (2003): 23–28. Cohen warns that tanning beds "can be just as dangerous as the sun's rays" (23). The writer explains that tanning salons are not well regulated, so the amount of exposure can be really dangerous. The writer also explains how skin type affects tanning and the dangers of cancer.

Geller, Alan C., et al. "Use of Sunscreen, Sunburning Rates, and Tanning Bed Use Among More than 10,000 U.S. Children and Adolescents." Pediatrics 109 (2002): 1009–15. The objective of this study was to examine the psychosocial variables associated with teens seeking suntans. It collected data from questionnaires submitted by 10,079 boys and girls 12 to 18 years old. It concluded that many children are at risk for skin cancer because of failure to use sun screen.

Segilia, Amanda. "Sunscreens, Suntans, and Sun Health." American Cancer Society. Interview. 13 June 2000. 4 June 2003 <http://www.intelihealth.com/search>. This site features Harvard Medical School's Consumer Health Information. In this article, Amanda Segilia, a coordinator of Cancer Control Programs for the American Cancer Society, answers questions about tanning, including the use of sunscreen of SPF 15 or higher, use of suntan lotions, the effects of the sun, and the dangers of skin cancer.

"Skin Protection: My Teen Likes to Tan." St. Louis Children's Hospital. 2003. 3 June 2003 <http://www.stlouischildrens.org/articles/article_print.asp?ID-2670>. This site quotes Susan Mallory, the director of dermatology at St. Louis Children's Hospital, and registered nurse Ann Leonard, who both offer warnings against the use of tanning beds. Rather than damaging the skin with sun or tanning beds, the two experts suggest the use of tanning sprays or lotions.

"Teens and the Sun." Health Watch. The U of Texas Southwestern Medical Center at Dallas. 29 July 2002. 4 June 2003 <http://www3.utsouthwestern.edu/library/consumer/teen&sun02.htm>. This article warns teenagers against sun worship and skipping sunscreen. The experts suggest more public education and warnings. For example, teens should know that tanning damages the structure of the skin and promotes sagging skin and wrinkles in later life.

Zazinski, Janic. "A Legion of Ladies' Lesions." Research Briefs. Boston U. 11 Aug. 2000. 4 June 2003 <www.bu.edu/news/research/2000/8-11-suntans-chf.htm>. This article cites Dr. Marie-France Demierre, a professor of dermatology, who laments the use of tanning beds by young women. In truth, women are joining men in contracting and dying of melanoma, in great part because of tanning beds. Demierre and Zazinski warn youngsters against addiction to tanning beds and sun worship.

Preparing a Review of the Literature on a Topic

The *review of literature* presents a set of summaries in essay form for two purposes:

1. It helps you investigate the topic because it forces you to examine and then describe how each source addresses the problem.
2. It organizes and classifies the sources in some reasonable manner for the benefit of the reader.

Thus, you should relate each source to your central subject, and you should group the sources according to their support of your thesis. For example, the brief review that follows explores the literature on the subject of gender communication. It classifies the sources under a progression of headings: the issues, the causes (both environmental and biological), the consequences for both men and women, and possible solutions.

You also will need to arrange the sources according to your selected categories or to fit your preliminary outline. Sometimes this task is as simple as grouping those sources that favor a course or action and those that oppose it. In other cases—let's say, in a paper on F. Scott Fitzgerald's *The Great Gatsby*—you may need to summarize sources on critics who examine Gatsby's character, others who study Daisy, and still others who write about Nick Carraway.

Like Kaci Holz in the paper below, you may wish to use headings that identify your various sections.

Holz 1

Kaci Holz

Dr. Bekus

April 23, 2003

English 1010

Gender Communication: A Review of the Literature

Several theories exist about different male and female communication styles. These ideas have been categorized below to establish the issues, to show causes for communication failures, to describe the consequences for both men and women, and to suggest possible solutions.

The Issues

Deborah Tannen, Ph.D., is a professor of sociolinguistics at Georgetown University. In her book <u>You Just Don't Understand: Men and Women in Conversation</u>, 1990, she claims there are basic gender patterns or stereotypes that can be found. Tannen says that men participate in conversations to establish "a hierarchical social order," while women most often participate in conversations to establish "a network of connections" (Tannen, <u>Don't Understand</u> 24–25). She distinguishes between the way women use "rapport-talk" and the way men use "report-talk" (74).

In similar fashion, Susan Basow and Kimberly Rubenfeld, in "'Troubles Talk': Effects of Gender and Gender Typing," explore in detail the sex roles and how they determine and often control the speech of each gender. They notice that "women may engage in 'troubles talk' to enhance communication; men may avoid such talk to enhance autonomy and dominance" (186).

In addition, Phillip Yancey asserts that men and women "use conversation for quite different purposes" (71). He provides a "no" answer to the question in his title, "Do Men and Women Speak the Same Language?" He claims that women converse to develop and maintain connections, while men converse to claim their position in the hierarchy they see around them. Yancey asserts that women are less likely to speak publicly than are men because women often perceive such speaking as putting oneself on display. A man, on the other hand, is usually comfortable with speaking publicly because that is how he establishes his status among others (Yancey 71).

Similarly, most men are "less likely than androgynous individuals to feel grateful for advice" (Basow and Rubenfeld 186).

Julia T. Wood's book <u>Gendered Lives</u> claims that "male communication is characterized by assertion, independence, competitiveness, and confidence [while] female communication is characterized by deference, inclusivity, collaboration, and cooperation" (440). This list of differences describes why men and women have such opposing communication styles.

In another book, Tannen addresses the issue that boys, or men, "are more likely to take an oppositional stance toward other people and the world" and "are more likely to find opposition entertaining—to enjoy watching a good fight, or having one" (Tannen, <u>Argument</u> 166). Girls try to avoid fights.

Causes

Two theories suggest causes for gender differences—the environment and biology.

<u>Environmental Causes</u>. Tammy James and Bethan Cinelli in 2003 mention, "The way men and women are raised contributes to differences in conversation and communication . . . " (41). Another author, Susan Witt, in "Parental Influence on Children's Socialization to Gender Roles," discusses the various findings that support the idea that parents have a great influence on their children during the development of their self-concept. She states, "Children learn at a very early age what it means to be a boy or a girl in our society" (253). She

says that parents "[dress] infants in gender-specific colors, [give] gender-differentiated toys, and [expect] different behavior from boys and girls" (Witt 254).

Yancey notices a cultural gap, defining culture as "shared meaning" (68). He says, "Some problems come about because one spouse enters marriage with a different set of 'shared meanings' than the other" (69). The cultural gap affects the children. Yancey also talks about the "Battle of the Sexes" as seen in conflict between men and women. Reverting back to his "childhood gender pattern" theory, Yancey claims, "Men, who grew up in a hierarchical environment, are accustomed to conflict. Women, concerned more with relationship and connection, prefer the role of peacemaker" (71).

Like Yancey, Deborah Tannen also addresses the fact that men and women often come from different worlds and different influences. She says, "Even if they grow up in the same neighborhood, on the same block, or in the same house, girls and boys grow up in different worlds of words" (Tannen, <u>Don't Understand</u> 43).

<u>Biological Causes</u>. Though Tannen often addresses the environmental issue in much of her research, she also looks at the biological issue in her book <u>The Argument Culture</u>. Tannen states, "Surely a biological component plays a part in the greater use of antagonism among men, but cultural influence can override biological inheritance" (Tannen, <u>Argument</u> 205). She sums up the nature versus nurture issue by saying, "The patterns that typify women's and men's styles of opposition and conflict are the result of both biology and culture" (207).

Lillian Glass, another linguistics researcher, has a 1992 book called <u>He Says, She Says: Closing the Communication Gap Between the Sexes</u>. Glass addresses the issue that different hormones found in men and women's bodies make them act differently and therefore communicate differently. She also discusses how brain development has been found to relate to sex differences.

Judy Mann says, "Most experts now believe that what happens to boys and girls is a complex interaction between slight biological differences and tremendously powerful social forces that begin to manifest themselves the minute the parents find out whether they are going to have a boy or a girl" (qtd. in McCluskey 6).

Consequences of Gender Differences

Now that we have looked at different styles of gender communication and possible causes of gender communication, let us look at the possible results. Michelle Weiner-Davis is a marriage and family therapist who wrote the best-seller Divorce Busting. She says to the point, "Ignorance about the differences in gender communication has been a major contributor to divorce" (qtd. in Warren 106).

Through various studies, Tannen has concluded that men and women have different purposes for engaging in communication. In the open forum that Deborah Tannen and Robert Bly gave in New York in 1993, Tannen (on videotape) explains the different ways men and women handle communication throughout the day. She explains that a man constantly talks during his workday in order to impress those around him and to establish his status in the office. At home he wants peace and quiet. On the other hand, a woman is constantly cautious and guarded about what she says during her workday. Women try hard to avoid confrontation and avoid offending anyone with their language. So when a woman comes home from work, she expects to be able to talk freely without having to guard her words. The consequence? The woman expects conversation, but the man is tired of talking.

Solutions

Answers for better gender communication seem elusive. What can be done about this apparent gap in communication between genders? In his article published in Leadership, Jeffrey Arthurs offers the obvious suggestion that women should make an attempt to understand the male model of communication and that men should make an attempt to understand the female model of communication.

However, in his article "Speaking Across the Gender Gap," David Cohen mentions that experts didn't think it would be helpful to teach men to communicate more like women and women to communicate more like men. This attempt would prove unproductive because it would go against what men and women have been taught since birth. Rather than change the genders to be more like one another, we could simply try to "understand" each other better.

In addition, Richard Weaver makes this observation: "The idea that women should translate their experiences into the male code in order to express themselves effectively . . . is an outmoded, inconsistent, subservient notion that should no longer be given credibility in modern society" (439). He suggests three things we can change: 1. Change the norm by which leadership success is judged; 2. Redefine what we mean by power; and 3. Become more sensitive to the places and times when inequity and inequality occur (Weaver 439). Similarly, Yancey offers advice to help combat "cross-cultural" fights. He suggests: 1. Identify your fighting style; 2. Agree on rules of engagement; and 3. Identify the real issue behind the conflict (Yancey 71).

McCluskey claims men and women need honest communication that shows respect, and they must "manage conflict in a way that maintains the relationship and gets the job done" (5). She says, "To improve relationships and interactions between men and women, we must acknowledge the differences that do exist, understand how they develop, and discard dogma about what are the 'right' roles of women and men" (5).

Obviously, differences exist in the way men and women communicate, whether they are caused by biological or environmental factors. We can consider the possible causes, the consequences, and possible solutions. Using this knowledge, we should be able to more accurately interpret communication between the genders.

Works Cited

Arthurs, Jeffrey. "He Said, She Heard: Any Time You Speak to Both Men and Women, You're Facing Cross-Cultural Communication." Leadership 23.1 (Winter 2002): 49. InfoTrac. Austin Peay State U, Woodward Lib. 22 Sept. 2003 <http://www.galegroup.com/>.

Basow, Susan A., and Kimberly Rubenfeld. " 'Troubles Talk': Effects of Gender and Gender Typing." Sex Roles: A Journal of Research (2003): 183– . InfoTrac. Austin Peay State U, Woodward Lib. 24 Apr. 2003 <http://web5.infotrac.galegroup.com/search>.

Cohen, David. "Speaking Across the Gender Gap." New Scientist 131.1783 (1991): 36. InfoTrac. Austin Peay State U, Woodward Lib. 28 Sept 2003. <http://web5.infotrac.galegroup.com/>.

Deborah Tannen and Robert Bly: Men and Women: Talking Together. New York Open Center. 1991. Videocassette. Mystic Fire Video, 1993.

Glase, Lillian. He Says, She Says: Closing the Communication Gap between the Sexes. New York: G.P. Putnam's Sons, 1992.

James, Tammy, and Bethann Cinelli. "Exploring Gender-Based Communication Styles." Journal of School Health 73 (2003): 41–41.

McCluskey, Karen Curnow. "Gender at Work." Public Management 79.5 (1997): 5–10.

Tannen, Deborah. The Argument Culture: Moving from Debate to Dialogue. New York: Random House, 1998.

---. You Just Don't Understand: Women and Men in Conversation. New York: Ballantine, 1990.

Warren, Andrea. "How to Get Him to Listen." Ladies' Home Journal 113 (Mar. 1996): 106.

Weaver, Richard L. "Leadership for the Future: A New Set of Priorities." Vital Speeches of the Day 61 (1995): 438–441.

Witt, Susan D. "Parental Influence on Children's Socialization to Gender Roles." Adolescence 32 (1997): 253.

Woods, Julia T. Gendered Lives. San Francisco: Wadsworth, 2002.

Yancey, Phillip. "Do Men and Women Speak the Same Language?" Marriage Partnership 10 (1993): 68–73.

YOUR RESEARCH PROJECT

1. Examine your sources to test the validity of the list against the pyramid on page 238. Do you have enough sources from the upper tier of scholarly works? If not, go in search of journal articles and scholarly books to beef up the list. Do not depend on Internet articles entirely, even if every one is from a sponsored Web site.
2. Conduct a citation search on your topic, which will help you identify key people who have written on the subject several times and for several publications.
3. Examine the chart of primary and secondary sources. Look for your discipline—literature, government, history—and then determine if you are using a mix of primary and secondary sources.
4. Respond to one of your sources by writing two items: (1) a rough outline of the contents of the source, and (2) a brief summary of the source.

11 Organizing Ideas and Setting Goals

Initially, research is haphazard, and your workspace will be cluttered with bits of information scattered through your notes and on sheets of photocopied material or printouts from the Internet. After the initial search to confirm the availability of sources, you should organize your ideas so that reading and notetaking will relate directly to your specific needs. Careful organization and the presentation of evidence will augment your voice and give it a touch of authority, which will invite readers to share your position. Gathering, organizing, and notetaking occur simultaneously, so use this chapter in harmony with the next chapter, "Writing Notes," as you gather more and more material.

Your needs become clear when you draw plans such as a research proposal, a list of ideas, a set of questions, or a rough outline. In addition, the design of your study should match an appropriate organizational model, called a *paradigm*. You may also be required to create a final outline to keep your manuscript well ordered. The organizational ideas in this chapter should help you find your way through the maze.

Charting a Direction and Setting Goals

Instead of plunging too quickly into notetaking, first decide *what* to look for and *why* you need it. One or more of these exercises will help your organization:

- Chart the course of your work with a basic order.
- Revisit your research proposal, if you developed one, for essential issues.
- List keywords, ideas, and issues that you must explore in the paper.
- Rough out an initial outline.
- Ask a thorough set of questions.
- Use modes of development (e.g., definition or cause/effect) to identify key issues.
- Search issues across the curriculum (e.g., economics, psychology, biology).
- Let your thesis sentence point you toward the basic issues.

Each of these techniques is explored on the following pages.

Using a Basic, Dynamic Order to Chart the Course of Your Work

Your finished paper should trace the issues, defend and support a thesis, and provide dynamic progression of issues and concepts that point forward to the conclusion. The paper should provide these elements:

Identification of the problem or issue
A review of the literature on the topic
Your thesis or hypothesis
Analysis of the issues
Presentation of evidence
Interpretation and discussion of the findings

In every case, you must generate the dynamics of the paper by (1) building anticipation in the introduction, (2) investigating the issues in the body, and (3) providing a final judgment. In this way, you will satisfy the demands of the academic reader, who will expect you to:

- Examine a problem.
- Cite pertinent literature on it.
- Offer your ideas and interpretation of it.

All three are necessary in almost every instance. Consequently, your early organization will determine, in part, the success of your research paper.

Using Your Research Proposal to Direct Your Notetaking

Your research proposal, if you developed one, introduces issues worthy of research. For example, the last sentence of this research proposal names four topics:

I want to address this paper to everybody who thinks water is plentiful and will always be here. I'm afraid that water might soon replace oil as an economic resource most treasured by nations. We already have legal battles about the sharing of water, and we may one day have wars over it. Preliminary reading has shown that a growing world population faces a global water supply that is shrinking. Accordingly, this paper will examine some of the issues with regard to supply and demand, the political power struggles that are emerging, and the ethical and perhaps even moral implications engulfing the world's scattered supply of fresh water.

This writer will search the literature and write notes to build an environmental examination on those who have good supplies of water and those who don't.

Another writer sketched the following research proposal, which lists the types of evidence necessary to accomplish her project:

> This paper will study organ and tissue donation. It will expose the myths that prevail in the public's imagination and, hopefully, dispel them. It will explore the serious need of and benefits derived from donated organs and tissue. It will also itemize the organs and their use to rehabilitate the diseased and wounded. It will evaluate, but it will also be a proposal: Sign the donor card!

Listing Keywords and Phrases to Set Directions for Notetaking

Follow two fairly simple steps: (1) Jot down ideas or words in a rough list, and (2) expand the list to show a hierarchy of major and minor ideas. Student Norman Berkowitz started listing items that are affected by and depend on the world's water supply:

```
wildlife survival
sanitation and hygiene
irrigation of farms and the food supply
bioscience issues
water distribution
global warming
the Ogallala aquifer
```

Berkowitz could begin notetaking with this list and label each note with one of the phrases.

HINT: What you are looking for at this point are terms that will speed your search on the Internet and in the library's indexes.

Writing a Rough Outline

As early as possible, organize your key terminology in a brief outline, arranging the words and phrases in an ordered sequence, as shown in this next example. Jamie Johnston began research in the matter of prehistoric wars. He soon jotted down this rough outline:

```
Prehistoric wars
      Evidence of weapons
      Evidence from skeletal remains
```

Evidence of soldiers and fortresses

Reasons for early fighting

Resources

Slaves, concubines, and sacrificial victims

Gold, silver, bronze, copper

Revenge

Defend honor

Cause for human compulsion to fight

Biology

Culture

This outline, although sketchy, provides the terminology needed for keyword searches on the Internet and in your library's databases. Also, it's not too early to begin writing notes for the items on the list.

Using Questions to Identify Issues

Questions can invite you to develop answers in your notes. Early in her work, one student made this list of questions:

What is a functional food?

How does it serve the body in fighting disease?

Can healthy eating actually lower health care costs?

Can healthy eating truly prolong one's life?

Can we identify the components of nutritional foods that make them work effectively?

What is an antioxidant? a carcinogen? a free radical? a triglyceride?

She then went in search of answers and built a body of notes. One question might lead to others, and an answer to a question (Are nutritional foods new?) might produce a topic sentence for a paragraph:

> Although medical professionals are just beginning to open their minds and eyes to the medicinal power of food, others have known about food's healthful properties for centuries.

Setting Goals by Using the Modes of Development

Try to anticipate the kinds of development you will need to build effective paragraphs and to explore your topic fully. Then base your notes on the modes of development: *definition, comparison and contrast, process, illustration, cause and effect, classification, analysis,* and *description*. Here's a list by one student who studied the issues of organ and tissue donation.

> Define tissue donation.
>
> Contrast myths, religious views, and ethical considerations.
>
> Illustrate organ and tissue donation with several examples.
>
> Use statistics and scientific data.
>
> Search out causes for a person's reluctance to sign a donor card.
>
> Determine the consequences of donation with a focus on saving the lives of children.
>
> Read and use a case study on a child's death and organ donation by the public.
>
> Explore the step-by-step stages of the process of organ donation.
>
> Classify the types and analyze the problem.
>
> Give narrative examples of several people whose lives were saved.

With this list in hand, a writer can search for material to develop as *contrast, process, definition,* and so forth.

HINT: Try developing each important item on your list into a full paragraph. Write a definition paragraph. Write a paragraph to compare and contrast the attitudes expressed by people about organ donation. Write another paragraph that gives four or five examples. By doing so, you will be well on your way to developing the paper.

One student recorded this note that describes the subject:

> Organ and tissue donation is the gift of life. Each year, many people confront health problems due to diseases or congenital birth defects. Organ transplants give these people the chance to live a somewhat normal life. Organs that can be successfully transplanted include the heart, lungs, liver, kidneys, and pancreas (Barnill 1). Tissues that can be transplanted successfully include bone, corneas, skin, heart valves, veins, cartilage, and other connective tissues (Taddonio 1).

Using Approaches across the Curriculum to Chart Your Major Ideas

Each scholarly field gives a special insight into any given topic. Suppose, for example, that you wish to examine an event from U.S. history, such as the

Battle of Little Big Horn. Different academic disciplines will help you approach the topic in different ways.

Political science:	Was Custer too hasty in his quest for political glory?
Economics:	Did the government want to open the western lands for development that would enrich the nation?
Military science:	Was Custer's military strategy flawed?
Psychology:	Did General Custer's ego precipitate the massacre?
Geography:	Why did Custer stage a battle at this site?

These approaches can also produce valuable notes as the student searches out answers in the literature, as shown in this example:

> The year 1876 stands as a monument to the western policies of Congress and the President, but Sitting Bull and Custer seized their share of glory. Custer's egotism and political ambitions overpowered his military savvy (Lemming 6). Also, Sitting Bull's military tactics (he told his braves to kill rather than show off their bravery) proved devastating for Custer and his troops, who no longer had easy shots at "prancing, dancing Indians" (Potter 65).

Using Your Thesis to Chart the Direction of Your Research

Often, the thesis sentence sets the direction of the paper's development.

Arrangement by Issues

The thesis sentence might force the writer to address various issues and positions.

THESIS: Misunderstandings about organ donation distort reality and set serious limits on the availability of those persons who need an eye, a liver, or a healthy heart.

ISSUE 1. Many myths mislead people into believing that donation is unethical.

ISSUE 2. Some fear that as a patient they might be terminated early for their body parts.

ISSUE 3. Religious views sometimes get in the way of donation.

The outline above, though brief, gives this writer three categories that require detailed research in support of the thesis. The notetaking can be focused on these three issues.

Arrangement by Cause/Effect

In other cases, the thesis sentence suggests development by cause/effect issues. Notice that the next writer's thesis on television's educational values points the way to four very different areas worthy of investigation.

Formulating an effective thesis, Chapter 5.

THESIS: Television can have positive effects on a child's language development.

CONSEQUENCE 1. Television introduces new words.

CONSEQUENCE 2. Television reinforces word usage and proper syntax.

CONSEQUENCE 3. Literary classics come alive verbally on television.

CONSEQUENCE 4. Television provides the subtle rhythms and musical effects of accomplished speakers.

The outline above can help the writer produce a full discussion on television viewing.

Arrangement by Interpretation and Evaluation

Evaluation will evolve from thesis sentences that judge a subject by a set of criteria, such as your analysis of a poem, movie, or museum display. Notice how the next student's thesis sentence requires an interpretation of Hamlet's character.

THESIS: Shakespeare manipulates the stage settings for Hamlet's soliloquies to uncover his unstable nature and forecast his failure.

1. His soul is dark because of his mother's incest.
2. He appears impotent in comparison with the actor.
3. He is drawn by the magnetism of death.
4. He realizes he cannot perform cruel, unnatural acts.
5. He stands ashamed by his inactivity in comparison.

Arrangement by Comparison

Sometimes a thesis sentence stipulates a comparison on the value of two sides of an issue, as shown in one student's preliminary outline:

THESIS: Discipline often involves punishment, but child abuse adds another element: the gratification of the adult.

COMPARISON 1: A spanking has the interest of the child at heart but a beating or a caning has no redeeming value.

COMPARISON 2: Time-outs remind the child that relationships are important and to be cherished but lock-outs in a closet only promote hysteria and fear.

COMPARISON 3: The parent's ego and selfish interests often take precedence over the welfare of the child or children.

CHECKLIST

Evaluating Your Overall Plan

1. What is my thesis? Will my notes and records defend and illustrate my proposition? Is the evidence convincing?
2. Have I found the best plan for developing the thesis with elements of argument, evaluation, cause/effect, or comparison?
3. Should I use a combination of elements—that is, do I need to evaluate the subject, examine the causes and consequences, and then set out the argument?

Using Academic Models (Paradigms)

A paradigm is a universal outline, one that governs most papers of a given type. It is not content-specific; rather, it provides a general model, a broad scaffold, and a basic academic pattern of reasoning for all papers with a certain purpose. In contrast, a traditional outline, with its specific detail on various levels of subdivision, is useful for only one paper. Therefore, we recommend that you start with a paradigm, an ideal pattern for many papers, and finish with an outline, a content-oriented plan for one paper only—your paper.

A General All-Purpose Model

If you are uncertain about the design of your paper, start with this bare-bones model and expand it with your material. Readers, including your instructor, are accustomed to this sequence for research papers. It offers plenty of leeway.

Identify the subject.
    Explain the problem.
    Provide background information.
    Frame a thesis statement.
Analyze the subject.
    Examine the first major issue.

Examine the second major issue.
Examine the third major issue.
Discuss your findings.
Restate your thesis and point beyond it.
Interpret the findings.
Provide answers, solutions, or a final opinion.

To the introduction you can add a quotation, an anecdote, a definition, or comments from your source materials. Within the body, you can compare, analyze, give evidence, trace historical events, and handle other matters. In the conclusion, you can challenge an assumption, take exception to a prevailing point of view, and reaffirm your thesis. Flesh out each section, adding subheadings as necessary, to create an outline.

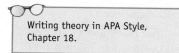

Developing introductions, bodies, and conclusions, Chapter 15.

Paradigm for Advancing Your Ideas and Theories

Writing theory in APA Style, Chapter 18.

If you want to advance a theory in your paper, use this next design, but adjust it to eliminate some items and add new elements as necessary.

Introduction:
Establish the problem or question.
Discuss its significance.
Provide the necessary background information.
Introduce experts who have addressed the problem.
Provide a thesis sentence that addresses the problem from a fresh perspective, if at all possible.
Body:
Evaluate the issues involved in the problem.
Develop a past-to-present examination.
Compare and analyze the details and minor issues.
Cite experts who have addressed the same problem.
Conclusion:
Advance and defend your theory as it grows out of evidence in the body.
Offer directives or a plan of action.
Suggest additional work and research that is needed.

Paradigm for the Analysis of Creative Works

If you plan to analyze musical, artistic, or literary works, such as an opera, a set of paintings, or a novel, adjust this next paradigm to your subject and purpose.

Introduction:
Identify the work.

Give a brief summary in one sentence.
Provide background information that relates to the thesis.
Offer biographical facts about the artist that relate to the specific issues.
Quote and paraphrase authorities to establish the scholarly traditions.
Write a thesis sentence that establishes your particular views of the literary work.

Body:
Provide evaluative analysis divided according to such elements as imagery, theme, character development, structure, symbolism, narration, and language.

Conclusion:
Keep a fundamental focus on the artist of the work, not just the elements of analysis as explained in the body.
Offer a conclusion that explores the contributions of the artist in accord with your thesis sentence.

Paradigm for Argument and Persuasion Papers

If you write persuasively or argue from a set position, your paper should conform in general to this next paradigm. Select the elements that fit your design.

Introduction:
In one statement, establish the problem or controversial issue your paper will examine.
Summarize the issues.
Define the key terminology.
Make concessions on some points of the argument.
Use quotations and paraphrases to clarify the controversial nature of the subject.
Provide background information to relate the past to the present.
Write a thesis to establish your position.

Body:
Develop arguments to defend one side of the subject.
Analyze the issues, both pro and con.
Give evidence from the sources, including quotations as appropriate.

Conclusion:
Expand your thesis into a conclusion that makes clear your position, which should be one that grows logically from your analysis and discussion of the issues.

Paradigm for Analysis of History

If you are writing a historical or political science paper that analyzes events and their causes and consequences, your paper should conform, in general, to the following plan.

Introduction:
- Identify the event.
- Provide the historical background leading up to the event.
- Offer quotations and paraphrases from experts.
- Give the thesis sentence.

Body:
- Analyze the background leading up to the event.
- Trace events from one historic episode to another.
- Offer a chronological sequence that explains how one event relates directly to the next.
- Cite authorities who have also investigated this event in history.

Conclusion:
- Reaffirm your thesis.
- Discuss the consequences of this event, explaining how it altered the course of history.

Paradigm for a Comparative Study

A comparative study requires that you examine two schools of thought, two issues, two works, or the positions taken by two persons. The paper examines the similarities and differences of the two subjects, generally using one of three arrangements for the body of the paper.

Introduction:
- Establish A.
- Establish B.
- Briefly compare the two.
- Introduce the central issues.
- Cite source materials on the subjects.
- Present your thesis.

Body (choose one):

Examine A. Examine B. Compare and contrast A and B.	Compare A and B. Contrast A and B. Discuss the central issues.	Issue 1 Discuss A and B. Issue 2 Discuss A and B. Issue 3 Discuss A and B.

Conclusion:
- Discuss the significant issues.
- Write a conclusion that ranks one side over the other, or
- Write a conclusion that rates the respective genius of each side.

Remember that the models provided above are general guidelines, not iron-clad rules. Adjust each as necessary to meet your special needs.

Writing a Formal Outline

Not all papers require a formal outline, nor do all researchers need one. A short research paper can be created from keywords, a list of issues, a rough outline, and a first draft. However, a formal outline can be important because it classifies the issues of your study into clear, logical categories with main headings and one or more levels of subheadings. An outline will change miscellaneous notes, computer drafts, and photocopied materials into an ordered progression of ideas.

> **HINT:** A formal outline is not rigid and inflexible; you may, and should, modify it while writing and revising. In every case, treat an outline or organizational chart as a tool. Like an architect's blueprint, it should contribute to, not inhibit, the construction of a finished product.

You may wish to experiment with the Outline feature of your computer software, which will allow you to view the paper at various levels of detail and to highlight and drop the essay into a different organization.

Using Standard Outline Symbols

List your major categories and subtopics in this form:

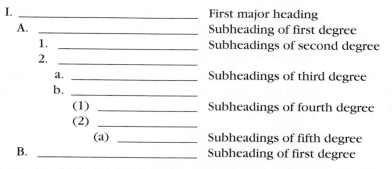

I. ______________________	First major heading
A. ____________________	Subheading of first degree
1. __________________	Subheadings of second degree
2. __________________	
a. ________________	Subheadings of third degree
b. ________________	
(1) ______________	Subheadings of fourth degree
(2) ______________	
(a) ____________	Subheadings of fifth degree
B. ____________________	Subheading of first degree

The degree to which you continue the subheads will depend, in part, on the complexity of the subject. Subheads in a research paper seldom carry beyond subheadings of the third degree, the first series of small letters.

An alternative form, especially for papers in business and the sciences, is the *decimal outline,* which divides material by numerical divisions:

1. ______________________
    1.1. ____________________
        1.1.1. ________________
        1.1.2. ________________
        1.1.3. ________________
    1.2. ____________________
        1.2.1. ________________
        1.2.2. ________________
2. ______________________

Writing a Formal Topic Outline

If your purpose is to arrange quickly the topics of your paper without detailing your data, build a topic outline of balanced phrases. The topic outline may use noun phrases:

```
III. The senses
     A. Receptors to detect light
        1. Rods of the retina
        2. Cones of the retina
```

It may also use gerund phrases:

```
III. Sensing the environment
     A. Detecting light
        1. Sensing dim light with retina rods
        2. Sensing bright light with retina cones
```

And it may also use infinitive phrases:

```
III. To use the senses
     A. To detect light
        1. To sense dim light
        2. To sense bright light
```

No matter which grammatical format you choose, you should follow it consistently throughout the outline. Student Sarah Bemis's topic outline follows. Her paper appears in Chapter 20.

```
 I. Diabetes defined
    A. A disease without control
       1. A disorder of the metabolism
       2. The search for a cure
    B. Types of diabetes
       1. Type 1, juvenile diabetes
       2. Type 2, adult-onset diabetes
II. Health complications
    A. The problem of hyperglycemia
       1. Signs and symptoms of the problem
       2. Lack of insulin
    B. The conflict of the kidneys and the liver
       1. Effects of ketoacidosis
       2. Effects of arteriosclerosis
```

III. Proper care and control

A. Blood sugar monitoring

1. Daily monitoring at home
2. Hemoglobin test at a laboratory

B. Medication for diabetes

1. Insulin injections
2. Hypoglycemia agents

C. Exercise programs

1. Walking
2. Swimming
3. Aerobic workouts

D. Diet and meal planning

1. Exchange plan
2. Carbohydrate counting

IV. Conclusion: Balance of all the factors

Writing a Formal Sentence Outline

The sentence outline requires full sentences for each heading and subheading. It has two advantages over the topic outline:

1. Many entries in a sentence outline can serve as topic sentences for paragraphs, thereby accelerating the writing process.
2. The subject/verb pattern establishes the logical direction of your thinking (for example, the phrase "Vocabulary development" becomes "Television viewing can improve a child's vocabulary").

Consequently, the sentence outline brings into the open any possible organizational problems rather than hiding them as a topic outline might do. The time invested writing a complete sentence outline, like writing complete, polished notes (see Chapter 12), will pay off when you write the rough draft and revise it.

Jamie Johnston's sentence outline is shown below. The complete paper can be found in Chapter 19. As shown below, the thesis sentence should appear as a separate item in the outline. It is the main idea of the entire paper, so try not to label it as Item I in the outline. Otherwise, you may search fruitlessly for parallel ideas to put in II, III, and IV. (See also Chapter 15 on using the thesis in the opening.)

Outline

Thesis: Prehistoric humans were motivated by biological instincts toward warfare rather than cultural demands for a share of limited resources.

I. The conflict of "noble savage" versus prehistoric warriors has surfaced in recent literature.
   A. Some literature has advocated the existence of harmony and peace among early tribes.
      1. Rousseau argued for a noble savage in the 1700s.
      2. The Bible speaks of the Garden of Eden.
   B. Recent research suggests that wars have existed since the dawn of life.
      1. LaBlanc cites evidence from the Southwest Indians.
      2. Yates reports on Chinese weapons from 28,000 BC.
      3. Ferrill has examined cave paintings.

II. The evidence points clearly to the existence of prehistoric wars.
   A. Anthropologists have uncovered skeletal remains of captives who were executed.
      1. Victims were skinned alive.
      2. Victims were decapitated.
      3. Massacres occurred in Europe, North and South America, Japan, and other parts of the world.
   B. Weapons of mass destruction (on their terms) have been unearthed along with fortifications.
      1. Clubs, slings, daggers, spears, and bows give testimony to early fighting.
      2. Fortress cities prove that villagers attempted to protect themselves from ravaging hordes.

III. Many reasons for prehistoric fighting have been advanced.
   A. Some fought to capture resources of various kinds.
      1. Humans were captured to serve as slaves, concubines, and sacrificial victims of religious ceremonies.
      2. Food, water, and cattle were targets of desperate tribes during famines.
      3. Gold, silver, bronze, and copper were prized commodities and worthy of a good battle.
      4. Trade routes and key locations were subject to dispute.

B. Some fought for personal reasons and points of honor.

1. Revenge was often a motivating factor for attacks on a village.

2. Religion motived warriors to search out not only religious icons but sacrificial victims.

3. Defending the tribe's honor was sometimes motivation for desperate battles.

IV. At issue is the primary motivating factor that prompted mass carnage at the dawn of civilization.

A. Some argue that society as a whole wants to preserve its culture and will fight to maintain it.

B. Others argue that human beings by nature are aggressive and love a good fight in the search for power over others.

Using a Research Journal to Enrich Your Organizational Plan

If you have kept a research journal, you have probably developed a number of notes in addition to the collection of printouts and photocopies. Therefore, review the collection and assign each piece to a section of your outline. Do this by making a note, such as "put in the conclusion," or by assigning an outline number, "use in II.A.1." Do the same thing with your other materials. Then assign them to a spot in your outline, as shown in this brief example from an outline:

A. Television viewing can improve the vocabulary of children.

1. Negative views
   Cite Powell; cite Winkeljohann.

2. Positive views
   Cite Rice and Woodsall; cite Singer; cite Postman.

In Chapter 12, we discuss methods for building notes from the various pieces you have collected.

YOUR RESEARCH PROJECT

1. Sketch out an outline for your project. List your general thesis and, below that, establish several divisions that will require careful and full development. Test more than one plan. Do you need several criteria of

judgment? causal issues? arguments? evidence from field research? Which seems to work best for you?

2. Select one of the paradigms, as found under the section, "Using Academic Models on page 269," and develop it fully with the information in your sketch outline (see #1 immediately above).
3. If you are familiar about the design of Web pages, you probably realize that the hierarchical ideas have value because readers can click on links that will carry them deeper into the files. Test your outline by constructing a plan like the one below, filling the blanks downward from the large block (thesis) to major issues (medium blocks) to evidence (small blocks). The chart, which you can redraw on a sheet of paper, looks something like this:

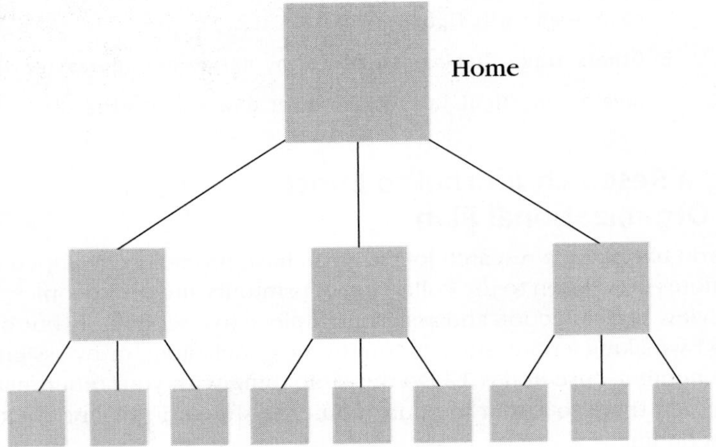

12 Writing Notes

The primary reason for writing from research is to announce and publicize new findings. A botanist explains the discovery of a new strain of ferns in Kentucky's Land between the Lakes. A medical scientist reports the results of her cancer research. A sociologist announces the results of a two-year pilot study of Native Americans in the Appalachian region.

Similarly, you will be asked to explain your findings from a geology field trip, disclose research on animal imagery in Robert Frost's poetry, or discuss the results of an investigation into overcrowding of school classrooms. The accurate notes from your personal research will join with your carefully paraphrased notes from experts on the topic to form the support for your thesis. Your goal is to share verifiable information, but others can verify your work only if good records are kept and reported.

Gathering Printouts, Photocopies, Scanned Images, and Downloaded Data

Today's technology makes it fairly easy to collect material quickly and in volume. You can print Internet articles or save them to a file. You can use a scanner to make digital images of graphics as well as text. Plus, photocopy machines enable you to carry home a few sheets of paper instead of an entire book.

Yet this convenience comes at a price: You will have a nice collection of articles and copied chapters from books, plus notes you have made along the way in your research journal, but *you must somehow make sense of it all*. Therefore, consult Chapter 11 often for tips on organizing and outlining the material.

Read each piece you have, make marginal notes on it, and assign it a place in your organization chart—be it an outline, a paradigm, or even a general list of issues. Identify a location for it in the overall layout. Then you have a choice: You can write notes from it now or wait to borrow from it during the drafting of the paper.

All this material will gradually make sense as you arrange it and use it. Warning: Keep *everything*. You will need to cite the source in the text and in a bibliography entry, so don't throw away a note, printout, or a photocopy.

Writing Notes of High Quality

Keeping accurate records and writing notes of high quality are essential steps in the research process. As you write, you will depend heavily on your notes. In like manner, your reader will rely on the precision of your information. For example, the inventor Thomas Edison built on documented research by others. How fortunate he was that his predecessors recorded their experiments and kept good notes. This chapter explains six types of notes.

- *Personal notes*, which express your own ideas or record data from field research.
- *Quotation notes*, which preserve the wisdom and distinguished syntax of an authority.
- *Paraphrase notes*, which interpret and restate what the authority has said.
- *Summary notes*, which distill factual data that has marginal value; you can return to the source later if necessary.
- *Précis notes*, which capture the essence of one writer's ideas in capsule form.
- *Field notes*, which record interviews, questionnaire tabulations, laboratory experiments, and other types of field research.

Creating Effective Notes

Whether you write notes on a computer or by hand, you should keep in mind some basic rules, summarized in the checklist below.

Honoring the Conventions of Research Style

Your notetaking will be more effective from the start if you practice the conventions of style for citing a source, as advocated by the Modern Language Association (MLA), American Psychological Association (APA), Council of Science Editors (CSE), or Chicago Manual of Style (CMS), and as shown briefly below and explained later in this book.

MLA: Lawrence Smith states, "The suicidal teen causes severe damage to the psychological condition of peers".

APA: Smith (1997) has commented, "The suicidal teen causes severe damage to the psychological condition of peers".

CMS footnote: Lawrence Smith states, "The suicidal teen causes severe damage to the psychological condition of peers."[3]

CSE number: Smith (4) has commented, "The suicidal teen causes severe damage to the psychological condition of peers."

CHECKLIST

Writing Effective Notes

1. Write one item per note to facilitate the shuffling and rearranging of the data as you develop your paper during all stages of organization. Several notes can be kept in a computer file if each is labeled clearly.
2. List the source with name, year, and page to be ready for in-text citations and/or bibliographic entries.
3. Label each note (for example, "objectivity on television").
4. Write a full note in well-developed sentences to speed the writing of your first draft.
5. Keep everything (photocopy, scribbled note) in order to authenticate dates, page numbers, and full names.
6. Label your personal notes with "my idea" or "personal note" to distinguish them from the sources.

Using a Computer for Notetaking

The computer affects notetaking strategies in several ways:

1. You can enter your notes into the word processor using one of two methods:
   a. Write each note as a separate temporary file in a common directory so each can be moved later into the appropriate section of your draft via the Copy and Paste commands.
   b. Write all notes in a single file. Begin each new note with a code word or phrase. When you begin the actual writing of the paper, you can begin writing at the top of the file, which will push the notes down as you write. As necessary, search out and bring up specific notes as you need them. In other situations, you might employ a split screen or use two windows so your draft is in one window and your notes are in another.

      Note: It might be wise to keep a copy of the original file(s) in case anything is lost or deleted while arranging materials.
2. You can record the bibliography information for each source you encounter by listing it in a BIBLIO file so that you build the necessary list of references in one alphabetical file. Chapters 17, 18, 19, and 20 give you the correct forms.

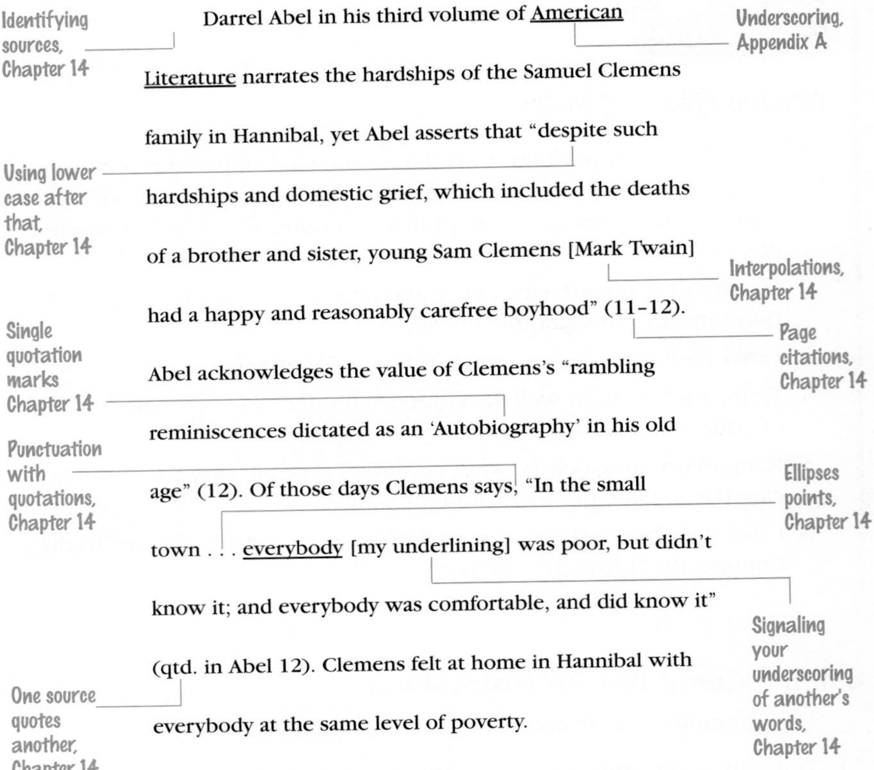

Identifying sources, Chapter 14
Underscoring, Appendix A
Darrel Abel in his third volume of American Literature narrates the hardships of the Samuel Clemens family in Hannibal, yet Abel asserts that "despite such hardships and domestic grief, which included the deaths of a brother and sister, young Sam Clemens [Mark Twain] had a happy and reasonably carefree boyhood" (11–12). Abel acknowledges the value of Clemens's "rambling reminiscences dictated as an 'Autobiography' in his old age" (12). Of those days Clemens says, "In the small town . . . everybody [my underlining] was poor, but didn't know it; and everybody was comfortable, and did know it" (qtd. in Abel 12). Clemens felt at home in Hannibal with everybody at the same level of poverty.
Using lower case after that, Chapter 14
Interpolations, Chapter 14
Page citations, Chapter 14
Single quotation marks Chapter 14
Punctuation with quotations, Chapter 14
Ellipses points, Chapter 14
Signaling your underscoring of another's words, Chapter 14
One source quotes another, Chapter 14

FIGURE 12.1 Conventions of style for writing notes.

HINT: Notetaking programs, such as *Take Note!*, and bibliography organizers, such as *Endnote,* can serve you well in this stage of developing your paper. Later, formatting software such as *StyleEase* can help you format the paper as you write it.

Developing Handwritten Notes

Handwritten notes should conform to these additional conventions:

- Write in ink, because penciled notes blur after repeated shuffling.
- Keep notes and the working bibliography separate.
- Write on one side of a sheet because information written on the back may be overlooked. Use the back side, if at all, for personal notes and observations, but mark the front with "OVER."
- Staple together two or more notes that document one item.

Writing Personal Notes

The content of a research paper is not a collection of ideas transmitted by experts in books and articles; it is an expression of your own ideas as supported by the scholarly evidence. Readers are primarily interested in *your* thesis sentence, *your* topic sentences, and *your* personal view of the issues. Therefore, during your research, record your thoughts on the issues by writing plenty of personal notes in your research journal, in your computer files, or on cards. Personal notes are essential because they allow you to:

- Record your discoveries.
- Reflect on the findings.
- Make connections.
- Explore another point of view.
- Identify prevailing views and patterns of thought.

Personal notes should conform to these three standards:

1. The idea on the note is yours.
2. The note is labeled with "my idea," "mine," or "personal thought" so that later you can be certain it has not been borrowed.
3. The note is a rough summary, a sketch of ideas, or, preferably, a complete sentence or two.

A sample of a personal note follows:

```
Personal thought

---

For me, organ donation might be a gift of life, so I have signed
my donor card. At least a part of me will continue to live if an
accident claims my life. My boyfriend says I'm gruesome, but I consider
it practical. Besides, he might be the one who benefits, and then what
will he say?
```

Writing Direct Quotation Notes

Copying the words of another person is the easiest type of note to write. Quotation notes are essential because they allow you to:

- Capture the authoritative voice of the experts on the topic.
- Feature essential statements.
- Provide proof that you have researched the subject carefully.
- Offer conflicting points of view.
- Show the dialog that exists about the topic.

In the process, you will need to follow basic conventions:

1. Select quoted material that is important and well-phrased, not something trivial or something that is common knowledge. NOT "John F. Kennedy was a Democrat from Massachusetts" (Rupert 233) BUT "John F. Kennedy's Peace Corps left a legacy of lasting compassion for the downtrodden" (Rupert 233).
2. Use quotation marks. Do not copy the words of a source into your paper in such a way that readers will think *you* wrote the material.
3. Use the exact words of the source.
4. Provide an in-text citation to author and page number, like this (Henson 34–35), or give the author's name at the beginning of the quotation and put the page number after the quotation, like this example in MLA style:

    Barnill says, "More than 400 people each month receive the gift of sight through yet another type of tissue donation—corneal transplants. In many cases, donors unsuitable for organ donation are eligible for tissue donation" (2).

5. The in-text citation goes *outside* the final quotation mark but *inside* the period.
6. Try to quote key sentences and short passages, not entire paragraphs. Find the essential statement and feature it; do not force your reader to fumble through a long quoted passage in search of the relevant statement. Make the brief quotation a part of your sentence, in this way:

    Many Americans, trying to mend their past eating habits, adopt functional foods as an essential step toward a more health-conscious future. This group of believers spends "an estimated $29 billion a year" on functional foods (Nelson 755).

7. Quote from both primary sources (the original words by a writer or speaker) and secondary sources (the comments after the fact about original works). The two types are discussed immediately below.

Quoting Primary Sources

Quote from primary sources for four specific reasons:

1. To draw on the wisdom of the original author
2. To let readers hear the precise words of the author
3. To copy exact lines of poetry and drama
4. To reproduce graphs, charts, and statistical data

Cite poetry, fiction, drama, letters, and interviews. In other cases, you may want to quote liberally from a presidential speech, cite the words of a

Selecting a Mix of Primary and Secondary Sources, Chapter 10.

businessman, or reproduce original data. As shown in the next example, quote exactly, retain spacing and margins, and spell words as in the original.

Images of Frustration Have a Prominent Role in Eliot's "Prufrock":

For I have known them all already,
known them all:—
Have known the evenings, mornings,
afternoons,
I have measured out my life with
coffee spoons;
I know the voices dying with a
dying fall
Beneath the music of a farther room.
So how should I presume?

Quoting Secondary Sources

Quote from secondary sources for three specific reasons:

1. To display excellence in ideas and expression by experts on the topic
2. To explain complex material
3. To set up a statement of your own, especially if it spins off, adds to, or takes exception to the source as quoted

The overuse of direct quotation from secondary sources indicates either (1) that you did not have a clear focus and copied verbatim just about everything related to the subject, or (2) that you had inadequate evidence and used numerous quotations as padding. Therefore, limit quotations from secondary sources by using only a phrase or a sentence, as shown here:

The geographical changes in Russia require "intensive political analysis" (Herman 611).

If you quote an entire sentence, make the quotation a direct object. It tells *what* the authority says. Headings on your notes will help you arrange them.

Geographic Changes in Russia

In response to the changes in Russia, one critic notes, "The American government must exercise caution and conduct intensive political analysis" (Herman 611).

More examples of handling quoted materials, Chapter 14.

Blend two or more quotations from different sources to build strong paragraphs, as shown here:

Functional foods are helping fight an economic battle against rising health care costs. Clare Hasler notes, "The U.S. population is getting older," which means more people are being diagnosed and treated for disease (68). These individuals are putting a huge financial strain on the health care system with their need for expensive antibiotics and hospital procedures. Dr. Herbert Pierson, director of the National Cancer Institute's $20 million functional food program, states, "The future is prevention, and looking for preventive agents in foods is more cost effective than looking for new drugs" (qtd. in Carper xxii).

Writing Paraphrased Notes

A paraphrase is the most difficult note to write. It requires you to restate, in your own words, the thought, meaning, and attitude of someone else. With *interpretation,* you act as a bridge between the source and the reader as you capture the wisdom of the source in approximately the same number of words. Use paraphrase for these reasons:

- To maintain your voice in the paper
- To sustain your style
- To avoid an endless string of direct quotations
- To interpret the source as you rewrite it

Keep in mind these five rules for paraphrasing a source:

1. Rewrite the original in about the same number of words.
2. Provide an in-text citation of the source (the author and page number in MLA style).
3. Retain exceptional words and phrases from the original by enclosing them within quotation marks.
4. Preserve the tone of the original by suggesting moods of satire, anger, humor, doubt, and so on. Show the author's attitude with appropriate verbs: "Edward Zigler condemns . . . defends . . . argues . . . explains . . . observes . . . defines."
5. Put the original aside while paraphrasing to avoid copying word for word. Compare the finished paraphrase with the original source to be certain the paraphrase truly restates the original and uses quotation marks with any phrasing or standout words retained from the original.

HINT: When instructors see an in-text citation but no quotations marks, they will assume that you are paraphrasing, not quoting. Be sure their assumption is true.

Here are examples that show the differences between a quotation note and a paraphrased one.

Quotation:

Heredity Hein 294

Fred Hein explains, "Except for identical twins, each person's heredity is unique" (294).

Paraphrase:

Heredity Hein 294

Fred Hein explains that heredity is special and distinct for each of us, unless a person is one of identical twins (294).

Quotation (more than four lines):

Heredity Hein 294

Fred Hein clarifies the phenomenon:

> Since only half of each parent's chromosomes are transmitted to a child and since this half represents a chance selection of those the child could inherit, only twins that develop from a single fertilized egg that splits in two have identical chromosomes. (294)

As shown above, MLA style requires a 10-space indention.

Paraphrase:

Heredity Hein

Hein specifies that twins have identical chromosomes because they grow from one egg that divides after it has been fertilized. He affirms that most brothers and sisters differ because of the "chance selection" of chromosomes transmitted by each parent (294).

As shown in the example above, place any key wording of the source within quotation marks.

Writing Summary Notes

You may write two types of summary notes: a quick sketch of material, as discussed here, and the more carefully drawn *précis*, as explained next in Writing Précis Notes.

The *summary note* describes and rewrites the source material without great concern for style or expression. Your purpose at the moment will be quick, concise writing without careful wording. If the information is needed, you can rewrite it later in a clear, appropriate prose style and, if necessary, return to the source for revision. Use summary notes for these reasons:

- To record material that has marginal value
- To preserve statistics that have questionable value for your study
- To note an interesting position of a source speaking on a closely related subject but not on your specific topic
- To reference several works that address the same issue, as shown in this example:

> The logistics and cost of implementing a recycling program have been examined in books by West and Loveless and in articles by Jones et al., Coffee and Street, and Abernathy.

Success with the summary requires the following:

1. Keep it short. It has marginal value, so don't waste time fine-tuning it.
2. Mark with quotation marks any key phrasing you cannot paraphrase.
3. Provide documentation to the author and page number. However, a page number is unnecessary when the note summarizes the entire article or book, not a specific passage.

> TV & reality Epstein's book
>
> -----
>
> Now dated but cited by various sources, the 1973 book by Epstein seems to lay the groundwork for criticism in case after case of distorted news broadcasts.

This sort of summary might find its way into the final draft, as shown here:

> Television viewers, engulfed in the world of communication, participate in the construction of symbolic reality by their perception of and belief in the presentation. Edward Jay Epstein laid the groundwork for such investigation in 1973 by showing in case after case how the networks distorted the news and did not, perhaps could not, represent reality.

Writing Précis Notes

A précis note differs from a quick summary note. It serves a specific purpose, so it deserves a polished style for transfer into the paper. It requires you to capture in just a few words the ideas of an entire paragraph, section, or chapter. Use the précis for these reasons:

- To review an article or book
- To annotate a bibliography entry
- To provide a plot summary
- To create an abstract

Success with the précis requires the following:

1. Condense the original with precision and directness. Reduce a long paragraph to a sentence, tighten an article to a brief paragraph, and summarize a book in one page.
2. Preserve the tone of the original. If the original is serious, suggest that tone in the précis. In the same way, retain moods of doubt, skepticism, optimism, and so forth.
3. Write the précis in your own language. However, retain exceptional phrases from the original, enclosing them in quotation marks. Guard against taking material out of context.
4. Provide documentation.

Use the Précis to Review Briefly an Article or Book

Note this example of the short review:

```
On the "Donor Initiative"          2003 Web site
-----
    The National Community of Organ and Tissue Sharing has a Web
site devoted to its initiatives. Its goal is to communicate the
problem—for example, more than 55,000 people are on the waiting
lists. It seeks a greater participation from the public.
```

With three sentences, the writer has made a précis of the entire article.

Use the Précis to Write an Annotated Bibliography

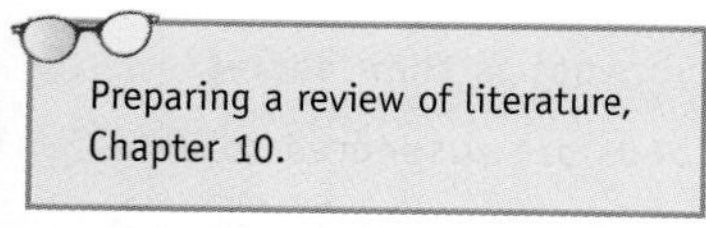
Preparing a review of literature, Chapter 10.

An annotation is a sentence or paragraph that offers explanatory or critical commentary on an article or book. It seldom extends beyond two or three sentences. The difficulty of this task is to capture the main idea of the source.

"Top Ten Myths about Donation and Transplantation." (N.d.). October 10, 2000 <http://www.transweb.org/myths/myths.htm>. This site dispels the many myths surrounding organ donation, showing that selling organs is illegal, that matching donor and recipient is highly complicated, and secret back room operations are almost impossible.

"Preparing an Annotated Bibliography," Chapter 10.

Use the Précis in a Plot Summary Note

In just a few sentences, a précis summarizes a novel, short story, drama, or similar literary work, as shown by this next note:

> Great Expectations by Dickens describes young Pip, who inherits money and can live the life of a gentleman. But he discovers that his "great expectations" have come from a criminal. With that knowledge, his attitude changes from one of vanity to one of compassion.

Furnish a plot summary in your paper as a courtesy to your readers to cue them about the contents of a work. The précis helps you avoid a full-blown retelling of the whole plot.

Use the Précis As the Form for an Abstract

An abstract is a brief description that appears at the beginning of an article to summarize the contents. It is, in truth, a précis. Usually, it is written by the article's author, and it helps readers make decisions about reading or skipping the article. You can find entire volumes devoted to abstracts, such as *Psychological Abstracts* and *Abstracts of English Studies*. An abstract is required for most papers in the social and natural sciences. Here's a sample:

Abstract using APA style, Chapter 18.

Abstract

The functional food revolution has begun! Functional foods, products that provide benefits beyond basic nutrition, are adding billions to the nation's economy each year. So what is their secret? Why are functional foods a hit? Functional foods are suspected to be a form of preventive medicine. This news has made the public swarm and food nutritionists salivate. Consumers hope that functional foods can calm some of their medical anxieties. Many researchers believe that functional foods may be the answer to the nation's prayers for lower health care costs. This paper goes behind the scenes, behind all the hype, in its attempt to determine if functional foods are an effective form of preventive medicine. The paper identifies several functional foods, locates the components that make them work, and explains the role that each plays in the body.

Writing Notes from Field Research

You sometimes will be expected to conduct field research. This work requires different kinds of notes kept on charts, cards, notepads, laboratory notebooks, a research journal, or the computer.

The report of empirical research, Chapter 8.

If you **interview** knowledgeable people, make careful notes during the interview and transcribe those notes to your draft in a polished form. A tape recorder can serve as a backup to your notetaking.

If you conduct a **questionnaire,** the results will become valuable data for developing notes and graphs and charts for your research paper.

If you conduct **experiments, tests,** and **measurements,** the findings serve as your notes for the results section of the report and will give you the basis for the discussion section.

YOUR RESEARCH PROJECT

1. Look carefully at each of the sources you have collected so far—books, photocopies of journal articles, and Internet printouts. Try writing a summary or précis of each one. At the same time, make decisions about material worthy of direct quotation and material that you wish to paraphrase or summarize.
2. Decide how you will keep your notes—in a research journal, on handwritten note cards, or in computer files. *Note*: The computer files will serve you well because you can transfer them into your text and save typing time.
3. Write various types of notes—that is, write a few that use direct quotations, some that paraphrase, and some that summarize.
4. Conscientiously and with dedication, write as many personal notes as possible. These will be your ideas, and they will establish your voice and position. Don't let the sources speak for you; let them support your position.
5. If you have access to Take Note! or some other notetaking program, take the time to consider its special features. You can create notes, store them in folders, and even search your own files by keyword, category, and reference.

13 Drafting the Paper in an Academic Style

As you draft, your voice should flow from one idea to the next smoothly and logically. You should adopt an academic style, understanding that such a style requires precision but not necessarily long, polysyllabic words pulled from a thesaurus. Therefore, treat the initial draft as exploratory, one that searches for the exact word, not just a long word. Every discipline has its own specialized words, and this matter is discussed in more detail later in this chapter under, "Using the Language of the Discipline."

Try to present a fair, balanced treatment of the subject. Do not load the paper with favorable citations at the expense of contradictory evidence. In fact, mentioning opposing viewpoints early in a report gives you something to work against and may strengthen the conclusion. Also, the claims made should be supportable. The writer who says, "Robert Frost exhibits a death wish in many of his poems," must be ready to cite both from the poems and from well-researched biographical data.

A research paper may examine a subject in depth, but it also examines *your* knowledge and the strength of *your* evidence. You may need to retrace previous steps—reading, researching, and notetaking. Ask your instructor to examine the draft, not so much for line editing but for the big picture, to see if you have met the assignment and not oversimplified the issues.

Be practical

- Write what you know and feel, not what you think somebody wants to hear.
- Write portions of the paper when you are ready, not only when you arrive there by outline sequence.
- If necessary, leave blank spots on the page to remind you that more evidence is required.
- Skip entire sections if you are ready to develop later paragraphs.

Be uninhibited

- Initial drafts must be attempts to get words on the page rather than to create a polished document.
- Write without fear or delay.
- Cite the names of the sources in your notes and text.
- Enclose quotations in your notes and text.
- Preserve the page numbers of the sources.

Your early draft is a time for discovery. Later, during the revision period, you can strengthen skimpy paragraphs, refine your prose, and rearrange material to maintain the momentum of your argument. Revision techniques are examined in Chapter 16.

Begin with these tasks:

1. Focus your argument.
2. Refine your thesis sentence.
3. Write a title that identifies your key terms.
4. Begin writing from your notes and outline.

Focusing Your Argument

Your writing style in a research paper should be factual, but it should also reflect your take on the topic. Your draft will evolve more quickly if you focus on the central issue(s). Each paragraph then amplifies your primary claim. Your aim or purpose is the key to discovering an argument. Do you wish to persuade, inquire, or negotiate?

Persuasion means convincing the reader that your position is valid and, perhaps, asking the reader to take action. For example:

> We need to establish green zones in every city of this country to control urban sprawl and to protect a segment of the natural habitat for the animals.

Inquiry is an exploratory approach to a problem in which you examine the issues without the insistence of persuasion. It is a truth-seeking adventure. For example:

> Many suburban home dwellers complain that deer, raccoons, and other wild animals ravage their gardens, flowerbeds, and garbage cans; however, the animals were there first. Thus, we may need a task force to examine the rights of each side of this conflict.

Negotiation is a search for a solution. It means you attempt to resolve a conflict by inventing options or a mediated solution. For example:

> Suburban neighbors need to find ways to embrace the wild animals that have been displaced rather than voice anger at the animals or the county government. Perhaps green zones and wilderness trails would solve some of the problems; however, such a solution would require serious negotiations with real estate developers who want to use every square foot of every development.

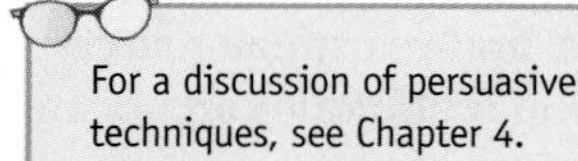

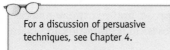

For a discussion of persuasive techniques, see Chapter 4.

Often, the instructor's research assignment will tell you whether you want to persuade, inquire, or negotiate. But if it doesn't, try to determine early in the process where your research is heading.

Maintaining a Focus on Objective Facts and Subjective Ideas

As an objective writer, you should examine the problem, make your claim in a thesis statement, and provide supporting evidence. As a subjective writer, you should argue with a touch of passion; you must believe in your position on the issues. For this reason, complete objectivity is unlikely in any research paper that puts forth an intellectual argument in the thesis statement. Of course, you must avoid being overly subjective, as by demanding, insisting, and quibbling. Moderation of your voice, even during argument, suggests control of the situation, both emotionally and intellectually.

Your objective and subjective analysis alerts the audience to your point of view in two ways:

Ethical appeal. If you project the image of one who knows and cares about the topic, the reader will recognize and respect your deep interest in the subject and your carefully crafted argument. The reader will also appreciate your attention to research conventions.

Logical appeal. For readers to believe in your position, you must provide sufficient evidence in the form of statistics, paraphrases, and direct quotations from authorities on the subject.

For example, in his examination of the world's water supply (see pages 372–383), Norman Berkowitz remained objective and logical in presenting his evidence and statistics. Even so, the ethical problem remained close to the surface, for he recognized the crisis as a global concern affecting most nations.

Refining the Thesis Sentence

A thesis statement expresses a theory you hope to support with your evidence and arguments. It is a proposition you want to maintain, analyze, and prove. It performs three tasks:

1. It sets the argument to control and focus the entire paper.
2. It provides unity and a sense of direction.
3. It specifies to the reader the point of the research.

For example, one student started with the topic "exorbitant tuition." He narrowed his work to "tuition fees put parents in debt." Ultimately, he crafted this thesis:

> The exorbitant tuition at America's colleges is forcing out the poor and promoting an elitist class.

This statement, a conclusion he must defend, focuses the argument on the fees and their effects on enrollment. Without such focus, the student might have drifted into other areas, confusing himself and his readers.

These same issues apply also to the use of the enthymeme or the hypothesis, as discussed earlier.

ENTHYMEME: America's colleges are promoting an elitist class because exorbitant tuition forces out the poor and limits their access to higher education.

HYPOTHESIS: This study will gather evidence on this proposition: Poor students are being locked out of higher education by the rapidly rising costs of tuition and registration fees.

Writing a thesis, enthymeme, or hypothesis, Chapter 5.

Using Questions to Focus the Thesis

If you have trouble focusing on a thesis sentence, ask yourself a few questions. One of the answers might serve as the thesis.

- What is the point of my research?

  THESIS: A delicate balance of medicine, diet, and exercise can control diabetes mellitus to offer a comfortable lifestyle for millions.

  ENTHYMEME: Because diabetes attacks the body in several ways, a person needs a careful balance of medicine, diet, and exercise.

  HYPOTHESIS: The objective of this study is to examine the effects of a balanced program of medication, diet, and exercise for a victim of diabetes.

- What do I want this paper to do?

  THESIS: The public needs to understand that advertisers who use blatant sexual images have little regard for moral scruples and ordinary decency.

- Can I tell the reader anything new or different?

  THESIS: The evidence indicates clearly that most well water in the county is unsafe for drinking.

- Do I have a solution to the problem?

  THESIS: Public support for safe houses will provide a haven for children who are abused by their parents.

- Do I have a new slant and new approach to the issue?

  THESIS: Personal economics is a force to be reckoned with, so poverty, not greed, forces many youngsters into a life of crime.

- Should I take the minority view of this matter?

  THESIS: Give credit where it is due: Custer may have lost the battle at Little Bighorn, but Crazy Horse and his men, with inspiration from Sitting Bull, *won* the battle.

- What exactly is my theory about this subject?

  THESIS: Because they have certain medicinal powers, functional foods can become an economic weapon in the battle against rising health care costs.

- Will an enthymeme serve my purpose by making a claim in a *because* clause?

  ENTHYMEME: Sufficient organ and tissue donation, enough to satisfy the demand, remains almost impossible because negative myths and religious concerns dominate the minds of many people.

- Will a hypothesis serve my purposes?

  HYPOTHESIS: An education program to dispel negative myths and religious concerns will build a greater base of organ and tissue donors.

- What are the keywords surrounding this issue that I might use in framing the thesis sentence?

  HYPOTHESIS: The objective is examination of issues with regard to supply and demand, the political power struggles that are emerging, and the ethical and perhaps even moral implication engulfing the world's scattered supply of fresh water.

Adjust or Change Your Thesis During Research if Necessary

Be willing to abandon your preliminary thesis if research leads you to new and different issues. For example, one writer began research on

CHECKLIST

Writing the Final Thesis

You should be able to answer "yes" to each question that follows.

Does the thesis:

1. Express your position in a full, declarative statement that is not a question, not a statement of purpose, and not merely a topic?
2. Limit the subject to a narrow focus that grows out of research?
3. Establish an investigative, inventive edge to the discovery, interpretation, or theoretical presentation?
4. Point forward to the conclusion?
5. Conform to the title and the evidence you have gathered?

child abuse with this preliminary thesis: "A need for a cure to child abuse faces society each day." Investigation, however, narrowed her focus: "Parents who abuse their children should be treated as victims, not criminals." The writer moved, in effect, to a specific position from which to argue that social organizations should serve abusing parents in addition to helping abused children.

Writing an Academic Title

A clearly expressed title, like a good thesis sentence, will control your writing and keep you on course. Although writing a final title may not be feasible until the paper is written, the preliminary title can provide specific words of identification to keep you on track. For example, one writer began with this title: "Diabetes." Then, to make it more specific, the writer added another word: "Diabetes Management." As research developed and she realized the role of medicine, diet, and exercise for victims, she refined the title even more: "Diabetes Management: A Delicate Balance of Medicine, Diet, and Exercise." Thereby, she and her readers had a clear idea of what the paper was to do—that is, explore methods for managing diabetes. Note that long titles are standard in scholarly writing. Consider the following strategies for writing your title.

1. Name a general subject, followed by a colon and a phrase that focuses or shows your slant on the subject.

```
    Organ and Tissue Donation and Transplantation: Myths, Ethical
Issues, and Lives Saved

    The World's Water Supply: The Ethics of Distribution
```

2. Name a general subject and narrow it with a prepositional phrase.

   Gothic Madness in Three Southern Writers

3. Name a general subject and cite a specific work that illuminates the topic.

   Analysis of Verbal Irony in Swift's A Modest Proposal

4. Name a general subject and follow it by a colon and a phrase that describes the type of study.

   Black Dialect in Maya Angelou's Poetry: A Language Study

5. Name a general subject and follow it by a colon and a question.

   AIDS: Where Did It Come From?

6. Establish a specific comparison.

   Religious Imagery in N. Scott Momaday's The Names and Heronimous Storm's Seven Arrows

As you develop a title, be sure to avoid fancy literary titles that fail to label issues under discussion.

Poor:	"Foods, Fads, and Fat"
Better:	"Nutritional Foods: A Survey"
Best:	"Nutritional Foods: A Powerful Step on the Path of Preventive Medicine"

For placement of the title, see "Title Page or Opening Page," Chapter 16.

Drafting the Paper from Your Research Journal, Notes, and Computer Files

To begin writing your research essay, you may work systematically through a preliminary plan or outline. You may also begin by writing what you know at the time. Either way, keep the pieces of your manuscript under control; your notes will usually keep you focused on the subject, and your thesis statement will control the flow and direction of your argument. Yet you must let the writing find its own way, guided but not controlled by your preliminary plans. Consult the paradigm (see Chapter 11, pages 269–272) that best fits your design.

Writing from Your Notes

Use your notes and research journal to:

1. Transfer personal notes, with modification, into the draft.
2. Transcribe précis notes and paraphrased materials directly into the text.
3. Quote primary sources.
4. Quote secondary sources from notes.

Weave source material into the paper to support *your* ideas, not as filler. Your notes will let the essay grow, blossom, and reach up to new levels of knowledge. You can do this in several ways, and you may even have a method beyond the four mentioned here.

Method one requires separate note files within a specially named directory. During the drafting stage, you can use the Insert, Copy, or Read command to transfer your notes into your text.

Method two assumes you have placed all your notes in one file. Begin writing your paper in a new file. As you need a note, minimize this text file and maximize your file of notes, or use two windows. Find the note you wish to transfer, highlight it, copy it, and then paste it into your file.

Method three assumes you have placed all your notes within one file and labeled each with a code word or title. Begin drafting your paper at the top of this file, which will push the notes down as you write. When you need a note, find it, copy it, and paste it into your text.

Method four requires the complete outline on file so you can enter information under any of the outline headings as you develop ideas (see Chapter 11 for details on outlining). You can import your notes to a specific location of the outline. This technique allows you to work anywhere within the paper to match your interest of the moment with a section of your outline. In effect, you expand your outline into the first draft of your research paper.

In the initial draft, leave plenty of space as you write. Keep the margins wide, use double spacing, and leave blank spaces between paragraphs. The open areas will invite your revisions and additions later on. The process is simplified when you use a computer because you will keyboard the paper the first time and revise directly within the file.

When working with pages copied from articles, books, or Internet sites, use caution. You will be tempted to borrow too much. Quote or paraphrase key phrases and sentences; do not quote an entire paragraph unless it is crucial to your discussion and you cannot easily reduce it to a précis. Moreover, any information you borrow should come from a credible source that has a scholarly or educational basis.

HINT: Drafting a paragraph or two by using different methods of development is one way to build the body of your paper, but only if each part fits the purpose and design of your work. Write a comparison paragraph, classify and analyze one or two issues, show cause and effect, and ask a question and answer it. Sooner than you think, you will have drafted the body of the paper. See Chapter 15 for detailed discussion of these methods of development.

Writing with Unity and Coherence

Unity refers to exploring one topic in depth to give your writing a single vision. With unity, each paragraph carefully expands on a single aspect of the narrowed subject. *Coherence* connects the parts logically by:

- Repetition of keywords and sentence structures

- The judicious use of pronouns and synonyms
- The effective placement of transitional words and phrases (e.g., *also, furthermore, therefore, in addition*, and *thus*).

The next passage reads with unity (it keeps its focus) and coherence (it repeats keywords and uses transitions effectively, as shown in boldface type).

> Talk shows are spectacles and forms of **dramatic** entertainment; **therefore,** members of the studio audience are **acting** out parts in the **drama,** like a Greek chorus, just as the host, the guest, and the television viewers are **actors** as well. **Furthermore,** some sort of interaction with the "characters" in this made-for-television **"drama"** happens all the time. If we read a book or attend a play, **we question** the text, **we question** the presentation, and **we determine** for ourselves what it means to us.

Writing in the Proper Tense

Verb tense often distinguishes a paper in the humanities from one in the natural and social sciences. MLA style requires the present tense to cite an author's work (e.g., "Patel *explains*" or "the work of Scoggin and Roberts *shows*"). The CMS footnote style also asks for present tense.

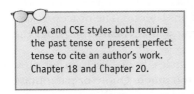

APA and CSE styles both require the past tense or present perfect tense to cite an author's work. Chapter 18 and Chapter 20.

MLA style requires that you use the present tense for your own comments and those of your sources because the ideas and the words of the writers remain in print and continue to be true in the universal present. Therefore, when writing a paper in the humanities, use the historical present tense, as shown here:

> "It was the best of times, it was the worst of times," writes Charles Dickens about the eighteenth century.
>
> Johnson argues that sociologist Norman Wayman has a "narrow-minded view of clerics and their role in the community" (64).

Use the past tense in a humanities paper only for reporting historical events. In the next example, past tense is appropriate for all sentences except the last:

> In 1876 Alexander Graham Bell invented the telephone. Signals, sounds, and music had been sent by wire before, but Bell's instrument

was the first to transmit speech. Bell's story is a lesson in determination, one worthy of study by any would-be inventor.

Using the Language of the Discipline

Every discipline and every topic has its own vocabulary. Therefore, while reading and taking notes, jot down words and phrases relevant to your research study. Get comfortable with them so you can use them effectively. For example, a child abuse topic requires the language of sociology and psychology, thereby demanding an acquaintance with these terms:

social worker	maltreatment	aggressive behavior
poverty levels	behavioral patterns	incestuous relations
stress	hostility	battered child
formative years	recurrence	guardians

Similarly, a poetry paper might require such terms as *symbolism, imagery, rhythm, persona,* and *rhyme*. Many writers create a terminology list to strengthen their command of appropriate nouns and verbs. However, nothing will betray a writer's ignorance of the subject matter more quickly than awkward and distorted technical terminology. For example, the following sentence uses big words, but it distorts and scrambles the language:

> The enhancement of learning opportunities is often impeded by a pathological disruption in a child's mental processes.

The words may be large, but what does the passage mean? Probably this:

> Education is often interrupted by a child's abnormal behavior.

Using Source Material to Enhance Your Writing

Readers want to see your thoughts and ideas on a subject. For this reason, a paragraph should seldom contain source material only; it must contain a topic sentence to establish a point for the research evidence. Every paragraph should explain, analyze, and support a thesis, not merely string together a set of quotations.

The following passage cites effectively two sources.

> Organ and tissue donation is the gift of life. Each year many people confront health problems due to diseases or congenital birth defects. Tom Taddonia explains that tissues such as skin, veins, and valves can be used to correct congenital defects, blindness, visual

impairment, trauma, burns, dental defects, arthritis, cancer, and vascular and heart disease (23). Steve Barnill says, "More than 400 people each month receive the gift of sight through yet another type of tissue donation—corneal transplants. In many cases, donors unsuitable for organ donation are eligible for tissue donation" (356). Barnill notes that tissues are now used in orthopedic surgery, cardiovascular surgery, plastic surgery, dentistry, and podiatry (358). Even so, not enough people are willing to donate organs and tissues.

This passage illustrates four points. A writer should:

1. Weave the sources effectively into a whole.
2. Use the sources as a natural extension of the discussion.
3. Cite each source separately, one at a time.
4. Provide separate in-text citations to pages or footnote numerals.

This means you must read carefully so you can select key ideas and phrasing. It also means you should be accurate and precise.

Writing in the Third Person

Write your paper with third-person narration that avoids "I believe" and "It is my opinion." Rather than saying, "I think objectivity on television is nothing more than an ideal," drop the opening two words and say, "Objectivity on television is nothing more than an ideal." Readers will understand that the statement is your thought. However, attribute human functions to yourself or other persons, not to nonhuman sources:

WRONG: The study considered several findings.

CORRECT: The study reported the findings of several sources.

The study can report its findings, but it can't consider them.

Writing with the Passive Voice in an Appropriate Manner

Instructors often caution young writers against using the passive voice, which is often less forceful than an active verb. However, research writers sometimes need to shift the focus from the actor to the receiver, as shown here:

PASSIVE: Forty-three students of a third-grade class at Barksdale School were observed for two weeks.

ACTIVE: I observed forty-three students of a third-grade class at Barksdale school.

In the examples above, the passive voice is preferred because it keeps the focus on the subject of the research, not the writer. Also, as a general rule, avoid the first person in research papers. Here are additional examples of the effective use of the passive voice:

```
    The soil was examined for traces of mercury.
    President Jackson was attacked repeatedly for his Indian policy
by his enemies in Congress.
    Children with attention disorders are often targeted for drug
treatment.
```

As you see, the sentences place the focus on the soil, the President, and the children.

Placing Graphics Effectively in a Research Essay

Graphics enable you to analyze trends and relationships in numerical data. Use them to support your text. Most computers allow you to create tables, line graphs, and pie charts as well as diagrams, maps, and other original designs. You may also import tables and illustrations from your sources. Place these graphics as close as possible to the parts of the text to which they relate. It is acceptable to use full-color art if your printer prints in colors; however, use black for the captions and date.

For more help with visuals, see Appendix A.

Place a full-page graphic design on a separate sheet after making a textual reference to it (e.g., "see Table 7"). Place graphic designs in an appendix when you have several complex items that might distract the reader from your textual message.

Avoiding Sexist and Biased Language

Racial and gender fairness is one mark of the mature writer. The best writers exercise caution against words that may stereotype any person, regardless of gender, race, nationality, creed, age, or disability. If the writing is precise, readers will not make assumptions about race, age, and disabilities. Therefore, do not freely mention sexual orientation, marital status, ethnic or racial identity, or a person's disability. The following guidelines will help you avoid discriminatory language:

Age

Review the accuracy of your statement. It is appropriate to use *boy* and *girl* for children of high school age and under. *Young man* and *young woman* or *male adolescent* and *female adolescent* can be appropriate, but *teenager* carries a certain bias. Avoid *elderly* as a noun; use *older persons,* as in "Fifteen older patients suffered senile dementia of the Alzheimer's type.

Gender

Gender is a matter of our culture that identifies men and women within their social groups. *Sex* tends to be a biological factor (see below for a discussion of sexual orientation).

1. Use plural subjects so that nonspecific, plural pronouns are grammatically correct. For example, do you intend to specify that Judy Jones maintains *her* lab equipment in sterile condition or to indicate that technicians, in general, maintain *their* own equipment?
2. Reword the sentence so a pronoun is unnecessary:

   Correct: The doctor prepared the necessary surgical [not *his*] equipment without interference.

   Correct: Each technician must maintain the laboratory [not *her*] equipment in sterile condition.

3. Use pronouns denoting gender only when necessary to specify gender or when gender has been previously established.

   Mary, as a new laboratory technician, must learn to maintain *her* equipment in sterile condition.

4. The use of *woman* and *female* as adjectives varies, as in *female athlete* and *woman athlete.* Use *woman* or *women* in most instances (e.g., *a woman's intuition*) and *female* for species and statistics, (e.g., *four female subjects, 10 males and 23 females, a female chimpanzee*). The word *lady* has fallen from favor (i.e., avoid *lady pilot*).
5. The first mention of a person requires the full name (e.g., Ernest Hemingway, Joan Didion) and thereafter requires only the use of the surname (e.g., Hemingway, Didion). At first mention, use Emily Brontë, but thereafter use Brontë, *not* Miss Brontë. In general, avoid formal titles (e.g., Dr., Gen., Mrs., Ms., Lt., or Professor). Avoid their equivalents in other languages (e.g., Mme, Dame, Monsieur).
6. Avoid *man and wife* and *7 men and 16 females.* Keep the terms parallel by saying *husband and wife* or *man and woman* and *7 male rats and 16 female rats.*

Sexual Orientation

The term *sexual orientation* is preferred over the term *sexual preference.* It is preferable to use the terms *lesbians* and *gay men* rather than *homosexuals.* The terms *heterosexual, homosexual,* and *bisexual* can be used to describe both the identity and the behavior of subjects.

Ethnic and Racial Identity

Some people prefer the term *Black,* others prefer *African American,* and still others prefer *person of color*. The terms *Negro* and *Afro-American* are now dated and inappropriate. Use *Black* and *White,* not the lowercase *black* and *white*. In like manner, some individuals may prefer *Hispanic, Latino, Mexican,* or *Chicano*. Use the term *Asian* or *Asian American* rather than *Oriental*. *Native American* is a broad term that includes *Samoans, Hawaiians,* and *American Indians*. A good rule of thumb is to specify a person's nationality, tribe, or ethnic group when it is known (*Mexican, Korean, Comanche,* or *Nigerian*).

Disability

In general, place people first, not their disability. Rather than *disabled person* or *retarded child,* say *a person who has scoliosis* or *a child with Down's syndrome*. Avoid saying *a challenged person* or *a special child* in favor of *a person with* _____ or *a child with* _____. Remember that a *disability* is a physical quality, while a *handicap* is a limitation that might be imposed by nonphysical factors, such as stairs, poverty, or social attitudes.

Drafting Electronic Research Papers

Because creating an electronic research paper can be more complicated than creating a traditional paper, it's important to plan your project carefully.

Creating a Plan for Your Research Paper

- **Assignment.** Does your instructor have specific requirements for this assignment that you should keep in mind?
- **Project description.** What topic will you be writing on?
- **Purpose.** What are your reasons for creating an electronic project? Are you going to blend photographs of the 1960s with an essay on the civil rights movement? Will you provide audio examples in an essay on John F. Kennedy's speeches?
- **Audience.** Are you writing for the instructor, or will you have a broader audience such as classmates or readers on the Web?
- **Format.** Will your research paper be a word-processed document, an electronic presentation, or a Web site?
- **Multimedia content.** What information, other than text, will you present? Do you have the tools to scan or import multimedia?
- **Structure.** How will you organize your document?

Designing Your Electronic Research Paper

Reading any kind of electronic document can be difficult unless you take special care in designing it, so be sure to offer:

- **A consistent looks and feel.** Make your research paper looks consistent throughout. Presentation software usually includes ready-made templates that help you create a professional feel

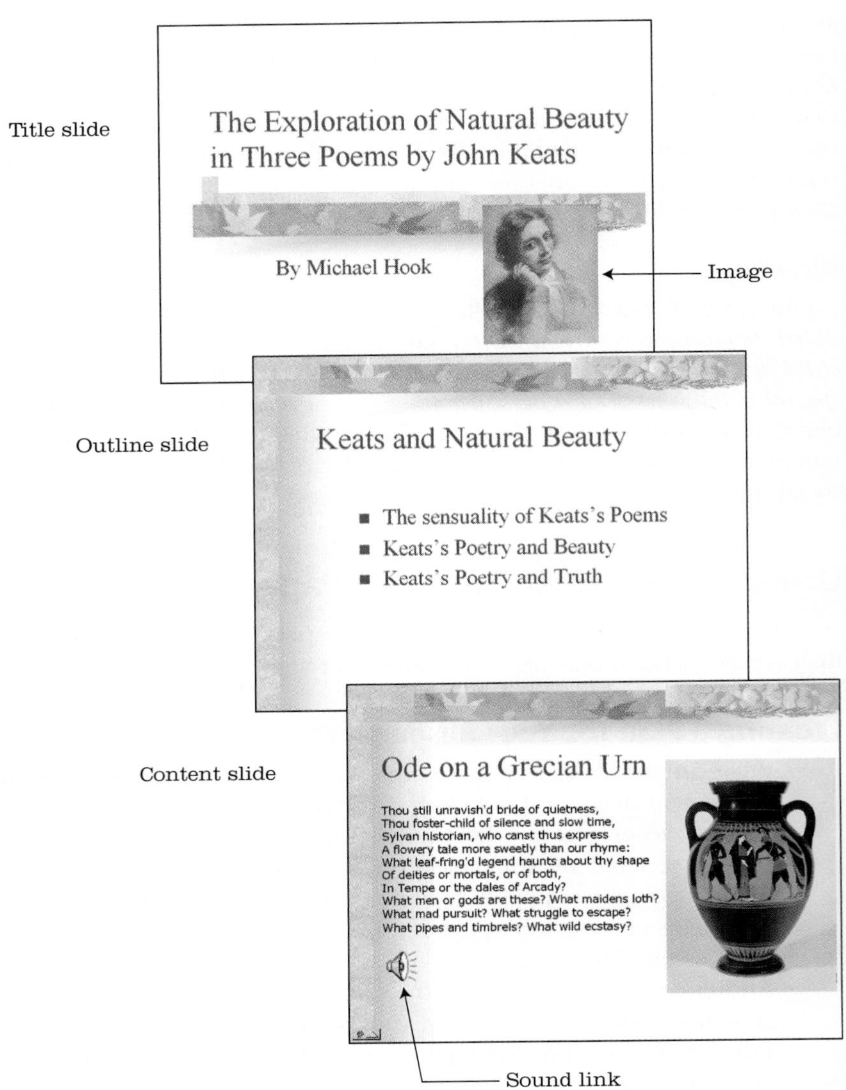

FIGURE 13.1 Research paper slide presentation.

(see Figure 13.1, which uses a ready-made template design for a presentation).

- **A subtle design.** It's easy to create a Web site or presentation that includes all the bells and whistles—but such documents are hard to navigate and even harder to read. Avoid distractions like blinking text, garish colors, and unnecessary animations (see Figure 13.2 for an example of a subtly designed Web site).

Research paper home page

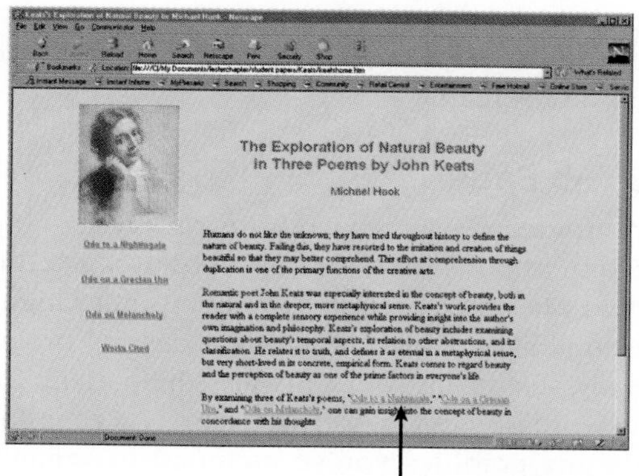

Hyperlinks for navigation

Text page

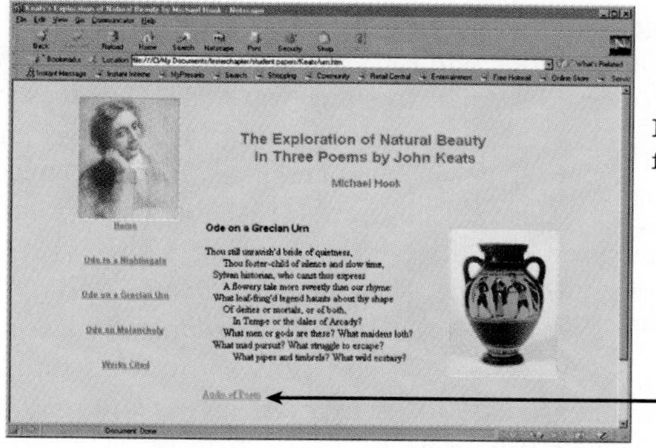

References or Works Cited page

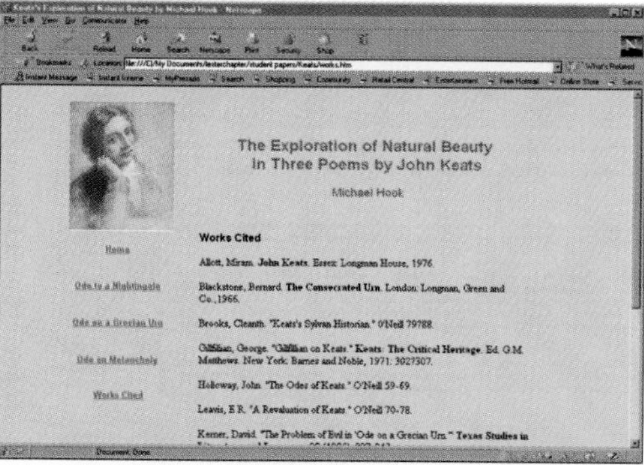

FIGURE 13.2 Three pages from a sample research paper Web site.

- **Ease of navigation.** Include consistent navigation tools so readers can see where they are and where they can go next (see the navigation links in Figure 13.2).
- **Legibility.** Because readers often access electronic documents via a computer, screen legibility is important. Make the contrast between

your text and background colors strong enough that readers can see the text easily. Avoid using the italic fonts, which are difficult to read on a computer screen.

Creating a Web Page

If you want to create a Web page from your research paper, the easiest but most limited method is to save your word-processed research paper in HTML (Hypertext Markup Language, the computer language that controls what Web sites look like). Different word-processing programs perform this process differently, so consult your software's help menu for specific instructions. When the word-processing software converts your document to HTML, it also converts any graphics you've included to separate graphics files. Together, your text and the graphics can be viewed in a Web browser like any other Web page (see Figure 13.3).

Your research paper will look somewhat different in HTML format than in its word-processed format. In some ways, HTML is less flexible than word processing, but you can still use word-processing software to make changes to your new HTML-formatted paper.

> For more information on Web design, see the following site:
> Yale CAIM WWW Style Guide
> http://info.med.yale.edu/caim/manual/contents.html.

Creating a site with multiple pages is more complicated and requires careful planning and organization. A multiple-page Web site allows you to assemble a large number of short pages that are easy for readers to access and read. Start with a home page that includes a title, a basic description of your project, and an index

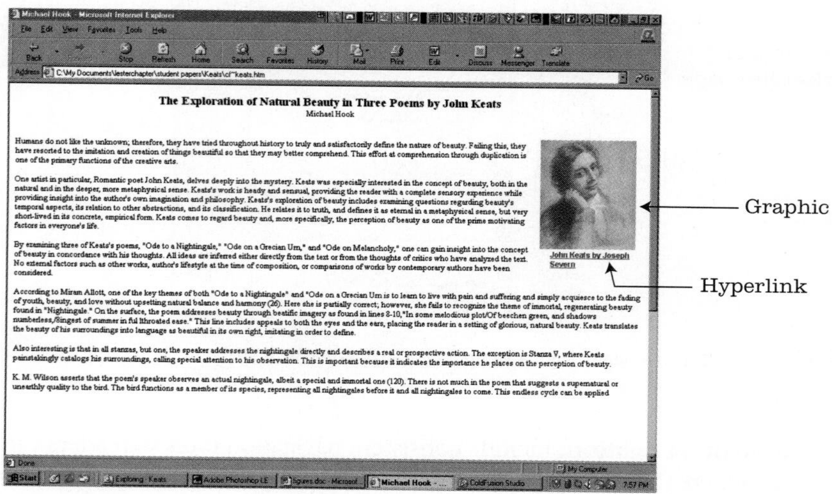

The Exploration of Natural Beauty in Three Poems by John Keats

Michael Hook

Humans do not like the unknown; therefore, they have tried throughout history to truly and satisfactorily define the nature of beauty. Failing this, they have resorted to the imitation and creation of things beautiful so that they may better comprehend. This effort at comprehension through duplication is one of the primary functions of the creative arts.

One artist in particular, Romantic poet John Keats, delves deeply into the mystery. Keats was especially interested in the concept of beauty, both in the natural and in the deeper, more metaphysical sense. Keats's work is heady and sensual, providing the reader with a complete sensory experience while providing insight into the author's own imagination and philosophy. Keats's exploration of beauty includes examining questions regarding beauty's temporal aspects, its relation to other abstractions, and its classification. He relates it to truth, and defines it as eternal in a metaphysical sense, but very short-lived in its concrete, empirical form. Keats comes to regard beauty and, more specifically, the perception of beauty as one of the prime motivating factors in everyone's life.

By examining three of Keats's poems, "Ode to a Nightingale," "Ode on a Grecian Urn," and "Ode on Melancholy," one can gain insight into the concept of beauty in concordance with his thoughts. All ideas are inferred either directly from the text or from the thoughts of critics who have analyzed the text. No external factors such as other works, author's lifestyle at the time of composition, or comparisons of works by contemporary authors have been considered.

According to Miram Allott, one of the key themes of both "Ode to a Nightingale" and "Ode on a Grecian Urn is to learn to live with pain and suffering and simply acquiesce to the fading of youth, beauty, and love without upsetting natural balance and harmony (26). Here she is partially correct; however, she fails to recognize the theme of immortal, regenerating beauty found in "Nightingale." On the surface, the poem addresses beauty through beatific imagery as found in lines 8-10,"In some melodious plot/Of beechen green, and shadows numberless,/Singest of summer in ful lthroated ease." This line includes appeals to both the eyes and the ears, placing the reader in a setting of glorious, natural beauty. Keats translates the beauty of his surroundings into language as beautiful in its own right, imitating in order to define.

Also interesting is that in all stanzas, but one, the speaker addresses the nightingale directly and describes a real or prospective action. The exception is Stanza V, where Keats painstakingly catalogs his surroundings, calling special attention to his observation. This is important because it indicates the importance he places on the perception of beauty.

K. M. Wilson asserts that the poem's speaker observes an actual nightingale, albeit a special and immortal one (120). There is not much in the poem that suggests a supernatural or unearthly quality to the bird. The bird functions as a member of its species, representing all nightingales before it and all nightingales to come. This endless cycle can be applied

FIGURE 13.3 Single Web page research paper.

CHECKLIST

Delivering Your Electronic Research Paper

- **Floppy disk.** Floppy disks are a convenient way to share information. However, they are unreliable, and papers with graphics, sound, or video may not fit on them.
- **Zip disk.** Zip disks and other proprietary-format disks hold much larger files than floppies do, but your reader/professor must own a drive that can read them.
- **CD-ROM disk.** These disks hold large amounts of data and thus work well for transmitting graphics, sound, and video files. However, you must own or have access to a CD-R (Compact Disk Recordable) or CD-RW (Compact Disk Recordable/Writeable) drive. Most readers have regular CD-ROM drives that can read your disks, but you might want to confirm this beforehand.
- **E-mail.** E-mailing your file as an attachment is the fastest way to deliver your electronic research paper; however, this approach works best if you have a single file, like a word-processed research paper, rather than a collection of related files, like a Web site.
- **Web site.** If you've created a Web site or Web page, you can upload your work to a Web server so readers can access your work on the Internet. Procedures for uploading Web sites vary from school to school and server to server; work closely with your instructor and Webmaster to perform this process successfully. Regardless of what method you choose, be sure to follow your instructor's directions and requirements.

with hyperlinks to the contents of your site. Navigational elements, like links to the home page and other major pages of your site, provide a way for readers to "turn the pages" of your report.

Delivering Your Electronic Research Paper to Readers

Follow your instructor's requirements for delivering your electronic research paper, or use one of the techniques in the checklist above.

YOUR RESEARCH PROJECT

1. Examine your own thesis using the Final Thesis Checklist. Revise your thesis as necessary.

2. Consider your focus to determine if you will persuade, inquire, negotiate or perhaps use a focus as explained in Chapter 4: evaluation, definition, proposal, causal argument, analogy, precedence.
3. Write an academic title for your paper—one that clearly describes the nature of your work.
4. After you draft a significant portion of the paper, review it carefully for each of these items: coherence, proper tense, third-person voice, and the language of the discipline.

14 Blending Reference Material into Your Writing by Using MLA Style

Your in-text citations should conform to standards announced by your instructor. This chapter explains the MLA style, as established by the Modern Language Association. It governs papers in freshman composition, literature, English usage, and foreign languages.

MLA style, Chapter 17
APA style, Chapter 18
CMS style, Chapter 19
CSE style, Chapter 20

The MLA style puts great emphasis on the writer of the source, asking for the full name of the scholar on first mention but last name only thereafter and last name only in parenthetical citations. Other styles emphasize the year of publication as well as the author. Still other styles use merely a number in order to emphasize the material, not the author or date.

Blending Reference Citations into Your Text

As you might expect, writing a research paper carries with it certain obligations. You should gather scholarly material on the topic and display it prominently in your writing. In addition, you should identify each source used with the authority's name or the title of the work with a page number, except unprinted sources and most Internet sources will not require a page number. As a general policy, keep citations brief. Remember, your readers will have full documentation to each source on the Works Cited page (see Chapter 17).

Making a General Reference without a Page Number

Sometimes you will need no parenthetical citation.

> The women of Thomas Hardy's novels are the special focus of three essays by Nancy Norris, Judith Mitchell, and James Scott.

Beginning with the Author and Ending with a Page Number

Introduce a quotation or a paraphrase with the author's name and close it with a page number, placed inside the parentheses. Try always to use this standard citation because it informs the reader of the beginning and the end of borrowed materials, as shown here:

> Herbert Norfleet states that the use of video games by children improves their hand and eye coordination (45).

In the following example, the reader can easily trace the origin of the ideas.

> Video games for children have opponents and advocates. Herbert Norfleet defends the use of video games by children. He says it improves their hand and eye coordination and that it exercises their minds as they work their way through various puzzles and barriers. Norfleet states, "The mental gymnastics of video games and the competition with fellow players are important to young children for their physical, social, and mental development" (45). Yet some authorities disagree with Norfleet for several reasons.

Putting the Page Number Immediately after the Name

Sometimes, notes at the end of a quotation make it expeditious to place the page number immediately after the name.

> Boughman (46) urges car makers to "direct the force of automotive airbags upward against the windshield" (emphasis added).

Putting the Name and Page Number at the End of Borrowed Material

You can, if you like, put cited names with the page number at the end of a quotation or paraphrase.

> "Each DNA strand provides the pattern of bases for a new strand to form, resulting in two complete molecules" (Justice, Moody, and Graves 462).

In the case of a paraphrase, you should give your reader a signal to show when the borrowing begins, as shown next:

> One source explains that the DNA in the chromosomes must be copied perfectly during cell reproduction (Justice, Moody, and Graves 462).

Use last names only within the parenthetical citation *unless your list contains more than one author with same last name,* in which case you should add the author's first initial—for example, (H. Norfleet 45) and (W. Norfleet 432). If the first initial is also shared, use the full first name: (Herbert Norfleet 45).

HINT: In MLA style, do not place a comma between the name and the page number.

Citing a Source When No Author Is Listed

When no author is shown on a title page, cite the title of the article, the name of the magazine, the name of a bulletin or book, or the name of the publishing organization. You should abbreviate or use an acronym (e.g., BBC, NASA).

HINT: Search for the author's name at the bottom of the opening page, at the end of the article, at an Internet home page, or an e-mail address.

Citing the Title of a Magazine Article

Use a shorted version of the title when no author is listed:

At various foundations of their homes, Americans are threatened by chemistry and its attacks on the human system. The dangers of Chlordane and the problems with Dursban are explored in one article ("Terminating Termites"), but termites just grab the headlines. There are many more dangers lurking in the crevices of the average home.

The Works Cited entry would read:

"Terminating Termites." Southern Living July 2000: 110.

Citing the Title of a Report

One bank showed a significant decline in assets despite an increase in its number of depositors (Annual Report, 2003, 23).

Citing the Name of a Publisher or a Corporate Body

The report by the Clarion County School Board endorsed the use of Channel One in the school system and said that "students will benefit by the news reports more than they will be adversely affected by advertising" (CCSB 3-4).

Citing Nonprint Sources That Have No Page Number

On occasion you may need to identify nonprint sources, such as a speech, the song lyrics from a CD, an interview, or a television program. Since no page number exists, omit the parenthetical citation. Instead, introduce the type of source—for example, lecture, letter, interview—so readers do not expect a page number.

> Thompson's lecture defined impulse as "an action triggered by the nerves without thought for the consequences."

> Mrs. Peggy Meacham said in her phone interview that prejudice against young black women is not as severe as that against young black males.

Citing Internet Sources

Identify the Source with Name or Title

Whenever possible, identify the author of an Internet article. Usually, no page number is listed.

> Hershel Winthrop interprets Hawthorne's stories as the search for holiness in a corrupt Puritan society.

If you can't identify an author, give the article title or Web site information.

> One Web site claims that any diet that avoids carbohydrates will avoid some sugars that are essential for the body ("Fad Diets").

Identify the Nature of the Information and Its Credibility

As a service to your reader, indicate your best estimate of the scholarly value of an Internet source. For example, the next citation explains the role of the Center for Communications Policy:

> The UCLA Center for Communication Policy, which conducted an intensive study of television violence, has advised against making the television industry the "scapegoat for violence" by advocating a focus

on "deadlier and more significant causes: inadequate parenting, drugs, underclass rage, unemployment and availability of weaponry."

Here's another example of an introduction that establishes credibility:

John Armstrong, a spokesperson for Public Electronic Access to Knowledge (PEAK), states:

> As we venture into this age of biotechnology, many people predict gene manipulation will be a powerful tool for improving the quality of life. They foresee plants engineered to resist pests, animals designed to produce large quantities of rare medicinals, and humans treated by gene therapy to relieve suffering.

HINT: To learn more about the source of an Internet article, as in the case immediately above, learn to search out a home page. The address for Armstrong's article is <http://www.peak.org/~armstroj/america.html#Aims>.

By truncating the address to <http://www.peak.org/>, you can learn about the organization Armstrong represents.

If you are not certain about the credibility of a source—that is, it seemingly has no scholarly or educational basis—do not cite it, or describe the source so readers can make their own judgments:

An Iowa non-profit organization, the Mothers for Natural Law, says—but offers no proof—that eight major crops are affected by genetically engineered organisms—canola, corn, cotton, dairy products, potatoes, soybeans, tomatoes, and yellow crook-neck squash ("What's on the Market").

Omitting Page and Paragraph Numbers to Internet Citations

In general, you should not list a page number, paragraph number, or screen number to an Internet site.

- You cannot list a screen number because monitors differ.
- You cannot list a page number of a downloaded document because computer printers differ.
- Unless they are numbered in the document, you cannot list paragraph numbers. Besides, you would have to go through and count every paragraph.

The marvelous feature of electronic text is that it is searchable, so your readers can find your quotation quickly with the Find or Search features. Suppose you have written the following:

> The Television Violence Report advices against making the television industry the "scapegoat for violence" by advocating a focus on "deadlier and more significant causes: inadequate parenting, drugs, underclass rage, unemployment and availability of weaponry."

A reader who wants to investigate further can consult your Works Cited page, find the Internet address (URL), use a browser to locate the article, and use Find for a phrase, such as "scapegoat for violence." That's much easier on you than numbering all the paragraphs and easier on the reader than counting them.

Some academic societies are urging scholars who publish on the Internet to number their paragraphs, and that practice may catch on quickly. Therefore, you should provide a paragraph number if the author of the Internet article has numbered each paragraph.

> The Insurance Institute for Highway Safety emphasizes restraint first, saying, "Riding unrestrained or improperly restrained in a motor vehicle always has been the greatest hazard for children" (IIHS, par. 13).

Provide a page number only if you find original page numbers buried within the electronic article. For example, a database like JSTOR reproduces original images of works and thereby provides original page numbers, as with the article by Harold R. Walley shown in Figure 14.1. Cite these pages just as you would a printed source.

> One source says the "moralizing and philosophical speculation" in Hamlet is worthy of examination, but to Shakespeare these were "distinctly subsidiary to plot and stage business . . . " (Walley 778).

Citing Indirect Sources

Sometimes the writer of a book or article quotes another person from an interview or personal correspondence, and you may want to use that same quotation. For example, in a newspaper article in *USA Today,* Karen S. Peterson writes this passage in which she quotes two people:

> Sexuality, popularity, and athletic competition will create anxiety for junior high kids and high schoolers. Eileen Shiff says, "Bring up the topics. Don't wait for them to do it; they are nervous and they want to appear cool." Monitor the amount of time high schoolers spend working for money, she suggests. "Work is important, but school

XL
SHAKESPEARE'S CONCEPTION OF *HAMLET*

What was Shakespeare's conception of *Hamlet?* That is the question. It is one which inevitably resolves itself into a reconstruction of the materials at his disposal, the dramatic problems with which he had to deal, and the means whereby he sought to satisfy contemporary dramatic taste. For such a reconstruction modern scholarship provides abundant information about both the theatrical practices and intellectual interests of the time and Shakespeare's habits as a craftsman. In particular should be noted his exceptional preoccupation with character portrayal and the scrupulous motivation of action; his conformity with changing theatrical fashion, yet at the same time his reluctance to pioneer in experiment; his sensitive, if sketchy, acquaintance with matters of contemporary interest; and his success as a skilled and inspired adapter rather than as an innovator. In the application of this knowledge two principles are fundamental. First, *Hamlet* must not be viewed as isolation, but in close conjunction with the theatrical environment which produced it. Second, Shakespeare must be recognized as primarily a practical playwright, a business man of the theater with obligations to fulfill, specific theatrical conditions to meet, and an audience to divert. For the rest, it is a pleasant exercise for the recreative imagination to try to think oneself into Shakespeare's mind, to face the problem of *Hamlet* as he faced it, and to trace the solution as he must have found it.

I

Shakespeare's *Hamlet* is a philosophical melodrama. Theatrically it is one of his most spectacular plays. For all its discursiveness it is crammed with action of the most sensational sort. Ghosts walk and cry "Revenge!" Murder is foully done. Conspirators plot and counterplot. Two characters go mad. A queen is terrified nearly to death. A play breaks up in a near-riot. An insurrection batters the palace gates. A brawl desecrates a suicide's grave. A duel explodes into murder and general butchery. There are poison, incest, war, and debauchery. This is not closet drama for the philosopher's study; it is blood and thunder for the popular stage.

Nevertheless, *Hamlet* is also one of Shakespeare's most thoughtful plays. Permeated with moralizing and philosophical speculation, it presents in its center character a most elaborate psychological study. As for the reader these are unquestionably the most enduring elements, so to the elucidation of these criticism has devoted most of its attention.

777

778 *Shakespeare's Conception of "Hamlet"*

Indeed, not infrequently is it implied that the play exists for the express purpose of expounding Shakespeare's views on life and death, or that the play is primarily a peg upon which to hang the character of Hamlet. Such a view, however, scarcely squares with the known practice of Shakespeare, or, for that matter, of any successful playwright. The one play of the period which openly advertised itself as a philosophical character study–Chapman's *Revenge of Bussy D'Ambois*–was an inglorious failure. Contrast with this the extraordinary popularity of *Hamlet*, and one may see how much of it depends upon the scrupulous subordination of those very philosophical elements which make Chapman's play so insufferably dull to the modern reader. To Shakespeare, doubtless, both character study and philosophical speculation were distinctly subsidiary to plot and stage business; and in the excised version, which must have been necessary for stage presentation, they probably interfered little with the more congenial business of swift melodrama.[1]

Harold R. Walley 779

session with a few restricted preoccupations. The peculiarity of Hamlet's madness is that, no matter how insane his ravings may seem to his hearers, without exception they contain *double entendre* and make perfect sense from Hamlet's point of view. The method is substantially that which underlies the contemporaneous intellectual conceit; namely, the surprise association of apparently incongruous elements linked by a submerged chain of thought. Thus whatever madness Hamlet exhibits is an integral part of his own mental attitude.

This mental obsession, which issues in the evidences of Hamlet's supposed madness, is intimately connected with two other important features of the play. Hamlet is much concerned with his inability to carry forward his revenge. This delay is essential to the plot; that it is a delay for which Hamlet is himself responsible Shakespeare makes clear throughout.[2] Much, however, as Hamlet endeavors to understand the reason, he is incapable of explaining it to himself; it is an ingrained part

You may cite these page numbers because JSTOR photocopies the original publications.

FIGURE 14.1 You may cite these page numbers.

must be the priority." Parental intervention in a child's school career that worked in junior high may not work in high school, psychiatrist Martin Greenburg adds. "The interventions can be construed by the adolescent as negative, overburdening and interfering with the child's ability to care for himself." He adds, "Be encouraging, not critical. Criticism can be devastating for the teenager."

Suppose you want to use the quotation above by Martin Greenburg. You must quote the words of Greenburg *and* put Peterson's name in the parenthetical citation as the person who wrote the article, as shown in the following:

> After students get beyond middle school, they begin to resent interference by their parents, especially in school activities. They need some space from Mom and Dad. Martin Greenburg says, "The interventions can be construed by the adolescent as negative, overburdening and interfering with the child's ability to care for himself" (qtd. in Peterson 9A).

CHECKLIST

Using Links to Document Internet Sources

If you are publishing your project on your own Web page, you have the opportunity to send your readers to other sites via hypertext links. If you do so, follow these guidelines:

1. You may activate a hot key (hypertext link) in your document that will automatically send your reader to one of your sources.
2. Identify the linked source clearly so readers know where the link will take them.
3. Be selective; don't sprinkle your document with excessive links. You want the reader to stay with you, not wander around on the Internet.
4. The links are part of your documentation, so cite these linked sources in your Works Cited list.

On the Works Cited page, you will list Peterson's name with the bibliography entry for her article, but you will not list Greenburg's name there because he is not the author of the article.

In other words, in the text you need a double reference that introduces the speaker and includes a clear reference to the book or article where you found the quotation or the paraphrased material. Without the reference to Peterson, nobody could find the article. Without the reference to Greenburg, readers would assume Peterson spoke the words.

HINT: If you can locate the original source of the quotation, cite it rather than use the double reference.

Citing Frequent Page References to the Same Work

If you quote more than once from the same page within a paragraph and no other citations intervene, you may provide one citation at the end for all the references.

When the character Beneatha denies the existence of God in Hansberry's A Raisin in the Sun, Mama slaps her in the face and forces her to repeat after her, "In my mother's house there is still God." Then Mama adds, "There are some ideas we ain't going to have in this house. Not long as I am at the head of the family" (37).

Also, when you make frequent references to the same source, you need not repeat the author's name in every instance. Note the following example:

The consumption of "healing foods," such as those that reduce blood pressure, grows in popularity each year. Clare Hasler says that when the medicinal properties of functional food gain the support of clinical evidence, functional foods can become an economical weapon in the battle against rising health care costs. In addition, functional foods may be a promising addition to the diet of people who suffer from deadly disease. As executive director of the Functional Foods for Health Program at the University of Illinois, she claims, "Six of the ten leading causes of death in the United State are believed to be related to diet: cancer, coronary heart disease, stroke, diabetes, atherosclerosis, and liver disease" ("Western Perspective" 66).

HINT: If you are citing from two or more novels in your paper—let's say John Steinbeck's *East of Eden* and *Of Mice and Men*—provide both title (abbreviated) and page(s) unless the reference is clear: (*Eden* 56) and (*Mice* 12–13).

Citing Material from Textbooks and Large Anthologies

Reproduced below is a poem you might find in many literary textbooks.

The Red Wheelbarrow
so much depends
upon
a red wheel
barrow
glazed with rain
water
beside the white chickens
William Carlos Williams

If you quote lines of the poem, and if that is all you quote from the anthology, cite the author and page in the text and put a comprehensive entry in the Works Cited list.

Text:

For Williams, "so much depends" on the red wheel barrow as it sits "glazed with rain water beside the white chickens" (926–27).

Bibliography Entry:

Williams, William Carlos. "The Red Wheelbarrow." The Norton Anthology of American Literature. Ed. Nina Baym et al. New York: Norton, 1999. 926–27.

Suppose, however, that you also take quotations from other poems in the textbook.

Robert Frost calls for escape into the pleasures of nature, saying "I'm going out to clean the pasture spring; / I'll only stop to rake the leaves away" and invites us to join in, "You come too" (859).

Carl Sandburg describes the morning fog as being a "little cat" that looks over the city as it rests on "silent haunches / and then moves on" (816).

More on citing anthologies, Chapter 17.

Now, with three citations to the same anthology, you should list in your Works Cited the anthology used, as edited by Baym et al., and also list shortened citations for Williams, Frost, and Sandburg with each referring to the lead editor's name, in this case *Baym*.

Baym, Nina, et al., eds. The Norton Anthology of American Literature. New York: Norton, 1999.

Frost, Robert. "The Pasture." Baym et al. 859.

Sandberg, Carl. "Fog." Baym et al. 887.

Williams, William Carlos. "The Red Wheelbarrow." Baym et al. 926–27.

Adding Extra Information to In-Text Citations

As a courtesy to your reader, add extra information within the citation. Show parts of books, different titles by the same writer, or several works by different writers. For example, your reader may have a different anthology than yours, so a clear reference, such as (*Great Expectations* 681; chap. 4), will enable the reader to locate the passage. The same is true with a reference to (*Romeo and Juliet* 2.3.65–68). The reader will find the passage in almost any edition of Shakespeare's play. Here's a reference to Herman Melville's *Moby-Dick* that shows both page and chapter:

Melville uncovers the superstitious nature of Ishmael by stressing Ishmael's fascination with Yojo, the little totem god of Queequeg (71; chap. 16).

One of Several Volumes

These next two citations provide three vital facts: (1) an abbreviation for the title, (2) the volume used, and (3) the page number(s). The Works Cited entry will list the total number of volumes (see "Volumes," Chapter 17).

> In a letter to his Tennessee Volunteers in 1812 General Jackson chastised the "mutinous and disorderly conduct" of some of his troops (Papers 2: 348–49).

> Joseph Campbell suggests that man is a slave yet also the master of all the gods (Masks 2: 472).

However, if you use only one volume of a multivolume work, you need give only page numbers in the parenthetical reference. Then include the volume number in the Works Cited entry (see Chapter 17):

> Don Quixote's strange adventure with the Knight of the Mirrors is one of Cervantes's brilliant short tales (1,908–14).

If you refer to an entire volume, there is no need for page numbers:

> The Norton Anthology includes masterpieces of the ancient world, the Middle Ages, and the Renaissance (Mack et al., vol. 1).

Two or More Works by the Same Writer

In this example, the writer makes reference to two novels, both abbreviated. The full titles are *Tess of the D'Urbervilles* and *The Mayor of Casterbridge.*

> Thomas Hardy reminds readers in his prefaces that "a novel is an impression, not an argument" and that a novel should be read as "a study of man's deeds and character" (Tess xxii; Mayor 1).

If the author appears in the parenthetical citation, place a comma after the name: (Hardy, *Tess* xxii; Hardy, *Mayor* 1). If anything other than a page number appears after the title, follow the title with a comma: (Worth, "Computing," par. 6).

The complete titles of the two works by Campbell referenced in the following example are *The Hero with a Thousand Faces* and *The Masks of God,* a four-volume work.

> Because he stresses the nobility of man, Joseph Campbell suggests that the mythic hero is symbolic of the "divine creative and redemptive image which is hidden within us all . . . " (Hero 39). The

> hero elevates the human mind to an "ultimate mythogenetic zone—the creator and destroyer, the slave and yet the master, of all the gods" (Masks 1: 472).

Several Authors in One Citation

You may wish to cite several sources that treat the same topic. Put them in alphabetical order to match that of the Works Cited page, or place them in the order of importance to the issue at hand. Separate them with semicolons.

> Several sources have addressed this aspect of gang warfare as a fight for survival, not just for control of the local neighborhood or "turf" (Robertson 98–134; Rollins 34; Templass 561–65).

Additional Information with the Page Number

Your citations can refer to special parts of a page—for example, footnote, appendix, graph, table—and can also specify emphasis on particular pages.

> Horton (22, n. 3) suggests that Melville forced the symbolism, but Welston (199–248, esp. 234) reaches an opposite conclusion.

However, use a semicolon to separate the page number from the edition used, a chapter number, or other identifying information: (Wollstonecraft 185; ch. 13, sec. 2).

Punctuating Citations Properly and Consistently

Keep page citations outside quotation marks but inside the final period, as shown here:

> "The benefits of cloning far exceed any harm that might occur" (Smith 34).

In MLA style, use no comma between the name and the page within the citation (for example, Jones 16–17, *not* Jones, 16–17). Do not use *p.* or *pp.* with the page number(s) in MLA style. However, if an author's name begins a citation to paragraph numbers or screen numbers, *do* include a comma after the author's name (Richards, par. 4) or (Thompson, screens 6–7).

Commas and Periods

Place commas and periods inside quotation marks unless the page citation intervenes. The example below shows: (1) how to put the mark inside the quotation marks, (2) how to interrupt a quotation to insert the speaker, (3) how to use single quotation marks within the regular quotation marks, and (4) how to place the period after a page citation.

> "Modern advertising," says Rachel Murphy, "not only creates a marketplace, it determines values." She adds, "I resist the advertiser's argument that they 'awaken, not create desires'" (192).

Sometimes you may need to change the closing period to a comma. Suppose you decide to quote this sentence: "Scientific cloning poses no threat to the human species." If you start your sentence with the quotation, you will need to change the period to a comma, as shown:

> "Scientific cloning poses no threat to the human species," declares Joseph Wineberg in a recent article (357).

However, retain question marks or exclamation marks; no comma is required:

> "Does scientific cloning pose a threat to the human species?" wonders Mark Durham (546).

Let's look at other examples. Suppose this is the original material:

> The Russians had obviously anticipated neither the quick discovery of the bases nor the quick imposition of the quarantine. Their diplomats across the world were displaying all the symptoms of improvisation, as if they had been told nothing of the placement of the missiles and had received no instructions what to say about them.—From: Arthur M. Schlesinger, Jr., *A Thousand Days* (New York: Houghton, 1965), 820.

Punctuate citations from this source in one of the following methods in accordance with MLA style:

> "The Russians," writes Schlesinger, "had obviously anticipated neither the quick discovery of the [missile] bases nor the quick imposition of the quarantine" (820).

> Schlesinger notes, "Their diplomats across the world were displaying all the symptoms of improvisation . . . " (820).

> Schlesinger observes that the Russian failure to anticipate an American discovery of Cuban missiles caused "their diplomats across the world" to improvise answers as "if they had been told nothing of the placement of the missiles . . . " (820).

Note that the last example correctly changes the capital *T* of "their" to lower case to match the grammar of the restructured sentence, and it does not use ellipsis points before "if" because the phrase flows smoothly into the text.

Semicolons and Colons

Both semicolons and colons go outside the quotation marks, as illustrated by these three examples:

> Zigler admits that "the extended family is now rare in contemporary society"; however, he stresses the greatest loss as the "wisdom and daily support of older, more experienced family members" (42).

> Zigler laments the demise of the "extended family": that is, the family suffers by loss of the "wisdom and daily support of older, more experienced family members" (42).

> Brian Sutton-Smith says, "Adults don't worry whether <u>their</u> toys are educational" (64); nevertheless, parents want to keep their children in a learning mode.

The third example, immediately above, shows how to place the page citation after a quotation and before a semicolon.

Use the semicolon to separate two or more works in a single parenthetical reference:

> (Roman, <u>Dallas</u> 16; Manfred 345)
>
> (Steinbeck, <u>Grapes</u> 24; Stuben xii)

Question Marks and Exclamation Marks

When a question mark or an exclamation mark serves as part of the quotation, keep it inside the quotation mark. Put the page citation immediately after the name of the source to avoid conflict with the punctuation mark.

> Thompson (16) passionately shouted to union members, "We can bring order into our lives even though we face hostility from every quarter!"

If you place the page number at the of the quotation, retain the original exclamation mark or question mark, follow with the page reference, and then a sentence period outside the citation.

> Thompson passionately shouted to union members, "We can bring order into our lives even though we face hostility from every quarter!" (16).

Retain questions marks and exclamation marks when the quotation begins a sentence; no comma is required.

> "We face hostility from every quarter!" declared the union leader.

Question marks appear inside the closing quotation mark when they are part of the original quotation; otherwise, they go outside.

> The philosopher Brackenridge (16) asks, "How should we order our lives?"

and

> The philosopher Brackenridge asks, "How should we order our lives?" (16).

but

> Did Brackenridge say that we might encounter "hostility from every quarter"(16)?

Single Quotation Marks

When a quotation appears within another quotation, use single quotation marks with the shorter one. The period goes inside both closing quotation marks.

> George Loffler (32) confirms that "the unconscious carries the best of human thought and gives man great dignity, but it also has the dark side so that we cry, in the words of Shakespeare's Macbeth, 'Hence, horrible shadow! Unreal mockery, hence.'"

Remember that the period always goes inside quotation marks unless the page citation intervenes, as shown below:

> George Loffler confirms that "the unconscious carries the best of human thought and gives man great dignity, but it also has the dark side so that we cry, in the words of Shakespeare's Macbeth, 'Hence, horrible shadow! Unreal mockery, hence'" (32).

Indenting Long Quotations

Set off long prose quotations of four lines or more by indenting 1 inch or 10 spaces, which is usually two clicks of the tab key. Do not enclose the indented material within quotation marks. If you quote only one paragraph or the beginning of one, do *not* indent the first line an extra five spaces. Maintain normal double spacing between your text and the quoted materials. Place the parenthetical citation *after* the final mark of punctuation. As shown below, the parenthetical citation might be a title to an Internet article rather than to page numbers:

The number of people who need transplants continues to increase, but the number of donors fails to meet these needs. In 1999 the National Organ and Tissue Donation Initiative asserted:

> Approximately 55 people each day receive life-enhancing organ transplants; another 10 people die each day on the national list waiting for a donated organ. In September 1997, more than 55,000 people were on the list, which grows by about 500 monthly. Most Americans approve of organ donation, but few give this gift of life to others. ("Organ")

With the ever increasing number of organ donors needed, why don't people give of themselves? The most recognized reason for the shortage of donors is directly related to the myths that are associated with organ and tissue donation.

If you quote more than one paragraph, indent all paragraphs an extra three (3) spaces or a quarter-inch. However, if the first sentence quoted does not begin a paragraph in the original source, do not indent it an extra three spaces.

Zigler makes this observation:

> With many others, I am nevertheless optimistic that our nation will eventually display its inherent greatness and successfully correct the many ills that I have touched upon here.
>
> Of course, much remains that could and should be done, including increased efforts in the area of family planning, the widespread implementation of Education for Parenthood programs, an increase in the availability of homemaker and child care services, and a reexamination of our commitment to doing what is in the best interest of every child in America.(42)

Citing Poetry

Quoting Two Lines of Poetry or Less

Incorporate short quotations of poetry (one or two lines) into your text.

In Part 3, Eliot's "The Waste Land" (1922) remains a springtime search for nourishing water: "Sweet Thames, run softly, for I speak not loud or long" (line 12) says the speaker in "The Fire Sermon," while in Part 5 the speaker of "What the Thunder Said" yearns for "a damp gust/ Bringing rain" (73–74).

As the example demonstrates:

1. Set off the material with quotation marks.
2. Indicate separate lines by using a virgule (/) with a space before and after it.
3. Place line documentation within parentheses immediately following the quotation mark and inside the period. Do not use the abbreviations *l.* or *ll.*, which might be confused with page numbers; use *lines* initially to establish that the numbers represent lines of poetry, and thereafter use only the numbers.
4. Use Arabic numerals for books, parts, volumes, and chapters of works; acts, scenes, and lines of plays; and cantos, stanzas, and lines of poetry.

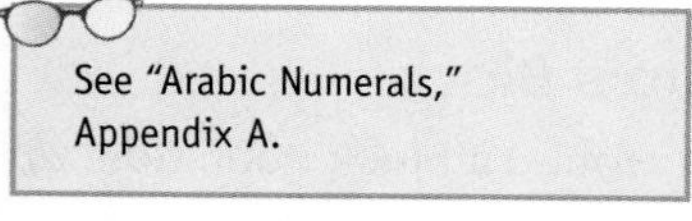
See "Arabic Numerals," Appendix A.

Quoting Three Lines of Poetry or More

Set off three or more lines of poetry by indenting 1 inch or 10 spaces, as shown below. Use double-spaced lines. A parenthetical citation to the lines of indented verse follows the last line of the quotation. If the parenthetical citation will not fit on the last line, place it on the next line, flush with the right margin of the poetry text.

The king cautions Prince Henry:

Thy place in council thou has rudely lost,
Which by thy younger brother is supplied,
And art almost an alien to the hearts
Of all the court and princes of my blood.
(3.2.32–35)

Refer to act, scene, and lines only after you have established Shakespeare's *Henry IV, Part 1* as the central topic of your study; otherwise, write (IH4 3.2.32-35). If you are citing from more than one play, always add an abbreviation for the play (1H4 1.1.15-18).

Indenting Turnovers for Long Lines of Poetry

When quoting a line of poetry that is too long for your right margin, indent the continuation line 3 spaces or a quarter-inch more than the greatest indentation.

Plath opens her poem with these lines:

Love set you going like a fat gold watch.
The midwife slapped your footsoles,
  and your bald cry
Took its place among the elements. (lines 1–3)

You may also indent less to make room for the words:

Plath opens her poem with these lines:

Love set you going like a fat gold watch.
The midwife slapped your footsoles, and your bald cry
Took its place among the elements. (lines 1–3)

Retaining Internal Quotations within a Block

While you should not use quotation marks around a block quotation, *do* retain any internal quotation marks:

With his sonnet "Spring," Shakespeare playfully describes the cry of the cuckoo bird:

The cuckoo then, on every tree,
Mocks married men; for thus sings he, "Cuckoo!
Cuckoo, cuckoo!" O word of fear,
Unpleasing to a married ear! (524)

Providing Translations

When a quotation is run into the text, use double quotation marks for translations placed within parentheses but single quotations around a translation without the parentheses:

Chaucer's setting is Spring, when "zephyrs ("west winds") have breathed softly all about . . . " (line 5).

Chaucer's setting is Spring, when "zephyrs 'west winds' have breathed softly all about . . . " (line 5).

Do not place quotation marks around quotations and translations set off from the text in a block. Place the block of translation below the block of poetry.

Ramon Magrans has translated this Lorca poem in a literal manner:

Alto pinar!

Cuatro palomas por el aire van.
Cuatro palomas
Vuelan y tornan
Llevan heridas
sus cuatro sombras

Bajo pinar!
Cuatro palomas en la tierra están.

Above the pine trees
four pigeons fly through the air.

Four pigeons
fly and turn around
Wounded, they carry
their four shadows.

Below the pine trees
four pigeons lie on the earth.

Handling Quotations from a Play

Set off from your text any dialog of two or more characters. Begin with the character's name, indented one inch and written in all capital letters. Follow the name with a period, and then start the character's lines of dialog. Indent subsequent lines of dialog an additional quarter-inch or three spaces.

At the end of Oedipus Rex, Kreon chastises Oedipus, reminding him that he no longer has control over his own life nor that of his children.

KREON. Come now and leave your children.
OEDIPUS. No! Do not take them from me!
KREON. Think no longer
That you are in command here, but rather think
How, when you were, you served your own
destruction.

Altering Initial Capitals in Quoted Matter

In general, you should reproduce quoted materials exactly, yet one exception is permitted for logical reasons. Restrictive connectors, such as *that* and *because,* create restrictive clauses and eliminate a need for the comma. Without a comma, the capital letter is unnecessary. In the following example, "The," which is capitalized as the first word in the original sentence, is changed to lower case because it continues the grammatical flow of the student's sentence.

> Another writer argues that "the single greatest impediment to our improving the lives of America's children is the myth that we are a child-oriented society" (Zigler 39).

Otherwise, write:

> Another writer argues, "The single greatest. . . . "

Omitting Quoted Matter with Ellipsis Points

You may omit portions of quoted material with three spaced ellipsis points, as shown in the examples below.

Context

In omitting passages, be fair to the author. Do not change the meaning or take a quotation out of context.

Correctness

Maintain the grammatical correctness of your sentences—that is, avoid fragments and misplaced modifiers. You don't want your readers to misunderstand the structure of the original. When you quote only a phrase, readers will understand that you omitted most of the original sentence, so no ellipsis is necessary.

> Phil Withim recognizes the weakness in Captain Vere's "intelligence and insight" into the significance of his decisions regarding Billy Budd (118).

Omission within a Sentence

Use three ellipsis points (periods) with a space before each and a space after the last.

> Phil Withim objects to the idea that "such episodes are intended to demonstrate that Vere . . . has the intelligence and insight to perceive the deeper issue" (118).

Omission at the End of a Sentence

If an ellipsis occurs at the end of your sentence, use three periods with a space before each following a sentence period—that is, you will have four periods with no space before the first or after the last. A closing quotation mark finishes the punctuation.

> R. W. B. Lewis (62) declares that "if Hester has sinned, she has done so as an affirmation of life, and her sin is the source of life. . . ."

However, if a page citation also appears at the end in conjunction with the ellipsis, use three periods with a space before each and put the sentence period after the final parenthesis. Thus, you will have three ellipsis points with a space before each, the closing quotation mark followed by a space, the parenthetical citation, and the period.

> R. W. B. Lewis declares that "if Hester has sinned, she has done so as an affirmation of life, and her sin is the source of life . . . " (62).

Omission at the Beginning of a Sentence

Most style guides discourage the use of ellipsis points for material omitted from the beginning of a source, as shown here:

> He states: ". . . the new parent has lost the wisdom and daily support of older, more experienced family members" (Zigler 34).

The passage would read better without the ellipsis points:

> He states that "the new parent has lost the wisdom and daily support of older, more experienced family members" (Zigler 34).

Another option is this one, as stipulated by the *Chicago Manual of Style:* "If a quotation that is only part of a sentence in the original forms a complete sentence as quoted, an initial lower case letter may be changed to a capital where the structure of the text suggests it."

> He states: "The new parent has lost the wisdom and daily support of older, more experienced family members" (Zigler 34).

Here's another example:

> R. W. B. Lewis declares, "If Hester has sinned, she has done so as an affirmation of life, and her sin is the source of life . . . " (62).

Omission of Complete Sentences and Paragraphs

Use a closing punctuation mark and three spaced ellipsis points when omitting one or more sentences from within a long quotation. Here's an omission in which one sentence ends, another sentence or more is omitted, and a full sentence ends the passage.

> Zigler reminds us that "child abuse is found more frequently in a single (female) parent home in which the mother is working. . . . The unavailability of quality day care can only make this situation more stressful" (42).

Here's an omission from the middle of one sentence to the middle of another:

> Zigler reminds us that "child abuse is found more frequently in a single (female) parent home in which the mother is working, . . . so the unavailability of quality day care can only make this situation more stressful" (42).

Omissions in Poetry

If you omit a word or phrase in a quotation of poetry, indicate the omission with three or four ellipsis points, just as you would with omissions in a prose passage. However, if you omit a complete line or more from the poem, indicate the omission by a line of spaced periods that equals the average length of the lines. Note that the parenthetical citation shows two sets of lines.

Elizabeth Barrett Browning asks:

> Do ye hear the children weeping, O my brothers,
>   Ere the sorrow comes with years?
> They are leaning their young heads against their mothers,
>   And <u>that</u> cannot stop their tears.
> . . . .
> They are weeping in the playtime of the others,
> In the country of the free. (1–4, 11–12)

Avoid Excessive Use of Ellipsis Points

Many times, you can be more effective if you incorporate short phrases rather than quote the whole sprinkled with many ellipsis points. Note how this next passage incorporates quotations without the use of ellipsis.

> The long-distance marriage, according to William Nichols, "works best when there are no minor-aged children to be considered," the two people are "equipped by temperament and personality to spend a considerable amount of time alone," and both are able to "function in a mature, highly independent fashion" (54).

Ellipsis in the Original

If the original passage has ellipsis by the author, and you wish to cut additional words, place brackets around your ellipsis points to distinguish them from the author's ellipsis points. If the original says:

> Shakespeare's innovative techniques in working with revenge tragedy are important in *Hamlet* . . . while the use of a Senecan ghost is a convention of revenge tragedy, a ghost full of meaningful contradictions in calling for revenge is part of Shakespare's dramatic suspense.

If you cut the middle phrase, use this form:

> One writer says, "Shakespeare's innovative techniques in working with revenge tragedy are important in Hamlet, . . . [. . .] a ghost full of meaningful contradictions in calling for revenge is part of Shakespare's dramatic suspense."

Altering Quotations with Parentheses and Brackets

You will sometimes need to alter a quotation to emphasize a point or to make something clear. You might add material, italicize an important word, or use the word *sic* (Latin for "thus" or "so") to alert readers that you have properly reproduced the material even though the logic or the spelling of the original might appear to be in error. Use parentheses or brackets according to these basic rules.

Parentheses

Use parentheses to enclose your comments or explanations that fall outside a quotation, shown in these examples:

> The problem with airbags is that children (even those in protective seats) can be killed by the force as the airbag explodes. Boughman (46) urges car makers to "direct the force of automotive airbags upward against the windshield" (emphasis added).

> Roberts (22) comments that "politicians suffer a conflict with honoure" (sic).

Brackets

Use brackets for interpolation, which means inserting your own comment into a text or quotation. The use of brackets signals the insertion. Note the following rules.

Use Brackets to Clarify

This same critic indicates that "we must avoid the temptation to read it [The Scarlet Letter] heretically" (118).

Use Brackets to Establish Correct Grammar within an Abridged Quotation

"John F. Kennedy [was] an immortal figure of courage and dignity in the hearts of most Americans," notes one historian (Jones 82).

He states: "[The] new parent has lost the wisdom and daily support of older, more experienced family members" (Zigler 34).

Use Brackets to Note the Addition of Underlining

He says, for instance, that the "extended family is now rare in contemporary society, and with its demise the new parent has lost the wisdom [my emphasis] and daily support of older, more experienced family members" (Zigler 42).

Use Brackets to Substitute a Proper Name for a Pronoun

"As we all know, he [Kennedy] implored us to serve the country, not take from it" (Jones 432).

Use Brackets with Sic to Indicate Errors in the Original

Lovell says, "John F. Kennedy, assassinated in November of 1964 [sic], became overnight an immortal figure of courage and dignity in the hearts of most Americans" (62).

HINT: The assassination occurred in 1963. However, do not burden your text with the use of "sic" for historical matter in which outmoded spellings are obvious, as with: "Faire seemely pleasauance each to other makes."

Use Brackets with Ellipsis Points

See the example on page 333.

YOUR RESEARCH PROJECT

1. Make a critical journey through your draft with one purpose: to examine your handling of the sources. Have you introduced them clearly so the reader will know when the borrowing began? Have you closed them with a page citation, as appropriate? Have you placed quotation marks at the beginning and the end of borrowed phrases as well as borrowed sentences?
2. If you have used Internet sources, look at them again to see if the paragraphs on the Internet site are numbered. If so, use the paragraph numbers in your citation(s); if not, use no numbers—not the numbers on any printout and not paragraph numbers if you must count them.
3. Look at your source material to find a table, graph, figure, or photograph you might insert into your paper as additional evidence. Then consult Appendix A to be certain that you have labeled it correctly (see Chapter 16 for examples).
4. Make a critical journey through your text to be certain you have made an informed choice about the documentation style you need. Normally, instructors will inform you. In general, use MLA style for papers in freshman composition and literature classes; use APA style for papers in the social sciences; use the footnote style for papers in history and the fine arts; use CSE number style for papers in the applied sciences.

15 Writing the Introduction, Body, and Conclusion

The three parts of your paper—the introduction, the body, and the conclusion—demand special considerations. For most papers, follow the guidelines offered below. However, some scientific papers will demand different elements (see Chapter 18).

Writing the Introduction of the Paper

Use the first few paragraphs of your paper to establish the nature of your study. In brief, the introduction should establish the problem, the body should present the evidence, and the conclusion should arrive at answers, judgments, proposals, and closure. Most important, let the introduction and body work *toward* a demonstrative conclusion. The introduction should be long enough to establish the required elements described in the checklist below.

For additional discussion of thesis sentence, enthymeme, and hypothesis, see Chapter 5.

How you work these essential elements into the framework of your opening will depend on your style of writing. They need not appear in this order, nor should you cram all these items into a short opening paragraph. Feel free to write two or three paragraphs of introduction, letting it run over onto page 2, if necessary. When crafting your introduction, use more than one of the techniques described in the following approaches.

Provide the Thesis Statement, Enthymeme, or Hypothesis

Generally, the controlling statement will appear early in the introduction to establish the agenda for the paper or appear late in the introduction to set the stage for the analysis to come in the body. For example, this opening features the thesis first:

Thesis

Shoplifting in stores all over America has reached the point that all shoppers are suspects; each of us is photographed, followed, and watched. The people who use

CHECKLIST

Writing the Introduction

Subject Identify your specific topic, and then define, limit, and narrow it to one issue.

Background Provide relevant historical data. Discuss a few key sources that touch on your specific issue. If writing about a major figure, give relevant biographical facts, but not an encyclopedia-type survey. (See "Providing Background Information.")

Problem The point of a research paper is to explore or resolve a problem, so identify and explain the complications you see. The examples shown below demonstrate this technique.

Thesis Within the first few paragraphs, use your thesis sentence to establish the direction of the study and to point your readers toward your eventual conclusions. (See below, "Opening with Your Thesis Sentence.")

the "five-finger discount" come from all walks of life—the unemployed, sure, but also doctors, lawyers, and even public officials. As a result, clerks in many retail stores look at us with ill will, not friendliness, and they treat us with suspicion, not trust.

Provide the Enthymeme

The enthymeme, as explained in Chapter 5, uses a *because* clause to make a claim. It also determines the direction your paper will take. Notice the enthymeme that closes this opening paragraph:

Here we are, a civilized world with reasonably educated people, yet we constantly fight with each other. These are not sibling squabbles either; people die in terrible ways. We wonder, then, if there was ever a time when men and women lived in harmony with one another and with nature and the environment. The Bible speaks of the Garden of Eden, and the French philosopher Jean-Jacques Rousseau advanced the idea in the 1700s of the "noble savage," and that "nothing could be more gentle" than an ancient colony of people (LaBlanc 15). Wrong! There has never been a "noble savage," as such, because even prehistoric human beings fought frequent wars for numerous reasons.

Enthymeme

Provide a Hypothesis

The hypothesis is a theory that needs testing in the lab, in the literature, and/or by field research to prove its validity. Writers may list it as an objective, as in this example:

Diabetes is a disease that affects approximately 11 million people in the U.S. alone. Its complications lead to approximately 350,000 deaths per year and cost the nation $20,373 billion per year in medical care, in the direct cost of complications, and in the indirect costs of loss of productivity related to the disease (Guthrie and Guthrie 1). The condition can produce devastating side effects and a multitude of chronic health problems. Diabetes currently has no known cure, but it can be controlled. The objective of this study is to examine how well diabetes can be controlled by a combination of medication, monitoring, diet, and exercise.

Hypothesis

Relate to the Well Known

The next passage will appeal to the popular interest and knowledge of the reader:

Television flashes images into our living rooms, radios invade the confines of our automobiles, and local newspapers flash their headlines to us daily. However, one medium that has gained great popularity and influence within the past decade is the specialized magazine.

Popular appeal

Provide Background Information

Writers may trace the historical nature of a topic, give biographical data about a person, or provide a geographic description. A summary of a novel, long poem, or other work can refresh a reader's memory about details of plot, character, and so forth.

> First published in 1915, Spoon River Anthology by Edgar Lee Masters gives readers candid glimpses into the life of a small town at the turn of the twentieth century. Speaking from beyond the grave, the narrator of each poem gives a portrait of happy, fulfilled people or draws pictures of lives filled with sadness and melancholy.

Background

This passage offers *essential* background matter, not information irrelevant to the thesis. For example, explaining that Eudora Welty was born in Jackson, Mississippi, in 1909 would contribute little to the following opening:

> In 1941 Eudora Welty published her first book of short stories, A Curtain of Green. That group of stories was followed by The Wide Net (1943) and The Bride of the Innisfallen (1955). Each collection brought her critical acclaim, but taken together the three volumes established her as one of America's premier short story writers.

Background

Review the Literature

Cite a few books and articles relevant to the specific issue to introduce literature connected with the topic. This paragraph gives distinction to your introduction because it establishes the scholarship on the subject. It also distinguishes your point of view by explaining the logical connections and differences between previous research and your work:

> Throughout his novella Billy Budd, Herman Melville intentionally uses biblical references as a means of presenting different moral principles by which people may govern their lives. The story depicts the "loss of Paradise" (Arvin 294); it serves as a gospel story (Weaver 37-38); and it hints at a moral and solemn purpose (Watson 319). The story explores the biblical passions of one man's confrontation with good and evil (Howard 327-328; Mumford 248). This paper will examine the biblical references.

Review of literature

Review the History and Background of the Subject

This opening passage normally reviews the history of the topic, often with quotations from the sources, as shown below in APA style:

> Autism, a neurological dysfunction of the brain which commences before the age of thirty months, was identified by Leo Kanner (1943). Kanner studied eleven cases, all of which showed a specific type of childhood psychosis that was different from other childhood disorders, although each was similar to childhood schizophrenia. Kanner described the characteristics of the infantile syndrome as:
>
> 1. Extreme autistic aloneness
> 2. Language abnormalities
> 3. Obsessive desire for the maintenance of sameness
> 4. Good cognitive potential
> 5. Normal physical development
> 6. Highly intelligent, obsessive, and cold parents
>
> Medical studies have reduced these symptoms to four criteria: onset within thirty months of birth, poor social development, late language development, and a preference for regular, stereotyped activity (Rutter, 1978; Watson, 1997; Waller, Smith, and Lambert, 2000). In the United States, autism affects one out of 2,500 children, and is not usually diagnosed until the child is between two and five years of age (Lambert & Smith, 2000).

Background information

Take Exception to Critical Views

This opening procedure identifies the subject, establishes a basic view taken by the literature, and then differs with or takes exception to the critical position of other writers, as shown in the following example:

> Lorraine Hansberry's popular and successful A Raisin in the Sun, which first appeared on Broadway in 1959, is a problem play of a black family's determination to escape a Chicago ghetto to a better life in the suburbs. There is agreement that this escape theme explains the drama's conflict and its role in the black movement (e.g., Oliver,

Archer, and especially Knight, who describes the Youngers as "an entire family that has become aware of, and is determined to combat, racial discrimination in a supposedly democratic land" [34]). Yet another issue lies at the heart of the drama. Hansberry develops a modern view of black matriarchy in order to examine both the cohesive and the conflict-producing effects it has on the individual members of the Younger family.

Exception to prevailing views

Challenge an Assumption

This type of introduction presents a well-known idea or general theory in order to question it, analyze it, challenge it, or refute it.

Christianity dominates the religious life of most Americans to the point that many assume that it dominates the world population as well. However, despite the denominational missionaries who have reached out to every corner of the globe, only one out of every four people on the globe is a Christian, and far fewer than that practice their faith. In truth, Christianity does not dominate religious beliefs around the globe.

Challenge to an assumption

Provide a Brief Summary

When the subject is a literary work, historic event, educational theory, or similar item, a brief summary will refresh the reader's memory.

The chief legacy of the two Bush administrations might well be one of waging war. George Bush liberated Kuwait with the 1991 war against Iraq, but he withdraw after accomplishing that mission rather than overthrow Saddam Hussein and his government in Baghdad. Later, George W. Bush retaliated against the Taliban of Afghanistan in late 2001 after the 9/11 tragedy. Then, in 2003, George W. Bush attacked Iraq again to remove Saddam Hussein from power. This study will examine the literature to confirm the hypothesis that Bush and Bush will be remembered as war presidents.

Summary

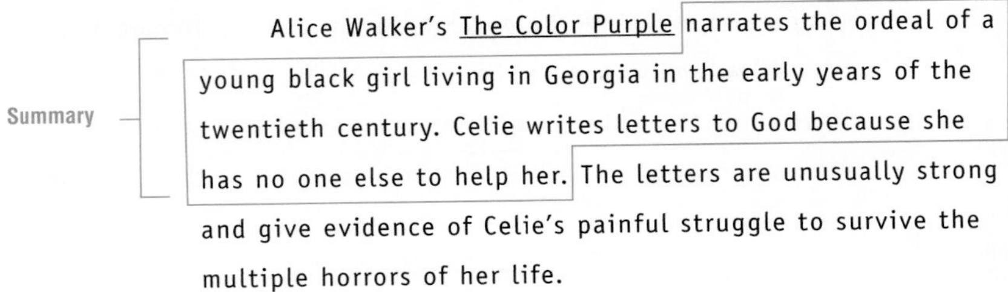

Summary
Alice Walker's The Color Purple narrates the ordeal of a young black girl living in Georgia in the early years of the twentieth century. Celie writes letters to God because she has no one else to help her. The letters are unusually strong and give evidence of Celie's painful struggle to survive the multiple horrors of her life.

Define Key Terms

Sometimes an opening passage must explain difficult terminology, as in the following example:

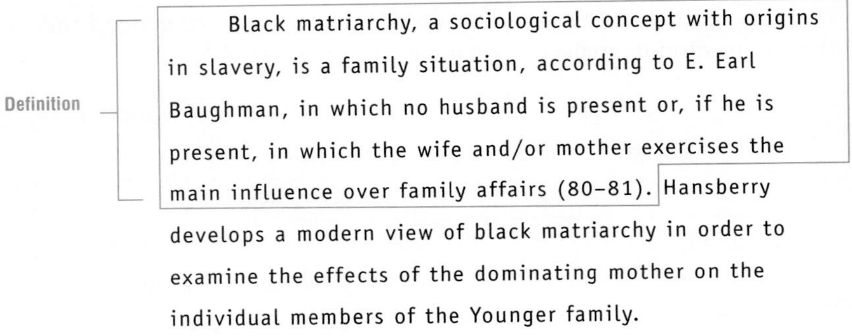

Definition
Black matriarchy, a sociological concept with origins in slavery, is a family situation, according to E. Earl Baughman, in which no husband is present or, if he is present, in which the wife and/or mother exercises the main influence over family affairs (80–81). Hansberry develops a modern view of black matriarchy in order to examine the effects of the dominating mother on the individual members of the Younger family.

Supply Data, Statistics, and Special Evidence

Concrete evidence can attract the reader and establish the subject. For example, a student working with demographic data might compare the birth and death rates of certain sections of the world. In Europe, the rates are almost constant, while the African nations have birth rates that are 30 percent higher than the death rates. Such statistical evidence can be a useful tool in many papers. Just remember to support the data with clear, textual discussion. The paper by Norman Berkowitz, Chapter 16, displays a table and two maps to support his research.

Sample introduction in a student paper using these techniques, Chapter 20.

Writing the Body of the Research Paper

When writing the body of the paper, you should classify, compare, and analyze the issues. Keep in mind three key elements, as shown in the checklist below.

Sample research papers with well-developed paragraphs, Chapter 16.

The length of your paragraphs ought to be from four sentences up to twelve or even fifteen. You can accomplish this task only by writing good topic sentences and by developing them fully. The techniques described in the following paragraphs demonstrate how to build substantive paragraphs for your paper.

Relate a Time Sequence

Use *chronology* and *plot summary* to trace historical events and to survey a story or novel. You should, almost always, discuss the significance of the events. This first example traces historical events.

Time sequence established

Following the death of President Roosevelt in April 1945, Harry S. Truman succeeded to the Presidency. Although he was an experienced politician, Truman "was ill prepared to direct a foreign policy," especially one that "called for the use of the atomic bomb to bring World War II to an end" (Jeffers 56). Consideration must be directed at the circumstances of the time, which led up to Truman's decision that took the lives of over 100,000 individuals and destroyed four square miles of the city of Hiroshima. Consideration must be given to the impact that this decision had on the

CHECKLIST

Avoiding Certain Mistakes in the Opening

Avoid a purpose statement, such as "The purpose of this study is . . . " unless you are writing reports of empirical research, in which case you *should* explain the purpose of your study (see Chapter 18, "Writing in APA Style").

Avoid repetition of the title, which should appear on the first page of the text anyway.

Avoid complex language or difficult questions that may puzzle the reader. However, general rhetorical questions are acceptable.

Avoid simple dictionary definitions, such as "Webster defines *monogamy* as marriage with only one person at a time."

Avoid humor, unless the subject deals with humor or satire.

Avoid hand-drawn artwork, clip art, and cute lettering unless the paper's subject matter requires it (for example, "The Circle as Advertising Symbol"). *Do* use computer graphics, tables, illustrations, and other designs that are appropriate to your subject.

CHECKLIST

Writing the Body of the Paper

Analysis Classify the major issues of the study and provide a careful analysis of each in defense of your thesis.

Presentation Provide well-reasoned statements at the beginning of your paragraphs, and supply evidence of support with proper documentation.

Paragraphs Offer a variety of development to compare, show process, narrate the history of the subject, show causes, and so forth.

war, on Japan, and on the rest of the world. Consideration must be directed at the man who brought the twentieth century into the atomic age.

The next passage shows the use of plot summary.

Quick plot summary

John Updike's "A & P" is a short story about a young grocery clerk named Sammy who feels trapped by the artificial values of the small town where he lives and, in an emotional moment, quits his job. The store manager, Lengel, is the voice of the conservative values in the community. For him, the girls in swimsuits pose a disturbance to his store, so he expresses his displeasure by reminding the girls that the A & P is not the beach (1088). Sammy, a liberal, believes the girls may be out of place in the A & P only because of its "fluorescent lights," "stacked packages," and "checkerboard green-and-cream rubber-tile floor," all artificial things (1086).

HINT: Keep the plot summary short and relate it to your thesis, as shown by the first sentence in the passage above. Do not allow the plot summary to extend beyond one paragraph; otherwise, you may retell the entire story. Your task is to make a point, not retell the story.

Compare or Contrast Issues, Critical Views, and Literary Characters

Employ *comparison* and *contrast* to show the two sides of a subject, to compare two characters, to compare the past with the present, or to compare positive and negative issues. The next passage compares and contrasts differences in forest conservation techniques.

Comparison and contrast

When a "controlled burn" gets out of hand and burns an entire town, defenders of controlled burns have a serious public relations problem. Thus, to burn or not to burn the natural forests in the national parks is the question. The pyrophobic public voices its protests while environmentalists praise the rejuvenating effects of a good forest fire. It is difficult to convince people that not all fire is bad. The public has visions of Smokey the Bear campaigns and mental images of Bambi and Thumper fleeing the roaring flames. Perhaps the public could learn to see beauty in fresh green shoots, like Bambi and Faline do as they returned to raise their young. Chris Bolgiano explains that federal policy evolved slowly "from the basic impulse to douse all fires immediately to a sophisticated decision matrix based on the functions of any given unit of land" (22). Bolgiano declares that "timber production, grazing, recreation, and wilderness preservation elicit different fire-management approaches" (23).

Develop Cause and Effect

Write *cause-and-effect* paragraphs to develop the reasons for a circumstance or to examine its consequences. An example is shown here that not only explains with cause and effect but also uses the device of *analogy,* or metaphoric comparison—in this case, of bread dough and the uniform expansion of the universe.

Analogy

To see how the Hubble Law implies uniform, centerless expansion of a universe, imagine that you want to make a loaf of raisin bread. As the dough rises, the expansion pushes the raisins away from each other. Two raisins that were originally about one centimeter apart separate more slowly than raisins that were about four centimeters apart. The uniform expansion of the dough causes the raisins to move apart at speeds proportional to their distances. Helen

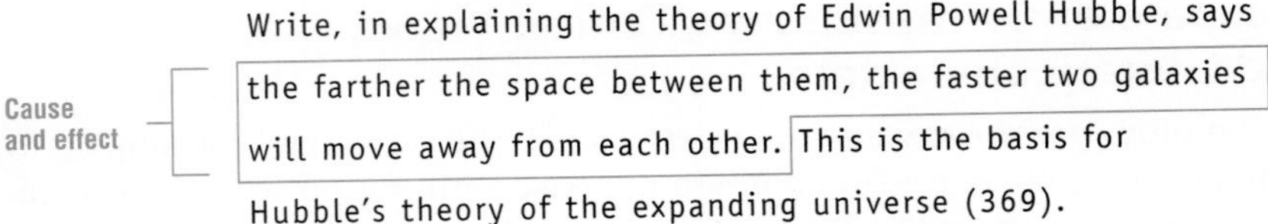

Cause and effect

Write, in explaining the theory of Edwin Powell Hubble, says the farther the space between them, the faster two galaxies will move away from each other. This is the basis for Hubble's theory of the expanding universe (369).

Define Your Key Terminology

Use *definition* to explain and expand upon a complex subject. This next example, by Katie Hebert, defines *functional foods:*

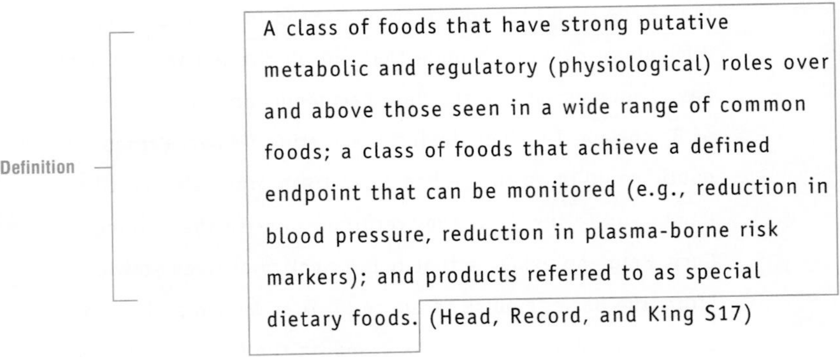

Definition

Functional foods, as defined by the Australian National Food Authority, are:

> A class of foods that have strong putative metabolic and regulatory (physiological) roles over and above those seen in a wide range of common foods; a class of foods that achieve a defined endpoint that can be monitored (e.g., reduction in blood pressure, reduction in plasma-borne risk markers); and products referred to as special dietary foods. (Head, Record, and King S17)

Explain a Process

Draft a *process* paragraph that explains, one by one, the steps necessary to achieve a desired end:

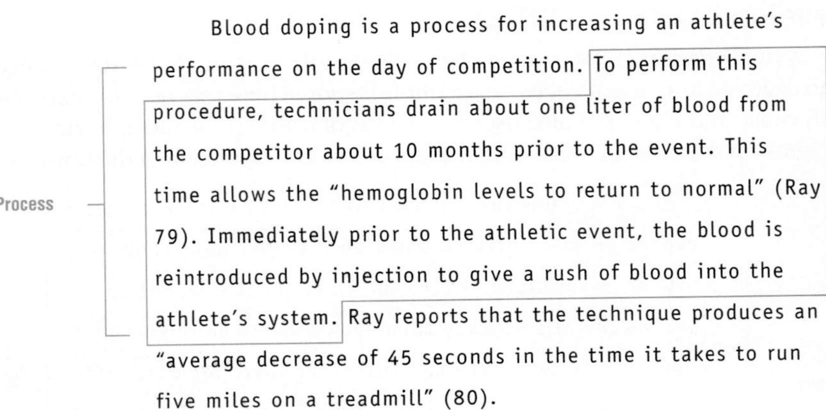

Process

Blood doping is a process for increasing an athlete's performance on the day of competition. To perform this procedure, technicians drain about one liter of blood from the competitor about 10 months prior to the event. This time allows the "hemoglobin levels to return to normal" (Ray 79). Immediately prior to the athletic event, the blood is reintroduced by injection to give a rush of blood into the athlete's system. Ray reports that the technique produces an "average decrease of 45 seconds in the time it takes to run five miles on a treadmill" (80).

Ask Questions and Provide Answers

Framing a question as a topic sentence gives you the opportunity to develop a thorough answer with specific details and evidence. Look at how this approach is used in this example:

Question

Does America have enough park lands? The lands now designated as national and state parks, forests, and wild land total in excess of 33 million acres. Yet environmentalists call for additional protected land. They warn of imbalances in the environment. Dean Fraser, in his book, The People Problem, addresses the question of whether we have enough park land:

> Yosemite, in the summer, is not unlike Macy's the week before Christmas. In 1965 it had over 1.6 million visitors; Yellowstone over 2 million. The total area of federal plus state-owned parks is now something like 33 million acres, which sounds impressive until it is divided by the total number of annual visitors of something over 400 million. . . . (33)

Answer

We are running short of green space, which is being devoured by highways, housing projects, and industrial development.

Cite Evidence from the Source Materials

Citing evidence from authorities in the form of quotations, paraphrases, and summaries to support your topic sentence is another excellent way to build a paragraph. This next passage combines commentary by a critic and a poet to explore Thomas Hardy's pessimism in fiction and poetry.

Several critics reject the impression of Thomas Hardy as a pessimist. He is instead a realist who tends toward optimism. Thomas Parrott and Willard Thorp make this comment about Hardy in Poetry of the Transition:

Evidence from a source

> There has been a tendency in the criticism of Hardy's work to consider him as a philosopher rather than as a poet and to stigmatize him as a gloomy pessimist. This is quite wrong.(413)

The author himself felt incorrectly labeled, for he has written his own description:

> As to pessimism. My motto is, first correctly diagnose the complaint—in this case human ills—and ascertain the cause: then set about finding a remedy if one exists. The motto of optimists is: Blind the eyes to the real malady, and use empirical panaceas to suppress the symptoms. (Life 383)

Hardy is dismayed by these "optimists," so he has no desire to be lumped within such a narrow perspective.

Use a Variety of Other Methods

Many methods exist for developing paragraphs; among them are *description* of a scene in a novel, *statistics* in support of an argument, *historical evidence* in support of a hypothesis, *psychological theory*, and others. You must make the choices, basing your decision on your subject and your notes. Employ the following methods as appropriate to your project.

- Use *classification* to identify several key issues of the topic, and then use *analysis* to examine each issue in detail. For example, you might classify several types of fungus infections, such as athlete's foot, dermatophytosis, and ringworm, and then analyze each.
- Use specific *criteria of judgment* to examine performances and works of art. For example, analyze the films of George Lucas with a critical response to story, theme, editing, photography, sound track, special effects, and so forth.
- Use *structure* to control papers on architecture, poetry, fiction, and biological forms. For example, a short story might have six distinct parts you can examine in sequence.
- Use *location* and *setting* for arranging papers in which geography and locale are key ingredients. For example, examine the settings of several novels by William Faulkner, or build an environmental study around land features (e.g., lakes, springs, sinkholes).
- Use *critical responses to an issue* to evaluate a course of action. For example, an examination of President Truman's decision to use the atomic bomb in World War II would invite you to consider several minor reasons and then to study Truman's major reason(s) for his decision.
- Dividing the body by important *issues* is standard fare in many research papers. One student examined the major issues of diabetes (see Chapter 20), and another developed the major issues about the water supplies (see Chapter 16).

Writing the Conclusion of the Research Paper

The conclusion of a research paper should offer the reader more than a mere summary. Use the checklist at the bottom of the page to review your conclusion.

How you work these elements into your conclusion will depend on your style of writing. They need not appear in this order, nor should you crowd all the items into one paragraph. The conclusion can extend over several paragraphs and require more than one page. When drafting the conclusion, consider using several of the techniques described here.

Restate the Thesis and Reach beyond It

As a general rule, restate your thesis sentence; however, do not stop and assume that your reader will generate final conclusions about the issues. Instead, establish the essential mission of your study. In the example below, one student opens her conclusion by reestablishing her thesis sentence and then moves quickly to her persuasive, concluding judgments.

Thesis restated in the conclusion

Functional foods appear to exert a strong preventive effect on the two diseases that take most American lives than any other—coronary heart disease and cancer. High cholesterol levels cause coronary heart disease, the factor responsible for 24 percent of the fatalities that occur in the United States (Blumberg 3). Foods high in antioxidants (i.e., Vitamin C, E, and betacarotene), omega-e fatty acids, and soluble fiber, along with green and black tea have been proven to be an

CHECKLIST

Writing the Conclusion

Thesis	Reaffirm your thesis statement.
Judgment	Reach a decision or judgment about the merits of the subject, be it a work of art, an author's writing, a historical moment, or a social position.
Discussion	Discuss the implications of your findings.
Directive	Offer a plan of action or a proposal that will put into effect your ideas. (Not required of every paper.)
Ending	Use the final paragraph, especially the final sentence, to bring the paper to closure.

effective form of preventive medicine for individuals at risk of developing coronary heart disease. Second only to coronary heart disease, "cancer is the cause of death in 22 percent of Americans" (4). Functional foods have exhibited similar strength in the fight for cancer prevention. By incorporating functional foods, such as insoluble fiber, garlic, and green and black tea into the diet, an individual can lower his or her risk of being diagnosed with cancer. Although this finding does not mean one should cancel all future doctor appointments, it has shown that individuals who eat functional foods are a step ahead in the battle for disease prevention.

Close with an Effective Quotation

Sometimes a source may provide a striking commentary that deserves special placement, as shown by this example:

W. C. Fields had a successful career that extended from vaudeville to musical comedy and finally to the movies. In his private life, he loathed children and animals, and he fought with bankers, landladies, and the police. Off screen, he maintained his private image as a vulgar, hard-drinking cynic until his death in 1946. On the screen, he won the hearts of two generations of fans. He was beloved by audiences primarily for acting out their own contempt for authority. The movies prolonged his popularity "as a dexterous comedian with expert timing and a look of bibulous rascality," but Fields had two personalities, "one jolly and one diabolical" (Kennedy 990).

Effective quotation

Return the Focus of a Literary Study to the Author

While the body of a literary paper should analyze characters, images, and plot, the conclusion should explain the author's accomplishments. The following closing shows how one writer focused on the author:

As to the issues of the country versus the city and the impact of a market economy, Jonathan Swift advances the conservative position of the early eighteenth century, which lamented the loss of the rural, agrarian society, with its

Focus on the author

adherence to tradition and a stable social hierarchy. His position focused on the social outcomes: unemployment, displacement, and the disenfranchisement of a significant portion of the populace. Unlike his London contemporaries, Swift resided in the economic hinterland of Ireland, so he had a more direct view of the destructive population shifts from rural to urban.

Focus on the author

Ultimately, Swift's commentary in A Modest Proposal is important because it records a consciousness of a continuing problem, one that worsens with the intensification of the urban rather than rural growth. It continues to plague the twenty-first-century world, from America to Africa and from Russia to Latin America.

Compare the Past to the Present

You can use the conclusion rather than the opening to compare past research to the present study or to compare the historic past with the contemporary scene. For example, after explaining the history of two schools of treatment for autism, one writer switches to the present, as shown in this excerpt:

Future in contrast to the present

There is hope in the future that both the cause and the cure for autism will be found. For the present, new drug therapies and behavior modification offer some hope for the abnormal, SIB actions of a person with autistism. Since autism is sometimes outgrown, childhood treatment offers the best hope for the autistic person who must try to survive in an alien environment.

Offer a Directive or Solution

After analyzing a problem and synthesizing issues, offer your theory or solution, as demonstrated immediately above in the example in which the writer suggests that "childhood treatment offers the best hope for the autistic person who must try to survive in an alien environment." Note also this closing:

A directive or solution

All of the aspects of diabetes management can be summed up in one word: balance. Diabetes itself is caused by a lack of balance of insulin and glucose in the body. In order to restore that balance, a diabetic must juggle medication, monitoring, diet, and exercise. Managing diabetes is not an easy task, but a long and healthy life is very possible when the delicate balance is carefully maintained.

Discuss Test Results

In scientific writing (see Chapters 18 and 20), your conclusion, labeled "discussion," must explain the ramifications of your findings and identify any limitations of your scientific study, as shown:

Test results

The results of this experiment were similar to expectations, but perhaps the statistical significance, because of the small subject size, was biased toward the delayed conditions of the curve. The subjects were, perhaps, not representative of the total population because of their prior exposure to test procedures. Another factor that may have affected the curves was the presentation of the data. The images on the screen were available for five seconds, and that amount of time may have enabled the subjects to store each image effectively. If the time period for each image were reduced to one or two seconds, there could be lower recall scores, thereby reducing the differences between the control group and the experimental group.

CHECKLIST

Avoiding Certain Mistakes in the Conclusion

- **Avoid** afterthoughts or additional ideas. Now is the time to end the paper, not begin a new thought. If new ideas occur to you as you write your conclusion, don't ignore them. Explore them fully in the context of your thesis and consider adding them to the body of your paper or modifying your thesis. Scientific studies often discuss options and possible alterations that might affect test results (see "Discuss Test Results," immediately above).
- **Avoid** the use of "thus," "in conclusion," and "finally" at the beginning of the last paragraph. Readers can see plainly the end of the paper.
- **Avoid** ending the paper without a sense of closure.
- **Avoid** questions that raise new issues; however, rhetorical questions that restate the issues are acceptable.
- **Avoid** fancy artwork.

YOUR RESEARCH PROJECT

1. Review your opening to determine whether it builds the argument and sets the stage for analysis to come in the body. Consider adding paragraphs like those described at the beginning of this chapter: Relate the well known, provide background information, review the literature, review the history of the subject, take exception to prevailing views, challenge an assumption, provide a summary of the issues, define key terms, supply statistical evidence.
2. After finishing the first draft, review the body of your paper. Has your analysis touched on all the issues? Have you built paragraphs of substance? Judge the draft against the checklist for the body on page 344.
3. Evaluate your conclusion according to the checklist on page 349. If you feel it's necessary, build the conclusion by these techniques: Elaborate on the thesis, use an effective quotation, focus on a key person, compare the past and the present, offer a directive or solution, or discuss test results.

16 Revising, Proofreading, and Formatting the Rough Draft

Once you have the complete paper in a rough draft, the serious business of editing begins. First, revise the paper on a global scale, moving blocks of material to the best advantage and into the proper format. Second, edit the draft with a line-by-line examination of wording and technical excellence. Third, proofread the final version to ensure your words are spelled correctly and the text is grammatically sound.

Conducting a Global Revision

For discussion of developing the introduction, see Chapter 15.

Revision can turn a passable paper into an excellent one and change an excellent one into a radiant one. First, revise the whole manuscript by performing the tasks in the checklist as shown below.

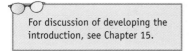

Revising the Introduction

Examine your opening for the presence of several items:

- Your thesis
- A clear sense of direction or plan of development
- A sense of involvement that invites the reader into your investigation of a problem

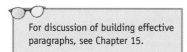

For discussion of building effective paragraphs, see Chapter 15.

Revising the Body

Use the following bulleted list as a guide for revising each individual paragraph of the body of your paper.

- Cut out wordiness and irrelevant thoughts, even to the point of deleting entire sentences that contribute nothing to the dynamics of the paper.
- Combine short paragraphs with others or build one of greater substance.

CHECKLIST

Global Revision

1. Skim through the paper to check its unity. Does the paper maintain a central proposition from paragraph to paragraph?
2. Transplant paragraphs, moving them to more relevant and effective positions.
3. Delete sentences that do not further your cause.
4. As you cut, copy, and paste, remember to rewrite and blend the words into your text.
5. If your outline must be submitted with your draft, revise it to reflect these global revisions.

- Revise long, difficult paragraphs by dividing them or by using transitions effectively (see "Writing with Unity and Coherence," pages 299–300).
- For paragraphs that seem short, shallow, or weak, add more commentary and more evidence, especially quotations from the primary source or critical citations from secondary sources.
- Add your own input to paragraphs that rely too heavily on the source materials.
- Examine your paragraphs for transitions that move the reader effectively from one paragraph to the next.

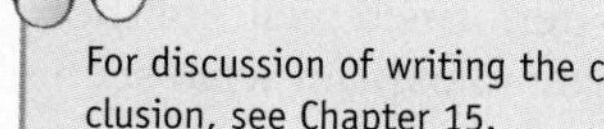
For discussion of writing the conclusion, see Chapter 15.

Revising the Conclusion

Examine the conclusion to see that it meets these criteria:

- It is drawn from the evidence.
- It is developed logically from the introduction and the body.
- It expresses your position on the issues.

Participating in Peer Review

Part of the revision process for many writers, both students and professionals, is peer review. This has two sides. First, it means handing your paper to a friend or classmate, asking for opinions and suggestions. Second, it means reviewing a classmate's research paper. You can learn by reviewing as well as by writing.

Since this task asks you to make judgments, you need a set of criteria. Your instructor may supply a peer review sheet, or you can use the checklist

CHECKLIST

Peer Review

1. Are the subject and the accompanying issues introduced early?
2. Is the writer's critical approach to the problem stated clearly in a thesis sentence? Is it placed effectively in the introduction?
3. Do the paragraphs of the body have individual unity? That is, does each one develop an important idea and only one idea? Does each paragraph relate to the thesis?
4. Are sources introduced, usually with the name of the expert, and then cited by a page number within parentheses? Keep in mind that Internet sources, in most cases, do not have page numbers.
5. Is it clear where a paraphrase begins and where it ends?
6. Are the sources relevant to the argument?
7. Does the writer weave quotations into the text effectively while avoiding long quotations that look like filler instead of substance?
8. Does the conclusion arrive at a resolution about the central issue?
9. Does the title describe clearly what you have found in the contents of the research paper?

shown above. Criticize the paper constructively on each point. If you can answer each question with a *yes,* your classmate has performed well. For those questions you answer *no,* you owe it to your classmate to explain what seems wrong. Make suggestions. Offer tips. Try to help!

Formatting the Paper to MLA Style

The format of a research paper consists of the following parts:

1. Title page
2. Outline
3. Abstract
4. The text of the paper
5. Content notes
6. Appendix
7. Works Cited

Items 4 and 7 are required for a paper in the MLA style; use the other items to meet the needs of your research. *Note:* A paper in APA style (see Chapter 18) requires items 1, 3, 4, and 7, and the order differs for items 5–7.

Title Page or Opening Page

A research paper in MLA style does not need a separate title page unless you include an outline, abstract, or other prefatory matter. Place your identification in the upper left corner of your opening page, as shown here:

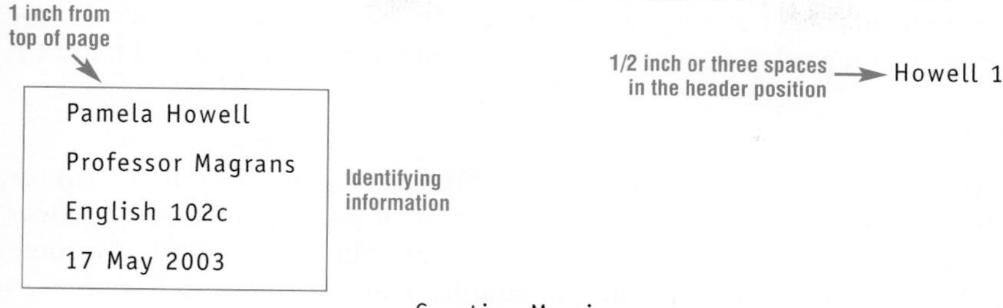

Howell 1

Pamela Howell

Professor Magrans

English 102c

17 May 2003

Creative Marriages

Judging by recent divorce rates, it would seem that the traditional marriage fails to meet the needs . . . .

> *Note*: APA style requires a different setup for the title page; see "Formatting an APA Paper" section in Chapter 18.

If you do include prefatory matter, such as an outline, you need the title page with centered divisions for the title, the author, and the course identification.

An Interpretation of Melville's

Use of Biblical Characters

in Billy Budd

by

Doris Singleton

Freshman English II, Section 108b

Dr. Crampton

April 23, 2004

Follow these guidelines for writing a title page in MLA style:

1. Use an inverted pyramid to balance two or more lines.
2. Use capitals and lowercase letters without underlining and without quotation marks. Published works that appear as part of your title require underlining (books) or quotation marks (short stories). Do not use a period after a centered heading.
3. Place your full name below the title, usually in the center of the page.
4. Employ separate lines, centered, to provide the course information, institution, instructor, date, or program (e.g., Honors Program).
5. Provide balanced, 2-inch margins for all sides of the title page.
6. Use your computer to print a border on this page, if you so desire, but not on any other pages.

Outline

Print your outline with the finished manuscript only if your instructor requires it. Place it after the title page on separate pages and number these pages with small Roman numerals, beginning with ii (for example, ii, iii, iv, v), at the top right-hand corner of the page, just after your last name (e.g., Spence iii). For information on writing an outline and sample outlines, see Chapters 11 and 19.

Abstract

Include an abstract for a paper in MLA style only if your instructor requires it. An abstract provides a brief digest of the paper's essential ideas in about 100 words. To that end, borrow from your introduction, use some of the topic sentences from your paragraphs, and use one or two sentences from your conclusion.

In MLA style, place the abstract on the first page of text (page 1) one double-space below the title and before the first lines of the text. Indent the abstract five spaces as a block, and indent the first line an additional five spaces. Use quadruple spacing at the end of the abstract to set it off from the text, which follows immediately after. You may also place the abstract on a separate page between the title page and first page of text.

For more on the abstract and examples, see Chapter 18.

Remember that the abstract is usually read first and may be the *only* part read; therefore, make it accurate, specific, objective, and self-contained (i.e., it makes sense alone without references to the main text). Note this example:

Walker 1

Child Abuse: A View of the Victims

Abstract

This study examines the problems of child abuse, especially the fact that families receive attention after abuse occurs, not before. With abuse statistics on the rise, efforts devoted to prevention rather than coping should focus on parents in order to discover those adults most likely to commit abuse because of heredity, their own childhood, the economy, and other causes of depression. Viewing the parent as a victim, not just a criminal, will enable social agencies to institute preventive programs that may control abuse and hold together family units.

Quadruple space →

Family troubles will most likely affect the delicate members of

Text → our society, the children. The recognition of causal elements . . .

The Text of the Paper

Double-space throughout the entire paper except for the title page (page 357) and the separation of the abstract from the first line of text (page 358). In general, you should *not* use subtitles or numbered divisions for your paper, even if it becomes twenty pages long. Instead, use continuous paragraphing without subdivisions or headings. However, some scientific and business reports require subheads (see chapters 18 and 20).

If the closing page of your text runs short, leave the remainder of the page blank. Do not write "The End" or provide artwork as a closing signal. Do not start Notes or Works Cited on this final page of text.

Content Endnotes Page

Label this page with the word *Notes* centered at the top edge of the sheet, at least one double-space below your page-numbering sequence in the upper right corner. Double-space between the *Notes* heading and the first note. Number the notes in sequence with raised superscript numerals to match those within your text. Double-space all entries and double-space between them.

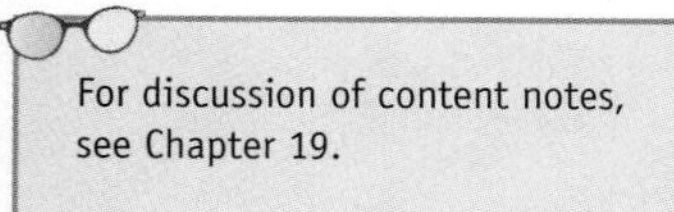

For discussion of content notes, see Chapter 19.

Appendix

Place additional material, if necessary, in an appendix preceding the Works Cited page. This is the logical location for numerous tables and illustrations, computer data, questionnaire results, complicated statistics, mathematical proofs, and detailed descriptions of special equipment. Double-space appendixes and begin each appendix on a new sheet. Continue your page numbering sequence in the upper right corner of the sheet. Label the page *Appendix,* centered at the top of the sheet. If you have more than one appendix, use *Appendix A, Appendix B,* and so forth.

See Chapter 17, "Works Cited," and sample Works Cited on pages 371 and 382–383.

Works Cited

Center the heading *Works Cited* 1 inch from the top edge of the sheet. Continue the page-numbering sequence in the upper right corner. Double-space throughout. Set the first line of each entry flush left and indent subsequent lines five spaces. If your software supports it, use the hanging indent.

Editing before Typing or Printing the Final Manuscript

For discussion of unity, coherence, and effective writing, see Chapter 13.

The cut-and-paste revision period is complemented by careful editing of paragraphs, sentences, and individual words. Travel through the paper to study your sentences and word choice. Look for ways to tighten and condense. Below is a checklist.

Note the editing by one student in Figure 16.1. As shown, this writer conscientiously deleted unnecessary material, added supporting statements, related facts to one another, rearranged data, added new ideas, and rewrote for clarity.

CHECKLIST

Editing

1. Cut phrases and sentences that do not advance your main ideas or that merely repeat what your sources have already stated.
2. Determine that coordinated, balanced ideas are appropriately expressed and that minor ideas are properly subordinated.
3. Change most of your *to be* verbs (is, are, was) to stronger active verbs.
4. Maintain the present tense in most verbs.
5. Convert passive structures to active if possible.
6. Confirm that you have introduced paraphrases and quotations so that they flow smoothly into your text. Use a variety of verbs for the instructions (*Winston argues, Thomas reminds, Morganfield offers*).
7. Use formal, academic style, and guard against clusters of monosyllabic words that fail to advance ideas. Examine your wording for its effectiveness within the context of your subject.

In some cases is see
~~One critic calls~~ television "junk food" (Fransecky

717), and ~~I think~~ excessive viewing ~~does~~ distracts
(see esp. Paul Witty as qtd. in Postman 41)
from other activities, yet television can and does
and shows of our best
bring cultural programs some ~~good~~ novels. It does,
according to the evidence,
improve children's vocabularies, encourages their
and school
reading, and inspires their writing. Television should
s the traditional classroom curriculum
not be ~~an~~ antagonist; ~~it should complement school~~
should seek and find harmony with the preschool television
~~work~~.
curriculum.

FIGURE 16.1 Example of editing on a manuscript page.

Using the Computer to Edit Your Text

Remember to click on Tools and use the spelling and grammar checkers to spot spelling errors and to perform several tasks related to grammar and mechanics—for example, looking for parentheses you have opened but not closed, unpaired quotation marks, passive verbs, and other items. Pay attention to these caution flags. Caution: the spellchecker will not discern incorrect usage of "its" and "it's." However, you must edit and adjust your paper by *your* standards with due respect to the computer analysis. Remember, it is your paper, not the computer's. You may need to use some long words and write some long sentences, or you may prefer the passive voice to emphasize the receiver of the action, not the actor.

Proofreading on the Screen and on the Printed Manuscript

First, proofread your paper on the screen with a program that will check your spelling, grammar, and style, as mentioned above. Check your formatting for double-spacing, 1-inch margins, running heads, page numbers, and so forth.

Check the entries in your Works Cited section for precision and completeness in the citations. Also, be sure that each is formatted with a hanging indention.

> Consult Appendix A, "Glossary: Preparing the Manuscript in MLA Style," for instructions on handling abbreviations, margins, tables, numbering, punctuation, content notes, and other matters.

After editing the text on screen to your satisfaction, print out a hard copy of the manuscript. You should proofread this final paper version with great care because the software will not have caught every error. Be sure your in-text citations are correct and confirm that you have a corresponding bibliography entry for each.

CHECKLIST

Proofreading

1. Check for errors in sentence structure, spelling, and punctuation.
2. Check for correct hyphenation and word division. Remember that *no* words should be hyphenated at the ends of lines. If you are using a computer, turn off the automatic hyphenation option.
3. Read each quotation for the accuracy of your own wording and of the words within your quoted materials. Look, too, for your correct use of quotations marks.
4. Be certain that in-text citations are correct and that each corresponding source is listed on your Works Cited page.
5. Double-check the format—the title page, margins, spacing, content notes, and many other elements, as explained earlier and in the glossary in Appendix A.

YOUR RESEARCH PROJECT

1. Examine once again the intellectual argument of your first draft. Is it clearly established in the opening and then reaffirmed in the closing?
2. Do the paragraphs of the body develop systematically the evidence to support your claim or thesis? Examine each paragraph for relevance.
3. Examine again your title. Does it meet the criteria set forth in the MLA Guidelines?
4. If you participated in a peer review, consider carefully the recommendations and judgments of your reviewer. There's always a tendency to dismiss words of criticism, but you need to learn that constructive criticism exists at all levels of collegiate and professional life.
5. Read aloud to yourself a portion of the paper. Does it have an academic style? If not, read Chapter 13 and begin editing.
6. Read through the two papers that follow next in this chapter, to get a feel for the academic style of writing. Try to duplicate that style.

Sample Papers in MLA Style

Literary Research Paper

Melinda Mosier accepted the challenge to write a literary paper on Shakespeare's play *Hamlet.* This task required her to find a focus for her work, so she chose to examine the soliloquies of the title character. In these speeches, she hoped to find a pattern that might focus the direction of her research and writing. She had read the entire play, so now she reread and studied the soliloquies. At the same time, she began her search of the source material—in the library stacks for books, on the library's electronic databases (e.g., InfoTrac), and on the Internet. Eventually, she settled her study on the settings within which the soliloquies are spoken by Hamlet. She examined each, found comparisons, cited a number of sources, and arrived at her conclusion: "Shakespeare leaves Hamlet alone on stage in the soliloquies to act out his anguish because he could not act otherwise. Each setting for each soliloquy was a pivotal but stifling moment."

Read the essay with care, noting the academic style of writing, the careful in-text citations to sources, the citations to the primary source—*Hamlet*—and the way Melinda moves carefully and methodically to her conclusion.

Mosier 1

Melinda Mosier

Professor Thompson

Humanities 1020

6 April 2003

Listening to Hamlet: The Soliloquies

A soliloquy is a dramatic form of discourse in which a person reveals inner thoughts and feelings while alone on stage or while unaware that others might be within the range of their voice. But then, the person might also deliver such a speech while knowing full well that somebody is listening. Thus, the dramatic convention has complications, and when Shakespeare uses it with a complex character like Hamlet, it appears in a variety of forms. Critical authorities have agreed that the soliloquies reveal the inner feelings of Hamlet (Auden, Bloom, and Wilson), yet they disagree somewhat in their interpretations. This study, however, will examine the settings within which the soliloquies occur and interpret the direction of Hamlet's remarks inward to himself and outward to a perceived listener.

Mosier opens with a definition.

Mosier establishes the concept she will explore.

The first soliloquy occurs in act 1, scene 2, lines 133–164, immediately after King Claudius and Queen Gertrude have left in a flourish. His mother has just admonished Hamlet for wearing black after these many days following the death of his father,

Lines of the play are indented, line breaks are maintained, and the act, scene, and lines are listed.

Two lines from the play can be quoted in the text, separated by a slash.

This section displays the manner in which Mosier interprets one of the soliloquies, citing from it and explaining the implications in light of the drama's setting.

Mosier 2

and he has responded with a play on the word <u>seems</u>, indicating in lines 79–89 that his mourning clothes are "but the trappings and the suits of woe," but that he has within a mournful spirit that is so deep it "passes show." He is stricken to his core by sadness. Then he is left alone and cries out:

> Oh, that this too too sullied flesh would melt,
> Thaw, and resolve itself into a dew,
> Or that the Everlasting had not fixed
> His canon 'gainst self-slaughter. O God, God,
> How weary, stale, flat and unprofitable
> Seem to me all the uses of this world! (1.2.133-38)[1]

This opening gives its obvious nod toward suicide and to the inner darkness of his soul, which even black clothing cannot show in full force. But Shakespeare uses this soliloquy for another important purpose--the son's verbal attack on his mother, Gertrude. She has just left in a flourish with the king, her new husband. Hamlet reveals his disgust with her because she has moved with "most wicked speed" (1.2.161) to marry Claudius, her dead husband's brother. Hamlet sees the union as incest and closes the soliloquy by saying: "It is not, nor it cannot come to good: / But break, my heart, for I must hold my tongue!" (1.2.163-64). Some critics, like Ernest Jones, would suggest that Hamlet is jealous of Claudius for winning a love that he (Hamlet) wanted, but that idea is severely weakened by Hamlet's damning words against her dexterity within "<u>incestuous sheets</u>" (my emphasis).

The second soliloquy occurs in act 2, scene 2, lines 576–634. The setting again has great relevance to Hamlet's words. An actor has just described how his company would portray the anguished and agonized cries of Hecuba, who must

[1]Quotations from the text come from the Folger Library edition.

Mosier 3

watch as her husband, Priam, the king of Troy, is hacked to death. Now, Hamlet is dismayed because a mere actor can show such passion in a fictional portrayal:

> O, what a rogue and peasant slave am I!
> Is it not monstrous that this player here,
> But in a fiction, in a dream of passion,
> Could force his soul so to his own conceit
> That from her working all his visage wanned,
> Tears in his eyes, distraction in his aspect,
> A broken voice, and his whole function suiting
> With forms to his conceit? And all for nothing!
> For Hecuba!
> What's Hecuba to him, or he to Hecuba,
> That he should weep for her? (2.2.576-86)

Comparing himself with the actor, Hamlet calls himself a "dull and muddy-mettled rascal" who "can say nothing; no, not for a king, / Upon whose property and most dear life / A damn'd defeat was made. Am I a coward?" (2.2.594-98). Hamlet is tortured in regard to his mother, who is his version of Hecuba. Next, Shakespeare uses the soliloquy to set out another comparison--one between a "pigeon-livered" (2.2.604) Prince Hamlet and an active and crafty Prince Hamlet. He recognizes his failure:

> Why, what an ass am I! This is most brave,
> That I, the son of a dear father murdered,
> Prompted to my revenge by heaven and hell,
> Must, like a whore, unpack my heart with words
> And fall a-cursing, like a very drab,
> A scullion!
> Fie upon 't! (2.2.611–16)

But suddenly, Hamlet changes his attitude, saying, "About, my brain!" This means, get busy, brain, and go to work! So now he

Mosier 4

plots the play within a play, saying, "The play's the thing / Wherein I'll catch the conscience of the king" (2.2.633–34).

In short, this soliloquy has three parts, all tied to the setting--praise for a performer who can act with passion, disgust with himself for his failure to act, and then his cunning plan for tricking the king by using the actors. Yet throughout the soliloquy he seems to be acting, and Shakespeare scholar Harold Bloom stresses that idea, saying:

> So histrionic is all of Hamlet that we need to develop our auditory consciousness to a new pitch, if we catch the prince's precise accent here. Where all is theatricality, our grounds for judgment must shift. Hamlet's hyperboles mock theater itself, in "drown the stage with tears." The soliloquy becomes a hyperparody of soliloquy . . . (30).

Mosier cites the authorities on Shakespeare in brief but effective ways.

The critic W. H. Auden will echo that sense of "theater" later in this paper, and Charles Cannon argues that "Hamlet is a play about the play-like deceit of much that poses for reality" (206).

The third soliloquy, and the most famous, again has a setting of great import. This time the king has called for Ophelia to meet with Hamlet while he and Polonius eavesdrop nearby. Although Shakespeare has given no stage instructions, it seems reasonable that Hamlet knows the plot, knows Ophelia is their foil, and knows they are listening. Thus, this suicidal monologue could be deception on his part, not a call for Prozac or death or any mind-altering alternative. Notice these words:

> To die, to sleep--
> To sleep--perchance to dream: ay, there's the rub,
> For in that sleep of death what dreams may come
> When we have shuffled off this mortal coil,
> Must give us pause. . . . (3.1.72–76)

Mosier 5

He hesitates about rushing into "the undiscovered country from whose bourn / No traveler returns" (3.1.87–88), and admits that "conscience does make cowards of us all . . . " (3.1.91). He does not wish to lose his chance for action, even though some critics, like Goethe, say a call to action has been "laid upon a soul unfit for the performance of it" (154). Thereafter, he performs his own little drama with Ophelia, knowing that the king is watching. W. H. Auden has observed that Hamlet is always "conscious of acting" (161). Hamlet's words and actions convince Ophelia, the king, and Polonius that he, Hamlet, has lost his sanity:

> Ophelia: O, what a noble mind is here o'erthrown!
> The courtier's, soldier's, scholar's, eye, tongue, sword:
> The expectancy and rose of the fair state,
> The glass of fashion and the mould of form,
> Th' observed of all observers, quite, quite down!
> (3.1.163–67)

Apparently insane, Hamlet can now act decisively in seeking his revenge. Youngson applies the Ganser syndrome to Hamlet, saying the prince has something "notable to gain from being thought mad" so he gives the appearance of psychiatric symptoms (1).

In the fourth soliloquy, which begins "'Tis now the very witching time of night" (3.2.419), Hamlet contrasts himself with Nero, a brutal Roman emperor, saying:

> Soft, now to my mother,
> O heart, lose not they nature, let not ever
> The soul of Nero enter this firm bosom,
> Let me be cruel not unnatural.
> I will speak daggers to her, but use none. (3.2.425–29)

The ghost of his father, after all, has asked him to spare Gertrude but not Claudius. Hamlet is diverted from his task but admits, by the comparison to Nero, that he does not have the stomach for the cruel and unnatural. J. Dover Wilson says his "murderous impulses must be kept in leash. True, she deserves the worst he can find it in his heart to say to her; she may even deserve death, but it is not for him to exact it" (244).

Mosier shows how the setting on a plain in Denmark allows a comparison of Hamlet and Fortinbras.

We see Hamlet in his fifth soliloquy still motivating himself, and again Shakespeare uses a comparison to force the issue--a prince of Norway versus the prince of Denmark. The setting is a plain in Denmark where Fortinbras, the nephew of the Norwegian king, leads an army across Denmark to attack a small section of Poland, fortified by 20,000 soldiers, but in truth the piece of land is not of great value. The Norwegian Captain explains, "We go to gain a little patch of ground / That hath in it no profit but the name. / To pay five ducats, five, I would not farm it . . . " (4.4.19–21). Hamlet recognizes the irony in the contrast--Fortinbras brazenly fights for what he deems his even though it has little value, but Hamlet refuses to fight in revenge for the very real death of his father.

> Witness this army of such mass and charge,
> Led by a delicate and tender prince,
> Whose spirit, with divine ambition puffed,
> Makes mouths at the invisible event,
> Exposing what is mortal and unsure
> To all that fortune, death, and danger dare,
> Even for an eggshell. (4.4.50–56)
> . . . .
> How stand I then,
> That have a father killed, a mother stained,
> Excitements of my reason and my blood,
> And let all sleep, while to my shame I see
> The imminent death of twenty thousand men

Mosier 7

That for a fantasy and trick of fame
Go to their graves like beds, fight for a plot
Whereon the numbers cannot try the cause,
Which is not tomb enough and continent
To hide the slain? (4.4.59–68)

Hamlet envisions 20,000 men going to slaughter and then buried on a plot of land so small it can't contain all the bodies. They will fight and die for a worthless cause while he procrastinates. "O, from this time forth," he cries, "My thoughts be bloody, or be nothing worth!" (4.4.69–70).

Thus, Shakespeare has carefully crafted a setting for each soliloquy, and the device of comparison plays a key role. In the first, Hamlet cries out that his soul is darker even than the black funeral garb he wears because of his mother's incestuous behavior. In the second, his behavior seems impotent (and perhaps that's a valid term) in comparison with the actor who cries so passionately for Hecuba, a distant historic figure far removed from Hamlet's recent loss of a father. In the third, he compares and contrasts the magnetism of death against "the dread of something after death, / The undiscovered country, from whose bourn / No traveler returns . . . " (3.1.86–87). In the fourth soliloquy, he reminds himself that he cannot perform cruel, unnatural acts like Nero. In the fifth, he stands ashamed of his inactivity in comparison to an aggressive Norwegian prince.

Mosier reviews briefly the elements of the five soliloquies to show how Hamlet compares himself to someone else.

In every instance Hamlet compares himself to someone else--a white knight; a passionate actor; a vibrant, throbbing human being; a Nero figure; or an aggressive soldier. Perhaps W. H. Auden expresses it best:

> Hamlet lacks faith in God and in himself. Consequently he must define his existence in terms of others, e.g., I am the man whose mother married

Mosier 8

> his uncle who murdered his father. He would like to become what the Greek tragic hero is, a creature of situation. Hence his inability to act, for he can only "act," i.e., play at possibilities. He is fundamentally <u>bored</u>, and for that reason he acts theatrically. (164)

Mosier reaches her conclusion about the stifling moments that affected Hamlet.

Shakespeare leaves Hamlet alone on stage in the soliloquies to act out his anguish because he could not act otherwise. Each setting for each soliloquy was a pivotal but stifling moment. If we have only the soliloquies before us, we can see that Hamlet will fail and "prophesy the election lights / on Fortinbras" (5.2.392–93), the man of action, not a man of "acting."

Mosier 9

Works Cited

Auden, W. H. Lectures on Shakespeare. Ed. Arthur Kirsch. Princeton: Princeton UP, 2000.

Bloom, Harold. Hamlet: Poem Unlimited. New York: Riverhead-Penguin, 2003.

Cannon, Charles K. "'As in a Theater'": Hamlet in the Light of Calvin's Doctrine of Predestination." Studies in English Literature, 1500–1600 11 (1971): 203–22. JSTOR. 8 Apr. 2003 <http://www.jstor.org/search>.

Goethe, Johann Wolfgang. "A Soul Unfit." Wilhelm Meister's Apprenticeship. Trans. Thomas Carlyle. Hamlet: A Norton Critical Edition. Ed. Cyrus Hoy. 2nd ed. New York: Norton, 1992.

Jones, Ernest. "The Oedipus-Complex as an Explanation of Hamlet's Mystery: A Study in Motive." The American Journal of Psychology 21.1 (1910): 72–113. Shakespeare Navigators. 8 Apr. 2003 <http://www.clicknotes.com/jones>.

Shakespeare, William. The Tragedy of Hamlet, Prince of Denmark. The New Folger Library Shakespeare. Ed. Barbara A. Mowat and Paul Werstine. New York: Washington Square P, 1992.

Wilson, Dover. What Happens in Hamlet. 1935. Cambridge, UK: Cambridge UP, 2001.

Youngson, Robert M. The Madness of Hamlet and Other Extraordinary States of Mind. New York: Carroll & Graf, 1999.

Form for a book.

A citation to a database's search page.

A work in an anthology.

Citation to a Web site.

Citation to the edition used and cited in the paper.

Sample Research Paper

Norman Berkowitz decided to explore the topic of the world's pending water crisis in his research paper. His paper, on the following pages, includes a table, two maps, and an appendix.

A title page is not required, but provide your name, instructor's name, date, and course.

Opening quotations may be centered, but normally they are indented 10 spaces from the left margin.

Berkowitz suggests a hypothesis that would require empirical proof, but he rejects it in favor of a theoretical study.

Berkowitz 1

Norman Berkowitz

Professor Zimmerman

April 9, 2004

English 1010

The World's Water Supply: The Ethics of Distribution

"Water, water, everywhere,
And all the boards did shrink,
Water, water, everywhere,
Nor any drop to drink"

--Samuel Taylor Coleridge, "The Rime of the Ancient Mariner"

The British poet Coleridge created a ghostly scene that might serve as a forecast for our children. The world is running out of fresh water while we, unthinking, enjoy a sip from our Evian. But wait, the bottled water craze should be a signal--why do we need bottled water? What's happened to good, fresh tap water?

The truth is, we have a crisis on our hands, and it grows more serious all the time. In fact, some authorities now forecast world wars over water rights. It's like the old western movies with ranchers squabbling over water rights, only now the squabbling is worldwide.

The crisis has not gone unnoticed. Hundreds of articles crowd the magazines and journals in many disciplines, from economics to environmental science and from sociology to physics. The issue of water touches almost every facet of life--religious rituals, food supply, political stability, disease, to name only a few. We might frame this hypothesis: Water will soon replace oil as the economic resource most treasured by nations of the world. However, that assertion would prove difficult to defend and may not be true at all. Rather, we need to look elsewhere, at human behavior, and at human responsibility for preserving the environment for our children.

Accordingly, the water crisis calls for examination of the issues with regard to supply and demand, the political power struggles that are emerging, and the ethical and perhaps even moral implications engulfing the world's scattered supply of fresh water.

A brief review of the literature reveals the extent of the complications. On one side we have the scientific community, as represented by Sandra Postel with articles in BioScience and her book entitled Last Oasis: Facing Water Scarcity, and by Mark Townsend in the journal Geographical. On another side we have the religious element of water, as presented by such articles as "The Liquid of the Gods" by Camille Talkeu Tounounga and "Sacred Land Film Project" by Christopher McLeod in Earth Island Journal.

The writer provides a brief review of the literature on the topic in the next two paragraphs.

Then there are the local environmental issues, such as Michael Misner's "Wild Wetlands of New York," which describes the urban wildlife preserve in Jamaica Bay near New York City, and "The End of Lake Powell" in Earth First! And in International Wildlife, Don Hinrichsen writes, "Down to the Last Drop—The Fate of Wildlife Is Linked to Water, But Too Many People Are Sucking It Up." As you might also expect, we have political commentators, such as Sandra K. Davis in The Social Science Journal, who writes on "The Politics of Water Scarcity in the Western States," and Ines Capdevila, with "Rising Population Faces Shrinking Water Supply" in Insight on the News.

The jungle of fragmentation seems bewildering as special interest groups advance their agenda--wildlife, irrigation, ecology, sanitation, hygiene, and so forth. Ultimately, the world community must come together, find answers, develop water resources across the entire earth, and the momentum for such a

Here Berkowitz establishes his thesis for the paper, which will be echoed in his final paragraph.

Berkowitz 3

revolution may be the responsibility and the task of the youth, not the established political base.

First, we should examine the shortages of water in key places around the globe. To begin, Table 1 displays the water of the earth and its distribution. As this chart from the Department

For tables, type both label and caption flush left on separate lines above the table in capital letters as in a title (not in all capital letters).

Table 1

Water Supply of the World

	Surface area (sq mi)	Volume (cu mi)	Percentage of total
Salt water			
The oceans	139,500,000	317,000,000	97.2%
Inland seas and saline lakes	270,000	25,000	0.008
Fresh water			
Freshwater lakes	330,000	30,000	0.009
All rivers (average level)	--	300	0.0001
Antarctic ice cap	6,000,000	6,300,000	1.9
Arctic ice cap and glaciers	900,000	680,000	0.21
Water in the atmosphere	197,000,000	3,100	0.001
Groundwater within half a mile of surface	--	1,000,000	0.31
Deep-lying ground water	--	1,000,000	0.31
Total (rounded)	--	326,000,000	100.00

Source: Department of the Interior, Geological Survey (Washington: GPO, 2002); rpt. in Science. 4 May 2003 <http://www.factmonster.com/ipka/Aooo4674.html>.

Give the source of a table below the table.

Berkowitz 4

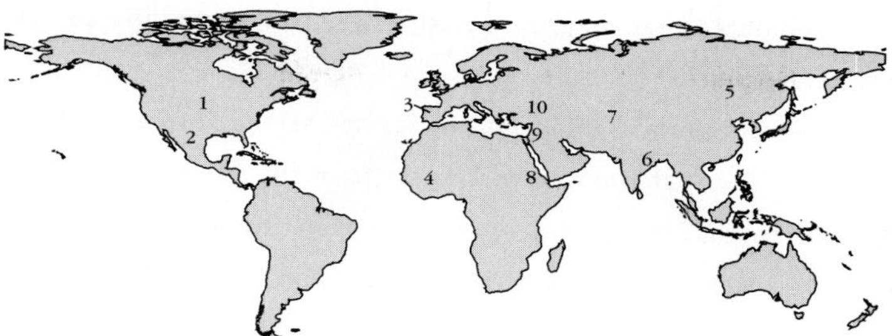

Fig. 1 Water problem Spots: My sketch that shows 10 water flashpoints around the globe.

A line drawing, photograph, map, or graph should be labeled *Figure*, usually abbreviated, assigned a number, and given a caption or title: "Fig. 12: Moon stones." The label appears below the figure.

of the Interior shows, the fresh water available for human consumption is only one-third of 1 percent of the total supply of water. The salt water of the oceans makes up the majority, 97.2 percent. The Antarctic ice cap holds an enormous amount of fresh water, 1.9 percent, but it is far removed from areas of need. BBC News warns that the "world's supply of fresh water is running out." The news bureau makes this assertion: "Already one person in five has no access to safe drinking water." Thus, we need to examine briefly ten regions that have been identified as crisis centers (BBC News, "World Water Crisis"). Figure 1 shows these locations.

1. The Ogallala, which is North America's largest aquifer (an underground bed) that stretches from Nebraska to Colorado, Kansas, Oklahoma, New Mexico, and down into Texas. According to BBC News, it is "being depleted at a rate of 12 billion cubic metres (bcm) a year" (BBC News). That equals the annual flow of the Colorado River 18 times. The High Plains of America are in trouble.
2. Mexico City, which is slowly sinking because of water pumped from under its foundations. It was at one time a land of lakes with cities built on islands, but now this large city, over

A numbered list in the text corresponds to the numbers in Figure 1.

populated, has reached a crisis--the "risk of running out of clean water" (BBC News).

3. In Cantalonia, Spain, authorities are asking France to allow a pipeline that would divert water from the Rhone River to Barcelona. It would give relief to 4.5 million people.
4. West Africa suffers massive shortages in Ghana, Mali, and Nigeria.
5. China's northern plain has three severely polluted rivers that are in danger of running dry, and the Yellow River was dry for 226 days in 1997.
6. In India, the sacred Ganges River is depleted and contains, in places, dangerous levels of arsenic.
7. The Aral Sea in Kazakhstan, Central Asia, at one time was the fourth-largest lake in the world, but its water level has dropped 16 meters, it is polluted, and the region now has high infant mortality rates.
8. The Nile River feeds Cairo and Egypt, but it also runs through Ethiopia and Sudan, two countries that could swallow the fresh water before it gets to Cairo. War looms if that happens.
9. The Middle East, already a hotbed of political differences, has tensions over fresh water usage from the River Jordan, the River Litani, and the Sea of Galilee. Any truce between the Palestine and Israel needs to include water rights.
10. Turkey has built dams along the Euphrates and Tigris rivers, to the anger of Syria and Iraq, denying those two countries of fully flowing rivers. Turkey also has plans for selling its water to parched countries in the Middle East.

Those ten spots are identified as the worst, but many others exist. The waters of the Colorado River, for example, are now totally absorbed by the basin's demand from ranches and farms, Las Vegas, and southern California. Twenty-five million people

Berkowitz 6

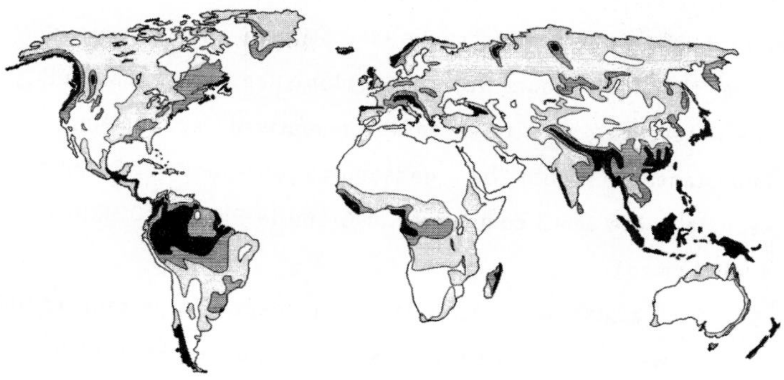

Fig. 2 The World's Renewable Water Supply showing annual precipitation minus evaporation from driest in white to the wettest in black with two degrees of gray in between, from Atlas of World Water Balance (Paris: UNESCO, 1977); rpt. in Postel 26.

are "plumbed into its system," more than twenty dams store its rich resources, yet at the very end of the river bed nothing is left; not even a trickle reaches the Gulf of California (Sprig 24).

After tracing that gloomy picture of the water shortages, we should also look at the supply side. Canada lucked out with about 20 percent of the world's supply of fresh water (O'Malley and Bowman), but that depends "on how one defines 'freshwater'--whether it means 'available,' 'usable,' or merely 'existing.'" Brazil, Russia, portions of China, and the Antarctic ice cap are other rich sources of water. See Figure 2 drawn from Atlas of World Water Balance. The United States has an abundance, thanks to the Great Lakes. The abundance in some places and scarcity in others provokes this question: Can those with plenty somehow share with others?

Make a reference in the text to any table or figure provided nearby and on the same page if possible.

Canada has become the focus of the debate on sharing water, which centers on the story of one man--Gerry White. According to reports by Martin O'Malley and John Bowman, White is trying to sell water from Newfoundland's Gisborne Lake. He would skim each week from the lake 500,000 cubic meters of water that in 10 hours would be replenished. Shipped in bulk, the water would give relief to water-deprived nations. More importantly, it would "be a godsend to jobs-poor Newfoundland, especially the small community of Grand le Pierre" (O'Malley and Bowman).

Such a plan seems more than reasonable. Large tankers full of fresh water could sail the seas with the oil tankers. At least when one of them cracked open, we'd only have a "water" spill. However, like so many good ideas--and Newfoundland embraced the idea wholeheartedly--opposition quickly appeared. Environmentalists argue that water is a "vital resource" like air (but not like oil, gas, or timber) and therefore cannot be sold else it become a "commodity." As a commodity it would be subject to the terms of the General Agreement on Tariffs and Trade (GATT) and the North American Free Trade Agreement (NAFTA). At the same time, Marq de Villiers, a Canadian who won a Governor General's Award for nonfiction with his book Water, says the international demand for Canadian water does not exist and that collecting and shipping the water would be "far more expensive than drinkable water recovered by new-generation desalination plants" (qtd. in O'Malley and Bowman). He even declares, "Water is not an issue."

Berkowitz explores the contentious problems facing those who have water and those who do not.

While the two sides debate, the premier of Newfoundland, Roger Grimes, thinks Newfoundland might "go it alone and damn the federal torpedoes" (qtd. in O'Malley and Bowman). So while one side says water is not an issue, Mayor Fizzard of Grand Le Pierre would welcome an economic boost from Lake Gisborne's rich supply of water.

The water is needed, and it is an issue. Gar Smith in "Water Wars, Water Cures" reports that Saudi Arabia purchases half of its

Berkowitz 8

water, Israel buys 87 percent of its water, and Jordan imports 91 percent (30). Smith predicts, "In another 25 years, 48 countries with more than one-third of the world's population will suffer from water starvation."

The political implications are obvious. Each nation with water will resist selling even though natural resources have been sold for years. In fact, timber sales have contributed to the disappearance of rain forests. Turkey talks like it will sell water. Major corporations are moving in and may corner the market--Bechtel (U.S.), Vivendi Universal (France), RWE/Thames (Germany/UK)--with financial help from the World Bank (Sprig). The world economy is such that a need will be met--for a price! That price may put poorer countries in peril, but the distribution is coming.

The writer explores both the political and ethical implications of water issues.

The ethical implications are something entirely different. What responsibilities do the rich nations, especially the United States, have to assure the fair and equitable distribution of water resources? Some might say that the economic forces will solve the problem, but that probably means the rich will capitalize. Meanwhile, the poor mother in Basra or New Delhi will still walk for miles in hopes of filling a jug to carry home for her children. Environmentalist Ray Dasmann puts it like this:

> We know how to solve these problems, without a doubt. To begin with, I believe we must restore a sense of individual responsibility and involvement, and get away from the idea that conservation is the responsibility of somebody else—the federal government, the state, the corporations, the rich. We must each face up to the need to develop an ecologically sustainable way of living; we need to look at our patterns of consumption and behavior, and shed those practices that contribute to the continuing destruction of nature. (48)

The page reference for an indented quotation goes outside the final period.

Berkowitz 9

Global warming is a fact, not a myth. Desertification continues and cannot correct itself without worldwide conservation. Americans consume an average of 300-plus liters of water per day per capita while the average person needs only 20 to 40 liters (O'Malley and Bowman). Postel reminds us that water is "a living system that drives the workings of a natural world we depend on" (Last Oasis 19). She declares: "A new water era has begun" (24). The great prairies of the world will dry up, including America's. When Americans notice the drought, then maybe something will happen. Meanwhile, a massive amount of water is locked in glaciers.

Berkowitz reaffirms his thesis in the final paragraph.

We young people have an ethical obligation to do small things now and anticipate the day when we will have political clout, maybe even by holding public office. For now, we can endorse electric automobiles, use less water, be politically active by joining conservation groups (see the Appendix, pages 10–11), and most of all by spreading the word--water is abundant in certain places but some have not a drop to drink.

Berkowitz 10

Appendix

Ways to Get Involved

An appendix is the place for extra information that is not germane to the principle discussion. Begin it on a new page.

1. **EarthWatch Institute** offers a rich program of activities that take small groups around the world for field research and humanitarian programs. Most teams are composed of 6 to 10 people, and the share of your cost for the trip ranges from $1,000 up to $5,000.

    There are fifteen or so expeditions for the various continents--Africa, Asia, Central America/Caribbean, Europe,

Berkowitz 11

North America, Australia/New Zealand, and South America. Most trips are for two weeks. Here are just three of 122 field trips for 2003:

- South African Penguins: Team size 4; Rendezvous site: Cape Town, South Africa; Cost $1,950; Task is to tag and monitor a threatened penguin population.
- Guatemala's Ancient Maya: Team size 10; Rendezvous site: Guatemala City, Guatemala; Cost $1,995; Task is to survey and map Mayan mounds near Chocola.
- Jackson Hole Bison Dig: Team size 12; Rendezvous site: Jackson Hole, Wyoming; Cost $1,595; Task is excavation, mapping, sorting, labeling, and documenting artifacts uncovered at the site of prehistoric bison kills. Visit EarthWatch Institute at <www.earthwatch.org>.

2. **Earth Island Journal** hosts an annual SolFest, which celebrates the sun, renewable energy, and sustainable living. It's held each year in August at the Real Goods Solar Living Center 90 minutes north of San Francisco. Check it out at <www.solfest.org>.
3. **Earth First magazine** sponsors numerous action camps throughout the year and all across the nation, such as nonviolent activities to protect the flora and fauna as well as the forests and wetlands. Visit this site at <www.earthfirstjournal.org>.
4. **World Water Day** is held on March 22 of each year. The United National Environment Program was the leading agency for World Water Day 2003, held in Kyoto, Japan. The goal is to inspire political and community action and encourage greater global understanding of the need for more responsible water use and conservation. Visit this site at <www.worldwaterday.org>.

Berkowitz 12

Begin the Works Cited on a new page.

Works Cited

A source from a library's electronic database.

Capdevila, Ines. "Rising Population Faces Shrinking Water Supply." Insight on the News 16 (2000): 30- . Expanded Academic ASAP. InfoTrac. Vanderbilt U, Heard Lib. 9 Apr. 2003 <http://www.galegroup.com/>.

An interview found in a journal.

Dasmann, Ray. "Voices." Interview with David Kupfer. Earth Island Journal 18 (2003): 48.

Davis, Sandra K. "The Politics of Water Scarcity in the Western States." The Social Science Journal 38 (2002): 527- . Expanded Academic ASAP. InfoTrac. Vanderbilt U, Heard Lib. 9 Apr. 2003 <http://www.galegroup.com/>.

Hinrichsen, Don. "Down to the Last Drop: The Fate of Wildlife Is Linked to Water, But Too Many People Are Sucking It Up." International Wildlife Nov.-Dec. 2001. Expanded Academic ASAP. InfoTrac. Vanderbilt U, Heard Lib. 9 Apr. 2003 <http://www.galegroup.com/>.

An article from an academic journal.

McLeod, Christopher. "Sacred Land Film Project." Earth Island Journal 18 (2003): 16-17.

Misner, Michael. "Wild Wetland of New York." Earth Island Journal 18 (2003): 46-47.

O'Malley, Martin, and John Bowman. "Selling Canada's Water." CBC News Online. June 2001. 9 Apr. 2003 <http://www.cbc.ca/news/indepth/water/>.

Postel, Sandra L. Last Oasis: Facing Water Scarcity. New York: Norton, 1992.

When a writer has two works, use three hyphens after the first in place of the name.

---. "Water for Food Production: Will There Be Enough in 2925?" BioScience 48 (1998): 629-. Expanded Academic ASAP. InfoTrac. Vanderbilt U, Heard Lib. 9 Apr. 2003 <http://www.galegroup.com/>.

No author listed.

"Research Expeditions 2003." EarthWatch Institute 21 (2003): 8-85.

Berkowitz 13

Sprig, [no first name listed]. "The End of Lake Powell." Earth First! 1 May 2003: 24-25.

Smith, Gar. "Water Wars, Water Cures." Earth Island Journal 15 (2000): 30-32.

Tounounga, Camile Taldeu. "The Liquid of the Gods." UNESCO Courier May 1993: 38-39.

Townsend, Mark. "Water Fight Is Looming: Water--Or the Lack of It--Threatens to Become One of the Single Biggest Factors Opposing World Peace." Geographical 74 (2002): 10- . Expanded Academic ASAP. InfoTrac. Vanderbilt U, Heard Lib. 9 Apr. 2003 <http://www.galegroup.com/>.

"World Water Crisis." BBC News. 2000. 9 Apr. 2003 <http://news.bbc.co.uk/hi/english/static/in_depth/world/2000/world_water_crisis/default.stm>.

"World Water Day." IRC International Water and Sanitation Centre. 2003. 9 Apr. 2003 <http://www.worldwaterday.org/>.

Use brackets to insert your words.

Internet sources require the date of access preceding the URL.

17 Works Cited: MLA Style

After writing your paper, you should begin to finalize your Works Cited page to list your reference materials. List only those sources actually used in your manuscript, including works mentioned within content endnotes and in captions to tables and illustrations. Preparing the Works Cited will be relatively simple if you carefully developed your working bibliography as a computer file. It will be difficult only if you have not kept publication data on each source cited in the paper.

> Sample Works Cited pages, Chapter 16.
> Sample annotated bibliography, Chapter 10.

Keep in mind that others might use your bibliography for research of their own. A documentation system, such as the MLA style, gives all scholars in the field a consistent way to consult the sources. Inaccurate records might prevent an easy retracing of your steps.

Select a heading that indicates the nature of your list.

Works Cited for a list of works including books, articles, films, recordings, Internet sources, and so on that are quoted or paraphrased in the research paper.

Works Consulted if your list includes nonprint items such as interviews, letters, or speeches as well as printed works.

Annotated Bibliography for a list of references that includes a description of the contents of each source (see pages 252–254).

Selected Bibliography for a list of readings on the subject.

> Other bibliography forms:
> APA, Chapter 18;
> CMS footnote style, Chapter 19;
> CSE number style, Chapter 20.

Works pertinent to the paper but not quoted or paraphrased, such as an article on related matters, can be mentioned in a content endnote (see pages 482–485) and then listed in the Works Cited.

Formatting the Works Cited Page

Arrange items in alphabetic order by the surname of the author using the letter-by-letter system. Ignore spaces in the author's surname. Consider the first names only when two or more surnames are identical. Note how the following examples are alphabetized letter by letter.

Bandercloth, Morgan
Dempsey, William R.
Lawrence, Jacob
Lawrence, Melissa
McPherson, James Alan
Saint-Exupéry, Antoine de
St. James, Christopher

When two or more entries cite coauthors that begin with the same name, alphabetize by the last names of the second authors:

Huggins, Marjorie, and Devan Blythe
Huggins, Marjorie, and Stephen Fisher

When no author is listed, alphabetize by the first important word of the title. Imagine lettered spelling for unusual items. For example, "#2 Red Dye" should be alphabetized as though it were "Number 2 Red Dye."

The list of sources may also be divided into separate alphabetized sections for primary and secondary sources, for different media (articles, books, Internet sources), for different subject matter (biography, autobiography, letters), for different periods (Neoclassic period, Romantic period), and for different areas (German viewpoints, French viewpoints, American viewpoints).

Place the first line of each entry flush with the left margin and indent succeeding lines one inch—which is usually one tab space on the computer or five spaces. Double-space each entry, and double-space between entries. Use one space after periods and other marks of punctuation.

Set the title "Works Cited" one inch down from the top of the sheet and double-space between it and the first entry. A sample page is illustrated below.

> **HINT:** Check your instructor's preference before using italics in place of underlining. If in doubt, use underlining because it prevents ambiguity by its distinctive marking of words and titles.

Masterson 12

Works Cited

Amato, Peter. "Hobbes, Darwinism, and Conceptions of Human Nature." Minerva: An Internet Journal of Philosophy 6 (2002). 22 Sept. 2003 <http://www.ul.ie/~philos/vol6/hobbes.html>.

Boyd, Robert, and Joan B. Silk. How Humans Evolved. 3rd ed. New York: Norton, 2003.

Campbell, Joseph. The Hero with a Thousand Faces. New York: Fine, 1996.

---, The Masks of God. 4 vols. New York: Viking, 1970.

Ehringhaus, Susan, and David Korn. "Conflicts of Interest in Human Subjects Research." Issues in Science and Technology Online 19.2 (2002). 20 Sept. 2003 <http://www.nap.edu/issues/19.2/ ehringhaus.htm>.

Jenkins, Philip. "Catch Me before I Kill More: Seriality as Modern Monstrosity." Cultural Analysis 3 (2002). 20 Sept. 2003 <http://socrates.berkeley.edu/%7Ecaforum/volume3/ vol_article1.html>.

Kourany, Janet A. "A Philosophy of Science for the Twenty-First Century." Philosophy of Science 70.1 (2003): 1-14.

Martin, Thomas R. "Religion, Myth, and Community." An Overview of Classical Greek History from Homer to Alexander. 3 Apr. 1999. 18 Sept. 2003 <http:// www.Perseus.tufts.edu/cgi-bin/ ptext?doc=Parsees%Adeste%3A1999.04.0009%3Ahead%3D%2328>.

Morford, Mark P. O., and Robert J. Lenardon. Classical Mythology. 7th ed. New York: Oxford UP, 2002.

"North American Mythology." 20 Aug. 2002. 17 Sept. 2003 <http://www.mythome.org/NorthAm.html>.

Index to Bibliographic Models: MLA Style

Bibliography Form—Books

Author's Name 391

Author, Anonymous 391

Author, Anonymous but Name Supplied 391

Author, Pseudonymous but Name Supplied 392

Author, Listed by Initials with Name Supplied 392

Authors, Two 392

Authors, Three 392

Authors, More Than Three 392

Author, Corporation or Institution 392

Author, Two or More Books by the Same Author 393

Author, Two or More Books by the Same Authors 393

Alphabetized Works, Encyclopedias, and Biographical Dictionaries 393

Anthology, Component Part 394

Index to Bibliographic Models: MLA Style

The Bible 395

A Book Published before 1900 395

Chapter or Part of a Book 396

Classical Works 396

Collection, Component Part 396

Cross-References to Works in a Collection 396

Edition 397

Editor, Translator, Illustrator, or Compiler 398

Encyclopedia and Reference Book 398

Introduction, Preface, Foreword, Afterword 398

Manuscript or Typescript 399

Page Number(s) to a Section of a Book 399

Play, Classical 399

Play, Modern 400

Poem, Classical 400

Poem, Modern Collection 400

Publication Information: Place, Publisher, and Date 401

Republished Book 402

Screenplay 402

Series, Numbered and Unnumbered 402

Sourcebooks and Casebooks 403

Title of the Book 403

Title of a Book in Another Language 403

Translator 404

Volumes 404

Bibliography Form—Periodicals

Abstract in an Abstracts Journal 405

Author 406

Author, Anonymous 406

Interview, Published 406

Journal, with All Issues for a Year Paged Continuously 406

Journal, with Each Issue Paged Anew 406

Loose-Leaf Collection 407

Magazine 407

Microform 408

Name of the Periodical 408

Notes, Editorials, Queries, Reports, Comments, Letters 408

Reprint of a Journal Article 409

Review in a Magazine, Newspaper, or Journal 409

Series 409

Special Issue 410

Speech or Address, Published 410

Title of the Article 410

Title, Quotation within the Article's Title 410

Title, within the Article's Title 410

Index to Bibliographic Models: MLA Style

Title, Foreign 410

Volume, Issue, and Page Numbers for Journals 411

Bibliography Form—Newspapers

Newspaper in One Section 411

Newspaper with Lettered Sections 411

Newspaper with Numbered Sections 411

Newspaper Editorial with No Author Listed 412

Newspaper Column, Cartoon, Comic Strip, Advertisement, Etc. 412

Newspaper Article with City Added 412

Newspaper Edition or Section 412

Newspaper in a Foreign Language 412

Bibliography Form—Government Documents

Congressional Papers 413

Executive Branch Documents 413

Documents of State Governments 414

Legal Citations and Public Statutes 414

Bibliography Form—Internet Sources

Citing Sources Found on the Internet 414

World Wide Web Sites 415

Abstract 415

Advertisement 415

Anonymous Article 415

Archive or Scholarly Project 415

Article from an Online Magazine 415

Article from a Scholarly Journal 416

Article Written for the Internet 416

Audio Program Online 416

Cartoon 416

Chapter or Portion of a Book 416

Article at a Library's Online Service with a Listed URL 416

Article with Only a Starting Page Number of the Original Print Version 417

Article from an Online Service to Which You Personally Subscribe 417

Article from an Online Service with an Unlisted or Scrambled URL 417

Article at a Library's Online Service with No URL listed 417

E-mail 418

Encyclopedia Article Online 418

ERIC Database 418

Film, Video, or Film Clip Online 418

FTP, TELNET, and GOPHER Sites 418

Home Page for a Course 418

Index to Bibliographic Models: MLA Style

Home Page for an Academic Department 419

Home Page for a Personal Web Site 419

Home Page for an Academic Site 419

Interview 419

Journal Article 419

Letter 419

Linkage Data (An Accessed File) 419

Manuscript 420

Map 420

MOO, MUD, and Other Chat Rooms 420

Newsgroup, Usenet News, Forum 420

Newsletter 420

Newspaper Article, Column, Editorial 421

Novel or Book Online 421

Online Posting for E-mail Discussion Groups 421

Photo, Painting, Sculpture 421

Poem, Song, or Story 422

Review 422

Report 422

Serialized Article 422

Song 422

Sound Clip or Audio Recording 422

Story 423

Synchronous Communication 423

Television or Radio Program 423

University Posting, Online Article 423

Video 423

Web Site, General Reference 423

Work in an Indeterminate Medium 423

Working Papers 423

Bibliography Form—Sources Found on CD-ROM

Full-Text Articles with Publication Information for the Printed Source 424

Full-Text Articles with No Publication Information for a Printed Source 424

Complete Books and Other Publications on CD-ROM 425

Abstracts to Books and Articles Provided on CD-ROM by National Distributors 425

Nonperiodical Publication on CD-ROM, Diskette, or Magnetic Tape 426

Encyclopedia Article 426

Multidisc Publication 426

Bibliography Form—Other Electronic Sources

Citing a Source You Access in More Than One Medium 426

Citing a Source Found on an Online Database 427

Bibliography Form—Other Sources

Advertisement 427

Art work 427

Bulletin 428

Cartoon 428

Index to Bibliographic Models: MLA Style

Computer Software 429
Conference Proceedings 429
Dissertation, Published 429
Dissertation, Unpublished 429
Film, Videocassette, or DVD 429
Interview 430
Lecture 430
Letter, Personal 430
Letter, Published 430
Loose-Leaf Collections 431
Manuscripts (ms.) and typescripts (ts.) 431
Map 431
Microfilm or Microfiche 431
Miscellaneous Materials (Program, Leaflet, Poster, Announcement) 432
Musical Composition 432
Pamphlet 432
Performance 432
Public Address or Lecture 433
Recording on Record, Tape, or Disk 433
Report 434
Reproductions, Photographs, and Photocopies 434
Table, Illustration, Chart, or Graph 434
Television or Radio Program 434
Thesis 435
Transparency 435
Unpublished Paper 435
Voice Mail 435

Bibliography Form—Books

Enter information for books in the following order. Items 1, 3, and 8 are usually required; add other items according to the circumstances explained in the text that follows.

1. Author(s)
2. Chapter or part of book
3. Title of the book
4. Editor, translator, or compiler
5. Edition
6. Number(s) of volume(s) used
7. Name of the series
8. Place, publisher, and date
9. Page numbers
10. Extra bibliographic information

The following list in alphabetical order explains and gives examples of the correct form for books.

Author's Name

List the author's name, surname first, followed by given name or initials, and then a period:

Winchester, Simon. Krakatoa. New York: Harper, 2003.

Always give authors' names in the fullest possible form—for example, "Grierson, Robert A." rather than "Grierson, R. A."—unless, as indicated on the title page of the book, the author prefers initials. However, APA style (see Chapter 18) requires last name and initials only (e.g., Grierson, R. A.). If you spell out an abbreviated name, put square brackets around the material added:

Lewis, C[live] S[taples].

With pseudonyms you may add the real name, enclosing the addition in brackets.

Carroll, Lewis [Charles Lutwidge Dodgson].

Omit titles, affiliations, and degrees that appear with the author's name on the title page.

If the title page says:	*In the Works Cited use:*
Sir Edmund Hillary	Hillary, Edmund
Sister Margaret Nelson	Nelson, Margaret
Barton O'Connor, Ph.D.	O'Connor, Barton

However, do provide an essential suffix that is part of a person's name:

Justin, Walter, Jr.
Peterson, Robert J., III

Author, Anonymous

Begin with the title. Do not use *anonymous* or *anon.* Alphabetize by the title, ignoring initial articles, *A, An,* or *The.*

The Song of Roland. Trans. W. S. Merwin. New York: Random, 2001.

Author, Anonymous But Name Supplied

Alphabetize by the supplied name, set in square brackets.

[Madison, James.] All Impressments Unlawful and Inadmissible. Boston: Pelham, 1804.

Author, Pseudonymous But Name Supplied

Slender, Robert [Freneau, Philip]. Letters on Various and Important Subjects. Philadelphia: Hogan, 1799.

Author, Listed by Initials with Name Supplied

Rowling, J[oanne] K[athleen]. Harry Potter and the Order of the Phoenix. New York: Scholastic, 2003.

Authors, Two

Loehr, Jim, and Tony Schwartz. The Power of Full Engagement. New York: Free, 2003.

Authors, Three

Be sure to list the authors in the same order they appear on the title page.

Slywotzky, Adrian, Richard Wise, and Karl Weber. How to Grow When Markets Don't. New York: Warner, 2003.

Authors, More Than Three

Use "et al.," which means "and others," or list all the authors. See the two examples that follow:

Clark, Duncan, et al. Classical Music. 3rd ed. New York: Rough, 2001.

Senge, Peter, Nelda Cambron-McCabe, Timothy Lucas, Bryan Smith, Janis Dutton, and Art Kleiner. Schools That Learn. New York: Doubleday, 2000.

Author, Corporation or Institution

A corporate author can be an association, a committee, or any group or institution when the title page does not identify the names of the members.

American Medical Association. Health Professions Career and Education Directory 2003-2004. New York: Random, 2003.

List a corporation as the author even when the organization is also the publisher, as in this example:

Consumer Reports. Best Buys for Your Home. New York: Consumer Reports, 2003.

Author, Two or More Books by the Same Author

When your works cited page includes two or more works by the same author, give the name in the first entry only. Thereafter, insert a continuous three-hyphen line flush with the left margin, followed by a period. Also, list the works alphabetically by the title (ignoring *a, an,* and *the*), not by the year of publication. In the following example, the *B* of *Bird's-Eye* precedes the *K* of *Key.*

Freedman, J. F. Above the Law. New York: Signet, 2001.

---. Bird's-Eye View. New York: Warner, 2001.

---. Key Witness. New York: Signet, 1998.

The three hyphens stand for exactly the same name(s) as in the preceding entry. However, do not substitute three hyphens for an author who has two or more works in the bibliography when one is written in collaboration with someone else:

Sagan, Carl. Contact. New York: Pocket, 1997.

---. Cosmos. New York: Ballantine, 1985.

Sagan, Carl, and Ann Druyan. Shadows of Forgotten Ancestors: A Search for Who We Are. New York: Random, 1993.

If the person edited, compiled, or translated the work that follows on the list, place a comma after the three hyphens and write *ed., comp.*, or *trans.* before you give the title. This label does not affect the alphabetic order by title.

Finneran, Richard J. Editing Yeats's Poems. New York: St. Martin's, 1983.

---, ed. Yeats Reader. New York: Scribner, 2002.

Author, Two or More Books by the Same Multiple Authors

When you cite two or more books by the same multiple authors, provide the names in the first entry only. Thereafter, use three hyphens, followed by a period.

Axelrod, Rise B., and Charles R. Cooper. Concise Guide to Writing. 3rd ed. Boston: St. Martin's, 2002.

---. Reading Critically, Writing Well. 6th ed. Boston: St. Martin's, 2002.

Alphabetized Works, Encyclopedias, and Biographical Dictionaries

Treat works arranged alphabetically as you would an anthology or collection, but omit the name of the editor(s), the volume number, place of publication, publisher, and page number(s). If the author is listed, begin the entry with the author's name; otherwise, begin with the title of the article. If the article is signed with initials, look elsewhere in the work for a complete name. Well-known works, such as the first two examples that follow, need only the edition and the year of publication.

"Kiosk: Word History." The American Heritage Dictionary of the English Language. 4th ed. 2000.

Moran, Joseph. "Weather." The World Book Encyclopedia. 2003 ed.

If you cite a specific definition from among several, add *Def.* (Definition), followed by the appropriate number/letter of the definition.

"Level." Def. 4a. The American Heritage Dictionary of the English Language. 4th ed. 2000.

Less-familiar reference works need a full citation, as shown in this next example:

"Infections." The American Medical Association Family Medical Guide. Ed. Charles B. Clayman. New York: Random, 1994.

Place within quotation marks the titles of a synopsis or description of a novel or drama when that title is the name of the entry in the alphabetized reference book, even though it would normally be underscored or italicized.

"Oedipus the King." The Compact Bedford Introduction to Literature. Ed. Michael Meyer. Boston: St. Martin's, 2003. 975-76.

Anthology, Component Part

In general, works in an anthology have been published previously and collected by an editor. Supply the names of authors as well as editors. Almost always cite the author first. Many times the prior publication data on a specific work may not be readily available; therefore, use this form:

Reagon, Bernice. "Black Music in Our Hands." The Conscious Reader. Eds. Caroline Shrodes, Harry Finestone, and Michael Shugrue. 8th ed. Boston: Allyn, 2001. 345-49.

> If you use several works from the same anthology, you can shorten the citation by using cross references; see "Cross-References," on pages 396–397.

Provide the inclusive page numbers for the piece, not just the page or pages you cited in the text.

Use the following form if you can quickly identify original publication information. Note that the page numbers in the *The New Yorker* were unavailable in the reprint:

"Soup." The New Yorker. Jan. 1989: n.p. Rpt. in The St. Martin's Guide to Writing. Eds. Rise B. Axelrod and Charles R. Cooper. Short 6th ed. Boston: Bedford, 2001. 132-34.

Conform to the rules given in these examples:

Elder, Lonne. "Ceremonies in Dark Old Men." New Black Playwrights: An Anthology. Ed. William Couch, Jr. Baton Rouge: Louisiana State UP, 1968. 55-72.

If you cite material from a chapter of one volume in a multivolume set, write an entry like these:

Child, Harold. "Jane Austen." The Cambridge History of English Literature. Ed. A. W. Ward and A. R. Waller. Vol. 12. London: Cambridge UP, 1927.

Although not required, you may also provide the total number of volumes:

Saintsbury, George. "Dickens." The Cambridge History of English Literature. Ed. A. W. Ward and A. R. Waller. Vol. 13. New York: Putnam's, 1917. 14 vols.

The Bible

Do not underscore or italicize the word *Bible* or the books of the Bible. Common editions need no publication information, but do underscore or italicize special editions of the Bible.

The Bible. [Denotes King James version]

The Bible. The Old Testament. CD-ROM. Audio Bible, 2003.

The Bible. Revised Standard Version.

The Geneva Bible. 1560. Facsim. rpt. Madison: U of Wisconsin P, 1961.

NIV [New International Version] Study Bible. Personal Size Rev. Ed. n.p.: Zondervan, 2002.

A Book Published before 1900

For older books that are now out of print, you may omit the publisher. Use a comma, not a colon, to separate the place of publication from the year. If no date is listed, use "n.d." If no place of publication is mentioned, use "n.p."

Dewey, John. The School and Society. Chicago, 1899.

Chapter or Part of a Book

List a chapter or part of a book on the Works Cited page only when it is separately edited, translated, or written. For example, if you quote from a specific chapter of a book, let's say Chapter 6 of Brian Hall's book, the entry should read:

Hall, Brian. I Should Be Extremely Happy in Your Company: A Novel of Lewis and Clark. New York: Viking, 2003.

Your in-text citation will have listed specific page numbers, so there is no reason to mention a specific chapter, even though it is the only portion of Hall's book that you read.

Classical Works

Homer. The Odyssey. Trans. Stanley Lombardo. Indianapolis: Hackett, 2000.

You are more likely to find a classic work in an anthology, which would require this citation:

Homer. The Odyssey. Trans. Robert Fitzgerald. The Norton Anthology of World Masterpieces. Ed. Maynard Mack, et al. New York: Norton, 1997. 96-336.

Collection, Component Part

If you cite from one work in a collection of works by the same author, provide the specific name of the work and the corresponding page numbers. This next entry cites one story from a collection of stories by the same author:

Sedaris, David. "Next of Kin." Naked. Boston: Back Bay, 1997. 40-45.

Cross-References to Works in a Collection

If you are citing several selections from one anthology or collection, provide a full reference to the anthology (as explained on pages 394–395) and then provide references to the individual selections by providing the author and title of the work, the last name of the editor of the collection, and the inclusive page numbers used from the anthology.

Elbow, Peter, and Pat Belanoff. Being a Writer. Boston: McGraw, 2003.

Koo, Eunsook. "Exploring the Writing Process." Elbow and Belanoff 181.

Spencer, Beth. "The Act of Writing as Prayer." Elbow and Belanoff 126–28.

Wilbur, Richard. "The Writer." Elbow and Belanoff 220.

Note also the following examples in which the first entry refers to the one that follows:

Eliot, George. "Art and Belles Lettres." Westminster Review. USA ed. April 1856. Partly rpt. Eliot, A Writer's Notebook.

---. A Writer's Notebook, 1854-1879, and Uncollected Writings. Ed. Joseph Wiesenfarth. Charlottesville: UP of Virginia, 1981.

Add an abbreviated title to the cross-reference if you list two or more works under the editor's name.

Angelou, Maya. "Uncle Willie." Axelrod and Cooper, Guide 82-86.

Axelrod, Rise B., and Charles R. Cooper. Reading Critically, Writing Well. 5th ed. New York: St. Martin's, 1999.

---. The St. Martin's Guide to Writing. Short 6th ed. Boston: Bedford, 1997.

Forster, E. M. "My Wood." Axelrod and Cooper, Reading 111-14.

Wolff, Tobias. "On Being a Real Westerner." Axelrod and Cooper, Guide 33-35.

Edition

Indicate the edition used, whenever it is not the first, in Arabic numerals ("3rd ed."), by name ("Rev. ed.," "Abr. ed."), or by year ("1999 ed."), without further punctuation:

Acredolo, Linda P., Susan Goodwyn, and Douglas Abrams. Baby Signs. Rev. ed. Boston: McGraw, 2002.

Indicate that a work has been prepared by an editor, not the original author:

Melville, Herman. Moby-Dick. Ed. with Intro. by Alfred Kazin. 2nd ed. Boston: Houghton, 1956.

If you wish to show the original date of the publication, place the year immediately after the title, followed by a period. *Note:* The title of an edition in a series is capitalized.

Hardy Thomas. Far from the Madding Crowd. 1874. Ed. Rosemarie Morgan and Shannon Russell. A Penguin Classic ed. New York: Penguin, 2003.

Editor, Translator, Illustrator, or Compiler

If the name of the editor or compiler appears on the title page of an anthology or compilation, place it first:

Trappl, Robert, Sabine Payr, and Paolo Petta, eds. Emotions in Human Artifacts. Cambridge, MA: MIT P, 2003.

If your in-text citation refers to the work of the editor, illustrator, or translator (e.g., "The Ciardi edition caused debate among Dante scholars" or "The note by Bevington"), use this form with the original author listed after the work, preceded by the word *By*:

Hollander, Robert, and Jean Hollander, trans. The Purgatorio. By Dante. New York: Doubleday, 2003.

Anderson, Wayne, illus. Year of the Dragon: Legends and Lore. By Nigel Suckling. New York: Barnes, 2000.

Bevington, David, ed. The Complete Works of Shakespeare. 5th ed. New York: Longman, 2004.

The in-text citation should explain the editorial content cited, e.g. "(Bevington, 316n)." Otherwise, mention an editor *after* the title:

Yeats, W. B. Yeats Reader. Ed. Richard J. Finneran. New York: Scribner, 2002.

Encyclopedia and Reference Book

Ward, Norman. "Saskatchewan." Encyclopedia Americana. 2003 ed.

See also "Alphabetized Works, Encyclopedias, and Biographical Dictionaries" and "Citing Sources Found on CD-ROM".

Introduction, Preface, Foreword, Afterword

If you are citing the introduction to a work, start with the name of the person who wrote it if other than the author of the work itself. Give the name of the part being cited, neither underscored nor enclosed within quotation marks. Place the name of the author in normal order after the title, preceded by the word *By*. Follow with publication information and end with the inclusive page numbers.

Barkley, Charles. Foreword. The Life of Really. By Rick Really. New York: Time, 2003. 5-6.

Jamison, Kay Redfield. Introduction. Unholy Ghost. By Nell Casey. New York: Perennial, 2001. 1-7.

If the author of the work is also the author of the prefatory matter, use only the last name after the word *By*.

Takes, C. W. Prologue. Ballpark Blues. By Takes. New York: Doubleday, 2003. 1-6.

Use the form above only if you cite from the prologue and not the main text.

Manuscript or Typescript

Martin, Wesley A. "Venice at Night." Unpublished essay, 2003.

Chaucer, Geoffrey. The Canterbury Tales. Harley ms. 7334. British Lib., London.

For more details about this type of citation, see "Chapter or Part of a Book," and "Anthologies".

Page Number(s) to a Section of a Book

Cite pages to help a reader find a particular section of a book.

Coyne, Kevin. "The Home Front, 1942-1944." Marching Home. New York: Viking, 2003. 75-88.

Play, Classical

Shakespeare, William. Titus Andronicus. Ed. Thomas L. Berger. Rpt. of the 1594 ed. Shakespeare Quartos. New York: Oxford UP, 2003.

Performances of a play will include the director and, if appropriate, the actor(s).

As You Like It. By William Shakespeare. Dir. Sir Peter Hall. Shubert Theatre, New Haven, CT. 24 Oct. 2003.

Today, classical plays are usually found in anthologies, which will require this form:

Shakespeare, William. Othello, The Moor of Venice. The Norton Anthology of World Masterpieces. Ed. Sarah Lawall et al. New York: Norton, 1999. 2,115-92.

Play, Modern

Contemporary plays may be published independently or as part of a collection.

Mamet, David. Oleanna. New York: Random, 1993.

Eliot, T. S. The Cocktail Party. The Complete Poems and Plays: 1909-1950. New York: Harcourt, 1952. 295-387.

> If you cite the translator's or editor's preface or notes to the text, put the name of the translator or editor first.

Poem, Classical

Classical poems are usually translated, so you will often need to list a translator and/or editor. If the work is one part of a collection, show which anthology you used.

Dante. The Divine Comedy. Trans. John Ciardi. New York: NAL, 2003.

Dante. Inferno. The Divine Comedy. Trans. John Ciardi. The Norton Anthology of World Masterpieces. Ed. Sarah Lawall et al. New York: Norton, 1999. 1303-1429.

Poem, Modern Collection

If you cite one short poem from a collection, use this form, which cites the inclusive page numbers.

Walker, Alice. "Goddess." Absolute Trust in the Goodness of the Earth. New York: Random, 2003. 154-55.

Use this next form if you cite from one book-length poem:

Eliot, T. S. Four Quartets. The Complete Poems and Plays 1909-1950. New York: Harcourt, 1952. 115-45.

Do not cite specific poems and pages if you cite several poems of the collection. Your in-text citations should cite the specific poems and line numbers (see pages 326–329). Your Works Cited entry would then list only the name of the collection.

Eliot, T. S. The Complete Poems and Plays 1909-1950. New York: Harcourt, 1952.

Publication Information: Place, Publisher, and Date

Indicate the place of publication, the publisher, and the year of publication:

Safire, William. No Uncertain Terms. New York: Simon, 2003.

Include the abbreviation for the state or country only if necessary for clarity:

Stone, Ruth. In the Next Galaxy. Port Townsend, WA: Copper, 2002.

If more than one place of publication appears on the title page, the first city mentioned is sufficient. If successive copyright dates are given, use the most recent (unless your study is specifically concerned with an earlier, perhaps definitive, edition). A new printing does not constitute a new edition. For example, if the text has a 1940 copyright date and a 1975 printing, use 1940 unless other information is given, such as "facsimile printing" or "1975 third printing rev."

Bell, Charles Bailey, and Harriett P. Miller. The Bell Witch: A Mysterious Spirit. 1934. Facsim. ed. Nashville: Elder, 1972.

If the place, publisher, date of publication, or pages are not provided, use one of these abbreviations:

n.p.	No place of publication listed
n.p.	No publisher listed
n.d.	No date of publication listed
n. pag.	No pagination listed

Lewes, George Henry. The Life and Works of Goethe. 1855. 2 vols. Rpt. as vols. 13 and 14 of The Works J. W. von Goethe. Ed. Nathan Haskell Dole. London: Nicolls, n.d. 14 vols.

Fleiss, Heidi. "Heidi Fleiss the Antichrist." Pandering. Los Angeles: 1 Hour, 2002. N. pag.

Some abbreviations to publisher's names are listed in Appendix A.

Provide the publisher's name in a shortened form, such as "Bobbs" rather than "Bobbs-Merrill Co., Inc." A publisher's special imprint name should be joined with the official name, for example, Anchor-Doubleday, Jove-Berkley, Ace-Grossett, Del Rey-Ballantine, Mentor-NAL.

Faulkner, William. "Spotted Horses." Three Famous Short Stories. New York: Vintage-Random, 1963.

Republished Book

If you are citing from a republished book, such as a paperback version of a book published originally in hardback, provide the original publication date after the title and then provide the publication information for the book from which you are citing.

Vonnegut, Kurt. Breakfast of Champions. 1973. New York: Delta, 1999.

Although it is not required, you may wish to provide supplementary information. Give the type of reproduction to explain that the republished work is, for example, a facsimile reprinting of the text:

Hooker, Richard. Of the Lawes of Ecclesiasticall Politie. 1594. Facsim. rpt. Amsterdam: Teatrum Orbis Terrarum, 1971.

Give facts about the original publication if the information will serve the reader. In this next example, the republished book was originally published under a different title:

Arnold, Matthew. "The Study of Poetry." Essays: English and American. Ed. Charles W. Eliot. 1886. New York: Collier, 1910. Rpt. of the General Introduction to The English Poets. Ed. T. H. Ward. 1880.

Screenplay

Kaufman, Donald, and Charlie Kaufman. Adaptation. Screenplay. New York: Newmarket, 2003.

Series, Numbered and Unnumbered

If the work is one in a published series, show the name of the series, abbreviated, without quotation marks or underscoring, the number of this work in Arabic numerals, and a period:

Jefferson, D. W. " 'All, all of a piece throughout': Thoughts on Dryden's Dramatic Poetry." Restoration Theatre. Ed. J. R. Brown and Bernard Harris. Stratford-upon-Avon Studies 6. London: Arnold, 1965. 159-76.

Wallerstein, Ruth C. Richard Crashaw: A Study in Style and Poetic Development. U of Wisconsin Studies in Lang. and Lit. 37. Madison: U of Wisconsin P, 1935.

Sourcebooks and Casebooks

Elbow, Peter, and Pat Belanoff. "Reflecting on Your Writing." Being a Writer: A Community of Writers Revisited. Boston: McGraw, 2003. 329–50.

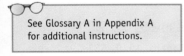

> If you cite more than one article from a casebook, use cross-references.

If you can identify the original facts of publication, include that information also:

Ellmann, Richard. "Reality." Yeats: The Man and the Masks. New York: Macmillan, 1948. Rpt. in Yeats: A Collection of Critical Essays. Ed. John Unterecker. Twentieth Century Views. Englewood Cliffs: Prentice, 1963. 163-74.

Title of the Book

Show the title of the work, underscored or italicized, followed by a period. Separate any subtitle from the primary title by a colon and one space even when the title page has no mark of punctuation or the card catalog entry has a semicolon:

Hai, LeChristine. In the Arms of Grace: One Saved Child's Journey--A Memoir of Healing. Atlanta: Univoice, 2003.

> See Glossary A in Appendix A for additional instructions.

If an underscored title to a book incorporates another title that normally receives underscoring, do not underscore or italicize the shorter title nor place it within quotation marks. In the title below, *Absalom and Acidophil* is the shorter title; it does not receive underscoring.

Schilling, Bernard N. Dryden and the Conservative Myth: A Reading of Absalom and Acidophil. New Haven: Yale UP, 1961.

Title of a Book in Another Language

In general, use lowercase letters for foreign titles except for the first major word and proper names. Provide a translation in brackets if you think it necessary (e.g., Étranger [The Stranger] or Praha [Prague]).

Eco, Umberto. La Isla Del Dia de Antes. New York: Sites, 2000.

Castex, P. G. Le rouge et le noir de Stendhal. Paris: Sedes, 1967.

Note: Le rouge et le noir is the shorter title within a long title, thus it does not receive underscoring; compare with the title at the top of the next page, which requires underscoring because there is no additional title within the title.

Levowitz-treu, Micheline. L'amour et la mort chez Stendhal. Aran: Editions du Grand Chène, 1978.

Translator

List the translator's name first only if the translator's work (preface, foreword, afterword, notes) is the focus of your study, for example, (Condé note 6).

Condé, Maryse. Segu. Trans. Barbara Bray. New York: Penguin, 1996.

Jowett, Benjamin, trans. The Republic. By Plato. Mineola, NY: Dover, 2000.

Volumes

If you are citing from only one volume of a multivolume work, provide the number of that volume in the Works Cited entry with information for that volume only. In your text, you will need to specify only page numbers—for example, (Borgese 45–46).

Borgese, Elisabeth Mann. Ocean Yearbook. Vol. 17. Chicago: U of Chicago P, 2003.

Although additional information is not required, you may provide the inclusive page numbers, the total number of volumes, and the inclusive dates of publication.

Daiches, David. "The Restoration." A Critical History of English Literature. 2nd ed. Vol. 2. New York: Ronald, 1970. 537-89. 2 vols.

If you are citing from two or more volumes of a multivolume work, your in-text citation must specify volume and page (2: 320–321); then the Works Cited entry must show the total number of volumes in Arabic numerals, as shown here:

Hersen, Michel. Comprehensive Handbook of Psychological Assessment. 4 vols. Indianapolis: Wiley, 2003.

If you are citing from volumes that were published over a period of years, provide the inclusive dates at the end of the citation. Should the volumes still be in production, write *to date* after the number of volumes and leave a space after the hyphen that follows the initial date.

Parrington, Vernon L. Main Currents in American Thought. 3 vols. New York: Harcourt, 1927-32.

Cassidy, Frederic, ed. Dictionary of American Regional English. 3 vols. to date. Cambridge: Belknap-Harvard UP, 1985- .

Handle the republishing of volumes in this manner:

Seivers, Harry J. Benjamin Harrison: Hoosier Warrior. 3 vols. 1952-68. Rpt. of vol. 1. Newtown, CT: American Political Biography Press, 1997.

If you are using only one volume of a multivolume work and the volume has an individual title, you can cite the one work without mentioning the other volumes in the set.

Crane, Stephen. Wounds in the Rain. Stephen Crane: Tales of War. Charlottesville: UP of Virginia, 1970. 95-284.

As a courtesy to the reader, you may include supplementary information about an entire edition.

Crane, Stephen. Wounds in the Rain. Stephen Crane: Tales of War. Charlottesville: UP of Virginia, 1970. Vol. 6 of The University of Virginia Edition of the Works of Stephen Crane. Ed. Fredson Bowers. 95-284. 10 vols. 1969-76.

Bibliography Form—Periodicals

For journal or magazine articles, use the following order:

1. Author(s)
2. Title of the article
3. Name of the periodical
4. Series number (if it is relevant)
5. Volume number (for journals)
6. Issue number (if needed)
7. Date of publication
8. Page numbers

These items are explained and illustrated in the following alphabetized list.

Abstract in an Abstracts Journal

If you have cited from an abstract found in a journal devoted to abstracts, not full articles, begin the citation with information on the original work and then give information on the abstracts journal. Use either item number or page number, according to how the journal provides the abstracts. Add the word *Abstract* if the title does not make clear you have used an abstract, not a full article.

> Ferguson, Tamara J., and Susan L. Crowley. "Gender Differences in the Organization of Guilt and Shame." Sex Roles 37 (1997): 19-44. Psychological Abstracts 85 (1998): item 4265.

Use the next form when you cite from *Dissertation Abstracts International (DAI)*. The page number features A, B, or C to designate the specific series: A Humanities, B Sciences, C European dissertations. Before volume 30 (1969) the title was *Dissertation Abstracts,* so use *DA* for those early volumes.

See page 429 for how to cite from the full text of a dissertation. See "Abstract", page 415, and Articles at a Library's Online Service, page 416.

> Shore, Zandra Lesley. "Girls Reading Culture: Autobiography as Inquiry into Teaching the Body, the Romance, and the Economy of Love." Diss. U of Toronto, 1999. DAI 60 (1999): 1657A.

Author(s)

Show the author's name flush with the left margin, without a numeral and with succeeding lines indented five spaces. Enter the surname first, followed by a comma, followed by a given name or initials, followed by a period:

> Feldman, Stanley. "Enforcing Social Conformity: A Theory of Authoritarianism." Political Psychology 24.1 (March 2003): 41-74.

Author, Anonymous

> "British Muslims: R.I.P. for Recruitment to Jihad." The Week 16 May 2003: 15.

Interview, Published

> Vonnegut, Kurt. Interview with David Hoppe. "Still Vonnegut." Utne Reader June 2003: 86-89.

Journal, with All Issues for a Year Paged Continuously

> Bartley, William. "Imagining the Future in The Awakening." College English 62 (2000): 719-46.

Journal, with Each Issue Paged Anew

Add the issue number after the volume number because page numbers alone are not sufficient to locate the article within a volume of six or twelve issues when each issue has separate pagination. Adding the month or season with the year will also serve the researcher.

Dawisha, Adeed, and Karen Dawisha. "How to Build a Democratic Iraq." Foreign Affairs 82.3 (May/June 2003): 36-50.

If a journal uses only an issue number, treat it as a volume number:

Simmons, Anna. "The Death of Conquest." National Interest 71 (Spring 2003): 41-49.

Loose-Leaf Collection

If the article is reprinted in an information service that gathers several articles on a common topic, as part of a series, use the form shown in the following example.

Cox, Rachel S. "Protecting the National Parks." The Environment. CQ Researcher ser. 23 (2000): 523+.

If the service reprints articles from other sources, use this next form, which shows original publication data and then information on the SIRS booklet—title, editor, and volume number.

Hodge, Paul. "The Andromeda Galaxy." Mercury July/ Aug. 1993: 98+. Physical Science. Ed. Eleanor Goldstein. Vol. 2. Boca Raton: SIRS, 1994. Art. 24.

Magazine

With magazines, the volume number offers little help for finding an article. For example, one volume of *Time* (52 issues) will have page 16 repeated 52 times. For this reason, you need to insert an exact date (month and day) for weekly and fortnightly (every two weeks) publications. Do not list the volume and issue numbers.

Walsh, Kenneth T. "Air Force One." U.S. News & World Report 19 May 2003: 26-35.

The month suffices for monthly and bimonthly publications:

Maliszewski, Paul, and Hadley Ross. "We Happy Few." Harper's May 2003: 56-57.

Supply inclusive page numbers (202–09, 85–115, or 1112–24), but if an article is paged here and there throughout the issue, write only the first page number and a plus sign with no intervening space:

Sim, Jillian. "Monroe Trotter: Profile in Protest." American Legacy Summer 2003: 73+.

Microform

Some reference sources, such as *NewsBank,* republish articles on microfiche. If you use such a microform, enter the original publication information first and then add the pertinent information about the microform, as shown next.

Chapman, Dan. "Panel Could Help Protect Children." Winston-Salem Journal 14 Jan 1990: 14. Newsbank: Welfare and Social Problems 12 (1990): fiche 1, grids A8-11.

Name of the Periodical

Give the name of the journal or magazine in full, underscored or italicized, and with no following punctuation. Omit any introductory article, such as *The*.

Tenner, Edward. "Body Smarts." Wisconsin Quarterly Spring 2003: 12-15.

Notes, Editorials, Queries, Reports, Comments, Letters

Magazine and journals publish many pieces that are not full-fledged articles. Identify this type of material if the title of the article or the name of the journal does not make clear the nature of the material (e.g., "Letter" or "Comment").

Trainor, Jennifer Seibel, and Deborah Klein. Comment and Response. College English 62 (2000): 767-72.

"Challenges to Intellectual Freedom Rise by Seven Percent." Bulletin. Library Journal 1 March 1994: 13.

Davey, Barbara J. Letter from the Editor. Mystery Review 11.3 (Spring 2003): 5.

Maltby, Richard E., Jr. "Save One for Me." Puzzle. Harper's June 2003: 87.

On occasion, an editor will reply to a reader's letter or comment. Identify such a response in this manner:

Goodman, Leisa. "A Letter from the Church of Scientology." Reply to article of Stephen A. Kent. Marburg Journal of Religion 6.2 (2001): 1-4.

Reprint of a Journal Article

Simonds, Robert L. "The Religious Right Explains the Religious Right." School Administrator 9 (Oct. 1993): 19–22. Education Digest Mar. 1994: 62-65.

Review, in a Magazine, Newspaper, or Journal

Name the reviewer and the title of the review. Then write *Rev. of* and the title of the work being reviewed, followed by a comma and the name of the author or producer. If necessary, identify the nature of the work within brackets immediately after the title.

Grant, Angelynn. "Differentiate or Die." Rev. of Differentiate or Die, by Jack Trout. Communication Arts 45.2 (May/June 2003): 140+.

If the name of reviewer is not provided, begin the entry with the title of the review.

"Sharp VL-MC500U." Rev. of Sharp VL-MC500U. E-design Feb. 2003: 27.

If the review has no title, omit it from the entry.

Tappin, Nigel. Rev. of Murder on the Caronia, by Conrad Allen. Mystery Review 11.3 (Spring 2003): 15.

If the review is neither signed nor titled, begin the entry with *Rev. of* and alphabetize the entry under the title of the work reviewed.

Rev. of By the Lake, by John McGahern. New Yorker 6 May 2002: 135.

Series

Between the name of the publication and the volume number, identify a numbered series with an ordinal suffix (2nd, 3rd) followed by the abbreviation *ser.* For publications divided between the original series and a new series, show the series with *os* or *ns*, respectively.

Hill, Christopher. "Sex, Marriage and the Family in England." Economic History Review 2nd ser. 31 (1978): 450-63.

Terry, Richard. "Swift's Use of 'Personate' to Indicate Parody." Notes and Queries ns 41.2 (June 1994): 196-98.

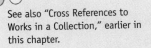

See also "Cross References to Works in a Collection," earlier in this chapter.

Special Issue

If you cite one article from a special issue of a journal, you may indicate the nature of this special issue, as shown next:

Ackerman, James. "Leonardo da Vinci: Art in Science." Science and Culture. Spec. Issue of Daedalus 127.1 (1998): 207-24.

Speech or Address, Published

Agnew, Karen. "Finding and Supporting Instructors in Continuing Education." Address to Conference on Continuing Education. Topeka, KS. 26 Apr. 2003. Rpt. in part Continuing Education Review 9.2 June 2003: 19-22.

United States. President. "Healthy Forests Initiative." 20 May 2003. Rpt. in Weekly Compilation of Presidential Documents 39.21 (26 May 2003): 621-57.

Title of the Article

Show the title within quotation marks followed by a period inside the closing quotation marks:

Schmidgen, Wolfram. "Robinson Crusoe, Enumerating, and the Merchantile Fetish." Eighteenth Century Studies 35.1 (2001): 19-39.

Title, Quotation within the Article's Title

Cornils, Ingo. " 'The Martians Are Coming!' War, Peace, Love, and Scientific Progress in H.G. Wells's The War of the Worlds and Kurd Labwitz's Auf Zwei Planeten." Comparative Literature 55.1 (Winter 2003): 24-41.

Title, within the Article's Title

Gatta, John J. "The Scarlet Letter as Pre-text for Flannery O'Connor's 'Good Country People.'" Nathaniel Hawthorne Review 16 (1990): 6-9.

Title, Foreign

Aranguez, Teresa. "Por la puerta grande." People En Espanol Junio Del 2003: 75-77.

Stivale, Charles J. "Le vraisemblable temporel dans Le Rouge et le noir." Stendhal Club 84 (1979): 299-313.

Volume, Issue, and Page Numbers for Journals

Most journals are paged continuously through all issues of an entire year, so listing the month of publication is unnecessary. For example, page numbers and a volume number are sufficient for you to find an article in *Eighteenth-Century Studies* or *English Literary Renaissance*. However, some journals have separate pagination for each issue. In this case, you will need to add an issue number following the volume number, separated by a period:

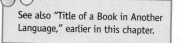

See also "Title of a Book in Another Language," earlier in this chapter.

Bedrossian, Rebecca. "Great Ideas on Limited Budgets." Communication Arts 45.2 (2003): 40–55.

Add the month also to ease the search for the article: "20.5 (Nov. 2003): 4–12."

Bibliography Form—Newspapers

Provide the name of the author; the title of the article; the name of the newspaper as it appears on the masthead, omitting any introductory article (e.g., *Wall Street Journal*, not *The Wall Street Journal*); and the complete date—day, month (abbreviated), and year. Omit volume and issue numbers.

Provide a page number as listed (e.g., 21, B-7, 13C, D4). For example, *USA Today* uses "6A" but the *New York Times* uses "A6." There is no uniformity among newspapers on this matter, so list the page accurately as an aid to your reader. If the article is not printed on consecutive pages (for example, if it begins on page 1 and skips to page 8), write the first page number and a plus (+) sign with no space before or after the (+) sign (see the entry below).

Newspaper in One Section

Reedy, Justin. "Axle Grease and Guitar Strings." Clayton News Daily 30 May 2003: 1+.

Newspaper with Lettered Sections

Maxwell, John. "Learn, Grow, and Succeed through Mistakes." Atlanta Business Chronicle 30 May 2003: 3A.

Newspaper with Numbered Sections

Jones, Tim. "New Media May Excite, While Old Media Attract." Chicago Tribune 28 July 1997, sec. 4: 2.

Newspaper Editorial with No Author Listed

"New Ballparks Sporting Lots of Empty Seats." Editorial. Atlanta Business Chronicle 30 May 2003: 32A.

Newspaper Column, Cartoon, Comic Strip, Advertisement, Etc.

Add a description to the entry to explain that the citation refers to something other than a regular news story.

Donlan, Thomas G. "Fine Tuning." Column. Barron's 26 May 2003: 31.

Newspaper Article with City Added

In the case of locally published newspapers, add the city in square brackets.

Youngman, Sam. "Lottery Bill Sails after Surprise Deal." Commercial Appeal [Memphis] 30 May 2003: A1.

Newspaper Edition or Section

When the masthead lists an edition, add a comma after the date and name the edition (late ed., city ed.), followed by a colon and then the page number.

Hakim, Danny. "Where Adults Go to Play in the Mud." New York Times 30 May 2003, national ed.: D1+.

The *New York Times* presents two types of pagination, depending on the day. On Monday through Saturday, it usually has four sections, A, B, C, D, with each having separate pagination, such as page C1 through page C24.

Myre, Greg. "A Young Man Radicalized by His Months in Jail." New York Times 30 May 2003: A1+.

The Sunday edition of the *New York Times* has numbered sections, individually paged, to cover art, business, travel, and so forth. If you cite from one of these sections, provide the section number.

Kifner, John. "The Holiest City, the Toughest Conflict." New York Times 23 July 2000, sec. 4: 1+.

Newspaper in a Foreign Language

"Les grands de ce monde reunis a Saint-Petersbourg." Le Monde 30 mai 2003: 1.

Bibliography Form—Government Documents

Since the nature of public documents is so varied, the form of the entry cannot be standardized. Therefore, your goal should be to provide sufficient information for the reader to easily locate the reference. As a general rule, place information in the bibliographic entry in this order (but see below if you know the author, editor, or compiler of the document):

1. Government
2. Body or agency
3. Subsidiary body
4. Title of document
5. Identifying numbers
6. Publication facts

When you cite two or more works by the same government, substitute three hyphens for the name of each government or body you repeat:

United States. Cong. House.

---. ---. Senate.

---. Dept. of Justice.

Congressional Papers

Senate and House sections are identified by an *S* or an *H* with document numbers (e.g., S. Res. 16) and page numbers (e.g., H2345–47).

United States. Cong. Senate. Subcommittee on Juvenile Justice of the Committee on the Judiciary. Juvenile Justice: A New Focus on Prevention. 102nd Cong., 2nd sess. S. Hearing 102-1045. Washington: GPO, 1992.

---. ---. ---. Violent Crime Control Act 1991. 102d Cong., 1st sess. S. 1241. Washington: GPO, 1991.

If you provide a citation to the *Congressional Record,* you should abbreviate it and provide only the date and page numbers.

Cong. Rec. 23 May 2003: S7101-05.

Executive Branch Documents

United States. Dept. of State. Foreign Relations of the United States: Diplomatic Papers, 1943. 5 vols. Washington: GPO, 1943-44.

---. President. 2003 Economic Report of the President. Washington: GPO, 2003.

Documents of State Governments

Publication information on state papers varies widely, so provide sufficient data for your reader to find the document.

2002-2003 Statistical Report. Nashville: Tennessee Board of Regents, 2003. TBR A-001-03.

Tennessee Election Returns, 1796-1825. Microfilm. Nashville: Tennessee State Library and Archives, n.d. M-Film JK 5292 T46.

"Giles County." 2002-2003 Directory of Public Schools. Nashville: State Dept. of Educ., n.d. 61.

Legal Citations and Public Statutes

Familiar historical documents and the United States Code can be documented with parenthetical citations in your text ("U.S. Const., art. 2, sec. 4" or "15 U.S.C. 78, 1964"). Use the following examples as guidelines for developing your citations. Laws and law cases, because of length, can be cited on the Works Cited page.

Illinois. Revised Statutes Annotated. Sec. 16-7-81. 1980.

Noise Control Act of 1972. Pub. L. 92-574. 1972. Stat. 86.

People v. McIntosh. California 321 P.3d 876, 2001-6. 1970.

State v. Lane. Minnesota 263 N. W. 608. 1935.

Bibliography Form—Internet Sources

Modern technology makes it possible for you to access information at your computer. In particular, the Internet opens a cornucopia of information from millions of sources. Other electronic sources include e-mail and databases.

Citing Sources Found on the Internet

Include these items as appropriate to the source:

1. Author/editor name
2. Title of the article within quotation marks, or the title of a posting to a discussion list or forum followed by the words *online posting,* followed by a period.
3. If the document has a printed version, publication information and date.
4. Information on the electronic publication, such as the title of the site, the date of the posting, and the sponsoring organization.
5. Date of your access, not followed by a comma or period.

6. URL (Uniform Resource Locator), within angle brackets, followed by a period. If you must divide the URL at the end of a line, break it only after a slash.

For discussion of the Internet's special format, see pages 170–177. For making judgments about the validity of Internet sources, see pages 169–170.

Note: Do not include page numbers unless the Internet article shows original page numbers from the printed version of the journal or magazine. Do not include the total number of paragraphs nor specific paragraph numbers unless the original Internet article provides them.

World Wide Web Sites

Titles of books and journals may be shown either in italics or with underlining. They are shown in this section with underlining.

Abstract

Riso, Lawrence P., et al. "Cognitive Aspects of Chronic Depression." Journal of Abnormal Psychology 112 (2003). Abstract. 10 May 2003 <http://www.apa.org/journals/abn/0203ab.html#7>.

Advertisement

Titanic: The Artifact Exhibit. Advertisement. 2001. 10 June 2003 <http://www.casciencedtr.org/Exhibits/Weingart/Titanic/Titanic.php>.

Anonymous Article, Nonprint Version

"Child Passenger Safety." National Highway Traffic Safety Administration. n.d. 11 Sept. 2003 <http://www.nhtsa.dot.gov/people/injury/childps/>.

Archive or Scholarly Project

British Poetry Archive. Ed. Jerome McGann and David Seaman. 2003. U of Virginia Lib. 19 Aug. 2003 <http://etext.lib.virginia.edu/britpo.html>.

Dorson, Richard M. "The Eclipse of Solar Mythology." Journal of American Folklore 68 (1955): 393-416. JSTOR 7 June 2003 <http://www.jstor.org/search>.

Article from an Online Magazine

"Controlling Anger--Before It Controls You." APA Online. 22 Sept. 2003 <http://www.apa.org/pubinfo/anger.html>.

Koretz, Gene. "Out of Work, Out of the Loop." BusinessWeek Online 15 May 2003. 2 Oct. 2003 <http://asia.businessweek.com/careers/content/may2003/ca20030515_2074_ca004.htm>.

Article from a Scholarly Journal

Fillmore, K. M., W. C. Kerr, and A. Bostrom. "Changes in Drinking Status, Serious Illness and Mortality." Journal of Studies on Alcohol 64 (2003): 278-85. 22 Sept. 2003 <http://www.rci.rutgers.edu/~cas2/journal/march03/>.

Article Written for the Internet

"History of Elba." Elba on line. Sept. 2002. 8 July 2003 <http://www.elba-on-line.com/Informazioni/elba.html>.

Audio Program Online

See the entry for "Television or Radio Program." page 423.

Cartoon

Parker, Brant. "My Son, the King." Cartoon. Wizard of Id. 11 May 2003. 29 Oct. 2003 <http://umweb2.unitedmedia.com/creators/wizardofid/archive/wizardofid-20030511.html>.

Chapter or Portion of a Book

Add the name of the chapter after the author's name:

Dewey, John. "Waste in Education." The School and Society. Chicago: U of Chicago P, 1907. 4 Feb. 2003 <http://spartan.ac.brocku.ca/~lward/dewey/Dewey_1907/Dewey_1907c.html>.

Article at a Library's Online Service with a Listed URL

Most libraries have converted their computer searches to online databases, such as Lexis-Nexis, ProQuest Direct, EBSCOhost, Electric Library, InfoTrac, and others. If the source provides the URL, omit the identifying numbers for the database or the keyword used in the search and include the URL. Here's an example from InfoTrac:

Lee, Catherine C. "The South in Toni Morrison's Song of Solomon: Initiation, Healing, and Home." Studies in the Literary Imagination 31 (1998): 109-23. Abstract. InfoTrac. U of Tennessee, Hodges Lib. 19 Sept. 2003 <http://firstsearch.oclc.org/next=NEXTCMD>.

You will know the database is online when you see the full URL at the top or bottom of the printout.

Article with Only a Starting Page Number of the Original Print Version

Worthen, W. B. "Recent Studies in Tudor and Stuart Drama." Review. Studies in English Literature, 1500-1900 42 (2002): 399- .

Note: Leave a space after the hyphen and before the period.

Article from an Online Service to Which You Personally Subscribe

Many students research topics from their homes, where they use such services as American Online or Netscape. If the URL is provided, use the form of this next example, which shows the name of the service.

"Nutrition and Cancer." Discovery Health. America Online. 1 May 2000. 30 Sept. 2003 <http://www.discoveryhealth.com.Sc000/8096/164609.html>.

Article from an Online Service with an Unlisted or Scrambled URL

Two possible forms are available to you when the online service provides no URL.

1. *Keyword.* If you access the site by using a keyword, provide a citation that gives the name of the service, the date of access, and the keyword:

   Esslin, Martin. "Theater of the Absurd." Grolier Multimedia Encyclopedia. 1995 ed. Netscape. 22 Aug. 2003. Keyword: Theater of the Absurd.

2. *Path.* If you follow a series of topic labels to reach the article, and no URL is provided, write the word *Path* followed by the sequence of topic labels that you followed to obtain the article. Use a semicolon to separate each topic.

   Kate Chopin: A Re-Awakening. 23 June 1999. PBS. College Webivore. Netscape. 24 Jan. 2003. Path: US Literature; 19th Century; Women Authors; Chopin, Kate (1850-1904).

Article at a Library's Online Service with No URL listed

On rare occasions you may access online material in the library that has no URL, or the URL on your printout is scrambled or incomplete, or the URL is so long as to make typing it difficult. In such a case, make a citation to the source, then give the name of the database, underlined (if known); the name of the service; the library; and the date of access. Provide the URL of the service's home page in angle brackets after your date of access. You can also list the site's search engine (e.g., <http://www.jstor.org/search>.)

Brezina, Timothy. "Teenage Violence toward Parents as an Adaptation to Family Strain: Evidence from a National Survey of Male Adolescents." Youth and Society 30 (1999): 416-44. MasterFILE Elite. EBSCOhost. Clarksville Montgomery County Library, Clarksville, Tn. 23 Nov. 2003 <http://www.ebsco.com/home/>.

E-mail

Wright, Ellen. "Online Composition Courses." E-mail to the author. 24 Sept. 2003.

Encyclopedia Article Online

"Coleridge, Samuel Taylor." Encyclopedia Britannica Online. Vers. 99.1. 1994-99. Encyclopedia Britannica. 19 Aug. 2003 <http://www.eb.com/bol/topic?eu=25136&sctn=1>.

ERIC Database

"America's Children: Key National Indicators of Well-Being." Federal Interagency Forum on Child and Family Statistics. 1999. ERIC. University of Tennessee, Hodges Lib. 15 Sept. 2003 <http://www.goarch.org/goa/departments/gotel/online_videos.html#LIGHT>.

Film, Video, or Film Clip Online

"The Glory Suffered: The Transfiguration of the Cross." The History of the Orthodox Christian Church. 2003. GoTelecom Online. 24 Oct. 2003 <http://www.goarch.org/en/multimedia/video/#transfiguration>.

FTP, TELNET, and GOPHER Sites

Most ftp, telnet, and gopher sites are now found on the World Wide Web:

"Modern Irish Language and Culture Internet FTP Site." Ed. Lisa L. Spangenberg. 4 Jan. 2003. 3 June 2003 <http://www.digitalmedievalist.com/urls/irish.html>.

Home Page for a Course

When citing a home page for a course, begin with the instructor's name and the title of the course, neither underlined nor in quotation marks. Continue with a description such as *Course Home Page,* neither underlined nor in quotation marks, the dates of the course, the department, name of the institution, date of access, and the URL.

Wilkins, John, Shelley Palmer, and Tom Barrett. Writing and Speaking about Physics and Astronomy. Summer 2003. Dept. of Physics, Ohio State U. 15 June 2003 <http://www.physics.ohio-state.edu/~wilkins/writing/>.

Home Page for an Academic Department

Department of Humanities. Dept. home page. Clayton College & State U School of Arts & Sciences. 19 Sept. 2003 <http://a-s.clayton.edu/humanities/>.

Home Page for a Personal Web Site

Miller, Alan R. Home page. 8 May 2003. 29 Oct. 2003 <http://www.nmt.edu/~armiller/>.

Home Page for an Academic Site

Since you are not citing a specific article, you can give the reader the address of an academic site, such as the following:

Robert Penn Warren: 1905-1989. 15 Oct. 2003 <http://www.english.uiuc.edu/maps/poets/s_z/warren/warren.htm>.

Interview

Strassman, Marc. "Is Journalism Dead?" Interview with Pete Hamill. Strassman Files. BookRadio 1998. 24 Nov. 2002 <http://www.bookradio.com/>.

Journal Article

See "Article from a Scholarly Journal," page 416.

Letter

Charter, Steve, and Jeanne Charter. Letter to the Editor. Billings Outpost Online 30 May 2003. 2 June 2003 <http://www.billingsnews.com/story?storyid=65&issue=6>.

Linkage Data (An Accessed File)

"What Happens to Recycled Plastics?" Online posting. Lkd. Better World Discussion Topics at Recycling Discussion Group nd. 18 June 2003 <http://www.betterworld.com/BWZ/9602/learn.htm>.

Manuscript

Girondo, Oliverio. Scarecrow & Other Anomalies. Trans. Gilbert Alter-Gilbert. Manuscript, 2002. 24 Aug. 2003 <http://www.xenosbooks.com/scarecrow.html>.

Map

"Virginia--1785." Map. U.S. County Formation Maps 1643-Present. Genealogy, Inc. 1999. 24 Sept. 2003 <http://www.segenealogy.com/virginia/va_maps/va_cf.htm>.

MOO, MUD, and Other Chat Rooms

"Virtual Conference on Mary Shelley's The Last Man." 13 Sept. 1997. Villa Diodati at EmoryMOO. 28 Oct. 2003 <http://www.rc.umd.edu/villa/vc97/ Shelley_9_13_97.html>.

Chat rooms seldom have great value, but on occasion you might find something you wish to cite; if so, use this form:

"Australia: The Olympics 2000." 30 May 2000. Yahoo! Chat. 30 May 2000 <http://chat.yahoo.com/?room=Australia::160032654&identity=chat>.

Newsgroup, Usenet News, Forum

Kalb, Jim. "Conservatism FAQ." Online Posting. 1 June 2003. Environment Newsgroup. 11 Sept. 2003 <http://nwww.faqs.org/faqs/conservatism/faq/>.

Add additional data to cite a document that has been forwarded.

Kalb, Jim. "Conservatism FAQ." 1 June 2003. Fwd. by Gwen Everett. Online posting. 12 June 2003. Environment Newsgroup. 13 June 2003 <http://nwww.faqs.org/faqs/conservatism/faq/>.

Newsletter

"MSU Grant to Help Improve Cancer Care." MSU News Bulletin 34.18 (29 May 2003). 3 June 2003 <http://www.newsbulletin.msu.edu/>.

Newspaper Article, Column, Editorial

Prater, Connie. "Small Study Offers Big Hope for Diabetics." Miami Herald 2 June 2003. 2 June 2003 <http://www.miami.com/mld/miamiherald/living/5999174.htm>.

Novel or Book Online

Lawrence, D. H. Lady Chatterly's Lover. 1928. 26 Sept. 2003 <http://bibliomania.com/0/-/frameset.html>.

Online Posting for E-mail Discussion Groups

List the Internet site, if known; otherwise show the e-mail address of the list's moderator.

Chapman, David. "Reforming the Tax and Benefit System to Reduce Unemployment." Online Posting. 25 Feb. 1998. Democracy Design Forum. 27 May 2003 <http://www.democdesignforum.demon.co.uk/unemp.nexus.html>.

Chapman, David. "Reforming the Tax and Benefit System to Reduce Unemployment." Online Posting. 25 Feb. 1998. Democracy Design Forum. 27 May 2003 <chapman@democdesignforumj.demon.co.uk>.

Photograph, Painting, Sculpture

MLA style does not require you to label the type of work, as shown in the first example of a photograph. Usually the text will have established the nature of the work. However, if you feel that clarification is necessary, as in the case of "The Blessed Damozel," which is both a painting and a poem, you may wish to designate the form.

Farrar, Ray. "Leadenhall Market." 2003. 29 Aug. 2003 <http://www.jrfarrar.fsnet.co.uk/lon1/image17.htm>.

Rossetti, Dante. "The Blessed Damozel." 1875-78. Painting. Rossetti Archive. U of Virginia Lib. 9 June 1999. 3 Sept. 2003 <http://www.engl.virginia.edu/~bpn2f/rossetti/tourf.html>.

"Leaping Gazelle, 1936." Bronze Sculpture. Marshall M. Fredericks Sculpture Museum. 2001. 29 Aug. 2003 <http://www.svsu.edu/mfsm/collections.htm>.

Poem, Song, or Story

Hardy, Thomas. "To a Lady." Wessex Poems and Other Verses. 1898. Project Bartleby. 2000 Great Books Online. 10 July 2003 <http://www.bartleby.com/121/40.html>.

Review

Ebert, Roger. Rev. of Capturing the Friedmans, dir. Andrew Jarecki. Chicago Sun-Times Online 6 June 2003. 16 June 2003 <http://www.suntimes.com/output/ebert1/wkp-news-friedmans06f.html>.

Report

"Auditor's General Report on Reintegration of Male Offenders." Correctional Service of Canada. 28 May 2003. 12 Sept. 2003 <http://www.csc-scc.gc.ca/text/ne/4_e.shtml>.

Serialized Article

Frank, Laura. "Worker: 'I Didn't Get That at Home.'" Tennessean.com 9 Feb. 1997. Pt. 1 of a series, An Investigation into Illnesses around the Nation's Nuclear Weapons Sites, begun 9 Feb. 1997. 20 Oct. 2003 <http://www.tennessean.com/special/oakridge/part3/frames/html>.

Thomas, Susan. "Oak Ridge Workers Offered Medical Screening." Tennessean.com 21 Jan. 1999. Pt. 2 of a series, An Investigation into Illnesses around the Nation's Nuclear Weapons Sites, begun 9 Feb. 1997. 20 Oct. 2003 <http://www.tennessean.com/special/oakridge/part3/frames/html>.

Thomas, Susan, Laura Frank, and Anne Paine. "Taking the Poison." Tennessean.com 9 Feb. 1997. Pt. 3 of a series, An Investigation into Illnesses around the Nation's Nuclear Weapons Sites, begun 9 Feb. 1997. 20 Oct. 2003 <http://www.tennessean.com/special/oakridge/part3/frames/html>.

Song

See "Poem, Song, or Story."

Sound Clip or Audio Recording

See "Television or Radio Program."

Story

See "Poem, Song, or Story."

Synchronous Communication

See "MOO, MUD, and Other Chat Rooms."

Television or Radio Program

Keillor, Garrison. "Writer and Radio Personality Garrison Keillor." Fresh Air Audio. NPR Online. 18 Oct. 2002. 22 Apr. 2003 <http://discover.npr.org/features/feature.jhtml?wfId=1151873>.

University Posting, Online Article

Chambers, Aaron. "Pedophiles to Pornographers." Online Posting. May 2003. U of Illinois at Springfield. 28 July 2003 <http://illinoisissues.uis.edu/features/2003may/offender.html>.

Video

See "Film, Video, or Film Clip Online."

Web Site, General Reference

As long as you are not citing a specific article but merely making reference to a site, provide the address in your text, *not* on the Works Cited page.

Further information about this program can be found at the Web site for the Department of Psychology at the University of Wisconsin-Parkside <http://www.uwp.edu/academic/ psychology>.

Work in an Indeterminate Medium

If the medium of a source cannot be determined, use the designation *Electronic* for the medium. For example, if you access material through a local network and cannot tell whether the work is on a CD-ROM or on the central computer's hard drive, designate it as *Electronic*. Give whatever relevant publication information you can, as well as the name of the network or of its sponsoring organization and the date of access.

Lubiano, Wahneema. "Toni Morrison." African American Writers. Valerie Smith, gen. ed. 2nd ed. Vol. 2. New York: Scribner's, 1999. 321-33. Electronic. Gale, 2001. Alabama Virtual Lib. 24 Apr. 2001.

Working Papers

Cutler, David M. "How Much Should the Tobacco Companies Have Paid?" Working Paper #00-004, Harvard Business School, 1999-2000. 30 July 2000 <http://www.hbs.edu/units/marketing/research.htm>.

Bibliography Form—Sources Found on CD-ROM

CD-ROM technology provides information in four ways, each of which requires an adjustment in the form of the entry for your Works Cited page.

Full-Text Articles with Publication Information for the Printed Source

Full-text articles are available from national distributors such as Information Access Company (InfoTrac), UMI-Proquest (Proquest), Silverplatter, and SIRS CD-ROM Information Systems. (*Note:* Most of these sources are also available online.) Conform to the examples that follow:

Grych, John H. "Patterns of Adjustment among Children of Battered Women." Journal of Consulting and Clinical Psychology 68 (2000): 84-94. Abstract. PsycLIT. CD-ROM. Silverplatter. 23 July 2003.

DePalma, Antony. "Mexicans Renew Their Pact on the Economy, Retaining the Emphasis on Stability." New York Times 25 Sept. 1994: 4. New York Times Ondisc. CD-ROM. UMI-Proquest. Jan. 1995.

Mann, Thomas E., and Norman J. Ornstein. "Shipshape? A Progress Report on Congressional Reform." Brookings Review Spring 1994: 40-45. SIRS Researcher. CD-ROM. Boca Raton: SIRS, 1994. Art. 57.

HINT: Complete information may not be readily available—for example, the original publication data may be missing. In such cases, provide what *is* available:

Silver, Daniel J. "The Battle of the Books." Rev. of The Western Canon: The Books and School of the Ages, by Harold Bloom. Resource/One. CD-ROM. UMI-ProQuest. Feb. 1995.

Full-Text Articles with No Publication Information for a Printed Source

Sometimes the original printed source of an article or report is not provided by the distributor of the CD-ROM database. In such a case, conform to the examples that follow, which provide limited data:

"Faulkner Biography." Discovering Authors. CD-ROM. Detroit: Gale, 1999.

"U.S. Population by Age: Urban and Urbanized Areas." 1999 U.S. Census of Population and Housing. CD-ROM. US Bureau of the Census. 2000.

Complete Books and Other Publications on CD-ROM

Cite this type of source as you would a book, and then provide information about the electronic source you accessed.

The Bible. The Old Testament. CD-ROM. Parsippany, NJ: Bureau Development, 1999.

English Poetry Full-Text Database. Magnetic Tape. Rel. 2. Cambridge, Eng.: Chadwyck, 1993.

"John F. Kennedy." InfoPedia. CD-ROM. n.p.: Future Vision, n.d.

Poe, Edgar Allan. "Fall of the House of Usher." Electronic Classical Library. CD-ROM. Garden Grove, CA: World Library, 1999.

Chaucer, Geoffrey. "The Wife of Bath's Tale." Canterbury Tales. CD-ROM facsimile text. Princeton: Films for the Humanities and Sciences, 2000.

Abstracts to Books and Articles Provided on CD-ROM by National Distributors

As a service to readers, the national distributors have members of their staff write abstracts of articles and books if the original authors have not provided such abstracts. As a result, an abstract found on InfoTrac and ProQuest may not be written by the original author, so you should not quote such abstracts. (You may quote from abstracts that say, "Abstract written by the author.") Silverplatter databases *do* have abstracts written by the original authors. In either case, you need to show in the Works Cited entry that you have cited from the abstract, so conform to the example that follows, which provides name, title, publication information, the word *abstract,* the name of the database underlined, the medium (CD-ROM), the name of the vendor, and—if available to you—the electronic publication date (month and year).

Figueredo, Aurelio J., and Laura Ann McCloskey. "Sex, Money, and Paternity: The Evolutionary Psychology of Domestic Violence." Ethnology and Sociobiology 14 (1993): 353-79. Abstract. PsycLIT. CD-ROM. Silverplatter. 12 Jan. 2003.

Nonperiodical Publication on CD-ROM, Diskette, or Magnetic Tape

Cite a CD-ROM, diskette, or magnetic tape as you would a book, with the addition of a descriptive word. If relevant, show edition (3rd ed.), release (Rel. 2), or version (Ver. 3). Conform to the examples that follow:

Lester, James D. Introduction to Greek Mythology: Computer Slide Show. 12 lessons on CD-ROM. Clarksville, TN: Austin Peay State U, 2003.

"Nuclear Medicine Technologist." Guidance Information System. 17th ed. Diskette. Cambridge: Riverside-Houghton, 1992.

Statistics on Child Abuse--Montgomery County, Tennessee. Rel. 2. Magnetic tape. Clarksville, TN: Harriett Cohn Mental Health Center, 2001.

Encyclopedia Article

For an encyclopedia article on a CD-ROM, use the following form:

"Abolitionist Movement." Compton's Interactive Encyclopedia. CD-ROM. Novato, CA: The Learning Company, 1999.

Multidisc Publication

When citing a multidisc publication, follow the term *CD-ROM* with the total number of discs or with the disc that you cited from:

Parsees 2.0: Interactive Sources and Studies on Ancient Greece. CD-ROM. Disc 3. New Haven: Yale UP, 2000.

Bibliography Form—Other Electronic Sources

Citing a Source You Access in More Than One Medium

Some distributors issue packages that include several media, such as CD-ROM and accompanying microfiche or a diskette and an accompanying videotape. Cite such publications as you would a nonperiodical publication on CD-ROM (see above, top of the page) with the addition of the media available with this product.

Franking, Holly. The Martensville Nightmare. Vers. 1.0. Diskette, CD-ROM. Prairie Village: Diskotech, 1997.

Jolly, Peggy. "A Question of Style." Exercise Exchange 26.2 (1982): 39-40. ERIC. CD-ROM, microfiche. Silverplatter. Feb. 17, 1995. ED236601, fiche 1.

Silver, Daniel J. "The Battle of the Books." Rev. of The Western Canon: The Books and School of the Ages, by Harold Bloom. Resource/One. CD-ROM, microfiche S-637. UMI-Proquest. Feb. 1995.

Chaucer, Geoffrey. "Prologue." Canterbury Tales. Videocassette, CD-ROM facsimile text. Princeton: Films for the Humanities and Sciences, 2000.

Citing an Entire Internet Site

To cite an online database, such as Dialog, conform to the style shown in these samples:

Grolier Online. 2003. Grolier Multimedia Encyclopedia. 6 Nov. 2003 <http://auth.grolier.com>.

NSDl. 2003. National Science Digital Library. 6 Nov. 2003 <http://www.nsdl.org>.

NBC.com. 2003. National Broadcasting Company. 6 Nov. 2003 <http://www.nbc.com>.

Bibliography Form—Other Sources

Advertisement

Provide the title of the advertisement, within quotation marks, or the name of the product or company, *not* within quotation marks, the label *Advertisement,* and publication information.

"A Brilliant Selection, a Vivid Promise." Advertisement. Pozzi Wood Windows. Home July 2003: 55.

OnStar. Advertisement. CNNLive. 4 Aug. 2003.

Carmax. Billboard advertisement. Stockbridge, GA. Aug. 2003.

Artwork

If you actually experience the work itself, use the form shown in the next two entries:

Remington, Frederic. Mountain Man. Metropolitan Museum of Art, New York.

Wyeth, Andrew. Hay Ledge. Private Collection of Mr. and Mrs. Joseph E. Levine.

If the artwork is a special showing at a museum, use the form of this next example.

"Elie Nadelman: Sculptor of Modern Life." Whitney Museum of American Art, New York. 4 June 2003.

Polidori, Robert. "Color Photographs of Aging Structures in Chernobyl." Pace/Macgill Gallery, New York. 13 June 2003.

Use this next form to cite reproductions in books and journals.

Lee-Smith, Hughie. Temptation. 1991. A History of African-American Artists: From 1792 to the Present. Ed. Romare Bearden and Harry Henderson. New York: Pantheon, 1993.

Raphael. School of Athens. The Vatican, Rome. The World Book Encyclopedia. 2003 ed.

If you show the date of the original, place it immediately after the title.

Raphael. School of Athens. 1510-1511. The Vatican, Rome. The World Book Encyclopedia. 2003 ed.

Bulletin

A bulletin is a brief publication, usually softbound, that you should treat as a book.

The South Carolina Market Bulletin. Columbia, SC: South Carolina Department of Agriculture, 15 May 2003.

Maryland State Bar Association's Public Awareness Committee. Appointing a Guardian. Baltimore: Maryland State Bar Association. 2003.

Cartoon

If you cannot decipher the name of the cartoonist and cannot find a title, use this form:

Cartoon. New Yorker 2 June 2003: 69.

Sometimes you will have the artist's name but not the name of the cartoon:

Bower, Tim. Cartoon. Harper's June 2003: 35.

Some cartoons are reprinted in magazines:

Ramirez. "Peace." Cartoon. Rpt. in Weekly Standard 2 June 2003: 13.

Adams, Scott. "Dilbert." Comic strip. Mercury News [San Jose] 10 June 2003: E7.

Computer Software

Publisher Deluxe 2002. CD-ROM. Redmond, WA: Microsoft, 2002.

Conference Proceedings

Beachley, Barbara, Amanda Brown, and Frances Conlin, eds. BUCLD-27: Proceedings of the Twenty-Seventh Boston University Conference on Language Development, April 2003. Somerville, MA: Cascadilla, 2003.

Dissertation, Published

Nilsson, Mattias. Essays in Empirical Corporate Finance and Governance. Diss. Lund U, 2002. Stockholm: EFI, 2002.

Dissertation, Unpublished

Park, No-Wook. "Decentralization As an Activator of Distributive Politics: Theory and Evidence from Korea." Diss. U of Michigan, 2002.

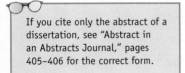

> If you cite only the abstract of a dissertation, see "Abstract in an Abstracts Journal," pages 405–406 for the correct form.

Film, Videocassette, or DVD

Cite the title of a film, the director, the distributor, and the year.

My Big Fat Greek Wedding. Dir. Joel Zwick. HBO Video, 2002.

If relevant to your study, add the names of performers, writers, or producers after the name of the director.

Ice Age. Dir. Chris Wedge. Screenplay by Michael J. Wilson. 20th Century Fox, 2002.

If the film is a DVD, videocassette, filmstrip, slide program, or videodisc, add the type of medium before the name of the distributor. Add the date of the original film, if relevant, before the name of the medium.

Citizen Kane. Dir. Orson Welles. 1941. DVD. Warner, 2002.

Crimmins, Morton. "Robert Lowell: American Poet." Lecture. Videocassette. Western State U, 2003.

If you are citing the accomplishments of the director or a performer, begin the citation with that person's name.

Jackson, Peter, dir. Lord of the Rings: The Fellowship of the Ring. Perf. Elijah Wood, Ian McKellen, and Ian Holm. Warner, 2001.

If you cannot find certain information, such as the original date of the film, cite what is available.

Altman, Robert, dir. The Room. Perf. Julian Sands, Linda Hunt, Annie Lennox. Videocassette. Prism.

Interview

For an interview you conduct, name the person interviewed, the type of interview (e.g., telephone interview, personal interview, e-mail interview), and the date.

Carter, Emma. "Growing Georgia Greens." Telephone interview. 5 Mar. 2003.

For broadcast interviews, cite all relevant information, including the broadcast source.

Gray, Jim. "NBA Coaching Vacancies." Interview. ESPN. 4 June 2003.

Foote, Shelby. Interview. Shelby Foote on Faulkner. C-SPAN. Videocassette. National Cable, 2003.

Lecture

See "Public Address," page 433.

Letter, Personal

Knight, Charles. Letter to the author. 21 Aug. 2003.

Letter, Published

Eisenhower, Dwight. Letter to Richard Nixon. 20 April 1968. Memoirs of Richard Nixon. By Richard Nixon. New York: Grosset, 1978.

Loose-Leaf Collections

If you cite an article from *SIRS, Opposing Viewpoints*, or other loose-leaf collections, provide both the original publication data and then add information for the loose-leaf volume, as shown in these next examples:

"The Human Genetic Code." Illustration. Facts on File 29 June 2000: 437-38.

Hodge, Paul. "The Andromeda Galaxy." Mercury July/Aug. 1993: 98+. Physical Science. Ed. Eleanor Goldstein. Vol. 2. Boca Raton: SIRS, 1994. Art. 24.

Cox, Rachel S. "Protecting the National Parks." The Environment. CQ Researcher ser. 23 (2000): 523+. Washington: Congressional Quarterly Inc., 2000.

Manuscripts (ms.) and Typescripts (ts.)

Glass, Malcolm. Journal 3, ms. M. Glass Private Papers, Clarksville, TN.

Tanner. Ms. 346. Bodleian Library, Oxford, Eng.

Williams, Ralph. Notebook 15, ts. Williams Papers. Vanderbilt U, Nashville.

Map

Treat a map as you would an anonymous work, but add a descriptive label, such as *map, chart, survey*, unless the title describes the medium.

County Boundaries and Names. United States Base Map GE-50, No. 86. Washington, DC: GPO, 2001.

Pennsylvania. Map. Chicago: Rand, 2003.

Microfilm or Microfiche

Chapman, Dan. "Panel Could Help Protect Children." Winston-Salem Journal 14 Jan. 1990: 14. Newsbank: Welfare and Social Problems 12 (1990): fiche 1, grids A8-11.

Jolly, Peggy. "A Question of Style." Exercise Exchange 26.2 (1982): 39-40. ERIC ED2336601, fiche 1.

Tuckerman, H. T. "James Fenimore Cooper." Microfilm. North American Review 89 (1859): 298-316.

Miscellaneous Materials (Program, Leaflet, Poster, Announcement)

"Earth Day." Poster. Louisville. 23 Mar. 2003.

"Spring Family Weekend." Program. Nashville: Fisk U 4 April 2003.

Musical Composition

For a musical composition, begin with the composer's name, followed by a period. Underline the title of an opera, ballet, or work of music identified by name, but do not underline or enclose within quotation marks the form, number, and key when these are used to identify the instrumental composition.

Mozart, Wolfgang A. Jupiter. Symphony No. 41.

Wagner, Richard. Lohengrin.

Treat a published score as you would a book.

Legrenzi, Giovanni. La Buscha. Sonata for Instruments. Historical Anthology of Music. Ed. Archibald T. Davison and Willi Apel. Cambridge: Harvard UP, 1950. 70-76.

Pamphlet

Treat a pamphlet as you would a book.

Federal Reserve Board. Consumer Handbook to Credit Protection Laws. Washington: GPO, 2003.

Westinghouse Advanced Power Systems. Nuclear Waste Management: A Manageable Task. Madison, PA: Author, n.d.

Performance

Treat a performance (e.g., play, opera, ballet, concert) as you would a film, but include the site (normally the theater and city) and the date of the performance.

Lakota Sioux Indian Dance Theatre. Cherokee Heritage Center, Tahlequah, OK. 12 May 2002.

The Merchant of Venice. By William Shakespeare. Pearl Theatre, New York. 25 Oct. 2003.

Tosca. By Puccini. Perf. Jennifer Welch-Babbidge and Gregory Turay. Opera Theatre, St. Louis. 24 May 2003.

If your text emphasizes the work of a particular individual, begin with the appropriate name(s).

Hoang, Haivan, and Doug Dangler. "Getting to Know You: Database Information for Writing Centers." Conf. on Coll. Composition and Communication. Hilton Hotel, New York, 19 March, 2003.

Mason, Jackie, comedian. Zanies, Chicago. 5 June 2003.

Buchbinder, Rudolph. "Gershwin Piano Concerto in F." New York Philharmonic. Avery Fisher Hall, New York. 5 June 2003.

Public Address

Identify the nature of the address (e.g., lecture, reading), include the site (normally the lecture hall and city), and the date of the performance.

Darrish, Murray B. "Documenting an Early Missouri Family." Lecture. St. Louis Genealogical Soc., St. Louis. 9 Sept. 2003.

Mong-Lan. Readings of Song of the Cicadas. Bolling Center at Earlham College. Richmond, IN. 15 April 2003.

Recording on Record, Tape, or Disk

If you are not citing a compact disc, indicate the medium (e.g., audiocassette, audiotape [reel-to-reel tape], or LP [long-playing record]).

"Chaucer: The Nun's Priest's Tale." Canterbury Tales. Narr. in Middle English by Alex Edmonds. Audiocassette. London, 2003.

Reich, Robert B. Locked in the Cabinet: A Political Memoir. 4 audiocassettes abridged. New York: Random Audio, 1997.

Dion, Celine. "I Drove All Night." One Heart. CD. Sony, 2003.

Tchaikovsky. Romeo and Juliet. Fantasy-Overture after Shakespeare. New Philharmonica Orchestra London. Cond. Lawrence Siegel. DVD. Classical Masters, 2000.

Do not underscore, italicize, or enclose within quotation marks a private recording or tape. However, you should include the date, if available, as well as the location and the identifying number.

Walpert, Wanda A. Folk Stories of the Smokey Mountains. Rec. Feb. 1995. Audiotape. U of Knoxville. Knoxville, TN. UTF.34.82.

Cite a libretto, liner notes, or booklet that accompanies a recording in the form shown in the following example.

Nelson, Willie. Booklet. The Great Divide. By Willie Nelson. UMG, 2002.

Report

Unbound reports are placed within quotation marks; bound reports are treated as books:

Coca-Cola Company. 2003 Annual Report. Atlanta: Author, 2003.

Franco, Lynn. "Confidence Slips Amid Fragile Economy." Report. The Conference Board. New York: CBS/Broadcast Group, 28 Jan. 2003.

Reproduction, Photograph, Photocopy

Kemmelmeyer, Frederick. Washington Reviewing the Western Army at Fort Cumberland. Winterthur Museum, Winterthur, DE. The American Presidency. By Lonnie G. Bunch III et al. Washington: Smithsonian, 2000. 7.

White, T. H. "The Young Arthur and His Tutor, Merlyn." The World of King Arthur. By Christopher Snyder. London: Thames & Hudson, 2000. 167.

Table, Illustration, Chart, Graph

Tables or illustrations of any kind published within works need a detailed label (chart, table, figure, photograph, and so on):

"Financial Indicators: Money and Interest Rates." Table. Economist 8 July 2000: 105.

Alphabet. Chart. Columbus: Scholastic, 2003.

Television or Radio Program

If available or relevant, provide information in this order: the episode (in quotation marks), the title of the program (underscored or italicized), title of the series (not underscored nor in quotation marks), name of the network, call letters and city of the local station, and broadcast date. Add other information (such as narrator) after the title of the episode or program. Place the number of episodes, if relevant, before the title of the series.

The Way We Live Now. By Anthony Trollope. Adapt. Andrew Davies. Dir. David Yates. Perf. David Suchet, Matthew Macfadyen, Paloma Baeza, and Cheryl Campbell. 4 episodes. Masterpiece Theatre. Introd. Russell Baker. PBS. WCDN, Nashville. 1 June 2003.

"Should the 22nd Amendment Be Repealed?" Crossfire. Hosts James Carville, Paul Begala, Tucker Carlson, and Bob Novak. CNN. 30 May 2003.

Prairie Home Companion. NPR. WABE, Atlanta. 7 June 2003.

"Distance Learning Class: The Cable Center at the U of Denver." Host: Brian Lamb. Washington Journal. C-SPAN. 6 June 2003.

Thesis

See "Dissertation, Unpublished," page 295.

Transparency

Sharp, La Vaughn, and William E. Loeche. The Patient and Circulatory Disorders: A Guide for Instructors. 54 transparencies, 99 overlays. Philadelphia: Lorrenzo, 2001.

Unpublished Paper

Schuler, Wren. "Prufrock and His Cat." Unpublished essay, 2003.

Voice Mail

Nerbarger, Henry. Memo to Lester. Voice mail to the author. 6 Jan. 2004.

18 Writing in APA Style

Your instructor may require you to write the research paper in APA style, which is governed by *The Publication Manual of the American Psychological Association,* 5th edition, 2001. This style has gained wide acceptance in the social sciences, and versions similar to it are used in the biological sciences, business, and earth sciences. Research is paramount in the sciences; in fact, the APA style guide says, "No amount of skill in writing can disguise research that is poorly designed or managed." Thus, you will need to execute your project with precision.

Writing Theory, Reporting Test Results, or Reviewing Literature

In the sciences, you may choose between three types of articles, or your instructor will specify one of these:

- Theoretical articles
- Reports of empirical studies
- Review articles

Theoretical Article

For a sample theoretical article, see the student paper which examines some of the prevailing theories on arranged marriages through online dating services.

The theoretical article draws on existing research to examine a topic. This is the type of paper you will most likely write as a first-year or second-year student. You will need to trace the development of a theory or compare theories by examining the literature to arrive at the current thinking about topics such as autism, criminal behavior, dysfunctional families, and learning disorders. The theoretical article generally accomplishes four aims:

1. Identifies a problem or hypothesis that has historical implications in the scientific community.
2. Traces the development and history of the evolution of the theory.
3. Provides a systematic analysis of the articles that have explored the problem.
4. Arrives at a judgment and discussion of the prevailing theory.

Report of an Empirical Study

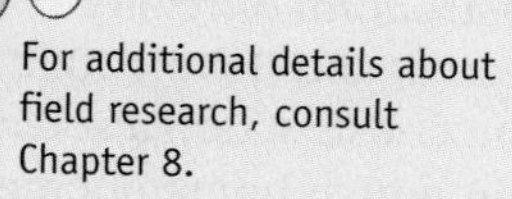

For additional details about field research, consult Chapter 8.

When you conduct field research and perform laboratory testing, you must report the details of your original research. The empirical report accomplishes these four purposes:

1. Introduces the problem or hypothesis investigated and explains the purpose of the work.
2. Describes the method used to conduct the research.
3. Reports the results and the basic findings.
4. Discusses, interprets, and explores the implications of the findings.

You will need to work closely with your instructor to accomplish each of these stages.

Review Article

See Chapter 10 for a sample review of literature.

You may be required to write a critical evaluation of a published article, a book, or a set of articles on a common topic. The purpose is to examine the state of current research—and, in some cases, to determine if additional work might be in order. A review article sets out to accomplish several goals:

1. Define a problem or issue that is the subject of discussion.
2. Summarize the article(s) or book(s) under review.
3. Analyze the literature to discover strengths, weaknesses, or inconsistencies in the research.
4. Recommend additional research that might grow logically from the work under review.

Writing in the Proper Tense for an APA Paper

Verb tense is an indicator that distinguishes papers in the humanities from those in the natural and social sciences. MLA style, as shown in previous chapters, requires you to use present tense when you refer to a cited work ("Jeffries *stipulates*" or "the work of Mills and Maguire *shows*"). In contrast, APA style requires you to use past tense or present perfect tense ("Jeffries *stipulated*" or "the work of Mills and Maguire *has demonstrated*"). The APA style does require present tense when you discuss the results (e.g., "*the results confirm*" or "*the study indicates*") and when you mention established knowledge (e.g., "*the therapy offers some hope*" or "*salt contributes to hypertension*"). The paragraphs below, side by side, show the differences in verb tenses for MLA and APA styles.

MLA style:
The scholarly issue at work here is the construction of reality. Cohen, Adoni, and Bantz label the construction a social process "in which human beings act both as the creators and products of the social world" (34). These writers identify three categories (34–35).

APA style:
The scholarly issue at work here is the construction of reality. Cohen, Adoni, and Bantz (2002) labeled the construction a social process "in which human beings act both as the creators and products of the social world" (p. 34). These writers have identified three categories.

APA style, shown on the right, requires that you use the present tense for generalizations and references to stable conditions, but it requires the present perfect tense or the past tense for sources cited (e.g., the sources *have tested* a hypothesis or the sources *reported* the results of a test). This next sentence uses tense correctly for APA style:

> The danger of steroid use exists for every age group, even youngsters. Lloyd and Mercer (2003) reported on six incidents of liver damage to 14-year-old swimmers who used steroids.

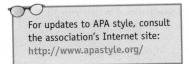

For updates to APA style, consult the association's Internet site: http://www.apastyle.org/

As shown above in the example, use the present tense (*exists*) for established knowledge and the present perfect (*has reported*) or the past tense (*reported*) for a citation.

Using In-Text Citations in APA Style

APA style uses the following conventions for in-text citations:

- Cites last names only.
- Cites the year, within parentheses, immediately after the name of the author. Include only the year in the text citation even if the reference includes a month.
- Cites page numbers with a direct quotation but not with a paraphrase.
- Uses "p." or "pp." before page numbers.

Citing Last Name Only and the Year of Publication

An in-text citation in APA style requires the last name of the author and the year of publication.

> Devlin (2002) has advanced the idea of combining the social sciences and mathematics to chart human behavior.

If you do not use the author's name in your text, place the name(s) within the parenthetical citation.

One study has advanced the idea of combining the social sciences and mathematics to chart human behavior (Devlin, 2002).

Providing a Page Number

If you quote the exact words of a source, provide a page number and use "p." or "pp." Place the page number in one of two places: after the year (2003, p. B4) or at the end of the quotation.

Devlin (2002) has advanced the idea of "soft mathematics," which is the practice of "applying mathematics to study people's behavior" (p. B4).

Citing a Block of Material

Present a quotation of forty words or more as a separate block, indented five spaces or ½ inch from the left margin. (*Note:* MLA style uses ten spaces or one inch). Because it is set off from the text in a distinctive block, do not enclose it with quotation marks. Do not indent the first line an extra five spaces; however, *do* indent the first line of any additional paragraphs that appear in the block an extra five spaces—that is, ten spaces from the left margin. Set parenthetical citations outside the last period.

Albert (2003) reported the following:

> Whenever these pathogenic organisms attack the human body and begin to multiply, the infection is set in motion. The host responds to this parasitic invasion with efforts to cleanse itself of the invading agents. When rejection efforts of the host become visible (fever, sneezing, congestion), the disease status exists. (pp. 314-315)

Citing a Work with More Than One Author

When one work has two or more authors, use *and* in the text but use *&* in the citation.

Werner and Throckmorton (2003) offered statistics on the toxic levels of water samples from six rivers.

but

It has been reported (Werner & Throckmorton, 2003) that toxic levels exceeded the maximum allowed each year since 1983.

For three to five authors, name them all in the first entry (e.g., Torgerson, Andrews, Smith, Lawrence, & Dunlap, 2003), but thereafter use "et al." (e.g.,

Torgerson et al., 2003). For six or more authors, employ "et al." in the first and in all subsequent instances (e.g., Fredericks et al., 2002).

Citing More Than One Work by an Author

Use lowercase letters (a, b, c) to identify two or more works published in the same year by the same author—for example, (Thompson, 2002a) and (Thompson, 2002b). Then use "2002a" and "2002b" in your List of References. If necessary, specify additional information:

> Horton (2001; cf. Thomas, 2002a, p. 89, and 2003b, p. 426) suggested an intercorrelation of these testing devices, but after multiple-group analysis, Welston (2002, esp. p. 211) reached an opposite conclusion.

Citing Indirect Sources

Use a double reference to cite a person who has been quoted in a book or article—that is, use the original author(s) in the text and cite your source for the information in the parenthetical citation.

> In other research, Massie and Rosenthal (2002) studied home movies of children diagnosed with autism, but determining criteria was difficult due to the differences in quality and dating of the available videotapes (cited in Osterling & Dawson, 2003, p. 248).

Citing from a Textbook or Anthology

If you make an in-text citation to an article or chapter of a textbook, casebook, or anthology, use the in-text citation to refer only to the person(s) you cite:

> One writer stressed that two out of every three new jobs in this decade will go to women (Rogers 2003).

The list of references will clarify the nature of this reference to Rogers.

Citing Classical Works

If an ancient work has no date of publication, cite the author's name followed by n.d. within parentheses.

> Seeing psychic emotions as . . . (Sophocles, n.d.).

Cite the year of any translation you have used, preceded by *trans.*, and give the date of the version used, followed by *version.*

Plato (trans. 1963) offered a morality that . . .

Plato's Phaedrus (1982 version) explored . . .

If you know the original date of publication, include it before the date of the translation or version you have used.

In his "Poetics," Aristotle (350 B.C.) viewed the structure of the plot as a requisite to a good poem.

Note: Entries on your References page need not cite major classical works and the Bible. Therefore, identify in your text the version used and the book, chapter, line, verse, or canto.

In Exodus 24:3-4 Moses erects an altar and "twelve pillars according to the twelve tribes of Israel" (King James Version).

The Epic of Gilgamesh shows, in part, the search for everlasting life (Part 4).

In the Iliad, Homer takes great efforts in describing the shield of Achilles (18:558-709).

Abbreviating Corporate Authors in the Text

The names of groups that serve as authors, such as corporations, associations, and government agencies, are usually spelled out each time they appear. The names of some corporate authors may be abbreviated after a first, full reference:

One source questioned the results of the use of aspirin for arthritis treatment in children (American Medical Association [AMA], 2001).

Thereafter, refer to the corporate author by initials: (AMA, 2001). It is important to give enough information in the text citation for the reader to locate the entry in the reference list without difficulty.

Citing a Work with No Author

When a work has no author listed, cite the title as part of the in-text citation (or use the first few words of the material).

The cost per individual student has continued to rise rapidly ("Money Concerns," 2003, p. 2).

Citing Personal Communications

E-mail, telephone conversations, memos, and conversations do not provide recoverable data, so APA style excludes them from the list of references. Consequently, you should cite personal communications in the text only. In so doing, give the initials as well as the last name of the source, provide the date, and briefly describe the nature of the communication.

> M. Gaither (personal communication, August 24, 2003) described the symptoms of Wilson's disease.

Citing Internet Sources in Your Text

As with MLA style, material from electronic sources presents special problems when you are writing in APA style. Currently, most Internet sources have no prescribed page numbers or numbered paragraphs. You cannot list a screen number because monitors differ. You cannot list the page numbers of a downloaded document because computer printers differ. Therefore, in most cases do not list a page number or a paragraph number. Here are basic rules.

Omit a page or paragraph number. The marvelous feature of electronic text is that it is searchable, so your readers can find your quotation quickly with the Find feature. Suppose you have written the following:

> The UCLA Internet Report (2003) advised policy makers with "a better understanding of the impact the Internet is having in our society."

A reader who wants to investigate further will find your complete citation, including the Internet address of the article, in your References list. After finding the article via a browser (e.g., Netscape or Internet Explorer), the investigator can press Edit, then Find, and type in a key phrase, such as *better understanding of the impact.* The software will immediately move the cursor to the passage shown above. That is much easier than counting through forty-six paragraphs.

Provide a paragraph number. Some scholars who write on the Internet number their paragraphs. Therefore, if you find an online article that has numbered paragraphs, by all means supply that information in your citation.

> The Insurance Institute for Highway Safety (2003) has emphasized restraint first, and said, "A federal rule requiring special attachments to anchor infant and child restraints in vehicles is making installation easier, but not all child restraints fit easily in all vehicles" (par. 1).

> Recommendations for treating non-insulin-dependent diabetes mellitus (NIDDM), the most common type of diabetes, include a diet that is rich in carbohydrates, "predominantly from whole grains, fruit, vegetables, and low-fat milk" (Yang, 2003, par. 3).

Provide a page number. In a few instances, you will find page numbers buried within brackets here and there throughout an article. These refer to the page numbers of the printed version of the document. In these cases, you should cite the page just as you would a printed source. Here is the Internet source with the page numbers buried within the text to signal the break between page 17 and page 18:

> What is required is a careful reading of Chekhov's subtext, that elusive [pp17-18] literature that lingers in psychological nuances of the words, not the exact words themselves.—Ward

The page number may be included in the citation:

One source argued the merits of Chekhov's subtext and its "psychological nuances of the words" (Ward, 2001, p. 18).

World Wide Web Site

Internet article

Commenting on the distinction between a Congressional calendar day and a legislative day, Dove (2003) stated that "a legislative day is the period of time following an adjournment of the Senate until another adjournment."

"Reports of abuses in the interrogation of suspected terrorists raise the question of how--or whether--we should limit the interrogation of a suspected terrorist when our national security may be at stake" (Parry & White, 2003, abstract).

HyperNews posting

Ochberg (2003) commented on the use of algae in paper that "initially has a green tint to it, but unlike bleached paper which turns yellow with age, this algae paper becomes whiter with age."

Online magazine

BusinessWeek Online (2002) reported that the idea of peer-to-peer computing is a precursor to new Web applications.

Government document

The Web site *Thomas* (2003) has outlined the amendments to the *Homeland Security Act of 2002*, which will implement the READICall emergency alert system.

Other Electronic Sources

E-mail

The Publication Manual of the American Psychological Association stipulates that personal communications, which others cannot retrieve, should be cited in the text only and not mentioned at all in the bibliography.

One technical writing instructor (March 8, 2003) has bemoaned the inability of hardware developers to maintain pace with the ingenuity of software developers. In his e-mail message, he indicated that educational institutions cannot keep pace with the hardware developers. Thus, "students nationwide suffer with antiquated equipment, even though it's only a few years old" (ClemmerJ@APSU.edu).

Listserv (e-mail discussion group)

Listserv groups have gained legitimacy in recent years, so in your text you might wish to give an exact date and provide the email address *only* if the citation has scholarly relevance and *only* if the list has an academic sponsor, such as an instructor of an online class.

T. L. Blackmore (online discussion, May 7, 2003) has identified the book *Echoes of Glory* for those interested in detailed battlefield maps of the American Civil War.

A. G. Funder (April 5, 2002) argued against the "judgmental process."

FTP sites

Del Reyes (2003) has shown in the following graph that "enrollment in radiology programs of study has increased by 67% in the past ten years."

CD-ROM

Grolier's Multimedia Encyclopedia (2003) explained that in recent decades huge swaths of the rain forest have been toppled; as the trees disappeared, so, too, did the flora and fauna that thrived under their canopy.

Preparing the List of References

Use the title *References* for your bibliography page. Like the body of the paper, your reference list should be double-spaced throughout. Alphabetize

Index to Bibliographic Models: APA Style

Book

Book 446

Part of a Book 447

Encyclopedia or Dictionary 447

Book with Corporate Author 447

Periodical

Journal 447

Article Retrieved from InfoTrac, Silverplatter, ProQuest, or Other Server 448

Magazine 448

Newspaper 448

Abstract

Abstract as the Cited Source 448

Abstract of an Unpublished Work 448

Abstract Retrieved from InfoTrac, Silverplatter, ProQuest, or Other Server 449

Review 449

Report 449

Nonprint Material

Computer Program 449

DVD, Videotape, Film 449

Interviews, Letters, and Memos 449

Unpublished Raw Data from a Study, Untitled Work 449

World Wide Web Sites

Article from Online Journal 450

Article from a Printed Journal, Reproduced Online 450

Article from an Internet-Only Newsletter 451

Document Created by a Private Organization, No Date 451

Chapter or Section in an Internet Document 451

Standalone Document, No Author Identified, No Date 451

Document from a University Program or Department 451

Report from a University, Available on a Private Organization's Web Site 451

Abstract 452

Article from a Printed Magazine, Reproduced Online 452

Article from an Online Magazine, No Author Listed 452

Article from an Online Newspaper 452

Bulletins and Government Documents 452–453

Message Posted to an Online Discussion Group or Forum 453

Message Posted to an Electronic Mailing List 453

Newsgroups, Message 453

Virtual Conference, report 453

Symposium, report 453

Usenet, Telnet, FTP, message 454

Library Database 454

CD-ROM

Abstract 454

Encyclopedia Article 454

Full-Text Article 454

the entries letter by letter—remembering, for example, that Adkins, Y. R., precedes Adkinson, A. G., even though *o* precedes the *y* for the first entry. Every reference used in your text, except personal communications and major classical works, should appear in your alphabetical list of references at the end of the paper. Type the first line of each entry flush left and indent succeeding lines five spaces. You may italicize or underscore names of books, periodicals, and volume numbers. Underline the punctuation mark at the end of names and volume numbers.

Book

Turlington, C. (2003). *Living yoga: Creating a life practice.*
New York: Hyperion.

List the author (surname first and then initials for given names), year of publication within parentheses, title of the book italicized or underscored and with only first word of the title and any subtitle capitalized (but do capitalize proper nouns), place of publication, and publisher. In the publisher's name omit the words *Publishing, Company*, and *Inc.*, but otherwise give a full name: Florida State University Press; Addison, Wesley, Longman; HarperCollins.

List chronologically, not alphabetically, two or more works by the same author—for example, Fitzgerald's 2002 publication would precede the 2003 publication.

Fitzgerald, R. A. (2002). Crimson glow . . .

Fitzgerald, R. A. (2003). Walking . . .

References with the same author in the same year are alphabetized and marked with lowercase letters—*a, b, c*—immediately after the date:

Murphy, T. B. (2002a). Buying trends . . .

Murphy, T. B. (2002b). Market matters . . .

Entries of a single author precede multiple-author entries beginning with the same surname without regard for the dates:

Martin, D. C. (2003). Principles . . .

Martin, D. C., & Smyth, A. F. (2001). Crimes . . .

References with the same first author and different second or third authors should be alphabetized by the surname of the second author:

Bacon, D. E., & Smithson, C. A. (2002). Arctic explorers . . .

Bacon, D. E., & Williamson, T. (2003). Seasons in . . .

If, *and only if,* the work is signed *Anonymous,* the entry begins with the word *Anonymous* spelled out, and the entry is alphabetized as if *Anonymous* were a true name. If no author is given, the title moves to the author position, and the entry is alphabetized by the first significant word of the title.

Part of a Book

List author(s), date, chapter or section title, editor (with name in normal order) preceded by "In" and followed by "(Ed.)" or "(Eds.)," the name of the book (underscored or italicized), page numbers to the specific section of the book cited (placed within parentheses), place of publication, and publisher.

Graham, K. (2003). The male bashing stereotype. In P. Elbow & P. Belanoff, *Being a writer* (pp. 249-254). New York: McGraw Hill.

If no author is listed, begin with the title of the article.

Obadiah. (1999). *Who was who in the Bible.* Nashville: Nelson.

Encyclopedia or Dictionary

Moran, J. (2002). Weather. In *World book encyclopedia* (Vol. 21, pp. 201–209). Chicago: Field Enterprises.

Book with Corporate Author

American Medical Association. (2003). *American Medical Association complete medical encyclopedia.* New York: Random House.

Periodical

Journal

List author(s), year, title of the article without quotation marks and with only the first word (and any proper nouns) capitalized, name of the journal underscored or italicized and with all major words capitalized, volume number underscored or italicized, inclusive page numbers *not* preceded by "p." or "pp."

Smiler, A. P., Gagne, D. D., & Stine-Morrow, E. A. L. (2003). Aging, memory load, and resource allocation during reading. *Psychology and Aging, 18,* 203-209.

Article Retrieved from InfoTrac, Silverplatter, ProQuest, and Other Servers

Wakschlag, L. S., & Leventhal, B. L. (1996). Consultation with young autistic children and their families. *Journal of the American Academy of Child and Adolescent Psychiatry, 35,* 963–965. Retrieved August 8, 1999, from *Expanded Academic Index* database.

Magazine

List author, the date of publication—year, month without abbreviation, and the specific day for magazines published weekly and fortnightly (every two weeks)—title of the article without quotation marks and with only the first word capitalized, name of the magazine underlined with all major words capitalized, the volume number if it is readily available, and inclusive page numbers preceded by "p." or "pp." if you do not provide the volume number. If a magazine prints the article on discontinuous pages, include all page numbers.

Creedon, Jeremiah. (2003, May/June). The greening of Tony Soprano. *Utne,* pp. 73-77.

Harman, T. D. (2003, August). The unchanging plan. *Civil War Times, 42,* 43-47.

Newspaper

List author, date (year, month, and day), title of article with only first word and proper nouns capitalized, complete name of newspaper in capitals and underlined, and the section with all discontinuous page numbers.

Haynes, T. (2003, June 10). Saving the Columbia. *Boston Globe,* p. C12.

Abstract

Abstract as the Cited Source

Pannewitz, S., Schlensog, M., Green, T. G. A., Sancho, L. G., & Schroeter, B. (2003). Are lichens active under snow in continental Antarctica? [Abstract]. *Oecologia, 135,* 30-38.

Abstract of an Unpublished Work

Darma, J. (2003). *Political institutions under dictatorship* [Abstract]. Unpublished manuscript, Knoxville: University of Tennessee.

Abstract Retrieved from InfoTrac, Silverplatter, ProQuest, or Other Servers

Gryeh, J. H., et al. (2000). Patterns of adjustment among children of battered women. *Journal of Consulting and Clinical Psychology, 68,* 84-94. Abstract retrieved August 15, 2003 from *PsycINFO* database.

Review

Sharpe, K. (2003, Summer). The whole world in your hands [Review of the book *World Atlas of Biodiversity*]. *Nature Conservancy, 53,* 86.

Report

Gorman, L.(2003). Why pay more? Simple insurance reform would save Coloradians millions (Report No. 2003-2). Golden, CO: Independence Institute.

Nonprint Material

Computer Program

Excel 2003. (2003). [Computer program]. Redmond, WA: Microsoft.

DVD, Videotape, Film

Ford, B., & Ford, S. (Producers). (2003). *Choreography on the Fly: Robert Royston & Lauree Baldovi* [Videotape]. Brentwood, CA: Images in Motion.

Interviews, Letters, and Memos

Barstow, I. (2003, May 22). "Palm reading as prediction" [Interview]. Chattanooga, TN.

Unpublished Raw Data from a Study, Untitled Work

Nathan, M., & Eller, B. J. (2003). [Homophone errors in essays of 100 9th grade writers]. Unpublished raw data.

Internet Sources

The following information conforms to the instructions of APA style. When citing sources in the References of your APA-style paper, provide this information if available:

1. Author/editor last name, followed by a comma, the initials, and a period.
2. Year of publication, followed by a comma, then month and day for magazines and newspapers, within parentheses, followed by a period.
3. Title of the article, not within quotations and not underscored, with the first word and proper nouns capitalized, followed by the total number of paragraphs within brackets only if that information is provided. *Note:* You need not count the paragraphs yourself; in fact, it's better that you don't. This is also the place to describe the work within brackets, as with [Abstract] or [Letter to the editor].
4. Name of the book, journal, or complete work, underscored or italicized, if one is listed.
5. Volume number, if listed, underscored or italicized.
6. Page numbers only if you have that data from a printed version of the journal or magazine. If the periodical has no volume number, use "p." or "pp." before the numbers; if the journal has a volume number, omit "p." or "pp.").
7. The word *Retrieved,* followed by the date of access.
8. The URL. (URLs can be quite long, but you will need to provide full data for other researchers to find the source.)

World Wide Web Sites

Article from an Online Journal

Clune, A. C. (2002). Mental disorder and its cause. *Psycoloquy, 13.* Retrieved September 23, 2003, from tp://psycprints.ecs.soton.ac.uk/archive/00000210/

Article from a Printed Journal, Reproduced Online

Many articles online are the exact duplicates of their print versions, so if you view an article in its electronic form and are confident that the electronic form is identical to the printed version, add within brackets *Electronic version*. This allows you to omit the URL.

Bowler, D. M., & Thommen, E. (2000). Attribution of mechanical and social causality to animated displays by children with autism [Electronic version]. Autism, *4*, 147-171.

Add the URL and date of access if page numbers are not indicated, as shown in this next entry:

Leshy, M. (2000). Missouri's savannas and woodlands. *Missouri Conservationist, 61*. Retrieved August 30, 2003, from http://www.conservation.state.mo.ua/nonmag/2000/08/1.htm

Article from an Internet-Only Newsletter

Tau, M. (2000, August 16). Data-jacking prevention for the psychologist. *Telehealth News.* Retrieved July 18, 2003, from http://telehealth.net/articles/datajacking.html

Document Created by a Private Organization, No Date

National Broadband Task Force. (n.d.). *An action plan for achieving basic broadband access by 2004*. Retrieved October 17, 2003, from http://broadband.gc.ca/Broadband-document/english/recommendations.htm

Chapter or Section in an Internet Document

Benton Foundation. (2003). *What is the initiative's purpose in 21st Century Skills Initiative* (sec. 1). Retrieved June 25, 2003, from http://www.benton.org/initiatives/skillsinitiative.html#Q1

Standalone Document, No Author Identified, No Date

Remember to begin the reference with the title of the document if the author of the document is not identified.

GVU's 10th WWW user survey. (n.d.). Retrieved September 11, 2003, from http://www.gvu.gatech.edu/user_surveys/survey-1998-10/

Document from a University Program or Department

Spence, S. (2003). *Department of Humanities: Writing Criteria.* Retrieved August 25, 2003, from Clayton College and State University, Department of Humanities Web site: http://a-s.clayton.edu/humanities/

Report from a University, Available on a Private Organization's Web Site

University of Illinois at Chicago, Health Research and Policy Centers. (2000). *Partners with tobacco use research centers: Advancing transdisciplinary science and policy studies.* Retrieved September 9, 2003, from the Robert Wood Johnson Foundation Web site: http://www.rwjf.org/programs/npoDetail.jsp?id=TRC

Abstract

Townsend, J. W. (2003). Reproductive behavior in the context of global population [Abstract]. *American Psychologist, 58*. Retrieved October 13, 2003, from http://www.apa.org/journals/amp/303ab.html#2

Article from a Printed Magazine, Reproduced Online

Allmon, J. (2003, March). Grow native! For beautifully resilient, drought-tolerant landscapes. *Kansas City Gardener.* Retrieved June 17, 2003, from http://www.grownative.org/index.cfm?fuseaction=resources.articleDetail&articleID=21

Creedon. (2003, May/June). The greening of Tony Soprano. *Utne.* Retrieved July 19, 2003, from ttp://www.utne.com/pub/2003_117/promo/10500-1.html

Article from an Online Magazine, No Author Listed

Housing market fueled by rising consumer confidence, low rates. (2003, June 12). *Builder Online.* Retrieved June 12, 2003, from http://www.builderonline.com/pages/builderonline/Story.nsp?story_id=39428052&ID=builderonline&scategory=Computers&type=news

Note: Avoid listing page numbers for online articles.

Article from an Online Newspaper

Ippolito, M. (2003, June 12). Delta Moon rising locally. *Atlanta Journal-Constitution Online.* Retrieved June 12, 2003, from http://www.accessatlanta.com/hp/content/entertainment/features/0603/12delta.html

Zaino, J. S. Learning a little discipline. (2003, June 12). *Chronicle of Higher Education*. Retrieved June 12, 2003, from http://chronicle.com/jobs/2003/06/2003061201c.htm

Bulletin

Bulletins are brief reports and brochures, usually printed in paperback form, which you should treat as a book.

Murphy, F. L., (2003). *What you don't know can hurt you.* Retrieved October 19, 2003, from the Preventive Health Center Web site: http://www.mdphc.com/education/fiber.html

Government Document

U.S. Cong. House. (2003, January 7). *Unlawful Internet gambling funding prohibition act.* House Resolution 21. Retrieved September 18, 2003, from http://thomas.loc.gov/cgi-bin/query/D?c108:2:./temp/~c108k7golG::

Message Posted to an Online Discussion Group or Forum

Lettevall, E. (2003, January 7). Analysis of small population size [Msg. 12]. Message posted to Population Discussion Group at http://canuck.dnr.cornell.edu/HyperNews/get/marked/marked/289/1.html

Message Posted to an Electronic Mailing List

Cheramy, R. (2003, April 18). Inexpensive and easy site hosting. Message posted to Fogo mailing list, archived at http://impressive.net/archives/fogo/20030418170059.GA23011@bougan.org

Newsgroup, Message

Burke, G. V. (2003, November 5). Narrative bibliography [Msg. 33]. Message posted to jvmacmillan@mail.csu.edu

Virtual Conference, Report

A virtual conference occurs entirely online, so there is no geographic location. Treat a report as a book.

Verhey, S. D., Stefanides, S., & Pinkart, H. C. *Genomics and Education: An Undergraduate Genome Project.* Paper presented at the Second Virtual Conference on Genomics and Bioinformatics. Retrieved October 1, 2003, from http://www.ndsu.nodak.edu/virtual-genomics/Proc_VCGB2002.pdf

Symposium, Report

Eisenfeld, B. 2003, October 19). *Tutorial: CRM 101: The Basics.* Paper presented at the Gartner Symposium ITxpo, Orlando, Florida.

Abstract retrieved October 22, 2003, from http://www.gartner.com/2_events/symposium/2003/asset_46841.jsp

Usenet, Telnet, FTP, message

Haas, H. (2000, August 5) Link checker that works with cold fusion [Msg. 34]. Message posted to impressive.net/archives/fogo/200000805113615.AI4381@w3.org

Library Databases

University servers give you access to many sources stored in large databases, such as PsycInfo, ERIC, and netLibrary. Use this next form, which gives the date of your retrieval, the name of the database, and if readily available the item number within parentheses. If you cite only from the abstract, mention that fact in your reference entry (see the Kang entry below).

Colemen, L. & Coleman J. (2002). The measurement of puberty: A review. *Journal of Adolescence, 25,* 535-550. Retrieved April 2, 2003, from ERIC database (EJ65060).

Kang, H. S. (2002). What is missing in interlanguage: Acquisition of determiners by Korean learners of English. *Working Papers in Educational Linguistics, 18.* Abstract retrieved April 2, 2003, from ERIC database.

CD-ROM

Material cited from a CD-ROM requires different forms.

Abstract

Figueredo, A. J., & McCloskey, L. A. (1993). Sex, money, and paternity: The evolutionary psychology of domestic violence [CD-ROM]. *Ethnology and Sociobiology, 14,* 353-79. Abstract from Silverplatter File: *PsychLIT* database (81-3654).

Encyclopedia Article

African American history: Abolitionist movement [CD-ROM]. (2003). *Encarta encyclopedia.* Redmond, WA: Microsoft.

Full-Text Article

Firestone, D. (2000, August 10). The south comes of age on religion and politics [CD-ROM]. *New York Times,* p. A-17. Available from UMI-ProQuest file (Item 3602-108).

Variations on the APA Style for Other Disciplines in the Social Sciences

Use APA style as explained in pages 436–454 for the following disciplines:

Education
Geography
Home Economics
Physical Education
Political Science

Alternative styles may be used for papers in Linguistics and Sociology, as explained next.

Linguistics

In-Text Citation

In-text citations for linguistic studies almost always include a specific page reference to the work along with the date, separated by a colon—for example, "Jones 2003: 12–18" or "Gifford's recent reference (2002: 162)." Therefore, follow basic standards for the name and year system (see pages 438–444) with a colon to separate the year and the page number(s).

References List

As shown below, label the list as *References* and alphabetize the entries. Use full names for authors if available. Place the year immediately after the author's name. For journal entries, use a period rather than a colon or comma to separate volume and page. There is *no* underlining. Linguistic journals are abbreviated (e.g., Lg for Linguistics); others are not. A sample list follows:

References

Bauschatz, Paul. 2003. Rhyme and the structure of English consonants. [Abstract]. English Language and Lg. 7. Retrieved September 19, 2003, from the World Wide Web: http://titles.cambridge.org/journals/journal_article.asp?mnemonic=ELL&pii=S1360674303001035

Blot, Richard K. (Ed). Language and social identity. Westport, CT: Greenwood Publishing.

Caballero, Rosario. 2003. Metaphor and genre: The presence and role of metaphor in the building review. Applied Lg. 24.145–167.

Fischer, Steven Roger. A history of language. London: Reaktion, 2003.

Nesselhauf, Nadja. 2003. The use of collocations by advanced learners of English and some implications for teaching. Applied Lg. 24.223-242.

Och, Franz Josef, & Ney, Hermann. 2003. A systematic comparison of various statistical alignment models. Computational Lg. 29.19-51.

Unsworth, Sharon. 2000. Review of the acquisition of second language syntax, by Susan M. Braidi. Web Journal of Modern Language Lg. 4-5. Retrieved September 18, 2003, from the World Wide Web: http://wjmll.ncl.ac.uk/issue04-05/unsworth_braidi.htm

Note: The form of these entries conforms in general to that advocated by the Linguistic Society of America, <**http://www.lsadc.org/language/langstyl.html**>. Updates to the language style sheet are published annually in the journal *Language* in the December issue.

Sociology and Social Work

In-Text Citation

Use the name and year system as explained in Using In-Text Citations in APA Style beginning on page 438.

References List

Use the format shown below, which duplicates the style of the *American Journal of Sociology*, or use APA style. This style is similar to MLA style, except that the date follows the author.

References

Brannen, Julia. 2003. "Towards a Typology of Intergenerational Relations: Continuities and Change in Families." *Sociological Research Online, 8*. 28 June 2003 <http://www.socresonline.org.uk/8/2/brannen.html>.

Eason, Amy. 2003. "There's a Disorder or Syndrome for Everyone." *News Daily*. [Jonesboro, GA] 11 June: 3B.

Frazier, James W. 2003. *Race and Place: Equity Issues in Urban America*. New York: Westview.

Gerteis, Joseph. 2002. "The Possession of Civic Virtue: Movement Narratives of Race and Class in the Knights of Labor." *American Journal of Sociology, 108:* 580-615. Abstract.

Shilling, Chris. 2003. *The Body and Social Theory*. Thousand Oaks, CA: Sage.

Formatting an APA Paper

APA style applies to three types of papers: theoretical articles, reports of empirical studies, and review articles (as explained earlier). Each requires a different arrangement of the various parts of the paper.

Theoretical Paper

The theoretical paper should be arranged much like a typical research paper, with the additional use of centered side heads and italicized side heads to divide the sections.

The introduction should:

- Establish the problem under examination.
- Discuss its significance to the scientific community.
- Provide a review of the literature (see Chapter 10 for more information).
- Quote the experts who have commented on the issue.
- Provide a thesis sentence that gives your initial perspective on the issue.

The body of the theoretical paper should:

- Trace the various issues.
- Establish a past-to-present perspective.
- Compare and analyze the various aspects of the theories.
- Cite extensively from the literature on the subject.

The conclusion of the theoretical paper should:

- Defend one theory as it grows from the evidence in the body.
- Discuss the implications of the theory.
- Suggest additional work that might be launched in this area.

Report of Empirical Research

The general design of a report of original research, an empirical study, should conform to the following general plan.

The introduction should:

- Establish the problem or topic to be examined.

- Provide background information, including a review of literature on the subject.
- Give the purpose and rationale for the study, including the hypothesis that serves as the motivation for the experiment.

The body of the report of empirical research should:

- Provide a methods section for explaining the design of the study with respect to subjects, apparatus, and procedure.
- Offer a results section for listing in detail the statistical findings of the study.

The conclusion of a report of empirical research should:

- Interpret the results and discuss the implications of the findings in relation to the hypothesis and to other research on the subject.

Review Article

The review article is usually a shorter paper because it examines a published work or two without extensive research on the part of the review writer.

The introduction of the review should:

- Identify the problem or subject under study and its significance.
- Summarize the article(s) under review.

The body of the review should:

- Provide a systematic analysis of the article(s), the findings, and the apparent significance of the results.

The conclusion of the review should:

- Discuss the implications of the findings and make judgments as appropriate.

Writing the Abstract

You should provide an abstract with every paper written in APA style. An abstract is a quick but thorough summary of the contents of your paper. It is read first and may be the only part read, so it must be:

1. *Accurate,* in order to reflect both the purpose and content of the paper.
2. *Self-contained,* so that it (1) explains the precise problem and defines terminology, (2) describes briefly both the methods used and the findings, and (3) gives an overview of your conclusions—but see item 4 below.
3. *Concise and specific,* in order to remain within a range of 80 to 150 words.
4. *Nonevaluative,* in order to report information, not to appraise or assess the value of the work.
5. *Coherent and readable,* in a style that uses an active, vigorous syntax and that uses the present tense to describe results (e.g., the findings confirm) but the past tense to describe testing procedures (e.g., I attempted to identify).

For theoretical papers, the abstract should include:

- The topic in one sentence, if possible
- The purpose, thesis, and scope of the paper
- A brief reference to the sources used (e.g., published articles, books, personal observation)
- Your conclusions and the implications of the study

For a report of an empirical study (see also Chapter 8), the abstract should include the four items listed above for theoretical papers, plus three more:

- The problem and hypothesis in one sentence if possible
- A description of the subjects (e.g., species, number, age, type)
- The method of study, including procedures and apparatus

Sample Paper in APA Style

The following paper demonstrates the format and style of a paper written to the standards of APA style. The paper requires a title page that establishes the running head, an abstract, in-text citations to the name and year of each source used, and a list of references. Marginal notations, below, explain specific requirements.

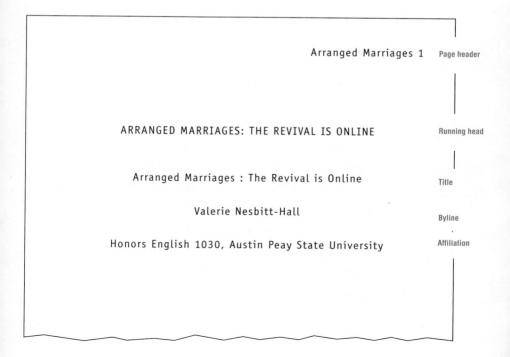

Arranged Marriages 1 **Page header**

ARRANGED MARRIAGES: THE REVIVAL IS ONLINE **Running head**

Arranged Marriages : The Revival is Online **Title**

Valerie Nesbitt-Hall **Byline**

Honors English 1030, Austin Peay State University **Affiliation**

Abstract

Computer match making was investigated to examine the theoretical implications of marriages arranged in part by online dating. The goal was to determine the effect of Internet activity on the private lives of participants. The social and psychological implications were determined by an examination of the literature, a profile of the participants, and a case study that interviewed an affected couple. Results were mixed with failures balanced against successful matches. The social implications affect the workplace as well as the private lives of the men and women who are active in chat rooms and dating services. The psychological implications involve infidelity, damage to self-esteem, the need for psychotherapy, but—importantly—a chance for true and lasting love.

Arranged Marriages: The Revival Is Online

Establish the topic along with social and or psychological issues that will be examined.

Arranged marriages are back, but with a twist. Online dating services provide today, among other things, an opportunity for people to meet, chat, reveal things about themselves, and--as one source has expressed it--"play the role of patriarchal grandfathers, searching for good matches based on any number of criteria that you select" (Razdan, 2003, p. 71). In addition, listserv groups by the thousands bring people together by the millions. Thus, computer matchmaking has social and psychological implications that are being examined more and more by psychologists. This paper will examine the theoretical implications of marriages arranged in part by online dating.

Figures vary greatly on the amount of activity. One source (Cha, 2003) reported that 37 million people used online matchmaking services in April 2003, but another source (Nussbaum, 2002) said only 15 million visited a dating site in all of 2002. Nevertheless, the figure is in the millions, and that is substantial. *People Weekly* (1999) reported that 50 million Americans were registered online, and that figure has climbed considerably since 1999. People have visited, many have found a mate, and some have even married. Match.com's and America Online's dating areas boast about hundreds of marriages that began as personal online messages. Can it be called a social revolution? Some have said "yes" to that question because about one-fifth of all singles in the country are online, prearranging their meetings and their lives, assuring themselves a better match than can be found in an evening's trip to a local nightclub. For example, Cooper (2002) has argued that online dating has the potential to lower the nation's divorce rate. Kass (2003) has identified the "distanced nearness" of a chat room that encourages self-revelation while maintaining personal boundaries" (cited in Razdan, 2003, p. 71). Epstein (2003) has argued that many arranged marriages, whether planned by parents or in cyberspace, have produced enduring love because of rational deliberation performed before moments of passionate impulse.

A theoretical study depends heavily upon the literature, which must be cited in correct APA form.

With the divorce rate at 50 percent, any marriage is already a roll of the dice, so experts have begun to agree that online dating reverts to the prearranged meetings of two young people whom the families have identified as compatible for economic, political, religious, and social reasons. Persons online can enjoy distance, even hiding their real names for a while, to enjoy "an intimate but protected (cyber)space" (Kass, 2003, cited in Razdan, p. 71). Participants online can erect and maintain personal fences of privacy but at the same time reveal private feelings that they might never express in face-to-face meetings.

Center major headings.

Method

The Internet dating services have made romance a commodity (Brooks, 2003). Match.com, founded in 1995 and now located in 27 countries, offers a subscription-based business model. Subscribers may place a personal advertisement for free, but to participate and send e-mail they must be members and pay about $20 per month. With several million active members, Match.com profits greatly from its primary commodity--romance. American Online, Yahoo!, Netscape--all the network servers offer the search machines--for a price, of course. "If you are prepared to pay a little--or a lot--it has never been easier to meet a partner," Brooks (2003) said. But Brooks has also asked, "So why are so many people still single?" And then Brooks supplied this answer: "Perhaps the commodification of *romance* hasn't been as good for our hearts as it has for business."

Scientific papers demand your explanation of procedures used in the study.

Subjects

Subheads are italicized and set flush left margin.

The people who participate in online romance run the whole range of human subjects. Sanz (1994) identified the typical subject as "male, college educated, affluent and, contrary to popular opinion, not a nerd." The case studies, seen below in the Results section, seem to confirm this finding, but in nine years since the study women have crowded into cyberspace in great numbers. Millions now consider meeting someone over the Internet like phoning them or sending a fax. It has become an everyday thing to send dozens of e-mails, so the next logical step is finding romance on the Internet.

A detailed description of the subjects is a normal part of scientific investigation.

High-profile subjects now appear as participants, and with success. Rush Limbaugh, the right-wing radio commentator, met his bride, Marta Fitzgerald, on the Internet. Cyberdating for subjects of high or low profile has a measure of safety while the people conduct a typical human courtship. This courtship, according to Kass (1999), is aimed at finding and winning over an ideal mate.

Persons on both keyboards can move as quickly or as slowly as they wish to find someone. Then the process of winning understanding and affection can also be measured. Each person is involved in an arranged courtship, and it's arranged on his or her terms for the heterosexual or the homosexual, for persons of the Jewish faith, for horse lovers, and for skiing buffs.

The Internet also serves the modest person. In this age of liberated sexual activity there still exist many women, and men, who remain modest and cautious. Sexual self-restraint by women in this day and age may even be a magnet for men. We should witness the fact that *The Rules* by Fein and Schneider (1995) was a best-seller because it offered, for example, "Rule 15: Don't Rush into Sex and Other Rules for Intimacy" and "Rule 3: Don't Stare at Men or Talk Too Much." Fein and Schneider (2002) have also targeted online dating with their *Rules for Online Dating*, which offers such rules as "Rule 1: Don't Answer Men's Ads or E-mail Them First" and "Rule 8: Block Yourself from Instant Messages." The books are catalogs on how to be modest. Kass (1999) said in a speech:

> Modesty not only spurred a man to love; equally important, it empowered a woman by defending her against the hazards of her own considerable erotic desires. She had more at stake in sex than did the man. (In fact, even in our age of female contraception and easy abortion, pregnancy remains a concern mainly for women--indeed, arguably, more so than ever, albeit for different reasons: the law now lodges responsibility and choice regarding pregnancy and childbirth entirely with

Use present tense verbs (*serves, exist*) for what happens or can happen now.

Use the present perfect tense (*have targeted*) for actions completed and for actions continued into the present time.

Use the past tense (*was, said*) with this rule in mind—*Use the past tense to express actions that occurred at a specific time in the past, as in "Kass (1999) said."*

Indent block quotations five spaces.

her; in consequence, men are no longer under social pressure to marry a woman should she become pregnant with or give birth to his child.)

The chaste or modest person can protect herself or himself by the walls of Internet protection--usernames, passwords, and other security measures.

Schneider and Weiss (2001) list some of the advantages of online romance: It links people miles apart; impressions are made by words, not looks; there is time to contemplate a message; there is time to compose a well-written response; and messages can be reviewed and revised before transmission (p. 66).

Procedures

The *method* section of the paper should include a description of the study's design as well as the tools used, if appropriate, and the procedures followed by you and/or by those you cite.

The process for logging on and sending messages is similar at all the sites, but the nature of the matchmaking differs. Emode had a group of PhDs design a personality test to measure participants' styles, temperaments, independence, romanticism, importance of wealth, and other factors (Cha, 2003). Participants in a pool of 1 million are matched carefully. Emode's spokesperson said, "Our goal is for you to go into the first date knowing much more than you would after three or four dates" (C. Johnson, cited in Cha, 2003, p. A01). Emode and Match.com permit users to search by scores on various tests. Once a person puts in a profile, the search engines go to work at Match.com or Yahoo! and begin to send the participant the usernames of possible matches. Another service is eHarmony, which offers scientific matchmaking but does not permit users to search or view ads. Instead, eHarmony requires a 45-minute, 500-question compatibility test and permits the user to contact only screened, compatible people (Cha, 2003).

Procedures to access a matching partner are varied, yet each has one thing in common--to bring two compatible people together on the Web. There they can e-mail each other, participate in instant messaging (IM) chats, send attachments of favorite songs or personal photographs, and eventually exchange real names, phone numbers, and addresses. Newsgroups work in a similar fashion with back-and-forth discussion, even argument, about a variety of topics.

Case Study

Research uncovered a match that resulted in marriage. The two subjects, Jennifer and Steven, were interviewed on the matter of cyber romance. What follows is a brief summary of the interview, which is on file. The couple met online in September 1996 in a chat room, not on a matching service. Steven initiated the first contact, and they chatted anonymously for nine months before Jennifer initiated an exchange of phone numbers, addresses, and photographs. Steven initiated the first meeting in person after 11 months, inviting Jennifer to travel from the United States to Glasgow, Scotland. Seven months later they married; it was 1.5 years from the time they met at the Internet newsgroup.

See pages 211–213 for more details on concluding interviews.

When asked if online romance gave her protection of her privacy and time to prearrange things, Jennifer answered in the affirmative with emphasis. When asked who was more aggressive in pushing forward the romance, Steven said it was a mutual thing. Both agreed that when they finally met in person, they really knew each other--spiritually, emotionally, and intellectually. The matter of different nationalities also played a role on two fronts--immigration matters and the concern of Jennifer's parents that she would fly to Scotland to see someone she had never met.

When asked if the relationship had been excellent to this point, both replied with affirmative answers. When asked if they would recommend online dating to others who are seeking mates, Steven and Jennifer said, yes, under the right circumstances--"be cautious and take your time."

Results

In many cases, the results section will include tables and charts and statistics.

Results of online romance can be positive or negative. First the negative, Miller (1996) said:

> There's a big group of married baby boomers. When we look at ourselves in the mirror in our 40's, we wonder, "Am I still sexy?" Some women get facelifts; men get sports cars. Online infatuations can be another antidote . . . . From my research, only about one in four online relationships turns out happy. People get into this bodice-ripping mentality in the beginning. But after you've had "sex" with someone the virtual way, there's a real desire to actually be intimate. When the two do meet, the relationship can't handle reality. Either the affair ends or it destroys their marriages. (p.39)

Yet, as shown by the case studies, online romances can have happy endings.

Discussion

The effects of online romance reach into the workplace as well as the personal lives of men and women in a variety of ways, both socially and psychologically.

Social Implications

Indented paragraph headings should be italicized and end with a period.

The workplace. BusinessWeek (1999) reported: "There's no question cybersex is invading the workplace. A recent survey from Stanford University found that roughly 20% of those going online for sexual material use their office computers to do so" (p. 27B). What many workers fail to realize is that the computer belongs to the company, and the hard drive can be examined, even if the user thinks he or she has erased the files. In this writer's opinion, the best avenue for safety of privacy is to take out the hard drive and destroy it with a hammer.

Marital counseling. Al Cooper (2002), a psychologist at Stanford University, has explained that marital counseling because of cybersex dalliances is "exploding" (cited in *BusinessWeek*, 27B). Cooper cited the attraction of the Web's access, anonymity, and cost as promoting sexual compulsions for married individuals, couples, and singles.

Adultery. Miller (1996) has examined affairs on the Internet chat rooms and at dating services, and he has commented on their threat to marriages:

> Affairs [in the virtual world] often progress quickly to the point where they're considerably more intimate than a one-night stand. Are they adultery? As a writer, I think it's a gray area. It's something that lawyers and men and women of the cloth need to decide. (p. 39)

Virtual sex chat that sometimes involves the exchange of pictures has no physical contact between the two people, so can it be adultery? The courts may be deciding that question as we speak because divorces are occurring regularly as one spouse discovers what's on the other's computer hard drive.

The woman's role. The woman must identify her role in a relationship to the men in her life. In that regard, Bloom (1993) said:

> Even the most independent-minded erotic man becomes dependent on the judgment of a woman, and a serious woman, one who is looking not only for an attractive man but for one who will love her and protect her, may be the best possible judge of a man's virtues and thus be regarded by even the most serious man as the supreme tribunal of his worth. (p. 104)

Cooper has observed that "the medium forces potential partners to talk, which," he says, "is something women in particular seem to want to do" (cited in "Intimacy and the Internet," 1996). Thus, although more men frequent the Web sites, the women may benefit at a higher rate, in part because they are more cautious and because anonymity gives them time to prearrange any meeting.

The man's role. Times they are a-changing. Women as much as men are cruising the Internet, and they are more serious than the men. The typical male enters the Internet dating service thinking about sex, but he encounters women thinking about a relationship. The two are not entirely antithetical, but the timing varies, and the man discovers on the Internet that the woman controls much of the timing. "They do not realize," Kass (1999) has explained, "that what they need is courtship or something like it." Perhaps that's what men have begun to learn by online romance.

Psychological Implications

It is too soon, perhaps, to understand the full ramifications of online romance. Certainly, people have been severely wounded, both psychologically and physically, by venturing onto the Internet and getting trapped into damaging and fatal liaisons. At the same time, the ability to prearrange a meeting after weeks and months of conversation has its benefits, as shown by the case study. A man or woman who ventures onto the Internet will expose himself or herself to some of the same dangers as a blind date, except for the built-in firewalls between a username on the Web and somebody actually knocking on the door, ready for a date.

Online infidelity. Young et al. (2000) have suggested that electronic communication can lead to marital discord, separation, and possible divorce. The ACE model (Anonymity, Convenience,

Escape) has served as a driving force behind "cybersexual addiction," and it explains the dynamics of virtual adultery.

Escape and damage to self-esteem. "Affairs can be a betrayal of the self and can imply that a person is avoiding knowing himself/herself or the partner when substituting fantasy sex online for a real relationship" (Maheu, 1999). A woman at midnight escapes into her addiction with an online lover, a man she has never met who may not even be a man, and she pretends the next day as she serves breakfast to her family that all is well. The damage to her psyche is like the early morning "walk of shame" that some young women experience--that return alone to their rooms from some encounter while the man curls up in bed with a smile on his face.

Psychotherapy. Participants in the online dating game can become depressed, angry, lose self-esteem, and go in search of psychotherapy. Cooper (2002), who is director of the San Jose Marital and Sexuality Centre, has reported that marital counseling is "exploding" because of fallouts from one partner's enticement into sex on the Internet, either the pornography or the online romance or the all-night chat sessions. In addition, the machinery continues to entice more people into sexual adventures; Klaffke (2003) reported recently that software now exists that "allows singles to post personal profiles and peruse those of others through text messaging on their cell phones," and as you may know, cell phones can now transfer photographs.

In conclusion, the world of online romance is growing at a staggering rate, with millions signing on each year and with thousands finding happiness and with thousands more finding sexual chaos and dangerous liaisons. Yet little research is being done in this area. My search of the literature produced a surprisingly limited number of journal articles. Maheu (1999) has

The conclusion will often include a statement on the state of research in the area of the study.

discussed methods of helping clients, even to the point of counseling in cyberspace itself, which would establish professional relationships online. Schneider and Weiss (2001) describe online addiction but offer little psychoanalysis. Cooper (2002) has an excellent collection of articles in his guidebook for clinicians. Counseling must be in place for persons who substitute fantasy sex online for a true relationship. However, numerous case studies also show that online romance can produce healthy relationships and successful marriages.

References

References begin on a new page.

Citation for a part of a book.

Citation for a book.

Citation for an article from a library's database.

Barak, A., & Fisher, W. A. The future of sexuality. In A. Cooper (Ed.). *Sex and the Internet: A guidebook for clinicians* (pp. 263-280). New York: Brunner-Routledge.

Bloom, A. (1993). *Love and friendship*. New York: Simon & Schuster.

Cha, A. E. (2003, May 4). ISO romance? Online matchmakers put love to the test. *Washington Post*, p. A01. Retrieved April 9, 2003, from Lexis-Nexis database.

Cooper, A. (Ed.). (2002). *Sex and the Internet: A guidebook for clinicians*. New York: Brunner-Routledge.

Fein, E., & Schneider, S. (1995). *The rules*. New York: Time-Warner.

Fein, E., & Schneider, S. (2002). *The rules for online dating*. New York: Pocket Books.

Intimacy and the Internet. (1996). *Contemporary sexuality, 30*. Retrieved April 10, 2003, from http://www.sex-centre.com/InternetandSex/Index_Internt_Sex.htm

Kass, A. A. (1999). A case for courtship (working paper No. 73). Address delivered to the Institute for American Values. New York: IAV.

Kass, A. A., & Kass, L. R. (Eds.). (2000). *Wing to wing, oar to oar: Readings on courting and marrying.* South Bend, Indiana: University of Notre Dame Press.

Klaffke, P. (2003, April 28). Never be lonely: Look dates over on a cellphone. *Calgary Herald* (Alberta, Canada), p. D3. Retrieved April 4, 2003, from Lexis-Nexis database.

Leiblum, S., & Döring, N. (2002). Internet sexuality: Known risks and fresh chances for women. In A. Cooper (Ed.). *Sex and the Internet: A guidebook for clinicians* (pp. 19-45). New York: Brunner-Routledge.

Maheu, M. M. (1999). Women's Internet behavior: Providing psychotherapy offline and online for cyber-infidelity. Paper presented at the Annual Conference of the American Psychological Association, Boston, MA. Abstract retrieved April 9, 2003, from http://telehealth.net/articles/women/internet.html

Miller, M. (1996, April 8). Love at first byte. *People Weekly, 45,* 39. Retrieved April 5, 2003, from InfoTrac database.

Nussbaum, E. (2002, December 15). The year in ideas: Online personals are cool. *New York Times*, sec. 6, p. 106. Retrieved April 8, 2003, from http://www.nytimes.com

Razdan, A. (2003, May-June). What's love got to do with it? *Utne*, pp. 69-71.

Ross, M. W., & Kauth, M. R. Men who have sex with men, and the Internet: Emerging clinical issues and their management. In A. Cooper (Ed.). *Sex and the Internet: A guidebook for clinicians* (pp. 263-280). New York: Brunner-Routledge.

Sanz, C. (1994, February 21). Where has love gone? *People Weekly*, 41, 40-44.

Citation for a conference presentation.

Citation for a magazine article.

Schneider, J., & Weiss, R. (2001). *Cybersex exposed: Simple fantasy or obsession?* Center City, Minnesota: Hazelden.

They've got love. (1999, February 15). *People Weekly, 51*, 46-52. Retrieved April 4, 2003, from InfoTrac database.

When Cupid uses a cursor. (1999, February 22). *Business Week.* Retrieved April 5, 2003, from InfoTrac database.

Young, K., Griffin, S., Shelley, E., Cooper, A., O'Mara, J., & Buchanan, J. (2002). Online infidelity: A new dimension in couple relationships with implications for evaluation and treatment. *Sexual Addiction and Compulsivity, 7*: 59-74. Abstract retrieved April 4, 2003, from InfoTrac database.

19 The Footnote System: CMS Style

The fine arts and some fields in the humanities (but not literature) use traditional footnotes, which should conform to standards set by *The Chicago Manual of Style* (CMS), 15th ed., 2003. In the CMS system, you must place superscript numerals within the text (like this[15]), and place documentary footnotes on corresponding pages.

If you wish to group all your notes into one list, see the instructions on pages 281–282.

The discussion below assumes that notes will appear as footnotes; however, some instructors accept endnotes—that is, all notes appear together at the end of the paper, not at the bottom of individual pages.

There are two types of footnotes: One documents your sources with bibliographic information, but the other can discuss related matters, explain your methods of research, suggest related literature, provide biographical information, or offer information not immediately pertinent to your discussion.

To see examples of content notes as opposed to documentation notes, see pages 282–285.

If available, use the footnote or endnote feature of your software. It will not only insert the raised superscript number but also keep your footnotes arranged properly at the bottom of each page or keep your endnotes in a correct list. In most instances, the software will insert the superscript numeral, but it will not write the note automatically; you must type in the essential data in the correct style.

Inserting a Superscript Numeral in Your Text

Use Arabic numerals typed slightly above the line (like this[12]). In both Microsoft Word and WordPerfect, go to Font and select Superscript or go to Insert and select Footnote. Place a superscript numeral at the end of each quotation or paraphrase, with the number following immediately without a space after the final word or mark of punctuation, as in this sample:

> Steven A. LeBlanc, an archaeologist at Harvard University, along with several other scholars, argues instead that "humans have been at

each others' throats since the dawn of the species."[1] Robin Yates, for example, says the ancient ancestors of the Chinese used "long-range projectile weapons" as long ago as 28,000 BC for both hunting and "intrahuman conflict."[2] Arthur Ferrill observes, "When man first learned how to write, he already had war to write about."[3] Ferrill adds, "In prehistoric times man was a hunter and a killer of other men. The killer instinct in the prehistoric male is clearly attested by archaeology in fortifications, weapons, cave paintings, and skeletal remains."[4]

The footnotes that relate to these in-text superscript numerals will appear at the bottom of the page, as shown here:

1. Steven A. LeBlanc, "Prehistory of Warfare," *Archaeology* (May/June, 2003), 18.

2. Robin Yates, "Early China," in *War and Society in the Ancient and Medieval Worlds*, ed. Kurt Raaflaub and Nathan Rosenstein (Cambridge, Mass.: Center for Hellenic Studies, 1999): 9.

3. Arthur Ferrill, "Neolithic Warfare," Frontline Educational Foundation, http://eserver.org/history/neolithic-war.txt.

4. Ibid.

However, you may place the notes at the back of your paper, so you should usually include a source's name in your text. The first example below implies a source that will be found in the footnote; the second expresses the name in the text. Some writers prefer the first approach, others the second.

Implied reference:

The organic basis of autism is generally agreed upon. Three possible causes for autism have been identified: behavioral syndrome, organic brain disorder, or a range of biological and psychosocial factors.[9]

Expressed reference:

Martin Rutter has acknowledged that the organic basis of autism is generally agreed upon. Rutter named three possible causes for autism: behavioral syndrome, organic brain disorder, or a range of biological and psychosocial factors.[10]

Index to Footnote Models

Book 476
Collection or Anthology 477
Journal Article 477
Magazine Article 477
Newspaper Article 477
Review Article 477
Nonprint Source 478
Encyclopedia 478
Government Documents 478
Television 478
Film or DVD 478
Musical Work 478
Biblical Reference 478
Scholarly Project 479
Article Online, Limited Information 479
Magazine Article Reproduced Online 479
Journal Article Online Reproduced Online 479
Journal Article Online with No Author Listed 479
Article from a Scientific Database 479
Article Access from a Database through the Library System 479
Book Online 480
CD-ROM Source 480
Electronic Mailing List, Archived 480
Article from an Online Service 480
E-mail 480

Writing Full or Abbreviated Notes

MLA style permits you to omit a bibliography page as long as you give full data to the sources in each of your initial footnotes.

1. James W. Hall, *Rough Draft* (New York: St. Martin's Press, 2000), 49.

However, you may provide a comprehensive bibliography to each source and abbreviate all footnotes entries, even the initial ones, since full data will be found in the bibliography.

1. Hall, *Rough Draft*, 4.

The bibliography entry would read this way:

Hall, James W. *Rough Draft*. New York: St. Martin's Press, 2000.

Consult with your instructor on this matter if you are uncertain about the proper format for a specific course.

Formatting and Writing the Footnotes

Place footnotes at the bottom of pages to correspond with superscript numerals (see immediately above). Some papers will require footnotes on almost every page. Follow these conventions:

1. **Spacing.** In academic papers not intended for publication, footnotes are commonly typed single-spaced and placed at the foot of the page, usually

with a line space between each note. Drafts and manuscript intended for publication in print or on the Web should have all notes double-spaced and placed together on one page at the end of the paper. The student example at the end of this chapter shows single-spaced footnotes. A Notes page with double spacing can be found later in this chapter.

2. **Indention.** Indent the first line of the note five spaces or one inch (usually one click of the tab key).
3. **Numbering.** Number the footnotes consecutively throughout the entire paper with an indented number, a period, and space, as shown in the examples throughout this chapter.
4. **Placement.** Collect at the bottom of each page all footnotes to citations made on that page.
5. **Distinguish footnotes from text.** Separate footnotes from the text by triple spacing or, if you prefer, by a twelve-space bar line from the left margin.
6. **Footnote form.** Basic forms of notes should conform to the following styles.

Book

List the author, followed by a comma, the title underlined or in italics, the publication data within parenthesis (city: publisher, year), followed by a comma and the page number(s). Unless ambiguity would result, the abbreviations *p.* and *pp.* may be omitted.

1. Steven A. LeBlanc, *Constant Battles: The Myth of the Peaceful, Noble Savage* (New York: St. Martin's Press, 2003), 20–23.

List two authors without a comma:

2. Doug Sulpy and Ray Schweighardt, *Get Back: The Unauthorized Chronicle of the Beatles "Let It Be" Disaster* (New York: St. Martins Press, 1997),18.

See pages 480–481 for further details about subsequent references and the use of Latinate phrases.

List three authors separated by commas. *Note:* Publisher's names are spelled out in full, but the words *Company* and *Inc.* are omitted. Reference to an edition follows the title or the editors, if listed (see footnote 6 on the next page).

3. James S. Mickelson, Karen S. Haynes, and Barbara Mikulski, *Affecting Change: Social Workers in the Political Arena*, 4th ed. (Boston: Allyn and Bacon, 2000), 340-41.

For more than three authors, use *et al.* after mention of the lead author:

4. Nina Baym et al., eds., "Introduction," *Norton Anthology of American Literature*, 6th ed. (New York: Norton, 2003), 4.

For a subsequent reference to an immediately preceding source, use "Ibid." in the roman typeface, not in italics and not underscored:

5. Ibid.

Collection or Anthology

6. Sandra Leiblum and Nicola Döring, "Internet Sexuality: Known Risks and Fresh Chances for Women," in *Sex and the Internet: A Guidebook for Clinicians*, ed. Al Cooper (New York: Brunner-Routledge, 2002), 20-21.

Journal Article

7. Gar Smith, "Water Wars, Water Cures," *Earth Island Journal* 15 (2003): 30.

Note: Use a colon before the page number of a journal but a comma before page numbers for magazines and books.

Magazine Article

8. Leslie Allen, "Comparing Notes with Lewis and Clark," *American Heritage*, May 2003, 45.

Newspaper Article

9. Rhonda Abrams, "Latest FCC Deregulation Move Hurts Small Businesses," *Tennessean* [Nashville], 18 May 2003, 3E.

10. John Kifner, "The Holiest City, the Toughest Conflict," *New York Times*, 23 July 2000, sec. 4, p. 1.

Note: the abbreviations *sec.* and *p.* are necessary to distinguish the 4 and the 1.

Review Article

11. Audrey Webb, review of *Change Activist: Make Big Things Happen Fast*, by Carmel McConnell, *Earth Island Journal* (Summer 2003): 41.

Nonprint Source: Lecture, Sermon, Speech, Oral Report

24. Dick Weber, "The Facts about Preparing Teens to Drive" (lecture, Morrow High School, Morrow, GA, April 16, 2003).

Encyclopedia

25. *The World Book Encyclopedia*, 2000 ed., s.v. "Raphael."

Note: "s.v." means *sub verbo*, "under the word(s)."

Government Documents

26. United States, Dept. of the Treasury, "Financial Operations of Government Agencies and Funds," *Treasury Bulletin*, Washington, DC, June 1974, 134-41.

27. U.S., *Constitution*, art. 1, sec. 4.

28. United Kingdom, *Coroner's Act, 1954*, 2 & 3 Eliz. 2, ch. 31.

29. State v. Lane, Minnesota 263 N. W. 608 (1935).

Television

30. Dan Rather, *CBS News*, September 2, 2003.

Film on DVD

31. *Titanic*, DVD, directed by James Cameron (1997, Hollywood, CA: Paramount Pictures, 1998).

Musical Work on VHS

32. Hanel, George Frederic, *Messiah*, selections, VHS, Atlanta Symphony Orchestra and Chamber Chorus, Robert Shaw, conductor (Batavia, OH: Video Treasures, 1999).

Biblical Reference

33. Matt. 10:5.

34. 1 Pet. 5:1-3 (New Revised Standard Version)

Writing Footnotes for Electronic Sources

To cite electronic sources, *The Chicago Manual of Style* includes a publication date and the URL but not the date of access. The models below show these requirements. Adjust your sources accordingly.

Scholarly Project

12. *British Poetry Archive*, ed. Jerome McGann and David Seaman (University Of Virginia Library, 1999), http://etext.lib.virginia.edu/britpo.html.

Article Online, Limited Information

13. Arthur Ferrill, "Neolithic Warfare Frontline Educational Foundation," http://eserver.org/history/neolithic-war.txt.

Magazine Article Reproduced Online

14. Ben Harder, "Ancient Peru Torture Deaths: Sacrifices or War Crimes?" *National Geographic News*, 29 April 2002, http://news.nationalgeographic.com/new/2002/04/0425_020426_mochekillings.html.

Journal Article Reproduced Online

15. B. A. Miller, N. J. Smyth, and P. J. Mudar, "Mothers' Alcohol and Other Drug Problems and Their Punitiveness toward Their Children," *Journal of Studies on Alcohol* 60 (1999): 632-42, http://www.ncbi.nlm.hih.gov.htbin.

Journal Article Online with No Author Listed

16. "Nutrition and Cancer," *Discovery Health* 1 May 2000, http://www.discoveryhealth.com.Sc000/8096/164609.html.

Article from a Scientific Database

At a minimum, show in this order the name of the database, the URL, a descriptive phrase or record locator (such as a number) to indicate the part of the database being cited, and an access date.

17. NASA/IPAC Extragalactic Database, http://nedwww.ipac.caltech.edu/ (object name IRAS F00400+4059; accessed August 1, 2001).

Article Accessed from a Database through the Library System

18. Victor Davis Hanson, "War Will Be War: No Matter the Era, No Matter the Weapons, and the Same Old Hell." *National Review* 54, 2002, http://web4.infotrac.galegroup.com.

Book Online

19. D. H. Lawrence, *Lady Chatterly's Lover*, 1928, http://bibliomania.com/fiction/dhl/chat.html.

CD-ROM Source

Place of publication and date may be omitted unless relevant.

20. The Old Testament, The Bible, CD-ROM, Bureau Development.

21. *Oxford English Dictionary*, 2nd ed. CD-ROM, version 2.0, Oxford University Press.

Electronic Mailing List, Archived

22. Warren Watts, e-mail to Victorian Association for Library Automation mailing list, September 23, 2003, http://www.vala.org.au/conf2004.htm.

Article from an Online Service

23. "Nutrition and Cancer," *Discovery Health*, May 1, 2000, http://www.discoveryhealth.com/Sc000/8096/164609.html.

E-mail

Since e-mail is not retrievable, do not document with a footnote or bibliography entry. Instead, mention the nature of the source within your text by saying something like this:

Walter Wallace argues that teen violence stems mainly from the breakup of the traditional family (e-mail to the author).

Writing Subsequent Footnote References

After a first full footnote, references to the same source should be shortened to the author's last name and page number. When an author has two works mentioned, employ a shortened version of the title, e.g., "3. Jones, *Paine*, 25." In general, avoid Latinate abbreviations such as *loc. cit.* and *op. cit.;* however, whenever a note refers to the source in the immediately preceding note, you may use "Ibid." alone or "Ibid." with a page number, as shown on the next page. If the subsequent note does not refer to the one immediately above it, do not use "Ibid." Instead, repeat the author's last name (note especially the difference between notes 4 and 6):

3. Jerrold Ladd, *Out of the Madness: From the Projects to a Life of Hope* (New York: Warner, 1994), 24.

4. Ibid., 27.

5. Michael Schulman and Eva Meckler, *Bringing Up a Moral Child*, rev. ed. (New York: Doubleday, 1994), 221.

6. Ladd, 24.

7. Ibid., 27.

Note: Single-space footnotes but double-space between each note.

Writing Endnotes Rather Than Footnotes

With the permission of your instructor, you may put all your notes together as a single group of endnotes to lessen the burden of typing the paper. Most computer software programs will help you with this task by inserting the superscript numerals and by allowing you to type the endnotes consecutively at the end of the text, not at the bottom of each page. Follow these conventions:

1. Begin notes on a new page at the end of the text.
2. Entitle the page "Notes," centered, and placed two inches from the top of the page.
3. Indent the first line of each note one-half inch or five spaces. Type the number of the note followed by a period.
4. Double-space the endnotes.
5. Triple-space between the heading and the first note.

Conform to the following example:

Notes

1. Jerrold Ladd, *Out of the Madness: From the Projects to a Life of Hope* (New York: Warner, 1994), 24.

2. Ibid., 27.

3. Michael Schulman and Eva Meckler, *Bringing Up a Moral Child*, rev. ed. (New York: Doubleday, 1994), 221.

4. W. V. Quine, *Word and Object* (Cambridge: MIT Press, 1966), 8.

5. Schulman and Meckler, 217.

6. Abraham J. Heschel, *Man Is Not Alone: A Philosophy of Religion* (New York: Farrar, Straus, and Young, 1951), 221.

7. Ladd, 24.

8. Ibid., 27.

9. Quine, 9–10.

10. Ladd, *Out of Madness*, 28.

Writing Content Footnotes or Content Endnotes

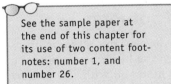

See the sample paper at the end of this chapter for its use of two content footnotes: number 1, and number 26.

As a general rule, put important matters in your text. Use a content note to explain research problems, conflicts in the testimony of the experts, matters of importance that are not germane to your discussion, interesting tidbits, credit to people and sources not mentioned in the text, and other matters that might interest readers.

HINT: After you have embedded most of your computer files in your draft, check the remaining files to find appropriate material for a few content endnotes.

Content notes should conform to these rules:

1. Content notes are *not* documentation notes; a full citation to any source mentioned in the note will appear elsewhere—in a documentation note or on the References page (see item 4.)
2. Content notes may be placed on a separate page(s) following the last page of text, but generally they appear as footnotes mixed among the documentation footnotes.
3. Content footnotes should be single-spaced, like your documentation footnotes. Content endnotes should be double-spaced, as shown in the next few examples.
4. Full information on sources mentioned in content notes must appear elsewhere in a footnote or in a separate Works Cited page at the end of the paper.
5. Unless ambiguity might result without them, do not use *p.* or *pp.* with page numbers.

The following samples demonstrate various types of content endnotes.

Related Matters Not Germane to the Text

1. The problems of politically correct language are explored in Adams, Tucker (4-5), Zalers, and also Young and Smith (583). These authorities cite the need for caution by administrators who would impose new measures on speech and behavior. Verbal abuse cannot be erased by a new set of unjust laws. Patrick German offers several guidelines for implementing an effective but reasonable program (170-72).

Blanket Citation

2. On this point see Giarrett (3-4), de Young (579), Kinard (405–07), and Young (119).

3. Cf. Campbell (*Masks* 1: 170–225; *Hero* 342-45), Frazer (312), and Baird (300–44).

Note: Cf. means *compare.*

Literature on a Related Topic

4. For additional study of the effects of alcoholics on children, see especially the *Journal of Studies on Alcohol* for the article by Wolin et al. and the bibliography on the topic by Orme and Rimmer (285-87). In addition, group therapy for children of alcoholics is examined in Hawley and Brown.

Major Source Requiring Frequent In-Text Citations

5. All citations to Shakespeare are to the Fogler Library edition.

6. Dryden's poems are cited from the California edition of his *Works* and documented in the text with first references to each poem listing volume, page, and lines and with subsequent references citing lines only.

Reference to Source Materials

7. See also James Baird, who argues that the whiteness of Melville's whale is "the sign of the all-encompassing God" (257). Baird

states: "It stands for what Melville calls at the conclusion of the thirty-fifth chapter of *Moby-Dick* 'the inscrutable tides of God'; and it is of these tides as well that the great White Whale himself is the quintessential emblem, the iconographic representation" (257).

NOTE: Either list Baird in the bibliography or include full bibliographic information with this footnote.

8. On this point see also the essay by Patricia Chaffee in which she examines the "house" as a primary image in the fiction of Eudora Welty.

Explanation of Tools, Methods, or Testing Procedures

9. Water samples were drawn from the identical spot each day at 8 a.m., noon, 4 p.m., and 8 p.m., with testing done immediately on site.

10. The control group continued normal dietary routines, but the experimental group was asked to consume nuts, sharp cheeses, and chocolates to test acne development of its members against that of the control group.

11. The initial sample was complete data on all twins born in Nebraska between 1920 and 1940. These dates were selected to provide test subjects 60 years of age or older.

NOTE: A report of an empirical study in APA style would require an explanation of tools and testing procedures in the text under "Methods." See the section entitled "Formatting an APA Paper" on pages 457–458.

Statistics

See also "Figures and Tables," pages A-13–A-15.

12. Database results show 27,000 pupil-athletes in 174 high schools with grades 0.075 above another group of 27,000 non-athletes at the same high schools. Details on the nature of various *reward structures* are unavailable.

Acknowledgments of Assistance or Support

13. Funds to finance this research were graciously provided by the Thompson-Monroe Foundation.

14. This writer wishes to acknowledge the research assistance of Pat Luther, graduate assistant, Physics Department.

Variables or Conflicts in the Evidence

15. Potlatch et al. included the following variables: the positive acquaintance, the equal status norm, the various social norms, the negative stereotypes, and sexual discrimination (415-20). However, racial barriers cannot be overlooked as one important variable.

16. The pilot study at Dunlap School, where sexual imbalance was noticed (62 percent males), differed sharply with test results of other schools. The male bias at Dunlap thereby caused the writer to eliminate those scores from the totals.

Using the Footnote System for Papers in the Humanities

Several disciplines in the humanities—history, philosophy, religion, and theology—use footnotes. The following list demonstrates the format for the types of notes you might need to write for papers on religion or history. They are shown as endnotes, which should be double-spaced.

Sample Page of Notes to a Paper on a Religious Topic

Notes

1. Elaine Pagels, *Beyond Belief: The Secret Gospel of Thomas* (New York: Random House, 2003), 23-27.

2. Jo Ann Hackett, "Can a Sexist Model Liberate Us? Ancient New Eastern 'Fertility' Goddesses," *Journal of Feminist Studies in Religion* 5 (1989): 457-58.

3. Claude Levi-Strauss, *The Savage Mind* (Chicago: University of Chicago Press, 1966), chap. 9, esp. p. 312.

4. Ibid., 314.

5. E. E. Evans-Pritchard, *Theories of Primitive Religion* (Oxford: Clarendon Press, 1965), chap. 2.

6. Evans-Pritchard, *Nuer Religion* (Oxford: Clarendon Press, 1956), 85.

7. Evans-Pritchard, *Primitive Religion*, 46.

8. Humphries, P. T., "Salvation Today, Not Tomorrow," Sermon (Bowling Green, KY: First Methodist Church, 2000).

9. Romans 6:2.

10. 1 Cor. 13:1-3.

11. *The Church and the Law of Nullity of Marriage*, Report of a Commission Appointed by the Archbishops of Canterbury and York in 1949 (London: Society for Promoting Christian Knowledge, 1955), 12-16.

Sample Page of Notes to a History Paper

Notes

1. Bill Bryson, *A Short History of Nearly Everything* (New York: Broadway Books, 2003), 34.

2. Thomas Jefferson, *Notes on the State of Virginia* (1784), ed. William Peden (Chapel Hill: University of North Carolina Press, 1955), 59.

3. Ralph Lerner, *Revolutions Revisited: Two Faces of the Politics of Enlightenment* (Chapel Hill: University of North Carolina Press, 1994), 56-60.

4. *Encyclopedia Britannica: Macropaedia*, 1974 ed., s.v. "Heidegger, Martin."

5. Henry Steele Commager, *The Nature and Study of History*, Social Science Seminar Series (Columbus, Ohio: Merrill, 1965), 10.

6. Dept. of the Treasury, "Financial Operations of Government Agencies and Funds," *Treasury Bulletin* (Washington, DC: GPO, June 1974), 134-41.

7. *Constitution*, Art. 1, sec. 4.

8. Great Britain, *Coroner's Act, 1954*, 2 & 3 Eliz. 2, ch. 31.

9. State v. Lane, Minnesota 263 N. W. 608 (1935).

10. Papers of Gen. A. J. Warner (P-973, Service Record and Short Autobiography), Western Reserve Historical Society.

11. *Ibid.*, clipping from the *Washington Chronicle*.

12. Gregory Claeys, "The Origins of the Rights of Labor: Republicanism, Commerce, and the Construction of Modern Social

Theory in Britain, 1796-1805." *The Journal of Modern History* 66 (1994): 249-90.

13. Lerner, 54-55.

Using the Footnote System for Papers in the Fine Arts

Several disciplines in the fine arts—art, dance, music, theater—use footnotes. The following list demonstrates the format for the types of footnotes you might need to write for topics that treat the fine arts.

Notes

1. Carolyn Damstra, "The Freer Gallery of Art," *Michigan History Magazine* 86 (2002): 46.

2. There are three copies of the papal brief in the archives of the German College, now situated on Via S. Nicola da Tolentino. The document is printed in Thomas D. Culley, *Jesuits and Music* (Rome and St. Louis, 1979), 1: 358-59.

3. Damstra, 47.

4. Denys Hay, ed., *The Age of the Renaissance* (New York, 1967): 286.

5. Aristophanes, *The Birds*, in *Five Comedies of Aristophanes*, trans. Benjamin B. Rogers (Garden City, N.Y.: Doubleday, 1955), 1.2.12-14.

6. Jean Bouret, *The Life and Work of Toulouse-Lautrec*, trans. Daphne Woodward (New York: Abrams, n.d.), 5.

7. Cyrus Hoy, "Fathers and Daughters in Shakespeare's Romances," in *Shakespeare's Romances Reconsidered*, ed. Carol McGinnis Kay and Henry E. Jacobs (Lincoln: Univ. of Nebraska Press, 1978), 77-78.

8. Lionello Venturi, *Botticelli* (Greenwich, Conn.: Fawcett, n.d.), plate 32, p. 214.

Note: Add *p.* for page only if needed for clarity.

9. Cotton Vitellius MSS, A., 15. British Museum.

10. *Ham.* 2.3.2.

11. George Henry Lewes, Review of "Letters on Christian Art," by Friedrich von Schlegel, *Athenaeum* no. 1117 (1849), 296.

12. Ron Stoppelmann, "Letters," *New York*, 23 August 1982, 8.

13. *The World Book Encyclopedia*, 1976 ed., s.v. "Raphael."

14. *Last Tango in Paris*, DVD. (1972; Studio City, CA: United Artists, 2001).

15. Wolfgang A. Mozart, *Jupiter*, Symphony No. 41.

16. William Blake, *Comus*, A photographic reproduction in Irene Taylor, "Blake's *Comus* Designs," *Blake Studies* 4 (Spring 1972): 61, plate 4.

17. Lawrence Topp, *The Artistry of Van Gogh* (New York: Matson, 1983), transparency 21.

18. Eric Sevareid, *CBS News* (New York: CBS-TV, 11 March 1975); Media Services Videotape 1975-142. (Nashville: Vanderbilt University, 1975).

19. Zipperer, Daniel, "The Alexander Technique as a Supplement to Voice Production," *Journal of Research in Singing* 14 (June 1991): 1-40.

Writing a Bibliography Page for a Paper That Uses Footnotes

In addition to footnotes or endnotes, you may be requested to supply a separate bibliography page that lists sources used in developing the paper. Use a heading that represents its contents, such as Selected Bibliography, Sources Consulted, or Works Cited.

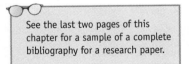

See the last two pages of this chapter for a sample of a complete bibliography for a research paper.

If your initial footnotes are completely documented, the bibliography is redundant. Check with your instructor before preparing one because it may not be required. Separate the title from the first entry with a triple space. Type the first line of each entry flush left; indent the second line and other succeeding lines five spaces or one inch. Alphabetize the list by last names of authors. Double-space the entries as shown below. List alphabetically by title two or more works by one author. The basic forms are:

Book

Bryson, Bill. *A Short History of Nearly Everything*. New York: Broadway Books, 2003.

Journal Article

Damstra, Carolyn. "The Freer Gallery of Art." *Michigan History Magazine* 86 (2002): 46.

Newspaper

Abrams, Rhonda. "Latest FCC Deregulation Move Hurts Small Businesses." *Tennessean* [Nashville] 18 May 2003, 3E.

Internet Article

Ferrill, Arthur. "Neolithic Warfare," Frontline Educational Foundation. http://eserver.org/history/neolithic-war.txt.

Sample Research Paper in the CMS Style

The essay that follows demonstrates the format and documentation style you should use for a research paper when the instructor asks that you use "footnotes," the Chicago style, or the CMS style, all of which refer to *The Chicago Manual of Style*. If permitted, notes may be placed at the end of the paper as double-spaced endnotes rather than at the bottom of the pages.

In the paper that follows, Jamie Johnston has researched the history of war back into prehistoric times. The student offers substantial evidence to prove that early tribes had a history of warfare and even brutality toward captives. The tools of war are reviewed, and then Johnston poses the crucial question: Why did early civilizations fight? He lists many reasons, such as fights for resources, slaves, precious metals, revenge, and honor. Ultimately, he poses the key issue: Was human behavior motivated by biology or culture? Johnston reaches an interesting conclusion, so read on.

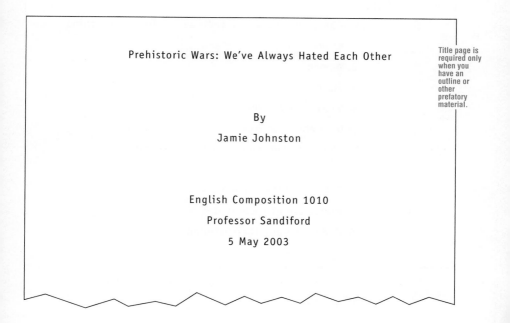

Prehistoric Wars: We've Always Hated Each Other

Title page is required only when you have an outline or other prefatory material.

By

Jamie Johnston

English Composition 1010

Professor Sandiford

5 May 2003

For information on writing an outline, see pages 273–277.

Johnston i

Prehistoric Wars

I. We are a civilized people, yet we love a good fight.
   A. Prehistory shows that we have always fought.
   B. The wars were often savage affairs.
   C. Evidence shows the truth about our love of fighting:
      1. Executions in Peru
      2. Wars among the Mayans
      3. Massacres in Europe
      4. Savagery in the Southwestern United States

II. We have always had weapons of mass destruction.
   A. Early tribes used clubs, arrows, spears, and slings.
   B. They made use of horses, mules, and even elephants.
   C. They developed large armies for aggression and protection.
   D. They left evidence of defensive barriers, such as walls and moats.

III. The crucial question that must be examined is, Why did we fight?
   A. Early humans used war in their search for several things:
      1. Food
      2. Women
      3. Slaves
      4. Sacrificial victims
      5. Gold and treasures
   B. Early humans also fought for these reasons:
      1. Revenge
      2. Defense of their honor
      3. Protection of trade routes
      4. Honor God and their religion

This writer uses a combination of sentences and phrases for the outline. See pages 274–275.

Johnston ii

IV. Ultimately, the cause for our warlike nature boils down to two primary causes.
   A. One group advances the theory that culture dictates our aggression.
      1. A desire for freedom demands war at times.
      2. Capitalism and world markets affect aggressive actions.
      3. Government and official control promote aggression.
   B. A second group advances the theory that biology is the motivating factor.
      1. Humans love a good fight.
      2. Tempers are explosive and sometimes uncontrollable.
      3. People want power over others.
      4. Civil law and moral behavior cannot be dictated to others.

One advantage of sentence outline is that the material can launch the drafting of the paper itself. See page 275.

Johnston 1

Prehistoric Wars: We've Always Hated Each Other

Here we are, a civilized world with reasonably educated people, yet we constantly fight with other. These are not sibling squabbles either; people die in terrible ways. We wonder, then, if there was ever a time when men and women lived in harmony with one another and with nature and the environment. The Bible speaks of the Garden of Eden, and the French philosopher Jean-Jacques Rousseau advanced the idea in the 1700s of the

Repeat the title on the opening page of text.

Johnston 2

"noble savage," and that "nothing could be more gentle" than an ancient colony of people.[1] Wrong!

The writer uses the introduction to discuss historical evidence.

Steven A. LeBlanc, an archaeologist at Harvard University, along with several other scholars, argues instead that "humans have been at each others' throats since the dawn of the species."[2] Robin Yates, for example, says the ancient ancestors of the Chinese used "long-range projectile weapons" as long ago as 28,000 B.C. for both hunting and "intrahuman conflict."[3] Arthur Ferrill observes, "When man first learned how to write, he already had war to write about."[4] Ferrill adds, "In prehistoric times man was a hunter and a killer of other men. The killer instinct in the prehistoric male is clearly attested by archaeology in fortifications, weapons, cave paintings, and skeletal remains."[5]

This section opens with the writer's thesis, and discusses reasons for prehistoric wars.

Evidence proves that savage fighting occurred in the ancient history of human beings. We have evidence of the types of weapons employed. We can also list reasons for the prehistoric fighting. This paper will examine those items, but the crux of the debate centers on the inducement or instinct. Were early

---

1. See Steven A. LeBlanc, *Constant Battles: The Myth of the Peaceful, Noble Savage* (New York: St. Martin's Press, 2003, 15, and also L. D. Cooper, *Rousseau, Nature, and the Problem of the Good Life* (University Park: Pennsylvania State Univ. Press, 1999.

Citation for a magazine.

2. Steven A. LeBlanc, "Prehistory of Warfare," *Archaeology* (May/June, 2003), 18.

Citation for a book.

3. Robin Yates, "Early China," in *War and Society in the Ancient and Medieval Worlds*, ed. Kurt Raaflaub and Nathan Rosenstein (Cambridge, Massachusetts: Center for Hellenic Studies, 1999), 9.

Citation for an Internet source.

4. Arthur Ferrill, "Neolithic Warfare," Frontline Educational Foundation, http://eserver.org/history/neolithic-war.txt.

5. Ibid.

Johnston 3

humans motivated by biological instincts or by cultural demands for a share of limited resources? That's the issue this paper will address.

First, we need to look briefly at the evidence. Ben Harder has reported on the work of one forensic anthropologist, John Verano, who has investigated a series of "grisly executions" in the valleys of Peru during the Moche civilization.[6] Victims "were apparently skinned alive. Others were drained of blood, decapitated, or bound tightly and left to be eaten by vultures."[7] Verano has the proof of the executions, but not the reason, although speculations center on religious ceremonies. UCLA anthropologist Christopher B. Donnan has studied Moche art and suggests "the suffering of the losers may have had a ritualistic meaning in Moche society much as the pain of Christ does in Christianity."[8] At the same time, Verano thinks the victims were prisoners of war and not the losers of ritual combat. In either case, the ancients were less than noble savages.

LeBlanc's book *Constant Battles* is a catalog of prehistoric fighting, David Webster describes the savage fighting of the ancient Mayans,[9] and Nick Thorpe in *British Archaeology* describes massacres that occurred in Europe over 8,500 years

---

6. Ben Harder, "Ancient Peru Torture Deaths: Sacrifices or War Crimes?" *National Geographic News*, 29 April 2002, http://news.nationalgeogrphic.com/news/2002/ 04/ 0425_020426_mochekillings.html.

7. Ibid.

8. Christopher Donnan, cited in Harder.

9. David Webster, "Ancient Maya Warfare," in *War and Society in the Ancient and Medieval Worlds*, ed. Kurt Raaflaub and Nathan Rosenstein (Cambridge, Massachusetts: Center for Hellenic Studies, 1999), 333-60.

The word *Ibid.* refers to the immediately preceding note.

ago—decapitation, scalping, axe blows, and other nasty methods.[10] Indeed, articles are now available on wars in ancient Japan, Egypt, Greece,[11] and the Southwestern areas of the United States.[12]

The weapons, too, have been uncovered: clubs, arrowheads, bows, slings, daggers, maces, and spears. Each weapon graduated upon the previous and served new purposes as armies gathered for combat. One source points out that "the bow and the sling were important for hunting, but the dagger and mace were most useful for fighting other humans."[13] The spear required close combat. The bow and arrow had a range of about 100 yards. The sling was a significant weapon because in the right hands it was accurate from long distances and very powerful with stones that could crush skulls. The mace gave way to the battle axe to cut through armor. Then with copper, bronze, and finally iron, the sword gained great popularity and remains a weapon of choice even today.[14]

Horses, mules, and even elephants gave primitive armies mobility. Ultimately, however, the primary weapon was the soldier, and over time the ragged fighting groups were organized into armies that could march in columns and lay siege to other villages and cities. Accordingly, archeologists have examined

---

10. Nick Thorpe, "Origins of War: Mesolithic Conflict in Europe," *British Archaeology* 52 (2000), http://www.birtarch.ac.uk/ba/ba52/ba52feat.html.

11. See Kurt Raaflaub and Nathan Rosenstein.

12. See LeBlanc, "Prehistory of Warfare," and also *Constant Battles*.

13. "Prehistoric Warfare," http://digilander.libero.it/tepec/prehistoric_warfare.htm.

14. Ibid.

walls, pits, ditches, moats, and barriers of all sorts, even villages with all the rooms built against each other, with access only from the roof.[15] Fortress cities were built on mountaintops, as with the Acropolis at Athens. And researchers have found an ancient Peruvian city high atop a mountain peak in the Andes.[16] Thus, archeologists have uncovered many offensive weapons but also gigantic earthen defenses, and the Great Wall of China springs forward as one great example.

Why fight? Many reasons have been advanced by different researchers, and we can take our pick from quite a list as armies went out in search of:

- Food, resources, water, and cattle
- Women for concubines and wives
- Slaves
- Sacrificial victims
- Gold, bronze, copper, and other valuable metals

This section of the paper examines the causes for prehistoric wars.

And they fought to:

- Seek revenge.
- Protect and secure the best trade routes.
- Honor their God and their religion.
- Defend their honor.

John Shy argues that early people, like today, fought to protect their culture and way of life.[17] Michael Adams says the four

---

15. LaBlanc, "Prehistory of Warfare," 20.

16. D.L. Parsell, "City Occupied by Inca Discovered on Andean Peak in Peru," *National Geographic News*, 21 March 2002, http://news.nationalgeographic.com/news/2002/03/0314_0318_vilcabamba.html.

17. John Shy, "The Cultural Approach to the History of War," Abstract, *The Journal of Military History* 57 (1993), http://web4.infotrac.galegroup.com.

Johnston 6

principles used by the Allies in World War II would serve all armies of all times—"freedom from want, freedom from fear, freedom of speech, freedom of religion."[18] Thorpe offers this theory:

> My own belief is that warfare, in earliest prehistory, arose over matters of personal honour—such as slights, insults, marriages going wrong, or theft. In a small hunter-gatherer community, everyone is related. An attack on one group member is an attack on the whole family. A personal feud may quickly involve the whole community. From there it is a small step to war.[19]

Use the computer's standard indention for block quotations.

Donald Kagan echoes that concept with his focus on the word *honor*: "If a state finds that its honor is at risk, that it is treated with contempt, the other two elements of the triad immediately become part of the story. Men get fearful that in light of this contempt others will take advantage and damage their real interests."[20] Yet I recall reading *Beowulf* for one of my classes, and Beowulf fought for *wergild* (money and riches), and he made no bones about it. Victory brings economic bonanzas. LaBlanc shows that ancient battles shifted from total annihilation of the enemy to economic control of villages, cities, and even large states. Conflict waged by complex societies results in a new twist. Warfare was controlled by the elite, and wealth and prestige began

---

18. Michael Adams, "The 'Good War' Myth and the Cult of Nostagia," *The Midwest Quarterly* 40 (1998), http://web4.infotrac.galegroup.com.

19. Thorpe.

20. Donald Kagan, "History's Largest Lessons" [interview by Fredric Smoler], *American Heritage* 48 (1997), http://web4.infotrac.galegroup.com.

to play a role. The commoners became valuable as a means to supply wealth to the elite, so warfare began to include conquest instead of annihilation as a goal.[21] Thus, we must add "the search for wealth" as a prime reason for war in primitive times and also the present because it was whispered about George W. Bush's conquest of Iraq—he did it for the oil.

Ultimately, the key question about the cause of war, whether ancient or current, centers on one's choice between biology and culture. On the one side we have the historian, like Victor Hanson, who argues, "Culture largely determines how people fight. The degree to which a society embraces freedom, secular rationalism, consensual government, and capitalism often determines—far more than its geography, climate, or population—whether its armies will be successful over the long term."[22] Hanson adds, "No nation has ever survived once its citizenry ceased to believe that its culture was worth saving."[23]

The society as a whole wants to preserve its culture, in peace if possible. In 500 B.C. Herodotus said, "No one is so foolish that he prefers war to peace. In peace sons bury their fathers, in war fathers their sons."[24]

Yet, in my opinion (I have to reach my own conclusion here), the biological history of men and women suggests that we love a good fight. I recall reading an article that said twins

---

21. LaBlanc, *Constant Battles*, 194.

22. Victor Davis Hanson, "War Will Be War: No Matter the Era, No Matter the Weapons, and the Same Old Hell," *National Review* 54 (2002), http://web4.infotrac.galegroup.com.

23. Ibid.

24. Qtd. in Peter Jones, "Ancient and Modern," *Spectator* 291 (2003), http://web4.infotrac.galegroup.com.

inside the womb actually fight, and one fetus might actually devour or absorb the other one. Siblings just naturally fight, as I did with my older sister and younger brother. His anger exploded one time, and he broke my arm by hitting me with a shovel. We all have witnessed the terrible fights at sporting events, and recently at Glenbrook North High School in Northbrook, Illinois, hazing turned into a terrible beating for some girls. Oh sure, we can give reasons for our eagerness to fight--to preserve our honor ("Don't diss me!"), to preserve our freedom ("Don't encroach!"), or because of fear ("Don't hit me 'cause I'll be hitting back even harder!"). Yet in a final analysis, people want power over others--men beat their wives, mothers overly spank their children, the better team overpowers an opponent, and, yes, a larger, stronger nation will demolish another if self-interest prevails.

The writer's conclusion connects his thesis to the modern emphasis on war and terrorism.

This is human nature. The men of Al Queda who flew their suicide missions into the World Trade Center and the Pentagon knew exactly what they were doing—exercising their power. In effect, they said, "We'll show the United States that we can inflict great damage." Professor Donald Kagan observes:

> In the end what people really go to war about is power, by which I simply mean the ability to have their will prevail. . . . Every being and every nation requires power for two purposes. The first is to be able to do what it wishes to and must do, some of which will be good and perfectly natural things. Second, one needs power to keep others from imposing their will, to prevent evil things from being done.[25]

The sport of boxing continues to thrive, despite attempts to end it because of its brutality. The fans have a vicarious thrill as one

25. Kagan.

Johnston 9

boxer gets pounded to the canvas. At NASCAR races the greatest shouts occur as the fenders crash and cars go tumbling topsy-turvy down the asphalt. The aggressive behavior of humans is not always a pretty sight, such as the eager willingness of some to loot and pilfer a neighborhood that has been hit by a tornado or other natural disaster.

At the same time, a country like ours governs itself, imposing order by law and moral behavior by religion.[26] Our government, our culture, and our sense of honor have prevailed in a world of nations gone berserk and lawless. Whether we should use our power to impose our sense of democracy on other countries is an international question without a clear answer. My brother, with the shovel in his hand, would say "yes."

---

26. When chaos develops, as in Baghdad during the 2003 war, lawless looting and violence emerge because neither the religious leaders nor an absent police force can maintain order. The breakdown of the culture opens a vacuum filled quickly by primitive behavior.

Johnston 10

Bibliography

A separate bibliography is not required if you write initial footnotes with full data.

Adams, Michael. "The 'Good War' Myth and the Cult of Nostalgia." *The Midwest Quarterly*, 40 (1998). http://web4.infotrac.galegroup.com.

Cooper, L. D. *Rousseau, Nature, and the Problem of the Good Life*. University Park: Pennsylvania State Univ. Press, 1999.

Ferrill, Arthur. "Neolithic Warfare," Frontline Educational Foundation. http://eserver.org/history/neolithic-war.txt.

Hanson, Victor Davis. "War Will Be War: No Matter the Era, No Matter the Weapons, and the Same Old Hell." *National Review*, 54 (2002). http://web4.infotrac.galegroup.com.

Harder, Ben. "Ancient Peru Torture Deaths: Sacrifices or War Crimes?" *National Geographic News*, 29 April 2002. http://news.nationalgeographic.com/news/2002/04/0425_020426_mochekillings.html.

Jones, Peter. "Ancient and Modern." *Spectator* 291 (2003). http://web4.infotrac.galegroup.com.

Kagan, Donald. "History's Largest Lessons." Interview by Fredric Smoler. *American Heritage* 48 (1997). http://web4.infotrac.galegroup.com.

LeBlanc, Steven A. *Constant Battles: The Myth of the Peaceful, Noble Savage*. New York: St. Martin's Press, 2003.

---. "Prehistory of Warfare," *Archaeology* May/June, 2003.

Parsell, D. L. "City Occupied by Inca Discovered on Andean Peak in Peru." *National Geographic News*, 21 March, 2002. http://news.nationalgeographic.com/news/2002/03/0314_0318_vilcabamba.html.

"Prehistoric Warfare." http://digilander.libero.it/tepec/prehistoric_warfare.htm.

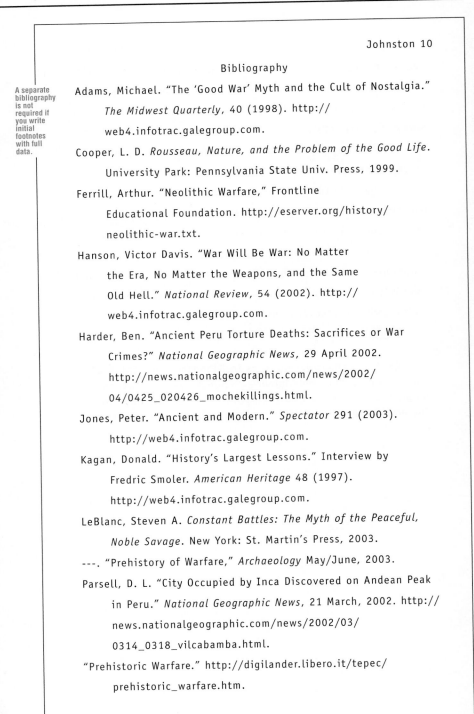

Johnston 11

Shy, John. "The Cultural Approach to the History of War." *The Journal of Military History*, 57 (1993). http://web4.nfotrac.galegroup.com.

Thorpe, Nick. "Origins of War: Mesolithic Conflict in Europe." *British Archaeology* 52 (2000). http://www.birtarch.ac.uk/ba/ba52/ba52feat.html.

Webster, David. "Ancient Maya Warfare." In *War and Society in the Ancient and Medieval Worlds*. Ed. Kurt Raaflaub and Nathan Rosenstein. Cambridge, Massachusetts: Center for Hellenic Studies, 1999.

Yates, Robin. "Early China." In *War and Society in the Ancient and Medieval Worlds*. Ed. Kurt Raaflaub and Nathan Rosenstein. Cambridge, Massachusetts: Center for Hellenic Studies, 1999.

20 CSE Style for the Natural and Applied Sciences

The Council of Biology Editors who produced the *CBE Style Manual* has changed its name recently to the Council of Science Editors. Thus, they are changing to the CSE Style for the natural and applied sciences in their 2004 edition. This governing body has established two forms for citing sources in scientific writing. One is the **number** system for writing in the applied sciences, such as chemistry, computer science, mathematics, physics, and medicine. The second is the **Name-Year** system for use in the biological and earth sciences; it duplicates the APA style as explained in Chapter 18.

Number

> The original description (3) contained precise taxonomic detail that differed with recent studies (4-6).

Name-Year

> The original description (Roberts 1999) contained precise taxonomic detail that differed with recent studies (McCormick 2000a, 2000b, and Tyson and others 1999).

There are advantages and disadvantages to each system. The number system saves space, and the numbers make minimal disruption to the reading of the text. But this system seldom mentions names, so readers must refer to the bibliography for the names of authors. Also, any disruption in the numbering sequence late in the composition may necessitate a renumbering of all references in the text and the bibliography.

The Name-Year system mentions authors' names in the text with the year to show timely application and historical perspective. Citations can be deleted or added without difficulty. But a long string of citations in the text can be more disruptive than numbers. In truth, the decision is usually not yours to make. The individual disciplines in the sciences have adopted one form or the other, as shown in the following chart.

Index to Bibliographic Models: CSE Style

Number System
Book 504
Article in a Journal 504
Internet Articles and Other Electronic Publications 505
Magazine or Newspaper Article 505
Proceedings and Conference Presentations 505
Article from a Loose-Leaf Collection 505

Name-Year System
Article in a Journal 508
Book 508
Internet Articles and Other Electronic Publications 509
Journal Article Reprinted on the Internet 509
Magazine or Newspaper Article 509
Proceedings and Conference Publications 509
Article from a Loose-Leaf Collection 510

Writing In-text Citations Using the CSE Number System

This system employs numbers to identify sources. Use this style with these disciplines: chemistry, computer science, mathematics, physics, and the medical sciences (medicine, nursing, and general health). In simple terms, the system requires an in-text *number*, rather than the year, and a list of Cited References that are numbered to correspond to the in-text citations.

After completing a list of references, assign a number to each entry. Use one of two methods for numbering the list: (1) arrange references in alphabetical order and number them consecutively (in which case the numbers will appear in random order in the text), or (2) number the references consecutively as you put them into your text, interrupting that order when entering references cited earlier.

The number serves as the key to the source, as numbered in the Cited References. Conform to the following regulations:

1. Place the number within parentheses (1) or brackets [2] or as a raised index numeral, like this.[5] A name is not required and is even discouraged, so try to arrange your wording accordingly. Full information on the author and the work will be placed in the references list.

```
    It is known (1) that the DNA concentration of a nucleus doubles
during interphase.

    A recent study [1] has raised interesting questions related to
photosynthesis, some of which have been answered [2].
```

In particular, a recent study[1] has raised many interesting questions related to photosynthesis, some of which have been answered.[2]

2. If you include the authority's name, add the number after the name.

Additional testing by Cooper (3) included alterations in carbohydrate metabolism and changes in ascorbic acid incorporation into the cell and adjoining membranes.

3. If necessary, add specific data to the entry:

"The use of photosynthesis in this application is crucial to the environment" (Skelton,[8] p 732).

The results of the respiration experiment published by Jones (3, Table 6, p 412) had been predicted earlier by Smith (5, Proposition 8).

Writing a Cited References Page

Supply a list of references at the end of your paper. Number the entries to correspond to sources as you cite them in the text. An alternate method is to alphabetize the list and then number it. Label the list *Cited References*. The form of the entries should follow the examples shown below.

Book

Provide a number and then list the author, title of the book, place of publication, publisher, year, and total number of pages (optional).

1. LeBlanc AN. Random family: Love, drugs, trouble and coming of age. New York: Simon & Schuster; 2003. 416 p.

Article in a Journal

Provide a number and then list the author, the title of the article, the name of the journal, the year and month if necessary, volume number and issue number if necessary, and inclusive pages. The month or an issue number is necessary for any journal that is paged anew with each issue (see item 3).

2. Bolli GB, Owens DR. Insulin glargine. Lancet 2000; 356:443-444.

3. Renner R. Drams of drugs and dregs. Scientific American 2002 May; 286(5):29.

Internet Articles and Other Electronic Publications

Add at the end of the citation an availability statement as well as the date you accessed the material. Use the form in number 4 for an article published on the Web. Use the form in number 5 for a periodical article reproduced on the Web.

4. Shane-McWhorter L. Complementary and alternative medicine (CAM) in diabetes. Complementary and Alternative Medicine [article online] 2002. Available from http://www.childrenwithdiabetes.com/clinic/alternative. Accessed 2003 Aug 8.

5. Insall R. Protein conformation: Through a lens, darkly. Biochem J [serial online] 2003;372:n.p. Available from http://www.biochemj.org//bj/372/bj3720033com.htm. Accessed 2003 May 18.

Magazine or Newspaper Article

Add a specific date and, for newspapers, cite a section letter or number.

6. Murphy C., Haggerty, R. Reinventing a river. American Heritage 2003 Apr/May:60-67.

7. [Anonymous]. FDA approval of drug gives diabetics a new choice. Los Angeles Times 2000 Aug 2;Sect A:4.

Proceedings and Conference Presentations

After supplying a number, give the name of the author or editor, the title of the presentation, name of the conference, type of work (report, proceedings, proceedings online, etc.), name of the organization or society, the date of the conference, and the place. If found on the Internet, add the URL and the date you accessed the information.

For a sample of a "Cited References" page using the number system, see pages 520–521.

8. Ashraf H, Banz W, Sundberg J. Soyful luncheon: Setting a healthful table for the community [abstract online]. In: Crossing Borders: Food and Agriculture in the Americas. Proceedings online of the Assn. for the Study of Food and Society; 1999 June 3-6; Toronto (ON). Available from http://www.acs.ryerson.ca/foodsec/foodsec/papers.html. Accessed 2003 Aug 8.

Article from a Loose-Leaf Collection

9. [Anonymous]. No-till farming shows skeptics the advantages of giving up the plow. CQ Researcher 1994;4:1066.

Writing In-text Citations with Name and Year

The CSE Name-Year style applies to these disciplines:

Agriculture	Anthropology	Archaeology
Astronomy	Biology	Botany
Geography	Geology	Zoology

When writing research papers in accordance with the Name-Year system, conform to the following rules:

1. Place the year within parentheses immediately after the authority's name:

   Smith (2002) ascribes no species-specific behavior to man. However, Adams (2003) presents data that tend to be contradictory.

2. If you do not mention the authority's name in your text, insert the name, year, and page numbers within the parentheses:

   One source found some supporting evidence for a portion of the questionable data (Marson & Brown 2003, pp 23-32) through point biserial correlation techniques.

3. For two authors, employ both names in your text and in the parenthetical citation:

   Torgerson and Andrews (2003)

   or

   (Torgerson and Andrews 2003)

   Note: Unlike APA style, the CSE style does not use the ampersand (&). For three or more authors, use the lead author's name with "and others." *Note:* CSE style prefers English terms and English abbreviations rather than Latin words and abbreviations, such as *et al.*

In the text:	Torgerson and others (2003)
In the parenthetical citation:	(Torgerson and others 2003)

4. Use lowercase letters (a, b, c) to identify two or more works published in the same year by the same author—for example, "Thompson (2003a)" and "Thompson (2003b)." Then use "2003a" and "2003b" in your List of References.

5. If necessary, supply additional information:

Horton (2003a, 2003b; cf. Thomas, 2002, p 89) suggests an intercorrelation of these testing devices. But after multiple-group analysis, Welston (2003, esp. p 211) reached an opposite conclusion.

6. In the case of a reference to a specific page, separate the page number from the year with a comma and a space. Do not use a period after the "p."
   a. A quotation or paraphrase in the middle of the sentence:

Jones stated, "These data of psychological development suggest that retarded adolescents are atypical in maturational growth" (2003, p 215), and Jones attached the data that were accumulated during the study.

   b. A quotation or paraphrase that falls at the end of a sentence:

Jones (2002) found that "these data of psychological development suggest that retarded adolescents are atypical in maturational growth" (p 215).

   c. A long quotation, indented with the tab key and set off from the text in a block (and therefore without quotation marks):

Albert (2003) found the following:

> Whenever these pathogenic organisms attack the human body and begin to multiply, the infection is set in motion. The host responds to this parasitic invasion with efforts to cleanse itself of the invading agents. When rejection efforts of the host become visible (fever, sneezing, congestion), the disease status exists. (pp 314–315)

7. Punctuate the citations according to the following stipulations:
   a. Use a comma followed by a space to separate citations of different references by the same author or authors in same-year or different-year references:

Supplemental studies (Johnson 2002a, 2002b, 2003) have shown. . . .

Supplemental studies (Randolph and Roberts 2002, 2003) have shown. . . .

b. Use a comma to separate two authors of the same work who have the same surname.

(Rudolph SL, and Rudolph CB, 2003)

Use commas with three or more authors:

(Smith, Jones, Thompson, and others 2003)

c. Use a semicolon followed by a space to separate citations to different authors:

Supplemental studies (Smith 2000; Barfield 2001, 2003; Barfield and Smith 1998; Wallace 2000) have shown. . . .

Using Name and Year with Bibliography Entries

Alphabetize the list and label it *Cited References*. Double-space the entries and use the hanging indention. When there are two to ten authors, all should be named in the reference listing. When there are eleven or more authors, the first ten are listed, followed by "and others." If the author is anonymous, insert "[Anonymous]. Place the year immediately after the author's name.

Article in a Journal

List the author, year, article title, journal title, volume number, and inclusive pages. Add an issue number for any journal that is paged anew with each issue.

Winickoff JP, Hillis VJ, Palfrey JS, Perrin JM, Rigotti NA. 2003. A smoking cessation intervention for parents of children who are hospitalized for respiratory illness: The Stop Tobacco Outreach Program. Pediatrics 111:140–146.

Book

List the author, year, title, place of publication, publisher, and total number of pages (optional).

Gershuny G, Smillie J. 1999. The soul of soil: A soil-building guide for master gardeners and farmers. White River Junction, Vt.: Chelsea Green. 173 p.

Internet Articles and Other Electronic Publications

Add at the end of the citation an availability statement as well as the date you accessed the material.

Watkins JE, Doupnik D, Kerr ED. 2003. Root and crown rot-Winterkill complex of winter wheat. NebGuide [article online]. Available from http:// www.ianr.unl.edu/pubs/plantdisease/g1097.htm. Accessed 2003 Aug 8.

Journal Article Reprinted on the Internet

Provide original publication data as well as the Internet address and the date you accessed the material. Label it as *serial online.*

Porter PM, Huggins DR, Perillo CA, Quiring SR, Crookston RK. 2003. Organic and other management strategies with two- and four-year crop rotations in Minnesota [abstract]. Agron J [serial online]; 95:233-244. Available from http://agron.scijournals.org/ current.shtml. Accessed 2002 Aug 8.

Magazine or Newspaper Article

Add a specific date and, if listed, a section letter or number.

Finck, C. 2003 Spring. A fit for fungicides. Farm Journal 124:B-4.

Teicher, SA. 2003 May 19. When social ills arrive at work. Christian Science Monitor 95:27.

Proceedings and Conference Publications

Give author, date, title of the presentation, name of conference, type of work (report, proceeding, proceedings online, etc.), name of the organization or society, and place of the conference. If found on the Internet, add the URL.

Ashraf H, Banz W, Sundberg J. 2003 June 3-6. Soyful luncheon: Setting a healthful table for the community [abstract online]. In: Crossing Borders: Food and Agriculture in the Americas. Proceedings of the Association for the Study of Food and Society]; Toronto (ON). Available http:// www.acs.ryerson.ca/ ~foodsec/foodsec/Papers.html. Accessed 2003 Aug 8.

Article from a Loose-Leaf Collection

[Anonymous]. 1994. No-till farming shows skeptics the advantages of giving up the plow. CQ Researcher 4:1066.

Arranging the Cited References List

The list of references should be placed in alphabetical order, as shown next.

Cited References

Finck C. 2003 Spring. A fit for fungicides. Farm Journal 124:B-4.

Porter PM, Huggins DR, Perillo CA, Quiring SR, Crookston RK. 2003. Organic and other management strategies with two- and four-year crop rotations in Minnesota [abstract]. Agron J [serial online]; 95:233-244. Available from http://agron.scijournals.org/current.shtml. Accessed 2003 Aug 8.

Teicher SA. 2003 May 19. When social ills arrive at work. Christian Science Monitor 95:27.

Winickoff JP, Hillis VJ, Palfrey JS, Perrin JM, Rigotti NA. 2003. A smoking cessation intervention for parents of children who are hospitalized for respiratory illness: The Stop Tobacco Outreach Program. Pediatrics 111:140-146.

Sample Paper Using the CSE Numbering System

Student Sarah Bemis has researched problems with managing diabetes and presented the paper using the CSE number system. As she cites a source in the text, she uses a number that also reappears on her Cited References page. Accordingly, the cited references are not in alphabetical order. As is standard with writing in the sciences, an abstract is provided.

Diabetes Management:

A Delicate Balance

By

Sarah E. Bemis

English 103: College Writing

Sister Winifred Morgan, O.P.

5 December 2003

Balance the title, name, and affiliation.

Bemis ii

Abstract

Diabetes affects approximately 11 million people in the U.S. alone, leading to $350 billion in medical costs. Two types, I and II, have debilitating effects. The body may tolerate hyperglycemia for a short time, but severe complications can occur, such as arteriosclerosis, heart disease, nerve damage, and cerebral diseases. New drugs continue to improve the lifestyle of a person with diabetes, but controlling blood sugar requires three elements working together--medication, diet, and exercise. This study examines the importance of each of the three. Patients need a controlled balance of the medication, diet, and exercise program.

An abstract of 100–200 words states the purpose, scope, and major findings of the report.

Bemis 1

Diabetes Management: A Delicate Balance

Use a number to register the use of a source.

Diabetes is a disease that affects approximately 17 million people in the U.S. alone (1), and its complications lead to numerous deaths per year and cost the nation millions in medical care for the direct cost of complications and for indirect costs of lost productivity related to the disease. The condition can produce devastating side effects and a multitude of chronic health problems. For this reason, it can be very frightening to those who do not understand the nature and treatment of the disease. Diabetes currently has no known cure, but it can be controlled. Diabetes research has made great advancements in recent years, but the most important insights into the management of this disease are those which seem the most simplistic. By instituting a healthy, balanced lifestyle, most persons with diabetes can live free of negative side effects.

The thesis or hypothesis is expressed at the end of the introduction.

Scientific writing requires careful definition, as shown here.

More than one source can be listed for one idea or concept.

Diabetes mellitus, according to several descriptions, is a disorder in which the body cannot properly metabolize glucose or sugar. The body's inability to produce or properly use insulin permits glucose to build up in the bloodstream. The excess sugar in the blood, or hyperglycemia, is what leads to the side effects of diabetes (2,3,4).

There are actually two types of diabetes. Type I, or juvenile diabetes, is the name given to the condition in which the pancreas produces very little or no insulin. It is normally discovered during childhood, but can occur at any age (3). Adult onset, or Type II diabetes, occurs when the pancreas produces usable insulin, but not enough to counteract the amount of glucose in the blood. This often results from obesity or poor diet.

In both Type I and Type II diabetes, the problem has been identified as hyperglycemia (5). This buildup of glucose in the

Bemis 2

bloodstream leads to a number of dangerous side effects. The initial effects and indicators of hyperglycemia are frequent urination, intense thirst, increased hunger, and fatigue. When glucose begins to build up in the blood, the kidneys begin to filter out the excess sugar into the urine. The amount of glucose the kidneys can filter varies with each person. In this process, all the water in the body's tissues is being used to produce urine to flush glucose from the kidneys. This is what leads to the intense thirst and frequent urination associated with hyperglycemia (5).

Causal analysis, as shown here, is a staple of scientific writing.

Because the body lacks the insulin needed to allow glucose into the cells, the glucose cannot be processed to produce energy. The cells signal the brain that they are not getting sugar, and this causes hunger. However, no matter how much a victim of hyperglycemic diabetes eats, the cells will not be producing energy (6).

It has been shown (4) that with hyperglycemia the kidneys try to compensate for the excess of sugar and lack of energy. While the kidneys attempt to filter the sugar from the blood, the liver tries to produce energy by burning fat and muscle to produce ketones, a protein that the body attempts to burn in place of glucose. Ketones do not provide the energy the body requires but do produce chemicals toxic to the body. When too many ketones are present in the blood, ketoacidosis occurs (4).

Refer to the sources with the past tense verb or the present participle.

Collins (1) has demonstrated that ketoacidosis is a condition caused by high levels of hydrogen in the blood. This leads initially to a high blood pH, depleted saline fluids, and dehydration. If untreated, it can lead to a shutdown of the central nervous system, coma, or even death. In fact, many diabetes-related deaths are caused by ketoacidosis that has reached a comatose state. Ketoacidosis is characterized by

In addition to the number, you may mention the name(s) of your sources.

frequent urination, dry mouth, extreme thirst, headache, rapid and deep respiration, increased heart rate, nausea, vomiting, disorientation, and lethargy (1).

Consumer Reports on Health (4) has reported that hyperglycemia can cause other, more subtle, side effects. Because the body is not receiving the nourishment it requires, a victim of hyperglycemic diabetes often experiences poor tissue growth and repair. This can cause problems with growth and development in children and wound healing in adults as well as children. It has also been reported (7) that the immune system is also affected and that victims experience infection more often and more severely than do persons without diabetes. Other conditions that frequently occur in conjunction with hyperglycemia in its early stages are depression and chronic fatigue (8). Many patients who experience hypoglycemia have difficulties controlling gain and loss of weight as well.

It has been shown (1) that the body may tolerate hyperglycemia over a short period. However, if untreated, it leads to other chronic and often fatal health conditions. Arteriosclerosis occurs in hyperglycemic diabetics over time, resulting in decreased circulation and eyesight. This also may lead to heart disease, angina, and heart attack, the most prevalent causes of death among diabetics (5). Also common is diabetic neuropathy, a degeneration of the nerves. This condition causes pain and loss of function in the extremities (6).

A person with diabetes is also at risk for many cerebral diseases. Both the large and small cerebral arteries of victims are prone to rupture, which can cause cerebral hemorrhage, thrombosis, or stroke. Blockages in the carotid arteries can decrease blood flow to the brain, causing episodes of lightheadedness and fainting (1, p 462-463).

You may add page numbers to the reference as a courtesy to the reader.

Diabetic nephropathy occurs when the kidneys are overloaded with glucose. Eventually, they begin to shut down. The kidneys of a person with uncontrolled diabetes are also susceptible to infection, resulting in decreased kidney function (1).

With all the complications victims experience, the outlook for a long and healthy life does not seem good for those diagnosed with the disease. However, all of these effects can be reduced, delayed, and even prevented with proper care and control. By monitoring blood sugar and reacting accordingly with medication, by special diets, and by exercise and a controlled lifestyle, persons with diabetes can avoid these serious health conditions (Brancati and others 9).

The first aspect of diabetes care is blood sugar monitoring and medication. The two go hand in hand in that the patient must have the appropriate type and dosage of medication and must know blood sugar values and patterns in order to determine the correct regimen. Two main types of monitoring are necessary for diabetes control. Patients must perform home glucose monitoring on a daily basis. Advancements in this area in recent years have made this relatively effortless. Several glucose monitoring kits are available to the general public. These consist of a small electronic machine that measures the amount of glucose in the blood, as well as the equipment necessary to obtain a small sample. With such equipment, patients can test and record blood sugars several times per day. This gives both short-term and long-term information by which they and their physicians can determine insulin dosages and meal plans.

Process analysis, as shown here, is often a staple of scientific writing.

In addition to daily monitoring, victims should visit their physician regularly. Doctors usually perform a test called a hemoglobin AIC, which gives a better indication of blood sugar control over a longer period of time than a home test. This should be done approximately every ninety days, as that is the time period over which blood cells are renewed. This test, along with consideration of daily glucose values, can help the physician determine overall control and effectiveness of the patient's routine. Regular visits also give the physician an opportunity to monitor the general health of the patient, including circulation, eyesight, infections, and organ infections.

The writer explores control element number one: methods of administering medication.

The treatment of diabetes usually involves medication. Since Type I diabetics produce very little or no insulin, insulin injections will always be necessary. For Type II, the treatment may be strictly dietary, dietary with oral hypoglycemic agents, or insulin therapy.

When insulin therapy is required, it is very important that the appropriate type and dosage be implemented. Many types of insulin are available. The main distinction among these types is in their action time, onset, peak-time, and duration. Different types of insulin begin to act at different rates. They also continue to act for different periods of time and hit peak effectiveness at different intervals (1). This is why it is important to have records of blood sugars at regular intervals over several weeks. From this it can be determined when and what type of insulin is needed most. Once it is determined what insulin regimen is appropriate, the patient must follow it closely. Routine is very important in controlling diabetes.

Patients with diabetes now have a few options when it comes to injection method. One may chose traditional manual injection, an injection aid, or an insulin pump. Injection aids can make using a needle easier and more comfortable or actually use air pressure to inject. The insulin pump is a device that offers convenience as well as improved control. The pump is a small battery-operated device that delivers insulin 24 hours a day through a small needle worn under the skin. The pump

Bemis 6

contains a computer chip that controls the amount of insulin delivered according to the wearer's personalized plan (10). The pump is meant for patients who do not wish to perform multiple injections but are willing to test blood sugars frequently. The pump can help patients who have some trouble controlling their blood sugars by providing insulin around the clock. It also provides an element of freedom for persons with busy schedules.

Some Type II patients can control the disease with a combination of diet, exercise, and an oral hypoglycemic agent. These drugs themselves contain no insulin. They traditionally lower blood glucose levels by stimulating the pancreas to produce insulin (1). Therefore, they are only appropriate for a patient whose pancreas is still producing some insulin. Diabetes research has advanced in recent years, however. Some new drugs may be coming available in the new millennium. Creators of the pharmaceuticals are able to increase sensitivity to insulin and suppress the secretion of hormones that raise blood sugar. A number of new drugs that are aimed at taking the place of insulin therapy are currently in the final stages of research and development. Glucovance has been advanced as a valuable new medication (11). For now, the oral medications that are available can aid in keeping better control when properly paired with an effective diet and exercise plan.

While it is important to have the proper medication, the backbone of diabetes management is the meal plan. By making wise choices in eating, persons with diabetes can reduce stress on the body and increase the effectiveness of their medication. The basis of a good meal plan is balanced nutrition and moderation. Eating a low-fat, low-sodium, low-sugar diet is the best way for a diabetic to ensure longevity and health. It is important for everyone to eat balanced meals on a routine

The writer now explores control element number two: methods of diet management.

schedule. For victims of diabetes, it can help in blood sugar control and in preventing heart disease and digestive problems.

Two established meal plans are recommended for patients: the Exchange Plan and carbohydrate counting (12, 13). Both are based on The Diabetes Food Pyramid (Nutrition). The Food Pyramid divides food into six groups. These resemble the traditional four food groups, except that they are arranged in a pyramid in which the bottom, or largest, section contains the foods that should be eaten most each day. The top, or smallest, section contains the foods that should be eaten least, if at all. With any diabetic meal plan, the patient should eat a variety of foods from all the food groups, except the sweets, fats, and alcohol group. New books by American Diabetic Association offer helpful and authoritative guidebooks to help victims cope with their meal planning (14, 15).

The Exchange Plan provides a very structured meal plan. Foods are divided into eight categories, which are more specific than those of the Food Pyramid. A dietician or physician determines a daily calorie range for the patient and, based on that range, decides how many servings she or he should eat from each category per meal. Portion sizes are determined and must be followed exactly. The patient then has the option to either choose foods that fit into the groups recommended for each meal or exchange foods from one group for foods from another.

Another meal plan patients can utilize is carbohydrate counting. This plan is less structured and gives the patient more flexibility in making meal choices. It also involves less planning. Once again, food is categorized, but into only three groups. The largest food group, carbohydrates, encompasses not only starches but dairy products, fruits, and vegetables as well. The dietician or physician again assigns a calorie range. With this plan,

Bemis 8

however, only the number of carbohydrates per meal is assigned, and even this is flexible. This plan is recommended for those who know how to make balanced meal choices but need to keep track of their food intake. Once again, portion sizes are important, and the patient must remember to eat the recommended amount of foods from each pyramid category (5, 11, 12).

The final element in successfully managing diabetes is exercise. It has been shown (14) that exercise can help stimulate the body to use glucose for energy, thus taking it out of the blood. Diabetic patients need regular exercise programs that suit their personal needs. Something as simple as a walking routine can significantly reduce blood glucose levels (14). Some patients may require as little as a fifteen-minute-per-day walk, whereas some may need a more involved workout. In each case, an exercise schedule works with meal plans, medication, and lifestyle. Also crucial to the success of an exercise routine is close monitoring of blood sugar. If glucose levels are too high or too low, exercise will have negative effects.

The writer now explores control element number three: methods of exercise.

The Internet also serves now as a source of information. Tsunehara and Gaster (17) have provided a detailed critical assessment of diabetes information on the Web, and Levey (18) has explained methods for searching the CINAHL database.

Help and information are available in many forms, but all of the aspects of diabetes management can be summed up in one word: balance. Diabetes itself is caused by a lack of balance of insulin and glucose in the body. In order to restore that balance, a person with diabetes must juggle medication, monitoring, diet, and exercise. Managing diabetes is not an easy task, but a long and healthy life is very possible when the delicate balance is carefully maintained. Intervention becomes a key word (19). Let the doctor intervene with both education and medication.

Citations on this page demonstrate the citation-sequence method, as explained on pages 504–505. For details on the year-date system, see pages 508–510.

Bemis 9

Cited References

1. Collins FM. Current treatment approaches to type 2 diabetes mellitus: Successes and shortcomings. Am J Managed Care [serial online] 2002;16:S460-471. Available from http://web5.silverplatter.com/webspirs/showFullRecondContent.ws. Accessed 2003 Aug. 20.
2. [Anonymous]. Diabetes insipidus. American Academy of Family Physicians [article online] 2002. Available from http://www.aafp.org/patientinfo/insipidu.html. Accessed 2003 Aug 10.
3. Clark CM, Fradkin JE, Hiss RG, Lorenz RA, Vinicor F, Warren-Boulton E. Promoting early diagnosis and treatment of type 2 diabetes. JAMA 2000;284:363-365.
4. [Anonymous]. Do you know your blood-sugar level? Consumer Reports on Health 2000;12(7):1-4.
5. Gehling E. The family and friends' guide to diabetes: Everything you need to know. New York: Wiley; 2000. 282 p.
6. Schlosberg S. The symptoms you should never ignore. Shape 2000 Aug;19:136-142.
7. Espenshade JE. Staff manual for teaching patients about diabetes mellitus. Chicago: Amer. Hospital Publ.; 1979. 192 p.
8. Roberts SS. The diabetes advisor. Diabetes Forecast [serial online] 2000;53:41-42. Available from http://www.diabetes.org/diabetesforecast/00August/default.asp. Accessed 2003 Aug 8.
9. Brancati FL, Kao WHL, Folsom AR, Watson RL, Szklo M. Incident type 2 diabetes mellitus in African American and white adults. JAMA 2000;283:2253-2259.
10. Schwartz S, Hitchcock J. Is pumping for you? Diabetes Monitor [article online] 1999. Available from http://www.diabetesmonitor.com/presentations/pumps/tsld0003.htm. Accessed 2003 Aug 11.

Bemis 10

11. [Anonymous]. Glucophage. Diabetes Healthsource [article online] 2002. Available from http://www.glucophage.com. Accessed 2003 Aug 11.
12. Donald RA. Endocrine disorders. Springhouse, PA: Marcel Dekker; 1984. 760 p.
13. Eades RE, Eades MD. Protein power. New York: Bantam Books; 1996. 320 p.
14. American Diabetes Association. The American diabetes association complete guide to diabetes. New York: McGraw-Hill; 2002. 544 p.
15. American Diabetes Association. Magic menues for people with diabetes. Alexandria, VA: ADA; 2003. 244 p.
16. [Anonymous]. Exercise. American Diabetes Association [article online] 2000. Available from http://www.diabetes.org/exercise. Accessed 2003 Aug 11.
17. Tsunehara ST, Gaster B. Professional development: A critical assessment of diabetes information on the Internet. Diabetes Education [serial online] 2002;28:186-188. Available from http://web5.silverplatter.com/webspirs/showFullRecordContent.ws. Accessed 2003 May 20.
18. Levy JR. Searching the CINAHL database part 2: Abstracts, cited references and full text. CINAHLnews [serial online] 2002;21(2):4,6,11. Available from http://web5.silverplatter.com/webspirs/showFullRecordContent.ws. Accessed 2003 May 20.
19. Renders CM, Valk GD, Griffin S, Wagner EH, van-Eijk JTM, Assendeift WJJ. Interventions to improve the mangement of diabetes mellitus in primary care, outpatient and community settings. CINAHL [database online] 2003. Available from http://web5.silverplatter.com/webspirs/showFullRecordContent.ws. Accessed 2003 May 20.

21 Rap Culture: Is It Too Negative?

Rap started in the cities, in poor, largely African-American neighborhoods. At parties, disc jockeys, or DJs, played records—the then-current music technology—and some began to experiment with moving the record back and forth under the needle, manipulating the beats on the record. Rap's basic paradigm was solidified when masters of ceremony, called MCs, picked up a microphone at those parties and began reciting rhyming poems. This spoken-word performance gave the new music the name of *rap.* Rap was a revolutionary music, and early performers such as Grandmaster Flash were interested in its power to reach black youth and expose the conditions in the inner cities. In the early 1990s, a form of rap called "gangsta rap" emerged out of Los Angeles and expressed the frustration evident in the inner cities. The stance of gangsta rappers included threatening the police (whom they saw as their enemies), dealing drugs, carrying guns, taking advantage of women, and expressing a callous attitude toward everything except money.

A controversy emerged: One side claimed that the violence and crime depicted in rap music is a realistic reflection of poor urban neighborhoods and that rappers, like all artists, aim to transform what they see into art. Those on the other side of the debate—especially but not exclusively media observers and politicians—see rap music as overly and unnecessarily negative and maintain that rap artists do more harm than good. These critics charge that rap glorifies violence and crime and alienates and provokes neighborhood police. The debate has raged for years and still rages.

In the first selection that follows, a college student argues that rap is moving the black community in the wrong direction. In the second selection, a magazine columnist insists that we should not call upon artists to censor themselves.

Greg Jones

Rap Fans Desire a More Positive Product

This selection appeared in the Daily Cougar, *the student newspaper for the University of Houston, in the summer of 2002. The writer, Greg Jones, was a communications major at the school. In this selection,*

Jones makes a distinction between "old school," conscience-raising hip-hop and what he perceives as the more negative message appearing in rap music today.

Prereading: Thinking About the Essay in Advance

Do you listen to rap music? Why or why not? What associations does rap music have for you? Do you agree with the title of this essay?

Words to Watch

materialism (par. 2) concern with money and possessions
disenfranchisement (par. 2) exclusion from power
ideology (par. 4) belief system
entrepreneurship (par. 6) position as owner of a business
reparations (par. 6) money as payment for suffering, as in slavery

1 In the early stage of rap music before the bling bling era, rap music was the CNN for poor and working-class blacks in America. Songs such as "The Message" and "Fight the Power" raised the conscience levels of people and the need for social change in America.

2 Then, in the early 1990s, greedy, out-of-touch record executives took control of the art form and made materialism the main priority, over the continued disenfranchisement of blacks, latinos, and poor whites.

3 I believe the billion-dollar rap industry, which has a great influence on American culture, needs to take a turn for the better by going back to its roots. Record executives use rap artists for major profits at the expense of the African-American poor and working-class people that actually experience what these rappers are rapping about.

4 Many people wonder why anyone should make a big deal out of negative rap music, because they believe it is only entertainment. Most fans know many of the artists such as Dr. Dre and Jay Z actually don't perform many of the activities they claim. This ideology is wrong and lacks serious thought. The reason we listen to music is because it makes us feel emotions such as joy, sadness, motivation, or even relaxation.

5 In other words, it affects the soul of an individual. The imbalance in rap music is consistently reflected on the radio and shown on the video programs such as "Rap City." The images presented are not an actual account of how blacks are living as a whole.

6 As a kid growing up on the West side of Chicago I saw many images I thought were good because I saw them over and over again. For example, I thought gang banging was good because it was around me. The same concept applies to music. Blacks in America have many concerns such as police brutality, entrepreneurship, reparations, election reform, employment, quality health care, and quality education. This is what the art form needs to reflect instead of promoting materialism and violence.

Black music has historically always voiced the concerns of issues in America that effect their way of living. Instead, rappers and even some R&B and rock artists admit to committing crimes consistently on records, thus promoting some of the worst elements our society has to offer. Songs such as "Hood Rich" or "My Neck/My Back" have become the norm. 7

Record executives such as Jimmy Iovine, L.A. Reid, Tommy Mottola, Andrew Herrera, Bryan Turner, Russell Simmons, Tony Brown, and Ted Fields don't want positive images seen or heard, because it will interfere with the millions they make off young, uneducated, and misled black rappers from the inner cities of America. 8

Female rapper Foxy Brown and former rapper Mase both have gone on record saying they portrayed negative images on albums and videos because the record executives forced them to do so in order to sell more records. This is the norm also for the entire music industry. Just look at Britney Spears. 9

What can cure the problems of negative images of Black America presented in rap and other forms of music? 10

Music fans of all backgrounds must e-mail and write letters to the major record company executives and voice their concerns. Also don't buy the music when you hear songs such as "Big Pimpin'." 11

Music fans can turn off the television and the radio when these images are displayed. Music listeners must e-mail and write the executives of the products that pay for advertising space on rap shows and in magazines such as *Vibe* and *The Source.* If companies such as the Coca-Cola Corporation do not take the concerns seriously, then music fans must stop buying their products. 12

Positive artists such as Common, Black Star, Dead Pres., KRS1, Mos Def, Gang Star, Goodie Mob, Pharoahe Monch, and The Roots must get more requests on the radio and rap video programs. 13

The most important aspect is to shift the focus from the rap artist and put the heat on the record executives who run the major distributors such as Universal and AOL/Time Warner. 14

The executives are responsible for what is seen and heard, not the artist. So the next time you have issues with a song such as "Money, Cash, Hoes," send Russell Simmons an e-mail, or just don't buy the album. 15

Building Vocabulary

The writer of this essay assumes knowledge of a few topical phrases relating to the world of music and rap music in particular. Identify the following terms, and explain their relevance to rap music:

1. bling bling (par. 1)
2. gang-banging (par. 6)
3. R&B (par. 7)

Thinking Critically About the Argument

Understanding the Writer's Argument

1. What does Jones mean in paragraph 1 when he writes that "rap music was the CNN for poor and working-class blacks in America"?
2. What change came over rap music in the early 1990s, according to Jones?
3. Why does Jones put so much emphasis on the financial situations of the record executives and the fans of rap music?
4. What are some of the issues facing blacks in America, according to Jones? Do you think rap music addresses some of these? How?
5. Why don't record executives want positive images in rap music, according to Jones? Why are the record executives responsible for the negative images in rap, as opposed to the artists, as Jones says in paragraph 15?
6. Which rap musicians does Jones cite for presenting a positive message? Whom does he cite as being negative?

Understanding the Writer's Techniques

1. Why does Jones start his essay with a short history of rap music?
2. What is Jones's major proposition? Is it simply his statement in paragraph 3, or is there another aspect to his argument? What minor proposition does Jones present to show that rap needs to "take a turn for the better"? What evidence does Jones give to support the minor proposition?
3. What is the writer's tone in this essay? Who is his audience, and how does that affect the tone? Explain your answer. This is an emotional issue for Jones, but do you sense emotion? Where? If not, why?
4. How effective is Jones's mini-recollection in paragraph 6? What purpose does it serve in his argument?
5. Jones's essay shifts strategy with his question in paragraph 10. What is the shift, and is his rhetorical question effective? Does his essay maintain coherence despite the shift?
6. In his conclusion, Jones returns to his major proposition, but there has been a change. What is that change, and is his conclusion effective?
7. What is your view of the title? If you could change it, would you? What would you call the essay?

Exploring the Writer's Argument

1. Jones implies in his first paragraph that "poor and working-class blacks in America" only get their identity and news from rap music and that music in general is the biggest influence on Americans. Do you think this is true? Why or why not?
2. This essay was written by a college student. Do you expect him to have these views? How does this fact alter your reception of his argument?

3. Are you convinced by Jones's argument in paragraph 7 regarding his opinion that rappers who admit to committing crimes promote "the worst elements our society has to offer"? Why or why not?
4. In paragraph 7, Jones cites the song "My Neck/My Back" as being one of the "worst elements" in society that rap glorifies. This song, however, is about two consenting adults having sex. Knowing this, do you accept or reject Jones's argument? Why?
5. Do you agree that record executives are responsible for the content of rap records but that the artists are not? Why or why not?
6. What in this essay's argument do you think is effective? Too simple or generalized? Which of Jones's points do you think are well reasoned? Open to question or serious disagreement?

Ideas for Writing Arguments

Prewriting

Jot down notes on what images you see on TV or in the movies and how they affect you negatively.

Writing a Guided Argument

A *genre* is a kind of artistic form. Write an essay in which you argue that some genre other than rap music is responsible for negative effects on children. Be specific. Don't just write about movies—write about action movies or horror films. Don't just write about TV shows—write about *South Park, The Simpsons,* or reality programming.

1. Begin your essay by explaining a little about the history of the particular medium.
2. Write your major proposition clearly and place it prominently in your essay.
3. Give at least two minor propositions for why you think your medium has negative effects on children.
4. Offer ample evidence for your minor propositions in the form of anecdotes or examples.
5. Decide who is mostly responsible for the continuing popularity of that genre.
6. Make sure to use proper transitions in your essay to ensure coherence.
7. In the conclusion of your essay, offer solutions that will minimize the damage done by your chosen offending genre.

Thinking, Arguing, and Writing Collaboratively

Play a song from the gangsta rap era in class, and in small groups analyze the music and lyrics for what you consider positive or helpful to society. Present your findings to the class and solicit their objections. Rebut their objections as a group.

Writing About the Text

Jones states in paragraph 5 that music "affects the soul of an individual." How well has he developed that idea? Do you think music has that much influence on people? Has the essay convinced you of that? Does Jones's argument depend on that statement being true? If so, and if it is not true, does the essay still work? Address these questions in an essay that analyzes "Rap Fans Desire a More Positive Product."

More Writing Ideas

1. In your journal, outline an essay about how you are personally affected by music.
2. Find the lyrics to one of the songs cited by Jones, and analyze it in a paragraph based on his ideas.
3. When novels were first becoming popular in the late 1700s, people accused the form of having a terrible effect on young people. When jazz became popular in the 1920s, critics leveled the same accusation at that music. In the 1950s, when rock and roll was becoming popular, the same thing happened. Research the history of the popular reception of one of these art forms. In an essay, compare the reaction against rap music with the reaction of those who thought novels, jazz, or rock and roll were going to have a negative effect on youth. How are the two situations similar? How are they different?

BARBARA EHRENREICH
Ice-T: The Issue Is Creative Freedom

Biologist Barbara Ehrenreich (who earned her Ph.D. from Rockefeller University in 1968) became involved in political activism during the Vietnam War and began writing on topics such as feminism, class in America, and health care. Her books include The American Health Empire: Power, Profits, and Politics (1970), The Hearts of Men: American Dreams and the Flight from Commitment (1983) and Blood Rites: Origins and History of the Passions of War (2001). She has written for the Progressive, In These Times, the Nation, Time, *and many other publications. In 1992, rap artist Ice-T released a rock song called "Cop Killer." The reaction among the public and politicians was swift and angry. As Ehrenreich mentions in this selection, even the president at the time, George H. Bush, offered his opinion that Ice-T was "sick." Ehrenreich's essay, which appeared in* Time *magazine that year, argues that everyone was overreacting.*

Prereading: Thinking About the Essay in Advance

What is the first emotion that comes to mind when you think of a song titled "Cop Killer"? What do you think Ehrenreich means by "the issue is creative freedom"?

Words to Watch

taboo (par. 1) against social customs
paroxysm (par. 2) attack of violent emotion
boycott (par. 2) protest that takes the form of refusing to take part in
sedition (par. 2) act of trying to overthrow those in power
hyperbole (par. 4) exaggeration
decorum (par. 5) the social norm
demagogues (par. 5) dangerously charismatic speakers
miscreants (par. 6) delinquents

Ice-T's song "Cop Killer" is as bad as they come. This is black anger—raw, rude, and cruel—and one reason the song's so shocking is that in postliberal America, black anger is virtually taboo. You won't find it on TV, not on the *McLaughlin Group* or *Crossfire,* and certainly not in the placid features of Arsenio Hall or Bernard Shaw. It's been beaten back into the outlaw subcultures of rap and rock, where, precisely because it is taboo, it sells. And the nastier it is, the faster it moves off the shelves. As Ice-T asks in another song on the same album, "Goddamn what a brotha gotta do / To get a message through / To the red, white, and blue?" 1

But there's a gross overreaction going on, building to a veritable paroxysm of white denial. A national boycott has been called, not just of the song or Ice-T, but of all Time Warner products. The president himself has denounced Time Warner as "wrong" and Ice-T as "sick." Ollie North's Freedom Alliance has started a petition drive aimed at bringing Time Warner executives to trial for "sedition and anarchy." 2

Much of this is posturing and requires no more courage than it takes to stand up in a VFW hall and condemn communism or crack. Yes, "Cop Killer" is irresponsible and vile. But Ice-T is as right about some things as he is righteous about the rest. And ultimately, he's not even dangerous—least of all to the white power structure his songs condemn. 3

The "danger" implicit in all the uproar is of empty-headed, suggestible black kids, crouching by their boom boxes, waiting for the word. But what Ice-T's fans know and his detractors obviously don't is that "Cop Killer" is just one more entry in pop music's long history of macho hyperbole and violent boast. Flip to the classic-rock station, and you might catch the Rolling Stones announcing "the time is right for violent revoloo-shun!" from their 1968 hit "Street Fighting Man." And where were the defenders of our 4 law-enforcement officers when a white British group, the Clash, taunted its fans with the lyrics: "When they kick open your front door / How you gonna come / With your hands on your head / Or on the trigger of your gun?"

5 "Die, Die, Die Pig" is strong speech, but the Constitution protects strong speech, and it's doing so this year more aggressively than ever. The Supreme Court has just downgraded cross burnings to the level of bonfires and ruled that it's no crime to throw around verbal grenades like "nigger" and "kike." Where are the defenders of decorum and social stability when prime-time demagogues like Howard Stern deride African Americans as "spear chuckers"?

6 More to the point, young African Americans are not so naive and suggestible that they have to depend on a compact disc for their sociology lessons. To paraphrase another song from another era, you don't need a rap song to tell which way the wind is blowing. Black youths know that the police are likely to see them through a filter of stereotypes as miscreants and potential "cop killers." They are aware that a black youth is seven times as likely to be charged with a felony as a white youth who has committed the same offense, and is much more likely to be imprisoned.

7 They know, too, that in a shameful number of cases, it is the police themselves who indulge in "anarchy" and violence. The U.S. Justice Department has received 47,000 complaints of police brutality in the past six years, and Amnesty International has just issued a report on police brutality in Los Angeles, documenting forty cases of "torture or cruel, inhuman, or degrading treatment."

8 Menacing as it sounds, the fantasy in "Cop Killer" is the fantasy of the powerless and beaten down—the black man who's been hassled once too often ("A pig stopped me for nothin'!"), spread-eagled against a police car, pushed around. It's not a "responsible" fantasy (fantasies seldom are). It's not even a very creative one. In fact, the sad thing about "Cop Killer" is that it falls for the cheapest, most conventional image of rebellion that our culture offers: the lone gunman spraying fire from his AK-47. This is not "sedition"; it's the familiar, all-American, Hollywood-style pornography of violence.

9 Which is why Ice-T is right to say he's no more dangerous than George Bush's pal Arnold Schwarzenegger, who wasted an army of cops in *Terminator 2.* Images of extraordinary cruelty and violence are marketed every day, many of far less artistic merit than "Cop Killer." This is our free market of ideas and images, and it shouldn't be any less free for a black man than for other purveyors of "irresponsible" sentiments, from David Duke to Andrew Dice Clay.

10 Just, please, don't dignify Ice-T's contribution with the word *sedition.* The past masters of sedition—men like George Washington, Toussaint L'Ouverture, Fidel Castro, or Mao Zedong, all of whom led and won armed insurrections—would be unimpressed by "Cop Killer" and probably saddened. They would shake their heads and mutter words like "infantile" and "adventurism." They might point out that the cops are hardly a noble target, being, for the most part, honest working stiffs who've got stuck with the job of patrolling ghettos ravaged by economic decline and official neglect.

Musician Ice-T explains to reporters his reasons for pulling "Cop Killer" from his "Body Count" album in Los Angeles, Calif., on July 28, 1992. Ice-T pulled "Cop Killer" from the album because of threats against Times Warner and Warner Bros.(Associated Press/Bob Galbraith)

There is a difference, the true seditionist would argue, between a revolution and a gesture of macho defiance. Gestures are cheap. They feel good, they blow off some rage. But revolutions, violent or otherwise, are made by people who have learned how to count very slowly to ten. 11

Building Vocabulary

1. For the following words, write definitions (attempt to understand their meanings from the context of the essay, or look them up in a dictionary), and write a sentence of your own using each word:
   a. placid (par. 1)
   b. subcultures (par. 1)
   c. veritable (par. 2)
   d. denounced (par. 2)
   e. posturing (par. 3)
   f. detractors (par. 4)
   g. indulge (par. 7)

h. ghettos (par. 10)
i. adventurism (par. 10)
j. defiance (par. 11)

2. Ehrenreich mentions a number of people and institutions from recent and distant history. Identify these people, and explain how they are relevant to Ehrenreich's argument:

   a. Arsenio Hall (par. 1)
   b. Bernard Shaw (par. 1)
   c. Time Warner (par. 2)
   d. Ollie (Oliver) North (par. 2)
   e. VFW (par. 3)
   f. Rolling Stones (par. 4)
   g. Howard Stern (par. 5)
   h. Amnesty International (par. 7)
   i. Arnold Schwarzenegger (par. 9)
   j. David Duke (par. 9)
   k. Andrew Dice Clay (par. 9)
   l. George Washington (par. 10)
   m. Toussaint L'Ouverture (par. 10)
   n. Fidel Castro (par. 10)
   o. Mao Zedong (par. 10)

Thinking Critically About the Argument

Understanding the Writer's Argument

1. Paraphrase the writer's first two sentences.
2. According to the writer, why does "angry" rap sell?
3. What is the writer's opinion of Ice-T's song "Cop Killer"? What is her opinion of the song's most outspoken critics?
4. How does the writer place Ice-T's song in the perspective of music history?
5. How does "Cop Killer" relate to the harsh realities of the criminal justice system and police brutality, according to the writer?
6. What is the writer's main criticism of "Cop Killer"?
7. What, according to the writer, is the difference between "revolution and a gesture of macho defiance"? Why is one more impressive than the other?

Understanding the Writer's Techniques

1. What is the intended argumentative effect of Ehrenreich's confrontational opening?
2. Where does Ehrenreich's introduction end? Where is her claim? Is it placed in her introduction? Explain.
3. What are the writer's minor propositions? Which makes her point most effectively? Which is weakest?

4. Compare and contrast the kinds of support Jones and Ehrenreich use to make their arguments. Do they both rely equally on reasonable propositions? Does one rely more on an emotional appeal? Explain your answers.
5. Analyze Ehrenreich's use of transitions. Which is most impressive?
6. What kinds of support does the writer use to bolster her minor propositions?
7. Why is the writer's conclusion effective? Explain your answer. How does it help the essay to cohere?

Exploring the Writer's Argument

1. How do you think Jones would react to Ehrenreich's points that Ice-T and his songs are "not even dangerous" (par. 3) and that "young African Americans are not so naive and suggestible that they have to depend on a compact disc for their sociology lessons" (par. 6)? What is your reaction to those statements?
2. Do you think Ehrenreich's placing Ice-T in the stream of music history in paragraph 4 is effective? Why or why not?
3. Do you find Ehrenreich's arguments in paragraph 9—that (1) rap is no more dangerous than action movies, and (2) there is free speech, so rap artists can say anything they want—compatible? Why or why not?
4. How effective is Ehrenreich's comparison of Ice-T to the "past masters of sedition"? Do you think this is a fair comparison? Is it an effective argumentative technique? Explain your answers.

Ideas for Writing Arguments

Prewriting

What other elements of popular culture might be considered dangerous, and why? What is your position?

Writing a Guided Argument

Choose an activity that many critics agree is dangerous, such as riding motorcycles or skydiving, and write an essay defending the right of people to do it.

1. Begin your essay by explaining your topic and summarizing the main objections on the grounds of its danger.
2. Write your major proposition clearly.
3. Use a tone that is similar to Ehrenreich's.
4. Offer at least three minor propositions to explain why critics of your chosen action are overreacting.
5. Support your ideas with vivid examples and, if possible, statistics.
6. For at least one of your minor propositions, explain that other activities that are not criticized are at least, if not more, dangerous.

7. Pick out one word that the critics would use to describe your chosen action (for example, some might call skydiving "suicidal"), and close your essay as Ehrenreich does, with a long analysis of how that word is not apt in describing the action.

Thinking, Arguing, and Writing Collaboratively

With the class divided into two arbitrary groups, have one group take Jones's position that rap music is dangerous and have the other group argue, as Ehrenreich does, that it is harmless. As a group, think of arguments and facts to add to those already explored by the writer whose position you are taking, and fix weaknesses in his or her argument. You may do research and bring in examples from home or the library. Take notes on your intragroup discussion, and use your notes to prepare for a debate on the issue of rap music. Present your position to the class as a group, with each member of the group presenting a certain aspect of your argument. As a class, discuss which group's argument was stronger, and explain why.

Writing About the Text

Compare Ehrenreich's argument in this essay with her argument in "From Stone Age to Phone Age" in Chapter 1. "Ice-T: The Issue Is Creative Freedom" was written in 1992, whereas "From Stone Age" was written in 1999. What development do you see in Ehrenreich's style? What is the difference in argumentative technique? How does the tone in her essays differ?

More Writing Ideas

1. In a journal entry, write notes about the word *sedition.* All the "past masters of sedition" Ehrenreich lists were seditious long ago. Can you think of any examples of true sedition or anarchy today?
2. In paragraph 3, Ehrenreich makes a point about American rhetoric, saying that arguing against rap music is "posturing and requires no more courage than it takes to stand up in a VFW hall and condemn communism or crack." In a paragraph, explain this quote, and give at least two examples of this kind of posturing and rhetoric that you have seen in the past year.
3. Write an essay in which you analyze an artistic medium other than music, such as movies, television, books, or radio. Explain how, as Ehrenreich notes, "precisely because it is taboo, it sells" (par. 1). How does the medium exploit the public's desire for "outlaw subcultures" or the shocking?

22 College Sports: Should We Seek Equal Rights Between the Sexes?

In 1972, President Richard Nixon signed into law legislation called the Education Amendments. Title IX of that legislation aimed to force equality between men's and women's sports in any school around the country that receives federal funds. The law says, simply: "No person in the United States shall, on the basis of sex, be excluded from participation in, be denied the benefits of, or be subjected to discrimination under any educational program or activity receiving Federal financial assistance." The law had an impact on all public schools in the country and most private schools and colleges, which receive funding through financial aid programs. Any school found in violation of Title IX would lose its federal funding.

By 1979, Title IX still languished without enforcement, so a Department of Education civil rights commission interpreted the law and issued the rule that would cause heated controversy in the years to come: the three-part test. To comply with Title IX, schools had to fulfill at least one of the following conditions: (1) make sure that the number of student athletes of each sex is roughly equivalent to enrollment percentages (the rule that would come to be known as the "proportionality" rule), (2) show a history and continuing practice of promoting women's sports, or (3) demonstrate that the campus fully and effectively accommodated the athletic interests and abilities of women.

In the years after the adoption of the three-part test, the courts have tested Title IX again and again. One such case, in 1996, involved Brown University, which tried to make the case that women shouldn't have an equal share in collegiate sports because they are not as involved in sports. Brown lost the case.

Critics accuse Title IX of supporting reverse discrimination and a form of unnecessary affirmative action. Supporters laud it for increasing equality for women in educational institutions. Most of the controversy has centered on sports, but note that Title IX covers "any educational program or activity." Americans are still debating the landmark law after more than 30 years.

In the following two selections, Billie Jean King, a retired world-class tennis player, and John Irving, a popular novelist, offer their positions on Title IX. King believes that the law does not go far enough; Irving maintains that although the intentions of the law are good, its interpretation, especially the three-part rule, have had unintentional negative side effects.

Billie Jean King

For All the Good Things It Has Done, Title IX Is Still Plagued by Myths

Tennis player Billie Jean King was born in 1943 in Long Beach, California. She had a long and spectacular career, winning the women's singles tournament at Wimbledon six times. In 1971 she became the first woman athlete to earn $100,000 in a year. In the famed "Battle of the Sexes" match in Texas in 1973, 30-year-old King beat 55-year-old Bobby Riggs in straight sets. King, who was captain of the women's tennis Olympic team in 1996 and 2000, has been an outspoken supporter of women's rights for many years, pushing especially for parity for the prize money that goes to women athletes. In this selection, King defends the Title IX legislation against widely held misconceptions.

Prereading: Thinking About the Essay in Advance

What do you think are the myths King is referring to in the title? What myths can you imagine exist about women's sports? How can those myths harm the future of women's sports?

Words to Watch

pit (par. 2) set up against each other
inception (par. 4) beginning
rhetoric (par. 5) insincere speech
irrefutably (par. 7) immune from criticism
hampered (par. 7) restricted
curtail (par. 7) restrain
proportionality (par. 12) system regulating amounts based on proportions
compliance (par. 12) conforming to requirements

1 When my brother Randy and I were growing up, we supported each other's dreams of being professional athletes. We both loved sports and we were there for each other as we went through the ups and downs of being athletes; he as a baseball player for the San Francisco Giants and me as an international tennis player.

2 As Title IX turns 30 today, there are those who want us to believe that this is a male-versus-female issue. There are those who want the public to believe that this is a "zero sum" game; that if women get a chance to play, men lose. This is no time for extremism and no time for anyone to pit men versus women or boys against girls. Those days are over. We are in this together—male and female athletes who love sports, and families who want their sons and daughters to play because of the health, confidence, and other benefits they will receive as a result of such participation. That's the bottom line and we had better not forget it. Also, there are a number of negative myths about Title IX that need to be addressed.

MYTH: Title IX requires cutting men's teams. 3

FACT: There is nothing in Title IX that requires schools to cut men's 4 teams. Men's sports participation in high school and college has increased since the law's inception 30 years ago. More important, two-thirds of the schools that have added women's sports to comply with Title IX did not eliminate any men's sports.

We can afford to maintain all of our exciting football and basketball pro- 5 grams, keep all men's minor sports and add new women's sports if schools exercise fiscal restraint and support each sport with a smaller piece of the budgetary pie. Financial responsibility is what we should be talking about, not weakening civil-rights laws. We simply cannot believe rhetoric claiming football will die if our daughters have an equal chance to play.

MYTH: Women are less interested in sports than men. 6

FACT: Development of women's interest in sports since the enactment 7 of Title IX shows irrefutably that interest reflects opportunity. While fewer than 30,000 women participated in college sports before Title IX, today that number exceeds 150,000—five times the pre-Title IX rate. Women's participation continues to be hampered simply by schools not sponsoring teams for them to play on. To accept the notion that women are less interested in sports than men would simply maintain existing discrimination and curtail opportunities at artificially limited levels.

Lets's face it, there will always be more kids interested in playing than 8 we have resources to provide them with opportunities. There are more than six million boys and girls playing high school sports today who are vying for fewer than half a million college athletic participation slots. All Title IX says is that if you have sports participation opportunities, you offer equal opportunity to men and women.

MYTH: Women are no longer the victims of discrimination in sports. 9

FACT: Despite Title IX's considerable successes, the playing field is far 10 from level. Spending on men's sports continues to vastly exceed spending on women's sports. Male athletes annually receive $133 million more in athletic scholarships than female athletes. Thirty years after Title IX, women still receive 30 percent fewer sports participation opportunities.

MYTH: Title IX requires quotas for women. 11

FACT: Title IX requires that women and girls be given equal opportuni- 12 ties to participate in athletics. Because Title IX allows sports teams to be segregated by gender, in essence it allows schools to decide how many teams they will sponsor and how many slots they will allocate for female, as compared to male, students. Title IX simply requires that schools allocate these slots in a nondiscriminatory manner. Title IX does not require "proportionality" or any other mathematical test, as some are alleging. There are many schools that are conducting athletic programs that are in compliance with Title IX with athletic program male/female participation numbers that are not proportional to the percentages of men and women in their general student bodies. Use of the word quota misleads the public.

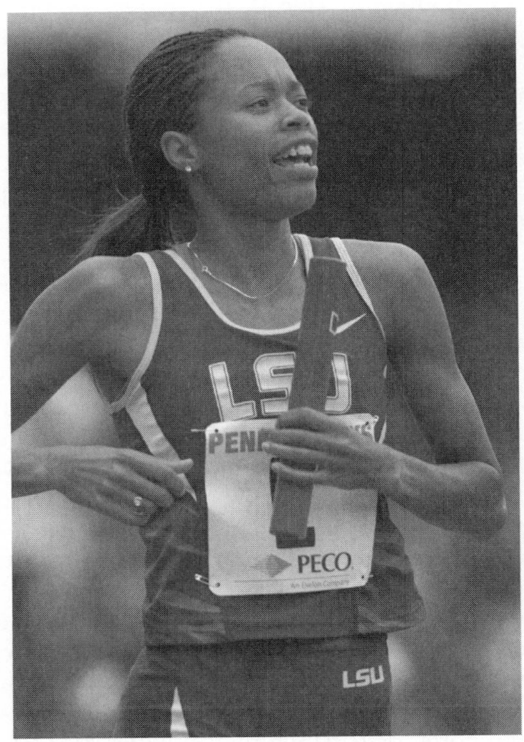

Louisiana State's Muna Lee holds the baton after anchoring LSU's college women's 800 relay team Saturday, April 26, 2003, at the Penn Relays in Philadelphia. LSU tied a meet record with four relay wins. LSU won the 800 in 1:29.78. (Associated Press/Douglas M. Bovitt)

13 Do I feel Title IX has worked in the intended way the law was created 30 years ago? I would say, judging by the 847 percent increase in high school athletic participation by girls, yes. But, Title IX needs stronger enforcement because girls are still receiving 1.1 million fewer chances to play high school sports than boys. Thirty years after the passage of Title IX, it's estimated that 80 percent of all schools and colleges are still out of compliance with the law.

14 The Bush administration needs to send a clear message that Title IX is valid and legal and women are entitled to full and equal rights to participate in federally funded education programs and activities. The public expects our government to strongly defend equal rights for men and women. Taxpayers expect their sons and daughters to receive equal educational opportunities, whether it's math, science, drama, or athletics. That's the bottom line. Let's go for it!

Building Vocabulary

In her essay, King uses figurative speech, but in most of those cases, her use of such language is clichéd. Look up the definition of cliché and explain why the following are clichés. What could you replace them with to make them more interesting?

1. went through the ups and downs (par. 1)
2. That's the bottom line (par. 2, 14)
3. smaller piece of the pie . . . (par. 5)
4. the playing field is far from level (par. 10)
5. send a clear message (par. 14)

Thinking Critically About the Argument

Understanding the Writer's Argument

1. Why, according to King, should people stop fighting over Title IX?
2. According to King, why does Title IX not mean that men's sports will disappear?
3. How are men's and women's sports still not equal after 30 years of Title IX, in King's view?
4. What is King's answer to opponents of Title IX who accuse the law of forcing quotas on schools?
5. What does King want the government to do now to improve the situation?

Understanding the Writer's Techniques

1. Where does King's introduction end? How do you know? What is her major proposition? What minor propositions does she use to support her major proposition?
2. What is the argumentative effect of using the words MYTH and FACT instead of other words? What is the effect of presenting them in uppercase letters?
3. The four myths that the writer highlights are really objections to Title IX that she rebuts. Make a list of the myths, and outline her rebuttals. Which is her most successful rebuttal? Which is her weakest? Explain your answers.
4. King uses statistics to help her case. How effective do you find them? What do you think is King's strongest piece of evidence?
5. Why does King use the word "segregated" in paragraph 12? What is the effect?
6. Do you think King's closing, including the use of the exclamation point, is persuasive? Why or why not?

Exploring the Writer's Argument

1. Is there any good argumentative reason why King includes her opening about her brother and her? If so, what is it? If not, how would you improve her introduction?
2. Do you find the structure of King's essay to be effective? Why or why not? Does the "MYTH/FACT" list format work for or against her argument?
3. King suggests in paragraph 2 that there are those who want to "pit men versus women," but she doesn't say who those people are. Does her vagueness hurt her argument? Justify your response.
4. King writes that both men's and women's sports have increased their numbers since 1972. She implies that this is because of Title IX. Can you think of any other explanation?
5. At the end of her essay, King implies that athletics are as important as the major subjects in school. Do you agree with her? Why or why not?

Ideas for Writing Arguments

Prewriting

Draft a brief outline arguing against misconceptions about a segment of the population on campus. What are the myths that circulate about them? What is the truth?

Writing a Guided Argument

Write an essay in which you dispel myths about a book, movie, television show, video game, or other technology. Choose something that you know a good deal about.

1. Begin your essay by recounting an anecdote in which you watch, read, or play with your chosen subject.
2. Connect your experience, using transitions, with the idea that there are common myths about your subject.
3. Write your major proposition.
4. Organize your minor propositions, rebuttals to myths, in an effective manner to maintain coherence in your argument.
5. Offer evidence in the form of statistics or facts to support your rebuttals.
6. Close your essay with a call for greater tolerance and understanding, explaining how the truth about your subject will benefit people.

Thinking, Arguing, and Writing Collaboratively

Exchange a draft of your Writing a Guided Argument assignment with a classmate. Review your partner's essay for its success in following the steps.

Does the writer express the major proposition as a choice? Is the major proposition reflected in the minor propositions? Is there sufficient evidence to back up the minor propositions? Write a paragraph evaluating the essay and suggesting revisions.

Writing About the Text

Read John Irving's essay below. Write an essay in which you compare and contrast King's and Irving's arguments. In what ways are the two writers in agreement, and where do they differ? Which do you think is the stronger argument? Use either writer's essay as a basis for the structure of your essay.

More Writing Ideas

1. In your journal, freewrite about the concept of a "'zero sum' game" (par. 2). Write for at least 15 minutes without editing your work. Then look over your journal entry and find any candidates for a major proposition.
2. Write two or three paragraphs that take issue with the way King uses statistics in her essay. What is suspect? Why?
3. John Irving writes in his essay that the Women's Sport Foundation and other women's groups are being "vindictive" in their faith in the success of Title IX and "their continuing endorsement of proportionality in collegiate athletics." King is the founder of the Women's Sport Foundation. Examine Irving's exact words, and write an essay in which you argue whether or not you think Irving's accusation of King and her organization is fair and in which you speculate as to how King might respond to Irving's accusation.

JOHN IRVING
Wrestling with Title IX

John Irving was born in Exeter, New Hampshire, in 1942. He was educated at Phillips Exeter Academy, a prep school, where he started to wrestle competitively, and later studied in Vienna, Austria, Pittsburgh, and at the prestigious Writer's Workshop at the University of Iowa. He is the author of several novels, including, Setting Free the Bears *(1968),* The World According to Garp *(1974),* The Cider House Rules *(1985), and* A Prayer for Owen Meany *(1989). He has been awarded many honors for his writing, including an American Book Award and a Guggenheim Fellowship. During the early part of his writing career, Irving supported himself by teaching and coaching wrestling. In this selection, the novelist and former wrestler explores the difference between the Title IX legislation and how it has been enforced over the years.*

Prereading: Thinking About the Essay in Advance

If you were to choose which college sports to abolish, which would you select? Explain your reasoning.

Words to Watch

disparate (par. 3) unfairly different
criteria (par. 4) requirements
proportionality (par. 4) system regulating amounts based on proportion
zealots (par. 6) overly enthusiastic believers
intramural (par. 8) occurring within an institution
equity (par. 12) equality
gulch (par. 16) ravine; small canyon

1 Title IX, the federal law that prohibits sex discrimination in educational programs receiving federal assistance, may be in for an overhaul. This week a committee appointed by the Bush administration will hold its final meetings before submitting its recommendations for changing the law to Secretary of Education Rod Paige. Since Title IX was enacted in 1972, it has been the subject of debate—much of it misguided—about its application to college athletics. At issue now is how to alter the law—or not—so that, as Secretary Paige has put it, we can find ways of "expanding opportunities to ensure fairness for all college athletes."

2 I hope the commission will realize that what's wrong with Title IX isn't Title IX. What's wrong is that, in practice, there are two Title IX's. The first Title IX was the one passed by Congress in 1972 to put an end to sex discrimination in schools—good for the original Title IX! The second Title IX, the one currently enforced, is the product of a policy interpretation in 1979 by the Department of Education's Office for Civil Rights (but never debated or approved by Congress)—and which is functioning as a gender quota law.

3 In its prohibition against sex discrimination, the 1972 law expressly states as "exceptions" any "preferential or disparate treatment because of imbalance in participation" or any "statistical evidence of imbalance." In English, this means that Congress recognized that the intent of Title IX was not to establish gender quotas or require preferential treatment as reparation for past discrimination. Smart thinking—after all, the legislation was intended to prohibit discrimination against either sex.

4 But what happened in 1979—and in subsequent re-evaluations of the law—has invited discrimination against male athletes. The 1979 interpretation required colleges to meet at least one of the following three criteria: that the number of athletes from each sex be roughly equivalent to the number of students enrolled; that colleges demonstrate a commitment to adding women's sports; and that they prove that the athletic interests of female students are effectively accommodated. The problems lie in complying with the first criterion. In order to achieve gender proportionality, men's collegiate sports are being undermined and eliminated. This was never the intention of Title IX.

The proportionality rule stipulates that the ratio of male to female athletes be proportionate to the ratio of male to female students at a particular college. On average, females make up about 56 percent of college enrollment, males 44 percent; for most colleges to be in compliance with proportionality, more than half the athletes on team rosters must be women. Can you imagine this rule being applied to all educational programs—classes in science, engineering, accounting, medicine or law? What about dance, drama or music—not to mention women's studies? 5

In 1996, the Department of Education further bolstered the proportionality zealots by requiring colleges to count every name on a team's roster—scholarship and nonscholarship athletes, starters and nonstarters. It is this ruling that has prompted a lawsuit by the National Wrestling Coaches Association, the Committee to Save Bucknell Wrestling, the Marquette Wrestling Club, the Yale Wrestling Association, and the National Coalition for Athletics Equity, all of whom argue that the 1996 rules exceed the Department of Education's statutory authority "by effectively mandating the very discrimination that Title IX prohibits." 6

Why are wrestlers so upset about this? The number of collegiate wrestling programs lost to Title IX compliance is staggering; this is especially alarming because, since 1993, wrestling has been a rapidly growing sport at the high-school level. Data compiled by Gary Abbott, director of special projects at USA Wrestling, indicates that in 2001, there were 244,984 athletes wrestling in high school; only 5,966 got to wrestle in the National Collegiate Athletic Association. Not to put too fine a point on it: there is only one N.C.A.A., spot for every 41 high-school wrestlers. The numbers have been going downhill for a while. In 1982, there were 363 N.C.A.A. wrestling teams with 7,914 wrestlers competing; in 2001, there were only 229 teams with fewer than 6,000 wrestlers. Yet, in that same period, the number of N.C.A.A. institutions has increased from 787 to 1,049. No wonder wrestlers are unhappy. 7

As for the virtual elimination of walk-ons (nonscholarship athletes) in many men's sports, and the unrealistic capping of male team rosters—again, to make the number of male athletes proportional to the number of females—the problem is that athletic programs are going to absurd lengths to fill the unfilled rosters for women's teams. But women, statistically, aren't interested in participating in intercollegiate athletics to the degree that men are. J. Robinson, wrestling coach at the University of Minnesota, cites intramural sports, which are wholly interest driven, as an example. In a column about Title IX published in the *Chronicle of Higher Education,* Robinson wrote that "men outnumber women 3-1 or 4-1 on the intramural field." 8

Don't we need to know the exact numbers for how many women are interested in playing college sports now? But the Women's Sports Foundation, an advocacy group that favors maintaining proportionality, opposes conducting surveys of incoming students—that is, expressly to gauge interest in athletics. These surveys, they say, would force "female athletes to prove their interest in sports in order to obtain the right to participate and be treated fairly." But men would fill out the same surveys. 9

10 One suggestion that the presidential commission is considering is counting the available spots on teams, rather than the actual participants. The Women's Sports Foundation rejects this idea, arguing that it counts "ghost female participants." However, the foundation has no objection to counting interest that isn't there.

11 In fact, those women's groups opposed to tampering with either the 1979 interpretation or the 1996 ruling, which endorses the proportionality arm of Title IX, often argue that there are three ways (at least on paper) for an institution to comply with Title IX—not just proportionality. But only proportionality can be measured concretely. A 1996 clarification letter from the Department of Education refers to the proportionality test as a "safe harbor"—meaning that this simple-to-apply numerical formula can assure an athletic director and a university president that their institution is in compliance and not subject to legal action. In other words, proportionality is not only wrong—it's lazy.

12 Some women's advocates argue that it is not proportionality that forces athletic directors to cut men's teams; they blame the budget excesses of Division I football and men's basketball. But there are countless examples where money was not the issue in the case or the sport that was dropped. Marquette University had a wrestling team that was completely financed by alumni and supporters; yet the sport was dropped in 2001, to comply with gender equity. (Marquette has no football team.)

13 Boston College dropped three sports that had only part-time coaches and offered no scholarships; these sports could easily have been sponsored by fund-raising. Keep in mind, too, that the majority of male college teams dropped in the 1990's were from Division II and Division III programs, which don't have big-time football or men's basketball.

14 Furthermore, many Division I football and basketball programs earn millions of dollars a year, enough to support all the other sports programs—men's and women's. Moreover, most schools with high-profile football programs are schools where women's teams have thrived. (Witness the Big 10, the S.E.C., the Big 12, and other Division I athletic conferences, which have produced both winning football teams as well as great women's teams in other sports.)

15 While eliminating men's sports like wrestling, where the interest in participation is increasing, athletic programs go begging to find women athletes to fill the vacancies on an ever-expanding number of women's teams.

16 One of the most ludicrous examples of this was the attempt by Arizona State University in Tempe—a cactus-studded campus in the middle of the Sonoran Desert—to add a competitive women's rowing team. There's not a lot of water in Arizona. But the school asked the city to create a body of water (by flooding a dry gulch) on which the team could practice. Because of a lack of funds, the school had to drop the plan. This is probably just as well; taxpayer dollars would have financed scholarships either to rowers from out of state or to teach Arizona women (most of whom have never held an oar) how to row. But Arizona State is to be commended. It not only worked to meet the numerical demands of proportionality, it tried to adhere to the

original spirit of Title IX by adding opportunities for women, not by cutting opportunities for men.

To apply the rule of proportionality to men's and women's collegiate athletics amounts to a feminist form of sex discrimination. And I won't be dismissed by that other argument I've heard (ad nauseam) from those women's advocates unwilling to let proportionality go—namely, that to oppose proportionality, or even the crudest enforcement of Title IX to eliminate men's sports programs, is tantamount to being antifeminist and hostile to women in sports. Don't try to lay that on me. 17

I *am* a women's advocate. I have long been active in the pro-choice movement; my principal political commitment is my longstanding and continuing role as an abortion-rights advocate. But I'm also an advocate of fairness. What is unfair is not Title IX—it is Title IX's enforcement of proportionality, which discriminates against men. 18

In 1992, Brian Picklo, a walk-on, asked the Michigan State Wrestling coach, Tom Minkel, if he could try out for the team. Picklo had wrestled for only two years in high school and never qualified for state tournaments. Minkel thought Picklo's chances of wrestling in the Big 10 were "slim to none." But Picklo became a two-time Division I All-American, and he won the Big 10 title at 190 pounds. In most wrestling programs across the country today, Brian Picklo wouldn't be allowed to be a walk-on. 19

Title IX, the original legislation, was conceived as a fairness-for-all law; it has been reinvented as a tool to treat men unfairly. Advocates of proportionality claim that universities that are not "proportional" are breaking the law, but they're not breaking the original law. 20

The Women's Sports Foundation has accused the presidential commission of politicizing Title IX. But Title IX was politicized by the Department of Education in 1979 and 1996—during Democratic administrations. Is it only now political because a Republican administration is taking a closer look at the way Title IX is applied? (I make this criticism, by the way, as a Democrat. I'd have a hard time being an abortion rights advocate in the Bush administration, wouldn't I?) 21

Based on 2001 membership data—raw data from the National Federation of State High Schools, and from the N.C.A.A.—for every single N.C.A.A. sports opportunity for a woman, there are 17 high school athletes available to fill the spot; for a man, there are 18. Isn't that equal enough? In fact, women have more opportunity to compete in college than men do. Yet the attitude represented by the Women's Sports Foundation, and other women's groups, is that women are far from achieving gender equity; by their continuing endorsement of proportionality in collegiate athletics, these women's advocates are being purely vindictive. 22

Years ago, I was playing in a Little League baseball game when an umpire made what I thought was a memorable mistake. Later, in another game, he made it again. I realized it was no mistake at all—he meant to say it. Instead of hollering "Play ball!" at the start of the game, this umpire shouted "Play fair!" 23

Keep Title IX; eliminate proportionality. Play fair. 24

Building Vocabulary

Define the following words and use each in a sentence of your own:

1. policy (par. 2)
2. criterion (par. 4)
3. bolstered (par. 6)
4. mandating (par. 6)
5. absurd (par. 8)
6. clarification (par. 11)
7. tantamount (par. 17)
8. vindictive (par. 22)

Thinking Critically About the Argument

Understanding the Writer's Argument

1. What, according to Irving, is the problem with Title IX? What does he mean when he writes that "there are two Title IX's"? (par. 2)
2. Why does Irving point out that the Department of Education's 1979 interpretation of Title IX was "never debated or approved by Congress"? (par. 2)
3. Paraphrase Irving's argument in paragraph 5.
4. What did the Department of Education do in 1996 concerning Title IX? Explain why Irving thinks it was a bad idea.
5. Who are "walk-ons," and why is it significant that they rarely make college teams anymore?
6. Why, according to Irving, would it be valuable to know the number of women who are interested in playing sports in college, and why is it difficult to get that number?
7. Why do colleges use the proportionality rule to comply with Title IX instead of one of the other two criteria?
8. How could money-starved college sports programs be funded, if not by the school, according to Irving?

Understanding the Writer's Techniques

1. How effective is Irving's opening? Explain.
2. What is Irving's major proposition? Make an outline of Irving's many minor propositions. Which is more effective? Which is the weakest? Explain your answers.
3. Why does Irving ask two rhetorical questions at the end of paragraph 5? How do they advance his argument?
4. Why does Irving write that "women, statistically, aren't interested in participating in intercollegiate athletics to the degree that men are"? (par. 8) How does he back up this point? King includes this in her essay as one of the myths of Title IX. How might she respond to Irving's statement?

5. Paraphrase Irving's point in paragraph 11. How effective is this point?
6. Irving shifts tone several times in this essay. Answer the following questions:
   a. Where in the essay does Irving use a tone of authority?
   b. Where in the essay does Irving switch to a sarcastic tone?
   c. Where in the essay does Irving use a sentimental tone?
   d. Can you identify any other tones?
   e. Why does he shift tone so much? How is the multiple shift in tone effective?
7. Paraphrase Irving's argument in paragraph 21. Do you find it to be effective? Why or why not?
8. Do you think that Irving's conclusion is effective? Explain your answer.

Exploring the Writer's Argument

1. Irving was a wrestler for many years and then coached for several years more. Does this give him enough authority to write about Title IX? Why or why not?
2. Do you think that Irving's essay is marred by too narrow a focus on wrestling? How could he widen the discussion? Where in his essay could you imagine he might refer to other men's sports that are less popular than football and basketball?
3. In her essay, King argues, that schools can save men's sports, even minor ones like wrestling, if they "exercise fiscal restraint and support each sport with a smaller piece of the budgetary pie." What would Irving's answer to this be? Do you agree with King? With Irving? Why?
4. Does Irving offer a solution to the problems he explores? If he does, what is it? If not, what do you think the solution is?

Ideas for Writing Arguments

Prewriting

Jot down some notes about other well-intentioned laws or rules that have caused problems. What was their original intention? What were the unintentional side effects? Were there any repercussions for the rule- or lawgiver?

Writing a Guided Argument

Write an essay that argues that colleges could easily comply with Title IX by using one of the criteria other than the proportionality rule. Pretend that you are preparing your paper as a speech to be given at a conference of collegiate athletic directors.

1. Begin your essay by explaining the problem, using quotes from either King's essay (about quotas) or Irving's essay (about the proportionality rule).

2. Acknowledge, in kind words, that most of the athletic directors, by using the proportionality rule, are, as Irving says in paragraph 11, "lazy." Do not use the word *lazy* so that you do not alienate your audience.
3. Shift your tone at some point to one of gentle accusation.
4. Write your major proposition.
5. Offer at least three minor propositions.
6. Support your minor propositions with examples and facts, using effective transitions to aid coherence.
7. Defend your own identity in the essay, making sure your audience has no question about your authority and integrity.
8. Close your essay with an anecdote that illustrates your major proposition.

Thinking, Arguing, and Writing Collaboratively

Break the class into four groups. Two groups will prepare an argument *for* the proportionality rule in Title IX, and the other two groups will prepare an argument *against* it. Both groups on each side should meet to come up with two good grounds to support their position, one for each group. Each group should prepare evidence to support its chosen ground. At the end of the preparation period, the groups should all come together and the four groups should present their argument, alternating between sides.

Writing About the Text

At a few points in Irving's essay, he defends himself personally against perceived objections from his reader. Write an essay analyzing those passages, explaining why you think he felt it necessary to go on the defensive.

More Writing Ideas

1. In your journal, write notes for an essay arguing that tuition money should not be used for college athletics at all.
2. Write an imaginary interview between King and Irving about women's tennis programs.
3. Investigate the way in which your school complies with Title IX (if it does comply), and write an essay on your findings. Explain how you think King and Irving would respond to your school's approach. If your school does not comply with Title IX, write a letter to the school's athletic director demanding the school does comply.

23 Animal Rights: Should They Compromise Human Needs?

In recent years the idea of *animal* rights has gained many supporters. Animal rights advocates believe that other species should exist without human interference. Modern researchers have argued that animals feel pain and emotions and, in some cases, are capable of reasoning. Organizations such as the People for the Ethical Treatment of Animals (PETA) go so far as to claim that drinking milk is immoral because it causes the cows suffering. Some animal rights advocates are more moderate and abstain from eating meat from big commercial farms or become vegetarians altogether. Some will not wear leather.

Most people, if pressed, will agree that we do not need to eat hamburgers to live, but what happens when it is a question of life and death? For example, what if the suffering of animals can help save the lives of humans who are sick with disease? Many drugs and procedures that humans rely on for health emerged through medical research on animals.

In the selections that follow, written by two writers of vastly different backgrounds and viewpoints, notice how emotional the arguments for or against animal experimentation can be.

JANE MCCABE

Is a Lab Rat's Fate More Poignant than a Child's?

Jane McCabe was a wife and mother living in northern California when she published this essay in Newsweek. *She is not a professional writer, nor is she a public person. Her only qualification for writing is that she believes strongly about animal experimentation and has a stake in the issue. Her daughter has an incurable disease, and hope for a cure lies mostly in the ability of scientists to continue doing experiments on animals. In this selection, McCabe argues passionately that animal experimentation must continue.*

Prereading: Thinking About the Essay in Advance

Think about the question posed in the title. Consider giving an answer to that question. What about the fate of a chimpanzee? A pet dog's fate? A cat's? Where would you personally draw the line and why?

Words to Watch

stark (par. 1) plain, harsh
cystic fibrosis (par. 1) a disease that appears in early childhood affecting the digestive system and the lungs
supplemental (par. 4) making up for something lacking
enzymes (par. 5) molecules that help biological function
antibiotics (par. 5) drugs designed to fight bacterial infection
diabetes (par. 5) a disease caused by a low level of insulin, the hormone in the body that controls the level of sugar in the blood
semblance (par. 6) an outward appearance or likeness
poignant (par. 7) deeply affecting the emotions
eloquent (par. 9) forcefully expressive and persuasive

1 I see the debate about using animals in medical research in stark terms. If you had to choose between saving a very cute dog or my equally cute, blond, brown-eyed daughter, whose life would you choose? It's not a difficult choice, is it? My daughter has cystic fibrosis. Her only hope for a normal life is that researchers, some of them using animals, will find a cure. Don't misunderstand. It's not that I don't love animals, it's just that I love Claire more.

2 Nine years ago I had no idea that I would be joining the fraternity of those who have a vital interest in seeing that medical research continues. I was a very pregnant woman in labor; with my husband beside me I gave birth to a 7-pound 1-ounce daughter. It all seemed so easy. But for the next four months she could not gain weight. She was a textbook case of failure to thrive. Finally a hospital test of the salt content in her sweat led to the diagnosis of cystic fibrosis.

3 The doctor gave us a little reason for hope. "Your daughter will not have a long life, but for most of the time, it will be a good life. Her life expectancy is about 13 years, though it could be longer or shorter. As research continues, we're keeping them alive longer."

4 "As research continues." It's not a lot to rely on but what's our alternative? We haven't waited passively. We learned how to take care of our little girl; her medical problems affect her digestion and lungs. We protected her from colds, learned about supplemental vitamins and antibiotics. We moved to California where the winters aren't so harsh and the cold and flu season isn't so severe. Our new doctor told us that the children at his center were surviving, on the average, to age 21. So far, our daughter is doing well. She is a fast runner and plays a mean first base. She loves her friends and is, in general, a happy little girl. All things considered, I feel very lucky.

5 How has research using animals helped those with CF? Three times a day my daughter uses enzymes from the pancreas of pigs to digest her food. She takes antibiotics tested on rats before they are tried on humans. As an adult, she will probably develop diabetes and need insulin—a drug developed by research on dogs and rabbits. If she ever needs a heart-lung transplant, one might be possible because of the cows that surgeons practiced on. There is no animal model to help CF research, but once the CF gene is

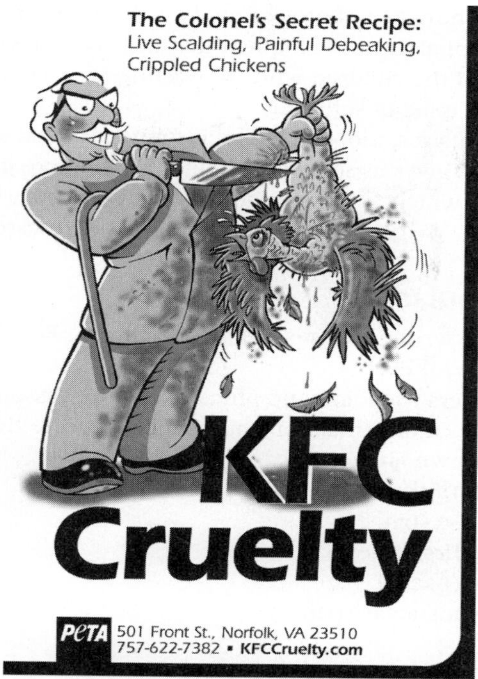
The Colonel's Secret Recipe:
Live Scalding, Painful Debeaking,
Crippled Chickens
KFC
Cruelty
PeTA
501 Front St., Norfolk, VA 23510
757-622-7382 • KFCCruelty.com

(People for the Ethical Treatment of Animals/AP)

located, new gene-splicing techniques may create a family of mice afflicted with the disease. Researchers would first learn to cure the mice with drugs, then cautiously try with humans.

There are only about 10,000 people with CF in the United States. But the number of people dependent on research is much larger. Walk with me through the Children's Hospital at Stanford University: here are the youngsters fighting cancer, rare genetic illnesses, immunological diseases. Amid their laughter and desperate attempts to retain a semblance of childhood, there is suffering. 6

I think the motivation of animal-rights activists is to cut down on the suffering in this world, but I have yet to hear them acknowledge that people—young and old—suffer, too. Why is a laboratory rat's fate more poignant than that of an incurably ill child? 7

There are advocates for animals who only seek to cut down on "unnecessary research." They don't specify how to decide what is unnecessary, but they do create an atmosphere in which doing medical research is seen as distasteful work. I think that's wrong. Researchers should be thanked, not hassled. 8

Every time I see a bumper sticker that says "Lab animals never have a nice day," a fantasy plays in my brain. I get out of my car, tap on the driver's window and ask to talk. In my fantasy, the other driver gets out, we find a 9 coffee shop and I show her photos of my kids. I ask her if she has ever visited Children's Hospital. I am so eloquent that her eyes fill with tears and she promises to think of the children who are wasting away as she considers the whole complicated issue of suffering.

10 I have other fantasies, too, that a cure is found for what ails my daughter, that she marries and gives us some grandchildren, and does great work in her chosen profession, which at this moment appears to be cartooning or computer programming. We can still hope—as long as the research continues.

Building Vocabulary

1. In this essay, the writer uses several medical terms. Find at least five and write definitions for each.
2. Sometimes, writers use idiomatic phrases that they assume their reader will either know or understand from context. Rewrite the following phrases in your own language:
   a. the fraternity of those (par. 2)
   b. a textbook case (par. 2)
   c. plays a mean first base (par. 4)
   d. cut down on (par. 7)
   e. who are wasting away (par. 9)

Thinking Critically About the Argument

Understanding the Writer's Argument

1. Why does McCabe begin her essay by admitting that she sees the issue of animal experimentation "in stark terms"? What does she mean? Why does she see the choice between child and animal as "stark"?
2. Why does McCabe place herself in the "fraternity of those who have a vital interest in seeing that medical research continues"? Why does she use the word "fraternity"? (par. 2)
3. In paragraph 4, McCabe mentions all the things that her husband and she have done for their daughter. What is she implying? In what ways has animal experimentation helped McCabe's daughter?
4. What other diseases can animal experimentation give hope for? Why does McCabe mention only children with diseases in paragraph 6?
5. In paragraph 7, McCabe repeats the title question, but in different words. What is the difference?
6. According to McCabe, what is the result of animal rights advocates making vague claims that research is "unnecessary"?
7. What is McCabe's reason for including her fantasy about confronting the driver? (par. 9)

Understanding the Writer's Techniques

1. What is McCabe's major proposition and where does she place it? Is it effective where it is? Explain.

2. What is the effect of McCabe's "stark" admission in paragraph 1? If this admission is part of the warrant behind her claim, why does she state it? Why can this warrant not remain implied?
3. What other implied or stated warrants affect McCabe's argument?
4. Who is McCabe's audience? How does her audience affect the tone of the essay?
5. Paraphrase McCabe's argument. Write one sentence for each paragraph explaining the function of that paragraph.
6. What examples does McCabe use to back up her major proposition?
7. McCabe's argument is emotional. What emotional appeals does she make?
8. Discuss the conclusion. Is it effective? Why or why not?
9. **(Mixing modes)** How does McCabe use narrative and illustration together? Does she do it successfully? Why or why not?

Exploring the Writer's Argument

1. What is your emotional reaction to the essay? Does she pull your "heart-strings" too much? Look at your list of emotional appeals from question 7, above. Which of McCabe's emotional appeals are unfair appeals?
2. What logical appeals could you think of to help out McCabe's argument?
3. McCabe writes that any criticism of animal experimentation is harmful. What reason does she give for this? What do you think of this argument?
4. McCabe offers examples of her daughter suffering, but never mentions the sufferings of the animals that are experimented upon. Is this a weakness in her argument? Why or why not?

Ideas for Writing Arguments

Prewriting

List the ways in which humans seem superior to animals. Are there ways in which humans are inferior to animals?

Writing a Guided Argument

Write an argument that supports animal experimentation, but assume that you, like McCabe, are a parent, friend, or relative of a seriously ill child who has been helped and perhaps can be cured by furthering animal experimentation.

1. Begin your essay by expressing the rules. What is your warrant, and what is your claim?
2. Address the expectations of the opposition.
3. State your first minor proposition to support your claim.
4. Support your first proposition with evidence.
5. State your second minor proposition.

6. Support your second proposition with evidence from McCabe's essay. Use her own words to prove your point.
7. End your essay by expressing, once again, how surprising your position is. Explain why your point of view lends your position more credibility.

Thinking, Arguing, and Writing Collaboratively

Work in small groups of three or four. List ways in which humans assert their superiority over animals. Which of these ways are acceptable ethically? Report the differences of opinion in your group, including reasons for your various claims.

Writing About the Text

Because McCabe is a parent, it is natural that she is going to argue for the value of her child's life over that of anonymous animals. Does her identity weaken her position because she will always be emotional about the topic? Does she anticipate this question in her essay? If not, how could she anticipate it? If so, could she do better and would doing so strengthen her argument?

More Writing Ideas

1. The most famous animal rights advocate, the contemporary philosopher Peter Singer, argues that the real question is one stated 150 years ago by Jeremy Bentham, a 19th-century English philosopher. Bentham, talking about the rights of animals, said, "The question is not, 'Can they reason?' nor, 'Can they talk?' But rather, 'Can they suffer?'" Do you agree with this view, or are the other questions he mentions worth considering? Write an essay agreeing or disagreeing with Singer and Bentham.
2. Some animals kill each other. Humans are, essentially, just animals with the ability to reason. If animals can kill each other for food, why can't we kill animals to prolong our own lives? Does our ability to reason take away our right to use animals for experimentation, food, or sport?
3. Many people wear leather or eat meat but still believe that animal experimentation is wrong. Write an essay about people wanting to have the issue of animal rights their own way. What is your position on the issue? Do you have a double standard? Justify your position.
4. Working with your list of claims and evidence from your collaborative work, write an essay in which you defend one human use of animals—for example, for food or in fashion. Choose a specific use, as in harvesting caviar or wearing leather belts.

JANE GOODALL
A Question of Ethics

Jane Goodall, born in 1934 in London, England, is best known for her work studying chimpanzees in the wild. In 1960, at the age of 26, with no college degree or formal training, she began to study chimps at the Gombe Stream Reserve in Tanzania in eastern Africa, working as a secretary to fund her work. By watching the chimps closely, she was able to gain their trust. Soon she saw differences between the individual chimps. She was the first scientist to note that chimps are not strictly vegetarian and that the species uses tools, something previously thought to be purely a human trait. Goodall wrote many books about her work, including My Friends the Wild Chimpanzees *(1967),* In the Shadow of Man *(1971),* The Chimpanzees of Gombe: Patterns of Behavior *(1986),* Through a Window: My Thirty Years with the Chimpanzees of Gombe *(1990), and* The Chimpanzee: The Living Link Between Man and Beast *(1992). She has received several awards for her research and for conservation, including the prestigious Albert Schweitzer Award. In this essay, Goodall displays her signature thoughtfulness and humanism.*

Prereading: Thinking About the Essay in Advance

Think about the word *ethics.* Ethics is the branch of philosophy that deals with moral obligations and duties. What is more ethical: protecting the rights and lives of animals or looking for cures for human diseases?

Words to Watch

fuzzy (par. 1) unclear
distinction (par. 1) difference
vaccines (par. 2) medicines that prevent a disease
surly (par. 2) bad tempered
sentient (par. 3) capable of feeling
dilemma (par. 3) problem with two unsatisfactory alternatives
vigorously (par. 4) with great energy
apathy (par. 5) lack of interest

David Greybeard first showed me how fuzzy the distinction between animals and humans can be. Forty years ago I befriended David, a chimpanzee, during my first field trip to Gombe in Tanzania. One day I offered him a nut in my open palm. He looked directly into my eyes, took the nut out of my hand and dropped it. At the same moment he very gently squeezed my hand as if to say, I don't want it, but I understand your motives. 1

Since chimpanzees are thought to be physiologically close to humans, researchers use them as test subjects for new drugs and vaccines. In the 2 labs, these very sociable creatures often live isolated from one another in 5-by-5-foot cages, where they grow surly and sometimes violent. Dogs, cats and rats are also kept in poor conditions and subjected to painful procedures. Many people would find it hard to sympathize with rats, but dogs and cats are part of our lives. Ten or 15 years ago, when the use of animals in medical testing was first brought to my attention, I decided to visit the labs myself. Many people working there had forced themselves to believe that animal testing is the only way forward for medical research.

3 Once we accept that animals are sentient beings, is it ethical to use them in research? From the point of view of the animals, it is quite simply wrong. From our standpoint, it seems ridiculous to equate a rat with a human being. If we clearly and honestly believe that using animals in research will, in the end, reduce massive human suffering, it would be difficult to argue that doing so is unethical. How do we find a way out of this dilemma?

4 One thing we can do is change our mind-set. We can begin by questioning the assumption that animals are essential to medical research. Scientists have concluded that chimpanzees are not useful for AIDS research because, even though their genetic makeup differs from ours by about 1 percent, their immune systems deal much differently with the AIDS virus. Many scientists test drugs and vaccines on animals simply because they are required to by law rather than out of scientific merit. This is a shame, because our medical technology is beginning to provide alternatives. We can perform many tests on cell and tissue cultures without recourse to systemic testing on animals. Computer simulations can also cut down on the number of animal tests we need to run. We aren't exploring these alternatives vigorously enough.

5 Ten or 15 years ago animal-rights activists resorted to violence against humans in their efforts to break through the public's terrible apathy and lack of imagination on this issue. This extremism is counterproductive. I believe that more and more people are becoming aware that to use animals thoughtlessly, without any anguish or making an effort to find another way, diminishes us as human beings.

Building Vocabulary

For each of the following words, write both a definition and a sentence of your own:

1. fuzzy (par. 1)
2. surly (par. 2)
3. sentient (par. 3)
4. dilemma (par. 3)
5. vigorously (par. 4)
6. apathy (par. 5)
7. counterproductive (par. 5)

Thinking Critically About the Argument

Understanding the Writer's Argument

1. Why does Goodall start her essay with the story of giving the nut to the chimp David Greybeard?
2. According to Goodall, how are lab animals treated, and what does this do to their behavior? What are other physical and emotional effects of experimentation on animals?
3. Why did Goodall visit the labs where animal experimentation was taking place? (par. 2)
4. In paragraph 3, Goodall questions whether it is "ethical" to use animals in medical research. What does she mean here by ethical? In your own words, what is the "dilemma" Goodall refers to in paragraph 3?
5. Goodall thinks that people should change their "mind-set" about animal experimentation. What is the current mind-set of people about the issue?
6. How can people change the way that they think about animal experimentation, according to Goodall?
7. Goodall says that extreme forms of protest are "counterproductive," alluding to violence by activists against people who use animals for medical research. What are *productive* ways of changing people's minds about the issue?

Understanding the Writer's Techniques

1. Which sentence in the essay states Goodall's claim?
2. Goodall is known as a scientist with a heart, a person who cares about all creatures of Earth. How does knowing this information influence how you perceive her argument?
3. What are Goodall's warrants for this essay? Who is her audience, and how does that affect the tone of the essay?
4. Make an outline of Goodall's essay, paraphrasing her argument.
5. What form of reasoning does Goodall use in this essay, deductive or inductive? What kind of evidence does she use?
6. Although this is mostly a reasoned argument, it is about an emotional issue. Can you locate the places where she appeals to her readers' emotions?

Exploring the Writer's Argument

1. Goodall makes many assumptions in her essay. For example, she interprets David Greybeard's behavior as a kindly, understanding response. Is this the only way we can interpret his behavior? What other assumptions does Goodall ask her readers to make?

2. The workers who worked at the labs, according to Goodall, "forced themselves" to believe that what they were doing was okay. Is this good logic? Do you see any logical fallacies here or elsewhere in her essay?
3. Goodall seems to offer solutions to the problem of animal experimentation when, in paragraph 3, she says that "if we clearly and honestly believe that using animals in research will, in the end, reduce massive human suffering, it would be difficult to argue that doing so is unethical." What burden does this place on her argument? Do you think she gives enough evidence for her own side?
4. In paragraph 4, Goodall states that people have to change their mindset, and then, in the last sentence, she writes that she thinks that people's minds are changing. Are these statements contradictory? Why or why not?

Ideas for Writing Arguments

Prewriting

List the moral, or ethical, arguments for and against the use of medical research on animals.

Writing a Guided Argument

In paragraph 3, Goodall poses a dilemma: We want to be ethical, but if animals suffer, how can it be ethical to harm them for any reason? Write a letter to Jane Goodall in which you satisfy Goodall's grounds for her own argument: She says that if we believe that animal experimentation will "reduce massive human suffering, it would be difficult to argue that doing so is unethical." Argue that animal experimentation is ethical because of this reason.

1. Start your essay by quoting Goodall from paragraph 3.
2. Next, state your major proposition, using Goodall's own words against her. Focus on establishing the correct tone in your first paragraph.
3. In the next paragraph, write your first minor proposition using a logical appeal.
4. Offer evidence to support your proposition.
5. Next, write a paragraph in which you offer another minor proposition, but this time use an emotional appeal.
6. Offer evidence to support your proposition.
7. In your concluding paragraph, make it clear to Goodall that you are correct on moral or ethical grounds, again repeating, for rhetorical reasons, her ideas.

Thinking, Arguing, and Writing Collaboratively

In small groups of four or five, discuss the dilemma explored in your Writing a Guided Argument paper. Where is the issue of animal experimentation headed in the future? Will people change their minds? Will protests lead to more violence, as Goodall warns against? Can animal experimentation ever end, realistically?

Writing About the Text

Goodall presents her essay as a reasoned argument, but much of what she writes is an emotional appeal presented as logic. Write an essay in which you explore the question of whether one can write about animal experimentation without an excess of emotion?

More Writing Ideas

1. Many people argue that animals can't understand their own death so their suffering is not as severe as human suffering. Do you agree or disagree? Outline your reasons in a persuasive essay.
2. David Greybeard showed Goodall "how fuzzy the distinction between animals and humans can be." What are other "fuzzy" distinctions between animals and humans? Are there clear distinctions?
3. On the basis of some research, write an essay about the similarities between the struggle for animal rights and other modern struggles for rights, such as the civil rights movement, the fight for gay rights, or the struggle for female suffrage.

24 Immigration: Should We Limit It?

The United States is a country of immigrants. All residents, except for Native American Indians and those descended from slaves, have ancestors who left another country to come to the United States to find a better life. However, immigrants have rarely trod an easy road. The Puritans settled here first, and all future immigrants have almost always been feared and hated. Before the Civil War, immigrants were mostly Protestants from Western Europe and Great Britain. After the war, when Eastern and Southern Europeans (mostly Catholic), along with Asians, came to the United States, they met with great resistance. Could they ever truly be Americans? Would they take jobs from citizens and ruin the society?

Despite the opposition, immigration grew. In the decade between 1900 and 1910, almost 1 million legal immigrants per year flooded the country. And with each new group of immigrants came a new attempt to limit their arrival through immigration laws. In the early 1920s, Congress passed litigation that limited the number of immigrants from Europe and barred immigration from Asia. These laws eventually prevented the entry of many Eastern Europeans who were threatened by Nazism before and during World War II. The laws highlight the ethical question surrounding immigration into the United States, which has always held itself up as a beacon of freedom and refuge, as symbolized by the Statue of Liberty. Since the end of World War II, immigration has steadily risen. In the 1980s and 1990s, more than 700,000 immigrants came to the United States per year. Since 1970, the number of immigrants in the United States has almost tripled. The numbers have changed, and the demographics have shifted—most immigrants today are Hispanic or Asian rather than European—but the problems for the new groups are the same as always: poverty, xenophobia from native-born Americans, unemployment, and overcrowding in the cities. Much immigration today is illegal immigration, which is often dangerous to the immigrants, especially Mexicans trying to escape through the desert into California or Arizona.

Immigration advocates point out the contributions that immigrants historically have made to the nation through hard work and that many immigrant families are interested in home ownership and in starting small businesses, which stimulate the economy. They say that immigrants help to revitalize previously neglected city neighborhoods and that if the United States limits immigration, it is going against the principles of freedom and liberty that America stands for. If people are in need of our help, should we turn them away? Those who think we should limit immigration say that the United States would not be betraying its principles. They point out that the situation today is different from the turn of the last century, when the country was developing. These critics say that there is great overpopulation here already, and immigration compounds those problems. Also, unskilled laborers from other countries take jobs from Americans who need them, and they drain resources from government programs paid with by tax dollars.

The following two selections offer disparate perspectives on the issue of immigration. Richard Rodriguez, a second-generation Mexican-American, explains why immigrants are better for America than native-born Americans. Mortimer B. Zuckerman explores the often dismal future today's immigrants face.

RICHARD RODRIGUEZ

Trouble Is, Native-Born Just Don't Measure Up

Richard Rodriguez was born to Mexican-American immigrants in 1944. He was educated at Stanford University and Columbia University. He won a Fulbright scholarship to England in 1972 when he was a doctoral student at the University of California at Berkeley. He is the author of The Hunger of Memory: The Education of Richard Rodriguez *(1982), in which he discusses his assimilation into American culture. His latest book is* Days of Obligation: An Argument with My Mexican Father. *His essays appear in many magazines and on* NewsHour with Jim Lehrer *on PBS. In this selection, Rodriguez takes to task those Americans who celebrate immigration while complaining about immigrants.*

Prereading: Thinking About the Essay in Advance

What did your ancestors have to do to allow you to be taking this college course?

Words to Watch

moratorium (par. 3) official halt
crucifixes (par. 4) image of Jesus Christ on the cross
sweatshops (par. 5) factories with poor working conditions
gleaned (par. 7) adopted
theological (par. 11) based in religion
mired (par. 14) stuck

"Come to Ellis Island," a friend said. "I will show you my Russian grandfather's name on the wall." 1

On a gray weekday morning, I went to Ellis Island with little armies of school children, in search of the past. But I was left thinking about the descendants of immigrants who came through that place. 2

Polls indicate that a majority of Americans favor a moratorium on immigration. Some even say that we should stop immigration altogether. 3

Americans conclude that we have an immigrant problem. No one wonders if perhaps America has a native-born problem. Does America need the native-born?

4 "We are a nation of immigrants," Americans like to say. We tend, however, to celebrate immigration after the fact. When the pavilions of Ellis Island were crowded at the turn of the century, most Americans probably didn't want foreigners, didn't like them—the way they looked, the way they spoke, their garlic and their crucifixes, their funny clothes.

5 Idealism prevailed. Pragmatism prevailed. America needed the cheap labor of Yiddish-speaking grandmothers in the sweatshops. We needed immigrants to build our bridges and carve the Great Plains. Out West, the Chinese were imported to build the railroads. Once the Chinese had finished, Americans wished they would go back to China.

6 But idealism also created Ellis Island. Americans in the 19th century understood the individual's right to flee the past. How could America resist these newcomers?

7 Just like immigrants, native-born Americans habitually are on the move—moving from Ohio to Kansas, moving from Dallas to Orlando, Portland to Boise. Our highways are crowded with the restlessness we gleaned from our immigrant ancestors.

8 The trouble is, we never measure up. We, the children of immigrants, are never as bold, never as driven, as our grandparents. That is why we become annoyed sometimes by immigrant ambition. In California—the destination of the majority of today's immigrants—people complain that the immigrants are coming for welfare dollars. The more interesting complaint one hears these days in California is that the immigrants work too hard.

9 One hears it particularly about illegal immigrants; they are taking our jobs. Or I remember the parent who told me—after his children failed to gain entrance into the University of California—that Asians were unfair because they worked so hard. Because of immigrants, Los Angeles has become a working town, no longer the golden, blond city of leisure. Immigrants are blamed for the change—the traffic, the bad air. Immigrants have turned L.A. into Cleveland.

10 The Puritans were America's first immigrants. They came, fleeing intolerance. Puritans ended up intolerant of other immigrants who came after. What the Puritans nonetheless planted on American soil was a Protestant faith: You can be born again.

11 In the 1840s, the Irish were America's major immigrant group. The nativist complaint against the Irish was theological. Today, we talk ethnicity and race. In the 19th century, it wasn't a question of Asians and Hispanics, but whether a Catholic could become a good American. Could a Jew?

12 The irony is that the Jews, the Orthodox Greeks, the Mennonites, the Irish Catholics who came through Ellis Island became the new Puritans, restoring the early Protestant determination, the founders' optimistic individualism.

13 Who doubts it now? The immigrants of Ellis Island created America. We, their children and grandchildren, inherited America. And this is the prob-

(© The New Yorker Collection 2004 Mick Stevens from cartoonbank.com. All Rights Reserved.)

lem. For the native-born, America is not a destination, it is our address. They tore down the forests; we become environmentalists. They were fiercely set on the new; we remember when it was possible to find a parking space in downtown L.A.

Who will say it? Native-born blacks are being outpaced by immigrant blacks from the Caribbean. I worry less about the newly arrived Mexican kid who is job-hunting today in Phoenix than I worry about the third generation "Chicano" undergraduate at UCLA who is mired in the despair of American pop culture. 14

Coming to Ellis Island, I expected the place to be haunted. Instead, I found a freshly painted irony. A few years ago, Ellis Island was restored by native-born Americans as a monument to the past. For those of us who are native-born Americans, Ellis Island is a historical landmark. But for the immigrants who came through this place, Ellis Island was only a stop on their way to the future. They rushed away. That is why Ellis Island is not haunted. 15

Building Vocabulary

Identify the following and explain how they relate to the topic of immigration:

1. Ellis Island (par. 1)
2. Great Plains (par. 5)
3. idealism (par. 5)

4. pragmatism (par. 5)
5. Yiddish (par. 5)
6. Puritans (par. 10)
7. Mennonites (par. 12)

Thinking Critically About the Argument

Understanding the Writer's Argument

1. What, according to the writer, is the public's majority view of immigration?
2. What does Rodriguez mean that we "celebrate immigration after the fact"? (par. 4) Why is that so?
3. Native-born Americans didn't want immigrants to come to America at the turn of the 20th century. Why did they let immigration take place, then?
4. How is America's immigrant past reflected in our present-day behavior?
5. Why, according to Rodriguez, are Americans today bothered by the ambition of immigrants? What are some common complaints against immigration, especially illegal immigration?
6. Explain what Rodriguez means when he says that it is ironic that Jewish, Irish Catholic, and other immigrants adopted the Puritan's work ethic and ambition? Why is this ironic?
7. Explain, in your own words, why the author thinks that native-born Americans are more of a problem for America than immigrants.

Understanding the Writer's Techniques

1. What is Rodriguez's major proposition?
2. Why does Rodriguez start his essay with the trip to Ellis Island? How does this connect with his major proposition?
3. How many minor propositions does Rodriguez use to support his major proposition? What are they?
4. Analyze the unusual structure of Rodriguez's essay by making an outline. How effective is the structure?
5. What kind of evidence does Rodriguez use most frequently to support his position? Where does he use sensory detail effectively?
6. How does Rodriguez support his assertion that he worries "less about the newly arrived Mexican kid . . . than I worry about the third generation 'Chicano' undergraduate at UCLA"? (par. 14)
7. How does Rodriguez's conclusion tie the essay together? Does it provide both closure and coherence? Explain your answer.

Exploring the Writer's Argument

1. Is it such a bad thing that "we tend . . . to celebrate immigration after the fact," as Rodriguez implies in paragraph 4? Why or why not?

2. Rodriguez says in paragraph 8 that we are "never as bold, never as driven, as our grandparents." Do you agree with him? Why or why not? Isn't that a vast generalization? What does that say about future generations?
3. In paragraph 13, Rodriguez makes the point that our experiences of American life are diluted. Do you think that's fair? Why or why not?
4. Answer question 6 in the "Understanding the Writer's Techniques" section, and write about why Rodriguez would worry so much about the third-generation undergraduate. What is he so worried about? Do you think his worrying is warranted? Why or why not?

Ideas for Writing Arguments

Prewriting

What was your family's history with immigration? Which generation, in your opinion, worked the hardest? What was the result of all that hard work? Which is the happiest generation?

Writing a Guided Argument

Think of an area of difference between you and a grandparent or someone you know well from you grandparent's generation (for example, consider the differences between your level of education, your experiences with dating or marriage, or your experiences working). Write an essay that outlines the various aspects of this difference, and explain the reasons for the difference.

1. Begin your essay with an experience that caused you to reflect on your chosen subject.
2. In the next section, introduce your grandparent or acquaintance.
3. State your major proposition clearly and directly.
4. Maintain a respectful and even tone throughout your essay.
5. Give two or three aspects of the difference in the form of clearly stated minor propositions.
6. Support your minor propositions with examples and cause analysis.
7. Close your essay with a new perspective on the experience with which you opened your essay.

Thinking, Arguing, and Writing Collaboratively

In small groups of four or five, talk to local longtime residents or merchants in your town. Collect quotes and comments about how the area has changed over the years in their memories and based on stories they have heard. Try to determine how much of this change is due to the influence of new people moving into town. Listen carefully to these people and take notes. Let them talk, and consider their judgment of the changes. Are they pleased, or are there complaints? Write up your findings in several paragraphs, and share your writing with the class.

Writing About the Text

Write an essay on question 3 in Exploring the Writer's Argument. Explain why you think the writer's assessment of native-born Americans is fair or not.

More Writing Ideas

1. In your journal, explore the ways in which you think American culture maintains a "Puritan" characteristic.
2. Write an extended paragraph about the circumstances that would have to exist for you to emigrate to another country from the United States.
3. Choose one immigrant group in America and go to the library to do research on their experiences upon arrival. Write an essay in which you explain how they and their descendents have both succeeded and struggled.

MORTIMER B. ZUCKERMAN
Our Rainbow Underclass

Mortimer B. Zuckerman is a graduate of Harvard Law School and used to teach at Harvard Business School. He is now chairman and copublisher of the New York Daily News *and the publisher and editor in chief of* U.S. News & World Report, *for which he frequently writes. In this selection, which appeared in that weekly magazine in 2002, eight years after Rodriguez's article appeared, Zuckerman tackles the issue many people don't want to talk about: the fact that many immigrants are terribly poor and remaining poor because of poor schooling opportunities.*

Prereading: Thinking About the Essay in Advance

Who was the first person in your family to go to college? How did that affect the fortunes of the family?

Words to Watch

linguistic (par. 3) relating to speech and language
infrastructure (par. 4) resources required for an activity
disquieting (par. 5) disturbing
myriad (par. 5) various
incalculable (par. 5) overwhelmingly large
consensus (par. 6) general agreement

1 The roll of honor read at the 9/11 ceremonies was a tapestry of America, of native-born Americans of all ethnic origins and more recent immigrants. Of course, we know too well that some of the assassins and others plotting against America were immigrants who betrayed our ideals, so it is natural that many peo-

ple feel we should now close the door altogether, beginning with immigrants from Muslim countries. Natural, and wrong. What is long overdue, however, is a sustained national dialogue on immigration.

Most politicians fear offending blocs of votes—a cowardice that does not serve the country well. Immigration has been out of control since 1965, when Sen. Edward Kennedy introduced a "reform" bill that ended the historic basis of the American melting pot. It was a bill remarkable for the fact that every single one of the assurances he and others gave proved wildly wrong—not because they wanted to mislead but because the bill unleashed forces they did not foresee. Indeed, the ensuing Immigration Reform Act triggered an immigration explosion, involving millions more than any other period, plus millions of illegals. There was a gross miscalculation of the effect of basing entry on "family reunification"; the criterion of "immediate relatives" was lost in the daisy-chain effect of brothers sponsoring brothers sponsoring cousins. It was said the goal was not to upset "the ethnic mix of this country," but the opposite occurred. Traditional immigrants from northern and western Europe were discriminated against in favor of Third World immigrants. 2

Schooling is the ticket. What is more disturbing is that the longer these new immigrants stay in the country the worse they do, reversing the history of upward mobility in previous waves of immigration. Why? Traditionally, there were well-paid manufacturing jobs for immigrants, enabling them to join the ranks of blue-collar workers who secured a middle-class lifestyle without much formal education. Those days are gone. Schooling is today's ticket for a better future—with a high school diploma as the minimum. The original European newcomers could also send their children to high-quality urban schools. Assimilation was swift. The immigrants, however numerous, were from many different countries, so they took to English more rapidly: There was no linguistic minority to dominate any large city the way Spanish speakers now dominate Miami and Los Angeles. Today Latino immigrants live in a subnation with their own radio and TV stations, newspapers, films, and magazines, stunting assimilation and diminishing economic opportunity. Mexican-born males, handicapped by low or nonexistent English ability, earn half of what non-Latino whites earn. Although Mexican immigrants are often perceived as highly reliable, disciplined workers, Harvard Prof. Christopher Jencks makes the point that "having the right attitude is often enough to get an $8-an-hour job; it is seldom enough to get one for $16 an hour." 3

A critical question that is almost never asked: What is the impact on the children, the second generation? Some thrive, but the majority do not. They form a rainbow underclass, caught in a cycle of downward assimilation, poverty combined with racial segregation. Often separated for long periods from their parents, especially their fathers, during the immigration process, they stop doing homework, reject their parents' values, and succumb to the dangers of an overcrowded inner-city culture. They face overwhelmed teachers, limited social service resources, and a decaying infrastructure, 4 and they often adopt the negative behavior pattern of their peer groups, such as academic indifference and substance abuse, leading to dropout rates three times as high as for native-born Americans. Even the stellar performance of Asian children declines—studies show that by the third generation, Chinese students no longer exceed whites in educational success.

5 There is another disquieting connection, the trifecta effect of rising immigrant fertility rates. Our population is projected to rise to over 500 million by 2050, roughly double what America is today—with post-1965 immigrants and their descendants making up about half. The effect of these numbers on myriad aspects of our environment, from rush-hour traffic to air and water pollution and social tensions, is incalculable.

6 How, then, should we proceed? No matter what, we must find more resources for the schools and other institutions that will support the development of second-generation children. Second, we must rebalance the number of visas provided for extended-family programs and add more to attract immigrants with skills transferable to the information economy. Third, we should slow down the process until we can thoroughly assess how the children of today's immigrants will fare as adults. Only through such measures can a national consensus on these issues begin to be forged.

Building Vocabulary

In this essay, the author uses a number of words and phrases from the world of sociology. Look up the following terms in a dictionary, and write out the definition. Then use each word or phrase in a sentence of your own having to do with immigration:

1. tapestry (par. 1)
2. melting pot (par. 2)
3. Third World (par. 2)
4. upward mobility (par. 3)
5. blue-collar workers (par. 3)
6. assimilation (par. 3)
7. underclass (par. 4)
8. fertility rates (par. 5)
9. visas (par. 6)

Thinking Critically About the Argument

Understanding the Writer's Argument

1. Why does Zuckerman think it's natural for Americans to want to stop immigration? What is his opinion of that viewpoint?
2. What was the intention of the 1965 Immigration Reform Act? What was the unintended result?

3. Why is the success of today's immigrant dependent on different factors than those that affected the immigrant of the early part of the 20th century?
4. Explain why Zuckerman thinks that earlier immigrants seemed to learn English more readily than today's immigrant? Why does he think this is important?
5. What is the effect of today's immigration trends on the first native-born generation, according to Zuckerman?
6. How can proper schooling help immigrants?

Understanding the Writer's Techniques

1. What is the argumentative effect of mentioning 9/11 and the terrorists in the beginning of the essay?
2. What is Zuckerman's major proposition? What does he explain to the reader before he offers his major proposition? Explain why, in your view, he takes this approach.
3. What is the writer's tone? Where does Zuckerman deviate from this tone for effect? Is it, in fact, effective?
4. What are Zuckerman's minor propositions?
5. What kinds of evidence does Zuckerman offer to promote his argument?
6. How does Zuckerman's prediction in paragraph 5 support his position?
7. What is your view of his proposed solutions to the problem in the conclusion? Are they useful suggestions? Why or why not?

Exploring the Writer's Argument

1. Zuckerman seems to believe that assimilation is a purely positive thing. Why does Zuckerman equate "stunting assimilation" with fewer economic opportunities for immigrants in paragraph 3? Do you agree with him? Does he support this idea with enough evidence? Is there anything about this idea that gives you pause? Explain your answer fully.
2. Analyze Zuckerman's use of transitions in this essay. Are they sufficient? Why or why not? How could you improve them to help his argument?
3. In his last paragraph, Zuckerman offers a number of solutions to the problems he addresses. Do you think his solutions are vague? Why or why not? Especially, his last solution seems like a tall order, but does not offer any suggestions for how to achieve this. Why is or why is this not a problem for his argument?

Ideas for Writing Arguments

Prewriting

How does language relate to ethnicity? Do you speak the language of your ancestors? In either case, how does that affect your experience as an American?

Writing a Guided Argument

The United States, unlike most countries, does not have an official language. Write an essay in which you argue that English should or should not be the official language of the United States. Before you write, search the online archives of *The New York Times* or other newspapers and magazines to acquaint yourself with the arguments on both sides.

1. Open your essay with an exploration of the issue, using your research to give some of the background.
2. Write your major proposition.
3. Have at least three minor propositions.
4. Organize your essay so that your most important point comes last.
5. Appeal to your reader's patriotism by making it clear in your argument that you are arguing for the best choice for the United States.
6. Support your minor propositions with examples and predictions for the future.
7. Include at least one opposing point. Rebut this point.
8. Conclude by restating your major proposition in light of the evidence. Use a quote from your research as your final piece of evidence.

Thinking, Arguing, and Writing Collaboratively

Hold a debate in class. Work in two groups. One group should prepare arguments that America is a "melting pot." The other group should argue that instead, America is what Bill Clinton used to call a "salad bowl." After about 20 minutes of preparation, mount a debate in which each side gets ten minutes to make their case, and then the other side gets 5 minutes to rebut their points.

Writing About the Text

How does your reading of Rodriguez's essay inform your reading of Zuckerman's? Write an essay in which you examine how the two arguments are related, and in what ways they disagree.

More Writing Ideas

1. In your journal, freewrite about this topic: assimilation. Do not edit your writing. Write nonstop for at least 15 minutes. When you finish, exchange journal entries with another student in the class. How do your responses compare? contrast?
2. How does the Internet change the lives of today's immigrants? Write a paragraph in which you develop an opinion and value judgment about this topic.
3. Write an essay expanding on Zuckerman's dire predictions in paragraph 5. What are other possible effects of overcrowding in the United States? Consider the question of any positive effects.

25 Affirmative Action: What Role Should It Play in Our Lives?

What does the government and other institutions owe women and minorities for previous years of discrimination?

Women were, in the past, locked out of many careers and did not even get the vote in this country until the 1920s. African Americans were slaves for centuries until the Emancipation Proclamation in 1865. But that did not cure all: True progress in civil rights did not become a reality until the 1960s. The policy of affirmative action is an attempt to make up for these past shortcomings by giving women and minorities special consideration in employment, education, and business decisions.

Proponents of affirmative action say that although the country made great strides in civil rights since the 1960s, the job of ending discrimination is not over, and although racism and sexism are not as overt as in the past, they are still a problem. Minorities and women still are not equally paid nor do they appear in proportionate numbers in high-paying jobs or positions of power. The defenders of affirmative action say that the policy can "level the playing field" until past wrongs are set right. Opponents of affirmative action say that the policy is reverse discrimination, in that it takes jobs away from more qualified candidates just because they happen to be white men. Another important argument from opponents (even opponents among the black community) is that the policy can have a negative effect on minorities and women by lowering their self-respect and respect from others because others see these minority groups as not having earned their positions. For decades, affirmative action has stood at the center of the argument over our "multicultural" society and about how we can advance the careers of future generations of minorities while still being fair and equitable to all.

Linda Chavez writes that affirmative action has a purely negative effect on the fabric of American society, whereas Nathan Glazer (who is a convert to affirmative action) insists that the United States must face up to its responsibility and realize that the time has not yet come to eliminate affirmative action. As you read the following selections, pay attention to how the writers appeal to your sense of fairness.

LINDA CHAVEZ
Affirmative Action Is Driving Us Apart

Linda Chavez was born in 1947 in Albuquerque, New Mexico. She is the author of Out of the Barrio: Toward a New Politics of Hispanic Assimilation *(2001). Since serving in President Ronald Reagan's Commission on Civil Rights, Chavez has worked to end various federal civil rights programs, including affirmative action and the minimum wage. She has promoted English as the official language of the United States. She is founder and president of the Center for Equal Opportunity, an organization that focuses on issues related to race, ethnicity, assimilation, and public policy. In 2000, the Library of Congress honored Chavez as a "Living Legend" for her contributions to America's cultural and historical legacy. In 2001, George W. Bush nominated Chavez to be the Secretary of Labor, but the Senate rejected the nomination because of her conservative views and opposition from organized labor. In this essay, which appeared in* USA Today *in 1996, Chavez argues that affirmative action and other racially and ethnically based programs tend to cause resentment and anger rather than solve problems.*

Prereading: Thinking About the Essay in Advance

Do you think that being identified by your race or ethnicity diminishes you or makes you less of an individual? Or does such identification strengthen you because of your part in a large group? What are the benefits of having a strong racial identity? What are the negative aspects?

Words to Watch

compensatory (par. 5) designed to make up for disadvantage
presumptive (par. 5) based on probability and assumption
morphology (par. 11) study of forms
alleviates (par. 13) reduces
imperative (par. 13) necessity
mores (par. 14) moral standards
linchpin (par. 14) crucial element
inextricable (par. 18) unable to be separated from
imbuing (par. 18) instilling
indoctrination (par. 19) teaching
exogamy (par. 21) marriage outside a specific group
cleavages (par. 28) breaks

1 In the name of eliminating discrimination, we continue to pursue policies that define people by color. In schools and universities, at work, at the polling place, even in the courts, race is an important, sometimes deciding, factor in admitting students or devising curricula, hiring or promoting employees, determining political representation, and selecting a jury. It is not only a

few white supremacists who promote such policies, but mainstream civil rights advocates as well.

The crux of the complaint against quotas or other forms of racial or ethnic preferences is that they force both benefactors and beneficiaries to elevate race and ethnicity in importance, which is fundamentally incompatible with reducing racism. It is not possible to argue that race or ethnicity alone entitles individuals to special consideration without also accepting that such characteristics are intrinsically significant. 2

Those who promote preferential affirmative action programs argue that race and ethnicity are important because they are the basis on which individuals have been, and continue to be, discriminated against. Setting employment or college admission quotas, by this reasoning, simply is a way of compensating for the discrimination that blacks, Hispanics, and some other minority groups face on the basis of their skin color. 3

However, most programs that confer special benefits to racial and ethnic minorities make no effort at all to determine whether the individuals who will receive them ever have been victims of discrimination. Indeed, the government regulations that govern Federal contractors state explicitly: "Individuals who certify that they are members of named groups (Black Americans, Hispanic Americans, Native Americans, Asian-Pacific Americans, Subcontinental Asian Americans) are to be considered socially and economically disadvantaged." 4

Such programs are not compensatory, but presumptive; they assume that race equals disadvantage. While there are many blacks, Hispanics, and Asians who have been discriminated against on the basis of their race or ethnicity, there are many others who have not, and still others for whom the discrimination either was trivial or, even if more serious, had no lasting consequences. 5

In 1995, at Indiana University following a debate in which I opposed affirmative action, a group of black and Hispanic students approached me to complain that I was not sensitive enough to the discrimination they said they faced daily on campus. I asked them to give me some examples. Only two spoke. The first, a young black woman, told me her father was a surgeon who makes more than $300,000 a year, but that her economic status doesn't protect her from the prejudice of her teachers. When I asked her to describe how that prejudice manifested itself, she said none of her professors would give above a "B" to any minority student. I pushed her a little further, asking whether that meant that a student who scored 98% on an exam would be given a "B" rather than a deserved "A." At that point, she dropped the issue with a dismissive, "You just don't understand." 6

A second student, a Mexican-American woman, said that she has to deal with discrimination every day. She cited as an example that her Spanish teacher expects her to do better than the other students because she is presumed to know Spanish. I was sympathetic with her frustration, since I am aware that most third-generation Hispanics speak only English—like third-generation Italians, Jews, Germans, and other ethnic groups in the 7

United States. Nevertheless, although being presumed to speak your ancestral language may be annoying, it hardly constitutes pernicious discrimination.

8 In fact, what ethnic or religious minority has not suffered its share of slights and prejudices? Certainly, Jews and Asians have faced significant levels of bigotry at certain points in their history in the United States. Jews often were the victims of private discriminatory actions, and Asians historically were the target of both private and state-sponsored exclusion and bias. The Chinese, for instance, were not allowed to become citizens, own property, or enter certain professions, or even to immigrate at all for certain periods of time. During World War II, Japanese-Americans had their property confiscated and were removed forcibly from their homes and interned in camps in the West. Nonetheless, despite persistent discrimination, these groups, on average, have excelled in this society, and it is difficult to argue that they are entitled to compensatory, preferential affirmative action on the basis of any current disadvantage.

9 It is true that blacks and, to a lesser degree, Hispanics are far more likely to face present disadvantage, some of it (though a declining share) the result of past discrimination. Again, though, many affirmative action programs make little effort to distinguish among potential beneficiaries on the basis of actual disadvantage, preferring instead to rely on race or ethnicity *per se* in awarding benefits.

10 Some of the most prestigious affirmative action slots—such as those at Ivy League universities, Fortune 500 corporations, or Wall Street law firms—go to middle- and upper-class blacks and Hispanics, who suffer no clear disadvantage compared with their white counterparts. For instance, a recent study at the University of California, Berkeley, found that, on average, black, Hispanic, and Asian students admitted through affirmative action guidelines come from families whose median income actually is *higher* than the national average. Affirmative action recipients frequently are the graduates of elite prep schools, universities, and professional schools. Increasingly, advocates of this select type of affirmative action eschew traditional arguments about discrimination or disadvantage, opting to emphasize the presumed benefits of racial and ethnic diversity.

11 What does this diversity imply? The current scientific consensus suggests that race or ethnicity is nothing more than a description of broad morphology of skin, hair, and eye color, bone structure, and hair type—hardly the basis for making moral claims or distinctions. If race and ethnicity, stripped of their power to demand retribution, represent nothing more than a common ancestry and similar physical attributes, culture, on the other hand, evinces something more controversial and enduring. Not surprisingly, practitioners of the politics of race have seized on culture as their new weapon. Americans—of all races—have grown tired of affirmative action. Many of those who still support racial preferences, such as Yale law professor Stephen Carter, admit that those preferences have been a mixed blessing for the beneficiaries, conferring tangible benefits, but often undermining self-confidence. The politics of race requires a new rationale and a new vocabulary. Multiculturalism supplies both.

Race-conscious policies now permeate not only employment and education, but also the courts and even the democratic process itself. Race or ethnicity often determines political representation and establishes voting procedures. In addition, the list of groups eligible to benefit continues to grow and now embraces even the most recent immigrants to America, who, by definition, have suffered no past discrimination. As the policies and the beneficiaries expand, so has their rationale. 12

The compensatory model has given way to one based on culture, which alleviates the necessity of proving past discrimination or present disadvantage. The demand to redress past or present wrongs evolves into the imperative to enhance and preserve culture. America becomes not simply a multi-racial, multi-ethnic society made up of individuals of different backgrounds—some of whom have suffered discrimination because of their color—but a *multicultural* nation. 13

The distinction is an important one. It implies that Americans differ not only in skin color and origin, but in values, mores, customs, temperament, language—all those attributes that endow culture with meaning. Indeed, multiculturalism questions the very concept of an *American* people. It replaces affirmative action as the linchpin in the politics of race with a much more profound power to shape how all Americans, not just racial and ethnic minorities, think of themselves and conceive the nation. 14

Multiculturalists insist on treating race or ethnicity as if they were synonymous with culture. They presume that skin color or national origin, which are immutable traits, determine values, mores, language, and other cultural attributes, which, of course, are learned. In the multiculturalists' world view, African-Americans, Puerto Ricans, or Chinese-Americans living in New York City, for instance, share more in common with persons of their ancestral group living in Lagos, San Juan, or Hong Kong than they do with other New Yorkers who are white. Culture becomes a fixed entity, transmitted, as it were, in the genes, rather than through experience. 15

Such convictions lead multiculturalists to conclude that, in the words of Molefi Kete Asante, a guru of the multicultural movement, "There is no common American culture." The logic is simple, if wrongheaded. Since Americans (or, more often, their forebears) hail from many different places, each with its own specific culture, the United States must be multicultural. Moreover, they claim, it is becoming more so every day as new immigrants bring their cultures with them when they come to the United States. 16

Indeed, multiculturalists hope to ride the immigrant wave to greater power and influence. They certainly have done so in education. The influx of non-English-speaking children into public schools has given added impetus to the multicultural movement. Approximately 2,300,000 youngsters who can not speak English well now attend public school, an increase of 1,000,000 since 1989. The Los Angeles Unified School District alone offers instruction to 160,000 students in Spanish, Armenian, Korean, Cantonese, Tagalog, Russian, and Japanese. In New York, students come from 167 different countries, speaking 120 separate languages. The costs for such programs are astronomical—more than $300,000,000 a year for 126,000 pupils in New York. 17

Multicultural advocates cite the presence of such children to demand bilingual education and other multicultural services. Federal and state governments literally spend billions of dollars on these initiatives, although an exact estimate of total outlay is difficult to obtain since it is allocated across several programs and layers of government.

18 The multiculturalists' emphasis on education, though, undercuts their own argument that culture is inextricable from race or national origin. The multiculturalists are acutely aware of just how fragile cultural identification is. If they were not, they would be less adamant about preserving and reinforcing it. The current emphasis on Afrocentric curricula for black elementary and secondary students, for instance, would be unnecessary if race itself conferred culture. Nor would multiculturalists insist on teaching immigrant children in their native language, instructing them in the history and customs of their native land, and imbuing them with reverence for their ancestral heroes, if ethnicity and national origin alone were antidotes to the appeal of American culture.

19 Multiculturalists haven't lost faith in the power of assimilation. If anything, they seem to believe that, without a heavy dose of multicultural indoctrination, immigrants won't be able to resist assimilation. They are right, though it remains to be seen whether anything, including the multiculturalists' crude methods, ultimately will detour immigrants from the assimilation path.

20 The urge to assimilate traditionally has been overpowering in the United States, especially among the children of immigrants. Only groups that maintain strict rules against intermarriage and other social contact with persons outside the group, such as Orthodox Jews and the Amish, ever have succeeded in preserving distinct, full-blown cultures within American society after one or two generations have been living here. It is interesting to note that religion seems to be a more effective deterrent to full assimilation than the secular elements of culture, including language.

21 Although many Americans worry that Hispanic immigrants, for example, are not learning English and therefore will fail to assimilate into the American mainstream, there is little evidence that this is the case. As already noted, a majority of Hispanics speak only English by the third generation in the United States, and are closer to other Americans on most measures of social and economic status than they are to Hispanic immigrants. On one of the most rigorous gauges of assimilation—intermarriage—Hispanics rank high. About one-third of young, third-generation Hispanics marry non-Hispanic whites, a pattern similar to that of young Asians. Even for blacks, exogamy rates, which have been quite low historically, are going up. About 3 percent of blacks now marry outside their group, though the rate in the western states is much higher—17 percent among black males marrying for the first time.

22 The impetus for multiculturalism is not coming from immigrants—even among groups such as Hispanics and Asians—but from their more affluent and (ironically) assimilated native-born counterparts in their ethnic commu-

nities. The proponents most often are the elite, best-educated, and most successful members of their respective racial and ethnic groups. Not surprisingly, college campuses are fertile recruiting grounds, where the most radical displays of multiculturalism take place.

In May, 1993, for instance, a group of Mexican-American students at 23
UCLA, frustrated that the university would not elevate the school's 23-year-old Chicano studies program to full department status, stormed the campus faculty center, breaking windows and furniture and causing $500,000 in damage. During the same month, a group of Asian-American students at the University of California, Irvine, went on a hunger strike to pressure administrators into hiring more professors to teach Asian-American studies courses there. These were not immigrants or even, by and large, disadvantaged students, but middle-class beneficiaries of their parents' or grandparents' successful assimilation into the American mainstream.

The protesters' actions had almost nothing to do with any effort to main- 24
tain their ethnic identity. For the most part, such students probably never thought of themselves as anything but American before they entered college. According to the Berkeley study cited earlier, most Hispanic and Asian students "discovered" their ethnic identity after they arrived on campus. Speaking of Asian students, the researchers reported: "After being around [the University of California] for one or two years, students who were integrated into predominantly white worlds of friendship and association in high school report a shift towards having predominantly Asian American friends, roommates, or affiliations with an Asian American organization."

The same was true for other groups as well, including blacks. "On arrival 25
on the Berkeley campus, these students are surprised to discover themselves no longer the 'token black person.' . . . These students experience a new kind of pressure: it comes from other African American students on campus, and it is experienced as pressure to make decisions about friends, networks, even who you sit with at lunch, on the basis of race."

Many of these students learn to define themselves as victims as well. As 26
one Mexican-American freshman summed it up, she was "unaware of the things that have been going on with our people, all the injustices we've suffered, how the world really is. I thought racism didn't exist here, you know, it just comes to light." The researchers went on to note that all "students of color" had difficulty pinpointing exactly what constituted this "subtle form of the new racism." Instead of empirical evidence, "There was much talk of certain facial expressions, or the way people look, and how white students 'take over the class' and speak past you."

If terms like racism and discrimination can be applied to such innocuous 27
behavior, what words can be used to describe the real thing? As author George Orwell said in his 1946 essay, "Politics and the English Language," "if thought corrupts language, language can also corrupt thought." Misusing words like racism undermines the very legitimacy of the concept.

The re-racialization of American society that is taking place in the name 28
of multiculturalism is not a progressive movement, but a step backward to

the America that existed before *Brown* v. *Board of Education* and the passage of the major civil rights laws of the 1960s. We are at a critical juncture in our history. Even if we are not, as the multiculturalists claim, about to become a majority minority nation, racial and ethnic diversity in our population is increasing. If we allow race and ethnicity to determine public policy, we invite the kind of cleavages that will oil one group against another in ways that cannot be good for the groups themselves or the society we all must live in.

29 The more diverse we become, the more crucial it is that we commit ourselves to a shared, civic culture. The distinguishing characteristic of American culture always has been its ability to incorporate so many disparate elements into a new whole. While conservative philosopher Russell Kirk was indisputably right that the United States owes much of its culture to Great Britain—our legal tradition, particularly the concept of the rule of law, our belief in representative government, and certainly our language and literatures—American assimilation always has entailed some give and take. American culture itself has been enriched by what individual groups brought to it.

30 Yet, it is more important that all of us—no matter where we come from or what circumstances brought us or our ancestors here—think of ourselves as Americans if we are to retain the sense that we are one people, not simply a conglomeration of different and competing groups. It is nonsense to think we can do so without being clear about our purposes.

31 We can by acknowledging that it is more important for immigrant children to learn English than to maintain their native language, although the two not necessarily are mutually exclusive. We should make sure that American students have a firm grasp of the history of this nation, the people who helped build it, and the institutions and principles on which the United States was founded. We should be careful not to repeat past errors, when American history courses conveniently excluded facts, but neither should history become simply an exercise in building the self-esteem of those who previously were left out. Finally, we need to get beyond the point where race and ethnicity are the most important factors in the way we identify ourselves or form allegiances. The principles and values that unite us remain far more important than our differences in ancestry, a lesson that bears repeating in our schools and universities.

Building Vocabulary

Write definitions and your own sentences for the following words:

1. **devising** (par. 1)
2. **crux** (par. 2)
3. **pernicious** (par. 7)
4. **eschew** (par. 10)
5. **evinces** (par. 11)
6. **redress** (par. 13)
7. **immutable** (par. 15)

8. **adamant** (par. 18)
9. **secular** (par. 20)
10. **innocuous** (par. 27)

Thinking Critically About the Argument

Understanding the Writer's Argument

1. What is the center of the argument against using race to decide preference, according to Chavez?
2. What does it mean that affirmative action programs "are not compensatory, but presumptive"? (par. 5) Why does Chavez think that's a bad idea?
3. Who is receiving the benefits of affirmative action who shouldn't, according to Chavez?
4. What, according to Chavez, does science tell us about race?
5. What is wrong, according to Chavez, with the multiculturalists calling for bilingual education?
6. What is one of the most reliable signs of assimilation?

Understanding the Writer's Techniques

1. What is Chavez's major proposition? Where do you find it in the essay? Is it in an effective location? Why or why not?
2. Outline the paragraphs leading up to the major proposition. What is their argumentative purpose?
3. What minor propositions does Chavez offer to help prove that affirmative action is not a realistic option?
4. How does Chavez support the perspective that multiculturalism threatens the idea of a unified American society? Explain the various ways in which Chavez says this happens.
5. What evidence does Chavez cite to support her claim that much of the call for multiculturalism comes not from immigrants, but from their second and third-generation descendents? Why does she think this is a problem? Is her explanation sufficient?
6. Where does Chavez's conclusion start? Is it effective? Why or why not?

Exploring the Writer's Argument

1. What is wrong with accepting that race and ethnicity are "intrinsically significant"? (par. 2)
2. Chavez says that the programs that offer preference to racial minorities don't determine whether the individuals have been discriminated against. Is she missing the point of affirmative action? Explain your answer.
3. In paragraph 11, Chavez writes that "Americans—of all races—have grown tired of affirmative action." Does she support this idea effectively? Why or why not? Is there another way to formulate this idea?

4. How successful is Chavez's argument in paragraphs 8 and 9 that affirmative action isn't a well made way of distributing money because every ethnic group has suffered discrimination? Is that a fair assessment? Why or why not?

Ideas for Writing Arguments

Prewriting

What evidence of affirmative action policy have you observed in American life? How has affirmative action policy affected you or others you know?

Writing a Guided Argument

Select a job or profession that you think particularly needs affirmative action programs to help minorities achieve equality. Write an essay arguing that affirmative action should apply to hiring or promotion in that profession or career.

1. Begin your essay by mentioning Chavez's essay and briefly summarizing her position on affirmative action.
2. Explain a little bit about the profession you have chosen to write about.
3. Write a major proposition in which you rebut Chavez and assert your own position.
4. Use clear and effective transitions to develop your ideas.
5. Write your minor propositions in the form of rebuttals to Chavez's points.
6. Make sure your argument is focused on your chosen subject.
7. Conclude by widening your argument and explaining how affirmative action, in your view, can help not only minorities in the profession you are writing about, but minorities in all jobs.

Thinking, Arguing, and Writing Collaboratively

Class members should divide into two groups, one of which will argue in favor of the quote by multiculturalist Molefi Kete Asante that Chavez includes in paragraph 16. He says that "There is no common American culture." The other group will argue Chavez's view that this is "wrongheaded." The group that supports the idea in the quote should think of arguments for that position, and the group that opposes the quote should come up with arguments to refute that idea. After debating the issue, come together as a class and discuss it.

Writing About the Text

Analyze Chavez's points in paragraph 10 about the current distribution of affirmative action benefits and argue that this point is either one of the strongest or one of the weakest in her argument.

More Writing Ideas

1. Write notes in your journal for an essay that supports or refutes Chavez's point that affirmative action programs should try to determine whether an individual has been discriminated against before bestowing benefits on that person.
2. Write two or three paragraphs that argue for or against the fact that some students in Los Angeles and other cities are taught their classes in Spanish and languages other than English.
3. Write an essay that explores the implications of the view that affirmative action might undermine self-confidence in minorities who received benefits.

NATHAN GLAZER
In Defense of Preference

Nathan Glazer was born in 1924, went to City College and the University of Pennsylvania, and earned his Ph.D. in sociology from Columbia University. For years he taught in the graduate school of education at Harvard University. He is the author of We Are All Multiculturalists Now *and* Beyond the Melting Pot. *He has written extensively on urban policy, education, and minority issues. In the 1970s, Glazer was against affirmative action and actually wrote a book arguing against it,* Affirmative Discrimination *(1975). Since the 1970s, Glazer has changed his mind about affirmative action. "I have definitely come to the conclusion that strict colorblindness is unrealistic and probably inadvisable," he has said. In this selection, Glazer argues that affirmative action is a crucial step in the road toward leveling the playing field for African Americans.*

Prereading: Thinking About the Essay in Advance

Write some notes on the idea of *preference*. What does that word mean to you? How does it relate to affirmative action? Glazer is arguing for preference, but does that word have any negative connotations? What are they?

Words to Watch

equanimity (par. 3) fairness
galvanized (par. 6) strengthened and bonded together
glacially (par. 6) slowly
vetted (par. 6) checked
elided (par. 12) reduced
egalitarian (par. 20) useless
discharged (par. 22) fulfilled
magistrates (par. 25) local official
demographically (par. 28) relating to population trends

1 The battle over affirmative action today is a contest between a clear principle on the one hand and a clear reality an the other. The principle is that ability, qualifications, and merit, independent of race, national origin, or sex, should prevail when one applies for a job or promotion, or for entry into selective institutions for higher education, or when one bids for contracts. The reality is that strict adherence to this principle would result in few African Americans getting jobs, admissions, and contracts. What makes the debate so confused is that the facts that make a compelling case for affirmative action are often obscured by the defenders of affirmative action themselves. They have resisted acknowledging how serious the gaps are between African Americans and others, how deep the preferences reach, how systematic they have become. Considerably more than a mild bend in the direction of diversity now exists, but it exists because painful facts make it necessary if blacks are to participate in more than token numbers in some key institutions of our society. The opponents of affirmative action can also be faulted: they have not fully confronted the consequences that must follow from the implementation of the principle that measured ability, qualification, merit, applied without regard to color, should be our only guide.

2 I argued for that principle in a 1975 book titled, provocatively, *Affirmative Discrimination.* It seemed obvious that that was what all of us, black and white, were aiming to achieve through the revolutionary civil rights legislation of the 1960s. That book dealt with affirmative action in employment, and with two other kinds of governmentally or judicially imposed "affirmative action," the equalization of the racial proportions in public schools and the integration of residential neighborhoods. I continued to argue and write regularly against governmentally required affirmative action, that is, racial preference, for the next two decades or more: it was against the spirit of the Constitution, the clear language of the civil rights acts, and the interests of all of us in the United States in achieving an integrated and just society.

3 It is not the unpopularity of this position in the world in which I live, liberal academia, that has led me to change my mind but, rather, developments that were unforeseen and unexpected in the wake of the successful civil rights movement. What was unforeseen and unexpected was that the gap between the educational performance of blacks and whites would persist and, in some respects, deepen despite the civil rights revolution and hugely expanded social and educational programs, that innercity schools would continue to decline, and that the black family would unravel to a remarkable degree, contributing to social conditions for large numbers of black children far worse than those in the 1960s. In the presence of those conditions, an insistence on color-blindness means the effective exclusion today of African Americans from positions of influence, wealth, and power. It is not a prospect that any of us can contemplate with equanimity. We have to rethink affirmative action.

4 In a sense, it is a surprise that a fierce national debate over affirmative action has not only persisted but intensified during the Clinton years. After

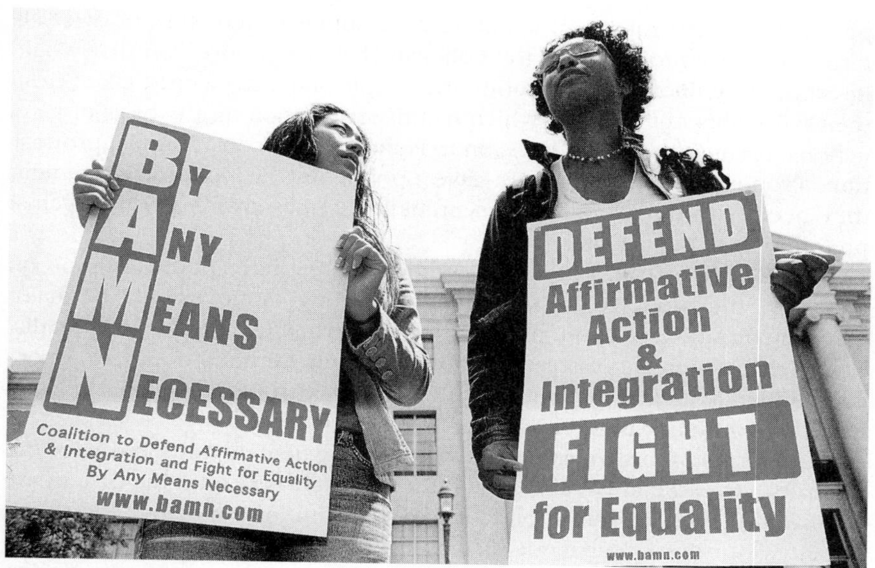

(AP Oakland Tribune.)

twelve years under two Republican presidents, Ronald Reagan and George Bush, who said they opposed affirmative action but did nothing to scale it back, the programs seemed secure. After all, affirmative action rests primarily on a presidential executive order dating back to the presidencies of Lyndon Johnson and Richard Nixon which requires "affirmative action" in employment practices from federal contractors—who include almost every large employer, university, and hospital. The legal basis for most of affirmative action could thus have been swept away, as so many noted at the time, with a "stroke of the pen" by the president. Yet two presidents who claimed to oppose affirmative action never wielded the pen.

Despite the popular majority that grumbles against affirmative action, 5
there was (and is) no major elite constituency strongly opposed to it: neither business nor organized labor, religious leaders nor university presidents, local officials nor serious presidential candidates are to be found in opposition. Big business used to fear that affirmative action would undermine the principle of employment and promotion on the basis of qualifications. It has since become a supporter. Along with mayors and other local officials (and of course the civil rights movement), it played a key role in stopping the Reagan administration from moving against affirmative action. Most city administrations have also made their peace with affirmative action.

Two developments outside the arena of presidential politics galvanized 6
both opponents and defenders of affirmative action. The Supreme Court changed glacially after successive Republican appointments—each of which, however, had been vetted by a Democratic Senate—and a number of circuit courts began to chip away at the edifice of affirmative action. But

playing the largest role was the politically unsophisticated effort of two California professors to place on the California ballot a proposition that would insert in the California Constitution the simple and clear words, taken from the Civil Rights Act of 1964, which ban discrimination on the basis of race, national origin, or sex. The decision to launch a state constitutional proposition, Proposition 209, suddenly gave opponents the political instrument they needed to tap the majority sentiment that has always existed against preferences.

7 While supporters of affirmative action do not have public opinion on their side, they do have the still-powerful civil rights movement, the major elites in education, religion, philanthropy, government, and the mass media. And their position is bolstered by a key fact: how far behind African Americans are when judged by the tests and measures that have become the common coin of American meritocracy.

8 The reality of this enormous gap is cleanest where the tests in use are the most objective, the most reliable, and the best validated, as in the case of the various tests used for admission to selective institutions of higher education, for entry into elite occupations such as law and medicine, or for civil service jobs. These tests have been developed over many years specifically for the purpose of eliminating biases in admissions and appointments. As defenders of affirmative action often point out, paper-and-pencil tests of information, reading comprehension, vocabulary, reasoning, and the like are not perfect indicators of individual ability. But they are the best measures we have for success in college and professional schools, which, after all, require just the skills the tests measure. And the tests can clearly differentiate the literate teacher from the illiterate one or the policeman who can make out a coherent arrest report from one who cannot.

9 To concentrate on the most hotly contested area of affirmative action—admission to selective institutions of higher education—and on the group in the center of the storm—African Americans: If the Scholastic Assessment Test were used for selection in a color-blind fashion, African Americans, who today make up about 6 percent of the student bodies in selective colleges and universities, would drop to less than 2 percent, according to a 1994 study by the editor of the *Journal of Blacks in Higher Education.*

10 Why is this so? According to studies summarized in Stephan and Abigail Thernstrom's book, *America in Black and White,* the average combined SAT score for entering freshmen in the nation's top 25 institutions is about 1300. White applicants generally need to score a minimum of 600 on the verbal portion of the test—a score obtained by 8 percent of the test-takers in 1995—and at least 650 on the mathematics section—a score obtained by 7 percent of the test-takers in 1995. In contrast, only 1.7 percent of black students scored over 600 on the verbal section in 1995, and only 2 percent scored over 650 on the math. This represents considerable progress over the last 15 years, but black students still lag distressingly far behind their white counterparts.

There is no way of getting around this reality. Perhaps the tests are irrelevant to success in college? That cannot be sustained. They have been improved and revised over decades and predict achievement in college better than any alternative. Some of the revisions have been carried out in a near-desperate effort to exclude items which would discriminate against blacks. Some institutions have decided they will not use the tests, not because they are invalid per se, but because they pose a barrier to the increased admission of black students. Nor would emphasizing other admissions criteria, such as high school grades, make a radical difference. In any case, there is considerable value to a uniform national standard, given the enormous differences among high schools. 11

Do qualifications at the time of admission matter? Isn't the important thing what the institutions manage to do with those they admit? If they graduate, are they not qualified? Yes, but many do not graduate. Two or three times as many African American students as white students drop out before graduation. And the tests for admission to graduate schools show the same radical disparities between blacks and others. Are there not also preferences for athletes, children of alumni, students gifted in some particular respect? Yes, but except for athletes, the disparities in academic aptitude that result from such preferences are not nearly as substantial as those which must be elided in order to reach target figures for black students. Can we not substitute for the tests other factors—such as the poverty and other hardships students have overcome to reach the point of applying to college? This might keep up the number of African Americans, but not by much, if the studies are to be believed. A good number of white and Asian applicants would also benefit from such "class-based" affirmative action. 12

(I have focused on the effect of affirmative action—and its possible abolition—on African Americans. But, of course, there are other beneficiaries. Through bureaucratic mindlessness, Asian Americans and Hispanics were also given affirmative action. But Asian Americans scarcely need it. Major groups—not all—of Hispanic Americans trail behind whites but mostly for reasons we understand: problems with the English language and the effect on immigrant children of the poor educational and economic status of their parents. We expect these to improve in time as they always have with immigrants to the United States. And, when it comes to women, there is simply no issue today when it comes to qualifying in equal numbers for selective institutions of higher and professional education.) 13

How, then, should we respond to this undeniable reality? The opponents of affirmative action say, "Let standards prevail whatever the result." So what if black students are reduced to two percent of our selective and elite student bodies? Those who gain entry will know that they are properly qualified for entry, that they have been selected without discrimination, and their classmates will know it too. The result will actually be improved race relations and a continuance of the improvements we have seen in black performance in recent decades. Fifteen years from now, perhaps three or four 14 percent of students in the top schools will be black. Until then, blacks can go to less competitive institutions of higher education, perhaps gaining greater advantage from their education in so doing. And, meanwhile, let us improve elementary and high school education—as we have been trying to do for the last 15 years or more.

15 Yet we cannot be quite so cavalier about the impact on public opinion—black and white—of a radical reduction in the number of black students at the Harvards, the Berkeleys, and the Amhersts. These institutions have become, for better or worse, the gateways to prominence, privilege, wealth, and power in American society. To admit blacks under affirmative action no doubt undermines the American meritocracy, but to exclude blacks from them by abolishing affirmative action would undermine the legitimacy of American democracy.

16 My argument is rooted in history. African Americans—and the struggle for their full and fair inclusion in U.S. society—have been a part of American history from the beginning. Our Constitution took special—but grossly unfair—account of their status, our greatest war was fought over their status, and our most important constitutional amendments were adopted because of the need to right past wrongs done to them. And, amid the civil rights revolution of the 1960s, affirmative action was instituted to compensate for the damage done to black achievement and life chances by almost 400 years of slavery, followed by state-sanctioned discrimination and massive prejudice.

17 Yet, today, a vast gulf of difference persists between the educational and occupational status of blacks and whites, a gulf that encompasses statistical measures of wealth, residential segregation, and social relationships with other Americans. Thirty years ago, with the passage of the great civil rights laws, one could have reasonably expected—as I did—that all would be set right by now. But today, even after taking account of substantial progress and change, it is borne upon us how continuous, rooted, and substantial the differences between African Americans and other Americans remain.

18 The judgment of the elites who support affirmative action—the college presidents and trustees, the religious leaders, the corporate executives—and the judgment even of many of those who oppose it but hesitate to act against it—the Republican leaders in Congress, for example—is that the banning of preference would be bad for the country. I agree. Not that everyone's motives are entirely admirable; many conservative congressmen, for example, are simply afraid of being portrayed as racists even if their opposition to affirmative action is based on a sincere desire to support meritocratic principle. The college presidents who support affirmative action, under the fashionable mantra of diversity, also undoubtedly fear the student demonstrations that would occur if they were to speak out against preferences.

19 But there are also good-faith motives in this stand, and there is something behind the argument for diversity. What kind of institutions of higher education would we have if blacks suddenly dropped from 6 or 7 percent of enrollment to 1 or 2 percent? The presence of blacks, in classes in social

studies and the humanities, immediately introduces another tone, another range of questions (often to the discomfort of black students who do not want this representational burden placed upon them). The tone may be one of embarrassment and hesitation and self-censorship among whites (students and faculty). But must we not all learn how to face these questions together with our fellow citizens? We should not be able to escape from this embarrassment by the reduction of black students to minuscule numbers.

The weakness in the "diversity" defense is that college presidents are 20
not much worried about the diversity that white working-class kids, or students of Italian or Slavic background, have to offer. Still, there is a reputable reason for that apparent discrepancy. It is that the varied ethnic and racial groups in the United States do not, to the same extent as African Americans, pose a test of the fairness of American institutions. These other groups have not been subjected to the same degree of persecution or exclusion. Their status is not, as the social status of African Americans is, the most enduring reproach to the egalitarian ideals of American society. And these other groups have made progress historically, and make progress today, at a rate that incorporates them into American society quickly compared to blacks.

This is the principal flaw in the critique of affirmative action. The critics 21
are defending a vitally important principle, indeed, the one that should be the governing principle of institutions of higher education: academic competence as the sole test for distinguishing among applicants and students. This principle, which was fought for so energetically during the 1940s and 1950s through laws banning discrimination in admission on the basis of race, national origin, or religion, should not be put aside lightly. But, at present, it would mean the near exclusion from our best educational institutions of a group that makes up 12 percent of the population. In time, I am convinced, this preference will not be needed. Our laws and customs and our primary and secondary educational systems will fully incorporate black Americans into American society, as other disadvantaged groups have been incorporated. The positive trends of recent decades will continue. But we are still, though less than in the past, "two nations," and one of the nations cannot be excluded so thoroughly from institutions that confer access to the positions of greatest prestige and power.

On what basis can we justify violating the principle that measured criteria 22
of merit should govern admission to selective institutions of higher education today? It is of some significance to begin with that we in the United States have always been looser in this respect than more examination-bound systems of higher education in, say, Western Europe: we have always left room for a large degree of freedom for institutions of higher education, public as well as private, to admit students based on nonacademic criteria. But I believe the main reasons we have to continue racial preferences for blacks are, first, because this country has a special obligation to blacks that has not been fully discharged, and second, because strict application of the principle of qualification would send a message of despair to many blacks, a message that the nation is indifferent to their difficulties and problems.

23 Many, including leading black advocates of eliminating preference, say no: the message would be, "Work harder and you can do it." Well, now that affirmative action is becoming a thing of the past in the public colleges and universities of California and Texas, we will have a chance to find out. Yet I wonder whether the message of affirmative action to black students today really ever has been, "Don't work hard; it doesn't matter for you because you're black; you will make it into college anyway." Colleges are indeed looking for black students, but they are also looking for some minimal degree of academic effort and accomplishment, and it is a rare ambitious African American student seeking college entry who relaxes because he believes his grades won't matter at all.

24 One of the chief arguments against racial preference in college and professional school admissions is that more blacks will drop out, the quality of blacks who complete the courses of instruction will be inferior, and they will make poorer lawyers, doctors, or businessmen. Dropping out is common in American higher education and does not necessarily mean that one's attendance was a total loss. Still, the average lower degree of academic performance has, and will continue to have, effects even for the successful: fewer graduating black doctors will go into research; more will go into practice and administration. More blacks in business corporations will be in personnel. Fewer graduating black lawyers will go into corporate law firms; more will work for government.

25 And more will become judges, because of another and less disputed form of affirmative action, politics. Few protest at the high number of black magistrates in cities with large black populations—we do not appoint judges by examination. Nor do we find it odd or objectionable that Democratic presidents will appoint more black lawyers as judges, or that even a Republican president will be sure to appoint one black Supreme Court justice. What is at work here is the principle of participation. It is a more legitimate principle in politics and government than it is for admission to selective institutions of higher education. But these are also gateways to power, and the principle of participation cannot be flatly ruled out for them.

26 Whatever the case one may make in general for affirmative action, many difficult issues remain: What kind, to what extent, how long, imposed by whom, by what decision-making process? It is important to bear in mind that affirmative action in higher education admissions is, for the most part, a policy that has been chosen (albeit sometimes under political pressure) by the institutions themselves. There are racial goals and targets for employment and promotion for all government contractors, including colleges and universities, set by government fiat, but targets on student admissions are not imposed by government, except for a few traditionally black or white institutions in the South.

27 Let us preserve this institutional autonomy. Just as I would resist governmentally imposed requirements that these institutions meet quotas of black admissions, so would I also oppose a judicial or legislative ban on the use of race in making decisions on admission. Ballot measures like Proposition 209 are more understandable given the abuses so common in systems of racial

preference. But it is revealing that so many other states appear to have had second thoughts and that the California vote is therefore not likely to be repeated. (A report in the *Chronicle of Higher Education* was headlined "LEGISLATURES SHOW LITTLE ENTHUSIASM FOR MEASURES TO END RACIAL PREFERENCES"; in this respect, the states are not unlike Congress.)

We should retain the freedom of institutions of higher and professional education to make these determinations for themselves. As we know, they would almost all make room for a larger percentage of black students than would otherwise qualify. This is what these institutions do today. They defend what they do with the argument that diversity is a good thing. I think what they really mean is that a large segment of the American population, significant not only demographically but historically and politically and morally, cannot be so thoroughly excluded. I agree with them. 28

I have discussed affirmative action only in the context of academic admissions policy. Other areas raise other questions, other problems. And, even in this one area of college and university admissions, affirmative action is not a simple and clear and uncomplicated solution. It can be implemented wisely or foolishly, and it is often done foolishly, as when college presidents make promises to protesting students that they cannot fulfill, or when institutions reach too far below their minimal standards with deleterious results for the academic success of the students they admit, for their grading practices, and for the legitimacy of the degrees they offer. No matter how affirmative action in admissions is dealt with, other issues remain or will emerge. More black students, for example, mean demands for more black faculty and administrators and for more black-oriented courses. Preference is no final answer (just as the elimination of preference is no final answer). It is rather what is necessary to respond to the reality that, for some years to come, yes, we are still two nations, and both nations must participate in the society to some reasonable degree. 29

Fortunately, those two nations, by and large, want to become more united. The United States is not Canada or Bosnia, Lebanon or Malaysia. But, for the foreseeable future, the strict use of certain generally reasonable tests as a benchmark criterion for admissions would mean the de facto exclusion of one of the two nations from a key, institutional system of the society, higher education. Higher education's governing principle is qualification—merit. Should it make room for another and quite different principle, equal participation? The latter should never become dominant. Racial proportional representation would be a disaster. But basically the answer is yes—the principle of equal participation can and should be given some role. This decision has costs. But the alternative is too grim to contemplate. 30

Building Vocabulary

1. In this essay, Glazer uses a number of words and phrases that have come into the English language from other languages, in most cases with the same spelling and meaning. Look up the following, identify the source

language, and write a definition for each:
   a. edifice (par. 6)
   b. philanthropy (par. 7)
   c. cavalier (par. 15)
   d. mantra (par. 18)
   e. albeit (par. 26)
   f. fiat (par. 26)
   g. de facto (par. 30)
2. Write definitions and your own sentences for each of the following:
   a. provocatively (par. 2)
   b. insistence (par. 3)
   c. constituency (par. 5)
   d. bureaucratic (par. 13)
   e. meritocracy (par. 15)
   f. autonomy (par. 27)
   g. deleterious (par. 29)

Thinking Critically About the Argument

Understanding the Writer's Argument

1. What makes the debate over affirmative action so confused, according to Glazer?
2. What made Glazer change his position on affirmative action?
3. If affirmative action was put into place through an executive order, how did the policy manage to survive despite the fact that later on two presidents opposed it?
4. What can the SATs and other tests tell us about the need for affirmative action?
5. What is the "principle flaw in the critique of affirmative action"? (par. 21)
6. How is "institutional autonomy" important for the success of affirmative action, according to Glazer?

Understanding the Writer's Techniques

1. Why does Glazer begin his essay with a summary of the arguments on both sides of the affirmative action debate?
2. What is the argumentative effect of Glazer's admission in paragraph 3 that he has changed sides in the debate?
3. What is Glazer's claim in this essay? Where does he articulate it most clearly?
4. Compare and contrast the kind of support Glazer and Chavez use to make their arguments. Do they both rely equally on logic? Does one make a more emotional appeal? Explain your answers.
5. Compare and contrast the tone Glazer takes in his essay with Chavez's in hers.

6. What evidence does Glazer cite to support his minor proposition that there is little real opposition to affirmative action?
7. How does Glazer support his point that abolishing affirmative action "would undermine the legitimacy of American democracy"? (par. 15)
8. How effective is Glazer's conclusion? Explain.

Exploring the Writer's Argument

1. Glazer acknowledges that one of the central tenets of the civil rights movement is the prohibition of discrimination based on race. How does he make a case for why affirmative action is not in violation of this principle? Explain.
2. What would Chavez say in response to Glazer's point that "the judgment of the elites who support affirmative action—the college presidents and trustees, the religious leaders, the corporate executives—and the judgment even of many of those who oppose it but hesitate to act against it—the Republican leaders in Congress, for example—is that the banning of preference would be bad for the country"? (par. 18)
3. In the course of his essay, Glazer uses the same statistic, the one introduced in paragraph 9, several times. He repeats the idea that if the SAT were used for admissions without looking at race, African Americans would go from 6 percent of students at top colleges to 2 percent. Where else in the essay does he mention this statistic, and what is the effect? What would happen to his argument if he didn't have this statistic?
4. Why do you think Chavez writes about minorities in general in her essay and Glazer, on the other hand, focuses on African Americans?

Ideas for Writing Arguments

Prewriting

In his conclusion, Glazer writes that affirmative action "has costs. But the alternative is too grim to contemplate." List the pros and cons of affirmative action.

Writing a Guided Argument

At the end of the 2003 term, the U.S. Supreme Court handed down two important decisions about affirmative action in Michigan: *Grutter v. Bollinger* and *Gratz v. Bollinger.* Find the text of the two decisions, read them, and choose one case and one of the justice's opinions (majority or dissenting) on that case. Write an essay that supports that position.

1. Open your essay with a summary of the Supreme Court case and its importance.
2. Explain which position you agree with, and write your major proposition.
3. Offer a minor proposition giving a ground for your position.

4. Support your minor proposition with facts from one of the essays in this chapter.
5. Write another minor proposition, and support it sufficiently.
6. Use strong transitions, and write another minor proposition if needed.
7. Bring your essay to a close by predicting what the consequences of the case will be and whether those consequences will be positive or negative.

Thinking, Arguing, and Writing Collaboratively

Divide into two equal groups, one taking Chavez's position and one taking Glazer's. As a group, think of arguments and facts to add to those already given by the writer whose position you are defending. Try to strengthen weaknesses you see in the original essays. Take notes on your discussion, and prepare an outline for a debate. Debate the issue, and then reconvene as a class and discuss the success of the respective arguments.

Writing About the Text

Write an essay that expands on questions 4 and 5 in the Understanding the Writer's Techniques section.

More Writing Ideas

1. Look up what has happened to Proposition 209 in California. What has been the result and the consequence? Collect notes on your research in your journal.
2. Write a paragraph about the fact that the United States has not fully repaid blacks for years of slavery. What other ways could the United States pay them back?
3. Find out your own college's affirmative action policy. Write an essay in support of or in opposition to the policy.

26 Capital Punishment: Should We Take a Human Life?

Does the government have the right to put one of its citizens to death for any reason? Does the death penalty violate the "cruel and unusual" punishment clause in the Eighth Amendment?

After World War II, many European and industrialized nations signed the *Universal Declaration of Human Rights* and banned the death penalty within their borders. The United States, however, kept the death penalty. The debate has intensified in this country over the fairness and humaneness of the punishment. One argument focuses on whether it is fair to execute a convict who is mentally ill or retarded. Another highlights the fact that a disproportionate number of people on death row are African Americans. A question here remains: Are blacks punished with execution more frequently than whites, and if so, why, and what does that say about our use of the death penalty? One other objection to capital punishment is that humans administer it and humans make mistakes. Innocent people have gone to their death.

Defenders of the death penalty, however, say that besides being a deterrent to people who might commit capital crimes in the future, execution fulfills a need by society for retribution—the public demands and deserves to see wrongdoers punished severely.

In the selections that follow, George Orwell, writing in the early 1930s, expresses his disgust for executions by showing one to his readers. His vivid and carefully chosen descriptions evoke a feeling of moral decay. David Gelernter, who was almost killed by a mail bomb sent by the Unabomber (a secretive terrorist who sent bombs by mail at the end of the 20th century), argues that we should administer the death penalty as the triumph of rationality over emotion. What do you think about the topic? As you read these two selections, consider why you feel the way you do about the death penalty. Is there a rational way to approach the subject, or are arguments only accessible through the emotions? How does that question affect these essays?

George Orwell
A Hanging

George Orwell (whose real name was Eric Blair) was born in India in 1903 and died in London at the age of 47. During his short life, he became famous for his political writing, especially his political novels.

Orwell's parents were members of the Indian Civil Service, and, after his education at Eton College in England, at the age of 19, Orwell joined the Indian Imperial Police in Burma, which he wrote about in his novel Burmese Days *(1934) and in various essays. One of those essays, "Killing an Elephant," expresses his disillusion with British colonialism. His politics shifted to the left and he became a socialist. He left Burma, traveled around Europe in self-enforced poverty, and wrote his first book about the experience,* Down and Out in Paris and London *(1933). Soon, in the mid-1930s, he joined many writers and intellectuals from all over the Western world in fighting with the Republicans against the Fascists in the Spanish Civil War.* Homage to Catalonia *(1938) tells of his experiences in the war. Orwell was wounded, and, when the Communists attempted to eliminate their allies on the far left, he fought against them and was forced to flee for his life.*

His most famous books, however, are Animal Farm *(1945), a modern fable that attacked the Soviet system of communism by setting the events among animals on a farm; and* 1984 *(1949), a novel about a frightening future.* 1984 *introduced the phrase "Big Brother" into the English language. In the years after his death, Orwell has become renowned for above all things his clarity of writing and his clarity of moral thought. In "A Hanging," written in 1931, Orwell tells of an experience watching an execution in Burma. The essay betrays his feelings about capital punishment, but he remains somewhat ambiguous. Elsewhere, Orwell wrote, "Society, apparently, cannot get along without capital punishment—for there are some people whom it is simply not safe to leave alive—and yet there is no one, when the pinch comes, who feels it right to kill another human being in cold blood."*

Prereading: Thinking About the Essay in Advance

Orwell's quote, that "society . . . cannot get along without capital punishment," has implications for the United States, one of the only industrial nations in the world that still executes prisoners. Why can't the United States get along without capital punishment?

Words to Watch

Dravidian (par. 4) a member of a group of southern Indians
spectacles (par. 4) glasses
magistrates (par. 6) local governmental officials
gambolled (par. 8) moved evasively
incuriously (par. 8) indifferent
timorously (par. 15) timidly
lathis (par. 17) batons
pannikin (par. 17) a small pan or cup
boxwallah (par. 18) peddler
refractory (par. 22) stubborn

It was in Burma, a sodden morning of the rains. A sickly light, like yellow tinfoil, was slanting over the high walls into the jail yard. We were waiting outside the condemned cells, a row of sheds fronted with double bars, like small animal cages. Each cell measured about ten feet by ten and was quite bare within except for a plank bed and a pot of drinking water. In some of them brown silent men were squatting at the inner bars, with their blankets draped round them. These were the condemned men, due to be hanged within the next week or two. 1

One prisoner had been brought out of his cell. He was a Hindu, a puny wisp of a man, with a shaven head and vague liquid eyes. He had a thick, sprouting moustache, absurdly too big for his body, rather like the moustache of a comic man on the films. Six tall Indian warders were guarding him and getting him ready for the gallows. Two of them stood by with rifles with fixed bayonets, while the others handcuffed him, passed a chain through his handcuffs and fixed it to their belts, and lashed his arms tight to his sides. They crowded very close about him, with their hands always on him in a careful, caressing grip, as though all the while feeling him to make sure he was there. It was like men handling a fish which is still alive and may jump back into the water. But he stood quite unresisting, yielding his arms limply to the ropes, as though he hardly noticed what was happening. 2

Eight o'clock struck and a bugle call, desolately thin in the wet air, floated from the distant barracks. The superintendent of the jail, who was standing apart from the rest of us, moodily prodding the gravel with his stick, raised his head at the sound. He was an army doctor, with a grey toothbrush moustache and a gruff voice. "For God's sake hurry up, Francis," he said irritably. "The man ought to have been dead by this time. Aren't you ready yet?" 3

Francis, the head jailer, a fat Dravidian in a white drill suit and gold spectacles, waved his black hand. "Yes sir, yes sir," he bubbled. "All iss satisfactorily prepared. The hangman iss waiting. We shall proceed." 4

"Well, quick march, then. The prisoners can't get their breakfast till this job's over." 5

We set out for the gallows. Two warders marched on either side of the prisoner, with their files at the slope; two others marched close against him, gripping him by arm and shoulder, as though at once pushing and supporting him. The rest of us, magistrates and the like, followed behind. Suddenly, when we had gone ten yards, the procession stopped short without any order or warning. A dreadful thing had happened—a dog, come goodness knows whence, had appeared in the yard. It came bounding among us with a loud volley of barks, and leapt round us wagging its whole body, wild with glee at finding so many human beings together. It was a large woolly dog, half Airedale, half pariah. For a moment it pranced round us, and then, before anyone could stop it, it had made a dash for the prisoner, and jumping up tried to lick his face. Everyone stood aghast, too taken aback even to grab at the dog. 6

"Who let that bloody brute in here?" said the superintendent angrily. "Catch it, someone!" 7

8 A warder, detached from the escort, charged clumsily after the dog, but it danced and gambolled just out of his reach, taking everything as part of the game. A young Eurasian jailer picked up a handful of gravel and tried to stone the dog away, but it dodged the stones and came after us again. Its yaps echoed from the jail walls. The prisoner, in the grasp of the two warders, looked on incuriously, as though this was another formality of the hanging. It was several minutes before someone managed to catch the dog. Then we put my handkerchief through its collar and moved off once more, with the dog still straining and whimpering.

9 It was about forty yards to the gallows. I watched the bare brown back of the prisoner marching in front of me. He walked clumsily with his bound arms, but quite steadily, with that bobbing gait of the Indian who never straightens his knees. At each step his muscles slid neatly into place, the lock of hair on his scalp danced up and down, his feet printed themselves on the wet gravel. And once, in spite of the men who gripped him by each shoulder, he stepped slightly aside to avoid a puddle on the path.

10 It is curious, but till that moment I had never realised what it means to destroy a healthy, conscious man. When I saw the prisoner step aside to avoid the puddle, I saw the mystery, the unspeakable wrongness, of cutting a life short when it is in full tide. This man was not dying, he was alive just as we were alive. All the organs of his body were working—bowels digesting food, skin renewing itself, nails growing, tissues forming—all toiling away in solemn foolery. His nails would still be growing when he stood on the drop, when he was falling through the air with a tenth of a second to live. His eyes saw the yellow gravel and the grey walls, and his brain still remembered, foresaw, reasoned—reasoned even about puddles. He and we were a party of men walking together, seeing, hearing, feeling, understanding the same world; and in two minutes, with a sudden snap, one of us would be gone—one mind less, one world less.

11 The gallows stood in a small yard, separate from the main grounds of the prison, and overgrown with tall prickly weeds. It was a brick erection like three sides of a shed, with planking on top, and above that two beams and a crossbar with the rope dangling. The hangman, a grey-haired convict in the white uniform of the prison, was waiting beside his machine. He greeted us with a servile crouch as we entered. At a word from Francis the two warders, gripping the prisoner more closely than ever, half led, half pushed him to the gallows and helped him clumsily up the ladder. Then the hangman climbed up and fixed the rope round the prisoner's neck.

12 We stood waiting, five yards away. The warders had formed in a rough circle round the gallows. And then, when the noose was fixed, the prisoner began crying out on his god. It was a high, reiterated cry of "Ram! Ram! Ram! Ram!", not urgent and fearful like a prayer or a cry for help, but steady, rhythmical, almost like the tolling of a bell. The dog answered the sound with a whine. The hangman, still standing on the gallows, produced a small cotton bag like a flour bag and drew it down over the prisoner's face. But the sound, muffled by the cloth, still persisted, over and over again: "Ram! Ram! Ram! Ram! Ram!"

The hangman climbed down and stood ready, holding the lever. Minutes seemed to pass. The steady, muffled crying from the prisoner went on and on, "Ram! Ram! Ram!" never faltering for an instant. The superintendent, his head on his chest, was slowly poking the ground with his stick; perhaps he was counting the cries, allowing the prisoner a fixed number—fifty, perhaps, or a hundred. Everyone had changed colour. The Indians had gone grey like bad coffee, and one or two of the bayonets were wavering. We looked at the lashed, hooded man on the drop, and listened to his cries—each cry another second of life; the same thought was in all our minds; oh, kill him quickly, get it over, stop that abominable noise! 13

Suddenly the superintendent made up his mind. Throwing up his head he made a swift motion with his stick. "Chalo!" he shouted almost fiercely. 14

There was a clanking noise, and then dead silence. The prisoner had vanished, and the rope was twisting on itself. I let go of the dog, and it galloped immediately to the back of the gallows; but when it got there it stopped short, barked, and then retreated into a corner of the yard, where it stood among the weeds, looking timorously out at us. We went round the gallows to inspect the prisoner's body. He was dangling with his toes pointed straight downwards, very slowly revolving, as dead as a stone. 15

The superintendent reached out with his stick and poked the bare body; it oscillated, slightly. "*He's* all right," said the superintendent. He backed out from under the gallows, and blew out a deep breath. The moody look had gone out of his face quite suddenly. He glanced at his wristwatch. "Eight minutes past eight. Well, that's all for this morning, thank God." 16

The warders unfixed bayonets and marched away. The dog, sobered and conscious of having misbehaved itself, slipped after them. We walked out of the gallows yard, past the condemned cells with their waiting prisoners, into the big central yard of the prison. The convicts, under the command of warders armed with lathis, were already receiving their breakfast. They squatted in long rows, each man holding a tin pannikin, while two warders with buckets marched round ladling out rice; it seemed quite a homely, jolly scene, after the hanging. An enormous relief had come upon us now that the job was done. One felt an impulse to sing, to break into a run, to snigger. All at once everyone began chattering gaily. 17

The Eurasian boy walking beside me nodded towards the way we had come, with a knowing smile: "Do you know, sir, our friend (he meant the dead man), when he heard his appeal had been dismissed, he pissed on the floor of his cell. From fright—Kindly take one of my cigarettes, sir. Do you not admire my new silver case, sir? From the boxwallah, two rupees eight annas. Classy European style." 18

Several people laughed—at what, nobody seemed certain. 19

Francis was walking by the superintendent, talking garrulously: "Well, sir, all hass passed off with the utmost satisfactoriness. It wass all finished—flick! like that. It iss not always so—oah, no! I have known cases where the doctor wass obliged to go beneath the gallows and pull the prisoner's legs to ensure decease. Most disagreeable!" 20

"Wriggling about, eh? That's bad," said the superintendent. 21

22 "Ach, sir, it iss worse when they become refractory! One man, I recall, clung to the bars of hiss cage when we went to take him out. You will scarcely credit, sir, that it took six warders to dislodge him, three pulling at each leg. We reasoned with him. 'My dear fellow,' we said, 'think of all the pain and trouble you are causing to us!' But no, he would not listen! Ach, he wass very troublesome!"

23 I found that I was laughing quite loudly. Everyone was laughing. Even the superintendent grinned in a tolerant way. "You'd better all come out and have a drink," he said quite genially. "I've got a bottle of whisky in the car. We could do with it."

24 We went through the big double gates of the prison, into the road. "Pulling at his legs!" exclaimed a Burmese magistrate suddenly, and burst into a loud chuckling. We all began laughing again. At that moment Francis's anecdote seemed extraordinarily funny. We all had a drink together, native and European alike, quite amicably. The dead man was a hundred yards away.

Building Vocabulary

Find the following words in the essay. Write brief definitions for each without using a dictionary. If the words are unfamiliar, try to figure out their meaning based on the context in which they appear:

1. sodden (par. 1)
2. desolately (par. 3)
3. aghast (par. 6)
4. solemn (par. 10)
5. abominable (par. 13)
6. oscillated (par. 16)
7. snigger (par. 17)
8. garrulously (par. 20)
9. genially (par. 23)
10. amicably (par. 24)

Thinking Critically About the Argument

Understanding the Writer's Argument

1. Recount, in outline form, the events in Orwell's essay.
2. How much does Orwell, as the narrator, actually participate in the hanging? Is he neutral or involved? Why do you think Orwell makes that choice for his essay?
3. What makes Orwell start thinking about the nature of the death penalty?
4. What does he mean in paragraph 10 by "solemn foolery"?
5. What is Orwell's speculation as to why the superintendent pokes the ground with his stick in paragraph 13?
6. Why does everyone laugh after the hanging, in your opinion?

Understanding the Writer's Techniques

1. What is Orwell's claim in this essay? Is there an explicit statement in which he states his claim? If not, how does the essay succeed without one?
2. Explain how Orwell's description of the jail and the weather help him to make his point. Give specific examples.
3. In paragraph 10, what is the argumentative effect of the phrase "one world less"? Why it is effective?
4. What is Orwell's tone? Point out his uses of irony in this essay. Explain how irony contributes to his argument.
5. Why does Orwell point out that the hangman is also a prisoner?
6. What is the significance of the dog for Orwell's argument?
7. What is the effect of Orwell's outburst at the end of paragraph 13?

Exploring the Writer's Argument

1. Between paragraphs 9 and 10, Orwell begins thinking about the morality of executing the prisoner. What triggers his thoughts? Is this an effective technique, or is it too abrupt and transparent a transition?
2. How does Orwell's description of the immediate aftermath of the execution affect his argument? Is it acceptable that he describes it so matter-of-factly? Why or why not?
3. How does the fact that Orwell writes this essay as a narrative help or harm his argument? What does his choice of form *not* allow him to do? What are the inherent limitations of this form?
4. What do you think the condemned man did to deserve his punishment?

Ideas for Writing Arguments

Prewriting

What ethical arguments do you see for and against the death penalty?

Writing a Guided Argument

One argument for the death penalty is often that it keeps other people who might be considering murder from doing it. Write an essay in which you argue that the death penalty is or is not a deterrent to future murders. Do some research on the topic, and find articles that address the issue of deterrence specifically before your make your choice. Title your essay "Death Penalty as a Deterrent."

1. Open your essay with a reference to an article that you have found in the course of your research, summarizing the opinion of a writer who agrees with your position.
2. Use a proper and effective transition to move into a well-articulated major proposition.

3. Have at least two reasons of your own to back up your position and express them as minor propositions.
4. Support your ideas with facts taken from your research.
5. Credit the articles you use.
6. In the next section, introduce one point made by the other side.
7. Rebut the opposing view.
8. Close your essay with an appeal to the reader's emotions.

Thinking, Arguing, and Writing Collaboratively

Divide into three equal groups. Each group should prepare for a debate on the use of the death penalty for the mentally retarded. You may conduct research on this issue in the library or on the Web. The aim of the preparation should be to win a debate through persuasion. Stage the debate, with one group arguing in favor of the death penalty and the second group arguing against it. The third group will act as jury (but should also prepare for the debate so the jury is familiar with all the basic arguments surrounding the topic). The jury will then vote on a winner and articulate its reasons to the class.

Writing About the Text

Watch a movie about the death penalty, such as Tim Robbins's *Dead Man Walking* or Clint Eastwood's *True Crime.* Write an essay that compares and contrasts the film's narrative techniques for being persuasive with Orwell's techniques.

More Writing Ideas

1. In your journal, consider how you might or might not change your views on capital punishment if someone in your circle of family and friends were murdered.
2. In the next essay you will read, David Gelernter writes that "Even when we resolve in principle to go ahead [with the death penalty], we have to steel ourselves." (par. 17) What does Gelernter mean, and how does Orwell's essay reflect this idea? Write two or three paragraphs answering these questions.
3. Write an essay that argues for or against the death penalty, purely on ethical grounds. If need be, investigate further the idea of ethics before you write.

DAVID GELERNTER

What Do Murderers Deserve?

David Gelernter is a professor of computer science at Yale. In 1991 he published a book, Mirror Worlds, *that some say predicted the Internet. In 1993, he was the victim of a letter bomb, and survived, but had a long rehabilitation period. He is a leading figure in the field of artificial intelligence. He is the author of three other books:* The Muse in the Machine *(1994),* 1939: The Lost World of the Fair *(1995), and* Drawing a Life: Surviving the Unabomber *(1998). His experience of almost getting killed informs this selection, in which he discusses what punishment murderers, including his would-be murderer (who did succeed in taking the lives of three people), deserve.*

Prereading: Thinking About the Essay in Advance

Why does a country have the right to execute one of its citizens? What is the political rational for keeping the death penalty?

Words to Watch

penitent (par. 1) those who ask for forgiveness
defiles (par. 4) morally stains
equivocation (par. 6) lack of commitment
reverting (par. 9) returning
inclination (par. 10) tendency
sanctity (par. 14) holiness
capricious (par. 15) impulsive
faculties (par. 18) abilities
bestiality (par. 22) animal-like behavior
smitten (par. 24) attacked

No civilized nation ever takes the death penalty for granted; two recent cases force us to consider it yet again. A Texas woman, Karla Faye Tucker, murdered two people with a pickaxe, was said to have repented in prison, and was put to death. A Montana man, Theodore Kaczynski, murdered three people with mail bombs, did not repent, and struck a bargain with the Justice Department; he pleaded guilty and will not be executed. (He also attempted to murder others and succeeded in wounding some, myself included.) Why did we execute the penitent and spare the impenitent? However we answer this question, we surely have a duty to ask it. 1

And we ask it—I do, anyway—with a sinking feeling, because in modern America, moral upside-downness is a specialty of the house. To eliminate race prejudice we discriminate by race. We promote the cultural assimilation of immigrant children by denying them schooling in English. We throw honest citizens in jail for child abuse, relying on testimony so phony any child could see through it. Orgasm studies are okay in public 2 high schools but the Ten Commandments are not. We make a point of admiring manly women and womanly men. None of which has anything to do with capital punishment directly, but it all obliges us to approach any question about morality in modern America in the larger context of this country's desperate confusion about elementary distinctions.

3 Why execute murderers? To deter? To avenge? Supporters of the death penalty often give the first answer, opponents the second. But neither can be the whole truth. If our main goal were deterring crime, we would insist on public executions—which are not on the political agenda, and not an item that many Americans are interested in promoting. If our main goal were vengeance, we would allow the grieving parties to decide the murderer's fate; if the victim had no family or friends to feel vengeful on his behalf, we would call the whole thing off.

4 In fact, we execute murderers in order to make a communal proclamation: that murder is intolerable. A deliberate murderer embodies evil so terrible that it defiles the community. Thus the late social philosopher Robert Nisbet: "Until a catharsis has been effected through trial, through the finding of guilt and then punishment, the community is anxious, fearful, apprehensive, and above all, contaminated."

5 Individual citizens have a right and sometimes a duty to speak. A community has the right, too, and sometimes the duty. The community certifies births and deaths, creates marriages, educates children, fights invaders. In laws, deeds, and ceremonies it lays down the boundary lines of civilized life, lines that are constantly getting scuffed and needing renewal.

6 When a murder takes place, the community is obliged, whether it feels like it or not, to clear its throat and step up to the microphone. Every murder demands a communal response. Among possible responses, the death penalty is uniquely powerful because it is permanent and can never be retracted or overturned. An execution forces the community to assume forever the burden of moral certainty; it is a form of absolute speech that allows no waffling or equivocation. Deliberate murder, the community announces, is absolutely evil and absolutely intolerable, period.

7 Of course, we could make the same point less emphatically if we wanted to—for example, by locking up murderers for life (as we sometimes do). The question then becomes: is the death penalty overdoing it? Should we make a less forceful proclamation instead?

8 The answer might be yes if we were a community in which murder was a shocking anomaly and thus in effect a solved problem. But we are not. Our big cities are full of murderers at large. "One can guesstimate," writes the criminologist and political scientist John J. Dilulio, Jr., "that we are nearing or may already have passed the day when 500,000 murderers, convicted and undetected, are living in American society."

9 Dilulio's statistics show an approach to murder so casual as to be depraved. We are reverting to a pre-civilized state of nature. Our natural bent in the face of murder is not to avenge the crime but to shrug it off, except in those rare cases when our own near and dear are involved. (And even then, it depends.)

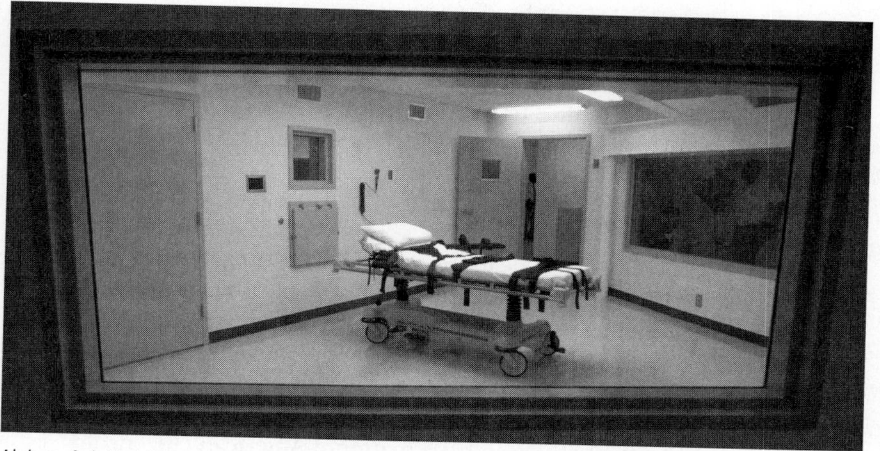

Alabama's lethal injection chamber at Holman Correctional Facility in Atmore, Ala. (Associated Press/Dave Martin)

This is an old story. Cain murders Abel and is brought in for questioning: where is Abel, your brother? The suspect's response: how should I know? "What am I, my brother's keeper?" It is one of the very first statements attributed to mankind in the Bible; voiced here by an interested party, it nonetheless expresses a powerful and universal inclination. Why mess in other people's problems? And murder is always, in the most immediate sense, someone else's problem, because the injured party is dead. 10

Murder in primitive societies called for a private settling of scores. The community as a whole stayed out of it. For murder to count, as it does in the Bible, as a crime not merely against one man but against the whole community and against God—that was a moral triumph that is still basic to our integrity, and that is never to be taken for granted. By executing murderers, the community reaffirms this moral understanding by restating the truth that absolute evil exists and must be punished. 11

Granted (some people say), the death penalty is a communal proclamation; it is nevertheless an incoherent one. If our goal is to affirm that human life is more precious than anything else, how can we make such a declaration by destroying life? 12

But declaring that human life is more precious than anything else is not our goal in imposing the death penalty. Nor is the proposition true. The founding fathers pledged their lives (and fortunes and sacred honor) to the cause of freedom; Americans have traditionally believed that some things are more precious than life. ("Living in a sanitary age, we are getting so we place too high a value on human life—which rightfully must always come second to human ideas." Thus E.B. White in 1938, pondering the Munich pact ensuring "peace in our time" between the Western powers and Hitler.) The point of capital punishment is not to pronounce on life in general but on the crime of murder. 13

14 Which is not to say that the sanctity of human life does not enter the picture. Taking a life, says the Talmud (in the course of discussing Cain and Abel), is equivalent to destroying a whole world. The rabbis used this statement to make a double point: to tell us why murder is the gravest of crimes, and to warn against false testimony in a murder trial. But to believe in the sanctity of human life does not mean, and the Talmud does not say it means, that capital punishment is ruled out.

15 A newer objection grows out of the seemingly random way in which we apply capital punishment. The death penalty might be a reasonable communal proclamation in principle, some critics say, but it has become so garbled in practice that it has lost all significance and ought to be dropped. Dilulio writes that "the ratio of persons murdered to persons executed for murder from 1977 to 1996 was in the ballpark of 1,000 to 1"; the death penalty has become in his view "arbitrary and capricious," a "state lottery" that is "unjust both as a matter of Judeo-Christian ethics and as a matter of American citizenship."

16 We can grant that, on the whole, we are doing a disgracefully bad job of administering the death penalty. After all, we are divided and confused on the issue. The community at large is strongly in favor of capital punishment; the cultural elite is strongly against it. Our attempts to speak with assurance as a community come out sounding in consequence like a man who is fighting off a choke-hold as he talks. But a community as cavalier about murder as we are has no right to back down. That we are botching things does not entitle us to give up.

17 Opponents of capital punishment tend to describe it as a surrender to our emotions—to grief, rage, fear, blood lust. For most supporters of the death penalty, this is exactly false. Even when we resolve in principle to go ahead, we have to steel ourselves. Many of us would find it hard to kill a dog, much less a man. Endorsing capital punishment means not that we yield to our emotions but that we overcome them. (Immanuel Kant, the great advocate of the death penalty precisely on moral grounds, makes this point in his reply to the anticapital-punishment reformer Cesare Beccaria—accusing Beccaria of being "moved by sympathetic sentimentality and an affectation of humanitarianism.") If we favor executing murderers it is not because we want to but because, however much we do not want to, we consider ourselves obliged to.

18 Many Americans, of course, no longer feel that obligation. The death penalty is hard for us as a community above all because of our moral evasiveness. For at least a generation, we have urged one another to switch off our moral faculties. "Don't be judgmental!" We have said it so many times, we are starting to believe it.

19 The death penalty is a proclamation about absolute evil, but many of us are no longer sure that evil even exists. We define evil out of existence by calling it "illness"—a tendency Aldous Huxley anticipated in his novel *Brave New World* (1932) and Robert Nisbet wrote about in 1982: "America has lost the villain, the evil one, who has now become one of the sick, the disturbed. . . . America has lost the moral value of guilt, lost it to the sickroom."

20 Our refusal to look evil in the face is no casual notion; it is a powerful drive. Thus we have (for example) the terrorist Theodore Kaczynski, who

planned and carried out a hugely complex campaign of violence with a clear goal in mind. It was the goal most terrorists have: to get famous and not die. He wanted public attention for his ideas about technology; he figured he could get it by attacking people with bombs.

He was right. His plan succeeded. It is hard to imagine a more compelling proof of mental competence than this planning and carrying out over decades of a complex, rational strategy. (Evil, yes; irrational, no; they are different things.) The man himself has said repeatedly that he is perfectly sane, knew what he was doing, and is proud of it. 21

To call such a man insane seems to me like deliberate perversity. But many people do. Some of them insist that his thoughts about technology constitute "delusions," though every terrorist holds strong beliefs that are wrong, and many nonterrorists do, too. Some insist that sending bombs through the mail is ipso facto proof of insanity—as if the 20th century had not taught us that there is no limit to the bestiality of which sane men are capable. 22

Where does this perversity come from? I said earlier that the community at large favors the death penalty, but intellectuals and the cultural elite tend to oppose it. This is not (I think) because they abhor killing more than other people do, but because the death penalty represents absolute speech from a position of moral certainty, and doubt is the black-lung disease of the intelligentsia—an occupational hazard now inflicted on the culture as a whole. 23

American intellectuals have long differed from the broader community—particularly on religion, crime and punishment, education, family, the sexes, race relations, American history, taxes and public spending, the size and scope of government, art, the environment, and the military. (Otherwise, I suppose, they and the public have been in perfect accord.) But not until the late 60's and 70's were intellectuals finally in a position to act on their convictions. Whereupon they attacked the community's moral certainties with the enthusiasm of guard dogs leaping at throats.* The result is an American community smitten with the disease of intellectual doubt—or, in this case, self-doubt. 24

The failure of our schools is a consequence of our self-doubt, of our inability to tell children that learning is not fun and they are required to master certain topics whether they want to or not. The tortured history of modern American race relations grows out of our self-doubt; we passed a civil-rights act in 1964, then lost confidence immediately in our ability to make a race-blind society work; racial preferences codify our refusal to believe in our own good faith. During the late stages of the cold war, many Americans laughed at the idea that the American way was morally superior or the Soviet Union was an "evil empire"; some are still laughing. Within their own community and the American community at large, doubting intellectuals have taken refuge (as doubters often do) in bullying, to the point where many of us are now so uncomfortable at the prospect of confronting evil that we turn away and change the subject. 25

---

*I have written about this before in "How the Intellectuals Took Over (And What to Do About It)," *Commentary*, March 1997.

26 Returning then to the penitent woman and the impenitent man: the Karla Faye Tucker case is the harder of the two. We are told that she repented of the vicious murders she committed. If that is true, we would still have had no business forgiving her, or forgiving any murderer. As Dennis Prager has written apropos this case, only the victim is entitled to forgive, and the victim is silent. But showing mercy to penitents is part of our religious tradition, and I cannot imagine renouncing it categorically.

27 Why was Cain not put to death, but condemned instead to wander the earth forever? Among the answers given by the rabbis in the Midrash is that he repented. The moral category of repentance is so important, they said, that it was created before the world itself. I would therefore consider myself morally obligated to think long and hard before executing a penitent. But a true penitent would have to have renounced (as Karla Faye Tucker did) all legal attempts to overturn the original conviction. If every legal avenue has been tried and has failed, the penitence window is closed. Of course, this still leaves the difficult problem of telling counterfeit penitence from the real thing, but everything associated with capital punishment is difficult.

28 As for Kaczynski, the prosecutors who accepted the murderer's plea-bargain say they got the best outcome they could, under the circumstances, and I believe them. But I also regard this failure to execute a cold-blooded impenitent terrorist murderer as a tragic abdication of moral responsibility. The tragedy lies in what, under our confused system, the prosecutors felt compelled to do. The community was called on to speak unambiguously. It flubbed its lines, shrugged its shoulders, and walked away.

29 Which brings me back to our moral condition as a community. I can describe our plight better in artistic than in philosophical terms. The most vivid illustrations I know of self-doubt and its consequences are the paintings and sculptures of Alberto Giacometti (who died in 1966). Giacometti was an artist of great integrity; he was consumed by intellectual and moral self-doubt, which he set down faithfully. His sculpted figures show elongated, shriveled human beings who seem corroded by acid, eaten-up to the bone, hurt and weakened past fragility nearly to death. They are painful to look at. And they are natural emblems of modem America. We ought to stick one on top of the Capitol and think it over.

30 In executing murderers, we declare that deliberate murder is absolutely evil and absolutely intolerable. This is a painfully difficult proclamation for a self-doubting community to make. But we dare not stop trying. Communities may exist in which capital punishment is no longer the necessary response to deliberate murder. America today is not one of them.

Building Vocabulary

1. In this essay, Gelernter uses several words and phrases that derive from other languages. Look up the following and write a definition for each:
   a. catharsis (par. 4)
   b. anomaly (par. 8)
   c. cavalier (par. 16)

d. ipso facto (par. 22)
e. apropos (par. 26)
f. abdication (par. 28)

2. Identify and define the following:
    a. assimilation (par. 2)
    b. retracted (par. 6)
    c. depraved (par. 9)
    d. integrity (par. 11)
    e. incoherent (par. 12)
    f. evasiveness (par. 18)
    g. abhor (par. 23)
    h. plea-bargain (par. 28)

Thinking Critically About the Argument

Understanding the Writer's Argument

1. Why does the writer choose the Tucker and Kaczynski cases to start his essay? Why does he think that in modern America, "moral upside-downness is a specialty of the house"? Explain this quote.
2. What is the rationale for executing murderers, according to Gelernter?
3. Why does John Dilulio's statistic in paragraph 8 "show an approach to murder so casual as to be depraved"?
4. How does the writer characterize the progress in crime and punishment from primitive society to today? (par. 11) What does he say to the objection that capital punishment is not administered effectively?
5. What is "bloodlust"? In your own words, summarize Gelernter's answer to the objection that being a supporter of the death penalty is "bloodlust."
6. What is perverse about calling a murderer insane? (par. 22)
7. Why is "self-doubt" such a problem in the United States, according to the writer?
8. What do Giacometti's sculptures have to do with the death penalty?

Understanding the Writer's Techniques

1. What sentence best states Gelernter's major proposition? What is his major argumentative purpose in this essay? Is he trying to convince the reader? Explain.
2. Paraphrase the writer's argument in paragraph 3.
3. What is the writer's overall tone? How and why does he develop this tone? Who is his audience?
4. What is the persuasive effect of the writer's argument in paragraph 9? Does it work? Explain your answer.
5. Analyze the writer's use of quotes from other writers. How well does he succeed in using them to advance his own claim?

6. Do you find effective the writer's argument in paragraph 13, that life isn't always the most precious thing? Explain.
7. Does paragraph 14 find the writer backing off from the earlier argument? Why or why not?
8. How effective is the conclusion?

Exploring the Writer's Argument

1. Analyze Gelernter's argument in paragraph 16. Do you think that his point is valid? Why or why not? What do you think of this statement: "That we are botching things does not entitle us to give up"? Do you think he's right? Explain.
2. Gelernter says that America is morally upside-down. He cites, for one, the fact that we try to right racial discrimination by affirmative action. Isn't calling for the death for murderers just as morally upside-down? Does he address this issue sufficiently? Explain your answers.
3. Gelernter was the victim of attempted murder by the hands of Theodore Kaczynski. To what degree do you think Gelernter's argument is affected by his experience? Explain your answer, addressing specifically the section in paragraphs 20 through 22.

Ideas for Writing Arguments

Prewriting

Freewrite for 15 minutes about the difference between your emotions about the death penalty and your intellectual consideration of the subject. Which do you trust more? Why?

Writing a Guided Argument

The Unabomber, Kaczynski, almost killed Gelernter and succeeded in killing three people. Investigate the Unabomber case and his trial. Why, despite the fact that Kaczynski never repented, did he not get the death penalty for his premeditated crimes? Write an essay in which you argue that it was right that he was spared and got the punishment he deserved, or that he should have been executed. Address Gelernter's statement in paragraph 28 that the community "flubbed its lines, shrugged its shoulders, and walked away."

1. Begin your essay with a summary of the case.
2. State your major proposition clearly.
3. Establish a tone of objectivity throughout your essay, while still being persuasive.
4. Offer at least three well-placed minor propositions to support your major proposition.
5. Support your minor propositions with examples and facts.
6. Refer to Gelernter's essay and argument at least twice.
7. Build up to what you think is your strongest minor proposition.
8. Close your essay with a classical argument for or against the death penalty in general, depending on your position.

Thinking, Arguing, and Writing Collaboratively

In small groups, exchange drafts of the paper you wrote for the Writing a Guided Argument assignment with a fellow student. Write a paragraph of comments to help your peer develop his or her argument. Exchange your paper with another student and compare the feedback. Are they consistent? Why or why not?

Writing About the Text

Write an essay expanding on your consideration of Gelernter's tone and analyzing how his tone affects his argumentative claim. Do you think it helps or hurts his argument? Pay attention, especially, to whether he ever gets cynical. What is his tone in paragraph 24?

More Writing Ideas

1. In your journal, write notes for an essay that examines whether or not you consider life imprisonment a "cruel and unusual" punishment.
2. Write a paragraph in which you argue for this idea: "Penitence doesn't matter—if someone does a crime, they must be punished."
3. Based on Gelernter's arguments on self-doubt and his comments in paragraphs 2 and 25, write an essay in which you argue that Gelernter would be against affirmative action, explaining why you think that is true.

27 The Internet: What Are the Prospects for Cyberspace?

In the past decade, we have witnessed a huge change in the way we live our lives. When the Internet started in the 1970s and 1980s, only governments and scientists used it in order to exchange information. In the early 1990s, consumer technology advanced and Marc Andreeson developed the extraordinary graphical browser, called Mosaic, which became Netscape Navigator. Soon, the World Wide Web was big news. We forget, but before the Internet, people had to shop in person at stores or through the use of catalogs. People wrote letters to each other. People got their news from the radio or newspapers. Now, because of the new technologies everything has changed, from basic communication between family members and friends to dating to politics. Almost all business done around the world involves the Internet at some point.

With the rise of such a revolutionary technology has come an army of writers trying to understand the change and trying to explain it to their readers. The following four selections suggest the wide range of arguments you will find about the Internet. In "I Surf, Therefore I Am," Judith Levine explores the dangers of students relying on the Internet in doing research. Dave Barry, on the other hand, in "ERROR, ERROR, ERROR," humorously conveys his very real frustration over having to switch to a digital workspace. Humor is a technique Barry and other humorists have shown to be a powerful and quite persuasive tool (in part because of the entertainment value—the reader stays interested). Another effective and stealthy way of being persuasive is to give advice. Beth Brophy writes about the variety of online dating problems in "Saturday Night and You're All Alone? Maybe You Need a Cyberdate" and is able to push her own point of view on the topic without being confrontational. Andrew Brown, on the other hand, makes it very clear what his argument is in "The Limits of Freedom," a selection that argues for censorship in some cases.

JUDITH LEVINE
I Surf, Therefore I Am

Author and journalist Judith Levine was born in 1952 in New York City. She is an activist for free speech and sex education, the founder of the feminist group No More Nice Girls, and is active in the National Writers Union. She has published many articles in

Ms., Mother Jones, *and* The Village Voice, *among other publications. She is the author of* My Enemy, My Love: Women, Men, and the Dilemmas of Gender *(1992) and, most recently, of* Harmful to Minors: The Perils of Protecting Children from Sex *(1999), a book that rethinks how we approach the topic of sexuality in children and teenagers. The book was quickly denounced by conservatives, who accused Levine of endorsing pedophilia. The following selection, which examines the content of what we read when we surf the Internet, appeared in the online magazine* Salon *in its Mothers Who Think column in 1997.*

Prereading: Thinking About the Essay in Advance

Is reading on the Web the same as reading in the book or magazine or newspaper? Does the information stick with you as long? What kind of reading leaves your head the quickest?

Words to Watch

bestowed (par. 1) donated
scant (par. 4) not sufficient
encumbrance (par. 5) a burden
corral (par. 5) organize
etiology (par. 5) cause, as of a disease
promiscuous (par. 5) casual
gleaned (par. 7) picked up, gathered
think tanks (par. 8) institutions often founded for political research
stratospheric (par. 12) extremely high
relinquishing (par. 12) giving up

"Obviously, I'm somebody who believes that personal computers are empowering tools," Bill Gates said after he bestowed a $200 million gift to America's public libraries so they could hook up to the Internet. 1

"People are entitled to disagree," Gates said. "But I would invite them to visit some of these libraries and see the impact on kids using this technology." 2

Well, I have seen the impact, and I disagree. Many of my students—undergraduate media and communications majors at a New York university—have access to the endless information bubbling through cyberspace, and *it is not* empowering. 3

Most of the data my students Net is like trash fish—and it is hard for them to tell a dead one-legged crab from a healthy sea bass. Scant on world knowledge and critical thinking skills, they are ill-equipped to interpret or judge the so-called facts, which they insert into their papers confidently but in no discernible order. 4

Their writing often "clicks" from info-bit to info-bit, their arguments free of that gluey, old-fashioned encumbrance—the transitional sentence. When I try to help them corral their impressions into coherent stories, I keep hearing 5 the same complaint: "I can't concentrate." I've diagnosed this phenomenon as epidemic attention deficit disorder. And I can't help but trace its etiology, at least in part, to the promiscuous pointing and clicking that has come to stand in for intellectual inquiry.

6 These students surf; therefore, they do not read. They do not read scholarly articles—which can be trusted because they are juried or challenged because they are footnoted. They do not read books—which tell stories and sustain arguments by placing idea and metaphor one on top of the other, so as to hold weight, like a stone wall. Even the journalism students read few magazines and even fewer newspapers, which are edited by people with recognizable and sometimes even admitted cultural and political biases and checked by fact-checkers using other edited sources.

7 On the Net, nobody knows if any particular "fact" is a dog. One student handed in a paper about tobacco companies' liability for smokers' health, which she had gleaned almost entirely from the Web pages of the Tobacco Institute. Did she know what the Tobacco Institute is? Apparently not, because she had done her research on the Net, and was deprived of the modifying clause, "a research organization supported by the tobacco industry," obligatory in any edited news article.

8 Another young woman, writing about teen pregnancy, used data generated by the Family Research Council, which, along with other right-wing Christian think tanks, dominates the links on many subjects related to family and sexuality and offers a decidedly one-sided view.

9 A teacher at another school told me one of her students had written a paper quoting a person who had a name but no identifying characteristics. "Who's this?" the professor asked. "Someone with a Web page," the young man said.

10 If there is no context on the Net, neither is there history. My friend who teaches biology told me her students propose research that was completed, and often discredited, 50 years ago. "They go online," she said, "where nothing has been indexed before 1980."

11 A San Francisco librarian interviewed on National Public Radio worried that, space and resources strained as they are, more computers will inevitably mean fewer books. Another commentator on the Gates gift suggested that the computers would not be very valuable without commensurate human resources—that is, trained workers to help people use them.

12 At New York's gleaming new Science, Industry, & Business Library (SIBL), you can sit in an ergonomically correct chair at one of several hundred lovely color computer terminals and call up, among hundreds of other databases, the powerful journalistic and legal service Nexis/Lexis. But since Nexis/Lexis is in great demand, you have about 45 minutes at the screen, half of which the inexperienced user will blow figuring out the system, because there is only one harassed staff person to assist all the computer-users. Then you'll learn that the library cannot afford the stratospheric fees for downloading the articles. So most users, I imagine, will manage to copy out quotes from a couple of articles before relinquishing the seat to the next person waiting for the cyber-kiosk.

Unlike a paper or microfilm version of the same pieces, which could be photocopied or copied at leisure onto a pad or laptop, the zillion articles available on the library's Nexis/Lexis are more or less unavailable—that is, to no avail. Useless. 13

Technology may empower, but how and to what end will that power be used? What else is necessary to use it well and wisely? I'd suggest, for a start, reading books—literature and history, poetry and politics—and listening to people who know what they're talking about. Otherwise, the brains of those kids in Gates' libraries will be glutted with "information" but bereft of ideas, rich in tools but clueless about what to build or how to build it. Like the search engines that retrieve more than 100,000 links or none at all, they will be awkward at discerning meaning, or discerning at all. 14

Building Vocabulary

Write definitions of the following and use them in sentences of your own:

1. discernible (par. 4)
2. epidemic (par. 5)
3. obligatory (par. 7)
4. ergonomically correct (par. 12)
5. glutted (par. 14)
6. bereft (par. 14)

Thinking Critically About the Argument

Understanding the Writer's Argument

1. What does Levine mean when she says in paragraph 4 that "most of the data my students Net is like trash fish"?
2. What is "the transitional sentence" (par. 5), and why is it important?
3. What is attention deficit disorder?
4. Why, according to Levine, is it important to read books, magazines, and newspapers?
5. Levine's student handed in a paper about tobacco for which she got research only from the Tobacco Institute. Why was Levine less than happy about this?
6. What is the risk, according to Levine, with adding so many computers to libraries?
7. What are the downsides to Lexis/Nexis at the public library?

Understanding the Writer's Techniques

1. What is the argumentative effect in the beginning of Levine's essay, when she openly disagrees with Bill Gates, chairman and founder of Microsoft and an expert of computers?
2. Where does Levine articulate her major proposition most clearly? What minor propositions does Levine offer to support her ideas?

3. Analyze why Levine places her minor propositions in the order she does. Is there a strategy at work? Explain your answer.
4. How would you characterize the tone that Levine uses in this essay? Is it effective in helping her argument?
5. What popular saying about computers does Levine satirize in the first sentence of paragraph 7?
6. What evidence does Levine use to support her idea that students today are not aware of the source of what they are reading online?
7. How effective is Levine's conclusion? Why does she return her discussion to Bill Gates's libraries?

Exploring the Writer's Argument

1. Levine wrote this article for *Salon* magazine, a publication that is only available on the Web. How can she publish an article criticizing online writing in an online magazine? How does that affect the writing? Explain your answer.
2. Prove Levine wrong. Pretend you are doing a research paper on a topic such as abortion or flag burning. Go to the Internet and print out four articles: two should be "trash fish," as Levine says in paragraph 4, and two should be from a respectable news source.
3. In paragraphs 12 and 13, it seems as if Levine relies too much on one example. What point is she trying to make? What could she do to improve this section? Explain fully.

Ideas for Writing Arguments

Prewriting

In your Web surfing time between classes, pay closer attention to your reading habits online. Write notes later analyzing whether what you read is worth reading.

Writing a Guided Argument

There is a debate among librarians and in communities around the country over the censorship of the Internet in libraries. Free Internet access in libraries is, in some communities, the only way for people to get online. However, through ease of availability everyone has access to pornography and information that could harm others. There are software filters that could stop viewers from visiting some sites, but the filters are imperfect and many find the idea of filters to violate First Amendment rights to free speech. Write an essay in which you argue that Internet access in libraries should or should not be censored. Do some research in the library (not online) to gather evidence for your position.

1. Open your essay by briefly outlining the issue.
2. Write your major proposition clearly and in strong language.

3. Affect a tone similar to Levine's.
4. Explain your minor propositions, offering ample support in the form of fact and examples.
5. Entertain one opposing view with a clear rebuttal.
6. Close your essay by referring in some useful way to the First Amendment.

Thinking, Arguing, and Writing Collaboratively

In small groups, exchange your Writing a Guided Argument papers with another student. Spend at least 15 minutes going through your classmate's paper, commenting on the following categories: (1) strength of basic argument, (2) argumentative effect of support, (3) grammar and quality of the prose, and (4) transitions. Write a short paragraph for your classmate about each of these categories, and give back the paper. Review your peer's comments, and discuss any questions you have.

Writing About the Text

Expand on question 4 in the Understanding the Writer's Techniques section. Levine seems to have a cynical edge to her tone. Write an essay that analyzes the use of cynicism and irony in her article.

More Writing Ideas

1. How has the way you get your news and information changed over the past few years? What do you rely on the Internet for? Answer these questions in a journal entry. Compare your answers with those of a classmate. Are your answers similar? Different? How?
2. Just how real is the threat to books by computers, the Internet, Web sites, e-mail, and so on? Write an extended paragraph to argue your position.
3. Write an essay in the form of a letter from Bill Gates to Judith Levine defending his decision to give $200 million to libraries to hook up to the Internet.

DAVE BARRY
Error Error Error

Humorist Dave Barry was born in Armonk, New York, in 1947 and, as he says, "has been steadily growing older ever since without ever actually reaching maturity." He was educated at Haverford College and worked as a reporter at a local Pennsylvania newspaper. From there he went to work in business, but he soon returned to the world of newspapers at the The Miami Herald. *He won the Pulitzer Prize for commentary in 1988 for his column, which is syndicated in several hundred newspapers. Barry is the author of* Babies and Other Hazards of Sex, Dave Barry Slept Here: A Sort of History of the United States, Dave Barry in Cyberspace, *and* Dave Barry Turns 40. *In this selection from his column, Barry, tongue firmly planted in cheek, explains why computers are far from the time-saving devices we think they are.*

Prereading: Thinking About the Essay in Advance

Do you think the personal computer has increased productivity, or has it just added another level of distraction and complication to our lives?

Words to Watch

wary (par. 6) suspiciously cautious
transmit (par. 8) send
mullet (par. 11) species of fish
pertinent (par. 13) to the point

1 Without question the most important invention in human history, next to frozen yogurt, is the computer. Without computers, it would be virtually impossible for us to accomploiwur xow;gkc,mf(&(

2 Hold it, there seems to be a keyboard problem here. Let me just try plugging this cable into . . .

3 ERROR ERROR ERROR ALL FILES HAVE BEEN DESTROYED YOU STUPID BAZOOTYHEAD

4 Ha ha! Considering what a wonderful invention computers are, they certainly have a way of making you sometimes feel like pouring coffee into their private parts and listening to them scream. Of course you should not do this. The first rule of data processing is: "Never pour hot beverages into a computer, unless it belongs to somebody else, such as your employer."

5 For many of us, the first "hands-on" experience with computers occurs in the workplace. This was certainly true in the newspaper business. One day we reporters came to work and discovered that our old, slow, horse-drawn typewriters had been replaced by sleek, efficient computers with keys that said mysterious scary things like "BREAK" and "NUM LOCK." Fortunately we were trained by highly skilled professional computer personnel who spoke no English. "Before you macro your ASCII, you have to format your RAM," they would advise us, in a tone of voice clearly suggesting that any member of the vegetable family should know this instinctively.

6 So we reporters were wary at first, but after just 175 weeks of training, we discovered that, instead of writing on clumsy, old-fashioned paper, we could create lengthy stories entirely on the computer screen, and then, simply by pushing a button, send them to the Planet Zembar. Or maybe even farther. We definitely couldn't find them anywhere in the building.

7 "WHERE THE HELL IS MY STORY??" we would say, shaking the computer personnel by their necks. But the lost stories always turned out to be

our own fault. We had invariably committed some basic bonehead data-processing error such as—you are going to laugh when I tell you this—failing to modem our ROM BIOS VGA megahertz cache.

But gradually we got the hang of it, and today we journalists routinely use highly sophisticated, multimillion-dollar computer systems to perform a function that is vital to the survival of a free society, namely, sending personal messages to each other. Walk into a newspaper office, and you'll see serious-looking journalists clattering away on their keyboards; it looks as though they're writing important stories about the plight of the Kurds, but in fact they're sending each other the joke about what the male giraffe said to the female giraffe in the bar. In the old days, journalists had to transmit jokes manually. 8

Also computers now have "spell-checkers," which enable us to catch and correct common misspellings such as "bazootiehead." 9

Of course there are some problems. You have probably read about computer "viruses," which computers get when they're left uncovered in drafty rooms. This is bad, because if you're working on an infected computer, it will periodically emit electronic sneezes, which unfortunately are not detectable by the naked eye—the word "ACHOO" appears on the screen for less than a millionth of a second—and you'll be showered with billions of tiny invisible pieces of electronic phlegm, called "bytes," which penetrate into your brain and gradually make you stupid. 10

This is definitely happening to me. I'll sit down at my home computer to write a thoughtful column about, say, foreign policy, and I'll type: "In view of the recent dramatic changes in the world geopolitical situation, it's time to play some solitaire." My computer has a solitaire-playing program on it, probably invented by the Japanese in an effort to sabotage the American economy. I used to think solitaire was boring, but now that my brain is clogged with computer boogers. I find it more fascinating than, say, the Sistine Chapel. I spend hours moving the little electronic cards around, staring at the screen with the same facial expression as a mullet, while the computer sneezes on me. None of this was possible just 15 years ago. 11

The computer is also a great teaching tool for young people. For example, my home computer has an educational program that enables you to control an entire simulated planet—its ecology, its technology, its weather, etc. My 10-year-old son and his friends use this program a lot, and we've all learned some important ecological lessons, the main one being: Never, ever put 10-year-old boys in charge of a planet ("Let's see what happens when you have volcanoes AND nuclear war!"). 12

So if you don't already have a home computer, I strongly recommend that you get one. Of course before you buy, you'll want to know the answers to some pertinent questions, especially: What DID the male giraffe say to the female giraffe in the bar? The answer—this'll kill you—is: "The higpowoifj &kjfkjO,dmjd ERROR ERROR ERROR." 13

Building Vocabulary

Although this is a humor essay, Barry uses computer terms because he assumes that his reader knows and understand them. This helps his jokes. Define the following terms and the purpose they serve in a computer:

1. NUM LOCK (par. 5)
2. macro (par. 5)
3. ASCII (par. 5)
4. RAM (par. 5)
5. modem (par. 7)
6. megahertz (par. 7)
7. cache (par. 7)
8. viruses (par. 10)

Thinking Critically About the Argument

Understanding the Writer's Argument

1. Why have newspaper reporters had a difficult time getting to know computers, according to Barry?
2. What, according to Barry, do journalists do with all this high-tech equipment?
3. What point is Barry making with his joke that when he sits down to write a serious article, he ends up playing solitaire? (par. 11)
4. What point does Barry make with his punchline, "None of this was possible just 15 years ago"? (par. 11)

Understanding the Writer's Techniques

1. Does Barry have a major proposition here? If so, what is it? If not, what is his argument about?
2. Barry's essay is obviously a series of jokes, but it has a serious point. How does Barry make his argument? Outline Barry's essay, listing his main points.
3. What is Barry's tone? Point out the instances when you notice him using irony.
4. Explain how jokes such as Barry's require the use of irony.
5. How does the scenario Barry describes in paragraph 11 help his argument?
6. Analyze Barry's closing. Why is it effective? Why is it funny?
7. How effective is the title of this essay? What does it achieve?

Exploring the Writer's Argument

1. Barry is a well-respected humorist, and his columns are always funny, but some say that his humor can be a little uneven. List at least three places where you think Barry has gone too far in his humor and earns a groan from his reader instead of a laugh. Explain your choices.

2. How does Barry's use of language and sentence structure help him achieve his goals?
3. To what degree is Barry's critique of computers fair? Which is the fairest argument? Which is the silliest complaint?

Ideas for Writing Arguments

Prewriting

What is the worst computer-glitch story you know?

Writing a Guided Argument

Write a humorous essay in which you argue that time-and-labor-saving computers have actually made *students'* lives more difficult.

1. Write your essay with a straightforward style. You should play it straight and allow your content to be funny.
2. Open your essay with the statement, "The computer has been the greatest thing to happen to students since . . ." (write your own comparison—for example, the keg).
3. Support your claim with at least three minor propositions.
4. Model your minor propositions on Barry's, as in paragraph 8.
5. Support your minor propositions by starting seriously and ending absurdly.
6. Balance long paragraphs with occasional short paragraphs.
7. Try to close your essay with a reprise of an earlier joke, as Barry reprises the "bazootiehead" joke.

Thinking, Arguing, and Writing Collaboratively

In small groups, share your stories from the Prewriting assignment, and help each other come up with potential subjects for extended paragraphs. Write the paragraphs, arguing for a lesson that you have learned from a computer-glitch horror story. Exchange the paragraphs with classmates, and give each other comments for revision.

Writing About the Text

On the Web or in the library, look up another two essays written by Dave Barry and compare and contrast them with "ERROR ERROR ERROR." What is consistent in his style? Do you see any differences? Write an essay analyzing the Barry style.

More Writing Ideas

1. Write a journal entry about spell-checkers in which you use as many large words and proper nouns as possible. Type your entry into a word-processing program and run a spell-check program. Accept each of the program's suggestions for spellings. Read your journal entry to the class. How has the spell-checker changed your meaning?

2. In a paragraph, describe how you think the future of entertainment will be affected by the Internet.
3. Write an essay in which you argue that trading music online is either morally wrong or morally acceptable. If necessary, do research to gather evidence for your argument.

Beth Brophy

Saturday Night and You're All Alone? Maybe You Need a Cyberdate

A Washington, D.C. journalist who has written for Forbes *magazine and* USA Today, *Beth Brophy is the author of* My Ex-Best Friend *(2003), a mystery novel about a suburban mother who solves a friend's murder. In this selection, which appeared in* U.S. News & World Report *in 1997, Brophy demystifies the subject of online dating by giving her take on everything from safety to the question of whether flirting online is actually cheating.*

Prereading: Thinking About the Essay in Advance

Have you tried online dating? Do you know anyone who has? What was your experience or your friend's experience? Was it a positive one? Negative? Why?

Words to Watch

infatuation (par. 3) romantic obsession
dalliance (par. 5) casual romance
clandestine (par. 6) secret
tryst (par. 6) illicit love affair
relented (par. 6) gave up
paradox (par. 7) something seemingly self-contradictory
personas (par. 7) personalities a person puts forth in front of other people

1 *Forget roses, candlelit dinners, pillow talk—or even two people in the same room. And read on for answers to those burning questions.*

2 **How is cyberdating different from meeting at a club?** It's a lot different. Everybody in cyberspace is tall, thin, blond, and rich—at least in theory. Without physical cues to provide a reality check—how someone looks or speaks, or whether he leaves his dirty socks on the floor—the person on the other end can be imagined as the ideal lover. The blank computer screen becomes a projection for hopes and dreams.

3 **I meet lots of people on the Net, but most of my romances last only a day or two. How come?** It's easy to deceive in cyberspace, but it's also easy to fall into premature intimacy. Revealing secrets to a stranger can be in-

toxicating and, like most stimulants, dangerous. The Internet "seems to be laced with truth serum," says therapist Marshall Jung, co-author of *Romancing the Net.* "All this truth-telling puts enormous pressure on fledgling relationships." So it's no wonder that the cycle of "love, infatuation, and disappointment may take three weeks," says MIT sociology professor Sherry Turkle, author of *Life on the Screen.*

Unlike real time, which involves annoying waits in traffic, time in cyberspace is compressed. Sometimes that leads to impulsive actions. Old-fashioned mail, on the other hand, allows time for reflection, for letting a passionate letter sit overnight, or even for tearing it up. 4

My husband says I spend too much time online. He's worried I'll find somebody else. Is he a control freak, or what? The relationship gurus of popular culture disagree as to whether extramarital cyber-romance is cheating or not. John Gray, omnipresent author of the bestseller *Men Are From Mars, Women Are From Venus,* gets huffy about online dalliance. "Indulging in sexual arousal is adultery as far as your partner is concerned," he says. "It's not innocent and harmless; it's a betrayal." Advice columnist Ann Landers is more pragmatic: "It's not adultery; it's just foolishness," she says, "and a little bit on the sick side." 5

Cyber-romance can strain a marriage, sometimes to the breaking point. One woman, an attractive professional in her mid-30s, compares chat rooms to the temptation of drugs. Her husband's clandestine four-month Internet romance with a married woman living in another state nearly wrecked their 10-year marriage. "He wouldn't have gone to a singles bar. A friend or client might have seen him," she says. When she asked him why their monthly bill for using the Net exceeded $200, she says, her husband told her, "I'm in love with the perfect woman and I'm leaving you." His "true love" was planning to leave her husband, but plans changed following an out-of-state tryst. "Each of them thought the other was the greatest—until they actually met," the woman says. Her husband begged to come back. She relented, and they're now in marriage counseling. So ask yourself why you're spending more time online than with your husband. 6

I met this woman on the Net two months ago. She thinks I'm "Cowboy," a daring Hollywood stuntman. But really I'm just a quiet, skinny accountant. Now she wants a face to face. Help! Meet her, come clean, and hope she's been lying, too. As Cowboy's dilemma illustrates, cyberspace can lead to a curious paradox: The anonymity of a computer screen makes people bolder and often leads them to try on more daring personas. At the same time, cyberspace allows users to exert tight control over information flow, which can lead to deception and disappointment. "Online is simply a starting point. You don't already have a relationship. You have a cyberflirtation," says Rosalind Resnick, host of the Web site *LoveSearch.com,* a combination dating site, personal data base, and advice column. 7

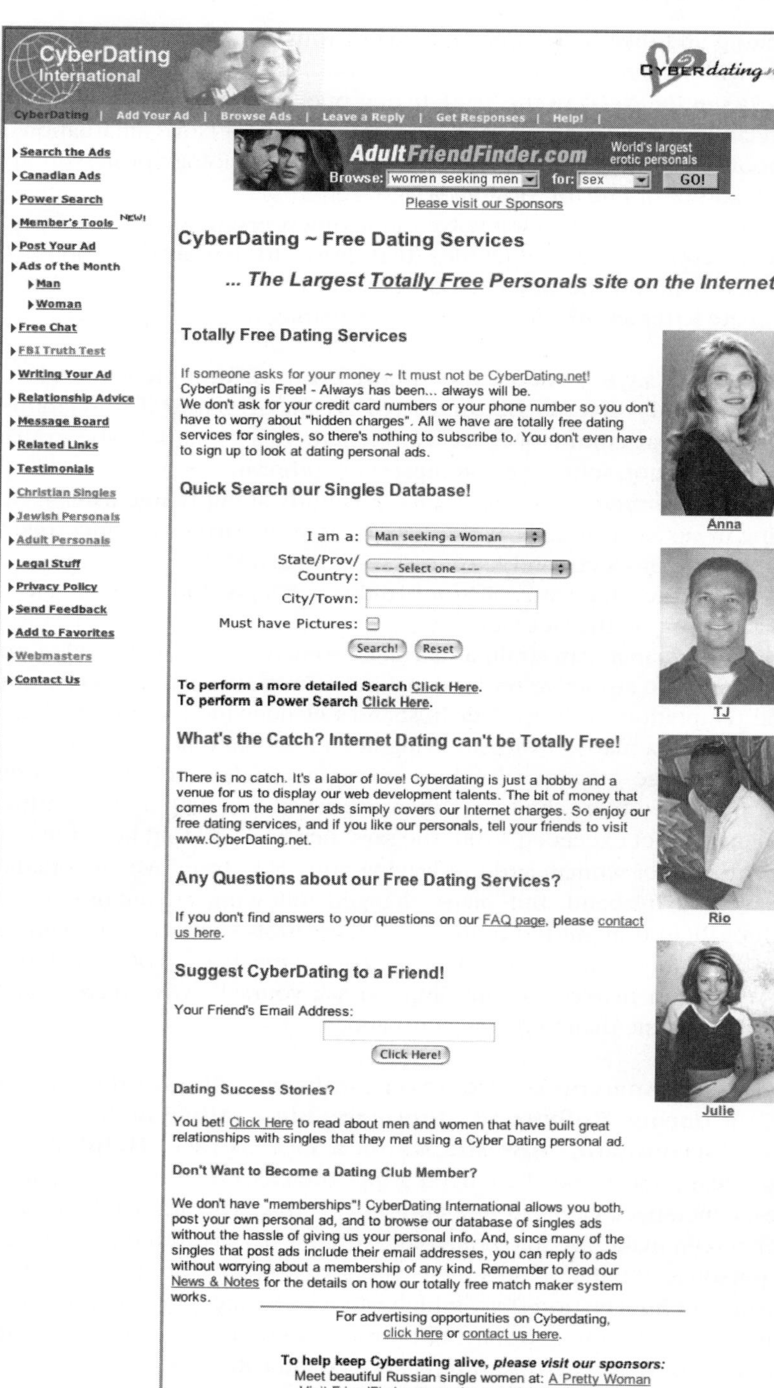

(Web site www.cyberdating.net)

I've been e-mailing somebody for three months who lives 60 miles away. I drop hints about a face to face, but he's slow on the uptake. Should I ask him directly? Sure, but be prepared for rejection. The sad fact is some people are better suited to being behind the screen—they don't want to reveal themselves in person. "True intimacy is not one aspect of the self, it's all aspects," Turkle says. "They may not be up for the lack of fantasy and the challenge of commitment." If that happens, say goodbye and try again. 8

I've heard there are weirdos on the Net, like the case of that woman who traded fantasies with a guy in an S&M chat room, met him in person and later was found strangled. Is online romance safe? Yes, there are some strange people online. But there are weirdos everywhere—in cyberspace, in singles bars, at parties, maybe even in the apartment next door. For some people, the Net offers an opportunity they despair of finding elsewhere. Melinda Stevenson who works for a Washington, D.C., international organization, says between her age and a long commute that left her exhausted at the end of the day, she'd stopped investing energy in dating. "I'm in my 40s," Stevenson says. "I'd given up." 9

But then she received an e-mail from "Bob," an avid sailor who lived in the Annapolis area. For six weeks, she and Bob e-mailed daily. Finally, Stevenson says, she "tossed out conventional wisdom" and invited him for dinner. He showed up 30 minutes later bearing "flowers, a bottle of wine, no ax—I checked." Their worst fears about each other (that she would be grossly overweight; that he would sport a comb-over hairdo) didn't materialize. Their first date lasted 10 hours—no touching, but "there was an electric sense between us," she says. After a few hours, he politely inquired if they could "share a bracket" (Web talk for hug). Three weeks later he said, "I love you." And five months after that, he proposed. The couple recently returned from their Hawaiian honeymoon. 10

I hear the Internet is a good place for shy people to meet others. Is it true? Cyberdating, says Frances Maier, general manager of Match.Com, an online personals ad service, "is not about lonely hearts. The Internet is a screener. Generally, the people on it have higher incomes and better jobs." Some shy people find that the Net allows them to meet someone outside their immediate geographic area. For example, attorney Heather Williams and 911 dispatcher Gerald Harrington, both divorced, lived 200 miles away from each other. After meeting in a chat room in December 1995, they e-mailed for two weeks, then talked on the phone. A month later Harrington drove to meet Williams. "I am a shy person who does not interact with people I do not know," he says, but the opportunity to build a relationship online first smoothed the way. "I felt totally at ease after several minutes and knew this was someone I could feel comfortable with." Within a few months, Harrington packed up his belongings and moved to Hollidaysburg, 11

Pa., to be with Williams. He proposed nine months later. They plan to marry in June.

12 Sound like a Valentine's Day fairy tale? In cyberspace, just as in face-to-face dating, things often don't work out so perfectly. Luckily, the Internet also has a Web site for divorce.

Building Vocabulary

1. Brophy uses phrases in her essay from the world of computers. Often, when a new technology is adopted, terminology from the technology it replaced seeps into its vocabulary. For example, we still say we "dial" the phone when the phone dial, the rotary phone, is long gone. Find at least three computer phrases in Brophy's essay with origins outside the world of computers, and explain why you think they were adopted.
2. In her essay, Brophy uses figurative language. In the following sentences, replace the italicized phrases with your own words:
   a. without physical cues to *provide a reality check* (par. 2)
   b. Is he *a control freak,* or what? (par. 5)
   c. I *drop hints* about a *face to face,* but he's *slow on the uptake.* (par. 8)
   d. she'd *stopped investing energy* in dating (par. 9)
   e. that he would *sport* a comb-over hairdo (par. 10)
   f. the opportunity to *build a relationship* online first *smoothed the way* (par. 11)

Thinking Critically About the Argument

Understanding the Writer's Argument

1. What is cyberdating?
2. Why can every person on a cyberdate be "the ideal lover"? (par. 2)
3. Why can cyberdating often be so intense and accelerated?
4. Does Brophy think that some online flirting is adultery? Explain.
5. Why is it that dating online makes people "bolder and often leads them to try on more daring personas"? (par. 7)
6. Does Brophy give any examples of success stories online? What are they?
7. In what way is the Internet a "screener"?

Understanding the Writer's Techniques

1. What is Brophy's major proposition? Does she have one? Explain.
2. What are the minor propositions in this essay? Make a list of the points Brophy makes.
3. Why do you think Brophy wrote this essay in the form of an advice column? How does the advice column format act as a series of rhetorical questions? Is it an effective way to cover her topic? Why or why not?
4. Who is Brophy's audience? How does that affect her tone?

5. How important is Brophy's use of quotes from experts in this essay? Do they help to convince you?
6. Evaluate Brophy's conclusion. Why does she end on the note she does? Explain.

Exploring the Writer's Argument

1. How good is Brophy's advice? What would you agree with? Disagree with? What would you add to her discussion? What would you like to see her address that she hasn't touched on?
2. Things move quickly on the Internet. Trends change almost weekly, it seems. Brophy's essay was written in 1997, ages ago in Internet years. Are any of her points outdated (so to speak)? Explain.
3. In paragraph 3, Brophy suggests that the Internet encourages people to tell the truth (too much), and in paragraph 7, she suggests that the Internet encourages people to lie about themselves. Is this a contradiction? Does it affect her argument? How? Explain your answers.

Ideas for Writing Arguments

Prewriting

How has e-mail changed the way people communicate?

Writing a Guided Argument

Write an essay that argues that people should write more letters (snail mail) and less e-mail.

1. Open your essay with an anecdote showing that e-mail can be a problem (for example, a misunderstanding or a message sent in anger).
2. Refer to paragraph 4 in Brophy's essay.
3. Move your argument into an articulation of your major proposition.
4. Offer a minor proposition that supports writing letters.
5. Expand on your idea with examples and other support.
6. Write a minor proposition in which you contrast e-mail with snail mail.
7. Repeat steps 4 through 6.
8. Adopt a tone of authority on the subject.
9. Close your essay with a positive anecdote about snail mail to counterbalance the anecdote you told at the beginning. You may refer to your intro if you like.

Thinking, Arguing, and Writing Collaboratively

In two or three paragraphs, write your own online personal ad. How can you persuade someone to answer your ad, purely through your description of yourself. Write your ad without lying about anything. When you are finished, exchange ads with a classmate. Is your classmate's ad persuasive? How are your ads similar? How are they different?

Writing About the Text

Write an essay that expands on this sentence by Brophy: "The blank computer screen becomes a projection for hopes and dreams."

More Writing Ideas

1. Find and print or cut out 10 personal ads, either from a local paper or online. In your journal, analyze the ads. Do you see any similarities? Differences?
2. Find an advice column in your local paper or online. Pick one of the questions and write your own advice to the writer in an extended paragraph.
3. Write an essay in which you argue that cyberdating is pathetic and that people should seek love in other, more social places.

ANDREW BROWN
The Limits of Freedom

Andrew Brown is a freelance journalist who writes for newspapers in his native England, including the Guardian, *the* Independent, *and the* Times, *as well as such American publications as* Vogue, The New York Times Review of Books, *and the online magazine* Salon. *He writes mostly about biology, religion, and technology, although he does not limit himself to those topics. He is the author of* Watching the Detectives *(1988), about the London police department,* The Darwin Wars *(2001), and, most recently,* In the Beginning Was the Worm *(2003), about the 30-year struggle to decode the complete DNA of a nematode worm. In this selection from* New Statesman, *Brown looks at the Internet and concludes that, sometimes, censorship is warranted.*

Prereading: Thinking About the Essay in Advance

Do you think freedom of speech, as protected in the First Amendment to the United States Constitution, is absolute, or are there times when it must be limited?

Words to Watch

libertarian (par. 1) one who believes in absolute liberty
perpetrators (par. 1) ones who committed a crime
mangled (par. 2) bent and broken
foetuses (par. 2) unborn child, also spelled "fetuses"
secular (par. 4) unrelated to religion
provenance (par. 5) origin, source
niggardly (par. 6) without generosity
stultifying (par. 6) causing stupidity
deprave (par. 7) make morally sick
subtle (par. 8) less forceful

There are two general truths about attitudes to *censoring* the Internet. The first is that hardly anyone admits to favouring it in principle. The second is that whoever you are, and however libertarian, it should never take more than five minutes at the keyboard to find something you believe should be removed from the net, and its perpetrators locked up in a criminal lunatic asylum. 1

Most of the truly disgusting stuff I have come across has been religious in inspiration: the Nuremberg Files website, whose perpetrators were fined $100 million by an Oregon jury last week, is one example. This is a site on which pictures of mangled foetuses mingle with photographs of doctors, usually framed by a line which increasingly drips blood. The doctors' names and addresses are published, and if they are murdered by anti-abortion fanatics, then an "X" is placed in front of their photographs. 2

This sort of thing may not harm children, but it clearly acts to corrupt and deprave the adults who take it seriously. The charmingly named www.godhatesfags.com stops short of incitement to murder, but it is not much of an advertisement for homo sapiens. There are also the various Holocaust-denying sites and the aryan churches of Idaho and western Montana. 3

Still, my collection of offensive religious sites is probably the result of a sampling error. I have a professional interest in being shocked by believers. A more balanced person could find plenty of secular things to censor: as well as the fairly obvious child porn there are some truly gut-wrenchingly awful displays of pornography with adults, too; and once a month someone with an account at the University of Michigan posts detailed and completely humourless instructions on how to have sexual intercourse with dogs and ponies (there's also something called "scaly sex," which I have not read up). 4

The provenance of these messages shows the first difficulty with censoring the Internet, which is that the First Amendment is held to allow anyone in a university to say anything at all. One might ask why American laws should apply in this country, or in Germany, and the answer is simple brute force. The only way you can enforce rules about the content of a website is by physically controlling it. Since it is trivially easy for anyone with Internet access to rent a website in the USA, it is American laws and standards that determine what is acceptable around the world. The result is that you are much more likely to be sent to jail for having a copy of Windows 98 on your website than a picture of a woman having sex with a pig. If there were a child involved, you might get into as much trouble but there wouldn't be nearly as many lawyers hunting you down. 5

The paradox in this is that individual American communities are extremely censorious: that is why American network television, which must appeal to all of them, is so bland, and why American textbooks, which dare not offend parents, are even worse for children than television is. But while almost every American community is in favour of censorship, or at least savage sanctions against unpopular speech, they all disapprove of different things. Some want to keep Darwin out of the schoolroom; others would 6 sack people for saying "niggardly." So the choice seems to lie between complete licence and stultifying conformity. Either you offend almost all community standards, or none.

7 If there has to be a choice, I would rather, I suppose, have anarchy than inoffensiveness. I make my living from words, and I would not want this trade threatened by a prison sentence just because I offended someone; and this would be the natural reflex of most of the people who write about the subject. But on reflection, it's less clear that we ought to be so smug. If words could not deprave and corrupt when abused, why would we bother using them in the first place? I'd still rather not suffer for my opinions, but I do hope that they can make my enemies wish I were suffering.

8 The libertarian case relies on a distinction between speech and act which is really quite hard to sustain when you look at it closely. An economist would point out that a journalist actually makes his living delivering readers to advertisers. This is true even when the advertisements are a great deal more subtle than simply crossing out the photographs of murdered doctors. No one who visited the Nuremberg Files site could have been in any doubt about the intention of the pictures and phone numbers there. There are times when censorship is a victory for civilisation: if speech is completely free, it is also valueless.

Building Vocabulary

Use a dictionary to look up any unfamiliar words in the phrases below from Brown's essay. Write a short explanation of each expression.

1. religious in inspiration (par. 2)
2. incitement to murder (par. 3)
3. Holocaust-denying (par. 3)
4. sampling error (par. 4)
5. gut-wrenchingly (par. 4)
6. brute force (par. 5)
7. sack people (par. 6)
8. natural reflex (par. 7)

Thinking Critically About the Argument

Understanding the Writer's Argument

1. What kinds of Web sites does Brown think warrant removal from the Internet?
2. Why does American law seem to dominate Internet law?
3. Why, according to Brown, are American television and textbooks so "bland"?
4. What are the implications of the blandness of American TV for the Internet?
5. Why would Brown rather "have anarchy than inoffensiveness"? (par. 7)
6. What is the "libertarian case" for not censoring the Internet?

Understanding the Writer's Techniques

1. What is Brown's major proposition? Where is it in the essay? Does he place it effectively? Why do you think he places it where he does?
2. What are Brown's minor propositions? Make a list of his points.
3. Analyze Brown's tone. How would you characterize it? Explain.
4. How well does Brown use transitions in his essay? Could you improve them? How?
5. Paraphrase Brown's argument in paragraph 5. Is it easy to understand? Why or why not? Explain.
6. How effective is Brown's conclusion?

Exploring the Writer's Argument

1. In paragraphs 2, 3, and 4, Brown gives examples of "disgusting stuff" on the Internet, both religious and secular. How do the materials he cites compare with each other? In other words, are they all equally disgusting? What is Brown's strategy here? Analyze these paragraphs and decide if, logically, his use of examples is coherent. Explain your answer.
2. Analyze Brown's argument in paragraph 6. Do you agree with his conclusion about American communities being censorious, that "Either you offend almost all community standards, or none"? Explain what he means and why he is right or wrong.
3. What is Brown's standard, finally, for censorship? Does he ever say? Why or why not? What programs on TV or movies or radio programs do you think Brown would want to censor, and why?
4. Brown's conclusion says that "the libertarian case relies on a distinction between speech and act which is really quite hard to sustain when you look at it closely." Do you agree with his assessment of the libertarian case? Does Brown's argument rely on the libertarian case being weak? Explain your answers fully.

Ideas for Writing Arguments

Prewriting

If Brown is right, why are Americans both against censorship and for censorship? Is it something specific in the American character? Is it based in American history? Explain.

Writing a Guided Argument

Write an essay titled "The Limits of . . ." in which you argue that limits should be placed on common elements in American life (for example, television, fast food, or the use of gasoline).

1. Begin your essay with an analysis of Americans' complicated relationship with your topic.
2. Analyze in a cursory way the various negative aspects of your chosen topic.
3. Write your major proposition clearly.

4. Offer at least three minor propositions.
5. Support your minor propositions with examples and narratives that highlight the reason why that product or activity should be curtailed.
6. Suggest a solution for the problem you have analyzed.
7. Write in a tone of cynical disgust.
8. Use effective transitions to build coherence.
9. Close your essay by stating that your solution will help America be more of what it can be.

Thinking, Arguing, and Writing Collaboratively

Write an extended paragraph explaining why Americans are so interested in their right of free speech. There are countries in the world that do not allow their citizens to speak out against the government. Americans have the right to say anything we want against the government. Why are we so concerned with fighting for peoples' rights to post animal pornography?

When you are finished with your paragraph, exchange it with someone else in the class and ask for comments on your paper.

Writing About the Text

Brown's argument is filled with an undercurrent of cynicism. Write an essay analyzing Brown's use of cynicism, explaining how that aspect of his essay helps or hurts the force of his argument.

More Writing Ideas

1. Find a widely used textbook in American elementary schools to teach history. Flip through it and write a journal entry about what in the textbook Brown would consider "even worse for children than television is." (par. 6)
2. Web sites devoted to health are popular, but they have been heavily criticized. Investigate the controversy, and write an extended paragraph that argues that online health sites shouldn't have diagnostic information on them.
3. In her essay, Levine writes that much on the Internet is junk. Write an essay that compares and contrasts Brown's argument with Levine's.

28 Work, Money, and Class: Who Benefits?

As economists tell us, the middle class in the United States is shrinking and the gulf that has always existed between the rich and the poor is getting wider. The rich are getting richer, the poor are getting poorer, and everybody is trying to figure out why. Although politicians pass tax cuts or raise and lower interest rates to help the economy, people suffer from poverty in our own country. Meanwhile, while poverty rises, Americans are still working harder. While many Europeans have 35-hour workweeks and four weeks of vacation a year, Americans are veritable workaholics. Although officially, we have a 40-hour workweek in this country, it is not unusual for people to work 50-, 60-, even 70-hour weeks on a regular basis.

How do our attitudes toward work and working affect our policies and our lives? In "The Case Against Chores," novelist Jane Smiley takes a leisurely look at how one's feelings toward work develop at home. She raises the interesting point that many people don't love what they do because they are taught not to as children. Conservative writer David Brooks takes on a mystery, explaining patiently in "The Triumph of Hope over Self-Interest" why the middle-class and poor don't vote for politicians who might make their lives easier. He argues that we just don't want to believe that we're not rich. If you criticize the wealthy, you criticize us all, this argument goes, because we all want to see ourselves as rich people. Some writers use their pen to try to expose what they see as injustice and inequality. Herbert J. Gans, in "Fitting the Poor into the Economy," doesn't like the attitude of Americans toward the poor. He says we have a notion of the poor as "too lazy or morally deficient to deserve assistance," an attitude, in Gans's opinion, that causes needless suffering. In "Vanishing Jobs," Jeremy Rifkin explores another aspect of the changing economy, the rise of computers as a way of life. He argues that we can't have blind faith in technology and progress, but that people inevitably get left behind. These four writers, all writing on a similar topic, show the range of approaches to the timeless issues of work, money, and class.

JANE SMILEY
The Case Against Chores

Novelist Jane Smiley was born in Los Angeles in 1950 and was reared near St. Louis, Missouri. She was educated at Vassar College and the

Writer's Workshop at the University of Iowa. Her novels include The Age of Grief *(1987),* A Thousand Acres *(1991), for which she won the Pulitzer Prize for fiction, and* Horse Heaven *(2000). She has written for many publications, including* The New Yorker, The New York Times Magazine, The Nation, *and, reflecting her interest in horses,* Practical Horseman. *This selection appeared in* Harper's *in 1995 and has an argument that most children would celebrate.*

Prereading: Thinking About the Essay in Advance

How can parents raise their children to appreciate the value of work? Do you know anyone who loves work? Hates work? Which applies to you?

Words to Watch

unrelenting (par. 1) not weakening in force
gleaned (par. 2) found out
pastimes (par. 2) activities
alienated (par. 2) separated from one's true interests
tack (par. 5) put on a horse's saddle and bridle
bales (par. 5) piles
humaneness (par. 5) basic kindness

1 I've lived in the upper Midwest for twenty-one years now, and I'm here to tell you that the pressure to put your children to work is unrelenting. So far I've squirmed out from under it, and my daughters have led a life of almost tropical idleness, much to their benefit. My son, however, may not be so lucky. His father was himself raised in Iowa and put to work at an early age, and you never know when, in spite of all my husband's best intentions, that early training might kick in.

2 Although "chores" are so sacred in my neck of the woods that almost no one ever discusses their purpose, I have over the years gleaned some of the reasons parents give for assigning them. I'm not impressed. Mostly the reasons have to do with developing good work habits or, in the absence of good work habits, at least habits of working. No such thing as a free lunch, any job worth doing is worth doing right, work before play, all of that. According to this reasoning, the world is full of jobs that no one wants to do. If we divide them up and get them over with, then we can go on to pastimes we like. If we do them "right," then we won't have to do them again. Lots of times, though, in a family, that *we* doesn't operate. The operative word is *you.* The practical result of almost every child-labor scheme that I've witnessed is the child doing the dirty work and the parent getting the fun: Mom cooks and Sis does the dishes; the parents plan and plant the garden, the kids weed it. To me, what this teaches the child is the lesson of alienated labor: not to love the work but to get it over with; not to feel pride in one's contribution but to feel resentment at the waste of one's time.

Another goal of chores: The child contributes to the work of maintaining the family. According to this rationale, the child comes to understand what it takes to have a family, and to feel that he or she is an important, even indispensable member of it. But come on. Would you really want to feel loved primarily because you're the one who gets the floors mopped? Wouldn't you rather feel that your family's love simply exists all around you, no matter what your contribution? And don't the parents love their children anyway, whether the children vacuum or not? Why lie about it just to get the housework done? Let's be frank about the other half of the equation too. In this day and age, it doesn't take much work at all to manage a household, at least in the middle class—maybe four hours a week to clean the house and another four to throw the laundry into the washing machine, move it to the dryer, and fold it. Is it really a good idea to set the sort of example my former neighbors used to set, of mopping the floor every two days, cleaning the toilets every week, vacuuming every day, dusting, dusting, dusting? Didn't they have anything better to do than serve their house? 3

Let me confess that I wasn't expected to lift a finger when I was growing up. Even when my mother had a full-time job, she cleaned up after me, as did my grandmother. Later there was a housekeeper. I would leave my room in a mess when I headed off for school and find it miraculously neat when I returned. Once in a while I vacuumed, just because I liked the pattern the Hoover made on the carpet. I did learn to run water in my cereal bowl before setting it in the sink. 4

Where I discovered work was at the stable, and, in fact, there is no housework like horsework. You've got to clean the horses' stalls, feed them, groom them, tack them up, wrap their legs, exercise them, turn them out, and catch them. You've got to clip them and shave them. You have to sweep the aisle, clean your tack and your boots, carry bales of hay and buckets of water. Minimal horsekeeping, rising just to the level of humaneness, requires many more hours than making a few beds, and horsework turned out to be a good preparation for the real work of adulthood, which is rearing children. It was a good preparation not only because it was similar in many ways but also because my desire to do it, and to do a good job of it, grew out of my love of and interest in my horse. I can't say that cleaning out her bucket when she manured in it was an actual joy, but I knew she wasn't going to do it herself. I saw the purpose of my labor, and I wasn't alienated from it. 5

Probably to the surprise of some of those who knew me as a child, I have turned out to be gainfully employed. I remember when I was in seventh grade, one of my teachers said to me, strongly disapproving, "The trouble with you is you do only what you want to do!" That continues to be the trouble with me, except that over the years I have wanted to do more and more. 6

My husband worked hard as a child, out-Iowa-ing the Iowans, if such a thing is possible. His dad had him mixing cement with a stick when he was five, pushing wheelbarrows not long after. It's a long sad tale on the order of 7 two miles to school and both ways uphill. The result is, he's a great worker, much better than I am, but all the while he's doing it he wishes he weren't. He thinks of it as work; he's torn between doing a good job and longing not to be doing it at all. Later, when he's out on the golf course, where he really wants to be, he feels a little guilty, knowing there's work that should have been done before he gave in and took advantage of the beautiful day.

8 Good work is not the work we assign children but the work they want to do, whether it's reading in bed (where would I be today if my parents had rousted me out and put me to scrubbing floors?) or cleaning their rooms or practicing the flute or making roasted potatoes with rosemary and Parmesan for the family dinner. It's good for a teenager to suddenly decide that the bathtub is so disgusting she'd better clean it herself. I admit that for the parent, this can involve years of waiting. But if she doesn't want to wait, she can always spend her time dusting.

Building Vocabulary

Explain these colloquialisms in Smiley's essay:

1. that early training might kick in (par. 1)
2. in my neck of the woods (par. 2)
3. I wasn't expected to lift a finger (par. 4)
4. I have turned out to be gainfully employed (par. 6)
5. he's torn between doing a good job (par. 7)

Thinking Critically About the Argument

Understanding the Writer's Argument

1. Why have Smiley's daughters got away with not doing any work, and why might her son not be so lucky?
2. What are the reasons people give chores to their children?
3. What does Smiley think is the result of giving kids the dirty work in a job?
4. What is "alienated labor"?
5. What is Smiley's answer to the rationale that putting kids to work "contributes to the work of maintaining the family"? (par. 3)
6. What activity kept Smiley from being alienated from work? How did this happen?
7. What was Smiley's husband's childhood like? What has been the result, as it relates to his work habits?

Understanding the Writer's Techniques

1. What is the major proposition of this essay?
2. This essay appeared in *Harper's,* a magazine that attracts a highly educated, relatively wealthy readership. How does that fact affect the writer's tone?
3. How does Smiley attempt to appeal to her readers' emotions in this essay?

4. How does Smiley rebut the arguments in favor of giving chores to children? How effective are her rebuttals?
5. What minor propositions does Smiley offer to support her argument against chores?
6. Which is Smiley's strongest paragraph? Explain your response.
7. Smiley writes about a subject she loves, horses, in paragraph 5. Analyze her use of language in that paragraph. How does she make the paragraph effective?
8. How effective is Smiley's conclusion? Explain.

Exploring the Writer's Argument

1. Smiley admits in paragraph 4 that the very thing she's arguing for is how she was raised. Does that make her argument suspect? Why or why not? If so, how? If not, how does she overcome that limitation in her argument?
2. Smiley writes at the beginning of her essay that her daughters "have led a life of almost tropical idleness." Later, at the end of her essay, she writes that kids should do work that is good for them (i.e., that doesn't alienate them from the work). Are these two statements contradictory? Why or why not?
3. Smiley writes that she lives in the Midwest, and she seems to imply that this is important to her argument. Do you think it is? Explain where she refers to her geographical location and how she makes her essay universal despite this focus.

Ideas for Writing Arguments

Prewriting

Jot some notes on the following questions: What did your parents, grandparents, or other family members do during your upbringing that you don't agree with? What did they do right?

Writing a Guided Argument

In her essay, Smiley is giving parental advice. Write an essay with the title "The Case Against . . ." in which you argue that parents should avoid doing something that you don't agree with. For example, argue against spankings, letting kids go out on bicycle rides by themselves, or attending rap concerts.

1. Begin your essay by explaining your own personal relationship with your chosen subject.
2. In the next section, lay out at least two arguments the opposition might have.
3. Write your major proposition.
4. Rebut the arguments with effective support.
5. Adopt an informal tone, much like Smiley's.
6. About halfway through your argument, write a personal reminiscence that illustrates the correct way to go about things.

7. Offer at least two minor propositions to support your argument.
8. Close your essay with a discussion of how you will approach the rearing of your children in relation to this topic.

Thinking, Arguing, and Writing Collaboratively

In groups of four or five, discuss alternate opposition arguments from those you present in your Writing a Guided Argument essay, and come up with possible rebuttals. Jot down notes and incorporate them into your essay's final draft.

Writing About the Text

Write an essay in which you analyze Smiley's informal style. What is informal here? How does she keep the reader relaxed? How does the fact that Smiley is a novelist come through in the essay?

More Writing Ideas

1. In your journal, freewrite about this topic: fun work. Do not edit your writing. Write for at least 15 minutes. When you are done, read over your unedited writing to see if there are any propositions that could be used as the basis for an essay.
2. What are your feelings about those people who have domestic help, such as maids, butlers, and chauffeurs? Is it really necessary to have that kind of help? Write an extended paragraph on the topic.
3. Write an essay in which you argue that children should stop receiving an allowance at age 14 and work for their own money.

DAVID BROOKS
The Triumph of Hope Over Self-Interest

David Brooks is a senior editor at the conservative magazine The Weekly Standard *and is the author of* Bobos in Paradise: The New Upper Class and How They Got There, *which was published in 2001. He is also a contributing editor at* Newsweek *and the* Atlantic Monthly, *writes for* The New York Times Magazine, *and recently began a twice weekly column in* The New York Times. *He is also a regular commentator on National Public Radio. He was educated at the University of Chicago, and started his career as a newspaper reporter. In this selection, Brooks explains why people don't vote for politicians who support policies that will help them.*

Prereading: Thinking About the Essay in Advance

What are your feelings about those who are more wealthy than you are? Do you envy them? Do you want to be like them? Do you resent them? Why do you react as you do?

Words to Watch

populist (par. 2) appealing to the common people
overdetermined (par. 3) having many reasons
savaged (par. 5) destroyed
appointed (par. 7) furnished
resentment (par. 8) feeling of anger and being injured
sommeliers (par. 10) waiter in a restaurant who helps customers choose wine
eau (par. 10) French for "water"
subsumes (par. 18) overwhelms

Why don't people vote their own self-interest? Every few years the Republicans propose a tax cut, and every few years the Democrats pull out their income distribution charts to show that much of the benefits of the Republican plan go to the richest 1 percent of Americans or thereabouts. And yet every few years a Republican plan wends its way through the legislative process and, with some trims and amendments, passes. 1

The Democrats couldn't even persuade people to oppose the repeal of the estate tax, which is explicitly for the mega-upper class. Al Gore, who ran a populist campaign, couldn't even win the votes of white males who didn't go to college, whose incomes have stagnated over the past decades and who were the explicit targets of his campaign. Why don't more Americans want to distribute more wealth down to people like themselves? 2

Well, as the academics would say, it's overdetermined. There are several reasons. 3

People vote their aspirations. 4

The most telling polling result from the 2000 election was from a *Time* magazine survey that asked people if they are in the top 1 percent of earners. Nineteen percent of Americans say they are in the richest 1 percent and a further 20 percent expect to be someday. So right away you have 39 percent of Americans who thought that when Mr. Gore savaged a plan that favored the top 1 percent, he was taking a direct shot at them. 5

It's not hard to see why they think this way. Americans live in a culture of abundance. They have always had a sense that great opportunities lie just over the horizon, in the next valley, with the next job or the next big thing. None of us is really poor; we're just pre-rich. 6

Americans read magazines for people more affluent than they are (*W, Cigar Aficionado, The New Yorker, Robb Report, Town and Country*) because they think that someday they could be that guy with the tastefully appointed horse farm. Democratic politicians proposing to take from the rich are just bashing the dreams of our imminent selves. 7

Income resentment is not a strong emotion in much of America. 8

If you earn $125,000 a year and live in Manhattan, certainly, you are surrounded by things you cannot afford. You have to walk by those buildings 9 on Central Park West with the 2,500-square-foot apartments that are empty three-quarters of the year because their evil owners are mostly living at their other houses in L.A.

10 But if you are a middle-class person in most of America, you are not brought into incessant contact with things you can't afford. There aren't Lexus dealerships on every corner. There are no snooty restaurants with water sommeliers to help you sort though the bottled eau selections. You can afford most of the things at Wal-Mart or Kohl's and the occasional meal at the Macaroni Grill. Moreover, it would be socially unacceptable for you to pull up to church in a Jaguar or to hire a caterer for your dinner party anyway. So you are not plagued by a nagging feeling of doing without.

11 **Many Americans admire the rich.**

12 They don't see society as a conflict zone between the rich and poor. It's taboo to say in a democratic culture, but do you think a nation that watches Katie Couric in the morning, Tom Hanks in the evening and Michael Jordan on weekends harbors deep animosity toward the affluent?

13 On the contrary. I'm writing this from Nashville, where one of the richest families, the Frists, is hugely admired for its entrepreneurial skill and community service. People don't want to tax the Frists—they want to elect them to the Senate. And they did.

14 Nor are Americans suffering from false consciousness. You go to a town where the factories have closed and people who once earned $14 an hour now work for $8 an hour. They've taken their hits. But odds are you will find their faith in hard work and self-reliance undiminished, and their suspicion of Washington unchanged.

15 **Americans resent social inequality more than income inequality.**

16 As the sociologist Jennifer Lopez has observed: "Don't be fooled by the rocks that I got, I'm just, I'm just Jenny from the block." As long as rich people "stay real," in Ms. Lopez's formulation, they are admired. Meanwhile, middle-class journalists and academics who seem to look down on megachurches, suburbia and hunters are resented. If Americans see the tax debate as being waged between the economic elite, led by President Bush, and the cultural elite, led by Barbra Streisand, they are going to side with Mr. Bush, who could come to any suburban barbershop and fit right in.

17 **Most Americans do not have Marxian categories in their heads.**

18 This is the most important reason Americans resist wealth redistribution, the reason that subsumes all others. Americans do not see society as a layer cake, with the rich on top, the middle class beneath them and the working class and underclass at the bottom. They see society as a high school cafeteria, with their community at one table and other communities at other tables. They are pretty sure that their community is the nicest, and filled with the best people, and they have a vague pity for all those poor souls who live in New York City or California and have a lot of money but no true neighbors and no free time.

19 All of this adds up to a terrain incredibly inhospitable to class-based politics. Every few years a group of millionaire Democratic presidential aspi-

rants pretends to be the people's warriors against the overclass. They look inauthentic, combative rather than unifying. Worst of all, their basic message is not optimistic.

They haven't learned what Franklin and Teddy Roosevelt and even Bill Clinton knew: that you can run against rich people, but only those who have betrayed the ideal of fair competition. You have to be more hopeful and growth-oriented than your opponent, and you cannot imply that we are a nation tragically and permanently divided by income. In the gospel of America, there are no permanent conflicts. 20

Building Vocabulary

Write out definitions for the following words from Brook's essay, and use them each in a sentence:

1. stagnated (par. 2)
2. abundance (par. 6)
3. affluent (par. 7)
4. imminent (par. 7)
5. incessant (par. 10)
6. taboo (par. 12)
7. animosity (par. 12)
8. aspirants (par. 19)

Thinking Critically About the Argument

Understanding the Writer's Argument

1. Why do Republicans want to cut the taxes of the richest 1 percent of Americans?
2. What is the estate tax? Who benefits from it?
3. Why do so many Americans think they're in the richest 1 percent? What does Brooks mean when he says that "none of us is really poor; we're just pre-rich"? (par. 6)
4. Why, according to Brooks, do Americans admire the rich?
5. What does Brooks mean by "Marxian categories"? (par. 17)
6. What, according to Brooks, did Franklin Roosevelt, Teddy Roosevelt, and Bill Clinton know that made them popular politicians?
7. What is the "gospel of America"? (par. 20)

Understanding the Writer's Techniques

1. What is Brooks's major proposition in this essay?
2. Why does Brooks start with a question?
3. Brooks only uses one statistic in his essay, the *Time* poll. Is this single information enough to help his case? Explain.
4. Does Brooks put his minor propositions in any strategic order? Explain.
5. Brooks uses causal analysis. How does he manage to use that rhetorical mode within his argument? Is it effective?

6. What is the argumentative effect of Brooks's section headings? Do they help or hurt his argument?
7. Analyze Brooks's analogies in paragraph 18. Are they effective? Why or why not?
8. How well done is Brooks's conclusion? What is its strongest element?

Exploring the Writer's Argument

1. Brooks is a conservative, yet he seems to work in this essay to give away one of the secrets of the Republican party's success: that often people who should vote Democratic do not. Why would he want to expose this secret?
2. In his essay, Brooks uses many vivid examples. Choose at least three that you find particularly effective and explain your choices.
3. Do you agree with Brooks's argument in paragraph 10 that people in middle-class America outside of New York City do not resent rich people? Why or why not?

Ideas for Writing Arguments

Prewriting

Are there any activities you take part in regularly that you know are counterproductive to your safety or health or to the safety or health of other people? Jot down some ideas for an essay on the topic.

Writing a Guided Argument

Write an essay that attempts to explain why someone might take part in an activity that not everyone would understand. For example, explain why people still smoke although they know it is bad for them or why people live in cities that are often hit with natural disasters.

1. Begin your essay with a rhetorical question.
2. Describe the activity you are going to explain.
3. State your major proposition.
4. Offer at least three reasons why people take part in the activity you've chosen to write about.
5. After each reason, support the idea with evidence in the form of examples.
6. In the next section, offer a solution to the problem: How can one stop doing the activity?
7. Close with a switch to a neutral, detached discussion of the issue.

Thinking, Arguing, and Writing Collaboratively

In groups of four or five, study one of the magazines Brooks mentions in paragraph 7, or find another magazine geared for a luxury readership. Each group should examine a different magazine. What images support Brooks's position that middle-class readers essentially are "wannabes" who see themselves in the places of the rich? Discuss the images, and present your findings to the class.

Writing About the Text

Write an essay that analyzes Brooks's use of irony. Choose at least three passages from Brooks's essay that you find particularly ironic. Explain how what Brooks says and what he means are two different things. How does irony fit into Brooks's overall tone, and how effective is it?

More Writing Ideas

1. In your journal, illustrate at least three times in the past few days when you observed class to be an issue between two or more people.
2. Write a paragraph or two that explores celebrity worship in our culture as the worship of the rich.
3. In an essay, argue that Americans should be more class conscious, and explain how this might come about.

HERBERT J. GANS
Fitting the Poor into the Economy

Herbert J. Gans, a professor of sociology at Columbia University, was born in Germany in 1927. The rise of the Nazis caused his family to flee to England in 1938. Gans came to America in 1940 and subsequently became a U.S. citizen. He went to the University of Chicago and then earned a Ph.D. at the University of Pennsylvania. He has been a professor at Pennsylvania Teachers College and M.I.T. Gans has written a number of books about class and culture in America, including The Levittowners *(1967),* People and Plans *(1968),* Popular Culture and High Culture *(1974),* Deciding What's News *(1979),* The War Against the Poor *(1995), and* Making Sense of America *(1999). In this selection, Gans examines the attitudes Americans have about the poor, especially the way in which people blame the poor for their own poverty.*

Prereading: Thinking About the Essay in Advance

What are the reasons for poverty in a rich country like America? Do people blame the poor for their poverty? Are there any realistic solutions to the problem?

Words to Watch

allocations (par. 1) money given for a specific purpose
affluent (par. 1) wealthy
onus (par. 2) responsibility
scapegoats (par. 2) those falsely blamed for a problem
antidote (par. 4) solution to a problem
inroads (par. 6) progress

paltry (par. 7) small, insignificant
dereliction (par. 8) serious shortcoming
spawned (par. 11) been the source for
utopian (par. 11) unrealistically idealistic

1 The notion of the poor as too lazy or morally deficient to deserve assistance seems to be indestructible. Public policies limit poor people to substandard services and incomes below the subsistence level, and Congress and state legislatures are tightening up even on these miserly allocations—holding those in the "underclass" responsible for their own sorry state. Indeed, labeling the poor as undeserving has lately become politically useful as a justification for the effort to eliminate much of the antipoverty safety net and permit tax cuts for the affluent people who do most of the voting.

2 Such misplaced blame offers mainstream society a convenient evasion of its own responsibility. Blaming poor men and women for not working, for example, takes the onus off both private enterprise and government for failing to supply employment. It is easier to charge poor unmarried mothers with lacking family values than to make sure that there are jobs for them and for the young men who are not marriageable because they are unable to support families. Indeed, the poor make excellent scapegoats for a range of social problems, such as street crime and drug and alcohol addiction. Never mind the reversal of cause and effect that underlies this point of view—for centuries crime, alcoholism, and single motherhood have risen whenever there has not been enough work and income to go around.

3 The undeserving underclass is also a useful notion for employers as the economy appears to be entering a period of long-term stagnation. Jobs are disappearing—some displaced by labor-saving technologies, others exported to newly industrializing, low-wage countries, others lost as companies "downsize" to face tougher global competition. Indeed, the true rate of unemployment—which includes involuntary part-time workers and long-term "discouraged" workers who have dropped out of the job market altogether—has remained in double digits for more than a generation and no longer seems to drop during times of economic strength. Labeling poor people as lacking the needed work ethic is a politically simple way of shedding them from a labor market that will most likely never need them again.

4 The most efficient antidote to poverty is not welfare but full employment. In the short run, therefore, today's war against the poor should be replaced with efforts to create jobs for now-surplus workers. New Deal-style programs of large-scale governmental employment, for example, can jump-start a slow economy. Besides being the fastest way to put people to work, a public-works program can improve the country's infrastructure, including highways, buildings, parks, and computer databases.

5 In addition, private enterprise and government should aim to stimulate the most promising labor-intensive economic activities and stop encouraging new technology that will further destroy jobs—reviving, for example, the practice of making cars and appliances partly by hand. A parallel policy

would tax companies for their use of labor-saving technology; the revenues from this tax would pay for alternative jobs for people in occupations that technology renders obsolete. This idea makes good business as well as social sense: human workers are needed as customers for the goods that machines now produce.

To distribute the jobs that do exist among more people, employers could shorten the work day, week, or year. Several large manufacturing companies in Western Europe already use worksharing to create a 35-hour week. Making significant inroads on U.S. joblessness may require reducing the work week to 30 hours. 6

A more generous welfare system would go a long way toward solving the problems of the remainder: those who cannot work or cannot find jobs. By persisting in the belief that poor people deserve their fate, society can easily justify a paltry and demeaning welfare system that pays recipients only about one-quarter of the median income. A system that paid closer to half the median income, by contrast, would enable those without work to remain full members of society and thus minimize the despair, anger, and various illnesses, as well as premature mortality, distinctive to the poor. 7

For such antipoverty policies to gain acceptance, mainstream America will have to unlearn the stereotype of poor people as immoral. Most of the poor are just as law-abiding as everyone else. (While a minority of poor people cheat on their welfare applications, an even larger minority of affluent people cheat on their tax returns—yet the notion of undeservingness is never applied to the middle or upper classes.) In admitting that the phenomena now explained as moral dereliction are actually traceable to poverty, Americans will force themselves to find solutions, not scapegoats, to the country's problems. 8

Most of the people assigned to today's undeserving underclass are the first victims of what is already being called the future "jobless economy." In the long run, if the cancer of joblessness spreads more widely among the population, large numbers of the present middle class will have to adapt to the reality that eventually most workers may no longer be employed full time. In that case, more drastic job-creation policies will be needed, including a ban on additional job-destroying technology and the establishment of permanent public employment modeled on the kind now associated with military spending. Worksharing would most likely be based on a 24-hour week. 9

At that point, everyone would in fact be working part time by today's standards, and new ways to maintain standards of living would have to be found. One approach, already being discussed in Europe, is a universal, subsistence-level income grant. This "demogrant," a twenty-first-century version of the $1,000-per-person allotment that presidential candidate George McGovern proposed in 1972, would be taxed away from people still working full time. In any case, private and government agencies should begin now to study what policies might be needed to preserve the American way of life when the full-time job will no longer be around to pay for the American Dream. 10

11 It is possible, of course, that new sources of economic growth will suddenly develop to revive the full employment and prosperity of the post–World War II decades. And some labor-saving technologies may, in the long run, create more jobs than they destroy; that may well be the case for computers, which have spawned a large sector of the economy. Such happy outcomes cannot be counted on to materialize, however, and there remains the danger that the war on the poor will continue as the politically most convenient path. We will undoubtedly find that when the economy begins to threaten the descendants of today's middle and even affluent classes with becoming poor, and then "undeserving," policies that today seem utopian will be demanded, and quickly.

Building Vocabulary

This selection assumes a general familiarity with basic economic and political terms and concepts. Identify and write definitions for the following:

1. subsistence level (par. 1)
2. safety net (par. 1)
3. private enterprise (par. 2)
4. underclass (par. 3)
5. stagnation (par. 3)
6. downsize (par. 3)
7. work ethic (par. 3)
8. welfare (par. 4)
9. New Deal (par. 4)

Thinking Critically About the Argument

Understanding the Writer's Argument

1. What responsibility does Gans say mainstream society has toward the poor? (par. 2)
2. Why, historically, are crime, alcoholism, and single motherhood common?
3. Why is the idea of an "undeserving underclass" something employers can use to shed responsibility, according to Gans?
4. What does Gans suggest in place of welfare, or does he think welfare is all right?
5. What are people on welfare paid in proportion to the average income? What does Gans think welfare recipients should be paid? Why?
6. How can shortening the 40-hour workweek reduce poverty, according to Gans?
7. What is a "demogrant"? How is it designed to help?

Understanding the Writer's Techniques

1. What is Gans's claim? Where does he express it best?
2. What grounds does Gans offer to support his claim?

3. Outline Gans's argument. How does he structure his points?
4. What is the nature of the switch in Gans's argument from paragraph 3 to paragraph 4?
5. How does Gans's position as a professor of sociology at Columbia University, an Ivy League school, help his essay? Explain.
6. What is the author's tone? Explain your answer fully, showing examples from the essay that led to your answer.
7. Is Gans's closing effective? Why or why not?

Exploring the Writer's Argument

1. Gans objects to society blaming the "underclass" for various social problems. He wants to take the responsibility off the poor. Is that, however, considering poor people as children who can't be held accountable for their actions? Is that what he's saying? Explain your answer fully. Do you agree?
2. In his essay (page 269), David Brooks writes about how people don't always act in their own political best interest. Do you see any arguments, implied or overt, in Brooks's essay that could help the poor with the problems Gans identifies? Explain.
3. Gans makes some radical suggestions to improve life in America. Do you think any of his suggestions are feasible? Why or why not?
4. In paragraph 8, Gans writes that if people change their minds about the poor, that will allow new policies to take shape. Do you agree with his assessment? Explain your answer.

Ideas for Writing Arguments

Prewriting

What are the effects, psychologically, of being unemployed? What are the psychological effects of making too little money in a job? Write notes on your thoughts.

Writing a Guided Argument

Write an essay arguing that a New Deal–style project, such as building a hypothetical high-speed highway from Los Angeles to New York (or some other comparably huge project of your own devising) would improve the economy.

1. Open your essay with a discussion of the problems of unemployment and poverty in our society, as described by Gans.
2. Write your major proposition, proposing your project.
3. Offer at least three minor propositions that explain why this project would benefit the economy.
4. Explain the long-term positive economic effects of full employment.
5. Use effective transitions to move from point to point.
6. Predict a possible objection to the project, and rebut that point.
7. Bring your essay to a close by illustrating how your project would provide a great convenience to everyone.

Thinking, Arguing, and Writing Collaboratively

After dividing into four equal groups, have members of each group read their essays from the Writing a Guided Argument assignment out loud. Select your group's strongest essay, and as a group help the writer to improve any weak points. List the strengths of the essay. Read the four strongest essays to the whole class, and discuss the strengths and weaknesses of each.

Writing About the Text

Write an essay that explores the concept of what it means to be "undeserving," as Gans defines it. Is this a useful concept? Does Gans make good use of it in his essay? What does it mean to "deserve" your economic fate? Do we have any control at all? Is there upward mobility in the United States?

More Writing Ideas

1. In your journal, speculate on what it would be like to live in poverty in a wealthy country like the United States.
2. In a paragraph or two, explore the responsibility you have personally as a citizen of this country to the poor of the country.
3. Write an essay in which you argue that the poor are actually *more* moral than the rich in the United States.

Jeremy Rifkin
Vanishing Jobs

Jeremy Rifkin has made a career out of wide-ranging activism. He is founder and president of the Foundation on Economic Trends, president of the Greenhouse Crisis Foundation, and head of the Beyond Beef Coalition. During the 1960s and 1970s, he was involved in the peace movement, founding the Citizens Commission, which was established to draw the public's attention to abuses of power in the war in Vietnam. Rifkin has also worked to place controls on biotechnology, including genetic engineering. He is the author of The Age of Access *(2002). In the following selection, Rifkin worries that as technology advances, the economy will leave many people, especially the unskilled poor, behind.*

Prereading: Thinking About the Essay in Advance

How has the advent of high technology and the Internet changed the workforce? What does it mean when the government says that jobs have been created or lost?

Words to Watch

sullen (par. 4) depressed
camp (par. 5) kitschy and ironic
malaise (par. 9) feeling of lack of mental wellness
incessantly (par. 11) without stopping
plethora (par. 14) wide variety
bellwether (par. 17) sign of things to come
progressive (par. 30) marked by a belief that government can cause social improvements
venerable (par. 31) respected because of longevity
discourse (par. 31) exchange of ideas
fledgling (par. 35) new

"Will there be a job for me in the new Information Age?" 1

This is the question that most worries American voters—and the question that American politicians seem most determined to sidestep. President Bill Clinton warns workers that they will have to be retrained six or seven times during their work lives to match the dizzying speed of technological change. Speaker of the House Newt Gingrich talks about the "end of the traditional job" and advises every American worker to become his or her own independent contractor. 2

But does the president really think 124 million Americans can reinvent themselves every five years to keep up with a high-tech marketplace? Does Gingrich honestly believe every American can become a freelance entrepreneur, continually hustling contracts for short-term work assignments? 3

Buffeted by these unrealistic employment expectations, American workers are increasingly sullen and pessimistic. Most Americans have yet to recover from the recovery of 1993–1995, which was essentially a "jobless" recovery. While corporate profits are heading through the roof, average families struggle to keep a roof over their heads. More than one-fifth of the workforce is trapped in temporary assignments or works only part time. Millions of others have slipped quietly out of the economy and into an underclass no longer counted in the permanent employment figures. A staggering 15 percent of the population now lives below the official poverty line. 4

Both Clinton and Gingrich have asked American workers to remain patient. They explain that declining incomes represent only short-term adjustments. Democrats and Republicans alike beseech the faithful to place their trust in the high-tech future—to journey with them into cyberspace and become pioneers on the new electronic frontier. Their enthusiasm for technological marvels has an almost camp ring to it. If you didn't know better, you might suspect Mickey and Pluto were taking you on a guided tour through the Epcot Center. 5

"I've stopped looking for work, which, I believe, helps the economic numbers."

6 Jittery and genuinely confused over the yawning gap between the official optimism of the politicians and their own personal plight, middle- and working-class American families seem to be holding on to a tiny thread of hope that the vast productivity gains of the high-tech revolution will somehow "trickle down" to them in the form of better jobs, wages, and benefits. That thread is likely to break by election time [November 1996] if, as I anticipate, the economy skids right by the soft landing predicted by the Federal Reserve Board and crashes headlong into a deep recession.

7 The Labor Department reported that payrolls sank by 101,000 workers in May 1995 alone—the largest drop in payrolls since April 1991, when the U.S. economy was deep in a recession. In June 1995, overall unemployment remained virtually unchanged, but manufacturing jobs declined by an additional 40,000. At the same time, inventories are up and consumer spending and confidence are down—sure signs of bad economic times ahead.

8 The psychological impact of a serious downturn coming so quickly upon the heels of the last one would be devastating. It is likely to set the framework for a politically wild roller-coaster ride for the rest of the 1990s, opening the door not only to new parties but to extralegal forms of politics.

9 Meanwhile, few politicians and economists are paying attention to the underlying causes of—dare we say it—the new "malaise" gripping the coun-

try. Throughout the current [1995] welfare reform debate, for example, members of both parties have trotted onto the House and Senate floors to urge an end to welfare and demand that all able-bodied men and women find jobs. Maverick Sen. Paul Simon (D-Ill.) has been virtually alone in raising the troubling question: "What jobs?"

The hard reality is that the global economy is in the midst of a transformation as significant as the Industrial Revolution. We are in the early stages of a shift from "mass labor" to highly skilled "elite labor," accompanied by increasing automation in the production of goods and the delivery of services. Sophisticated computers, robots, telecommunications, and other Information Age technologies are replacing human beings in nearly every sector. Factory workers, secretaries, receptionists, clerical workers, salesclerks, bank tellers, telephone operators, librarians, wholesalers, and middle managers are just a few of the many occupations destined for virtual extinction. In the United States alone, as many as 90 million jobs in a labor force of 124 million are potentially vulnerable to displacement by automation. 10

A few mainstream economists pin their hopes on increasing job opportunities in the knowledge sector. Secretary of Labor Robert Reich, for example, talks incessantly of the need for more highly skilled technicians, computer programmers, engineers, and professional workers. He barnstorms the country urging workers to retrain, retool, and reinvent themselves in time to gain a coveted place on the high-tech express. 11

The secretary ought to know better. Even if the entire workforce could be retrained for very skilled, high-tech jobs—which, of course, it can't—there will never be enough positions in the elite knowledge sector to absorb the millions let go as automation penetrates into every aspect of the production process. 12

It's not as if this is a revelation. For years the Alvin Tofflers and the John Naisbitts of the world have lectured the rest of us that the end of the industrial age also means the end of "mass production" and "mass labor," What they never mention is what "the masses" should do after they become redundant. 13

Laura D'Andrea Tyson, who now heads the National Economic Council, argues that the Information Age will bring a plethora of new technologies and products that we can't as yet even anticipate, and therefore it will create many new kinds of jobs. After a debate with me on CNN, Tyson noted that when the automobile replaced the horse and buggy, some people lost their jobs in the buggy trade but many more found work on the assembly line. Tyson believes that the same operating rules will govern the information era. 14

Tyson's argument is compelling. Still, I can't help but think that she may be wrong. Even if thousands of new products come along, they are likely to be manufactured in near-workerless factories and marketed by near-virtual companies requiring ever-smaller, more highly skilled workforces. 15

This steady decline of mass labor threatens to undermine the very foundations of the modern American state. For nearly 200 years, the heart of the 16 social contract and the measure of individual human worth have centered on the value of each person's labor. How does society even begin to adjust to a new era in which labor is devalued or even rendered worthless?

17 This is not the first time the issue of devalued human labor has arisen in the history of the United States. The first group of Americans to be marginalized by the automation revolution was black men, more than 40 years ago. Their story is a bellwether.

18 In the mid-1950s, automation began to take a toll on the nation's factories. Hardest hit were unskilled jobs in the industries where black workers concentrated. Between 1953 and 1962, 1.6 million blue-collar manufacturing jobs were lost. In an essay, "Problems of the Negro Movement," published in 1964, civil rights activist Tom Kahn quipped, "It's as if racism, having put the Negro in his economic place, stepped aside to watch technology destroy that 'place.'"

19 Millions of African-American workers and their families became part of a perpetually unemployed "underclass" whose unskilled labor was no longer required in the mainstream economy. Vanquished and forgotten, many urban blacks vented their frustration and anger by taking to the streets. The rioting began in Watts in 1965 and spread east to Detroit and other Northern industrial cities.

20 Today, the same technological and economic forces are beginning to affect large numbers of white male workers. Many of the disaffected white men who make up ultraright-wing organizations are high school or community college graduates with limited skills who are forced to compete for a diminishing number of agricultural, manufacturing, and service jobs. While they blame affirmative action programs, immigrant groups, and illegal aliens for their woes, these men miss the real cause of their plight—technological innovations that devalue their labor. Like African-American men in the 1960s, the new militants view the government and law enforcement agencies as the enemy. They see a grand conspiracy to deny them their basic freedoms and constitutional rights. And they are arming themselves for a revolution.

21 The Information Age may present difficulties for the captains of industry as well. By replacing more and more workers with machines, employers will eventually come up against the two economic Achilles' heels of the Information Age. The first is a simple problem of supply and demand: If mass numbers of people are underemployed or unemployed, who's going to buy the flood of products and services being churned out?

22 The second Achilles' heel for business—and one never talked about—is the effect on capital accumulation when vast numbers of employees are let go or hired on a temporary basis so that employers can avoid paying out benefits—especially pension fund benefits. As it turns out, pension funds, now worth more than $5 trillion in the United States alone, keep much of the capitalist system afloat. For nearly 25 years, the pension funds of millions of workers have served as a forced savings pool that has financed capital investments.

Pension funds account for 74 percent of net individual savings, more than one-third of all corporate equities, and nearly 40 percent of all corporate bonds. Pension assets exceed the assets of commercial banks and make up nearly one-third of the total financial assets of the U.S. economy. In 1993 alone, pension funds made new investments of between $1 trillion and $1.5 trillion. 23

If too many workers are let go or marginalized into jobs without pension benefits, the capitalist system is likely to collapse slowly in on itself as employers drain it of the workers' funds necessary for new capital investments. In the final analysis, sharing the vast productivity gains of the Information Age is absolutely essential to guarantee the well-being of management, stockholders, labor, and the economy as a whole. 24

Sadly, while our politicians gush over the great technological breakthroughs that lie ahead in cyberspace, not a single elected official, in either political party, is raising the critical question of how we can ensure that the productivity gains of the Information Age are shared equitably. 25

In the past, when new technology increased productivity—such as in the 1920s when oil and electricity replaced coal- and steam-powered plants—American workers organized collectively to demand a shorter workweek and better pay and benefits. Today, employers are shortening not the workweek, but the workforce—effectively preventing millions of American workers from enjoying the benefits of the technology revolution. 26

Organized labor has been weakened by 40 years of automation, a decline in union membership, and a growing temp workforce that is difficult to organize. In meetings with union officials, I have found that they are universally reluctant to deal with the notion that mass labor—the very basis of trade unionism—will continue to decline and may even disappear altogether. Several union leaders confided to me off the record that the labor movement is in survival mode and trying desperately to prevent a rollback of legislation governing basic rights to organize. Union leaders cannot conceive that they may have to rethink their mission in order to accommodate a fundamental change in the nature of work. But the unions' continued reluctance to grapple with a technology revolution that might eliminate mass labor could spell their own elimination from American life over the next three or four decades. 27

Working women may hold the key to whether organized labor can reinvent itself in time to survive the Information Age. Women now make up about half of the U.S. workforce, and a majority of employed women provide half or more of their household's income. 28

In addition to holding down a 40-hour job, working women often manage the household as well. Significantly, nearly 44 percent of all employed women say they would prefer more time with their family to more money. 29

This is one reason many progressive labor leaders believe the rebirth of the American labor movement hinges on organizing women workers. The call for a 30-hour workweek is a powerful rallying cry that could unite trade unions, women's groups, parenting organizations, churches, and synagogues. Unfortunately, the voice of trade union women is not often heard 30 inside the inner sanctum of the American Federation of Labor and Congress of Industrial Organizations (AFL-CIO) executive council. Of the 83 unions in the AFL-CIO, only one is headed by a woman.

31 The women's movement, trapped in struggles over abortion, discriminatory employment practices, and sexual harassment, has also failed to grasp the enormous opportunity brought on by the Information Age. Betty Friedan, the venerable founder of the modern women's movement and someone always a step or two ahead of the crowd, is convinced that the reduction of work hours offers a way to revitalize the women's movement, and take women's interests to the center of public policy discourse.

32 Of course, employers will argue that shortening the workweek is too costly and would threaten their ability to compete both domestically and abroad. That need not be so. Companies like Hewlett-Packard in France and BMW in Germany have reduced their workweek while continuing to pay workers at the same weekly rate. In return, the workers have agreed to work shifts. Management executives reason that, if they can operate the new high-tech plants on a 24-hour basis, they can double or triple productivity and thus afford to pay workers the same.

33 In France, government officials are playing with the idea of forgiving the payroll taxes for employers who voluntarily reduce their workweek. While the government will lose tax revenue, economists argue that fewer people will be on welfare, and the new workers will be taxpayers with purchasing power. Employers, workers, the economy, and the government all benefit.

34 In this country, generous tax credits could be extended to any company willing both to reduce its workweek voluntarily and implement a profit-sharing plan so that its employees will benefit directly from productivity gains.

35 The biggest surprise I've encountered in the fledgling debate over rethinking work has been the response of some business leaders. I have found genuine concern among a small but growing number of business executives over the critical question of what to do with the millions of people whose labor will be needed less, or not at all, in an increasingly automated age. Many executives have close friends who have been re-engineered out of a job—replaced by the new technologies of the Information Age. Others have had to take part in the painful process of letting employees go in order to optimize the bottom line. Some tell me they worry whether their own children will be able to find a job when they enter the high-tech labor market in a few years.

36 To be sure, I hear moans and groans from some corporate executives when I zero in on possible solutions—although there are also more than a few nods of agreement. But still, they are willing—even eager—to talk about these critical questions. They are hungry for engagement—the kind that has been absent in the public policy arena. Until now, politicians and economists have steadfastly refused to entertain a discussion of how we prepare for a new economic era characterized by the diminishing need for mass human labor. Until we have that conversation, the fear, anger, and frustration of millions of Americans are going to grow in intensity and become manifest through increasingly hostile and extreme social and political venues.

We are long overdue for public debate over the future of work and how to share the productivity gains of the Information Age. The 1996 election year offers the ideal time to begin talking with each other—both about our deep misgivings and our guarded hopes—as we journey into a new economic era. 37

Building Vocabulary

Explain the meaning of the following examples of figurative language. Rewrite the sentence by putting the figures of speech in your own words.

1. Jittery and genuinely confused over the *yawning* gap between the official optimism of the politicians and their own personal plight, middle- and working-class American families seem to be *holding on to a tiny thread of* hope that the vast productivity gains of the high-tech *revolution* will somehow "*trickle down*" to them in the form of better jobs, wages, and benefits. (par. 6)
2. It is likely to set the framework for a politically *wild roller-coaster ride* for the rest of the 1990s, *opening the door* not only to new parties but to extralegal forms of politics. (par. 8)
3. He *barnstorms* the country urging workers to retrain, retool, and reinvent themselves in time to gain a coveted place on the *high-tech express.* (par. 11)
4. By replacing more and more workers with machines, employers will eventually come up against the two economic *Achilles' heels* of the Information Age. (par. 21)
5. If too many workers are *let go* or marginalized into jobs without pension benefits, the capitalist system is likely to *collapse slowly in on itself* as employers *drain it* of the workers' funds necessary for new capital investments. (par. 24)
6. This is one reason many progressive labor leaders believe the rebirth of the American labor movement *hinges on* organizing women workers. (par. 30)

Thinking Critically About the Argument

Understanding the Writer's Argument

1. What was happening in the U.S. economy at the time this essay appeared in 1995? What was the hope for the future of the economy at that time? What did Rifkin think would happen to the economy soon after he published this essay?
2. What effect on jobs does Rifkin say the computer revolution is having?
3. What does Rifkin think about Laura Tyson's optimism as quoted in paragraph 14?
4. How can Americans learn about how technological change affects job markets over history? Who is always hurt the most?
5. Paraphrase Rifkin's argument about the loss of benefits starting in paragraph 22.

6. In the past, as Rifkin points out, unions joined together "to demand a shorter workweek and better pay." (par. 26) What was the status of organized labor when this essay appeared?
7. What are the economic benefits of a shorter workweek, according to Rifkin?
8. What, in Rifkin's view, is the reaction of business leaders when they hear his proposals to help the situation?

Understanding the Writer's Techniques

1. What claim does Rifkin make in this essay?
2. What is the argumentative effect of Rifkin's rhetorical questions in paragraph 3?
3. What is the argumentative function of each section Rifkin has created in the essay?
4. Which argument supporting Rifkin's claim is the strongest? Which is the weakest? Why?
5. Analyze the transitions Rifkin uses in his essay to link his various points.
6. How does Rifkin's concluding few paragraphs support his claim?

Exploring the Writer's Argument

1. This essay was written in 1995. Rifkin predicts that by late 1996, the economy would slide "headlong into a deep recession." (par. 6) However, until 2000 or so, the economy grew at unprecedented levels, in part because of technology. For you, does this knowledge undermine Rifkin's basic message? Explain.
2. In paragraph 10, Rifkin argues that a number of jobs are "destined for virtual extinction" because of the Information Revolution. Do you agree with him? If so, which jobs do you think will not survive? If you don't agree with his assessment, explain how the jobs he mentions will survive.
3. Are Rifkin's dire predictions about pension funds and benefits in paragraphs 22 to 24 persuasive? If so, how are they persuasive? If not, what is lacking?

Ideas for Writing Arguments

Prewriting

What problems do freelancers and most part-time workers have because of their employment status? Make an outline listing as many as you can think of.

Writing a Guided Argument

Write an essay in which you argue that the current trend toward employers using part-time and freelance workers is a dangerous problem for workers, who don't receive overtime or benefits. You might need to do some reading in the library or online to gather evidence and facts, especially statistics, if you can find them.

1. Open your essay with a rhetorical question posing the problem to the reader.
2. In the next paragraph, establish the history of the issue, explaining that this is a new trend in employment.
3. Write your major proposition.
4. Organize your minor propositions so that your strongest point comes last.
5. Support your minor propositions by offering examples from life to illustrate the hardship of this problem.
6. Develop a tone of cynicism that reflects the frustration you think these workers feel.
7. Close your essay by stating that you are a pessimist about the situation or an optimist.

Thinking, Arguing, and Writing Collaboratively

In groups of four or five class members, discuss the possible audience for Rifkin's essay. Come up with at least two passages you think are directed at each of the following audiences: (1) corporate executive and business leaders, (2) organized labor and union workers, (3) liberal intellectuals, (4) government workers. Explain why your group thinks each passage could be persuasive to that audience, then convene as a class and discuss your groups' answers.

Writing About the Text

Write an essay in which you evaluate Rifkin's use of statistics. Which are most impressive? Which are the weakest? What kind of statistics aren't here that you would like to see?

More Writing Ideas

1. Freewrite in your journal for 15 minutes on the subject of finding jobs on the Internet. Do not edit your work. When you are done, show your writing to a classmate and discuss possibilities for future essays.
2. Write one or two paragraphs analyzing how the time Rifkin describes (1995) is similar to and different from today.
3. Do some research on the Industrial Revolution. Which jobs disappeared when machines started to be used extensively? To take a well-known example, when the automobile replaced the horse and buggy, makers of horsewhips went out of business. Write an essay based on your research in which you argue that the Industrial Revolution was responsible for many lost jobs.

29 The Media: Do We Control It, or Does It Control Us?

In our media-saturated culture, there are hundreds of channels on cable television, from entertainment TV to sports to movies to music videos. How can the media *not* influence us? Almost every movie we want to watch is available at our local video store. Video cameras are getting smaller and cheaper, so that few events can escape taping. Since the early 1900s, when movies started, through the 1950s, when television became a popular medium (and advertisers discovered its power), the images created by Hollywood, the TV industries, and the advertising companies on Madison Avenue have become as familiar to us as our own family members. We watch for entertainment, but we are also aware that the media manipulate us at the same time.

Some would argue that even adults cannot resist the onslaught of images, but what about children? Children learn about the world, in part, by imitating what they see. Parents influence their children by offering themselves as behavioral models. But children today witness things that they normally wouldn't see in real life—on television and in the movies. What, for example, is the effect of video gunfights on children? This is the subject of one of the most bitterly fought debates today. In an age when children have gone to school with guns and shot their teachers and classmates, the question arises: How responsible are the media for these tragedies? And if they are responsible, can we really ask them to stop showing things people want to see? Violence and sex sell, and so that is what shows up on TV and in the movies. But are images of violence and sex enough to make youngsters imitate what they see, or are children media savvy enough today to have sufficient distance from what they view? How can parents protect their children?

Karen Springen, a parent of two girls, explores one response. She explains in "Why We Tuned Out" that she is simply not letting her children watch any TV or movies. To some, this might seem extreme. Gregg Easterbrook, in "Watch and Learn," makes a more scholarly attempt to argue about the influence of violence on youngsters. But talking about causes is one thing. Although she might disagree with Springen, Wendy Kaminer, like Springen, chooses to focus on solutions, with vastly different results. In "Toxic Media," Kaminer examines the danger of government censorship and finds that prospect to be scarier than the scariest slasher film.

Karen Springen
Why We Tuned Out

Karen Springen has written for Newsweek *since the 1980s, and focuses on health, social issues, and parenting. She has also written freelance articles for many magazines, including* Vegetarian Times, Working Woman, *and* Elle. *Springen was educated at Stanford University and got her master's degree in journalism from Columbia University, where she teaches journalism. She also teaches a reporting and writing class at Columbia College. Springen is a wife and the mother of two daughters who are the subjects of this selection about her and her husband's decision to keep their children from watching television.*

Prereading: Thinking About the Essay in Advance

Were you allowed to watch television when you were a child? What effect did it have on you, do you think?

Words to Watch

inquisitive (par. 2) asking a lot of questions
cartwheels (par. 2) a gymnastic move in which, arms and legs extended, one turns over sideways like a wheel
puritanical (par. 4) overly moral
outcasts (par. 4) those excluded from a group
cringed (par. 7) reacted out of pain or disgust
crusading (par. 7) acting as if on a mission
ridicule (par. 7) being made fun of, mockery

"What's your favorite TV show?" our girls' beloved ballet instructor asked each pint-size dancer in her class. Our oldest daughter, Jazzy, didn't know how to answer. She shrugged. Her moment of awkwardness results from a decision my husband, Mark, and I made five years ago. We don't allow our kids to watch TV. Period. Not at home, not at friends' houses; and they don't watch videos or movies, either. We want our daughters, Jazzy, now nearly 6, and Gigi, 3, to be as active as possible, physically and mentally. So when a babysitter asked whether Jazzy, then 1 year old, could watch TV, we thought about it—and said no. 1

When we look at our inquisitive, energetic daughters, we have no regrets. And our reading of the research makes us feel even better. Nielsen Media Research reports that American children 2 through 11 watch three hours and 16 minutes of television every day. Kids who watch more than 10 hours of TV each week are more likely to be overweight, aggressive and slow to learn in school, according to the American Medical Association. For 2

Tuning in. (www.mediawatch.com)

these reasons, the American Academy of Pediatrics recommends no TV for children younger than 2 and a maximum of two hours a day of "screen time" (TV, computers or videogames) for older kids. We are convinced that without TV, our daughters spend more time than other kids doing cartwheels, listening to stories and asking such interesting questions as "How old is God?" and "What makes my rubber ducks float?" They also aren't haunted by TV images of September 11—because they never saw them.

3 Going without TV in America has its difficult moments. When I called my sister, Lucy, to make arrangements for Thanksgiving, she warned that her husband was planning to spend the day watching football. We're going anyway. We'll just steer the girls toward the playroom. And some well-meaning friends tell us our girls may be missing out on good educational programming. Maybe. But that's not what most kids are watching. Nielsen Media Research reports that among children 2 through 11, the top-five TV shows in the new fall season were "The Wonderful World of Disney," "Survivor: Thailand," "Yu-Gi-Oh!", "Pokémon" and "Jackie Chan Adventures."

Will our happy, busy girls suffer because they're not participating in such a big part of the popular culture? Will they feel left out in school when they don't know who won on "Survivor"? "Kids are going to make fun of them," warns my mother-in-law. And a favorite child psychiatrist, Elizabeth Berger, author of "Raising Children With Character," cautions that maintaining a puritanical approach may make our kids into social outcasts. "Part of preparing your children for life is preparing them to be one of the girls," she says. "It's awful to be different from the other kids in fourth grade." 4

Our relatives all watch TV. So did we. I was born in 1961, the year Newton Minow, then the chairman of the U.S. Federal Communications Commission, called television a "vast wasteland." But I loved it. My sister, Katy, and I shared a first crush on the TV cartoon hero Speed Racer. Watching "Bewitched" and "The Brady Bunch" and, later, soap operas gave us an easy way to bond with our friends. Am I being selfish in not wanting the same for our children? 5

So far, our daughters don't seem to feel like misfits. We have no problem with the girls enjoying products based on TV characters. The girls wear Elmo pajamas and battle over who can sit on a big Clifford stuffed animal. From books, they also know about Big Bird, the Little Mermaid and Aladdin. And they haven't mentioned missing out on "Yu-Gi-Oh!" cartoon duels. Dr. Miriam Bar-on, who chairs the American Academy of Pediatrics committee on public education, says I'm helping our kids be creative, independent learners and calls our decision "awesome." And Mayo Clinic pediatrician Daniel Broughton, another group member, says that "there's no valid reason" the girls need to view television. 6

As the girls grow older, we can't completely shield them from TV anyway. We'll probably watch Olympic rhythmic gymnastics; the girls love it. And if Jazzy's favorite baseball team, the Cubs, ever make the World Series, we'll tune in. Last Monday Jazzy's music teacher showed "The Magic School Bus: Inside the Haunted House." Though "Magic School Bus" is a well-regarded Scholastic product, I still cringed, wondering why the kids weren't learning about vibrations and sounds by singing and banging on drums. But I kept silent; I'd never require my kids to abstain in school. Like Jean Lotus, the Oak Park, Ill., mom who founded the anti-TV group the White Dot and who also reluctantly allows her kids to view TV in school, I'm wary of being seen "as the crusading weirdo." But some public ridicule will be worth it if I help get even a few people to think twice before automatically turning on the tube. Now it's time for me to curl up with the girls and a well-worn copy of "Curious George." 7

Building Vocabulary

Identify and explain the following references, looking them up in reference works if necessary:

1. Nielsen Media Research (par. 2)
2. American Medical Association (par. 2)

3. *Survivor* (par. 4)
4. Federal Communications Commission (par. 5)
5. Mayo Clinic (par. 6)
6. Scholastic (par. 7)
7. *Curious George* (par. 7)

Thinking Critically About the Argument

Understanding the Writer's Argument

1. What is negative about the statistic that, on average, children watch more than three hours of television a day?
2. Why is it difficult to go without TV in America, according to Springen?
3. Why does Springen list the top five TV shows for children in the fall of 2002?
4. What did Newton Minow mean in 1961 when he called TV a "vast wasteland"?
5. Did Springen watch TV as a kid? What did she watch? How did it affect her?
6. Do Springen's girls know anything about what's on TV?
7. Will Springen always bar her children from watching TV? Explain.

Understanding the Writer's Techniques

1. What is Springen's major proposition? Where does she articulate it best in her essay?
2. What are Springen's minor propositions? List them in the form of an outline.
3. How does Springen use transitions effectively to build coherence in her essay? Analyze her use of transitions. Could you improve them? How?
4. What point is Springen making when she lists the top five TV shows for children ages 2 to 11 in paragraph 3?
5. What is the effect of Springen quoting Elizabeth Berger in paragraph 4? Why does she do this? Does it help or hurt her argument? Explain.
6. What is your reaction to paragraph 6? Do you find it persuasive? Why or why not?
7. Do you find the last paragraph persuasive? Why or why not?
8. What is the effect of the title? What meanings can you suggest for the phrase "tuned out"?

Exploring the Writer's Argument

1. Springen's daughters did not see images of the September 11 attacks. The children were young, and the images are disturbing. But if Springen's no-TV rule remains in place, her children will most likely miss out on the images that help shape American culture. Do you think that the children are missing out or will miss out on becoming involved Americans? Or are they better off without those images? Do we rely on those images today? Explain your answers.

2. Is Springen's essay presumptuous? Is she telling people how to rear their children or is she merely sharing her own experiences? Is she too self-congratulatory or appropriately proud? Explain your view of how Springen's argument is affected by how she presents her subject.
3. What does Springen's point about her children doing cartwheels and asking interesting questions contribute to the argument? Is a lack of TV the only reason they do these things? Explain your response. Do you know any children who are active and imaginative yet also watch TV? Explain your answers.

Ideas for Writing Arguments

Prewriting

What is it about television that you think has a *positive* effect on children? Are there any programs that kids like that are also educational and make them think? Jot down some notes on the topic.

Writing a Guided Argument

Write an essay in which you argue that television is good for children. You might have to do some research by watching television during those hours when children watch—Saturday mornings and weekday afternoons.

1. Begin with a paragraph that introduces your reader to the subject through an anecdote or interesting example.
2. Write your claim clearly.
3. Establish a tone early on of self-importance—make sure your reader understands that you are absolutely sure of your argument.
4. Allow two rhetorical questions that put voice to the opposition's viewpoint—for example, "Doesn't television make kids lazy?"
5. Answer the rhetorical questions with persuasive grounds to back up your claim.
6. Use effective transitions to maintain coherence.
7. Close your essay by asserting that you are going to let your children watch television.

Thinking, Arguing, and Writing Collaboratively

In small groups of three or four, exchange your Writing a Guided Argument papers. Offer suggestions in the form of a paragraph or two to help your classmate develop his or her essay. After revising the essay at home, meet with the same partner to discuss the success of the revisions.

Writing About the Text

Consider the weaknesses in Springen's essay. What are the major problems in her argument? Write an essay in the form of a letter to Springen in which you point out at least three criticisms you have of her essay.

More Writing Ideas

1. Write notes for an essay on the effect advertising has on children.
2. Write a paragraph or two that argues that even if TV isn't great for children, it's great for *parents.*
3. Write an essay that explores the idea of popular culture and its importance. What is popular culture, and what is its effect on our lives?

GREGG EASTERBROOK
Watch and Learn

Journalist and novelist Gregg Easterbrook is a senior editor at The New Republic *and a contributing editor for* Atlantic Monthly *and* Washington Monthly. *He is the author of nonfiction books* A Moment on the Earth *(1996), about environmentalism, and* Beside Still Waters: Searching for Meaning in an Age of Doubt *(1999), about faith in the modern world. He is also author of the novel* The Here and Now *(2002). In this selection, which appeared in* The New Republic *in 1999, Easterbrook calls the media to account for their glorification of violence. How much responsibility do they have?*

Prereading: Thinking About the Essay in Advance

How do you think TV and the movies can influence children?

Words to Watch

wry (par. 1) dryly humorous
provocative (par. 1) meant to elicit a strong response
carnage (par. 3) bloody violence
whimpering (par. 3) softly crying
gratuitously (par. 4) without good reason
dramatizations (par. 5) reenactments for a movie or TV show
psyche (par. 8) psychological term for the mind
calculus (par. 11) way of figuring out
absolve (par. 13) forgive
cohabitation (par. 19) living with someone before marriage

1 Millions of teens have seen the 1996 movie *Scream,* a box-office and home-rental hit. Critics adored the film. The *Washington Post* declared that it "deftly mixes irony, self-reference, and social wry commentary." The *Los Angeles Times* hailed it as "a bravura, provocative send-up." *Scream* opens with a scene in which a teenage girl is forced to watch her jock boyfriend tortured and then disemboweled by two fellow students who, it will eventually be learned, want revenge on anyone from high school who crossed them. After jock boy's stomach is shown cut open and he dies screaming, the killers stab and torture the girl, then cut her throat and hang her body from a tree so that Mom can discover it

when she drives up. A dozen students and teachers are graphically butchered in the film, while the characters make running jokes about murder. At one point, a boy tells a big-breasted friend she'd better be careful because the stacked girls always get it in horror films; in the next scene, she's grabbed, stabbed through the breasts, and murdered. Some provocative send-up, huh? The movie builds to a finale in which one of the killers announces that he and his accomplice started off by murdering strangers but then realized it was a lot more fun to kill their friends.

Now that two Colorado high schoolers have murdered twelve classmates and a teacher—often, it appears, first taunting their pleading victims, just like celebrity stars do in the movies!—some commentators have dismissed the role of violence in the images shown to the young, pointing out that horrific acts by children existed before celluloid or the phosphor screen. That is true—the Leopold-Loeb murder of 1924, for example. But mass murders by the young, once phenomenally rare, are suddenly on the increase. Can it be coincidence that this increase is happening at the same time that Hollywood has begun to market the notion that mass murder is fun? 2

For, in cinema's never-ending quest to up the ante on violence, murder as sport is the latest frontier. Slasher flicks began this trend; most portray carnage from the killer's point of view, showing the victim cowering, begging, screaming as the blade goes in, treating each death as a moment of festivity for the killer. (Many killers seek feelings of power over their victims, criminology finds; by reveling in the pleas of victims, slasher movies promote this base emotion.) The 1994 movie *Natural Born Killers* depicted slaying the helpless not only as a way to have a grand time but also as a way to become a celebrity; several dozen on-screen murders are shown in that film, along with a discussion of how great it makes you feel to just pick people out at random and kill them. The 1994 movie *Pulp Fiction* presented hit men as glamour figures having loads of interesting fun; the actors were mainstream stars like John Travolta. The 1995 movie *Seven,* starring Brad Pitt, portrayed a sort of contest to murder in unusually grotesque ways. (Screenwriters now actually discuss, and critics comment on, which film's killings are most amusing.) The 1995 movie *The Basketball Diaries* contains an extended dream sequence in which the title character, played by teen heartthrob Leonardo DiCaprio, methodically guns down whimpering, pleading classmates at his high school. A rock soundtrack pulses, and the character smiles as he kills. 3

The new Hollywood tack of portraying random murder as a form of recreation does not come from schlock-houses. Disney's Miramax division, the same mainstream studio that produced *Shakespeare in Love,* is responsible for *Scream* and *Pulp Fiction.* Time-Warner is to blame for *Natural Born Killers* and actually ran television ads promoting this film as "delirious, daredevil fun." (After it was criticized for calling murder "fun," Time-Warner tried to justify *Killers* as social commentary; if you believe that, you believe *Godzilla* was really about biodiversity protection.) Praise and publicity for 4 gratuitously violent movies come from the big media conglomerates, including the newspapers and networks that profit from advertising for films that glorify murder. Disney, now one of the leading promoters of violent images in American culture, even feels that what little kids need is more violence. Its Christmas 1998 children's movie *Mighty Foe Young* begins with an eight-year-old girl watching her mother being murdered. By the movie's end, it is 20 years later, and the killer has returned to stalk the grown daughter, pointing a gun in her face and announcing, "Now join your mother in hell." A Disney movie.

5 One reason Hollywood keeps reaching for ever-more-obscene levels of killing is that it must compete with television, which today routinely airs the kind of violence once considered shocking in theaters. According to studies conducted at Temple University, prime-time network (nonnews) shows now average up to five violent acts per hour. In February 1999, NBC ran in prime time the movie *Eraser,* not editing out an extremely graphic scene in which a killer pulls a gun on a bystander and blasts away. The latest TV movie based on *The Rockford Files,* which aired on CBS the night of the Colorado murders, opened with a scene of an eleven-year-old girl in short-shorts being stalked by a man in a black hood, grabbed, and dragged off, screaming. *The Rockford Files* is a comedy. Combining television and movies, the typical American boy or girl, studies find, will observe a stunning 40,000 dramatizations of killing by age 18.

6 In the days after the Colorado slaughter, discussion of violent images in American culture was dominated by the canned positions of the anti-Hollywood right and the mammon-is-our-God film lobby. The debate missed three vital points: the distinction between what adults should be allowed to see (anything) and what the inchoate minds of children and adolescents should see; the way in which important liberal battles to win free expression in art and literature have been perverted into an excuse for antisocial video brutality produced by cynical capitalists; and the difference between censorship and voluntary acts of responsibility.

7 The day after the Colorado shooting, Mike De Luca, an executive of New Line Cinema, maker of *The Basketball Diaries,* told *USA Today* that, when kids kill, "bad home life, bad parenting, having guns in the home" are "more of a factor than what we put out there for entertainment." Setting aside the disclosure that Hollywood now categorizes scenes of movie stars gunning down the innocent as "entertainment," De Luca is correct: studies do show that upbringing is more determinant of violent behavior than any other factor. But research also clearly shows that the viewing of violence can cause aggression and crime. So the question is, in a society already plagued by poor parenting and unlimited gun sales, why does the entertainment industry feel privileged to make violence even more prevalent?

8 Even when researchers factor out other influences such as parental attention, many peer-reviewed studies have found causal links between viewing phony violence and engaging in actual violence. A 1971 surgeon general's report asserted a broad relationship between the two. Studies by Brandon Cen-

terwall, an epidemiologist at the University of Wisconsin, have shown that the postwar murder rise in the United States began roughly a decade after TV viewing became common. Centerwall also found that, in South Africa, where television was not generally available until 1975, national murder rates started rising about a decade later. Violent computer games have not existed long enough to be the subject of many controlled studies, but experts expect it will be shown that playing such games in youth also correlates with destructive behavior. There's an eerie likelihood that violent movies and violent games amplify one another, the film and television images placing thoughts of carnage into the psyche while the games condition the trigger finger to act on those impulses.

Leonard Eron, a psychologist at the University of Michigan, has been 9 tracking video violence and actual violence for almost four decades. His initial studies, in 1960, found that even the occasional violence depicted in 1950s television—to which every parent would gladly return today—caused increased aggression among eight-year-olds. By the adult years, Eron's studies find, those who watched the most TV and movies in childhood were much more likely to have been arrested for, or convicted of, violent felonies. Eron believes that 10 percent of U.S. violent crime is caused by exposure to images of violence, meaning that 90 percent is not but that a 10 percent national reduction in violence might be achieved merely by moderating the content of television and movies. "Kids learn by observation," Eron says. "If what they observe is violent, that's what they learn." To cite a minor but telling example, the introduction of vulgar language into American public discourse traces, Eron thinks, largely to the point at which stars like Clark Gable began to swear onscreen, and kids then imitated swearing as normative.

Defenders of bloodshed in film, television, and writing often argue that 10 depictions of killing don't incite real violence because no one is really affected by what they see or read; it's all just water off a duck's back. At heart, this is an argument against free expression. The whole reason to have a First Amendment is that people are influenced by what they see and hear: words and images do change minds, so there must be free competition among them. If what we say, write, or show has no consequences, why bother to have free speech?

Defenders of Hollywood bloodshed also employ the argument that, 11 since millions of people watch screen mayhem and shrug, feigned violence has no causal relation to actual violence. After a horrific 1992 case in which a British gang acted out a scene from the slasher movie *Child's Play 3*, torturing a girl to death as the movie had shown, the novelist Martin Amis wrote dismissively in the *New Yorker* that he had rented *Child's Play 3* and watched the film, and it hadn't made him want to kill anyone, so what was the problem? But Amis isn't homicidal or unbalanced. For those on the psychological borderline, the calculus is different. There have, for example, been at least two instances of real-world shootings in which the guilty imitated scenes in *Natural Born Killers*.

12 Most telling, Amis wasn't affected by watching a slasher movie because Amis is not young. Except for the unbalanced, exposure to violence in video "is not so important for adults; adults can watch anything they want," Eron says. Younger minds are a different story. Children who don't yet understand the difference between illusion and reality may be highly affected by video violence. Between the ages of two and eight, hours of viewing violent TV programs and movies correlates closely to felonies later in life; the child comes to see hitting, stabbing, and shooting as normative acts. The link between watching violence and engaging in violence continues up to about the age of 19, Eron finds, after which most people's characters have been formed, and video mayhem no longer correlates to destructive behavior.

13 Trends in gun availability do not appear to explain the murder rise that has coincided with television and violent films. Research by John Lott Jr., of the University of Chicago Law School, shows that the percentage of homes with guns has changed little throughout the postwar era. What appears to have changed is the willingness of people to fire their guns at one another. Are adolescents now willing to use guns because violent images make killing seem acceptable or even cool? Following the Colorado slaughter, the *New York Times* ran a recounting of other postwar mass murders staged by the young, such as the 1966 Texas tower killings, and noted that they all happened before the advent of the Internet or shock rock, which seemed to the *Times* to absolve the modern media. But all the mass killings by the young occurred after 1950—after it became common to watch violence on television.

14 When horrific murders occur, the film and television industries routinely attempt to transfer criticism to the weapons used. Just after the Colorado shootings, for instance, TV talkshow host Rosie O'Donnell called for a constitutional amendment banning all firearms. How strange that O'Donnell didn't call instead for a boycott of Sony or its production company, Columbia Tristar—a film studio from which she has received generous paychecks and whose current offerings include *8MM,* which glamorizes the sexual murder of young women, and *The Replacement Killers,* whose hero is a hit man and which depicts dozens of gun murders. Handguns should be licensed, but that hardly excuses the convenient sanctimony of blaming the crime on the weapon, rather than on what resides in the human mind.

15 And, when it comes to promoting adoration of guns, Hollywood might as well be the National Rifle Association's (NRA) marketing arm. An ever-increasing share of film and television depicts the firearm as something the virile must have and use, if not an outright sexual aid. Check the theater section of any newspaper, and you will find an ever-higher percentage of movie ads in which the stars are prominently holding guns. Keanu Reeves, Uma Thurman, Laurence Fishburne, Geena Davis, Woody Harrelson, and Mark Wahlberg are just a few of the hip stars who have posed with guns for movie advertising. Hollywood endlessly congratulates itself for reducing the depiction of cigarettes in movies and movie ads. Cigarettes had to go, the film industry admitted, because glamorizing them gives the wrong idea to kids. But the glamor-

ization of firearms, which is far more dangerous, continues. Today, even female stars who otherwise consider themselves politically aware will model in sexualized poses with guns. Ads for the movie *Goodbye Lover* show star Patricia Arquette nearly nude, with very little between her and the viewer but her handgun.

But doesn't video violence merely depict a stark reality against which 16 the young need to be warned? American society is far too violent, yet the forms of brutality highlighted in the movies and on television—prominently "thrill" killings and serial murders—are pure distortion. Nearly 99 percent of real murders result from robberies, drug deals, and domestic disputes; figures from research affiliated with the FBI's behavioral sciences division show an average of only about 30 serial or "thrill" murders nationally per year. Thirty is plenty horrifying enough, but, at this point, each of the major networks and movie studios alone depicts more "thrill" and serial murders annually than that. By endlessly exploiting the notion of the "thrill" murder, Hollywood and television present to the young an entirely imaginary image of a society in which killing for pleasure is a common event. The publishing industry, including some [*New Republic*] advertisers, also distorts for profit the frequency of "thrill" murders.

The profitability of violent cinema is broadly dependent on the "down- 17 rating" of films—movies containing extreme violence being rated only R instead of NC-17 (the new name for X)—and the lax enforcement of age restrictions regarding movies. Teens are the best market segment for Hollywood; when moviemakers claim their violent movies are not meant to appeal to teens, they are simply lying. The millionaire status of actors, directors, and studio heads—and the returns of the mutual funds that invest in movie companies—depends on not restricting teen access to theaters or film rentals. Studios in effect control the movie ratings board and endlessly lobby it not to label extreme violence with an NC-17, the only form of rating that is actually enforced. *Natural Born Killers,* for example, received an R following Time-Warner lobbying, despite its repeated close-up murders and one charming scene in which the stars kidnap a high school girl and argue about whether it would be more fun to kill her before or after raping her. Since its inception, the movie ratings board has put its most restrictive rating on any realistic representation of lovemaking, while sanctioning ever-more-graphic depictions of murder and torture. In economic terms, the board's pro-violence bias gives studios an incentive to present more death and mayhem, confident that ratings officials will smile with approval.

When R-and-X battles were first fought, intellectual sentiment regarded 18 the ratings system as a way of blocking the young from seeing films with political content, such as *Easy Rider,* or discouraging depictions of sexuality; ratings were perceived as the rubes' counterattack against cinematic sophistication. But, in the 1960s, murder after murder after murder was not standard cinema fare. The most controversial violent film of that era, *A Clockwork*

Orange, depicted a total of one killing, which was heard but not on-camera. (*Clockwork Orange* also had genuine political content, unlike most of today's big-studio movies.) In an era of runaway screen violence, the '60s ideal that the young should be allowed to see what they want has been corrupted. In this, trends in video mirror the misuse of liberal ideals generally.

19 Anti-censorship battles of this century were fought on firm ground, advocating the right of films to tackle social and sexual issues (the 1930s Hays office forbid among other things cinematic mention of cohabitation) and free access to works of literature such as *Ulysses, Story of O,* and the original version of Norman Mailer's *The Naked and the Dead.* Struggles against censors established that suppression of film or writing is wrong.

20 But to say that nothing should be censored is very different from saying that everything should be shown. Today, Hollywood and television have twisted the First Amendment concept that occasional repulsive or worthless expression must be protected, so as to guarantee freedom for works of genuine political content or artistic merit, into a new standard in which constitutional freedoms are employed mainly to safeguard works that make no pretense of merit. In the new standard, the bulk of what's being protected is repulsive or worthless, with the meritorious work the rare exception.

21 Not only is there profit for the performers, producers, management, and shareholders of firms that glorify violence, so, too, is there profit for politicians. Many conservative or Republican politicians who denounce Hollywood eagerly accept its lucre. Bob Dole's 1995 anti-Hollywood speech was not followed up by any anti-Hollywood legislation or campaign-funds strategy. After the Colorado murders. President Clinton declared, "Parents should take this moment to ask what else they can do to shield children from violent images and experiences that warp young perceptions." But Clinton was careful to avoid criticizing Hollywood, one of the top sources of public backing and campaign contributions for him and his would-be successor, Vice President Al Gore. The president had nothing specific to propose on film violence—only that parents should try to figure out what to do.

22 When television producers say it is the parents' obligation to keep children away from the tube, they reach the self-satire point of warning that their own product is unsuitable for consumption. The situation will improve somewhat beginning in 2000, by which time all new TVs must be sold with the "V chip"—supported by Clinton and Gore—which will allow parents to block violent shows. But it will be at least a decade before the majority of the nation's sets include the chip, and who knows how adept young minds will prove at defeating it? Rather than relying on a technical fix that will take many years to achieve an effect, TV producers could simply stop churning out the gratuitous violence. Television could dramatically reduce its output of scenes of killing and still depict violence in news broadcasts, documentaries, and the occasional show in which the horrible is genuinely relevant. Reduction in violence is not censorship; it is placing social responsibility before profit.

The movie industry could practice the same kind of restraint without sacrificing profitability. In this regard, the big Hollywood studios, including Disney, look craven and exploitative compared to, of all things, the porn-video industry. Repulsive material occurs in underground porn, but, in the products sold by the mainstream triple-X distributors such as Vivid Video (the MGM of the erotica business), violence is never, ever, ever depicted—because that would be irresponsible. Women and men perform every conceivable explicit act in today's mainstream porn, but what is shown is always consensual and almost sunnily friendly. Scenes of rape or sexual menace never occur, and scenes of sexual murder are an absolute taboo. 23

It is beyond irony that today Sony and Time-Warner eagerly market explicit depictions of women being raped, sexually assaulted, and sexually murdered, while the mainstream porn industry would never dream of doing so. But, if money is all that matters, the point here is that mainstream porn is violence-free and yet risqué and highly profitable. Surely this shows that Hollywood could voluntarily step back from the abyss of glorifying violence and still retain its edge and its income. 24

Following the Colorado massacre, Republican presidential candidate Gary Bauer declared to a campaign audience, "In the America I want, all of these producers and directors, they would not be able to show their faces in public" because fingers "would be pointing at them and saying, 'Shame, shame.'" The statement sent chills through anyone fearing right-wing thought-control. But Bauer's final clause is correct—Hollywood and television do need to hear the words "shame, shame." The cause of the shame should be removed voluntarily, not to stave off censorship, but because it is the responsible thing to do. 25

Put it this way. The day after a teenager guns down the sons and daughters of studio executives in a high school in Bel Air or Westwood, Disney and Time-Warner will stop glamorizing murder. Do we have to wait until that day? 26

Building Vocabulary

Identify the following words, phrases, and references, and write a definition for each:

1. bravura (par. 1)
2. stacked (par. 1)
3. Leopold/Loeb case (par. 2)
4. slasher flicks (par. 3)
5. dream sequence (par. 3)
6. shlock (par. 4)
7. conglomerates (par. 4)
8. mammon (par. 6)
9. peer-reviewed (par. 8)
10. market segment (par. 17)

Thinking Critically About the Argument

Understanding the Writer's Argument

1. What events do you think prompted Easterbrook's essay?
2. What does the writer think is responsible for the rise in mass murders by young people?
3. What does the phrase "murder as sport is the final frontier" imply? Who, according to the writer, is responsible for movies that have the most violent content? Why do movies keep getting more violent?
4. Why does the writer quote Mike DeLuca of New Line Cinema, in paragraph 7?
5. What do the Wisconsin and Michigan studies show?
6. What, according to the writer, is the difference between the novelist Martin Amis and people who might be influenced to imitate violent acts?
7. What does the writer make of the *Times* report he mentions in paragraph 13?
8. What is the writer's opinion of the current movie ratings system?

Understanding the Writer's Techniques

1. What is the writer's major proposition? Where does it appear?
2. What argumentative function does the opening, describing the movie *Scream,* have?
3. What kinds of authoritative sources does Easterbrook use to support his argument? Which do you think are the most effective?
4. The writer relies heavily on examples. Which do you see as his most persuasive example? How does he make the example stronger by explaining it?
5. What is the writer's tone? Explain and offer examples to support your answer.
6. How do paragraphs 4 to 7 support the writer's major proposition?
7. Is the concluding paragraph effective? Why or why not?

Exploring the Writer's Argument

1. The beginning of Easterbrook's essay summarizes the shocking contents of the popular movie *Scream.* He includes the gory and graphic details, presumably for effect. Should he tone it down for his audience? Is he committing the same offense that he accuses the filmmakers of committing? Explain your answers.
2. Easterbrook uses loaded language in his essay. For example he writes that the movie *8MM* "glamorizes the sexual murder of young women." (paragraph 14) Obviously, the filmmakers do not think their movies were glamorizing murder. Find at least five more places in which Easterbrook uses such language to stack the debate in his favor. Do you think this kind of usage is fair? Explain your answer fully.
3. The argument Easterbrook makes is open to debate, but what about his audience? How persuasive can Easterbrook really be with his essay? Is

there any chance that this essay can persuade anyone? Who has the power to effect the changes he wants, and how could they truly be persuaded to change their minds and actions? Is it possible? Explain.

Ideas for Writing Arguments

Prewriting

Assuming that violence in movies is influential to children, are all images of violence in movies harmful? Write some notes for an essay about this topic.

Writing a Guided Argument

Write an essay arguing that some kinds of violence in the movies can actually have a positive effect on children.

1. Begin your essay with a vivid example of the kind of violence you are going to argue for.
2. Admit that this violence can influence children.
3. Surprise your reader by writing your claim that this kind of violence can have a positive effect on children.
4. Offer at least three kinds of film violence that can be beneficial.
5. Illustrate your points with good examples.
6. Use strong transitions to bind your argument.
7. Address at least one view from the opposition's perspective.
8. Rebut the opposition's argument.
9. Close your essay by reaffirming your claim.

Thinking, Arguing, and Writing Collaboratively

In groups of four or five students, exchange drafts of your Writing a Guided Argument essays with each member of your group, passing them around the group. Each student should read each other student's essay, marking notes directly on the essay and writing a short paragraph commenting on the success of the argument. Then collect your essay and use the comments as the basis for your final draft.

Writing About the Text

In his essay "The Limits of Freedom" in Chapter 10, Andrew Brown argues for occasional censorship of offensive and provocative content on the Internet. Write an essay that compares and contrasts both the content and the effectiveness of Brown's and Easterbrook's arguments.

More Writing Ideas

1. Watch the news on television and write a journal entry about how the TV news can contribute to violence in our society.
2. Write a paragraph or two that explore the implications of Easterbrook's sentence in paragraph 26: "The day after a teenager guns down the sons

and daughters of studio executives in a high school in Bel Air or Westwood, Disney and Time-Warner will stop glamorizing murder."

3. Recently, a great deal of controversy has arisen over the violence in video games like Duke Nukem and Grand Theft Auto. Write an essay in which you argue that violent video games are (or are not) much more likely to incite violence than the violence children see in the movies.

WENDY KAMINER
Toxic Media

Lawyer and writer Wendy Kaminer is a contributing editor for The Atlantic Monthly *and is on the board of the libertarian legal organization the American Civil Liberties Union. She is the author of* Sleeping with Extra-Terrestrials: I'm Dysfunctional, You're Dysfunctional *(1992),* It's All the Rage: Crime and Culture *(1995), and* The Rise of Irrationalism and Perils of Piety *(1999). She also writes freelance for* The New York Times, The Wall Street Journal, The Nation, *and* Newsweek. *This essay, which appeared in 2000 in* The American Prospect, *for which she is a senior correspondent, warns against the danger of censorship gone out of control.*

Prereading: Thinking About the Essay in Advance

Is there anything on television you'd like to see censored? What, and why?

Words to Watch

ceasefire (par. 1) a break in fighting
concomitant (par. 2) accompanying
centrist (par. 3) politically between the extremes of liberal and conservative
complemented (par. 3) made complete or matched up with
bipartisan (par. 4) having members from both parties
stringent (par. 8) strict and unbending
abhors (par. 9) hates
hyperbolic (par. 10) wildly exaggerated
dearth (par. 10) a lack of, insufficient amount
de facto (par. 12) in reality, even if not official

1 Like Claude Rains in Casablanca, Al Gore is shocked!, shocked! that the entertainment industry is marketing violent material to minors. Countering Hollywood's macho entertainments with some macho rhetoric of his own, he gave the industry six months to "clean up its act" and declare a "ceasefire" in what he apparently sees as the media's war against America's children.

2 No one should be surprised by the vice president's threat to impose government regulations on the marketing of popular entertainments, which im-

mediately followed the issuance of a new Federal Trade Commission (FTC) report on the subject. As his choice of running mate [Joseph Lieberman] made clear, Gore is positioning himself as the moral voice of the Democratic Party—replete with Godliness and a desire to cleanse the culture. With a concomitant promise to protect ordinary Americans from rapacious corporations, Gore is an early twenty-first-century version of a nineteenth-century female Progressive—a Godloving social purist with a soft spot for working families and, not so incidentally, women's rights.

Many Victorian women's rights activists, like Frances Willard of the Women's Christian Temperance Union and Julia Ward Howe, enthusiastically supported the suppression of "impure" or "vicious" literature, which was blamed for corrupting the nation's youth. "Books are feeders for brothels" according to the notorious nineteenth-century antivice crusader Anthony Comstock, for whom the nation's first obscenity law was named. Gun violence is fed by violent media, Al Gore, Joseph Lieberman, and others assert. The new FTC report was commissioned by President Clinton immediately after the 1999 shootings at Columbine High. That was when centrist politicians (and commentators) were touting the new "commonsense" view of youth violence: It was caused by both the availability of firearms and the availability of violent media. Gun control would be complemented by culture control. 3

So in June 1999, two Democratic senators, Lieberman and the usually thoughtful Kent Conrad of North Dakota, joined with [Senators] Trent Lott and John McCain in proposing federal legislation requiring the labeling of violent audio and visual media. These requirements, which were to be enforced by the FTC, were amendments to the cigarette labeling act. (When politicians revisit their bad ideas, critics like me repeat themselves. I discussed this proposed bill and the bipartisan drive to censor in a November 23, 1999, *American Prospect* column, "The Politics of Sanctimony.") 4

Advocates of censorship often charge that media can be "toxic" (as well as "addictive") like tobacco and other drugs. By describing whatever film or CD they disdain as a defective product, they undermine the view of it as speech. (We should regulate pornography the way we regulate exploding Ford Pintos, one feminist antiporn activist used to say; she seemed to consider *Playboy* an incendiary device.) In endorsing Internet filtering programs, Gore has remarked that minors should be protected from "dangerous places" on the Internet—in other words, "dangerous" speech. Some Web sites should effectively be locked up, just as medicine cabinets are locked up to protect children from poisons, the vice president remarked at a 1997 Internet summit. 5

Once you define violent or sexually explicit media as toxic products, it is not terribly difficult to justify regulating their advertising, at least, if not their distribution and production. Commercial speech generally enjoys constitutional protection, but as advocates of marketing restrictions assert, the First Amendment does not protect false or misleading advertising or ads promoting illegal activities. That's true but not necessarily relevant here. 6

Campaigns marketing violent entertainment to children may be sleazy, but they don't promote an illegal activity (the sale of violent material to minors is not generally criminal); and they're not deceptive or unfair (many popular entertainments are just as bad as they purport to be). Ratings are not determined or mandated by the government (not yet, anyway), so why should it be a federal offense for industry executives to violate the spirit of their own voluntary codes?

7 Effective regulation of media marketing campaigns would require new federal legislation that would entangle the government in the production of popular entertainments. What might this legislation entail? Ratings and labeling would be mandatory, supervised by the FTC (or some other federal agency), and any effort to subvert the ratings system would be a federal offense. Testifying before the Senate Commerce Committee on September 12, 2000, Lieberman promised that regulation of the entertainment industry would focus on "how they market, not what they produce," but that promise ignores the effect of marketing considerations on content.

8 Some may consider the decline of violent entertainments no great loss, imagining perhaps that slasher movies and violent video games will be the primary victims of a new federal labeling regime. But it's not hard to imagine a docudrama about domestic abuse or abortion, or a coming-of-age story about a gay teen, receiving the same restricted rating as a sleazy movie about a serial murderer. In any case, a stringent, federally mandated and monitored rating and labeling system will not enhance parental control; it's a vehicle for bureaucratic control. Federal officials, not parents, will determine what entertainment will be available to children when they devise and enforce the ratings.

9 Some claim that federal action is justified, nonetheless, by an overriding need to save lives. At the September 12 hearing inspired by the FTC report, several senators and other witnesses vigorously condemned the entertainment industry for "literally making a killing off of marketing to kids," in the words of Kansas Republican Sam Brownback. He called upon the industry to stop producing the entertainments he abhors. Lieberman charged that media violence was "part of a toxic mix that has turned some of our children into killers." Lynne Cheney, former head of the National Endowment for the Humanities, declared that "there is a problem with the product they market, no matter how they market it." Democratic Senator Fritz Hollings proposed giving the Federal Communications Commission the power to impose a partial ban on whatever programming it considers violent and harmful to minors.

10 What all this hyperbolic rhetoric obscured (or ignored) was the dearth of hard evidence that violent media actually turns "children into killers." In fact, the FTC study on which would-be censors rely found no clear causal connection between violent media and violent behavior. "Exposure to violent materials probably is not even the most important factor" in determining whether a child will turn violent, FTC Chairman Robert Pitofsky observed. The most he

would say was that exposure to violent media "does seem to correlate with aggressive attitudes, insensitivity toward violence, and an exaggerated view of how much violence occurs in the world."

This is not exactly a defense of media violence, but it may present a fairly balanced view of its effects, which do not justify limitations on speech. Living in a free society entails a commitment not to prohibit speech unless it clearly, directly, and intentionally causes violence. If violent entertainment can be regulated by the federal government because it allegedly causes violence, so can inflammatory political rhetoric, like assertions that abortion providers kill babies. Anti-abortion rhetoric probably has even a clearer connection to violence than any violent movie, but both must be protected. If Disney can be brought under the thumb of federal regulators, so can Cardinal Law when he denounces abortion as murder. 11

It's unfortunate and ironic that apparently amoral corporations, like Disney or Time-Warner, stand as champions and beneficiaries of First Amendment rights. As gatekeepers of the culture, they're not exactly committed to maintaining an open, diverse marketplace of ideas. Indeed, the de facto censorship engineered by media conglomerates may threaten public discourse nearly as much as federal regulation. And neither our discourse nor our culture is exactly enriched by gratuitously violent media. 12

But speech doesn't have to provide cultural enrichment to enjoy constitutional protection. We don't need a First Amendment to protect popular, inoffensive speech or speech that a majority of people believe has social value. We need it to protect speech that Lynne Cheney or Joseph Lieberman consider demeaning and degrading. Censorship campaigns often begin with a drive to protect children (or women), but they rarely end there. 13

Building Vocabulary

1. Write out the meanings of the following idioms:
   - **a.** the moral voice (par. 2)
   - **b.** cleanse the culture (par. 2)
   - **c.** a soft spot for working families (par. 2)
   - **d.** entangle the government (par. 7)
   - **e.** making a killing off (par. 9)
   - **f.** under the thumb (par. 11)
   - **g.** marketplace of ideas (par. 12)
2. Identify and define the following references, and explain their significance to American culture:
   - **a.** Federal Trade Commission (par. 2)
   - **b.** Victorian (par. 3)
   - **c.** Ford Pintos (par. 5)
   - **d.** slasher movies (par. 8)
   - **e.** National Endowment for the Humanities (par. 9)
   - **f.** Cardinal Law (par. 11)

Thinking Critically About the Argument

Understanding the Writer's Argument

1. What does it mean that Al Gore is "shocked! shocked!" about the entertainment industry's marketing of violence? What is the writer referring to here? Why is Kaminer not surprised by Gore's threat to the entertainment industry?
2. What is the history of labeling media? According to Kaminer, what are the risks of labeling entertainment?
3. What does the First Amendment not protect when it comes to advertising?
4. What is Kaminer's view of the politicians and their opinions as quoted in paragraph 9? What does Kaminer think is more of a risk to America than media violence?
5. What, according to Kaminer, is the problem with the argument that media violence is a direct cause of the rise in violence?
6. Why does Kaminer think it's odd that large media corporations "stand as champions and beneficiaries of First Amendment rights"? (par. 12)

Understanding the Writer's Techniques

1. What is Kaminer's major proposition? Where does it appear?
2. Why does the writer start her essay with the voices of politicians? How does she portray them? What argumentative effect does her opening have?
3. Why does Kaminer give the history of politicians' attempts to regulate media? What point is she making? Is it effectively done? Why or why not?
4. What tone is the writer taking in this essay? Give examples to explain your answer.
5. How do paragraphs 9 and 10 support Kaminer's position?
6. List two or three of her most effective transitions, and explain why they are effective.
7. Is the conclusion effective? What makes it so, or how could it be improved?

Exploring the Writer's Argument

1. In paragraph 6, Kaminer complains that "once you define violent or sexually explicit media as toxic products, it is not terribly difficult to justify regulating their advertising, at least, if not their distribution and production." Do you agree with her statement? Do you still think it is difficult, no matter what a politician or other public figure might say? Why or why not?
2. Do you think Kaminer's occasionally combative tone strengthens or weakens her argument? Explain your answer.
3. Although this essay was written recently, in 2000—after the shootings at Columbine High School in 1999 and after other school shootings—do

you think Kaminer would have any reason today to change her mind about her claim? Why or why not? Can you think of any reason Kaminer would change her mind? Explain your response.

Ideas for Writing Arguments

Prewriting

Warning labels now appear on video games and television shows to indicate violence, sexually explicit material, and so on. What is your opinion of those labels? Are they helpful? Why or why not? Write some notes on your feelings and the reasons for your feelings.

Writing a Guided Argument

Write an essay arguing for or against the warning labels on television shows. Do some research online or in the library to determine the origin of the labels. Who made the networks include them, or did the networks put them in on their own?

1. Open your essay with an account of watching television and noticing a label on a show.
2. Link your experience with your major proposition by using a transition.
3. Give the history of the labels and a partial list, for your reader's information, of the labels.
4. Explain in brief why you are for or against the labels.
5. In the next section, offer your minor propositions.
6. Support your minor propositions with examples and facts you gleaned from your research.
7. Address the issue of television as "toxic media."
8. Establish a tone that has some irony and cynicism.
9. Rebut at least one possible objection to your argument.
10. Close your essay with a discussion of how the television industry is doing things the right way, or offer a proposal to address the problem.

Thinking, Arguing, and Writing Collaboratively

Help to divide the class into two equal groups. One group should take Kaminer's position that violence in the media does not warrant censorship, and the other should take Easterbrook's position that violence at least warrants self-censorship. As a group, think of arguments and facts to add to those already given by the writer whose position you are taking and try to remedy weaknesses you might see. Take notes on your group discussion and prepare an outline for a debate. Debate the issue, and afterwards reconvene as a class to discuss the success of the structure of the debate and how effective the arguments your group added were. Discuss what you left out or improved.

Writing About the Text

Write an essay that expands on the following sentence by Kaminer: "Campaigns marketing violent entertainment to children may be sleazy, but they don't promote an illegal activity (the sale of violent material to minors is not generally criminal); and they're not deceptive or unfair (many popular entertainments are just as bad as they purport to be)." (par. 6)

More Writing Ideas

1. In your journal, write an entry about your feelings on the First Amendment.
2. If violent media is one possible risk that we face in an open society, what other risks are there? Write one or two paragraphs outlining the various dangers that arise from living as we do in a free country.
3. Find an item in the media (a song, a clip from a movie, a television show, a radio show, or a newspaper or magazine advertisement, for example) that you find particularly offensive and bad for society, then defend it in an essay. Defend the piece's right to be created, distributed, and marketed, addressing each of these rights in order.

30 Education: How Do We Teach and Learn?

As long as there are parents, they will argue about education. How can parents today make sure that their children are brought up with the values that the parents believe in? When children are 5, 4, or even 3 years old (parents are working more and more these days), they go out in the world and become the responsibility of teachers, who act *in loco parentis* (that is, as substitute parents). The future adults of society are molded in school, which is what makes education such a volatile topic. What is the best way to educate our children so that our society heads in the right direction? How do the issues change, if at all, when we're talking about high school and college?

In a wide variety of ways, newspapers, magazines, and books published across the country are answering these questions. Each writer engages the emotional issue with a different level of authority, a different set of credentials, a different point of view. For example, Ellen Goodman writes in "Religion in the Textbooks" about her dissatisfaction with what she sees as a loss of nerve among school officials. Religion is a part of almost everyone's life, yet schools are shying away from the topic and transforming it into something it's not. She calls for a braver approach. In "Their Cheating Hearts," William Raspberry approaches his topic, that of cheating in school, with a bemused interest. What's behind the fact that 80 percent of students have admitted to cheating? Raspberry is merely interested in finding answers, but along the way he manages to make an argument about what he thinks is the source. "The Dangerous Myth of Grade Inflation" by Alfie Kohn and "Curtailing High School: A Radical Proposal" by Leon Botstein are different takes on education, but both offer well-reasoned, forceful suggestions for changes that the authors think can improve schools in America. As you read the selections that follow, think about how these writers try to influence their readers.

ELLEN GOODMAN
Religion in the Textbooks

Pulitzer Prize–winning editor and journalist Ellen Goodman started her career as a researcher at Newsweek. *She began reporting for the* Detroit Free Press *in 1965, and then moved on to* The Boston Globe, *where the column she has written for many years has been praised for its lively writing and strong voice. Goodman was educated at Radcliffe*

College at Harvard, which is where she began writing her column. She is the author of Turning Points *(1979) and of several collections of her columns, including* Keeping in Touch *(1985),* Making Sense *(1989), and* Value Judgments *(1993). In this selection, Goodman explores the squeamishness Americans seem to have about teaching religion in public schools.*

Prereading: Thinking About the Essay in Advance

If you attended a public school, did you discuss religion in class? What were the content and tenor of those discussions? In what other settings did you discuss religion?

Words to Watch

crockery (par. 1) ceramic dishware
pluralistic (par. 4) theory that there should be many different groups coexisting
subtexts (par. 6) meanings that lie underneath the main content
masquerading (par. 7) pretending to be
taboo (par. 8) considered unacceptable by social or traditional standards
curriculum (par. 10) what is taught in a school course
incorporate (par. 10) include

1 There was a time when people who wanted to keep the peace and keep the crockery intact held to a strict dinner-table rule: Never argue about politics or religion. I don't know how well it worked in American dining rooms, but it worked pretty well in our schools. We dealt with religion by not arguing about it.

2 Children who came out of diverse homes might carve up the turf of their neighborhood and turn the playgrounds into a religious battlefield, but the public classroom was common ground. Intolerance wasn't tolerated.

3 In place of teaching one religion or another, the schools held to a common denominator of values. It was, in part, the notion of Horace Mann, the nineteenth-century father of the public-school system. He believed that the way to avoid religious conflicts was to extract what all religions agreed upon and allow this "non-religious" belief system into schools.

4 I wonder what Mann would think of that experiment now. Was it naive or sophisticated? Was it a successful or a failed attempt to avoid conflict in a pluralistic society?

5 Today, textbooks are the texts of public-school education and their publishers are, if anything, controversy-phobic. Textbooks are written and edited by publishing committees that follow elaborate guidelines to appease state and local education committees. They must avoid alienating either atheist or fundamentalist. And still these books have become centerpieces, controversial sources of evidence in courtrooms.

6 A judge in Tennessee recently allowed a group of students to "opt out" of reading class because the textbooks violated their religious beliefs. Their

parents had managed to read religious subtexts, even witchcraft, into such tales as "Goldilocks," "Cinderella" and "The Three Little Pigs." Nothing was safe enough or bland enough to please them.

At the same time, a group of parents in Alabama went to court protesting that textbooks are teaching a state religion masquerading as "secular humanism." Not to teach about God is to teach about no God. The attempt to keep religion out of the textbooks was no guarantee against controversy either. 7

There is still a third argument about religion in the public schools that doesn't come from fanatics but from educators. They maintain that the attempt to avoid conflict has pushed textbook publishers to excise religion altogether, even from history class. It is not just the teaching *of* religion that has become taboo, they claim. It is teaching *about* religion. 8

Sources as diverse as William Bennett's Department of Education and Norman Lear's People for the American Way have reported in the past year on the distortions that result. There is a history book that tells about Joan of Arc without mentioning her religious motives. Others explain Thanksgiving without discussing the religious beliefs of the Puritans or to Whom they were giving thanks. 9

"The result of wanting to avoid controversy is a kind of censorship," maintains Diane Ravitch of Columbia University. "It becomes too controversial to write about Christianity and Judaism." Ravitch is involved in creating a new history curriculum for California that would incorporate teaching about people's belief systems and their impact on society. It may be tricky, she admits, to teach about religion without teaching religion, but then all good teaching is risky. So is learning. And that's what is at stake. 10

11 The common ground of values, neutral turf in the religious strife, threatens to shrink to the size of a postage stamp. In Tennessee, the court agreed to protect the religious beliefs of a set of parents whose own beliefs included intolerance of other religions and the importance of binding a child's imagination. These are ideas that are profoundly hostile to the American concept of education.

12 If textbook publishers keep retreating to a shrinking patch of safe ground, they will end up editing chunks out of "The Three Little Pigs." The task is not to shy away from our diversity, but to teach it to our children, and proudly. The strength of our system, what's worth telling the young, is not that Americans deny their differences or always resolve them, but that we have managed, until now, to live with them.

Building Vocabulary

1. In this essay, Goodman uses a number of colloquial phrases. Identify them and come up with another way to write each.
   a. *religious battlefield (par. 2)*
   b. *common ground (par. 2)*
   c. *common denominator (par. 3)*
   d. *father of the public-school system (par. 3)*
   e. *threatens to shrink to the size of a postage stamp (par. 11)*
   f. *the task is not to shy away (par. 12)*
2. This essay assumes knowledge of several terms and references having to do with religion. Identify and explain each.
   a. *atheist (par. 5)*
   b. *fundamentalist (par. 5)*
   c. *secular humanism (par. 7)*
   d. *William Bennett (par. 9)*
   e. *People for the American Way (par. 9)*
   f. *Joan of Arc (par. 9)*
   g. *Puritans (par. 9)*

Thinking Critically About the Argument

Understanding the Writer's Argument

1. Why does the writer start with a look into the past?
2. Who was Horace Mann, and what does he have to do with the issue of religion in schools?
3. What was the rationale of the judge who allowed students to leave classes because the textbooks "violated their religious beliefs"? (par. 6) What does the writer think of his decision?
4. What do most educators want to do with religion in textbooks, according to Goodman?
5. What is wrong with teaching about the Puritans without mentioning their religious beliefs?

6. Paraphrase Diane Ravitch's argument in paragraph 10.
7. What does the writer see as the threat of religion being taken out of textbooks?

Understanding the Writer's Techniques

1. What is the writer's major proposition? Where is it located? Is it located in an effective place? Why do you think so?
2. Where does the writer's extended introduction end? What comes after the introduction?
3. Is the writer's structure in this essay effective? Explain.
4. Why does the writer present questions in paragraph 4? Is this technique effective or not?
5. What is the argumentative effect of showing the fighting on both sides of the issue of religion in the classroom? What is the writer trying to do by illustrating this infighting?
6. The word *appease* in paragraph 5 has historical connotations from the years before World War II. What are those connotations, and how do they affect your reading of this paragraph?
7. How effective are the author's transitions? Explain your answer.
8. Is the closing paragraph effective? Why or why not?

Exploring the Writer's Argument

1. Goodman quotes Diane Ravitch in paragraph 10 but never explicitly says whether she agrees with Ravitch. Do you think the writer agrees with Ravitch's sentiment or not? Why do you think that? What is your opinion of Ravitch's argument that "to avoid controversy is a kind of censorship"?
2. One solution to this problem might be to teach only about the history of religion, without mentioning the state of the religions today. Is that a possible solution? What would William Bennett say to that? What would Norman Lear say? What would Ellen Goodman say?
3. In paragraph 11, Goodman writes about a judge who protected the rights of parents whose children were brought up to be intolerant of other religions. She says that "These are ideas that are profoundly hostile to the American concept of education." Does citing an extreme case weaken her argument here or leave it strong? Explain your answer.

Ideas for Writing Arguments

Prewriting

Jot down some notes about prayer and other religious content in schools.

Writing a Guided Argument

Controversy often surrounds the question of whether religion has any place in public schools at all. Coaches leading prayers before a football game, the Ten Commandments posted in a school hallway, mandated moments of silence for prayer—all are hotly contested. Write an essay in which you argue that either there is no place for religious content in schools or that there are some areas in which religious topics are okay.

1. Open your essay with an illustration of religious activity that you are either going to argue for or against.
2. Take a position on the issue in the form of a major proposition.
3. Give a short history of the issue and give the reader an overview of the main players in the debate.
4. Address possible opposing points and rebut them.
5. Include at least two minor propositions that support your position.
6. Link paragraphs with effective transitions.
7. Establish an even, neutral-sounding tone.
8. Close your essay with a prediction about the future of religion in schools.

Thinking, Arguing, and Writing Collaboratively

Find a section of a textbook designed for public school instruction. In groups of three or four, read a section about religion out loud. Write notes based on your reading. Is the section overly bland? Does it leave out crucial information? Do you see anything that could possibly offend a parent? Convene as a class and discuss your findings.

Writing About the Text

Read Anna Quindlen's essay "One Nation, Indivisible? Wanna Bet?" from Chapter 1. Write an essay arguing that Quindlen's and Goodman's arguments reflect the same tendency in American culture to be confused on the issue of the separation of church and state.

More Writing Ideas

1. Write a journal entry addressing the following question: Which religions do you think would be most difficult to teach to schoolchildren? Which religions would it be most important to teach children in the United States about? Why?
2. Question 3 of "Exploring the Writer's Argument" refers to Goodman's statement that restrictive educational ideas are "profoundly hostile to the American concept of education." Do you think that is true? Write a paragraph or two arguing for one side or the other.
3. Look up the concept and history of "secular humanism." (par. 7) Write an essay in which you argue for or against the "faith" of secular humanism.

William Raspberry
Their Cheating Hearts

William Raspberry grew up in a small, segregated town in Mississippi. He served in the army and then joined the Washington Post, *where he worked his way up to being an editor and reporter. He now writes a column for the newspaper that is also syndicated in more than 100 newspapers around the country. He has received many honors for his work, including a Capital Press Club's "Journalist of the Year" award, a citation of merit in journalism from Lincoln University in Jefferson City, Missouri. In 1994 he received both the Pulitzer Prize and a Lifetime Achievement Award from the National Association of Black Journalists. Raspberry is also the Knight professor of the practice of communications and journalism at Duke University. In this selection, Raspberry, from his point of view as a teacher, tries to get to the bottom of the growing phenomenon of cheating among young people in America.*

Prereading: Thinking About the Essay in Advance

Have you or someone you know ever cheated on an exam or plagiarized an essay? If so, would you call the act a serious offense? If not, why not?

Words to Watch

infraction (par. 1) offense against a law or rule
lax (par. 4) not strict
pragmatic (par. 6) concerned with practical results rather than ideas
epiphany (par. 12) sudden realization
ambivalent (par. 12) having mixed feelings

By the time I arrived for my "Family and Community" class, I still was reeling from the results of a survey I'd just seen. A poll of more than 3,000 students listed in "Who's Who Among High School Students"—the cream of our scholastic crop—revealed that 80 percent had engaged in academic cheating and thought cheating was commonplace. Moreover, most saw cheating as a minor infraction. 1

Surely this couldn't be correct, I thought. 2

But close to half of my Duke University students (encouragingly less than 80 percent) acknowledged some high school cheating, though all of them insisted they'd outgrown the practice since they had entered college. I decided to spend the bulk of the period talking about it, and the result was one of the more interesting classes of the semester. 3

4 We began with a discussion of honor codes and their enforcement: stiff codes, such as the University of Virginia's, where students are required to report any cheating they observe and name the cheaters on pain of expulsion; softer codes such as Duke's, which requires students to report infractions but permits them, under some circumstances, to do so anonymously; or lax codes that amount to a no-cheating policy statement that says, in effect, don't get caught.

5 Most of the class—predictably—chose the middle ground. Nearly all said they would have walked away from a stolen answer sheet rather than use it to boost their college-entry SAT scores. Only a handful said they would have gone all the way and told school authorities what was being done and by whom. On the other hand, most said they were likelier to report cheating that put them at a competitive disadvantage.

6 The attitude toward reporting—and to a serious degree toward cheating—turned out to be remarkably pragmatic. Do it, or don't do it, because it works—to make life more fair, more comfortable, more predictable.

7 Then came what was for me the interesting part. The class was after all about community—about understanding and strengthening the institution that, along with family, is the foundation on which our society rests.

8 So I asked which sort of community they'd rather live in: one in which nearly everyone adhered to the highest ethical standards or one that embraced a live-and-let-live attitude. They were almost unanimous in preferring the high-standard community.

9 "You'd want neighbors with higher ethical standards than your own?" I asked. They would but also thought it likely that they'd raise their own standards to meet the community norm. "And also lower them to meet that norm?" They weren't sure, but fitting in did seem to count for something; isn't that what standards are about?

10 Then I asked them to imagine they had come up with a foolproof way of counterfeiting money. Would they be tempted? Not enough to ruin the economy, of course. Just, say, $100,000 in undetectable counterfeit. You could pay off your college loans, help out the family, get the jalopy fixed . . . and then destroy the plates. After all, you're no career criminal. Who would get hurt? Your family's better off, your debts are paid, the mechanic has a job he wouldn't have had. Maybe the trickle-down effect of your clever counterfeiting improves the local community.

11 And no one would do it. Ethics, they decided, wasn't only about pragmatism and getting along. Personal integrity mattered for its own sake. Who would be hurt? They would, they agreed.

12 I'm not alleging major epiphany in a single afternoon. Many of my students remain ambivalent (and unbelievably honest) about the temptation to lower their ethical standards, particularly in settings where lower standards are the norm. And if 80 percent of the brightest and best own up to cheating, those lower standards are the norm.

13 Nor is this some personal discovery of mine. Donald McCabe, the Princeton professor who conducted the survey that launched our discus-

sion, is the founding president of the Center for Academic Integrity, a consortium of some 200 colleges and universities (including Duke, where the center is based). This group is exploring ways not merely to reverse the rising tide of academic cheating and plagiarism, but, more important, to get students to embrace high ethical standards as a matter of personal integrity.

It won't be easy, as McCabe's survey makes clear. But it's hard to think of anything more worth whatever effort it will take. 14

Building Vocabulary

In his essay, Raspberry uses several idiomatic phrases. For each of the following, rewrite the sentences they come from into your own words without using the idiom:

1. the cream of our scholastic crop (par. 1)
2. insisted they'd outgrown the practice (par. 3)
3. the middle ground (par. 5)
4. nearly everyone adhered to the highest (par. 8)
5. the trickle-down effect (par. 10)
6. reverse the rising tide (par. 13)

Thinking Critically About the Argument

Understanding the Writer's Argument

1. In the beginning of his essay, why is Raspberry "reeling"?
2. What is an honor code?
3. What is the spectrum of different honor codes? Which does Duke University have?
4. What opinion do Raspberry's students have on reporting people they know to be cheating?
5. What part of the discussion about cheating does Raspberry find most interesting? Why?
6. What is the point of the hypothetical situation that Raspberry offers his class?
7. What is the purpose of the Center for Academic Integrity?

Understanding the Writer's Techniques

1. What is the author's claim? Where does he state it, if at all?
2. What are the implied warrants in this essay? Are there any explicit ones? Which are they?
3. What is the writer's tone? How does the tone support the author's argument?
4. What is the rhetorical effect of starting the essay with the beginning of Raspberry's "Family and Community" class? How does the first paragraph frame the argument?
5. Why does the writer progress through his ideas in the order that he does?

6. What is the argumentative effect of admitting that his "epiphany" is not a "personal discovery"?
7. How effective is the concluding paragraph? The title? Explain.

Exploring the Writer's Argument

1. In paragraph 7, Raspberry says that the implications of the community are for him "the interesting part." Do you think this is the most interesting part of this discussion? Explain your answer.
2. Is there any aspect of cheating that you think Raspberry fails to explain? What would you have liked him to address?
3. Explore the last sentence in paragraph 9. Is Raspberry being sarcastic here, or is he respectful of his students' answers? Explain your response.
4. Are you persuaded by the author when he says of cheating that "it's hard to think of anything more worth whatever effort it will take" (par. 14) to stop it? Why or why not?

Ideas for Writing Arguments

Prewriting

Make an outline of what you think are the causes of cheating among students.

Writing a Guided Argument

In his essay, Raspberry explores the implications of cheating and addresses the idea of integrity, but he doesn't really dig into the sources of cheating. If even half of Raspberry's students, almost definitely people with integrity, have cheated, then what is the root cause of cheating? Write an essay in which you argue for what you think are the real causes of cheating among students.

1. Open your essay with a moment that led you to think about the origins of cheating (for example, a time when you or someone you know cheated).
2. Continue by writing your major proposition clearly.
3. Explain further what it means to cheat and explain your minor propositions.
4. Cultivate a tone of professorial authority.
5. Support your minor propositions with examples and anecdotes as well as appropriate reasoning.
6. Do not hesitate to appeal to the reader's sense of decency and integrity.
7. Bring your essay to a close with a section that attempts to prescribe a solution to the causes you offered.

Thinking, Arguing, and Writing Collaboratively

In one of four equal groups, invent a hypothetical situation as Raspberry does in paragraph 10. Then, each group should poll the class on its hypothetical situation. Record the results, and talk as a group about what you think the implications are. Report what you think the results are to the class, and discuss them.

Writing About the Text

Raspberry is both a columnist and a professor, but this column feels very scholarly. Write an essay in which you tease out the ways in which Raspberry uses his style and word choice to make this seem like an intellectual enterprise that has a home in academia. How does his voice sound like a professor's voice rather than the voice of a newspaper columnist?

More Writing Ideas

1. Do you think that it is more likely or less likely that cheating occurs on the average test given at your school? Explain your answer in a journal entry.
2. In a paragraph or two, explain why nearly all of the students in Raspberry's class would refrain from cheating on the SATs, whereas half of them would cheat (and have cheated) on other exams.
3. Visit the Web site for the Center for Academic Integrity, or colleges' individual Web sites, and find at least three honor codes, one of which, if possible, is the honor code from your own school. Print them out and read them. Write an essay in which you argue for one honor code over the other two, exploring the issue of what you think is the proper balance between honesty and pragmatism.

ALFIE KOHN
The Dangerous Myth of Grade Inflation

Alfie Kohn is the author of No Contest: The Case Against Competition *(1986),* Punished By Rewards: The Trouble with Gold Stars, Incentive Plans, A's, Praise, and Other Bribes *(1993),* The Schools Our Children Deserve: Moving Beyond Traditional Classrooms and "Tougher Standards" *(1999), and* The Case Against Standardized Testing: Raising the Scores, Ruining the Schools *(2000). He has published articles in* The Nation, Harvard Business Review, *the* Atlantic Monthly, Parents, Psychology Today, The New York Times *and other publications.* Time *has called Kohn "perhaps the country's most outspoken critic of education's fixation on grades [and] test scores." In this selection, Kohn makes his case for why giving grades to students is bad for education.*

Prereading: Thinking About the Essay in Advance

Do you think your grades in school have always matched your effort and skill? Why or why not? Are there any alternatives to giving grades in school? What are they?

Words to Watch

harrumphing (par. 2) making comments of displeasure
indignation (par. 2) anger over unfairness
dubious (par. 4) suspiciously unreliable
lamentations (par. 5) expressions of sorrow
aggregate (par. 9) collected together to make a whole
epistemological (par. 13) having to do with the philosophy of knowledge
constituencies (par. 19) group of people with the same ideas or views
dichotomy (par. 28) separation into two divisions
candor (par. 29) absolute honesty
inducement (par. 36) something that gives someone a reason to do something

Grade inflation got started . . . in the late '60s and early '70s. . . . The grades that faculty members now give . . . deserve to be a scandal.

—Professor Harvey Mansfield, Harvard University, 2001

Grades A and B are sometimes given too readily—Grade A for work of no very high merit, and Grade B for work not far above mediocrity. . . . One of the chief obstacles to raising the standards of the degree is the readiness with which insincere students gain passable grades by sham work.

—Report of the Committee on Raising the Standard, Harvard University, 1894

1 Complaints about grade inflation have been around for a very long time. Every so often a fresh flurry of publicity pushes the issue to the foreground again, the latest example being a series of articles in *The Boston Globe* last year that disclosed—in a tone normally reserved for the discovery of entrenched corruption in state government—that a lot of students at Harvard were receiving A's and being graduated with honors.

2 The fact that people were offering the same complaints more than a century ago puts the latest bout of harrumphing in perspective, not unlike those quotations about the disgraceful values of the younger generation that turn out to be hundreds of years old. The long history of indignation also pretty well derails any attempts to place the blame for higher grades on a residue of bleeding-heart liberal professors hired in the '60s. (Unless, of course, there was a similar countercultural phenomenon in the *1860s.*)

3 Yet on campuses across America today, academe's usual requirements for supporting data and reasoned analysis have been suspended for some reason where this issue is concerned. It is largely accepted on faith that grade inflation—an upward shift in students' grade-point averages without a similar rise in achievement—exists, and that it is a bad thing. Meanwhile, the truly substantive issues surrounding grades and motivation have been obscured or ignored.

4 The fact is that it is hard to substantiate even the simple claim that grades have been rising. Depending on the time period we're talking about, that claim may well be false. In their book *When Hope and Fear Collide*

(Jossey-Bass, 1998), Arthur Levine and Jeanette Curteon tell us that more undergraduates in 1993 reported receiving A's (and fewer reported receiving grades of C or below) compared with their counterparts in 1969 and 1976 surveys. Unfortunately, self-reports are notoriously unreliable, and the numbers become even more dubious when only a self-selected, and possibly unrepresentative, segment bothers to return the questionnaires. (One out of three failed to do so in 1993; no information is offered about the return rates in the earlier surveys.)

To get a more accurate picture of whether grades have changed over the 5
years, one needs to look at official student transcripts. Clifford Adelman, a senior research analyst with the U.S. Department of Education, did just that, reviewing transcripts from more than 3,000 institutions and reporting his results in 1995. His finding: "Contrary to the widespread lamentations, grades actually declined slightly in the last two decades." Moreover, a report released just this year by the National Center for Education Statistics revealed that fully 33.5 percent of American undergraduates had a grade-point average of C or below in 1999-2000, a number that ought to quiet "all the furor over grade inflation," according to a spokesperson for the Association of American Colleges and Universities. (A review of other research suggests a comparable lack of support for claims of grade inflation at the high-school level.)

However, even where grades *are* higher now as compared with then— 6
which may well be true in the most selective institutions—that does not constitute proof that they are inflated. The burden rests with critics to demonstrate that those higher grades are undeserved, and one can cite any number of alternative explanations. Maybe students are turning in better assignments. Maybe instructors used to be too stingy with their marks and have become more reasonable. Maybe the concept of assessment itself has evolved, so that today it is more a means for allowing students to demonstrate what they know rather than for sorting them or "catching them out." (The real question, then, is why we spent so many years trying to make good students look bad.) Maybe students aren't forced to take as many courses outside their primary areas of interest in which they didn't fare as well. Maybe struggling students are now able to withdraw from a course before a poor grade appears on their transcripts. (Say what you will about that practice, it challenges the hypothesis that the grades students receive in the courses they complete are inflated.)

The bottom line: No one has ever demonstrated that students today get 7
A's for the same work that used to receive B's or C's. We simply do not have the data to support such a claim.

Consider the most recent, determined effort by a serious source to 8
prove that grades are inflated: "Evaluation and the Academy: Are We Doing the Right Thing?" a report released this year by the American Academy of Arts and Sciences. Its senior author is Henry Rosovsky, formerly Harvard's dean of the faculty. The first argument offered in support of the proposition that students couldn't possibly deserve higher grades is that SAT

scores have dropped during the same period that grades are supposed to have risen. But this is a patently inapt comparison, if only because the SAT is deeply flawed. It has never been much good even at predicting grades during the freshman year in college, to say nothing of more-important academic outcomes. A four-year analysis of almost 78,000 University of California students, published last year by the UC president's office, found that the test predicted only 13.3 percent of variation in freshman grades, a figure roughly consistent with hundreds of previous studies. (I outlined numerous other problems with the test in "Two Cheers for an End to the SAT," *The Chronicle*, March 9, 2001.)

9 Even if one believes that the SAT is a valid and valuable exam, however, the claim that scores are dropping is a poor basis for the assertion that grades are too high. First, it is difficult to argue that a standardized test taken in high school and grades for college course work are measuring the same thing. Second, changes in aggregate SAT scores mostly reflect the proportion of the eligible population that has chosen to take the test. The American Academy's report states that average SAT scores dropped slightly from 1969 to 1993. But over that period, the pool of test takers grew from about one-third to more than two-fifths of high-school graduates—an addition of more than 200,000 students.

10 Third, a decline in overall SAT scores is hardly the right benchmark against which to measure the grades earned at Harvard or other elite institutions. Every bit of evidence I could find—including a review of the SAT scores of entering students at Harvard over the past two decades, at the nation's most selective colleges over three and even four decades, and at all private colleges since 1985—uniformily confirms a virtually linear rise in both verbal and math scores, even after correcting for the renorming of the test in the mid-1990s. To cite just one example, the latest edition of "Trends in College Admissions" reports that the average verbal-SAT score of students enrolled in all private colleges rose from 543 in 1985 to 558 in 1999. Thus, those who regard SAT results as a basis for comparison should *expect* to see higher grades now rather than assume that they are inflated.

11 The other two arguments made by the authors of the American Academy's report rely on a similar sleight of hand. They note that more college students are now forced to take remedial courses, but offer no reason to think that this is especially true of the relevant student population—namely, those at the most selective colleges who are now receiving A's instead of B's.

12 Finally, they report that more states are adding high-school graduation tests and even standardized exams for admission to public universities. Yet that trend can be explained by political factors and offers no evidence of an objective decline in students' proficiency. For instance, scores on the National Assessment of Educational Progress, known as "the nation's report card" on elementary and secondary schooling, have shown very little change over the past couple of decades, and most of the change that has occurred has been for the better. As David Berliner and Bruce Biddle put it in their tellingly titled book *The Manufactured Crisis* (Addison-Wesley, 1995), the

data demonstrate that "today's students are at least as well informed as students in previous generations." The latest round of public-school bashing—and concomitant reliance on high-stakes testing—began with the Reagan administration's "Nation at Risk" report, featuring claims now widely viewed by researchers as exaggerated and misleading.

Beyond the absence of good evidence, the debate over grade inflation brings up knotty epistemological problems. To say that grades are not merely rising but inflated—and that they are consequently "less accurate" now, as the American Academy's report puts it—is to postulate the existence of an objectively correct evaluation of what a student (or an essay) deserves, the true grade that ought to be uncovered and honestly reported. It would be an understatement to say that this reflects a simplistic and outdated view of knowledge and of learning. 13

In fact, what is most remarkable is how rarely learning even figures into the discussion. The dominant disciplinary sensibility in commentaries on this topic is not that of education—an exploration of pedagogy or assessment—but rather of economics. That is clear from the very term "grade inflation," which is, of course, just a metaphor. Our understanding is necessarily limited if we confine ourselves to the vocabulary of inputs and outputs, incentives, resource distribution, and compensation. 14

Suppose, for the sake of the argument, we assumed the very worst—not only that students are getting better grades than did their counterparts of an earlier generation, but that the grades are too high. What does that mean, and why does it upset some people so? 15

To understand grade inflation in its proper context, we must acknowledge a truth that is rarely named: The crusade against it is led by conservative individuals and organizations who regard it as analogous—or even related—to such favorite whipping boys as multicultural education, the alleged radicalism of academe, "political correctness" (a label that permits the denigration of anything one doesn't like without having to offer a reasoned objection), and too much concern about students' self-esteem. Mainstream media outlets and college administrators have allowed themselves to be put on the defensive by accusations about grade inflation, as can be witnessed when deans at Harvard plead nolo contendere and dutifully tighten their grading policies. 16

What are the critics assuming about the nature of students' motivation to learn, about the purpose of evaluation and of education itself? (It is surely revealing when someone reserves time and energy to complain bitterly about how many students are getting A's—as opposed to expressing concern about, say, how many students have been trained to think that the point of going to school is to get A's.) 17

"In a healthy university, it would not be necessary to say what is wrong with grade inflation," Harvey Mansfield asserted in an opinion article last year (*The Chronicle,* April 6, 2001). That, to put it gently, is a novel view of health. It seems reasonable to expect those making an argument to be prepared to defend it, and also valuable to bring their hidden premises to light. 18

Here are the assumptions that seem to underlie the grave warnings about grade inflation:

19 **The professor's job is to sort students for employers or graduate schools.** Some are disturbed by grade inflation—or, more accurately, grade compression—because it then becomes harder to spread out students on a continuum, ranking them against one another for the benefit of postcollege constituencies. One professor asks, by way of analogy, "Why would anyone subscribe to *Consumers Digest* if every blender were rated a 'best buy'"?

20 But how appropriate is such a marketplace analogy? Is the professor's job to rate students like blenders for the convenience of corporations, or to offer feedback that will help students learn more skillfully and enthusiastically? (Notice, moreover, that even consumer magazines don't grade on a curve. They report the happy news if it turns out that every blender meets a reasonable set of performance criteria.)

21 Furthermore, the student-as-appliance approach assumes that grades provide useful information to those postcollege constituencies. Yet growing evidence—most recently in the fields of medicine and law, as cited in publications like *The Journal of the American Medical Association* and the *American Educational Research Journal*—suggests that grades and test scores do not in fact predict career success, or much of anything beyond subsequent grades and test scores.

22 **Students should be set against one another in a race for artificially scarce rewards.** "The essence of grading is exclusiveness," Mansfield said in one interview. Students "should have to compete with each other," he said in another.

23 In other words, even when no graduate-school admissions committee pushes for students to be sorted, they ought to be sorted anyway, with grades reflecting relative standing rather than absolute accomplishment. In effect, this means that the game should be rigged so that no matter how well students do, only a few can get A's. The question guiding evaluation in such a classroom is not "How well are they learning?" but "Who's beating whom?" The ultimate purpose of good colleges, this view holds, is not to maximize success, but to ensure that there will always be losers.

24 A bell curve may sometimes—but only sometimes—describe the range of knowledge in a roomful of students at the beginning of a course. When it's over, though, any responsible educator hopes that the results would skew drastically to the right, meaning that most students learned what they hadn't known before. Thus, in their important study, *Making Sense of College Grades* (Jossey-Bass, 1986), Ohmer Milton, Howard Pollio, and James Eison write, "It is not a symbol of rigor to have grades fall into a 'normal' distribution; rather, it is a symbol of failure—failure to teach well, failure to test well, and failure to have any influence at all on the intellectual lives of students." Making sure all students are continually re-sorted, with excellence turned into an artificially scarce commodity, is almost perverse.

25 What does relative success signal about student performance in any case? The number of peers that a student has bested tells us little about how

much she knows and is able to do. Moreover, such grading policies may create a competitive climate that is counter-productive for winners and losers alike, to the extent that it discourages a free exchange of ideas and a sense of community that's conducive to exploration.

Harder is better (or higher grades mean lower standards). Compounding the tendency to confuse excellence with victory is a tendency to confuse quality with difficulty—as evidenced in the accountability fad that has elementary and secondary education in its grip just now, with relentless talk of "rigor" and "raising the bar." The same confusion shows up in higher education when professors pride themselves not on the intellectual depth and value of their classes but merely on how much reading they assign, how hard their tests are, how rarely they award good grades, and so on. "You're going to have to *work* in here!" they announce, with more than a hint of machismo and self-congratulation. 26

Some people might defend that posture on the grounds that students will perform better if A's are harder to come by. In fact, the evidence on this question is decidedly mixed. Stringent grading sometimes has been shown to boost short-term retention as measured by multiple-choice exams—never to improve understanding or promote interest in learning. The most recent analysis, released in 2000 by Julian R. Betts and Jeff Grogger, professors of economics at the University of California at San Diego and at Los Angeles, respectively, found that tougher grading was initially correlated with higher test scores. But the long-term effects were negligible—with the exception of minority students, for whom the effects were negative. 27

It appears that something more than an empirical hypothesis is behind the "harder is better" credo, particularly when it is set up as a painfully false dichotomy: Those easy-grading professors are too lazy to care, or too worried about how students will evaluate them, or overly concerned about their students' self-esteem, whereas *we* are the last defenders of what used to matter in the good old days. High standards! Intellectual honesty! No free lunch! 28

The American Academy's report laments an absence of "candor" about this issue. Let us be candid, then. Those who grumble about undeserved grades sometimes exude a cranky impatience with—or even contempt for—the late adolescents and young adults who sit in their classrooms. Many people teaching in higher education, after all, see themselves primarily as researchers and regard teaching as an occupational hazard, something they're not very good at, were never trained for, and would rather avoid. It would be interesting to examine the correlation between one's view of teaching (or of students) and the intensity of one's feelings about grade inflation. Someone also might want to examine the personality profiles of those who become infuriated over the possibility that someone, somewhere, got an A without having earned it. 29

Grades motivate. With the exception of orthodox behaviorists, psychologists have come to realize that people can exhibit qualitatively different kinds of motivation: intrinsic, in which the task itself is seen as valuable, and extrinsic, in which the task is just a means to the end of gaining a reward or escaping 30 a punishment. The two are not only distinct but often inversely related. Scores of studies have demonstrated, for example, that the more people are rewarded, the more they come to lose interest in whatever had to be done in order to get the reward. (That conclusion is essentially reaffirmed by the latest major meta-analysis on the topic: a review of 128 studies, published in 1999 by Edward L. Deci, Richard Koestner, and Richard Ryan.)

31 Those unfamiliar with that basic distinction, let alone the supporting research, may be forgiven for pondering how to "motivate" students, then concluding that grades are often a good way of doing so, and consequently worrying about the impact of inflated grades. But the reality is that it doesn't matter how motivated students are; what matters is *how* students are motivated. A focus on grades creates, or at least perpetuates, an extrinsic orientation that is likely to undermine the love of learning we are presumably seeking to promote.

32 Three robust findings emerge from the empirical literature on the subject: Students who are given grades, or for whom grades are made particularly salient, tend to display less interest in what they are doing, fare worse on meaningful measures of learning, and avoid more-challenging tasks when given the opportunity—as compared with those in a nongraded comparison group. College instructors cannot help noticing, and presumably being disturbed by, such consequences, but they may lapse into blaming students ("grade grubbers") rather than understanding the systemic sources of the problem. A focus on whether too many students are getting A's suggests a tacit endorsement of grades that predictably produces just such a mind-set in students.

33 These fundamental questions are almost completely absent from discussions of grade inflation. The American Academy's report takes exactly one sentence—with no citations—to dismiss the argument that "lowering the anxiety over grades leads to better learning," ignoring the fact that much more is involved than anxiety. It is a matter of why a student learns, not only how much stress he feels. Nor is the point just that low grades hurt some students' feelings, but that grades, per se, hurt all students' engagement with learning. The meaningful contrast is not between an A and a B or C, but between an extrinsic and an intrinsic focus.

34 Precisely because that is true, a reconsideration of grade inflation leads us to explore alternatives to our (often unreflective) use of grades. Narrative comments and other ways by which faculty members can communicate their evaluations can be far more informative than letter or number grades, and much less destructive. Indeed, some colleges—for example, Hampshire, Evergreen State, Alverno, and New College of Florida—have eliminated grades entirely, as a critical step toward raising intellectual standards. Even the American Academy's report acknowledges that "relatively undifferentiated course grading has been a traditional practice in many graduate schools for a very long time." Has that policy produced lower-quality teaching and learning? Quite the contrary: Many people say they didn't begin to explore ideas deeply and passionately until graduate school began and the importance of grades diminished significantly.

If the continued use of grades rests on nothing more than tradition ("We've always done it that way"), a faulty understanding of motivation, or excessive deference to graduate-school admissions committees, then it may be time to balance those factors against the demonstrated harms of getting students to chase A's. Ohmer Milton and his colleagues discovered—and others have confirmed—that a "grade orientation" and a "learning orientation" on the part of students tend to be inversely related. That raises the disturbing possibility that some colleges are institutions of higher learning in name only, because the paramount question for students is not "What does this mean?" but "Do we have to know this?" 35

A grade-oriented student body is an invitation for the administration and faculty to ask hard questions: What unexamined assumptions keep traditional grading in place? What forms of assessment might be less destructive? How can professors minimize the salience of grades in their classrooms, so long as grades must still be given? And: If the artificial inducement of grades disappeared, what sort of teaching strategies might elicit authentic interest in a course? 36

To engage in this sort of inquiry, to observe real classrooms, and to review the relevant research is to arrive at one overriding conclusion: The real threat to excellence isn't grade inflation at all; it's grades. 37

Building Vocabulary

1. This essay assumes knowledge of a number of terms that you might find unfamiliar. For each of the following terms, define it and use it in a sentence of your own:
   a. *bleeding-heart liberal (par. 2)*
   b. *countercultural (par. 2)*
   c. *high-stakes testing (par. 12)*
   d. *whipping boys (par. 16)*
   e. *radicalism (par. 16)*
   f. *political correctness (par. 16)*
   g. *nolo contendere (par. 16)*
   h. *bell curve (par. 24)*
   i. *behaviorists (par. 30)*
   j. *meta-analysis (par. 30)*

2. Write a definition for each of the following words:
   a. *hypothesis (par. 6)*
   b. *inapt (par. 8)*
   c. *benchmark (par. 10)*
   d. *linear (par. 10)*
   e. *continuum (par. 19)*
   f. *scarce (par. 22)*
   g. *machismo (par. 26)*
   h. *stringent (par. 27)*
   i. *credo (par. 28)*

Thinking Critically About the Argument

Understanding the Writer's Argument

1. What is grade inflation? Why is the beginning of this essay concerned with Harvard University?
2. Why can we not blame grade inflation on political changes in the 1960s?
3. What makes Kohn doubt that grades have been inflated? What evidence does he show that says the opposite?
4. According to Kohn, what is the problem with the SAT?
5. What does Kohn mean when he writes that without "good evidence, the debate over grade inflation brings up knotty epistemological problems"? (par. 13)
6. What are the reasons Kohn outlines for why grades seem so important to everyone? What are the institutional barriers to dropping grades entirely?
7. What is Kohn's opinion of competition over grades in school?
8. What is the relationship between difficult classes and the quality of the education?
9. Does Kohn believe that grades motivate students to learn more? Explain. What does it mean that grades and the level of learning "tend to be inversely related"? (par. 35)

Understanding the Writer's Techniques

1. What is Kohn's claim in this essay? Where is it located? Does he state it in just one sentence? Explain.
2. What is the argumentative effect of starting his essay with epigraphs, the quotes that appear before the essay proper? Why do they both have to do with Harvard?
3. What is Kohn's tone in this essay? Offer examples to show why you answered as you did.
4. The writer divides the argument into sections. Make a list of the sections and the rhetorical strategy used in each section.
5. How much of Kohn's argument depends on the debunking of grade inflation in the first part of his essay? Explain.
6. Which point that Kohn makes in this essay do you find the most surprising? Why?
7. What point is Kohn making in paragraph 9 about the SAT as it relates to grades?
8. How effective is Kohn's conclusion? Explain your answer.

Exploring the Writer's Argument

1. Kohn tries to show that grade inflation cannot be proven. Does his argument convince you? Why or why not? What are the strengths and weaknesses of the argument?
2. Analyze Kohn's parenthetical comment in paragraph 17. Do you think he's right? His point is crucial to his argument. Why does he put it in parentheses? Does that weaken his argument? Explain your answers.

3. Kohn rebuts the arguments of various reports and professors. What is your opinion of his rebuttals? Are they effective? Which is the most effective rebuttal? Which is the weakest? Why?
4. Attempt to find an answer to Kohn's question in paragraph 36, "How can professors minimize the salience of grades in their classrooms, so long as grades must still be given?"
5. How does the fact that Kohn doesn't give any real solutions to the problem he exposes affect the essay's quality?

Ideas for Writing Arguments

Prewriting

How can seemingly innocent language, language we don't even think about being persuasive, be used to make a point? For example, the phrase "pro-life" seems innocent enough, but it implies that the other side might be considered "pro-death." List as many of these terms as you can.

Writing a Guided Argument

Kohn says in paragraph 16 that the term "political correctness" permits us to condemn anything we don't like without having to offer a reasoned objection. Public discourse in our day, it seems, contains phrases that allow us to condemn without having to offer a reasoned objection. Write an essay in which you explain the use and abuse of at least three of those phrases.

1. Begin your essay with an explanation of Kohn's point about the term "political correctness." Explain the term and its meaning.
2. Introduce your claim that other terms are used similarly.
3. Tell your reader the terms.
4. In the next section, explain where these terms are used most often (for example, television talk shows or politicians' speeches) and how.
5. Next, make your case for your first term or phrase.
6. Support your point with examples from your experience and from your reading.
7. Do the same with the other two phrases.
8. In your concluding section, argue that discourse is only hurt by phrases such as the ones explored in your essay.

Thinking, Arguing, and Writing Collaboratively

Divide the class into two groups. One group should adopt the position that grades are good for education and the other the position that they have a negative effect. Each group should amplify or refute the writer's main points.

Writing About the Text

Kohn's essay appeared in a weekly publication directed at college and university teachers and administrators. How does his language and sentence structure reflect an understanding of his audience?

More Writing Ideas

1. In your journal, consider the question of what alternatives there might be to giving grades in college. Would you like to eliminate grades? Why or why not?
2. Kohn raises the question of why students even go to college in the first place. In one or two paragraphs, explore the idea of what you believe is the most important reason to go to college, and determine if you are living up to that standard.
3. Some colleges have done away with grades. Do some research to determine which colleges have done this. Write an essay to evaluate the success of those schools. Are the students learning?

Leon Botstein
Curtailing High School: A Radical Proposal

The president of Bard College in upstate New York, Botstein is also the music director of the American Symphony Orchestra and is a well-respected conductor for most of the orchestra's concerts. He also is the music director and conductor of the Jerusalem Symphony Orchestra. He has traveled the world as a guest conductor and is a classically trained violinist, a scholar of music history, and an editor and a writer. He is also an education theorist and the author of Jefferson's Children: Education and the Promise of American Culture *(1997), which makes several suggestions about the future of public schools. This selection argues for one of those ideas, that high school should not last as long as it does today.*

Prereading: Thinking About the Essay in Advance

Why do you think American society keeps children in school until age 18? Is there some reason for that age, or is it arbitrary?

Words to Watch

pressing (par. 1) urgently important
evenhandedly (par. 1) fairly
immunization (par. 2) act of giving medicine to prevent disease
presumptions (par. 3) beliefs
aspire (par. 4) seek a higher goal
infantilize (par. 6) treat like a child

1 The most pressing concern for the future of the American high school is correcting the fatal flaw in the way we educate adolescents, revealed through its inability to deliver excellence evenhandedly over the past 40 years. It is that failure from which we must learn. The high school has outlived its usefulness to

the point of catastrophe, not only with respect to those least privileged who live in the inner cities and poor rural districts of America. It has also let down the children of families with sufficient incomes to move to suburbia in hopes of finding superior public education there.

The primary cause for the inadequacy of high school rests with irreversible changes in adolescent development. The current system of public education was designed when the onset of puberty was three years later than it is today. Over the past century, the age of physical maturation has steadily dropped as a result of immunization and nutritional standards. Before World War II, 18, the traditional age of high school graduation, was two or three years after maturation. That age also coincided with the onset of adult sexual activity. In the beginning of the 21st century, 16-year-old Americans are, in development and behavior, comparable to the 18-year-olds of a century ago. High school was designed to deal with large children. It is now faced with young adults whose adult behavior has already begun. 2

Neither the personnel, the buildings, the schedule nor the curriculum of high school can satisfy the presumptions of adulthood that today's high school age adolescents legitimately bring with them. The issue is not whether today's adolescents are more mature because of earlier development. The fact is they are *able* to act as adults whether they do so responsibly or not. They are treated by our consumer society as adults; the fashion industry and Hollywood recognize their role as consumers. Modern transportation and communication have given adolescents the freedom of movement we associate with adulthood. Neither community nor home effectively limits their freedom of movement. 3

Plans to extend the high school education to five years, or to expand its degree-granting range, fly in the face of social and biological facts. The freedom in learning, the dignity of serious study and the access to the deep command of subject matter that adulthood and higher education require are not available in the American high school today, nor can they be created within the current high school framework. The Advanced Placement courses that are taught, for example, are largely substandard and inferior to what is available in most colleges. The definition of what constitutes the Advanced Placement curriculum is dictated not by the teacher, but by a private testing agency. No university or college of standing permits such a system to define its standards. The professional preparation, autonomy and academic freedom characteristic of the faculty in American higher education do not exist and cannot flourish within the walls of the American high school. Yet these qualities are essential to the high standards in science, mathematics, history and all other subjects to which adolescents can aspire. 4

The future of the American high school rests with shifting its existing curriculum and practices to younger students and reforming these practices as the shift takes place. In other words, during the next decade, we should rationalize our education system into a two-part elementary and secondary system that ends at age 16. Already it is estimated that more than 1 million 5 young Americans complete their high school education outside the walls of the high school. The majority of college-bound seniors admit that their final year of high school is a waste of time. Increasingly, that criticism is being leveled at the last two years. The high school should, therefore, replace the junior high school and refocus its energies on a younger population, from the ages of 13 to 16.

6 In place of a high school that ends at age 18, the education system should offer multiple options for those between 16 and 19. With a high school diploma, a 16-year-old could choose to attend a community college, to enter a four-year college, or to engage in work, internships or other alternatives to formal school, as well as perhaps national service. We must maintain the democratic pattern of the American educational system by allowing individuals to start college at any time, not necessarily immediately after completing high school. The most important gain from shifting high school graduation to age 16 would be that we would no longer "infantilize" older adolescents and retard their intellectual development.

Building Vocabulary

This essay uses several words and terms from the world of education. Define the following:

1. curriculum (par. 3)
2. Advanced Placement (par. 4)
3. elementary (par. 5)
4. secondary (par. 5)
5. internships (par. 6)

Thinking Critically About the Argument

Understanding the Writer's Argument

1. What does Botstein think is the way that the inadequacy of the high school system in America reveals itself?
2. Has the system only been insufficient for a certain segment of the population? Explain.
3. What is the main reason high school has been inadequate, according to Botstein?
4. Other than physically, what other ways are teenagers today different from their predecessors?
5. What is the problem with Advanced Placement tests, according to Botstein?
6. What is Botstein's suggestion to reform the high school system?
7. What does Botstein say we can gain by adopting his suggestions?

Understanding the Writer's Techniques

1. What is Botstein's major proposition in this essay? Where does he state it?
2. Do you find the introductory paragraph to be effective? Why or why not?
3. How does Botstein support his major proposition? Write an outline that reflects the structure of his essay.
4. What evidence does Botstein offer to prove that teenagers have changed over the years?
5. Do you find the structure of his essay to be effective? Why or why not?
6. How does paragraph 3 help to support the writer's position?
7. Has the writer made his case about the Advanced Placement test? Explain your answer.
8. What is the writer's tone? Do you think it helps his argument? Explain.
9. How effective is the conclusion? Explain your answer.

Exploring the Writer's Argument

1. Botstein includes some scientific information about the onset of puberty today compared to before World War II. Are you convinced by his presentation of this evidence and his explanation of it? Why or why not?
2. Does Botstein persuade you that his suggestion for ending high school early is a good one? Does he persuade you that it is a feasible suggestion? What is the difference between these two questions? Explain your answers.
3. In paragraph 5, Botstein writes that high school seniors don't think much of the last two years of high school. From this, he concludes that educators need to focus on earlier years in their education. Are you convinced by this reasoning? Why or why not?
4. Do you think the end of Botstein's essay is satisfactory, bringing his argument to a natural close, or do you think it is too abrupt? Explain your answer fully.

Ideas for Writing Arguments

Prewriting

Botstein's essay might be easy to accept in the abstract, but how would you feel if your family was affected by his ideas? Jot some notes down about your feelings on the matter.

Writing a Guided Argument

Imagine that you are the parent of a 16-year-old child who has just read Botstein's essay and agrees with him. Your child now wants to quit school, get a GED, and travel and read for two years before college. Your child has articulated his or her views on the subject and has argued from Botstein's position. Write a letter to your child in response.

1. Begin by acknowledging your child's decision.
2. Explain your views on the subject and why you hold them.
3. Write your major proposition, either agreeing with your child or disagreeing.
4. Adopt a tone of patience and authority.
5. Present minor propositions to support your position.
6. Support your minor propositions by offering evidence from your own life and from Botstein's essay.
7. Close your essay with a pledge that your child can do whatever it is he or she wants to do, and that you either agree or disagree with the decision.

Thinking, Arguing, and Writing Collaboratively

Working in small groups, share with a classmate your paper that grew out of the Guided Argument assignment. On your classmate's paper, write a paragraph or two about the effectiveness of the student's argument. Are you convinced? Why or why not? Return your classmate's paper and discuss your classmate's comments with him or her.

Writing About the Text

In this essay, Botstein writes in an extremely clear, lucid style. Write an essay in which you analyze Botstein's style, explaining how he resists overwriting and instead uses prose that does not rely on unnecessary words or ideas.

More Writing Ideas

1. In your journal, freewrite on the idea of extending high school to a fifth year. Write for at least 15 minutes, and do not edit your writing until the time is up. Afterward, read your work and see if there is anything in what you have written that might be the basis for an argument.
2. In an extended paragraph, explore the implications of what Botstein writes in paragraph 1 of his essay, that what he is concerned about is high school's "inability to deliver excellence evenhandedly over the past 40 years."
3. Write an essay in which you argue for what is right about the present-day high school system. What does the public school system do well? How does it help students achieve their goals?

31 The Environment: How Can We Preserve It?

Will we leave any resources for our children and our children's children? That's the urgent question from the environmentalist movement. Humankind is the only species able to alter the climate artificially and pollute the land, water, and air, and we certainly have done that. The Industrial Revolution marked a move away from an agricultural economy to one dominated by machines and factories. Trains, running on coal fuel, belched out black smoke and fouled the atmosphere. Factories dumped chemicals into rivers and harbors. Not until relatively recently did scientists understand the extent to which 200 years of industrialization was damaging the world we live in.

Nature writers helped bring to light the diversity of plants and animals and moved readers to try to protect this diversity. Many writers mobilized to persuade people (especially legislators and politicians) to sit up and take notice and to understand that how they act affects the rest of the world. "Think globally, act locally" became one of the slogans of environmentalism. Much of the recent conversation has focused on global warming and trying to reduce greenhouse gases, which result from the burning of coal or gasoline. The gases warm the atmosphere and have upset Earth's climate. Scientists warn that if humanity doesn't stop global warming, many species will become extinct.

New York Times columnist Bob Herbert, in "No Margin for Error," attempts to frighten his readers into caring about the future of the coral reefs. Verlyn Klinkenborg, in "Out of the Wild," uses a different and more genteel strategy to underline the wonder of the natural world, telling the story of surprising a sick fox in the writer's barn. Barry Lopez in "Apologia" takes this sense of wonder to an extreme in his account of a road trip. Feeling guilty for all the animals he sees dead on the road, he takes his time to pay tribute to them. Fiction writer Wendell Berry, in "In Distrust of Movements," agrees with these writers, but he has no patience for the environmentalist movement or any other movement. In his essay, he circles his subject until arriving at a prescription—have respect for the Earth, and everything will be okay.

Bob Herbert

No Margin for Error

Bob Herbert was born in Brooklyn in 1945 and started his career as a reporter for The Star-Ledger, *a Newark, New Jersey, newspaper. He worked in television news for NBC before returning to newspaper writing in 1993 as a columnist for* The New York Times *op-ed page. He has won numerous awards, including the American Society of Newspaper Editors award for distinguished newspaper writing. He has taught journalism at Brooklyn College and the Columbia University Graduate School of Journalism. Herbert is known for having a strong moral compass in his columns, and in this selection, he takes a look at global warming and its effects on the world's coral reefs.*

Prereading: Thinking About the Essay in Advance

What do you think is the greatest threat to Earth as a result of global warming? What effects have we felt already as a result?

Words to Watch

disintegrate (par. 1) fall apart
emissions (par. 5) things released or given off
phenomena (par. 7) things that occur
indisputable (par. 9) impossible to doubt
catastrophic (par. 12) causing terrible damage
epochs (par. 14) long period of time

1 Global warming is already attacking the world's coral reefs and, if nothing is done soon, could begin a long-term assault on the vast West Antarctic Ice Sheet. If the ice sheet begins to disintegrate, the worldwide consequences over the next several centuries could well be disastrous.

2 Coral reefs are sometimes called the rain forests of the oceans because of the tremendous variety of animal and plant life that they support.

3 "They're the richest ocean ecosystem, and if they are destroyed or severely damaged, a lot of the biological diversity simply goes away," said Dr. Michael Oppenheimer, a professor of geosciences and international affairs at Princeton who is an expert on climate change.

4 Dr. Oppenheimer and Brian C. O'Neill, a professor at Brown, have an article in the current issue of *Science* magazine that addresses some of the long-term dangers that could result if nothing is done about global warming.

5 One of the things that is not widely understood about the greenhouse gases that are contributing to the warming of the planet is that once they are spewed into the atmosphere, they stay there for centuries, and in some cases, millenniums. So a delay of even a decade or so in reducing those emissions can make it much more difficult—and costly—to slow the momentum of the warming and avert the more extreme consequences.

In their article, Dr. Oppenheimer and Dr. O'Neill suggest that public officials and others trying to determine what levels of global warming would actually be dangerous could use the destruction of the world's coral reefs as one of their guides. 6

Coral reefs, which are breathtakingly beautiful natural phenomena, tend to thrive in water temperatures that are only slightly below the maximum temperature at which they can survive. There is not much margin for error. Even allowing for some genetic adaptation, a sustained increase in water temperatures of as little as a couple of degrees Fahrenheit can result in widespread coral reef destruction in just a few years. 7

A number of factors are already contributing to the destruction of coral reefs, and global warming is one of them. As the earth's temperature continues to rise, global warming will most likely become the chief enemy of what Dr. Oppenheimer calls "these wonderful sources of biological diversity." 8

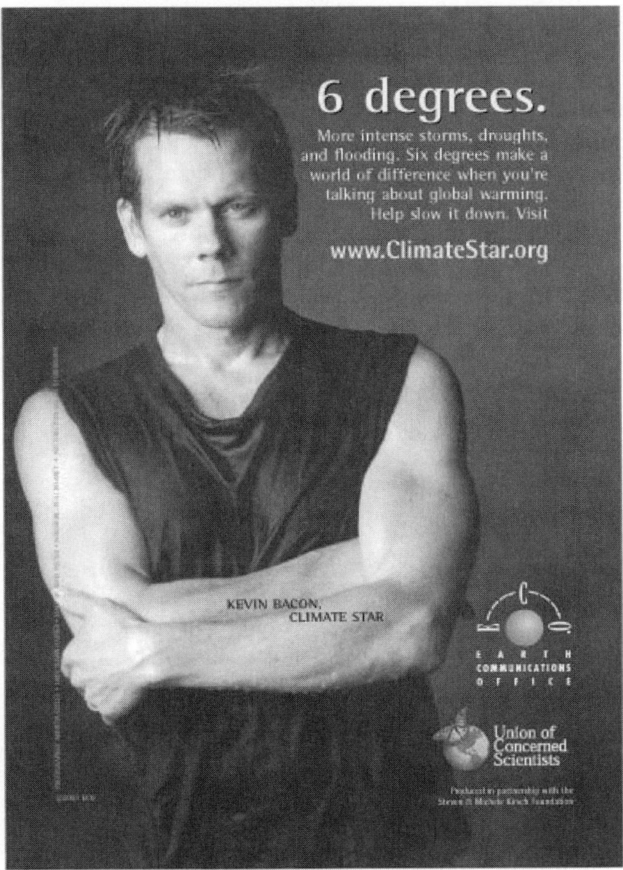

(www.ClimateStar.org)

9 The threat to coral reefs is clear and indisputable. Much less clear is the danger that global warming presents to the West Antarctic Ice Sheet.

10 "We really don't know with any level of certainty what amount of warming would destroy the ice sheet or how quickly that would happen," said Dr. Oppenheimer. He and Dr. O'Neill wrote, "In general, the probability is thought to be low during this century, increasing gradually thereafter."

11 There is not even agreement among scientists on the amount of warming necessary to begin the destruction. But what is clear is that if the ice sheet were to disintegrate, the consequences would be profound. So you don't want to play around with this. You want to make sure it doesn't happen.

12 "We know," said Dr. Oppenheimer, "that if the ice sheet were destroyed, sea levels would rise about five meters, which would be catastrophic for coastal regions. That would submerge much of Manhattan below Greenwich Village, for instance. It would drown the southern third of Florida, an area inhabited by about four million people."

13 Five meters is approximately 16 feet. Tremendous amounts of housing, wetlands and farming areas around the world would vanish. Large portions of a country like Bangladesh, on the Bay of Bengal, would disappear.

14 So what could actually set this potential catastrophe in motion? Dr. Oppenheimer has looked back at past geological epochs. "There is some evidence," he said, "that when the global temperature was warmer by about four degrees Fahrenheit than it is today the ice sheet disintegrated."

15 It is now estimated that if we do nothing to stem the rise of global warming, the increase in the earth's temperature over the course of this century will be between 3 and 10.5 degrees Fahrenheit. That is a level of warming that could initiate the disintegration of the ice sheet. And stopping that disintegration, once the planet gets warm, may be impossible.

Building Vocabulary

In this essay, Herbert uses several terms from the world of ecology and earth science. Identify and write definitions for the following:

1. global warming (par. 1)
2. rain forests (par. 2)
3. ecosystem (par. 3)
4. geosciences (par. 3)
5. climate change (par. 3)
6. greenhouse gases (par. 5)
7. wetlands (par. 13)

Thinking Critically About the Argument

Understanding the Writer's Argument

1. What are coral reefs? Why are they so special?
2. Why is time of the essence when dealing with issues of global warming?
3. How are coral reefs a good gauge of the destruction wrought by global warming?

4. What is the West Antarctic Ice Sheet, and why should we care what happens to it?
5. What is the main cause of global warming?

Understanding the Writer's Techniques

1. What is Herbert's major proposition? Where does he express it most clearly?
2. Why does Herbert begin his essay with such a confrontational paragraph? Explain how it affects his argument.
3. This essay lists the effects of global warming. Identify these effects in the order that Herbert presents them. Which is most surprising or powerful? Why?
4. Why does Herbert present his argument in the order that he does?
5. Why does Herbert pause in his argument to explain how many feet five meters is, after he has already mentioned much of the destruction that might occur if the ice sheet melts?
6. How does the concluding paragraph help to wrap up Herbert's argument?

Exploring the Writer's Argument

1. There are a few places in this short essay when Herbert repeats information. Why does he repeat himself? Is the strategy effective or it is a weakness in the essay?
2. Herbert doesn't spend much time explaining what his readers could do to help the coral reefs or the ice sheet. Is this a weakness in his essay? Explain your answer.
3. Herbert praises the coral reefs and explains why it would be terrible if they were lost, but at the end of his essay he doesn't mention them again. Why? Does this omission weaken his essay? Why or why not?

Ideas for Writing Arguments

Prewriting

Herbert says that people are the problem. What can you do yourself to help stop global warming, if it is such a problem?

Writing a Guided Argument

One of the sayings in the environmental movement is "think globally, act locally." Activists say that if many people do little things to conserve resources, then we will see the benefits worldwide. Write an essay in the form of an open letter to the other students in your college arguing that they can act locally to help the environment. (You might have to do a little bit of research to gather evidence.)

1. Open your essay with an explanation of the problem and why it is urgent that we protect the environment.
2. Write your major proposition, and explain how students can play a role in this effort.

3. Next, show how students can be wasteful and act in ways that harm the environment.
4. Offer your minor propositions in the next section, showing exactly what students can do to help protect the environment.
5. Support your minor propositions with facts and process analysis, giving your reader a "how-to" for each.
6. Affect a tone that reflects the seriousness and urgency of the topic.
7. Explain to your reader that students are important because they are the future leaders of the world.
8. Bring your essay to a close on an ominous note, explaining what might happen if students don't take a role.

Thinking, Arguing, and Writing Collaboratively

In groups of four or five, discuss the ideas presented in your Writing a Guided Argument assignment. Jot down notes, and incorporate your peers' opinions—making sure they suit your essay—in your final draft.

Writing About the Text

In this essay, Herbert depends for his evidence almost entirely on the single article in *Science* magazine by Drs. Michael Oppenheimer and Brian C. O'Neill. Where in Herbert's essay do you, as the reader, desire more varied evidence? Or do you not need more? Write an essay in which you analyze how Herbert's essay is either strengthened or weakened by having only one source?

More Writing Ideas

1. In your journal, write an entry assessing your own activities when it comes to saving or wasting natural resources.
2. Some people, despite all scientific evidence for global warming, have denied that it's happening at all. Do some research and in several paragraphs, summarize the arguments of those who don't believe in global warming.
3. Many countries have tried to reduce the effects of global warming. One of those efforts, the Kyoto Conference, was an international meeting brokered under the power of the United Nations. The conference drafted the Kyoto Protocol, which called for countries to reduce emissions and other greenhouse gases. Most industrial nations agreed to adhere to Kyoto, but the United States, which causes most of the emissions in the world, refused to agree. Do some research on the topic, and write an essay that argues either for or against the United States' agreeing to the Kyoto Protocol.

VERLYN KLINKENBORG
Out of the Wild

Verlyn Klinkenborg lives on a small farm in upstate New York, from which he writes his popular "The Rural Life" column on the editorial page of The New York Times. *He published a collection of the columns in 2003. Klinkenborg comes from a family of Iowa farmers. His unique vision as someone from the country who lived in the city and then returned to the country makes his essays poignant and touching. He is also the author of* Making Hay *(1986). A member of the editorial board of* The New York Times, *he has written for* The New Yorker, Harper's, Esquire, National Geographic, Mother Jones, *and* The New York Times Magazine, *among others. In this essay Klinkenborg narrates his face-to-face meeting with a wild animal and is forced to rethink his preconceptions.*

Prereading: Thinking About the Essay in Advance

Have you or someone you know ever encountered a wild animal? What was the reaction—fear, awe, surprise, respect, or some other emotion?

Words to Watch

bale (par. 1) pile bound together
transgression (par. 1) act of crossing a forbidden boundary
frigid (par. 3) bitterly cold
platonic (par. 4) perfect and idealistic in form
vertebrae (par. 5) backbones

The other morning I lifted a bale of hay from a loose pile of bales on the barn floor, and a fox jumped out from under it. The fox ran to the back of the barn and turned to watch me. It paced a few steps, uncertain, and then scurried under the door and out into the cold rain. It was a moment of pure transgression. All the old story lines broke apart—the ones about farmers and foxes and chickens—and just when the old story had been going so well. The fox had stolen a couple of our chickens. I had chased it off several times. It would lope up the hill in the middle pasture and sit on the ridge looking back at me, waiting for my next move. We hated to lose the chickens, and we hated the fox for taking them, but it was a conventional hatred, a part we knew we were supposed to play. 1

But there are no stories in which the fox sleeps overnight in the barn on a bed of hay only a few feet from three horses in a run-in shed and a big, campaigning dog in his kennel. In all the traditional tales the fox keeps its distance, a playful distance perhaps, always respecting the invisible boundary between wildness and not-wildness. But the other morning that fox ignored the boundary completely. 2

3 The reason was obvious. It was dying from a terrible case of sarcoptic mange, an all-too-common disease caused by mites that infest the skin and cause severe inflammation and hair loss. Foxes with mange die of malnutrition or they freeze to death. The night had been frigid, with a blowing, soaking rainfall. Even the driest den would have been insufferable, and so the fox took refuge in a burrow among hay bales in a dry barn.

4 My wife and I have been seeing foxes ever since we moved to this place. They skirted the far edge of the pasture at a businesslike trot, keeping watch as if they knew that someday we'd give in and get chickens. But because they always kept their distance, they were platonic foxes, storybook foxes with sharp muzzles and thick red fur and bushy tails and the gloss of wild health. They looked the way they were supposed to look, the way you imagine a fox looks. The binoculars only confirmed what we knew we'd find, the very idea of Vulpes vulpes. Every now and then a fox would get hit by a car on the nearby highway, and one of us would wonder aloud if it was our fox and we would miss it in advance. And yet there was always another fox crossing the pasture.

5 But seeing this nearly hairless fox shivering at the barn door, its tail a pitiful file of vertebrae under bare flesh, I couldn't help thinking what a thin concept of wildness I had been living with. The wild I imagined was where the archetypes lived, negotiating their survival. Each animal in the wild embodied its species, which means that it lived up to its portrait in "The Sibley Guide to Birds" or "Walker's Mammals of the World." And though I had a rough idea of how creatures died in the wild, I had never come across an animal driven out of the wild—across that taboo boundary and into my barn—by its suffering. The fox and I looked at each other, only a few feet apart. If it had been a dog I could have helped it. But even the pity in my eyes reminded it that it had come too close.

Building Vocabulary

Define and write a sentence of your own using each of the following words:

1. scurried (par. 1)
2. lope (par. 1)
3. businesslike (par. 4)
4. archetypes (par. 5)
5. embodied (par. 5)
6. taboo (par. 5)

Thinking Critically About the Argument

Understanding the Writer's Argument

1. What does the writer have against the fox at the beginning of his essay?
2. Why does Klinkenborg think it unusual that the fox was taking refuge in his barn?
3. Why *was* the fox in the barn?

4. What is the normal behavior of foxes around the writer's farm?
5. What is the writer's usual view of "wildness"? How has it changed after his run-in with the fox?

Understanding the Writer's Techniques

1. What is Klinkenborg's major proposition? Is it a clear statement? If so, what is it? If not, what do you think it is?
2. The essay is essentially a narrative and attempts to move its readers emotionally. How does the writer build an emotional appeal to his readers?
3. Analyze the use of transitions. How do they move the essay along?
4. This essay aims for an urban readership, and the writer must educate his readers about the rural life. How does Klinkenborg get this information into his essay?
5. What are the warrants in this essay? Are they implied or explicit?
6. Most of the writer's explicit argument is in the final paragraph. How effective is his conclusion?

Exploring the Writer's Argument

1. Klinkenborg writes that if the fox had been a dog, he "could have helped it." Do you think that makes him seem heartless? Or is he merely being realistic? Could he have helped the fox, do you think? Should he have?
2. The writer speaks as a gentleman-farmer, an observer of nature who is educated. Do you believe he is a real farmer? Is his voice authentic? Defend your answers.
3. What relation does the essay imply between humans and animals? Why might you agree or disagree with the relation as Klinkenborg suggests it?

Ideas for Writing Arguments

Prewriting

What did people have to do to domesticate animals like dogs, cats, pigs, and cows? Why did they do it? What do humans gain from domesticating animals?

Writing a Guided Argument

Many of us have pets for companionship and safety, and they are reliable and veritable members of the family. Every once in a while, however, we get a glimpse of just how much they are still animals. Write an essay in which you argue that a pet such as a dog or cat remains, in part, wild, no matter how domesticated it is.

1. Open your essay with a short narrative about a time when you saw the wild animal inside of a pet come through.
2. Next, write a major proposition that argues that pets are, in part, wild.

3. State at least two or three minor propositions to support your position.
4. Show examples to illustrate your minor propositions.
5. Establish a tone that shows how you are amused by the idea of pets being wild.
6. Somewhere near the end, break the normal tone of your essay to express that although it is amusing that pets can be wild, there is something a bit frightening about the fact.
7. Close your essay by reestablishing the normal tone.

Thinking, Arguing, and Writing Collaboratively

In groups of four or five students, share your papers that grew out of the Guided Argument assignment. Discuss the success of the opening narrative and the examples offered to support the minor propositions. Can the passages be improved by omission or rewriting? Can the argument be improved by altering the facts?

Writing About the Text

Write an essay in which you analyze Klinkenborg's style in "Out of the Wild." How does the writer succeed in creating an argument out of a situation he encounters on his farm? He is writing for a newspaper for the biggest city in the United States. How does his rural, laid-back style work?

More Writing Ideas

1. In your journal, freewrite on the topic of boundaries between humans and animals. Write for at least 15 minutes, but do not edit your work as you go. After the time is up, look at what you wrote, and take notes on anything that might be the basis for an essay.
2. Write a paragraph or two in which you explore how nature asserts itself in a city.
3. Write an essay in which you defend or challenge people's efforts to assist animals in the wild—a beached whale or an injured bird, for example. Should humankind help beasts in the wild, or should we leave them to the fate to which nature has led them?

BARRY LOPEZ
Apologia

Barry Lopez was born in 1945 in rural California and now lives in Oregon. He is a short story and nonfiction writer best known for his nature writing, especially Arctic Dreams *(1986), which won the National Book Award for nonfiction. He is also the author of* Crow and Weasel *(1990) and* Field Notes *(1994), among other books. In this selection, Lopez tells the story of a road trip turned deadly—for animals in the wild.*

Prereading: Thinking About the Essay in Advance

Have you ever run over an animal or seen one run over? What did you feel, if anything? Do you ever feel grief at seeing a dead animal on the road?

Words to Watch

maniacally (par. 1) in a crazy way
cornea (par. 2) the membrane that covers the eye
seers (par. 5) people who can see the future
carcass (par. 9) dead body of an animal
tawny (par. 11) of an orange-brown color
gunnysack (par. 11) a bag made from a rough material
cloister (par. 12) place in a monastery where monks live; considered secluded
macadam (par. 14) road surface made of asphalt mixed with rocks
fractious (par. 15) irritable and complaining
beryl (par. 16) a hard mineral consisting of many colors
mandibular (par. 18) relating to the jaw
limpid (par. 21) clear and calm
exculpation (par. 23) to free someone from blame
lavabo (par. 25) a ceremony in a Catholic mass in which a congregant ritually washes his hands

A few miles east of home in the Cascades I slow down and pull over for 1
two raccoons, sprawled still as stones in the road. I carry them to the side and lay them in sun-shot windblown grass in the barrow pit. In eastern Oregon along U.S. 20, black-tailed jackrabbits lie like welts of sod—three, four, then a fifth. By the bridge over Jordan Creek, just shy of the Idaho border in the drainage of the Owyhee River, a crumpled adolescent porcupine leers up almost maniacally over its blood-flecked teeth. I carry each one away from the pavement into a cover of grass or brush out of decency, I think. And worry. Who are these animals, their lights gone out? What journeys have fallen apart here?

I do not stop to remove each dark blister from the road. I wince before 2
the recently dead, feel my lips tighten, see something else, a fence post, in the spontaneous aversion of my eyes, and pull over. I imagine white silk threads of life still vibrating inside them, even if the body's husk is stretched out for yards, stuck like oiled muslin to the road. The energy that once held them erect leaves like a bullet, but the memory of that energy fades slowly from the wrinkled cornea, the bloodless fur.

The raccoons and, later, a red fox carry like sacks of wet gravel and 3
sand. Each animal is like a solitary child's shoe in the road.

Once a man asked, Why do you bother? 4

5 You never know, I said. The ones you give some semblance of burial, to whom you offer an apology, may have been like seers in a parallel culture. It is an act of respect, a technique of awareness.

6 In Idaho I hit a young sage sparrow—thwack against the right fender in the very split second I see it. Its companion rises from the same spot but a foot higher, slow as smoke, and sails off clean into the desert. I rest the walloped bird in my left hand, my right thumb pressed to its chest. I feel for the wail of the heart. Its eyes glisten like rain on crystal. Nothing but warmth. I shut the tiny eyelids and lay it beside a clump of bunchgrass. Beyond a barbed-wire fence the overgrazed range is littered with cow flops. The road curves away to the south. I nod before I go, a ridiculous gesture, out of simple grief.

7 I pass four spotted skunks. The swirling air is acrid with the rupture of each life.

8 Darkness rises in the valleys of Idaho. East of Grand View, south of the Snake River, nighthawks swoop the roads for gnats, silent on the wing as owls. On a descending curve I see two of them lying soft as clouds in the road. I turn around and come back. The sudden slowing down and my K-turn at the bottom of the hill draw the attention of a man who steps away from a tractor, a dozen yards from where the birds lie. I can tell by his step, the suspicious tilt of his head, that he is wary, vaguely proprietary. Offended, or irritated, he may throw the birds back into the road when I leave. So I wait, subdued like a penitent, a body in each hand.

9 He speaks first, a low voice, a deep murmur weighted with awe. He has been watching these flocks feeding just above the road for several evenings. He calls them whippoorwills. He gestures for a carcass. How odd, yes, the way they concentrate their hunting right on the road, I say. He runs a finger down the smooth arc of the belly and remarks on the small whiskered bill. He pulls one long wing out straight, but not roughly. He marvels. He glances at my car, baffled by this out-of-state courtesy. Two dozen nighthawks careen past, back and forth at arm's length, feeding at our height and lower. He asks if I would mind—as though I owned it—if he took the bird up to the house to show his wife. "She's never seen anything like this" He's fascinated. "Not close."

10 I trust, later, he will put it in the fields, not throw the body in the trash, a whirligig.

11 North of Pinedale in western Wyoming on U.S. 189, below the Gros Ventre Range, I see a big doe from a great distance, the low rays of first light gleaming in her tawny reddish hair. She rests askew, like a crushed tree. I drag her to the shoulder, then down a long slope by the petals of her ears. A gunnysack of plaster mud, ears cold as rain gutters. All of her doesn't come. I climb back up for the missing leg. The stain of her is darker than the black asphalt. The stains go north and off to the south as far as I can see.

12 On an afternoon trafficless, quiet as a cloister, headed across South Pass in the Wind River Range, I swerve violently but hit a bird, and then try to wrestle the gravel-spewing skid in a straight line along the lip of an embankment. I know even as I struggle for control the irony of this: I could easily

pitch off here to my own death. The bird is dead somewhere in the road behind me. Only a few seconds and I am safely back on the road, nauseated, light-headed.

It is hard to distinguish among younger gulls. I turn this one around slowly in my hands. It could be a western gull, a mew gull, a California gull. I do not remember well enough the bill markings, the color of the legs. I have no doubt about the vertebrae shattered beneath the seamless white of its ropy neck. 13

East of Lusk, Wyoming, in Nebraska, I stop for a badger. I squat on the macadam to admire the long claws, the perfect set of its teeth in the broken jaw, the ramulose shading of its fur—how it differs slightly, as does every badger's, from the drawings and pictures in the field guides. A car drifts toward us over the prairie, coming on in the other lane, a white 1962 Chevrolet station wagon. The driver slows to pass. In the bright sunlight I can't see his face, only an arm and the gesture of his thick left hand. It opens in a kind of shrug, hangs briefly in limp sadness, then extends itself in supplication. Gone past, it curls into itself against the car door and is still. 14

Farther on in western Nebraska I pick up the small bodies of mice and birds. While I wait to retrieve these creatures I do not meet the eyes of passing drivers. Whoever they are, I feel anger toward them, in spite of the sparrow and the gull I myself have killed. We treat the attrition of lives on the road like the attrition of lives in war: horrifying, unavoidable, justified. Accepting the slaughter leaves people momentarily fractious, embarrassed. South of Broken Bow, at dawn, I cannot avoid an immature barn swallow. It hangs by its head, motionless in the slats of the grille. 15

I stop for a rabbit on Nebraska 806 and find, only a few feet away, a garter snake. What else have I missed, too small, too narrow? What has gone under or past me while I stared at mountains, hay meadows, fencerows, the beryl surface of rivers? In Wyoming I could not help but see pronghorn antelope swollen big as barrels by the side of the road, their legs splayed rigidly aloft. For animals so large, people will stop. But how many have this habit of clearing the road of smaller creatures, people who would remove the ones I miss? I do not imagine I am alone. As much sorrow as the man's hand conveyed in Nebraska, it meant gratitude too for burying the dead. 16

Still, I do not wish to meet anyone's eyes. 17

In Southwestern Iowa, outside Clarinda, I haul a deer into high grass out of sight of the road and begin to examine it. It is still whole, but the destruction is breathtaking. The skull, I soon discover, is fractured in four places; the jaw, hanging by shreds of mandibular muscle, is broken at the symphysis, beneath the incisors. The pelvis is crushed, the left hind leg unsocketed. All but two ribs are dislocated along the vertebral column, which is complexly fractured. The intestines have been driven forward into the chest. The heart and lungs have ruptured the chest wall at the base of the neck. The signature of a tractor-trailer truck: 80,000 pounds at 65 mph. 18

In front of a motel room in Ottumwa I finger-scrape the dry, stiff carcasses of bumblebees, wasps, and butterflies from the grille and headlight 19 mountings, and I scrub with a wet cloth to soften and wipe away the nap of crumbles, the insects, the aerial plankton of spiders and mites. I am uneasy cleaning so many of the dead. The carnage is so obvious.

20 In Illinois, west of Kankakee, two raccoons as young as the ones in Oregon. In Indiana another raccoon, a gray squirrel. When I make the left turn into the driveway at the house of a friend outside South Bend, it is evening, hot and muggy. I can hear cicadas in a lone elm. I'm glad to be here.

21 From the driveway entrance I look back down Indiana 23, toward Indiana 8, remembering the farm roads of Illinois and Iowa. I remember how beautiful it was in the limpid air to drive Nebraska 2 through the sand hills, to see how far at dusk the land was etched east and west of Wyoming 28. I remember the imposition of the Wind River Range in a hard, blue sky beneath white ranks of buttonhook clouds, windy hay fields on the Snake River plain, the welcome of Russian olive trees and willows in western creek bottoms. The transformation of the heart such beauty engenders is not enough tonight to let me shed the heavier memory, a catalog too morbid to write out, too vivid to ignore.

22 I stand in the driveway now, listening to the cicadas whirring in the dark tree. My hands grip the sill of the open window at the driver's side, and I lean down as if to speak to someone still sitting there. The weight I wish to fall I cannot fathom, a sorrow over the world's dark hunger.

23 A light comes on over the porch. I hear a deadbolt thrown, the shiver of a door pulled free. The words of atonement I pronounce are too inept to offer me release. Or forgiveness. My friend is floating across the tree-shadowed lawn. What is to be done with the desire for exculpation?

24 "Later than we thought you'd be," he says.

25 I do not want the lavabo. I wish to make amends.

26 "I made more stops than I thought I would," I answer. "Well, bring in your things. And whatever I can take," he offers.

27 I anticipate, in the powerful antidote of our conversation, the reassurance of a human enterprise, the forgiving embrace of the rational. It waits within, beyond the slow tail-wagging of two dogs standing at the screen door.

Building Vocabulary

1. Go through this essay again and list at least ten of the animals mentioned. Write a short description of each, using reference works, if necessary.
2. For each of the following words, write a definition:
   - **a.** *leers (par. 1)*
   - **b.** *wince (par. 2)*
   - **c.** *semblance (par. 5)*
   - **d.** *walloped (par. 6)*
   - **e.** *acrid (par. 7)*
   - **f.** *penitent (par. 8)*
   - **g.** *supplication (par. 14)*
   - **h.** *atonement (par. 23)*

Thinking Critically About the Argument

Understanding the Writer's Argument

1. What are the Cascades? Why is Lopez driving east through them? Where is he going?
2. Why does Lopez carry the bodies of dead animals to the side of the road? What does Lopez mean by "What journeys have fallen apart here?" (par. 1) How do you know?
3. List the different encounters Lopez has with people along his trip, and explain the nature of each encounter.
4. What does Lopez mean in paragraph 5 that offering a "semblance of burial" to a dead animal on the road is "a technique of awareness"? Where does this phrase come from?
5. Why does Lopez write that his nod to the bird in paragraph 6 is a "ridiculous gesture"?
6. Why doesn't Lopez tell his friend what he had been thinking at the end of his essay?
7. Paraphrase the following sentence: "I anticipate, in the powerful antidote of our conversation, the reassurance of a human enterprise, the forgiving embrace of the rational." (par. 27)

Understanding the Writer's Techniques

1. This essay's argument is complicated. It is not as simple as it seems at first glance. What is Lopez's claim, and where does he state it? If he doesn't state it, why not?
2. Comment on Lopez's use of transitions. How do they contribute to the coherence of the essay and his portrayal of the passage of time?
3. Why does Lopez write about the man who asks him "Why do you bother?" in paragraph 4?
4. What tense does the writer use for the verbs is this essay? Why do you think Lopez uses this tense? Is it effective? Why or why not?
5. What is the effect of the transition between paragraphs 12 and 13? At first, the reader thinks Lopez has driven away from his near-accident, and then the reader realizes that Lopez has turned around. How does he explain this?
6. What three descriptions in Lopez's essay do you think help his position the most?
7. Why does Lopez describe the driver of the Chevrolet driving past him in paragraph 14?
8. Why does Lopez make paragraph 17 one sentence? Is it effective? If so, how, and if not, why not?
9. What is the rhetorical effect of the last section of the essay, after Lopez has pulled into his friend's driveway?
10. What is your opinion of the last paragraph? Is it effective? How does it contribute to the essay's message?

Exploring the Writer's Argument

1. Lopez describes carefully the dead animals he finds. What is your reaction to his descriptions? Do you find the descriptions beautiful? Repulsive? Attractive? Why would he make them so? Explain your answers.
2. The language that Lopez uses in this essay is lyrical, but some readers also might consider it unnecessarily flowery and overwritten. Which do you think it is? Do you think the language in this essay is appropriate? Why or why not?
3. Do you agree with Lopez's statement in paragraph 15 that "we treat the attrition of lives on the road like the attrition of lives in war: horrifying, unavoidable, justified." Is this an apt simile? Why or why not?

Ideas for Writing Arguments

Prewriting

What kind of purely legal and natural behavior do people engage in as a matter of course that we would have to apologize for or defend?

Writing a Guided Argument

Write a narrative argumentative essay also called "Apologia," in which you apologize for or defend some frequent action you take, or action you believe requires apology or defense. For example, you might apologize for last-minute, all-night vigils before a major test; for deciding to break off a relationship with someone you liked; or for refusing to give money to a homeless person begging for help.

1. Begin your narrative at the moment when you first start doing something that needs explaining. Do not start before this.
2. After you establish your story, fill in the back story, explaining anything your reader needs to know.
3. Attempt a lyrical style and tone in your essay, adding descriptions where appropriate.
4. Continue your story, breaking it up into episodes.
5. Offer your reader part of your argument after each episode.
6. Use effective transitions to move your essay along chronologically.
7. Close your essay with a section that ends the narrative and widens the discussion of the lesson you have learned (and which your reader can presumably learn) from your narrative.

Thinking, Arguing, and Writing Collaboratively

In groups of four or five, share experiences that you have had in nature when you felt either superior as humans (perhaps crushing a line of ants) or small as humans (perhaps watching a major storm). Make a list of the kinds of experiences that can make us feel one way or the other.

Writing About the Text

In this essay, Lopez uses many similes, such as in paragraph 11 when describing the dead deer: "She rests askew, like a crushed tree." Write an essay analyzing Lopez's use of figurative language, such as similes and metaphors, and how it helps his argument.

More Writing Ideas

1. In your journal, write a beautiful description of something not ordinarily seen as beautiful—such as withered trees, a sick old dog or cat, or a beaten-up automobile, for example.
2. Write a couple of paragraphs about a trip you took that led you to think about something you hadn't thought about before.
3. *Merriam-Webster Collegiate Dictionary* defines *apologia* as "a defense especially of one's opinions, position, or actions" but also lists it as a synonym of "apology." Does the definition surprise you? Do you think this essay is a defense at all, or an apology? Write an essay in which you analyze the extent to which this essay is an apologia as Webster's defines it, and to what extent it is an apology. What would Lopez be apologizing for? What would he be defending?

WENDELL BERRY
In Distrust of Movements

Prolific Kentucky writer Wendell Berry was born in 1934. He was educated at the University of Kentucky. He is the author of 32 books of essays, poetry, and fiction. His collections of poetry include There Is Singing Around Me *(1976)* Traveling at Home *(1989), and* Entries: Poems *(1994). His novels include* Remembering *(1988) and* A World Lost *(1996). He is also the author of essay collections* A Continuous Harmony *(1972),* Standing on Earth: Selected Essays *(1991),* Sex, Economy, Freedom, & Community *(1993), and* Another Turn of the Crank *(1995). He has taught English at New York University and his alma mater, University of Kentucky. Berry lives on a farm in Port Royal, Kentucky. In this selection, originally published in 1999, Berry expresses his impatience with organized environmental efforts and offers an alternative way to make a difference.*

Prereading: Thinking About the Essay in Advance

Have you ever given money to a cause? Why or why not? What do you think are the most respectable nonprofit organizations? Why?

Words to Watch

preemption (par. 3) action that comes before something else can happen
advocates (par. 3) people who support something
appropriate (par. 3) claim or use something as one's own
irradiation (par. 8) treating food with radiation to kill germs
reconciled (par. 4) have accepted that something is going to happen
erosion (par. 14) a wearing-away from water or air
watersheds (par. 4) area of land that drains into a body of water
husbandry (par. 10) science and art of farming
constituency (par. 11) group of possible voters
profound (par. 12) very great
timber (par. 13) wood to be used as lumber
reductionist (par. 16) oversimplified
hubris (par. 24) excessive arrogance and pride

1 I must burden my readers as I have burdened myself with the knowledge that I speak from a local, some might say a provincial, point of view. When I try to identify myself to myself I realize that, in my most immediate reasons and affections, I am less than an American, less than a Kentuckian, less even than a Henry Countian, but am a man most involved with and concerned about my family, my neighbors, and the land that is daily under my feet. It is this involvement that defines my citizenship in the larger entities. And so I will remember, and I ask you to remember, that I am not trying to say what is thinkable everywhere, but rather what it is possible to think on the westward bank of the lower Kentucky River in the summer of 1998.

2 Over the last twenty-five or thirty years I have been making and remaking different versions of the same argument. It is not "my" argument, really, but rather one that I inherited from a long line of familial, neighborly, literary, and scientific ancestors. We could call it "the agrarian argument." This argument can be summed up in as many ways as it can be made. One way to sum it up is to say that we humans can escape neither our dependence on nature nor our responsibility to nature—and that, precisely because of this condition of dependence *and* responsibility, we are also dependent upon and responsible for human culture.

3 Food, as I have argued at length, is both a natural (which is to say a divine) gift and a cultural product. Because we must *use* land and water and plants and animals to produce food, we are at once dependent on and responsible to what we use. We must know both how to use and how to care for what we use. This knowledge is the basis of human culture. If we do not know how to adapt our desires, our methods, and our technology to the nature of the places in which we are working, so as to make them productive *and to keep them so,* that is a cultural failure of the grossest and most dangerous kind. Poverty and starvation also can be cultural products—if the culture is wrong.

Though this argument, in my keeping, has lengthened and acquired branches, in its main assumptions it has stayed the same. What has changed—and I say this with a good deal of wonder and with much thankfulness—is the audience. Perhaps the audience will always include people who are not listening, or people who think the agrarian argument is merely an anachronism, a form of entertainment, or a nuisance to be waved away. But increasingly the audience also includes people who take this argument seriously, because they are involved in one or more of the tasks of agrarianism. They are trying to maintain a practical foothold on the earth for themselves or their families or their communities. They are trying to preserve and develop local land-based economies. They are trying to preserve or restore the health of local communities and ecosystems and watersheds. They are opposing the attempt of the great corporations to own and control all of Creation. 4

In short, the agrarian argument now has a significant number of friends. 5
As the political and ecological abuses of the so-called global economy become more noticeable and more threatening, the agrarian argument is going to have more friends than it has now. This being so, maybe the advocate's task needs to change. Maybe now, instead of merely propounding (and repeating) the agrarian argument, the advocate must also try to see that this argument does not win friends too easily. I think, myself, that this is the case. The tasks of agrarianism that we have undertaken are not going to be finished for a long time. To preserve the remnants of agrarian life, to oppose the abuses of industrial land use and finally correct them, and to develop the locally adapted economies and cultures that are necessary to our survival will require many lifetimes of dedicated work. This work does not need friends with illusions. And so I would like to speak—in a friendly way, of course—out of my distrust of "movements."

I have had with my friend Wes Jackson a number of useful conversations 6
about the necessity of getting out of movements—even movements that have seemed necessary and dear to us—when they have lapsed into self-righteousness and self-betrayal, as movements seem almost invariably to do. People in movements too readily learn to deny to others the rights and privileges they demand for themselves. They too easily become unable to mean their own language, as when a "peace movement" becomes violent. They often become too specialized, as if they cannot help taking refuge in the pinhole vision of the industrial intellectuals. They almost always fail to be radical enough, dealing finally in effects rather than causes. Or they deal with single issues or single solutions, as if to assure themselves that they will not be radical enough.

And so I must declare my dissatisfaction with movements to promote 7
soil conservation or clean water or clean air or wilderness preservation or sustainable agriculture or community health or the welfare of children. Worthy as these and other goals may be, they cannot be achieved alone.

They cannot be responsibly advocated alone. I am dissatisfied with such efforts because they are too specialized, they are not comprehensive enough, they are not radical enough, they virtually predict their own failure by implying that we can remedy or control effects while leaving the causes in place, Ultimately, I think, they are insincere; they propose that the trouble is caused by *other* people; they would like to change policy but not behavior.

8 The worst danger may be that a movement will lose its language either to its own confusion about meaning and practice, or to preemption by its enemies. I remember, for example, my naive confusion at learning that it was possible for advocates of organic agriculture to look upon the "organic method" as an end in itself. To me, organic farming was attractive both as a way of conserving nature and as a strategy of survival for small farmers. Imagine my surprise in discovering that there could be huge "organic" monocultures. And so I was somewhat prepared for the recent attempt of the United States Department of Agriculture to appropriate the "organic" label for food irradiation, genetic engineering, and other desecrations by the corporate food economy. Once we allow our language to mean anything that anybody wants it to mean, it becomes impossible to mean what we say. When "homemade" ceases to mean neither more nor less than "made at home," then it means anything, which is to say that it means nothing. The same decay is at work on words such as "conservation," "sustainable," "safe," "natural," "healthful," "sanitary," and "organic." The use of such words now requires the most exacting control of context and the use immediately of illustrative examples.

9 Real organic gardeners and farmers who market their produce locally are finding that, to a lot of people, "organic" means something like "trustworthy." And so, for a while, it will be useful for us to talk about the meaning and the economic usefulness of trust and trustworthiness. But we must be careful. Sooner or later, Trust Us Global Foods, Inc., will be upon us, advertising safe, sanitary, natural food irradiation. And then we must be prepared to raise another standard and move on.

10 As you see, I have good reasons for declining to name the movement I think I am a part of. I call it The Nameless Movement for Better Ways of Doing—which I hope is too long and uncute to be used as a bumper sticker. I know that movements tend to die with their names and slogans, and I believe that this Nameless Movement needs to live on and on. I am reconciled to the likelihood that from time to time it will name itself and have slogans, but I am not going to use its slogans or call it by any of its names. After this, I intend to stop calling it The Nameless Movement for Better Ways of Doing, for fear it will become the NMBWD and acquire a headquarters and a budget and an inventory of T-shirts covered with language that in a few years will be mere spelling.

11 Let us suppose, then, that we have a Nameless Movement for Better Land Use and that we know we must try to keep it active, responsive, and intelligent for a long time. What must we do?

What we must do above all, I think, is try to see the problem in its full size and difficulty. If we are concerned about land abuse, then we must see that this is an economic problem. Every economy is, by definition, a land-using economy. If we are using our land wrong, then something is wrong with our economy. This is difficult. It becomes more difficult when we recognize that, in modern times, every one of us is a member of the economy of everybody else. Every one of us has given many proxies to the economy to use the land (and the air, the water, and other natural gifts) on our behalf. Adequately supervising those proxies is at present impossible; withdrawing them is for virtually all of us, as things now stand, unthinkable. 12

But if we are concerned about land abuse, we have begun an extensive work of economic criticism. Study of the history of land use (and any local history will do) informs us that we have had for a long time an economy that thrives by undermining its own foundations. Industrialism, which is the name of our economy, and which is now virtually the only economy of the world, has been from its beginnings in a state of riot. It is based squarely upon the principle of violence toward everything on which it depends, and it has not mattered whether the form of industrialism was communist or capitalist, the violence toward nature, human communities, traditional agricultures, and local economies has been constant. The bad news is coming in from all over the world. Can such an economy somehow be fixed without being radically changed? I don't think it can. 13

The Captains of Industry have always counseled the rest of us to "be realistic." Let us, therefore, be realistic. Is it realistic to assume that the present economy would be just fine if only it would stop poisoning the earth, air, and water, or if only it would stop soil erosion, or if only it would stop degrading watersheds and forest ecosystems, or if only it would stop seducing children, or if only it would quit buying politicians, or if only it would give women and favored minorities an equitable share of the loot? Realism, I think, is a very limited program, but it informs us at least that we should not look for bird eggs in a cuckoo clock. 14

Or we can show the hopelessness of single-issue causes and single-issue movements by following a line of thought such as this: We need a continuous supply of uncontaminated water. Therefore, we need (among other things) soil-and-water-conserving ways of agriculture and forestry that are not dependent on monoculture, toxic chemicals, or the indifference and violence that always accompany big-scale industrial enterprises on the land. Therefore, we need diversified, small-scale land economies that are dependent on people. Therefore, we need people with the knowledge, skills, motives, and attitudes required by diversified, small-scale land economies. And all this is clear and comfortable enough, until we recognize the question we have come to: *Where are the people?* 15

Well, all of us who live in the suffering rural landscapes of the United States know that most people are available to those landscapes only recreationally. We see them bicycling or boating or hiking or camping or hunting 16 or fishing or driving along and looking around. They do not, in Mary Austin's phrase, "summer and winter with the land." They are unacquainted with the land's human and natural economies. Though people have not progressed beyond the need to eat food and drink water and wear clothes and live in houses, most people have progressed beyond the domestic arts—the husbandry and wifery of the world—by which those needful things are produced and conserved. In fact, the comparative few who still practice that necessary husbandry and wifery often are inclined to apologize for doing so, having been carefully taught in our education system that those arts are degrading and unworthy of people's talents. Educated minds, in the modern era, are unlikely to know anything about food and drink or clothing and shelter. In merely taking these things for granted, the modern educated mind reveals itself also to be as superstitious a mind as ever has existed in the world. What could be more superstitious than the idea that money brings forth food?

17 I am not suggesting, of course, that everybody ought to be a farmer or a forester. Heaven forbid! I *am* suggesting that most people now are living on the far side of a broken connection, and that this is potentially catastrophic. Most people are now fed, clothed, and sheltered from sources, in nature and in the work of other people, toward which they feel no gratitude and exercise no responsibility.

18 We are involved now in a profound failure of imagination. Most of us cannot imagine the wheat beyond the bread, or the farmer beyond the wheat, or the farm beyond the farmer, or the history (human or natural) beyond the farm. Most people cannot imagine the forest and the forest economy that produced their houses and furniture and paper; or the landscapes, the streams, and the weather that fill their pitchers and bathtubs and swimming pools with water. Most people appear to assume that when they have paid their money for these things they have entirely met their obligations. And that is, in fact, the conventional economic assumption. The problem is that it is possible to starve under the rule of the conventional economic assumption; some people are starving now under the rule of that assumption.

19 Money does not being forth food. Neither does the technology of the food system. Food comes from nature and from the work of people. If the supply of food is to be continuous for a long time, then people must work in harmony with nature. That means that people must find the right answers to a lot of questions. The same rules apply to forestry and the possibility of a continuous supply of forest products.

20 People grow the food that people eat. People produce the lumber that people use. People care properly or improperly for the forests and the farms that are the sources of those goods. People are necessarily at both ends of the process. The economy, always obsessed with its need to sell products, thinks obsessively and exclusively of the consumer. It mostly takes for granted or ignores those who do the damaging or the restorative and preserving work of agriculture and forestry. The economy pays poorly for this work, with the unsurprising result that the work is

mostly done poorly. But here we must ask a very realistic economic question: Can we afford to have this work done poorly? Those of us who know something about land stewardship know that we cannot afford to pay poorly for it, because that means simply that we will not get it. And we know that we cannot afford land use without land stewardship.

One way we could describe the task ahead of us is by saying that we need to enlarge the consciousness and the conscience of the economy. Our economy needs to know—and care—what it is doing. This is revolutionary, of course, if you have a taste for revolution, but it is also merely a matter of common sense. How could anybody seriously object to the possibility that the economy might eventually come to know what it is doing? 21

Undoubtedly some people will want to start a movement to bring this about. They probably will call it the Movement to Teach the Economy What It Is Doing—the MTEWIID. Despite my very considerable uneasiness, I will agree to participate, but on three conditions. 22

My first condition is that this movement should begin by giving up all hope and belief in piecemeal, one-shot solutions. The present scientific quest for odorless hog manure should give us sufficient proof that the specialist is no longer with us. Even now, after centuries of reductionist propaganda, the world is still intricate and vast, as dark as it is light, a place of mystery, where we cannot do one thing without doing many things, or put two things together without putting many things together. Water quality, for example, cannot be improved without improving farming and forestry, but farming and forestry cannot be improved without improving the education of consumers—and so on. 23

The proper business of a human economy is to make one whole thing of ourselves and this world. To make ourselves into a practical wholeness with the land under our feet is maybe not altogether possible—how would *we* know?—but, as a goal, it at least carries us beyond ***hubris,*** beyond the utterly groundless assumption that we can subdivide our present great failure into a thousand separate problems that can be fixed by a thousand task forces of academic and bureaucratic specialists. That program has been given more than a fair chance to prove itself, and we ought to know by now that it won't work. 24

My second condition is that the people in this movement (the MTEWIID) should take full responsibility for themselves as members of the economy. If we are going to teach the economy what it is doing, then we need to learn what *we* are doing. This is going to have to be a private movement as well as a public one. If it is unrealistic to expect wasteful industries to be conservers, then obviously we must lead in part the public life of complainers, petitioners, protesters, advocates and supporters of stricter regulations and saner policies. But that is not enough. If it is unrealistic to expect a bad economy to try to become a good one, then we must go to work to build a good economy. It is appropriate that this duty should fall to us, for good economic behavior is more possible for us than it is for the great corporations with their miseducated managers and their greedy and oblivious stockholders. 25

Because it is possible for us, we must try in every way we can to make good economic sense in our own lives, in our households, and in our communities. We must do more for ourselves and our neighbors. We must learn to spend our money with our friends and not with our enemies. But to do this, it is necessary to renew local economics, and revive the domestic arts. In seeking to change our economic use of the world, we are seeking inescapably to change our lives. The outward harmony that we desire between our economy and the world depends finally upon an inward harmony between our own hearts and the creative spirit that is the life of all creatures, a spirit as near us as our flesh and yet forever beyond the measures of this obsessively measuring age. We can grow good wheat and make good bread only if we understand that we do not live by bread alone.

26 My third condition is that this movement should content itself to be poor. We need to find cheap solutions, solutions within the reach of everybody, and the availability of a lot of money prevents the discovery of cheap solutions. The solutions of modern medicine and modern agriculture are all staggeringly expensive, and this is caused in part, and maybe altogether, by the availability of huge sums of money for medical and agricultural research.

27 Too much money, moreover, attracts administrators and experts as sugar attracts ants—look at what is happening in our universities. We should not envy rich movements that are organized and led by an alternative bureaucracy living on the problems it is supposed to solve. We want a movement that is a movement because it is advanced by all its members in their daily lives.

28 Now, having completed this very formidable list of the problems and difficulties, fears and fearful hopes that lie ahead of us, I am relieved to see that I have been preparing myself all along to end by saying something cheerful. What I have been talking about is the possibility of renewing human respect for this earth and all the good, useful, and beautiful things that come from it. I have made it clear, I hope, that I don't think this respect can be adequately enacted or conveyed by tipping our hats to nature or by representing natural loveliness in art or by prayers of thanksgiving or by preserving tracts of wilderness—though I recommend all those things. The respect I mean can be given only by using well the world's goods that are given to us. This good use, which renews respect—which is the only currency, so to speak, of respect—also renews our pleasure. The callings and disciplines that I have spoken of as the domestic arts are stationed all along the way from the farm to the prepared dinner, from the forest to the dinner table, from stewardship of the land to hospitality to friends and strangers. These arts are as demanding and gratifying, as instructive and as pleasing as the so-called fine arts. To learn them, to practice them, to honor, and reward them is, I believe, our profoundest calling. Our reward is that they will enrich our lives and make us glad.

Building Vocabulary

Write out a definition for each of the following words, then write a sentence using it:

1. invariably (par. 1)
2. naive (par. 3)
3. undermining (par. 7)
4. degrading (par. 10)
5. formidable (par. 11)
6. oblivious (par. 18)

Thinking Critically About the Argument

Understanding the Writer's Argument

1. Wes Jackson is the founder of the Land Institute, which does research on agriculture. Why does Berry mention Jackson at the beginning of his essay? How does this help you to understand the Nameless Movement for Better Land Use in paragraph 10?
2. What kinds of movements is Berry talking about in the title? What does he see as the main problems with movements? What does he say is the worst problem, and how does it have larger implications for society?
3. Who are the "Captains of Industry"? (par. 14) Why are they important to Berry's argument?
4. What does Berry mean when he writes that "we should not look for bird eggs in a cuckoo clock"?
5. Paraphrase Berry's crucial argument in paragraph 15.
6. Berry lives in the country. What cues does Berry give you to express that information?
7. What point is Berry making when he writes that "we are involved now in a profound failure of imagination"? (par. 18)
8. What is the Movement to Teach the Economy What It Is Doing? What does he demand from the movement?
9. What are the "domestic arts"? What do they have to do with Berry's argument?
10. Berry says in paragraph 28 that he has been preparing to say "something cheerful." What is that cheerful thing?

Understanding the Writer's Techniques

1. What is Berry's claim? In what sentence does he express it most clearly?
2. Berry organizes this essay in three sections. Make an outline in which you paraphrase the essential argument in each section, and then analyze how the argument moves from one to the other. How does he develop his claim?

3. Make a shorter outline in which you analyze the second section in Berry's essay. How does Berry move from identifying a problem in paragraph 15 to his demand for conditions starting in paragraph 22?
4. What is Berry's tone? Point out the uses of irony in the essay. How does irony contribute to Berry's intent?
5. Why doesn't Berry use the real names of movements? What is the effect of making up names for hypothetical movements?
6. What is the argumentative purpose of Berry's accusations regarding the "Captains of Industry"? Is it effective? How is it effective or how is it not?
7. Who is Berry's audience for this essay? What assumption about the audience does he imply in his conclusion?
8. Evaluate the success of Berry's concluding paragraph. Does he tie his essay together? If so, how? If not, why not?

Exploring the Writer's Argument

1. Berry's introduction lists "dealing . . . in effects rather than causes" (par. 6) as one of his grievances against movements. In what way does Berry take his own advice here and concentrate on causes rather than effects? In what way does he *not* take his own advice?
2. Why doesn't Berry argue against nonprofit organizations, which are the organizations working for these "single causes"? Instead, he targets "movements." What are the implications of the choice for his argument and for how you understand the essay?
3. How effective are Berry's arguments in support of his statement in paragraph 16, that in taking modern conveniences for granted "the modern educated mind reveals itself also to be as superstitious a mind as ever has existed in the world"?
4. Write a response to Berry's accusation that because people don't think of wheat when they eat bread, "we are involved now in a profound failure of imagination." (par. 18)

Ideas for Writing Arguments

Prewriting

How do you pay your respects to nature, or do you at all? What do you do that Berry states in his conclusion everyone should do?

Writing a Guided Argument

Write an essay that attempts to prove that you, a modern educated mind, are not alienated from the everyday items and activities that you consume or are engaged in and that you do what Berry asks in his conclusion, that you use "well the world's goods that are given to us."

1. Begin by explaining to your reader why you are writing this essay—to defend yourself against Wendell Berry's accusations.
2. Continue with a brief personal story in which you illustrate your lack of alienation from nature.

3. Link your illustration with a major proposition.
4. Support your main point with a number of minor propositions.
5. Expand each minor proposition with details and examples that explain your grounds for believing yourself to understand and live in accordance with Berry's demands.
6. End your essay with a paragraph that extends your use of goods to a larger philosophy of living.

Thinking, Arguing, and Writing Collaboratively

In small groups, share your papers that grew out of the Writing a Guided Argument assignment. Discuss possible weak examples of your respectful use of nature and possible objections that a reader might have. Brainstorm in your groups about how you might address these objections or weaknesses in your essay. Take notes, and incorporate your notes into your final draft.

Writing About the Text

All of the essays in this book are arguments of some sort. Some argue for simple policy changes, whereas Berry's essay is qualitatively different. He is calling for his readers to change their belief systems, to look at the world in a whole new way. Find another essay in this book that calls for the same kind of radical shift in thinking, and compare and contrast Berry's essay with that selection. How are the arguments similar? Different? Which is more successful, and why?

More Writing Ideas

1. In your journal, list the causes identified in paragraph 2 of this essay, and do some research to find which nonprofit organizations are the leaders of those movements. Which are you drawn to? Why?
2. In an extended paragraph, explore Berry's idea from paragraph 6 that "every one of us is a member of the economy of everybody else."
3. Write an essay in which you argue that even in private life, Berry's statement in paragraph 19 is true: "the availability of a lot of money prevents the discovery of cheap solutions."

32 Human Rights: Why Does Society Need Them?

In 1948, the United Nations adopted the Universal Declaration of Human Rights, a document meant to assert the natural rights of humankind. For example, Article 3 of the declaration says, "Everyone has the right to life, liberty and security of person." The remaining 29 articles outline other basic rights.

After World War II, the great colonial powers collapsed, freeing billions of people from oppression and giving hope. The declaration set a standard for all countries to refer to and instructed them on how they are to treat their citizens. But why do we need a document like the Universal Declaration? Governments believe that they cannot control their people if their people have all the rights, so many countries simply don't grant their citizens these rights. Organizations and movements rose up to try to shame countries into ensuring their people these basic freedoms, and writers have used their voices to raise consciences and explain the necessity of human rights standards and basic respect for human life.

The essential message behind human rights is simple, but as with other topics, writers choose to tackle their subject in many different ways. In this chapter, you will read former President Jimmy Carter's argument in "A World Criminal Court Is Urgently Needed." In a straightforward way, he offers his view as an elder statesman lending his authority to a cause. In "Let It Be," Jonathan Rauch, on the other hand, projects a wry cynicism to highlight what he sees as a way to remove a hindrance to human rights, religious fervency. Israeli writer Amos Oz, in "Two Stubborn Men, Many Dead," chooses to argue in highly emotional terms, in speaking of slain children and in calling for the end of the Israeli-Palestinian war. Terry Tempest Williams, in "The Clan of the One-Breasted Women," also uses emotional appeals to expose the plight of the victims of U.S. atomic testing in the desert in the 1950s. Each of these writers has a position to defend, but each uses a vastly different technique.

JIMMY CARTER

A World Criminal Court Is Urgently Needed

The 39th president of the United States of America, James Earl Carter was born in 1924 in Plains, Georgia, which has remained his home to this day. A devout Baptist, Carter spent seven years in the navy, serving on a nuclear submarine, before returning to Plains to take over the family business, peanut farming. After a successful business career, he turned to politics. He was elected the governor of Georgia in 1962 and was elected president in 1976 over Republican incumbent Gerald Ford. His administration struggled with the terrible inflation and unemployment that affected the country in the late 1970s. Carter worked to improve domestic affairs, including race relations and government efficiency. He worked toward peace in the Middle East and brokered the Camp David agreement of 1978 that marked an end of aggression between Israel and Egypt. A crisis overshadowed the end of his administration, however, when Iran took as hostages 52 members of the U.S. embassy in Tehran. Carter paid the price, and he was defeated by Ronald Reagan in the 1980 election. (Iran released the hostages on Carter's last day in office.)

Carter's career did not end with his presidency, however. He and his wife, Rosalyn, went back to Plains and started the Carter Center in 1982, which "seeks to prevent and resolve conflicts, enhance freedom and democracy, and improve health." The center acts as a neutral observer of elections around the world and works to eradicate diseases in Third World countries (they were successful in Africa with Guinea worm disease). Since the 1980s, Carter has been involved with Habitat for Humanity, a nonprofit organization that builds houses for people in need. Carter is the author of The Blood of Abraham *(1985), about the Middle East peace process,* An Outdoor Journal *(1988), and* An Hour Before Daylight *(2001). In 2002 he received the Nobel Peace Prize for "his decades of untiring efforts to find peaceful solutions to international conflict." In this selection, published in the* Los Angeles Times *in 1996, Carter lends his moral authority to what he sees as the need for a permanent international criminal court.*

Prereading: Thinking About the Essay in Advance

What possible arguments can you think of for not supporting a criminal court subject to international law?

Words to Watch

avert (par. 1) prevent
compliance (par. 1) agreement to do something
convene (par. 3) come together for an official reason
marred (par. 5) spoiled or took away from
acute (par. 8) very serious

undermine (par. 11) weaken
arbiter (par. 11) someone who has the power to decide
panacea (par. 12) cure-all for all problems
expeditiously (par. 13) quickly

1 Out of the horrors of World War II, world leaders collectively agreed that genocide and crimes against humanity represented a threat to international peace and security, above and beyond the populations directly affected. To avert future occurrences, mechanisms were devised, such as the Geneva and Genocide conventions, which place obligations on states engaged in warfare and the international community at large. Unfortunately, these have been inadequate in their ability to enforce state compliance. Genocide has been perpetrated twice within the last few years, in the former Yugoslavia and Rwanda.

2 Political efforts to address these crises failed for far too long. World leaders have been largely divided about what could have been done to prevent them, given the absence of enforceable protection procedures. One response to this concern has been the creation of special tribunals to prosecute the architects of genocidal policies and practices in the two countries.

3 Simultaneously, negotiations have been under way within the United Nations to create an International Criminal Court. This would be a permanent court for prosecuting suspected perpetrators of crimes against humanity when national courts are not able to do so, eliminating the need for special tribunals. In November 1996, these negotiations resulted in a landmark agreement to convene a diplomatic conference in 1998, during which a treaty establishing the court would be concluded.

4 These developments offer hope in the struggle to protect human rights, but will require greater care and attention in the coming years.

5 Since the creation of the two special tribunals, they have been marred with difficulties that provide lessons for the permanent court. Early on, financial resources were scarce. While this lack seems to have been solved for the time being, other matters threaten the tribunals' effectiveness.

6 After initial missteps, the Bosnia Tribunal has gradually addressed many of these issues, including performing more effective investigations of crimes of sexual violence against women. This required proper definitions of crimes in international law, adequate specialized training and arrangements for collection of evidence and testimonies as well as witness protection.

7 However, more general problems, such as failure to arrest and extradite the vast majority of those indicted by the tribunal, could undermine its prospects for successful prosecutions.

8 The Rwanda Tribunal suffers from more acute problems, including shortages of qualified personnel, limited training, faulty methodology and weak investigative procedures. The matter of investigating crimes of sexual violence against women has not been handled well and needs dedicated resources and expertise. In addition to indictments having been slow in emerging, as of December 1996 only three of the 21 of those indicted are in the custody of the Tribunal.

The responsibility falls upon the international community to ensure the effective functioning of the tribunals by investing in them resources and political will that until now, have fallen short of what is needed. One place to start is for all nations to enact laws that enable them to extradite indicted war criminals to The Hague. 9

The permanent court is needed so that any future cases can be brought forward quickly without waiting years for procedures and structures to be built, as has been the case with the special tribunals. Now that a date has been set for the court's establishment, the U.S. government should play a leadership role in ensuring that it will be constituted in a way that enables it to work independently from political pressures. We should reflect on our own experience which shows that a judicial process must not be vulnerable to politics or personal preferences. It must be guided by the law alone. 10

In that light, a U.S. proposal to grant the Security Council control over prosecutions in the court would undermine its very purpose. Such a move rightly would be seen by many nations as a means for serving only the interests of the permanent members of the Security Council rather than as an independent arbiter of justice. 11

The court will not be a panacea. As we have found in our own society, a criminal justice system does not ensure the absence of violence, but we would never consider eliminating it as a key ingredient in any strategy to protect civil rights and public safety in general. 12

The International Criminal Court will be good for America, and it will be good for the world. Meanwhile, all nations should consider it their duty to ensure that the existing tribunals overcome current difficulties and complete their work as expeditiously and effectively as possible. 13

Building Vocabulary

In this essay, Carter uses several words from the legal profession and the world surrounding it. Define the following words (looking them up in reference works, if necessary), and offer an example of each from outside the realm of the World Criminal Court:

1. genocide (par. 1)
2. perpetrated (par. 1)
3. tribunals (par. 2)
4. extradite (par. 7)
5. indicted (par. 8)

Thinking Critically About the Argument

Understanding the Writer's Argument

1. Which "horrors of World War II" is Carter referring to in paragraph 1?
2. What does Carter think we can do to help prevent genocide around the world?
3. What is the International Criminal Court?

4. What are the "two special tribunals" to which Carter refers in paragraph 5? What problems have they faced?
5. What does Carter mean when he writes that "The court will not be a panacea"? (par. 12)

Understanding the Writer's Techniques

1. What is Carter's major proposition? In which sentence does it appear?
2. What minor propositions does Carter present to show why a permanent international criminal court is needed? What details does he offer to back up those minor propositions?
3. In what order has Carter chosen to present his argument? Why do you think he chooses that order? Is it effective? Why do you think so?
4. Carter's style is extremely straightforward. Why does he choose this style? Is it appropriate? Explain.
5. Analyze how Carter maintains coherence in this essay. What techniques does he use?
6. Who do you think is Carter's audience for this essay? Why?
7. How effective is Carter's conclusion? Why does he close by mentioning the temporary courts if his essay is about the need for a permanent court?

Exploring the Writer's Argument

1. Do you agree with Carter that developing criminal courts to prosecute those accused of genocide "offer hope in the struggle to protect human rights"? Why or why not?
2. One of Carter's points is that temporary tribunals, for individual conflicts, do not work, and a permanent court is needed to do a good job. Does he convince you of this need, or are you still not sure if temporary courts would do a fine enough job?
3. Do you think it is appropriate for an ex-president of this country to be criticizing a U.S. proposal to the United Nations, as Carter does in paragraph 11? Why or why not?

Ideas for Writing Arguments

Prewriting

Can you think of any reasons why a country would not want to agree to the establishment of the International Criminal Court? List as many objections as you can come up with.

Writing a Guided Argument

Two years after Carter wrote this essay in 1996, a convention was held in Rome, Italy, officially beginning the process to establish the court Carter calls for in this essay. Then-President Bill Clinton agreed to adhere to the convention. His successor, President George W. Bush, has said that he would not allow the United States to be a party to the International Criminal Court. Do some research to learn the arguments of the Bush administration, and write an essay in which you argue that the United States will or will not eventually sign on to the court.

1. Open your essay with an update about the International Criminal Court since Carter's essay was published in December 1996.
2. Next, include a reference to the controversy over the court's founding, paying attention to the United States' recent arguments against it.
3. Assert your claim that the United States will or will not join on eventually.
4. Present the grounds for your claim in separate paragraphs.
5. Support the grounds for your position with evidence from your research and your own opinions.
6. Make reference to other international treaties the United States does not want to be a part of, or has left, and link this idea with the court.
7. Conclude with a summary of your own opinion about the International Criminal Court, and what you think the United States *should* do, based on your research.

Thinking, Arguing, and Writing Collaboratively

In groups of four or five, discuss what a proper punishment is for war crimes. Is it better to execute war criminals convicted of genocide, or is it better to keep them alive as an example? Your group might want to do some research to see what temporary tribunals have done with war criminals over the years.

Writing About the Text

During his presidency, Carter was caricatured as always having a huge grin and being too soft-spoken for the job. Carter's calm voice comes through in this essay. Write an essay in which you argue either that his flatness of style lacks the impact needed to influence anyone or that his voice is exactly the one that is needed in an argument of this type.

More Writing Ideas

1. Will humans ever succeed in ending genocide, or will there always be madmen with the means to achieve their goals? In your journal record your responses to this question.
2. Write a paragraph that explores the idea of human rights and how an International Criminal Court can advance the cause of human rights throughout the world.
3. Wendell Berry argues in his essay "In Distrust of Movements" that often people who act to help the world lose their way and don't help much at all. Read Berry's essay, and ascertain what he thinks can be done to help movements stay on track. Do some research on Jimmy Carter's Carter Center, and write an essay in which you argue that the Carter Center is (or is not) faithful to Berry's prescriptions.

JONATHAN RAUCH

Let It Be

Born in Phoenix, Arizona, in 1960, Jonathan Rauch attended Yale University before starting his career as a reporter and writer at the Winston-Salem Journal *in North Carolina. Rauch moved to Washington in 1984 for a stint as a staff writer for the* National Journal. *Since then he has written freelance for many magazines and newspapers on political and cultural issues, and since 1991 he has also written as an openly gay writer about gay rights. He is the author of* The Outnation *(1992),* Kindly Inquisitors *(1993),* Demosclerosis *(1994), and* Government's End: Why Washington Stopped Working *(1999). He currently writes a biweekly column for the* National Journal. *In this selection published in the* Atlantic Monthly *in 2002, Rauch argues in favor of an attitude toward religion that he calls "apatheism."*

Prereading: Thinking About the Essay in Advance

What religion were you brought up with? Do you still practice? Do you think organized religion makes the world a better place? Why or why not?

Words to Watch

induced (par. 1) caused by
disinclination (par. 2) reluctance to do something
ostensibly (par. 2) seeming to be true, but perhaps not
pious (par. 2) devoutly religious
quaint (par. 3) charmingly old-fashioned
unrepentantly (par. 7) in a way as not to apologize for something
divisive (par. 8) causing disagreements
volatile (par. 8) unstable
pragmatic (par. 9) concerned with practical results rather than ideas
snicker (par. 11) laugh condescendingly

1 It came to me recently in a blinding vision that I am an apatheist. Well, "blinding vision" may be an overstatement. "Wine-induced haze" might be more strictly accurate. This was after a couple of glasses of Merlot, when someone asked me about my religion. "Atheist," I was about to say, but I stopped myself. "I used to call myself an atheist," I said, "and I still don't believe in God, but the larger truth is that it has been years since I really cared one way or another. I'm"—that was when it hit me—"an . . . apatheist!"

2 That got a chuckle, but the point was serious. Apatheism—a disinclination to care all that much about one's own religion, and an even stronger disinclination to care about other people's—may or may not be something new in the world, but its modern flowering, particularly in ostensibly pious America, is worth getting excited about.

Apatheism concerns not what you believe but how. In that respect it differs from the standard concepts used to describe religious views and people. Atheism, for instance, is not at all like apatheism; the hot-blooded atheist cares as much about religion as does the evangelical Christian, but in the opposite direction. "Secularism" can refer to a simple absence of devoutness, but it more accurately refers to an ACLU-style disapproval of any profession of religion in public life—a disapproval that seems puritanical and quaint to apatheists. Tolerance is a magnificent concept, John Locke's inestimable gift to all mankind; but it assumes, as Locke did, that everyone brims with religious passions that everyone else must work hard to put up with. 3

And agnostics? True, most of them are apatheists, but most apatheists are not agnostics. Because—and this is an essential point—many apatheists are believers. 4

In America, as Thomas Byrne Edsall reported in these pages recently, the proportion of people who say they never go to church or synagogue has tripled since 1972, to 33 percent in 2000. Most of these people believe in God (professed atheists are very rare in the United States); they just don't care much about him. They do care a bit; but apatheism is an attitude, not a belief system, and the over-riding fact is that these people are relaxed about religion. 5

Even regular churchgoers can, and often do, rank quite high on the apatheism scale. There are a lot of reasons to attend religious services: to connect with a culture or a community, to socialize, to expose children to religion, to find the warming comfort of familiar ritual. The softer denominations in America are packed with apatheists. The apatheism of Reform Jews is so well known as to be a staple of synagogue humor. (Orthodox rabbi to Reform rabbi: "One of my congregants says his son wants a Harley for his bar mitzvah. What's a Harley?" Reform rabbi to Orthodox rabbi: "A Harley is a motorcycle. What's a bar mitzvah?") 6

Finally, and this may seem strangest of all, even true-believing godliness today often has an apatheistic flavor. I have Christian friends who organize their lives around an intense and personal relationship with God, but who betray no sign of caring that I am an unrepentantly atheistic Jewish homosexual. They are exponents, at least, of the second, more important part of apatheism: the part that doesn't mind what *other* people think about God. 7

I believe that the rise of apatheism is to be celebrated as nothing less than a major civilizational advance. Religion, as the events of September 11 and after have so brutally underscored, remains the most divisive and volatile of social forces. To be in the grip of religious zeal is the natural state of human beings, or at least of a great many human beings; that is how much of the species seems to be wired. Apatheism, therefore, should not be assumed to represent a lazy recumbency, like my collapse into a soft chair after a long day. Just the opposite: it is the product of a determined cultural effort to discipline the religious mindset, and often of an equally determined personal effort to master the spiritual passions. It is not a lapse. It is an achievement. 8

9 "A world of pragmatic atheists," the philosopher Richard Rorty once wrote, "would be a better, happier world than our present one." Perhaps. But best of all would be a world generously leavened with apatheists: people who feel at ease with religion even if they are irreligious; people who may themselves be members of religious communities, but who are neither controlled by godly passions nor concerned about the (nonviolent, noncoercive) religious beliefs of others. In my lifetime America has taken great strides in this direction and its example will be a source of strength, not weakness, in a world still beset by fanatical religiosity (al Qaeda) and tyrannical secularism (China).

10 Ronald Reagan used to insist that he was religious even though, as President, he hardly ever entered a church. It turns out he was in good company. Those Americans who tell pollsters they worship faithfully? Many of them are lying. John G. Stackhouse Jr., a professor of theology and culture, wrote recently in *American Outlook* magazine, "Beginning in the 1990s, a series of sociological studies has shown that many more Americans tell pollsters that they attend church regularly than can be found in church when teams actually count." In fact, he says, actual churchgoing may be at little more than half the professed rate. A great many Americans, like their fortieth President, apparently care about religion enough to say they are religious but not enough to go to church.

11 You can snicker at Reagan and the millions of others like him; you can call them hypocrites if you like. I say, God bless them, every one.

Building Vocabulary

1. Identify the following:
   a. ACLU (par. 3)
   b. John Locke (par. 3)
   c. The difference between Orthodox and Reform Judaism (par. 6)
   d. Richard Rorty (par. 9)
   e. pollsters (par. 10)
2. This essay explores different approaches to various aspects of religion. Identify and define the following religious terms:
   a. atheist (par. 1)
   b. evangelical Christian (par. 3)
   c. secularism (par. 3)
   d. puritanical (par. 3)
   e. agnostics (par. 4)
   f. denominations (par. 6)
   g. religious zeal (par. 8)

Thinking Critically About the Argument

Understanding the Writer's Argument

1. What is an *apatheist?* What two words does Rauch combine to get this word?
2. In paragraph 2, Rauch explains why apatheism is different from other ways people can be indifferent to religion. In your own words, explain the difference.

3. What are the "softer denominations" among the religions in America? (par. 6) List at least three.
4. In paragraph 7, Rauch describes himself as an "atheistic Jewish homosexual." How can he be atheistic and Jewish at the same time?
5. What does Rauch mean in paragraph 9 when he says that if there were many apatheists, the world would be "leavened"? Do you recognize the joke here? What is it?
6. Rauch quotes John G. Stackhouse as saying that perhaps half of the people who tell pollsters they go to church actually go. Why do you think people would lie to people taking polls?
7. Why does Rauch like Reagan's approach to religion?

Understanding the Writer's Techniques

1. What is Rauch's claim? In which paragraph does it appear?
2. What is the effect of Rauch in saying that he was mildly drunk when he came up with his idea?
3. What grounds does Rauch offer to back up his claim?
4. In what order does Rauch present his points? Why do you think he chose that order? Is it effective?
5. What is the effect of Rauch's joke in paragraph 6? Do you think it is appropriate? Why or why not? Does it help his essay? Explain.
6. How has Rauch used the strategy of definition here? What other rhetorical modes can you identify in this essay?
7. Do you like Rauch's conclusion? Do you think it's funny? Does it help his argument? If so, how? If not, why not?

Exploring the Writer's Argument

1. Some people suggest that with the loss of interest in religion comes the loss of something noble and exalted in the human mind. Do you think Rauch properly addresses this objection to his argument? Explain your answer.
2. In paragraph 7, Rauch makes the point that one aspect of apatheism is the fact that some people don't mind "what *other* people think about God." Do you think he fully explains why this is the "more important part of apatheism"? Explain your answer fully.
3. Do you agree with Rauch that apatheism is "the product of a determined cultural effort to discipline the religious mindset," (par. 8) or do you think it is just laziness? Why?

Ideas for Writing Arguments

Prewriting

Look up the word *neologism* in the dictionary. Brainstorm to come up with as many neologisms as you can, in the style of Rauch's *apatheism.*

Writing a Guided Argument

Write an essay in which you combine two words to create a new word, and then defend that word and its idea as a new, important concept that sheds light on a recent controversy. (For example, you might call people who illegally download music on the Internet but also buy music in stores "KaZumers," combining the popular program KaZaa and the word "consumers.")

1. Begin with a paragraph that dramatizes your discovery of the new word, modeled on Rauch's discovery of *apatheism*.
2. Explain how you were at first amused by your discovery but that in reality, your idea has serious implications.
3. In the body of your essay, explore at least three major implications of your new word.
4. Indicate your own beliefs about the issue that you are illustrating.
5. Link your paragraphs with appropriate transitions.
6. Write an appropriate conclusion, a quick jab of a paragraph that closes on a witty statement.

Thinking, Arguing, and Writing Collaboratively

In small groups, talk about what this essay has to do with human rights, and expand on how Rauch's idea can actually improve human rights around the United States and the world. On the basis of your discussion, write notes for an outline of possible minor propositions supporting this idea.

Writing About the Text

Concentrating on the fact that the message behind all religions is peace, and contrasting this with Rauch's judgments about the problems religion has caused, write an essay that takes issue with Rauch and defends religion against his charges.

More Writing Ideas

1. In paragraph 8, Rauch writes that "to be in the grip of religious zeal is the natural state of human beings." Write a journal entry explaining why you think that is.
2. Write a paragraph explaining why the title of Rauch's essay is ironic.
3. Turn the notes from your Thinking, Arguing, and Writing Collaboratively activity into an essay.

Amos Oz
Two Stubborn Men, Many Dead

Israeli writer and novelist Amos Oz was born in 1939 in Jerusalem. He studied literature at the Hebrew University in Jerusalem and has taught at Oxford University and Ben Gurion University of the Negev. He has published 18 books in Hebrew, including the novels My Michael *(1968),* Touch the Water, Touch the Wind *(1973),* Black Box *(1987), and* To Know a Woman *(1989), and collections of essays and fiction. Many of his works have been translated extensively. He has also published many essays in international magazines and newspapers. During the Six Day War in 1967 and in the 1973 Yom Kippur War, Oz fought for the Israeli Army as a soldier in a tank unit. He is involved in the movement for peace in the Middle East and writes often about the topic, supporting the idea of a Palestinian state in the West Bank and Gaza. In this selection, published as an op-ed piece in* The New York Times *in 2002, Oz takes the leaders of both Israel and Palestine to task for delaying the peace process while people die.*

Prereading: Thinking About the Essay in Advance

What keeps leaders of countries from making peace? Why do war and conflict between two countries often go on for years?

Words to Watch

accordance (par. 2) such a way as to conform
demographic (par. 2) having to do with patterns of populations
persona (par. 4) public personality
sovereign (par. 5) independent and self-governing
credentials (par. 7) official papers that show a person's position

On Saturday night a 9-month old baby girl, an Israeli, was murdered in Netanya by a group of Palestinian gunmen. A few days earlier another baby girl, a Palestinian, was blown up by an Israeli bomb. Innocent civilians are dying, killed on both sides nearly every day. They are dying not because there is no way of resolving the crisis, but, on the contrary, they are dying precisely because a way exists and is known very well by all. 1

Every Israeli in the street knows what the solution is, just as every Palestinian knows it. Even Ariel Sharon and Yasir Arafat know the solution: peace between two states, established by the partition of the land roughly in accordance with demographic realities based on Israel's pre-1967 borders. 2

During this period of long sleepless nights, I sometimes wish I could believe in ghosts. I turn and toss in bed and imagine being able to send the ghosts of all the dead children, Israeli and Palestinian, to haunt Mr. Sharon and Mr. Arafat. I imagine that I am able to assemble these innocents around 3

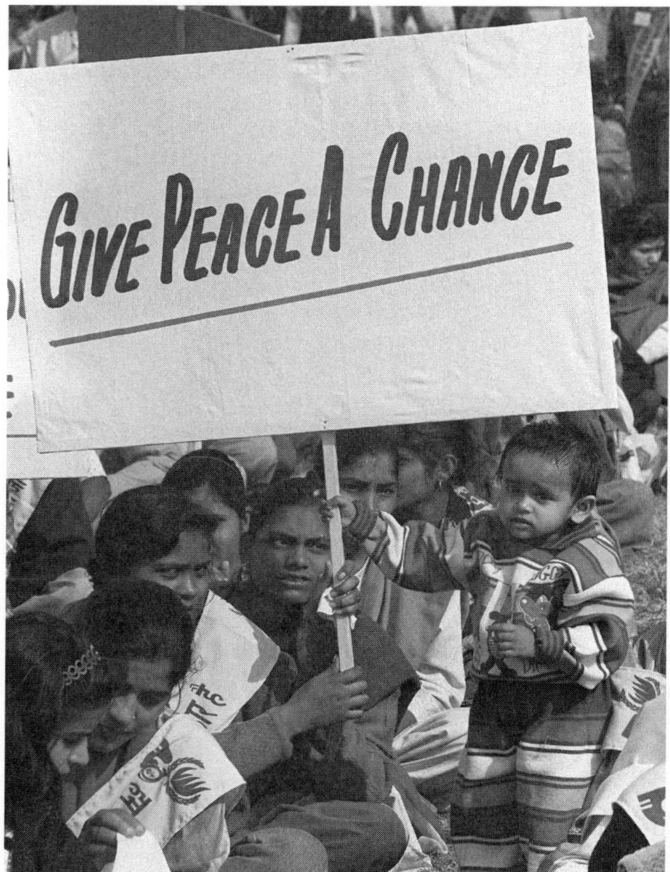

A child holds up a sign at the "Women on the Move" March Thursday, Dec. 10, 1998 in New Delhi, India during International Human Rights Day. (Associated Press/John McConnico)

the beds of the two leaders; two men, both more than 70 years old, each a prisoner of the other, each at the mercy of the other. Each ready to act every day exactly as the enemy foresees, to throw more fuel on the flames, to spill yet more blood.

4 Sometimes during these nights I see these two men fused into the persona of an ancient warrior, a wicked Nero, amusing himself by playing with fire, laughing savagely while stoking the flames. During the same troubled nights, I find myself hoping for the opposite, too—that Mr. Sharon and Mr. Arafat will not be haunted by the ghosts of the dead children, but will instead be sent away to sleep for weeks and months, to be awakened only after the signing of a peace treaty.

5 History will never forget their offenses, because the solution is here, visible, manifestly clear before us all. Every Israeli and every Palestinian

knows that this land will be divided into two sovereign nations and become like a semi-detached two-family house. Even those who loathe this future already know, deep in their hearts, that all this is inevitable.

I suspect that even the Siamese twins, Mr. Sharon and Mr. Arafat—I now 6
call them "Mr. Sharafat"—know this. But fear and stagnation stifle them both. They are living under the dominion of a bloodstained past. They are hostages to one another, so much so that the entire historical dynamic of the conflict of the Middle East has become captive to their fears, their immobility.

One day when the peace treaty is achieved, and the Palestinian ambas- 7
sador presents his credentials to the president of Israel in the Western section of Jerusalem, while the Israeli ambassador presents his to the Palestinian president in East Jerusalem, we shall all have to laugh at the stupidities of our past. Even as we laugh, we shall have to answer for the spilling of so much innocent blood. But the mothers and fathers of the dead will not be laughing.

Building Vocabulary

For each of the following words, write a definition that shows how Oz uses the word in his essay, and write an original sentence:

1. innocents (par. 3)
2. loathe (par. 5)
3. stagnation (par. 6)
4. dynamic (par. 6)
5. immobility (par. 6)

Thinking Critically About the Argument

Understanding the Writer's Argument

1. Why does Oz start his essay by referring to the two children who were killed?
2. What is the solution Oz refers to in the first paragraph?
3. Who are Sharon and Arafat?
4. Who was Nero, and why is Oz's image of Sharon and Arafat as Nero appropriate?
5. What does Oz mean when he says that Sharon and Arafat are "living under the dominion of a bloodstained past"?

Understanding the Writer's Techniques

1. What is Oz's claim? Where is it stated most clearly?
2. What warrants does Oz imply in this essay?
3. Outline the essay by paragraph, summarizing the purpose of each.
4. How does the portrait of Sharon and Arafat as being haunted help to focus the essay? More important, how does each succeeding image of the two men build on the last?

5. What is the argumentative effect of Oz's statement that "history will never forget their offences"? Explain.
6. Oz punctuates his essay with phrases and words intended to lend his argument emotional force, such as "laughing savagely" in paragraph 4. List three more examples of such words and phrases, and explain how they add to (or weaken) Oz's argument.
7. What do you think of Oz's conclusion? Is it effective? Why or why not?

Exploring the Writer's Argument

1. Does Oz do a good enough job of convincing you, the reader, that splitting the land into two separate countries is "inevitable"? Explain your answers.
2. What is Oz's aim in this essay? Is he trying to convince anyone in particular of anything? If so, who and what? Who is his audience? If he isn't trying to convince, then why does he bother to write? Explain.
3. Oz claims that Sharon and Arafat are afraid and that the peace process is stifled, as he says, by the fear of these two men. Does Oz explain what they are afraid of? Does he suggest anything? Explain.

Ideas for Writing Arguments

Prewriting

Write some notes on what effect the ongoing war in Israel is likely to have on future generations of Israeli and Palestinian children.

Writing a Guided Argument

In many ways, the Mideast peace process is like a bitter divorce. The two sides know they must split up, but they are fighting to the end to gain as much advantage as possible before the split is complete. Write an essay in which you write a letter to divorcing parents of two children, arguing that their fight is really hurting the children.

1. Begin your essay with an invocation of the children in the marriage and how the divorce is hurting them.
2. Explain that the divorce is inevitable, and that the parents must end it quickly to save their children.
3. In the next section, explain the effects the divorce is likely to have on the children. Feel free to invent details about the hypothetical children.
4. Organize the various effects on the children in a separate paragraph, taking your time to develop each one.
5. Use charged language to deepen the emotional appeal to the parents.
6. Establish a slightly cynical tone in your essay, while remaining objective and not placing the blame on either parent.
7. If you have them, use statistics to back up your points about the effects divorce has on children.
8. Close your essay with an unabashedly emotional plea to the parents to put aside their differences and think of their children.

Thinking, Arguing, and Writing Collaboratively

With the class divided into three groups, one group will represent the Israelis, one group will represent the Palestinians, and one group will represent the United States and European peacemakers. Each group should go to the library to do research on the positions each side holds. What do the Israelis want from the peace process? What do the Palestinians want? Then reconvene as a class and hold a mock peace conference in which you make proposals and concessions and draw up a plan that will lead to peace. What points are hardest to resolve?

Writing About the Text

Oz has a simple but powerful point to make in this essay. He must be rational to get his point across, but, as he writes, everyone knows what the solution is. So he depends on an emotional appeal to promote his position about peace. Write an essay in which you consider how Oz mixes the basic rational argument for peace with rhetorical emotional arguments. How do his emotional passages help or hurt his rational argument?

More Writing Ideas

1. In your journal, freewrite on the idea of innocents in war. Do not edit your work. Just write for at least 15 minutes. When you are finished, show your work to a classmate.
2. Arafat, of course, has been the leader of the Palestinians since there was a Palestinian movement, but he will eventually be replaced or die; Sharon is an elected official. Still, the peace process has been going on for a long time, without real peace, there has been no progress by these men since Oz wrote, militant groups seem to be in charge, and peace is elusive. Do some reading on the topic, and write an extended paragraph on how you think things could change if one or both of the men leave their positions of power.
3. In the past couple of years, a new plan has been drawn up for peace in Israel, a plan called the "roadmap" that mandates several deadlines for specific accomplishments along the way to peace. Do some research on the roadmap, and write an essay arguing that it is or is not the best hope for the region.

TERRY TEMPEST WILLIAMS

The Clan of the One-Breasted Women

Terry Tempest Williams grew up in Salt Lake City, Utah, and has worked to protect the natural landscape of that state. She was inducted into the Rachel Carson Honor Roll and has received the National Wildlife Federation's Conservation Award for Special Achievement. Williams is the author of several books, including Pieces of White Shell: A Journey to Navajoland *(1984),* Coyote's Canyon *(1989),*

Red: Patience and Passion in the Desert *(2001), and* Refuge: An Unnatural History of Family and Place *(1991), about the Great Salt Lake and the surrounding areas. She has published widely, in such magazines as* The New Yorker, The Nation, *and* The New England Review. *This selection, which is the epilogue from* Refuge, *deals with Williams's mother's cancer, believed to be caused by radioactive fallout from the nuclear tests in the Nevada desert in the 1950s and 1960s.*

Prereading: Thinking About the Essay in Advance

What is a citizen's responsibility to act when the government is not acting in its people's best interests?

Words to Watch

stoic (par. 6) showing patience and calmness in the face of problems
permeated (par. 13) spread throughout
deceit (par. 19) act of misleading
midwife (par. 32) literally, someone who helps to deliver babies
wax (par. 39) grow
wane (par. 39) shrink
mesa (par. 47) mostly flat elevated area that is usually found in the Southwest

1 I belong to a Clan of One-Breasted Women. My mother, my grandmothers, and six aunts have all had mastectomies. Seven are dead. The two who survive have just completed rounds of chemotherapy and radiation.

2 I've had my own problems: two biopsies for breast cancer and a small tumor between my ribs diagnosed as a "borderline malignancy."

3 This is my family history.

4 Most statistics tell us breast cancer is genetic, hereditary, with rising percentages attached to fatty diets, childlessness, or becoming pregnant after thirty. What they don't say is living in Utah may be the greatest hazard of all.

5 We are a Mormon family with roots in Utah since 1847. The "word of wisdom" in my family aligned us with good foods—no coffee, no tea, tobacco, or alcohol. For the most part, our women were finished having their babies by the time they were thirty. And only one faced breast cancer prior to 1960. Traditionally, as a group of people, Mormons have a low rate of cancer.

6 Is our family a cultural anomaly? The truth is, we didn't think about it. Those who did, usually the men, simply said, "bad genes." The women's attitude was stoic. Cancer was part of life. On February 16, 1971, the eve of my mother's surgery, I accidentally picked up the telephone and overheard her ask my grandmother what she could expect.

7 "Diane, it is one of the most spiritual experiences you will ever encounter."

8 I quietly put down the receiver.

Two days later, my father took my brothers and me to the hospital to visit her. She met us in the lobby in a wheelchair. No bandages were visible. I'll never forget her radiance, the way she held herself in a purple velvet robe, and how she gathered us around her. 9

"Children, I am fine. I want you to know I felt the arms of God around me." 10

We believed her. My father cried. Our mother, his wife, was thirty-eight years old. 11

A little over a year after Mother's death, Dad and I were having dinner together. He had just returned from St. George, where the Tempest Company was completing the gas lines that would service southern Utah. He spoke of his love for the country, the sandstoned landscape, bare-boned and beautiful. He had just finished hiking the Kolob trail in Zion National Park. We got caught up in reminiscing, recalling with fondness our walk up Angel's Landing on his fiftieth birthday and the years our family had vacationed there. 12

Over dessert, I shared a recurring dream of mine. I told my father that for years, as long as I could remember, I saw this flash of light in the night in the desert—that this image had so permeated my being that I could not venture south without seeing it again, on the horizon, illuminating buttes and mesas. 13

"You did see it," he said. 14

"Saw what?" 15

"The bomb. The cloud. We were driving home from Riverside, California. You were sitting on Diane's lap. She was pregnant. In fact, I remember the day, September 7, 1957. We had just gotten out of the Service. We were driving north, past Las Vegas. It was an hour or so before dawn, when this explosion went off. We not only heard it, but felt it. I thought the oil tanker in front of us had blown up. We pulled over and suddenly, rising from the desert floor, we saw it, clearly, this golden-stemmed cloud, the mushroom. The sky seemed to vibrate with an eerie pink glow. Within a few minutes, a light ash was raining on the car." 16

I stared at my father. 17

"I thought you knew that," he said. "It was a common occurrence in the fifties." 18

It was at this moment that I realized the deceit I had been living under. Children growing up in the American Southwest, drinking contaminated milk from contaminated cows, even from the contaminated breasts of their mothers, my mother—members, years later, of the Clan of One-Breasted Women. 19

It is a well-known story in the Desert West, "The Day We Bombed Utah," or more accurately, the years we bombed Utah: above ground atomic testing in Nevada took place from January 27, 1951, through July 11, 1962. Not only were the winds blowing north covering "low-use segments of the population" with fallout and leaving sheep dead in their tracks, but the climate was right. The United States of the 1950s was red, white, and blue. The Korean 20

War was raging. McCarthyism was rampant. Ike was it, and the cold war was hot. If you were against nuclear testing, you were for a communist regime.

21 Much has been written about this "American nuclear tragedy." Public health was secondary to national security. The Atomic Energy Commissioner, Thomas Murray, said, "Gentlemen, we must not let anything interfere with this series of tests, nothing."

22 Again and again, the American public was told by its government, in spite of burns, blisters, and nausea, "It has been found that the tests may be conducted with adequate assurance of safety under conditions prevailing at the bombing reservations." Assuaging public fears was simply a matter of public relations. "Your best action," an Atomic Energy Commission booklet read, "is not to be worried about fallout." A news release typical of the times stated, "We find no basis for concluding that harm to any individual has resulted from radioactive fallout."

23 On August 30, 1979, during Jimmy Carter's presidency, a suit was filed, *Irene Allen* v. *The United States of America.* Mrs. Allen's case was the first on an alphabetical list of twenty-four test cases, representative of nearly twelve hundred plaintiffs seeking compensation from the United States government for cancers caused by nuclear testing in Nevada.

24 Irene Allen lived in Hurricane, Utah. She was the mother of five children and had been widowed twice. Her first husband, with their two oldest boys, had watched the tests from the roof of the local high school. He died of leukemia in 1956. Her second husband died of pancreatic cancer in 1978.

25 In a town meeting conducted by Utah Senator Orrin Hatch, shortly before the suit was filed, Mrs. Allen said, "I am not blaming the government, I want you to know that, Senator Hatch. But I thought if my testimony could help in any way so this wouldn't happen again to any of the generations coming up after us . . . I am happy to be here this day to bear testimony of this."

26 God-fearing people. This is just one story in an anthology of thousands.

27 On May 10, 1984, Judge Bruce S. Jenkins handed down his opinion. Ten of the plaintiffs were awarded damages. It was the first time a federal court had determined that nuclear tests had been the cause of cancers. For the remaining fourteen test cases, the proof of causation was not sufficient. In spite of the split decision, it was considered a landmark ruling. It was not to remain so for long.

28 In April 1987, the Tenth Circuit Court of Appeals overturned Judge Jenkins's ruling on the ground that the United States was protected from suit by the legal doctrine of sovereign immunity, a centuries-old idea from England in the days of absolute monarchs.

29 In January 1988, the Supreme Court refused to review the Appeals Court decision. To our court system it does not matter whether the United States government was irresponsible, whether it lied to its citizens, or even that citizens died from the fallout of nuclear testing. What matters is that our government is immune: "The King can do no wrong."

In Mormon culture, authority is respected, obedience is revered, and in- 30
dependent thinking is not. I was taught as a young girl not to "make waves" or "rock the boat."

"Just let it go," Mother would say. "You know how you feel, that's what 31
counts."

For many years, I have done just that—listened, observed and quietly 32
formed my own opinions, in a culture that rarely asks questions because it has all the answers. But one by one, I have watched the women in my family die common, heroic deaths. We sat in waiting rooms hoping for good news, but always receiving the bad. I cared for them, bathed their scarred bodies, and kept their secrets. I watched beautiful women become bald as Cytoxan, Cisplatin, and Adriamycin were injected into their veins. I held their foreheads as they vomited green-black bile, and I shot them with morphine when the pain became inhuman. In the end, I witnessed their last peaceful breaths, becoming a midwife to the rebirth of their souls.

The price of obedience has become too high. 33

The fear and inability to question authority that ultimately killed rural 34
communities in Utah during atmospheric testing of atomic weapons is the same fear I saw in my mother's body. Sheep. Dead sheep. The evidence is buried.

I cannot prove that my mother, Diane Dixon Tempest, or my grand- 35
mothers, Lettie Romney Dixon and Kathryn Blackett Tempest, along with my aunts developed cancer from nuclear fallout in Utah. But I can't prove they didn't.

My father's memory was correct. The September blast we drove 36
through in 1957 was part of Operation Plumbbob, one of the most intensive series of bomb tests to be initiated. The flash of light in the night in the desert, which I had always thought was a dream, developed into a family nightmare. It took fourteen years, from 1957 to 1971, for cancer to manifest in my mother—the same time, Howard L. Andrews, an authority in radioactive fallout at the National Institutes of Health, says radiation cancer requires to become evident. The more I learn about what it means to be a "downwinder," the more questions I drown in.

What I do know, however, is that as a Mormon woman of the fifth gen- 37
eration of Latter-day Saints, I must question everything, even if it means losing my faith, even if it means becoming a member of a border tribe among my own people. Tolerating blind obedience in the name of patriotism or religion ultimately takes our lives.

When the Atomic Energy Commission described the country north of 38
the Nevada Test Site as "virtually uninhabited desert terrain," my family and the birds at Great Salt Lake were some of the "virtual uninhabitants."

One night, I dreamed women from all over the world circled a blazing 39
fire in the desert. They spoke of change, how they hold the moon in their bellies and wax and wane with its phases. They mocked the presumption of

even-tempered beings and made promises that they would never fear the witch inside themselves. The women danced wildly as sparks broke away from the flames and entered the night sky as stars.

40 And they sang a song given to them by Shoshone grandmothers:

Ah ne nah, nah	Consider the rabbits
nin nah nah—	How gently they walk on the earth—
ah ne nah, nah	Consider the rabbits
nin nah nah—	How gently they walk on the earth—
Nyaga mutzi	We remember them
oh ne nay—	We can walk gently also—
Nyaga mutzi	We remember them
oh ne nay—	We can walk gently also—

41 The women danced and drummed and sang for weeks, preparing themselves for what was to come. They would reclaim the desert for the sake of their children, for the sake of the land.

42 A few miles downwind from the fire circle, bombs were being tested. Rabbits felt the tremors. Their soft leather pads on paws and feet recognized the shaking sands, while the roots of mesquite and sage were smoldering. Rocks were hot from the inside out and dust devils hummed unnaturally. And each time there was another nuclear test, ravens watched the desert heave. Stretch marks appeared. The land was losing its muscle.

43 The women couldn't bear it any longer. They were mothers. They had suffered labor pains but always under the promise of birth. The red hot pains beneath the desert promised death only as each bomb became a stillborn. A contract had been made and broken between human beings and the land. A new contract was being drawn by the women, who understood the fate of the earth as their own.

44 Under the cover of darkness, ten women slipped under a barbed-wire fence and entered the contaminated country. They were trespassing. They walked toward the town of Mercury, in moonlight, taking their cues from coyote, kit fox, antelope squirrel, and quail. They moved quietly and deliberately through the maze of Joshua trees. When a hint of daylight appeared they rested, drinking tea and sharing their rations of food. The women closed their eyes. The time had come to protest with the heart that to deny one's genealogy with the earth was to commit treason against one's soul.

45 At dawn, the women draped themselves in mylar, wrapping long streamers of silver plastic around their arms to blow in the breeze. They wore clear masks, that became the faces of humanity. And when they arrived at the edge of Mercury, they carried all the butterflies of a summer day in their wombs. They paused to allow their courage to settle.

46 The town that forbids pregnant women and children to enter because of radiation risks was asleep. The women moved through the streets as winged messengers, twirling around each other in slow motion, peeking inside homes and watching the easy sleep of men and women. They were aston-

ished by such stillness and periodically would utter a shrill note or low cry just to verify life.

The residents finally awoke to these strange apparitions. Some simply stared. Others called authorities, and in time, the women were apprehended by wary soldiers dressed in desert fatigues. They were taken to a white, square building on the other edge of Mercury. When asked who they were and why they were there, the women replied, "We are mothers and we have come to reclaim the desert for our children." 47

The soldiers arrested them. As the ten women were blindfolded and handcuffed, they began singing: 48

You can't forbid us everything
You can't forbid us to think—
You can't forbid our tears to flow
And you can't stop the songs that we sing.

The women continued to sing louder and louder, until they heard the voices of their sisters moving across the mesa: 49

Ah ne nah, nah
nin nah nah—
Ah ne nah, nah
nin nah nah—
Nyaga mutzi
oh ne nay—
Nyaga mutzi
oh ne nay—

"Call for reinforcements," one soldier said. 50

"We have," interrupted one woman, "we have—and you have no idea of our numbers." 51

I crossed the line at the Nevada Test Site and was arrested with nine other Utahans for trespassing on military lands. They are still conducting nuclear tests in the desert. Ours was an act of civil disobedience. But as I walked toward the town of Mercury, it was more than a gesture of peace. It was a gesture on behalf of the Clan of One-Breasted Women. 52

As one officer cinched the handcuffs around my wrists, another frisked my body. She found a pen and a pad of paper tucked inside my left boot. 53

"And these?" she asked sternly. 54

"Weapons," I replied. 55

Our eyes met. I smiled. She pulled the leg of my trousers back over my boot. 56

"Step forward, please," she said as she took my arm. 57

We were booked under an afternoon sun and bused to Tonopah, Nevada. It was a two-hour ride. This was familiar country. The Joshua trees standing their ground had been named by my ancestors, who believed they looked like prophets pointing west to the Promised Land. These were 58 the same trees that bloomed each spring, flowers appearing like white flames in the Mojave. And I recalled a full moon in May, when Mother and I had walked among them, flushing out mourning doves and owls.

59 The bus stopped short of town. We were released.

60 The officials thought it was a cruel joke to leave us stranded in the desert with no way to get home. What they didn't realize was that we were home, soul-centered and strong, women who recognized the sweet smell of sage as fuel for our spirits.

Building Vocabulary

1. Williams uses several medical terms in this essay. Write out a definition for each. Try to figure out what each is from the context of the essay, and if you cannot identify it, use a reference book.
   - **a.** mastectomies (par. 1)
   - **b.** chemotherapy (par. 1)
   - **c.** hereditary (par. 4)
   - **d.** leukemia (par. 24)
   - **e.** bile (par. 32)
   - **f.** stillborn (par. 43)
2. This essay tells the story of government actions and their consequences. Explain at least five of the following terms from government and American history:
   - **a.** McCarthyism (par. 20)
   - **b.** cold war (par. 20)
   - **c.** national security (par. 21)
   - **d.** Atomic Energy Commission (par. 22)
   - **e.** sovereign immunity (par. 28)
   - **f.** Shoshone (par. 40)
   - **g.** desert fatigues (par. 47)
   - **h.** Promised Land (par. 58)

Thinking Critically About the Argument

Understanding the Writer's Argument

1. What does Williams mean by the "Clan of One-Breasted Women"?
2. Why is Williams sure that the people in her family didn't get sick from an unhealthy lifestyle?
3. What is Williams's sudden realization when she has dinner with her father as she describes in paragraphs 12 to 18?
4. What is Williams's double meaning in paragraph 20 when she uses the word "climate"?
5. Why did the U.S. Court of Appeals for the Tenth Circuit overturn Judge Jenkins's decision? How did the people involved respond?

6. Where in the essay does Williams indicate that she had decided not to sit quietly anymore about the government's atomic testing?
7. How does Williams's family's Mormon faith prevent them from fighting for their rights?
8. Why do the women in Williams's dream speak in a Native American language?
9. How does Williams connect her dream with her actual protest experience?
10. What is Williams's double meaning when she replies "Weapons" when asked by the police officer what her pen and pad are?

Understanding the Writer's Techniques

1. What is Williams's major proposition? Where is it located?
2. This essay is structured into three main sections. What happens in each one? How does the structure help Williams's argument?
3. What is the effect of Williams's withholding a clear statement that her mother died soon after surgery?
4. Certainly Williams has much to be cynical about, but do you think this shows up in her tone? If not, why not? If so, offer at least three examples where you think Williams is being cynical.
5. How does Williams connect rhetorically the fact that the Tenth Circuit overturned the Allen case with her family members dying of cancer?
6. Paraphrase Williams's argument in paragraph 34. What is the argumentative effect of including her mother's and grandmothers' names in paragraph 35?
7. Analyze Williams's dream. How is it persuasive here? What themes does she illustrate that previously she had only talked about in the abstract?
8. Do you think the conclusion of this essay is effective? Why or why not? What is your view of the title?

Exploring the Writer's Argument

1. What does Williams mean by the sentences in paragraph 43: "A contract had been made and broken between human beings and the land. A new contract was being drawn by the women who understood the fate of the earth as their own"?
2. Find information online or in the library about depleted uranium, which is a radioactive material used in bombs and ammunition by the U.S. military. What does depleted uranium have to do with the plight of the "downwinders" like Williams's family?
3. This essay's title focuses on women, and Williams mentions only women in her family who got sick. She describes women as being protectors of the land. But what about men, who got sick as well and protested against the government's atmospheric tests? Is she able to get men on her side? If so, how? If not, why not?

Ideas for Writing Arguments

Prewriting

Prepare a list of what you think are the most pressing issues in human rights. What can be done about each?

Writing a Guided Argument

Do some research on how people fight for human rights. Write an essay about human rights in which you argue for one country as the worst offender against human rights. Visit the Web site or read the annual report of a human rights group such as Human Rights Watch, and investigate what kinds of problems it focuses on. Which countries are the worst offenders? Is the United States an offender? How does the organization you looked at fight for human rights? Do you agree?

1. Open your essay with an illustration of an abuse of human rights drawn from your research.
2. Write a short summary of the extent of your research.
3. Offer your major proposition, that you have concluded that a particular country is the world's worst offender against human rights.
4. Establish a serious tone in the beginning that carries moral weight.
5. In separate paragraphs, write the minor propositions that will build your case against the country you are focusing on.
6. In the next section, explain what the hope is for ending the human rights abuses.
7. Conclude your essay with a section that examines in brief the United States's current problems with human rights? Are there any serious issues?
8. Finish with an emotional plea for human rights.

Thinking, Arguing, and Writing Collaboratively

In groups of four or five, explore Williams's use of imagery in this essay. In your group, make a list of at least five powerful images that she uses to help her argument, along with an explanation of why each is powerful. Choose the best two, and present them with your group to the class. As a class, discuss how this kind of imagery can advance an argument based on emotion and ethics.

Writing About the Text

Williams is writing about a very emotional topic, so she must not let her reader become too comfortable. She does rely on emotional situations, and she does have grotesque images, but she also uses her skills as a writer to do the job a bit more subtly. For example, in paragraph 1, her sentence, "Seven are dead" hits the reader hard, as does her statement that "living in Utah may be the greatest hazard of all" in paragraph 4. Write an essay about how Williams uses surprises and double meanings in her prose to keep her readers unsettled.

More Writing Ideas

1. In your journal act as devil's advocate and argue that the atmospheric tests might have harmed people in the desert, but they saved many more lives by helping the United States win the Cold War.
2. Read the Universal Declaration of Human Rights, which was adopted by the United Nations in 1948. Write a paragraph exploring the implications of having a document like that. What can it possibly do to help matters?
3. In part because of the efforts of Senator Hatch (par. 25), in 1990, the U.S. Congress passed and George H. W. Bush signed the Radiation Exposure Compensation Act. This law has led to monetary awards of more than $300 million to the people who lived downwind from the tests. Any "downwinder" who contracts a serious disease gets $50,000 from the government. The government also has apologized officially to the participants. Write an essay in which you argue that this is fair or that the government could have done (or can do) more.

33 Terrorism: How Should We Meet the Challenge?

The planes crash into the World Trade Center and the Pentagon on September 11, 2001, shocking what many saw as a complacent nation. All of a sudden, Americans are vulnerable to sneak attack. The country went into mourning. For whom? For what? For the dead, yes, the more than 2,700 murdered. It seemed that most of us had some direct or indirect connection to someone who died that day. But Americans have also mourned their innocence, their lost way of life. The world since 9/11 has grown darkly complex. Two wars later, we are trying to deal with many issues raised by the attacks: What is the nature of patriotism? How can we balance our open society and our civil liberties with national security? Is it possible to defend ourselves against terrorism at all? And if not, then how can we prepare for the next attacks? How do we heal? The questions go on and on, and there seem to be few answers.

There are viewpoints, though. Columnist Thomas L. Friedman in "Globalization, Alive and Well" argues that we have no choice but to go forward with the international economy, as it is inevitable—something he thinks is obvious since 9/11. Reshma Memon Yaqub, a Muslim-American writer expresses her fear of being blamed for terrorism in "You People Did This." She counsels education to counter the ignorance that leads to violence. In "Words Fail, Memory Blurs, Life Wins," novelist Joyce Carol Oates offers a humanist-reading of our response to terrorism. We'll all be okay, she says, if we trust life. Finally, Jeffrey Rosen in "Bad Luck," cautions us against exaggerating the terrorist threat. Sometimes argumentative essays can make hopeful claims!

THOMAS L. FRIEDMAN
Globalization, Alive and Well

Thomas L. Friedman has written for The New York Times *since 1981. He has reported for the paper from Beirut in Lebanon, Jerusalem in Israel, New York, and Washington, D.C. Since 1995 he has served as the paper's foreign-affairs columnist. In all he has won three Pulitzer Prizes. He is the author of* From Beirut to Jerusalem *(1989), which won the National Book Award for nonfiction, and* The Lexus and the Olive Tree: Understanding Globalization *(2000). Friedman was born in*

Minneapolis in 1953 and went to Brandeis University and Oxford University. In January 1989, Friedman took up a new assignment in Washington as the Times' *chief diplomatic correspondent. His sobering and intelligent columns on all topics touching American foreign policy and events around the world are read widely and are influential. In this column, published just after a year after the September 11 attacks, Friedman scoffs at those who said that 9/11 would end the process of globalization.*

Prereading: Thinking About the Essay in Advance

What is globalization? Do you see its effects in your life? What does globalization have to do with terrorism?

Words to Watch

integration (par. 1) act of combining
pampered (par. 3) comfortable financially
abject (par. 3) hopeless, complete
subsidies (par. 3) money given from a government to a company to help it function
ideology (par. 4) system of beliefs

If one were having a contest for the most wrongheaded prediction about the world after 9/11, the winner would be the declaration by the noted London School of Economics professor John Gray that 9/11 heralded the end of the era of globalization. Not only will Sept. 11 not be remembered for ending the process of global financial, trade and technological integration, but it may well be remembered for bringing some sobriety to the antiglobalization movement. 1

If one thing stands out from 9/11, it's the fact that the terrorists originated from the least globalized, least open, least integrated corners of the world: namely, Saudi Arabia, Yemen, Afghanistan and northwest Pakistan. Countries that don't trade in goods and services also tend not to trade in ideas, pluralism or tolerance. 2

But maybe the most important reason why globalization is alive and well post-9/11 is that while pampered college students and academics in the West continue to debate about whether countries should globalize, the two biggest countries in the world, India and China—who represent one-third of humanity—have long moved beyond that question. They have decided that opening their economies to trade in goods and services is the best way to lift their people out of abject poverty and are now focused simply on how to globalize in the most stable manner. Some prefer to go faster, and some prefer to phase out currency controls and subsidies gradually, but the debate about the direction they need to go is over. 3

"Globalization fatigue is still very much in evidence in Europe and America, while in places like China and India, you find a great desire for participation in the economic expansion processes," said Jairam Ramesh, the Indian 4

Congress Party's top economic adviser. ". . . Even those who are suspicious now want to find a way to participate, but in a way that manages the risks and the pace. So we're finding ways to 'globalize,' to do it our own way. It may mean a little slower growth to manage the social stability, but so be it. . . . I just spent a week in Germany and had to listen to all these people there telling me how globalization is destroying India and adding to poverty, and I just said to them, 'Look, if you want to argue about ideology, we can do that, but on the level of facts, you're just wrong.'"

5 That truth is most striking in Bangalore, India's Silicon Valley, where hundreds of thousands of young Indians, most from lower-middle-class families, suddenly have social mobility, motor scooters and apartments after going to technical colleges and joining the Indian software and engineering firms providing back-room support and research for the world's biggest firms—thanks to globalization. Bangalore officials say each tech job produces 6.5 support jobs, in construction and services.

6 "Information technology has made millionaires out of ordinary people [in India] because of their brainpower alone—not caste, not land, not heredity," said Sanjay Baru, editor of India's Financial Express. "India is just beginning to realize that this process of globalization is one where we have an inherent advantage."

7 Taking advantage of globalization to develop the Indian I.T. industry has been "a huge win in terms of foreign exchange [and in] self-confidence," added Nandan Nilekani, chief executive of Infosys, the Indian software giant. "So many Indians come and say to me that 'when I walk through immigration at J.F.K. or Heathrow, the immigration guys look at me with respect now.' The image of India changed from a third-world country of snake charmers and rope tricks to the software brainy guys."

8 Do a majority of Indians still live in poor villages? Of course. Do we still need to make globalization more fair by compelling the rich Western countries to open their markets more to those things that the poor countries are best able to sell: food and textiles? You bet.

9 But the point is this: The debate about globalization before 9/11 got really stupid. Two simple truths got lost: One, globalization has its upsides and downsides, but countries that come at it with the right institutions and governance can get the best out of it and cushion the worst. Two, countries that are globalizing sensibly but steadily are also the ones that are becoming politically more open, with more opportunities for their people, and with a young generation more interested in joining the world system than blowing it up.

Building Vocabulary

Friedman uses some common expressions in his essay to make his prose feel familiar. Use each of the following terms in a sentence of your own based on how they are used in the essay:

1. alive and well (par. 3)
2. pampered (par. 3)

3. abject poverty (par. 3)
4. phase out (par. 3)
5. in evidence (par. 4)
6. social mobility (par. 5)
7. back-room support (par. 5)
8. third-world country (par. 7)
9. simple truths (par. 9)

Thinking Critically About the Argument

Understanding the Writer's Argument

1. What is globalization in your own words?
2. Who is John Gray? What was his prediction after 9/11, and why is he wrong, according to Friedman?
3. Where were the 9/11 terrorists from? Why is that significant to Friedman?
4. What does Friedman mean when he says that China and India have moved past the question of whether globalization is alive and well?
5. What does Jairam Ramesh mean by the word "glocalize" (par. 4), and why is this desirable?
6. In Friedman's view, what effect is globalization having on India?
7. What effect does globalization have on how Indians are viewed around the world, according to Friedman? Explain.
8. What two truths about globalization were forgotten before 9/11, according to Friedman?

Understanding the Writer's Techniques

1. What is Friedman's major proposition?
2. How does Friedman structure his essay? Make an outline that reflects the flow of his argument.
3. What kinds of evidence does Friedman offer to back up his position?
4. Paraphrase Friedman's argument in paragraph 3. Is it effective?
5. What is the effect of the quotes Friedman offers? Are they persuasive? Why or why not?
6. Which quote is the most effective? Which is the least effective? Why?
7. What is Friedman's tone in this essay? How do you know?
8. How do paragraphs 8 and 9 work together to make up a complete conclusion? Explain.

Exploring the Writer's Argument

1. Friedman depends in this essay on India as a test country for his claim. Is this convincing enough? Why doesn't he include examples from other countries? Explain your answers.
2. What aspects (if any) of Friedman's argument cause you to have confidence in his conclusions? What aspects of his argument cause you to distrust him (if any)?

3. Friedman does not include in his argument the idea that there are many people in developing countries who do not want globalization because they resent the influence of more developed countries, like the United States. Why, do you think, does Friedman not discuss this point?

Ideas for Writing Arguments

Prewriting

What causes young men and women to resort to terrorism as a means of making their point?

Writing a Guided Argument

Write an essay in which you argue that the root causes of terrorism are mainly economic. Refer to Friedman's argument at least once in your essay.

1. Open your essay with a discussion of a hypothetical person who might turn to terrorism because of his or her economic situation.
2. Offer your claim in a clear statement.
3. Back up your claim with at least strong grounds for why economic problems might cause terrorism.
4. Use examples to demonstrate the grounds for your claim.
5. Link your paragraphs with strong transitions to improve the coherence of the essay.
6. End by restating your claim in other words.

Thinking, Arguing, and Writing Collaboratively

In groups of four or five, discuss how globalization has already deeply affected our lives and has for many years. List the ways in which this has happened, and choose the three most important ones to present to the class. As a class, discuss the future of globalization and how it will affect the United States.

Writing About the Text

Write an essay in which you explore the positive aspects of globalization as Friedman sees it. What are the "upsides," as he puts it? What are the main factors that will promote these upsides? How can the common person promote upsides? How does religion play a role?

More Writing Ideas

1. In your journal, freewrite about social mobility. Do not edit your writing. Write nonstop for at least 15 minutes. When you are done, exchange journal entries with another student in your class. How do your responses compare? Contrast?
2. Write a two- or three-paragraph letter in which you, as a "pampered college student," take issue with Friedman's statement that we shouldn't "debate about whether countries should globalize."

3. Antiglobalization groups have protested around the world, most famously in Seattle in 1999, when protesters smashed the facades of Starbucks stores. Read about the antiglobalization forces, and write an essay in which you argue that they are either justified in their protests or wrong and being unrealistic.

RESHMA MEMON YAQUB
You People Did This

Reshma Memon Yaqub is a writer living in Maryland who, after the attacks on America on September 11, found herself faced with a familiar prejudice. As a Muslim-American, she knew immediately that she would have to deal with people's misconceptions. Yaqub, a graduate of the University of Pennsylvania, is a writer for Worth *magazine and has written for the* St. Louis Post-Dispatch, *the* Washington Post, Parents, Men's Health, *and* Reader's Digest, *among other publications. She currently writes a monthly consumer-help column for* Good Housekeeping. *This selection, which contain her thoughts soon after the attacks, was published in* Rolling Stone.

Prereading: Thinking About the Essay in Advance

How much do you know about Islam? What were the different reactions to Muslims in the United States after the events of 9/11?

Words to Watch

miscarry (par. 4) lose a fetus, which is expelled dead
travesty (par. 5) a grotesque, twisted version of something
epithets (par. 6) abusive, insulting words
assailant (par. 6) attacker
decry (par. 8) express strong disapproval

As I ran through my neighborhood on the morning of September 11th, in search of my son, who had gone to the park with his baby sitter, I wasn't just afraid of another hijacked plane crashing into us. I was also afraid that someone else would get to my son first, someone wanting revenge against anyone who looks like they're from "that part of the world." Even if he is just one and a half years old. 1

I know I wasn't just afraid that the building where my husband works, a D.C. landmark, might fall on him. I was also afraid that another American might stop him on the street and harass him, or hurt him, demanding to know why "you people" did this. As soon as we heard the news, 7 million American Muslims wondered in terror, "Will America blame me?" 2

3 When our country is terrorized, American Muslims are victimized twice. First, as Americans, by the madmen who strike at our nation, at our physical, mental and emotional core. Then we're victimized again, as Muslims, by those Americans who believe that all Muslims are somehow accountable for the acts of some madmen, that our faith—that our God, the same peace-loving God worshiped by Jews and Christians—sanctions it.

4 It didn't matter when the federal building in Oklahoma City blew up that a Muslim didn't do it. That a Christian man was responsible for the devastation in Oklahoma City certainly didn't matter to the thugs who terrorized a Muslim woman there, nearly seven months pregnant, by attacking her home, breaking her windows, screaming religious slurs. It didn't matter to them that Sahar Al-Muwsawi, 26, would, as a result, miscarry her baby. That she would bury him in the cold ground, alongside other victims of the Oklahoma City bombing, after naming him Salaam, the Arabic word for "peace."

5 But that travesty and hundreds like it certainly were on my mind that Tuesday morning. And they were reinforced every time a friend called to check on my family and to sadly remind me, "It's over for us. Muslims are done for."

6 Even as we buckled under the same grief that every American was feeling that day, American Muslims had to endure the additional burden of worrying for our own safety, in our own hometowns, far from hijackers and skyscrapers. Shots would be fired into the Islamic Center of Irving, Texas; an Islamic bookstore in Virginia would have bricks thrown through its windows; a bag of pig's blood would be left on the doorstep of an Islamic community center in San Francisco; a mosque near Chicago would be marched on by 300 people shouting racist epithets. A Muslim of Pakistani origin would be gunned down in Dallas; a Sikh man would be shot and killed in Mesa, Arizona (possibly by the same assailant who would go on to spray bullets into the home of a local Afghani family).

7 And those were just the cases that were reported. I know I didn't report it when a ten-year-old neighborhood boy walked by and muttered, "Terrorist," as I got into my car. My neurosurgeon friend didn't report that a nurse at the prominent Washington hospital where they both work had announced in front of him that all Muslims and Arabs should be rounded up and put into camps, as Japanese were in World War II. My family didn't report that we're sick with worry about my mother-in-law, another sister-in-law and my niece, who are visiting Pakistan, with their return uncertain.

8 In the days to come, in the midst of the darkness, there is some light. A neighbor stops by to tell me that he doesn't think Muslims are responsible for the acts of madmen. Strangers in Starbucks are unusually friendly to me and my son, reaching out as if to say, "We know it's not your fault." The head of a church told me his congregation wants to come and put its arms around us, and to help in any way possible—by cleaning graffiti off a mosque, by hosting our Friday prayers, whatever we needed. President Bush warns Americans not to scapegoat Muslims and Arabs. He even visits a mosque, in a show of solidarity. Congress swiftly passes a resolution to up-

hold the civil rights of Muslims and Arabs, urging Americans to remain united. Jewish and Christian leaders publicly decry the violence against Muslims. At a mosque in Seattle, Muslim worshippers are greeted by members of other faiths bringing them flowers.

There's something America needs to understand about Islam. Like Judaism, like Christianity, Islam doesn't condone terrorism. It doesn't allow it. It doesn't accept it. Yet, somehow, the labels *jihad, holy war* and *suicide martyrs* are still thrown around. In fact, jihad doesn't even mean holy war. It's an Arabic word that means "struggle"—struggle to please God. And suicide itself is a forbidden act in Islam. How could anyone believe that Muslims consider it martyrdom when practiced in combination with killing thousands of innocents? Anyone who claims to commit a politically motivated violent act in the name of Islam has committed a hate crime against the world's 1.2 billion Muslims. 9

It is not jihad to hijack a plane and fly it into a building. But in fact there was jihad done that Tuesday. It was jihad when firemen ran into imploding buildings to rescue people they didn't know. It was jihad when Americans lined up and waited to donate the blood of their own bodies. It was jihad when strangers held and comforted one another in the streets. It was jihad when rescue workers struggled to put America back together, piece by piece. 10

Yes, there were martyrs made that Tuesday. But there were no terrorists among them. There were only Americans, of every race and religion, who, that Tuesday, took death for us. 11

Building Vocabulary

Define and use each of the following words in a sentence of your own, making sure that you use the word as Yaqub uses it in her essay.

1. core (par. 3)
2. sanctions (par. 3)
3. slurs (par. 4)
4. buckled (par. 6)
5. scapegoat (par. 8)
6. condone (par. 9)

Thinking Critically About the Argument

Understanding the Writer's Argument

1. In the beginning of her essay, why does Yaqub run to find her son on the morning of September 11, 2001? Why is she afraid for her husband?
2. Why and how do people harass Muslims in America when terrorism strikes America? What examples does Yaqub give of Muslims being harassed? Why aren't all incidents of harassment reported?
3. How does Yaqub show that not all people she comes into contact with harass her?

4. What do most people think *jihad* is? What is it, in fact?
5. What does Yaqub mean when she says that anybody who commits an act of terrorism "in the name of Islam has committed a hate crime" against all Muslims?

Understanding the Writer's Techniques

1. What is Yaqub's major proposition? Where in the essay does she state it?
2. Why does Yaqub mention that there are 7 million Muslims in the United States? She also states that there are 1.2 billion in the world. Is she setting up a deliberate comparison? Explain your answer.
3. Which examples that Yaqub gives of Muslims being harassed are the most effective? How does her title project the sense of harassment?
4. What is the emotional impact of Yaqub quoting her friend as saying, "It's over for us. Muslims are done for"?
5. How does Yaqub use transitions to maintain coherence in her essay? Are there any places you think need stronger transitions? Where?
6. In paragraph 10, Yaqub uses the word *jihad* over and over. What is the argumentative effect of this technique?
7. How effective is Yaqub's conclusion? Why?

Exploring the Writer's Argument

1. In what way does Yaqub's description convince you of her fears? Do you think they are warranted based on her essay? In what ways does she build your trust? Or do you distrust her? If so, why?
2. In paragraph 8, Yaqub mentions actions by the president and Congress to make sure that Americans show tolerance of Islam and Muslims. In what ways are their actions useful? Do you think that after 9/11, President George W. Bush's visits helped matters? Why or why not?
3. How do Yaqub's examples of *jihad* in paragraph 10 support her definition of the word?

Ideas for Writing Arguments

Prewriting

During and after the 9/11 attacks, men and women across the country took the opportunity to perform both great and completely rotten acts. Draw a line down the middle of the page and make two lists headed NOBLE and IGNOBLE. Fill in each column as best you can.

Writing a Guided Argument

Write an essay in which you argue that although times of adversity and crisis lead to displays of both the best humankind has to offer and the worst, one of these always dominates. Feel free to be as optimistic or pessimistic as you'd like.

1. Open your essay with a summary of the events of 9/11.
2. After this, give one example of a noble act and one example of an ignoble act.

3. Write your claim that one tendency is the dominant one.
4. Build your case by giving grounds for your claim.
5. Analyze what it is about human nature that led you to make your claim.
6. Offer examples to back up your case.
7. Link paragraphs with appropriate transitions.
8. In your conclusion, offer a suggestion for how to tilt people's behavior in the direction of nobility.

Thinking, Arguing, and Writing Collaboratively

Exchange draft versions of your Guided Argument assignment with a classmate. Review your partner's essay for its success in following the guidelines and how well it succeeds on its own. What are the paper's greatest strengths? Weaknesses? Write one or two paragraphs that will help your partner take the paper to the next draft.

Writing About the Text

In "Let It Be," Jonathan Rauch argues for a kind of attitude toward religion called apatheism. Read Rauch's essay and argue that he's right—that the kind of problems Yaqub faces here would be a thing of the past if apatheism were more widely practiced.

More Writing Ideas

1. Write in your journal about why you think the Department of Homeland Security's color coding terror alert system does more harm than good or more good than harm. Pick your side.
2. In a paragraph or two, explore the notion of how America's reaction to terrorism is bound to change if it becomes more common.
3. Read some accounts of how Germans and Japanese people in the United States were treated during World War II, how the Japanese were put into internment camps in California, and how, during the Vietnam and Korean wars, Asian Americans were treated. Compare any of those episodes in American history with the most recent episode of the treatment of Muslim Americans after 9/11.

JOYCE CAROL OATES
Words Fail, Memory Blurs, Life Wins

Novelist, short story writer, essayist, poet, and teacher Joyce Carol Oates was born in 1938 in Lockport in upstate New York. She has been writing novels since the age of 14, and she hasn't stopped since. She went to Syracuse University where she won the coveted Mademoiselle *fiction contest. She graduated at the top of her class at Syracuse and went to graduate school at the University of Wisconsin. During her career, she has published more than 75 books. To comments that she is a "workaholic," she has responded, "I am not conscious of working especially hard, or of 'working' at all. Writing and teaching have always been, for me, so richly rewarding that I don't think of them as work in the usual sense of the word." Her novels, which are noted for their unflinching eye on the noble as well as the profane aspects of human life, include* Them *(1969),* Bellefleur *(1980),* Solstice *(1984),* Black Water *(1992), and* Blonde *(2000), among many others. In this essay, from* The New York Times *on New Year's Eve 2001, Oates argues that terrorism cannot destroy basic human hope.*

Prereading: Thinking About the Essay in Advance

After September 11, 2001, people in the United States were nervous and on edge. How long did people's nerves remain raw? Are they still? How long does the grieving process take in the wake of such an event?

Words to Watch

demonized (par. 1) caused someone or something to seem evil
palliative (par. 2) soothing and alleviating pain
invests (par. 4) to give someone or something a characteristic
visceral (par. 6) directly from the emotions rather than from rational thought
aphorisms (par. 6) short statements representing a larger truth
crevices (par. 9) small openings in something
amnesia (par. 9) state of forgetfulness

1 Since Sept. 11, what might be called the secondary wave of the terrorist attacks has been nearly as traumatic to some of us as the attacks themselves: our discovery that we have been demonized and that because we are Americans, we are hated; because we are Americans, we are seen to be deserving of death. "Words fail us" was the predominant cliché in the days immediately after the attacks, but for some, even intellectuals in other secular democracies, words have been too easily and cheaply produced; they matter-of-factly declared, "The United States had it coming."

2 The closest I've knowingly come to a "senseless" violent death was during an airline flight from New Orleans to Newark when turbulence so rocked, shook, rattled the plane that it seemed the plane could not endure and would break into pieces. White-faced attendants were strapped into their seats, and the rest of us, wordless, very still except for the careenings and lurchings of the plane, sat with eyes fixed forward and hands clenched into fists. In the earlier, less alarming stages of the turbulence, the passenger beside me had remarked that turbulence "per se" rarely caused plane crashes, that crashes were caused by "mechanical failure" or bad takeoffs or landings. But now he was silent, for we'd passed beyond even the palliative value of words.

3 If I survive this, I vowed, I will never fly again. No doubt every passenger on the flight was making a similar vow. *If—survive!—never again.*

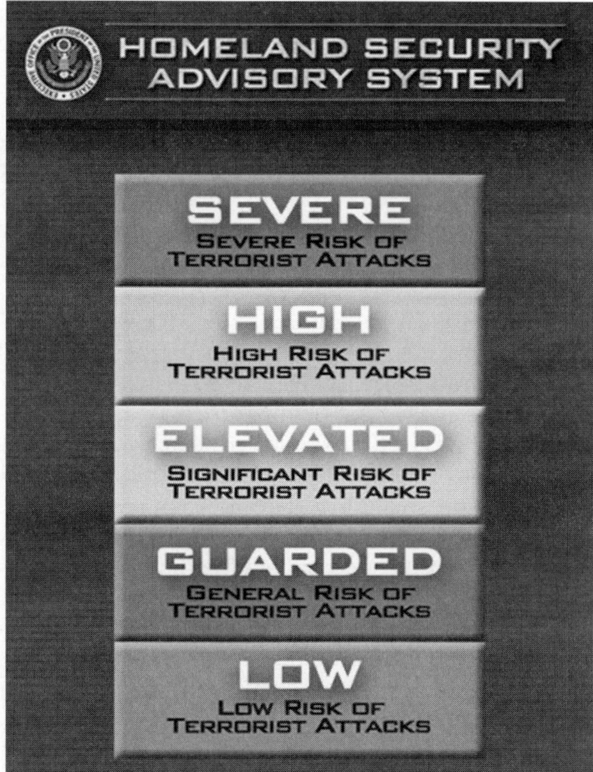

The color-coded terrorism warning system is shown Tuesday, March 12, 2002, in Washington. The five-level system is a response to public complaints that broad terror alerts issued by the government since the Sept. 11, 2001 attacks raised alarm without providing useful guidance. (AP Photo/Joe Marquette)

The utterly physical—visceral—adrenaline-charged—sensation that you may be about to die is so powerful that it invests the present tense with an extraordinary lucidity and significance. To imagine the next stage as it has been experienced by countless fellow human beings—when the plane actually disintegrates, or begins to fall, or, in the case of hijacked planes, nears the targets chosen by "martyrs" in the holy war—is to re-experience symptoms of anxiety that culminate in the mind simply blanking out: as words fail us in extremis, so do coherent sensations fail us. 4

We flew through the turbulence. If there was a narrative developing here it was not to be a narrative of tragedy or even melodrama but one that lends itself to a familiar American subgenre, the anecdote. 5

As soon as such an experience—whether anecdotal or tragic—is over, we begin the inevitable process of "healing": that is, forgetting. We extract from the helpless visceral sensation some measure of intellectual summary 6 or control. We lie to ourselves: we revise experience to make it lighthearted and amusing to others. For in what other way is terror to be tamed, except recycled as anecdotes or aphorisms, a sugary coating to hide the bitter pellet of truth within?

7 How many airplane flights I've taken since that day I vowed I would never fly again, I can't begin to estimate. Dozens, certainly. Perhaps more than 100. The promise I'd made to myself in extremis was quickly broken, though it was a reasonable promise and perhaps my terror-stricken mind was functioning more practically than my ordinary mind, uncharged by adrenaline.

8 Yet the fact is: Words fail us. There is the overwhelming wish to "sum up"—"summarize"—"put into perspective." As if typed-out words possessed such magic and could not, instead, lead to such glib summations as "The United States had it coming."

9 Admittedly, having survived that rocky airplane flight, I could not long retain its significance in my mind, still less in my emotions. Amnesia seeps into the crevices of our brains, and amnesia heals. The present tense is a needle's eye through which we thread ourselves—or are threaded—and what's past is irremediably past, to be recollected only in fragments. So, too, the collective American experience of the trauma of Sept. 11 has begun already to fade and will continue to fade, like previous collective traumas: the shock of Pearl Harbor, the shock of President John F. Kennedy's assassination.

10 The great narrative of our planet isn't human history but the history of evolving life. Environments alter, and only those species and individuals that alter with them can survive.

11 "Hope springs eternal in the human breast" may be a cliché, but it is also a profound insight. Perhaps unfairly, the future doesn't belong to those who only mourn, but to those who celebrate.

12 The future is ever-young, ever forgetting the gravest truths of the past.

13 Ideally we should retain the intellectual knowledge that such traumas as the terrorist attacks have given us, while assimilating and moving beyond the rawness of the emotional experience. In this season of unease, as ruins continue to smolder, we celebrate the fact of our existence, which pity, terror and visceral horror have made more precious, at least in our American eyes.

Building Vocabulary

1. Write a paragraph describing a car or train trip in which you use at least five words that help bring the events to life.
2. For each of the following words, write a definition and a sentence of your own:
   - **a.** turbulence (par. 2)
   - **b.** lucidity (par. 4)
   - **c.** melodrama (par. 5)
   - **d.** cliché (par. 11)
   - **e.** gravest (par. 13)

Thinking Critically About the Argument

Understanding the Writer's Argument

1. What does Oates mean by the "secondary wave of the terrorist attacks"? (par. 1)
2. Who, after the 9/11 attacks, said that America "had it coming"? Why doesn't Oates mention any of them?
3. How does Oates describe the feeling of impending death? What happens, in her opinion?
4. What does "in extremis" mean? How does Oates use it here?
5. According to Oates, what is the natural way people deal with harrowing situations?
6. What does Oates mean when she writes in paragraph 9 that "The present tense is a needle's eye through which we thread ourselves"? What does this have to do with 9/11?
7. How does hope come out of forgetfulness, according to Oates?

Understanding the Writer's Techniques

1. What is Oates's major proposition? Where does she state it most clearly?
2. Is her major proposition in an effective place? Why or why not?
3. What is Oates's rhetorical intent in this essay? Is she trying to convince her reader of something? If so, of what? If not, what is she trying to do?
4. How well does Oates's title reflect the argument in her essay?
5. How does Oates connect paragraph 1 with paragraph 2? There doesn't seem to be any transition. How does this affect her argument?
6. How does Oates's repetition of the phrase "words fail us" help to hold the essay together?
7. Analyze Oates's concluding paragraph. Is it effective? Why or why not?

Exploring the Writer's Argument

1. Do you agree with Oates that one can call the idea that Americans are to blame for terrorism "the secondary wave of the terrorist attacks"? Explain.
2. Oates says that the "future is ever-young," and that we forget quickly, thus gaining hope. Do you think that is always true with tragedies? Is that true for everyone? Explain your answers.
3. Do our minds always blur when we are in situations "in extremis"? How can we change that?
4. Do you think Oates's conclusion is too analytical for such an emotional topic, or do you think she gets the emotion across properly? Explain your answer.

Ideas for Writing Arguments

Prewriting

What did the United States do, if anything, to deserve the attacks on the World Trade Center and the Pentagon on 9/11? Write some notes on the subject.

Writing a Guided Argument

Write a letter in the form of an argumentative essay in which you take issue with those people who say about 9/11, "The United States had it coming."

1. Open your essay by summarizing the argument that the United States had it coming. Give at least three arguments that can be made for this position.
2. Write that you can understand why the opposition feels as it does, but that you disagree.
3. Write your major proposition.
4. For each of the opposition arguments, write a paragraph in rebuttal.
5. Explain how the opposition's idea can be dangerous.
6. In the next section, explain how the United States can change the minds of people around the world.
7. In your conclusion, restate your major proposition and assess how successful the United States is being in convincing the world that it is not responsible for being attacked.

Thinking, Arguing, and Writing Collaboratively

In groups of four or five, exchange drafts of the essays that grew out of your Writing a Guided Argument assignment. After making general comments about the success of your partner's paper, write a paragraph or two about the effectiveness of the conclusion. How well has your partner succeeded in tying the paper together? Is the conclusion appropriate?

Writing About the Text

How does Oates, as a novelist, use her gifts of description and narration (and her powers of imagination) to help her argument? Write an essay in which you analyze both (1) how Oates is led to her conclusion because she is a fiction writer and (2) how her fiction writing leads her to write this essay as it is written.

More Writing Ideas

1. In your journal, write about a "senseless violent death" that you may have witnessed or heard about.
2. Write a paragraph or two in which you explore the implications of Oates's assertion that "the future doesn't belong to those who only mourn, but to those who celebrate."
3. People who suffer tragedies and crises deal with lingering effects for years, or perhaps for their entire lives. In an essay, argue that, contrary to what Oates says, people never completely get over tragedies.

JEFFREY ROSEN
Bad Luck: Why Americans Exaggerate the Terrorist Threat

A teacher at George Washington Law School in Washington, D.C., Jeffrey Rosen holds degrees from Harvard, Balliol, and Oxford Universities. He is a staff writer for the New Republic, *in which this essay first appeared in November of 2001. He is the author of* The Unwanted Gaze: The Destruction of Privacy in America *(2000), in which he draws on a broad historical perspective to examine the right of privacy in a variety of cultures. In this essay, Rosen examines the response to terrorism in America. As you can see from the title, he finds our fears overblown.*

Prereading: Thinking About the Essay in Advance

What does the phrase "bad luck" suggest to you? What connections can you make between the notion of misfortune and terrorism?

Words to Watch

vulnerability (par. 3) weakness, helplessness
assaulted (par. 6) attacked
scenarios (par. 7) outlines of a plan of likely events
melodramatically (par. 7) in an exaggerated or over-emotional manner
arbitrary (par. 8) determined by chance or whim, not logic or reason
calamities (par.8) disasters; catastrophes
egregious (par. 9) extremely bad; shocking
inegalitarian (par. 11) not supporting equal political, economic, and legal rights for all human beings

The terrorist threat is all too real, but newspapers and TV stations around 1
the globe are still managing to exaggerate it. As new cases of anthrax infection continue to emerge, the World Health Organization is begging people not to panic. But tabloid headlines like this one from *The Mirror* in London send a different message: "panic." A Time/CNN poll found that nearly half of all Americans say they are "very" or "somewhat" concerned that they or their families will be exposed to anthrax, even though only a handful of politicians and journalists have been targeted so far.

This isn't surprising. Terrorism is unfamiliar, it strikes largely at random, 2
and it can't be easily avoided by individual precautions. Criminologists tell us that crimes with these features are the most likely to create hysteria. If America's ability to win the psychological war against terrorism depends upon our ability to remain calm in the face of random violence, our reaction to similar threats in the past is not entirely reassuring.

In the academic literature about crime, scholars have identified a para- 3
dox: "Most surveys discover that people apparently fear most being a victim of precisely those crimes they are least likely to be victims of," writes Jason

Ditton of the University of Sheffield. "Little old ladies apparently worry excessively about being mugged, but they are the least likely to be mugging victims." Women worry most about violent crime, though they have the lowest risk of being victims, while young men worry the least, though they have the highest risk. And because of their physical vulnerability, women tend to worry more about violence in general, even when the risk of experiencing a particular attack is evenly distributed. In a Gallup poll at the end of September, 62 percent of women said they were "very worried" that their families might be victimized by terrorist attacks. Only 35 percent of the men were similarly concerned.

4 Why are people most afraid of the crimes they are least likely to experience? According to Wesley Skogan of Northwestern University, "it may be the things we feel we can't control or influence, those uncontrollable risks, are the ones that make people most fearful." It's why people fear flying more than they fear being hit by a car. We think we can protect ourselves against cars by looking before crossing the street—and therefore underestimate the risk, even though it is actually higher than being killed in a plane crash.

5 People also overestimate the risk of crimes they have never experienced. The elderly are no more fearful than anyone else when asked how safe they feel when they go out at night. That's because many senior citizens don't go out at night, or they take precautions when they do. But when surveys ask how safe they would feel if they did go out at night more often, old people say they would be very afraid, since they have less experience to give them context. Instead they tend to assess risk based on media hype and rumors. "To be able to estimate the probability of an event occurring, you first have to know the underlying distribution of those events, and second the trend of those events—but when it comes to crime, people usually get both hugely wrong," writes Ditton.

6 The media is partly to blame. A survey by George Gerbner, former dean of the Annenberg School at the University of Pennsylvania, found that people who watch a lot of television are more likely than occasional viewers to overestimate their chances of being a victim of violence, to believe their neighborhood is unsafe, to say fear of crime is a very serious problem, to assume that crime is rising, and to buy locks, watchdogs, and guns. And this distortion isn't limited to television. Jason Ditton notes that 45 percent of crimes reported in the newspaper involve sex or violence, even though they only represent 3 percent of crimes overall. When interviewed about how many crimes involve sex or violence, people tend to overestimate it by a factor of three or four. People believe they are more likely to be assaulted or raped than robbed, even though the robbery rate is much higher.

7 Will sensationalistic reports of worst-case terrorist scenarios exaggerate people's fear of being caught in an attack? There's every reason to believe that they will because of the media's tendency to exaggerate the scope and probability of remote risks. In a book called *Random Violence,* Joel Best, then of Southern Illinois University, examined the "moral panics" about a series of new crimes that seized public attention in the 1980s and '90s: free-

way violence in 1987, wilding in 1989, stalking around 1990, kids and guns in 1991, and so forth. In each case, Best writes, television seized on two or three incidents of a dramatic crime, such as freeway shooting, and then claimed it was part of a broader trend. By taking the worst and most infrequent examples of criminal violence and melodramatically claiming they were typical, television created the false impression that everyone was equally at risk, thereby increasing its audience.

The risk of terrorism is more randomly distributed than the crimes the media has hyped in the past. This makes it even more frightening because it is hard to avoid through precautions. (The anthrax envelopes were more narrowly targeted than the World Trade Center attack, of course, but they still infected postal workers.) Contemporary Americans, in particular, are not well equipped to deal with arbitrary threats because, in so many realms of life, we refuse to accept the role of chance. In his nineteenth-century novel *The Gilded Age,* Mark Twain described a steamship accident that killed 22 people. The investigator's verdict: "nobody to blame." This attitude was reflected in nineteenth-century legal doctrines such as assumption of risk, which refused to compensate victims who behaved carelessly. In the twentieth century, by contrast, the United States developed what the legal historian Lawrence Friedman has called an expectation of "total justice"—namely, "the general expectation that somebody will pay for any and all calamities that happen to a person, provided only that it is not the victim's 'fault,' or at least not solely his fault." 8

This effort to guarantee total justice is reflected throughout American society—from the regulation of product safety to the elimination of legal doctrines like assumption of risk. Since September 11 the most egregious display of this total justice mentality has been the threat by various personal injury lawyers to sue the airlines, security officials, and the architects of the World Trade Center on behalf of the victims' families. One of their claims: Flaws in the design of the twin towers may have impeded escape. 9

Given America's difficulty in calculating and accepting unfamiliar risk, what can be done, after September 11, to minimize panic? Rather than self-censoring only when it comes to the ravings of Osama bin Laden, the broadcast media might try to curb its usual focus on worst-case scenarios. Wesley Skogan found that when people were accurately informed about the real risk, they adjusted their fears accordingly. Politicians also need to be careful about passing on unspecified but terrifying threats of future attacks. In the middle of October the Justice Department warned that a terrorist attack might be imminent, but didn't say what the attack might be, or where it might strike. The vagueness of the warning only increased public fear and caused people to cancel travel plans. But it didn't make anyone more secure. 10

While Americans learn to take sensible precautions, we need to also learn that there is no insurance against every calamity or compensation for every misfortune. There is something inegalitarian about risk: It singles out some people from the crowd for no good reason and treats them worse than everybody else. But even in the United States, there is no such 11 thing as perfect equality or total justice. If the first foreign attack on U.S. soil helps teach Americans how to live with risk, then perhaps we can emerge from this ordeal a stronger society as well as a stronger nation.

Building Vocabulary

Determine the meanings of the familiar words that follow by using your knowledge of prefixes, roots, and suffixes and your understanding of compound words—that is, two words put together to form a new word. Define each word in the list; then explain how the parts of the word contribute to the definition. Check your definitions in a dictionary.

1. criminologists (par. 2)
2. uncontrollable (par. 2)
3. underestimate (par. 2)
4. precautions (par. 5)
5. watchdogs (par. 6)
6. freeway (par. 7)
7. steamship (par, 8)
8. self-censoring (par. 10)
9. worst-case (par. 10)
10. misfortune (par 11)

Thinking Critically About the Argument

Understanding the Writer's Argument

1. Who, according to Rosen, is to blame for America's anxiety about different kinds of threats?
2. What paradox does Rosen identify in paragraph 3?
3. According to the writer, why are people afraid of the crimes they are least likely to experience? Why do they overestimate the risk of crimes that they never have experienced?
4. Why does the writer feel that "sensationalist reports of worst-case terrorist scenarios" will exaggerate people's fear of being caught in an attack?
5. Why are contemporary Americans not equipped to deal with arbitrary threats, according to Rosen?
6. What, according to the writer, can we do to minimize panic, given our difficulty to calculate and accept unfamiliar risk?

Understanding the Writer's Techniques

1. What is Rosen's major proposition? Which sentence or two do you think best sums it up? How would you state the proposition in your own words?
2. Why does the writer use the words "Bad Luck" as the opening of his title? How does the statement after the colon in the title help establish the writer's purpose in the essay?

3. How has Rosen used cause-and-effect strategies in this essay? In what way does the title establish the audience's expectations of a cause-and-effect analysis?
4. Rosen uses many external sources for expert testimony to support his argument. What is the effect of the statistical reports he cites? What is the effect of the quotes from scholars, writers, and university professors? What is the effect of the quotation drawn from Mark Twain in paragraph 8? In what ways do you find the evidence he presents convincing?
5. Rosen has considerable legal training. How does his knowledge of the law and legal issues contribute to the way he builds his case in this essay?
6. In what ways does the last paragraph serve as an effective conclusion to the essay? How does the last paragraph relate to the introductory paragraph?
7. How does Rosen maintain a tone of calm and logic despite the frightening topic of terrorism?

Exploring the Writer's Argument

1. Why might you agree or disagree with the idea that the media are exaggerating the terrorist threat? In what ways do the newspapers you read or the television news programs you watch contribute to your fears of terrorism? Or do you think that the media respond appropriately to terrorist threats?
2. How do you think that people can learn to remain calm in the face of random violence?
3. How effective is Rosen's point about why people fear flying more than they fear automobiles?
4. Why do you think Americans refuse to accept the role of chance? In what ways do you think our expectation of total justice is a good thing? A bad thing? How much should we support the 19th-century idea of "nobody to blame" when it comes to accidents?
5. Rosen complains about personal injury lawyers who try to sue airlines, security officials, and World Trade center architects on behalf of the 9/11 victims. Why might you agree or disagree with his position? How has the "total justice" belief affected recent controversies at fast-food restaurants like McDonald's? Accidental injuries or deaths in doctors' offices or hospitals? Automobile accidents?

Ideas for Writing Arguments

Prewriting

In what ways do you think that we have to take terrorist threats seriously, even when they are ambiguous?

Writing a Guided Argument

Terrorist threats have reached new highs across the world, and whereas nobody supports panic in response to them, many people—government authorities included—believe that we have to take these threats seriously, both as a society and as individuals. Write an essay in which you argue that we should take terrorist threats seriously—that is, write an essay opposing Rosen's proposition.

1. Open your essay with an introduction to the notion of terrorist threats, and cite one or two of the most recent examples.
2. Introduce and deal with the *opposing* argument—that most of the threats *are* exaggerated and that we should not panic when we hear about imminent threats.
3. State your major proposition about how the threats are not exaggerated and that we must take them seriously.
4. Offer at least two minor propositions to back up your major proposition. Draw on recent threats you know of that require more than "sensible precautions"—Rosen's point in the last paragraph. Offer suggestions about how we should respond in the light of threats and subsequent government warnings.
5. Present statistics, quotations, or cases to reinforce your argument.
6. Establish a calm tone that uses logic as opposed to emotional appeal.
7. Use appropriate transitions to link your points.

Thinking, Arguing, and Writing Collaboratively

In small groups, discuss the possibilities inherent in Rosen's tenth paragraph: that the broadcast media can and should "curb its usual focus on worst-case scenarios." In what ways might this idea, if acted upon, keep people calm? In what ways does the suggestion fringe on censorship on potentially misinforming the public?

Writing About the Text

Write a brief essay in which you analyze Rosen's use of expert testimony. How do the quotes, paraphrases, and survey data strengthen the piece? What shortfalls do you see in drawing on expert testimony in the way that Rosen has?

More Writing Ideas

1. Write a journal entry about your own response to a recent terrorist threat.
2. In an extended paragraph, define "random violence" as you understand the use of the term today.
3. Write an essay called "The Responsibilities of the Media" in which you argue that newspapers, radio, and television have important responsibilities in providing information to American citizens. Include your views on how well the media are meeting those responsibilities.

APPENDIX A

Glossary

Rules and Techniques for Preparing the Manuscript in MLA Style

The alphabetical glossary that follows will answer most of your questions about matters of form, such as margins, pagination, dates, and numbers. For matters not addressed below, consult the index, which will direct you to appropriate pages elsewhere in this text.

Abbreviations

Employ abbreviations often and consistently in notes and citations, but avoid them in the text.

In your citations, but not in your text, always abbreviate these items:

- technical terms and reference words (anon., e.g., diss.)
- institutions (acad., assn., Cong.)
- dates (Jan., Feb.)
- states and countries (OH, CA, U.S.A.)
- names of publishers (McGraw, UP of Florida)
- titles of well-known religious and literary works

See also "Names of Persons," page A-18, for comments on abbreviations of honorary titles.

A few general rules apply:

1. With abbreviations made up of capital letters, use neither periods nor spaces:

   DC   MS   JD   CD-ROM   AD
2. Do use periods and a space with initials used with personal names:

   J. R. Rowlings
3. Abbreviations that end in lowercase letters are usually followed by a period:

   assoc. fig. min. Sept. yr.
4. In abbreviations in which lowercase letters represent a word, a period usually follows each letter with no space after the period:

   p.m. e.g. n.p. v.

   but exceptions are common:

   n, nn (for note, notes)

   ns (for new series)

Abbreviations for Technical Terms and Institutions

abr. abridged
anon. anonymous
art., arts. article(s)
assn. association
assoc. associate, associated
bib. biblical
bibliog. bibliography, bibliographer, bibliographic
biog. biography, biographer, biographical
bk. bks. book(s)
bull. bulletin
ca., c. *circa* 'about'; used to indicate an approximate date, as in "ca. 1812"
cf. *confer* 'compare' (one source with another); not, however, to be used in place of "see" or "see also"
ch., chs. chapter(s), also shown as chap., chaps.
col., cols. column(s)
comp. compiled by or compiler
doc. document
ed., eds. editor(s), edition, or edited by
enl. enlarged, as in "enl. ed."
esp. especially, as in "312–15, esp. 313"
et al. *et alii* 'and others'; "John Smith et al." means John Smith and other authors
f., ff. page or pages following a given page; "8f." means page eight and the following page; but exact references are sometimes preferable, for example, "45–51, 55, 58" instead of "45ff." Acceptable also is "45 + ."
fl. *floruit* 'flourished'; which means a person reached greatness on these dates, as in "*fl.* 1420–50"; used when birth and death dates are unknown.
ibid. *ibidem* 'in the same place,' i.e., in the immediately preceding title, normally capitalized and underlined as in "Ibid., p. 34"
i.e. *id est* 'that is'; preceded and followed by a comma
infra 'below'; refers to a succeeding portion of the text; compare "supra." Generally, it is best to write "see below"
loc. cit. *loco citato* 'in the place (passage) cited'
ms., mss. manuscript(s) as in "(Cf. the mss. of Glass and Ford)"
n, nn note(s), as "23, n 2"
narr. narrated by
n.d. no date (in a book's title or copyright pages)
no., nos. number(s)
n.p. no place (of publication)
n. pag. no page
ns new series
op. cit. *opere citato* 'in the work cited'
p., pp. page(s); do not use "ps." for "pages"
proc. proceedings

pseud.	pseudonym
pt. pts.	part(s)
qtd.	quoted
rev.	revised, revised by, revision, review, or reviewed by
rpt.	reprint, reprinted
ser.	series
sic	'thus'; placed in brackets to indicate an error has been made in the quoted passage and the writer is quoting accurately.
st., sts.	stanza(s)
sup.	*supra* ("above"); used to refer to a preceding portion of the text; it is just as easy to write "above" or "see above"
supp.	supplement(s)
s.v.	*sub voce (verbo)* ("under the word or heading")
trans., (tr.)	translator, translated, translated by, or translation
ts., tss.	typescript, typescripts
viz.	*videlicet* (namely)
vol., vols.	volume(s) (e.g., vol. 3)
vs., (v.)	versus ("against"); used in citing legal cases

Abbreviations of Publishers' Names

Use the shortened forms below as guidelines for shortening all publishers names for MLA citations (but *not* for APA, CMS, or CSE styles).

Abrams	Harry N. Abrams, Inc.
Addison	Addison, Wesley, Longman
ALA	American Library Association
Allyn	Allyn and Bacon, Inc.
Barnes	Barnes and Noble Books
Bowker	R. R. Bowker Co.
Cambridge UP	Cambridge University Press
Free	The Free Press
GPO	Government Printing Office
Harvard UP	Harvard UP
Longman	Addison, Wesley, Longman
MIT P	The MIT Press
MLA	Modern Language Association
Scott	Scott, Foresman and Co.
Scribner's	Charles Scribner's Sons
U of Chicago P	University of Chicago Press
UP of Florida	University Press of Florida

Abbreviations of Biblical Works

Use parenthetical documentation for biblical references in the text—that is, place the entry within parentheses immediately after the quotation. For example:

> After the great flood God spoke to Noah, "And I will establish my covenant with you; neither shall all flesh be cut off any more by the waters of a flood; neither shall there any more be a flood to destroy the earth" (Gen. 9.11).

Do not italicize or underline titles of books of the Bible. Abbreviate books of the Bible, except some very short titles, such as Ezra and Mark, as shown in these examples.

Acts	Acts of the Apostles	Mal.	Malachi
1 and 2 Chron.	1 and 2 Chronicles	Matt.	Mathew
Col.	Colossians	Mic.	Micah
1 and 2 Cor.	1 and 2 Corinthians	Nah.	Nahum
Dan.	Daniel	Neh.	Nehemiah
Deut.	Deuteronomy	Num.	Numbers
Eccles.	Ecclesiastes	Obad.	Obadiah

Abbreviations for Literary Works

Shakespeare

In parenthetical documentation, use italicized or underscored abbreviations for titles of Shakespearean plays, as shown in this example:

> Too late, Capulet urges Montague to end their feud, "O brother Montague, give me thy hand" (Rom. 5.3.296).

Abbreviate as shown by these examples:

Ado	*Much Ado About Nothing*	*LLL*	*Love's Labour's Lost*
Ant.	*Antony and Cleopatra*	*Lr.*	*Lear*
AWW	*All's Well That Ends Well*	*Luc.*	*The Rape of Lucrece*
AYL	*As You Like It*	*Mac*	*Macbeth*
Cor.	*Coriolanus*	*MM*	*Measure for Measure*
Cym.	*Cymbeline*	*MND*	*A Midsummer's Night Dream*
Err.	*The Comedy of Errors*	*MV*	*Merchant of Venice*
F1	*First Folio Edition (1623)*	*Oth.*	*Othello*

Chaucer

Abbreviate in parenthetical documentation as shown by these examples. Italicize the book but not the individual tales:

BD	*The Book of the Duchess*	MLT	The Man of Law's Tale
CkT	The Cook's Tale	NPT	The Nun's Priest's Tale
ClT	The Clerk's Tale	PardT	The Pardoner's Tale
CT	*The Canterbury Tales*	ParsT	The Parson's Tale
CYT	The Canon's Yeoman's Tale	*PF*	*The Parliament of Fowls*

Other Literary Works

Wherever possible in your in-text citations, use the initial letters of the title. A reference to page 18 of Melville's *Moby-Dick: The White Whale* could appear as: (*MD* 18). Use the following italicized abbreviations as guidelines:

Aen.	*Aeneid* by Vergil	*LB*	*Lyrical Ballads* by Wordsworth
Ag.	*Agamemnon* by Aeschylus	*Lys.*	*Lysistrata* by Aristophanes
Ant.	*Antigone* by Sophocles	*MD*	*Moby-Dick* by Melville
Bac.	*Bacchae* by Euripides	*Med.*	*Medea* by Euripides
Beo.	*Beowulf*		

Accent Marks

When you quote, reproduce accents exactly as they appear in the original. You may need to use the character sets embedded within the computer software (see "Character Sets," page A-11). Write the mark in ink on the printout if your typewriter or word processor does not support the mark.

> "La tradición clásica en españa," according to Romana, remains strong and vibrant in public school instruction (16).

Acknowledgments

Generally, acknowledgments are unnecessary. Nor is a preface required. Use a superscript reference numeral to your first sentence and then place any obligatory acknowledgments or explanations in a content endnote (see pages 482–485). Acknowledge neither your instructor nor typist for help with your research paper, though such acknowledgments are standard with graduate theses and dissertations.

Ampersand

MLA Style

Avoid using the ampersand symbol "&" unless custom demands it (e.g., "A&P"). Use *and* for in-text citations in MLA style (e.g., Smith and Jones 213–14).

APA Style

Use "&" within citations (e.g., Spenser & Wilson, 1994, p. 73) but not in the text (Spenser and Wilson found the results in error.)

Annotated Bibliography

An annotation describes the essential details of a book or article. Place it just after the facts of publication. Provide enough information in about three sentences for a reader to have a fairly clear image of the work's purpose, contents, and special value. See pages 252–254 for a complete annotated bibliography.

Arabic Numerals

Both the MLA style and the APA style require Arabic numerals whenever possible: for volumes, books, parts, and chapters of works; acts, scenes, and lines of plays; cantos, stanzas, and lines of poetry.

Words or Numerals

Spell out numbers that you can write in one or two words (two, sixteen, fifty-six, two hundred, three million, 15th test, 12%) and use numerals to represent other numbers (154, 1,269, 31/4, 3.5 million, 6.234). However, for technical papers, use numerals for all numbers that precede technical units of measurement (*12 amperes*).

Inclusive Numbers

For inclusive numbers that indicate a range, give the second number in full for numbers through 99 (e.g., 3–5, 15–21, 70–96). In MLA style, with three digits or more give only the last two digits in the second number unless more digits are needed for clarity (e.g. 98–101, 110–12, 989–1001, 1030–33, 2766–854). In APA style, with three digits or more give all numbers (e.g., 110–112, 1030–1033, 2766–2854). Do not abbreviate the range of years that begin before AD 1 (748–749 BC). For years beginning AD 1 forward, follow basic rules for inclusive numbers (2000–03, 1787–88, 1787–1821). You may write "in 1997–99" and "from 1997 to 1999" but not "from 1997–99."

Commas in Numbers

Place commas between the third and fourth digits from the right, the sixth, and so on (1,200 or 1,200,000). Exceptions are page and line numbers, addresses, the year, and zip codes (page 1620, at 12116 Nova Road, New York, NY 10012, in 1985), but add commas for year numbers of five or more figures (15,000 BC).

Use the number 1 in every case for numbers, not the lowercase *l* or uppercase *L*, especially if you are typing on a word processor or computer.

Numbers at the Beginning of Sentences

Do not begin a sentence with a numeral.

Nineteen sixty-three ended the Camelot years of the Kennedy White House.

But

The year 1963 ended the Camelot years of the Kennedy White House.

Numbers with Abbreviations, Symbols, Dates, and Page References

Unless they begin the sentence, use figures (5 lbs., $7, 6:30 p.m., 56 George Avenue, 3 July 2003 or July 3, 2003, page 9).

Related Numbers

Use the same style for related numbers (4 through 6).

Dates and Times of the Day

Be consistent in using either 3 July 2003 or July 3, 2003. Use numerals for times of the day (3:30 p.m., the 10:00 a.m. lecture), but exceptions are made for quarter-hours, half-hours, and hours followed by *o'clock* (half past eight, a quarter to nine, seven o'clock). Spell out centuries (twenty-first century). Hyphenate century numbers when using them as adjectives (seventeenth-century literature and fourteenth- and fifteenth-century wars). Decades can be written out (the eighties) or expressed in figures (1960s or the '90s). The abbreviation BC follows the year, but AD precedes the year (240 BC, AD 456). Some writers now use the abbreviations BCE 'before the common era,' and CE 'common era,' and both follow the year (43 BCE or 1498 CE).

Percentages and Money

If your discussion infrequently uses numbers, spell out a percentage or an amount of money only if you can do so in three words or fewer (twelve dollars, fifty-five percent, six thousand dollars *but* $6,543).

The Numbers Zero and One

When used alone, spell them as words (zero-base budget planning, a one-line paragraph, one response *but* 1 of 15 responses).

Back-to-Back Modifiers

Write both spelled words and figures to distinguish back-to-back modifiers (twelve 6-year-olds or 12 six-year-olds, but not 12 6-year olds).

Numbers in Documentation

Use numbers with in-text citations and Works Cited entries according to the following examples:

(Ham. 5.3.16-18)
(Faust 2.140)
(2 Sam. 2.1-8)
(Fredericks 23-24) (MLA style)
(Fredericks, 1995, pp. 23-24) (APA and CSE style)
2 vols.
Rpt. as vols. 13 and 14
MS CCCC 210
102nd Cong., 1st sess. S. 2411
16 mm., 29 min., color
Monograph 1962-M2
College English 22 (Winter 2002): 3-6 (MLA style)
Memory and Cognition, 3, 562-590 (APA style)
Mol. Biol. 157:15-39; 2003 (CSE style)
Journal of Philosophy 36 (2002): 172-89 (CMS footnote style)

Asterisks

Do not use asterisks (*) for tables, content notes, or illustrations (see pages A-9–A-10). Use numbers for tables and figures (e.g., Table 2 or Figure 3) and use letters for content notes (see Figure A5, page A-14).

Bible

Use parenthetical documentation for biblical references in the text (e.g., 2 Chron. 18.13). Do not underline the books of the Bible. For abbreviations, see page A-5.

Borders

Computers offer you the opportunity to build borders around pages, paragraphs, and graphic designs. Place the title page within a full-page border if you like, but *not* pages of your text. Use a border with a fill pattern, if desired, for graphs, charts, highlighted text, and other material that deserves special emphasis. Use this feature with restraint. The content of your text reigns supreme, while design features only decorate. Usually, instructors look at the content and dismiss or ignore special effects such as color and unusual fonts.

Bullets, Numbers, and Indented Lists

Computers supply several bullet or number styles, which are indented lines that begin with a circle, square, diamond, triangle, number, or letter. Use this feature for a list:

- Observation 1: Kindergarten class
- Observation 2: First grade class
- Observation 3: Second grade class

Capitalization

Capitalize Some Titles

For books, journals, magazines, and newspapers, capitalize the first word, the last word, and all principal words, including words that follow hyphens in compound terms (e.g., French-Speaking Islands). Do not capitalize articles, prepositions that introduce phrases, conjunctions, and the *to* in infinitives when these words occur in the middle of the title (for example, *The Last of the Mohicans*). For titles of articles and parts of books, capitalize as for books (e.g., "Writing the Final Draft" and "Appendix 2"). If the first line of the poem serves as the title, reproduce it exactly as it appears in print:

> The paper will examine the poem "anyone lived in a pretty how town."

Use this feature with restraint.

Note: Some scholarly styles capitalize only the first word and proper names of reference titles (including the first word of subtitles). Study the appropriate style for your field, as found in chapters 17–20.

Capitalize after a Colon

Only when a rule, principle, or quotation follows a colon should you capitalize. When introducing a list or series, do not capitalize:

> The results of the testing suggest three possible changes: young girls need more education in science and math, more physical exercise, and a carefully monitored diet.

When introducing a definition or elaboration on the first clause, do not capitalize the first word after the colon:

> The consequences of this decision will be disastrous: each division of the corporation will be required to cut twenty percent of its budget within this fiscal year.

When introducing a rule or principle, do capitalize the first word after the colon:

> Benjamin Franklin's maxim should be changed for the modern age: A dollar saved is a dollar earned.

When introducing a quotation that is independent of your main sentence, capitalize the first word after the colon:

> Commenting on Carl Hiaasen's <u>Tourist Season</u>, one critic said: "Few novels combine violence and comedy so successfully."

See also pages 325–326, which demonstrates the use of the colon to introduce long, indented quotations.

Capitalize Some Compound Words

Capitalize the second part of a hyphenated compound word only when it is used in a heading with other capitalized words:

Low-Frequency Sound Equipment

but

Low-frequency sound distortion is caused by several factors.

Capitalize Trade Names

Use capitals for trade names such as: Pepsi, Plexiglas, Du Pont

Capitalize Proper Names

Capitalize proper names used as adjectives *but not* the words used with them: Marshall plan
Salk vaccine

Capitalize Specific Departments or Courses

Capitalize the specific names of departments or courses, but use lowercase when they are used in a general sense.

Department of Psychology *but* the psychology department
Psychology 314 *but* an advanced course in psychology

Capitalize Nouns Used before Numerals or Letters

Capitalize the noun when it denotes a specific place in a numbered series:

during Test 6   we observed Group C

However, do *not* capitalize nouns that name common parts of books or tables followed by numerals:

chapter 12   page ix   column 14

Character Sets

Most word processing programs provide characters that are unavailable on your keyboard. These are special letters, signs, and symbols, such as _, Σ, â, and ≻. The software instructions will help you find and utilize these marks and icons.

Clip Art

Pictures, figures, and drawings are available on many computers, but avoid the temptation to embed them in your document. Clip art, in general, conveys an informal, sometimes comic effect, one that is inappropriate to the serious nature of most research papers.

Copyright Law

"Fair use" of the materials of others is permitted. To protect your own work, keyboard in the upper right-hand corner of your manuscript, "Copyright © 20_ by _____." Fill the blanks with the proper year and your name. Then, to register a work, order a form from the U.S. Copyright Office, Library of Congress, Washington, D.C. 20559.

Covers and Binders

Most instructors prefer that you submit manuscript pages with one staple in the upper left corner. Unless required, do not use a cover or binder.

Dates

See "Arabic numerals," pages A-7–A-9.

Definitions

For definitions and translations within your text, use single quotation marks without intervening punctuation. For example:

> The use of <u>et alii</u> 'and others' has diminished in scholarly writing.

Electronic Presentations

If you have the expertise, many instructors will allow you to submit the research paper in one of these forms:

E-mail attachment
Floppy disk
CD
Slide show
Web page

Publishing your research paper electronically has a number of advantages:

- *It's easy*. The tools for creating electronic documents make the task as simple as saving the file.
- *It's inexpensive*. Your school probably has the resources for publishing your paper electronically. If not, you can do it with a typical home computer.
- *It's up to date*. It helps you show others, especially your instructors and prospective employers, that you have learned valuable skills on the cutting edge of technology.
- *It's easily conveyed*. You can send your work to your readers quickly through a variety of means—e-mail, diskette, cassette, slide show, Web site.
- *It has multimedia potential*. Unlike paper documents, electronic documents can include any material you can transfer to a digital form—text, illustrations, sound, and video.
- *It can offer links to further information*. You can direct your reader to additional sources of information and, on a Web site, provide the link that will carry the reader to new information.

However, consider this question: Is electronic publishing suitable for your research paper? Don't get so excited about the glamour of electronic publication that you forget to ask what your readers will gain from reading an electronic text rather than the traditional paper version.

Endnotes for Documentation of Sources

An instructor or supervisor may prefer traditional superscript numerals within the text and documentation notes at the end of paper. If so, see Chapter 19.

Figures and Tables

A table is a systematic presentation of materials, usually in columns. A figure is any nontext item that is not a table: blueprint, chart, diagram, drawing, graph, photo, photostat, map, and so on. Use graphs appropriately. A line graph serves a different purpose than a circle (pie) chart, and a bar graph plots different information than a scatter graph. Here are sample figures and tables.

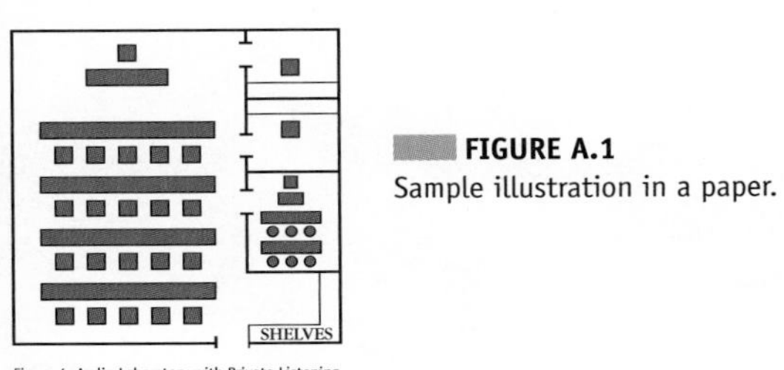

Figure 4: Audio Laboratory with Private Listening Rooms and a Small Group Room

FIGURE A.1
Sample illustration in a paper.

Table 1
Response by Class on Nuclear Energy Policy

	Freshmen	Sophomores	Juniors	Seniors
1. More nuclear power	150	301	75	120
2. Less nuclear power	195	137	111	203
3. Present policy is acceptedable	87	104	229	37

FIGURE A.2
Sample table in a paper.

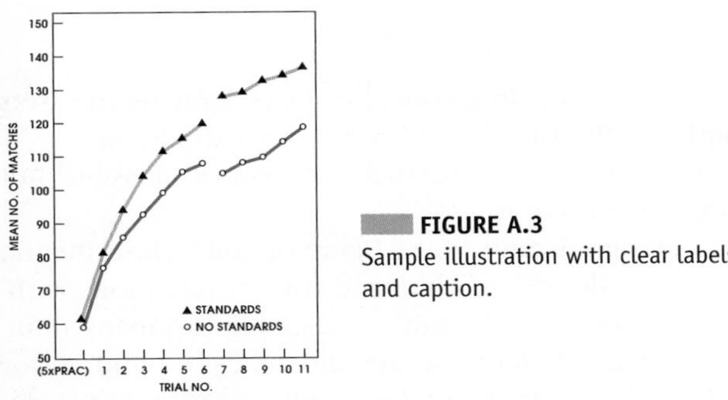

Figure 6: Mean Number of Matches by Subject with and without Standard (by Trial). Source: Lock and Bryan (289).

FIGURE A.3
Sample illustration with clear labels and caption.

A table is a systematic presentation of materials, usually in columns. A table is shown on the following page. Your figures and tables, as shown below and on following page, should conform to the following guidelines:

- Present only one kind of information in each figure or table, and make it as simple and as brief as possible. Frills and fancy artwork may distract rather than inform the reader.

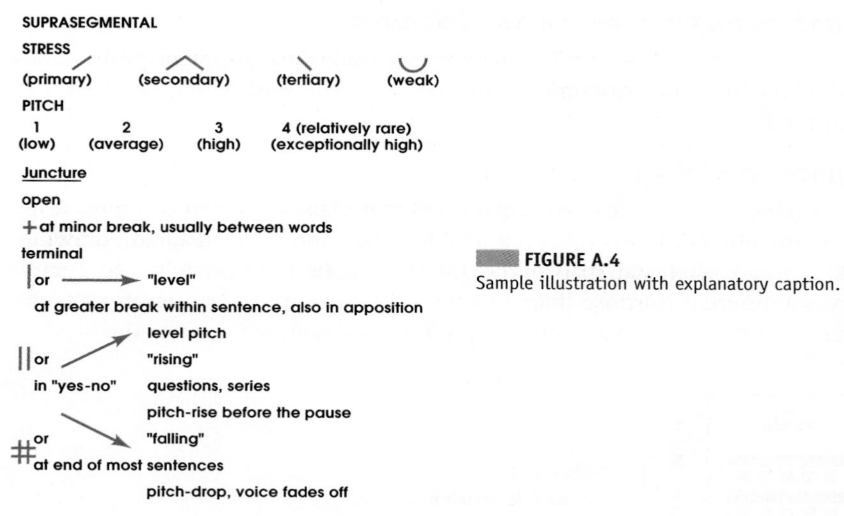

Figure 9: Phonemes of English. Generally this figure follows the Trager-Smith system, used widely in American linguistics. Source: Anna H. Live (1066).

FIGURE A.4
Sample illustration with explanatory caption.

Table 2[a]

Mean Sources of Six Values Held by College Students According to Sex

All Students		Men		Women	
Pol.	40.61	Pol.	43.22	Aesth.	43.86
Rel.	40.51	Theor.	43.09	Rel.	43.13
Aesth.	40.29	Econ.	42.05	Soc.	41.13
Econ.	39.45	Soc.	37.05	Econ.	36.85
Soc.	39.34	Aesth.	36.72	Theor.	36.50

[a]Carmen J. Finley, et al. (165).

FIGURE A.5
Sample table with in-text citation source.

- Place small figures and tables within your text; place large figures, sets of figures, or complex tables on separate pages in an appendix.
- Place the figure or table as near your textual discussion as possible, but not before your first mention of it.
- In the text, explain the significance of the figure or table. Describe the figure or table so your reader may understand your observations without reference to the figure or table, but avoid giving too many numbers and figures in your text. Refer to figures and tables by number (for example, "Figure 5") or by number and page reference ("Table 4, 16"). Do not use locational references (such as "the table above," "the following illustration," or "the chart below").
- Write a caption for the figure or table so your reader can understand it without reference to your discussion. Set it in full capital letters or in capitals and lowercase, but do not mix forms in the same paper.
- Number figures consecutively throughout the paper with Arabic numbers, preceded by "Fig." or "Figure" (for example, "Figure 4"). Place the figure number and the caption flush left *below* the figure, as shown in Figures A.1 and A.3.

- Number tables consecutively throughout the paper with Arabic numerals, preceded by "Table" (for example, "Table 2"). Place the numbered designation one doublespace flush left *above* the table.
- Insert a caption or number for each column of a table, centered above the column or, if necessary, inserted diagonally or vertically above it.
- When inserting an explanatory or reference note, place it below the table or figure, and then use a lowercase letter as the identifying superscript, not an Arabic numeral (see Figure A.5).
- Sources are abbreviated as in-text citations, and full documentation must appear on the Works Cited page.

Footnotes for Documentation

If your instructor requires you to use footnotes, see Chapter 19, for discussion and examples.

Fonts

Most computers offer a variety of typefaces. Courier **(Courier),** the typewriter font, is always a safe choice, but you may use others, such as a nonserif typeface like Ariel **(Ariel)** or a serif typeface like Times Roman **(Times Roman).** Use the same font consistently throughout for your text, but shift to different fonts if desired for tables, illustrations, and other matter. Use 12-point type size.

Foreign Cities

In general, spell the names of foreign cities as they are written in original sources. However, for purposes of clarity, you may substitute an English name or provide both with one in parentheses:

Köln (Cologne)	Braunschweig (Brunswick)
München (Munich)	Praha (Prague)

Foreign Languages

Underscore or italicize foreign words used in an English text:

Like his friend Olaf, he is aut Caesar, aut nihil, either overpowering perfection or ruin and destruction.

Do not underscore or italicize quotations of a foreign language:

Obviously, he uses it to exploit, in the words of Jean Laumon, "une admirable mine de themes poetiques."

Do not underscore or italicize foreign titles of magazine or journal articles, but *do* underline the names of the magazines or journals themselves:

Arrigoitia, Luis de. "Machismo, folklore y creación en Mario Vargas Llosa." Sin nombre 13.4 (1983): 19-25.

Do not underscore or italicize foreign words of places, institutions, proper names, or titles that precede proper names:

Racine became extremely fond of Mlle Champmeslé, who interpreted his works at the Hôtel de Bourgogne.

Graphics

If they will contribute in a demonstrable way to your research study, you may create graphic designs and import them into your document. Computer software offers various methods for performing this task. See "Figures and Tables," pages A-13–A-15, for basic rules; see also the paper by Norman Berkowitz, pages 375 and 377, for examples.

If you create an electronic text, graphics can provide exciting features that are foreign to the traditional research paper. They tend to be among the following types:

- *Decorative graphics* make the document look more attractive but seldom add to the paper's content. Examples include typographic symbols, such as bullets and arrows.
- *Identity graphics*, much like a corporate logo, give identity to a header for each Web page or each slide in a presentation. The logo is like a signpost for the reader.
- *Illustration graphics* provide a visual amplification of the text. For example, a photograph of John Keats would augment a research paper on the British poet.
- *Information graphics*, such as charts, graphs, or tables, provide data about your topic.

Making your own graphics file is a complex but rewarding undertaking. It adds a personal creativity to your research paper. Use one of the following techniques:

- *Use a graphics program,* such as Macromedia Freehand and Adobe Illustrator. With such software you can create a graphics file and save it in the JPEG or GIF format. Also useful are Adobe Photoshop and JASC Paintshop Pro, which are designed primarily for working with photographs.
- *Use a scanner* to copy your drawings, graphs, photographs, and other matter.
- *Create original photographs with a digital camera.* Consult your manual to learn how to create JPEGs or GIFs from your photographs.
- *Create your own information graphics* in Powerpoint or Microsoft Excel.

Headers and Footers

The software of your computer can automatically insert your name and the page number at the top right margin of each page for MLA style (e.g., Morris 3). Use a Numbering or Header command to set an automatic numbering sequence. For APA style use a shortened title and page number (see pages 460–461 for an example). Footers are seldom used.

Headings

Begin every major heading on a new page (title page, opening page, notes, appendix, Works Cited or references). Center the heading in capital and lowercase letters one inch from the top of the sheet. Use a doublespace between the heading and your first line of text. Number *all* text pages, including those with major headings. (See also "Spacing," later in this appendix.) Most papers require only major headings (A-level), but the advent of desktop publishing makes it possible for some research papers to gain the look of professional typesetting. Use the following guideline for writing subheads in your paper.

Writing a Research Paper	⟵	**A heading,** centered
Writing the First Draft	⟵	**B heading,** flush left with capital letters on each major word
Revising and editing the manuscript	⟵	**C heading,** flush left with only the first word capitalized
Proofreading. Every researcher . . .	⟵	**D heading,** run-in side head, underscored or italicized, to begin a paragraph

Indention

Indent paragraphs five spaces or a half-inch. Indent long quotations (four lines or more) ten spaces or one inch from the left margin. If you quote only one paragraph, do not indent the first line more than the rest. However, if you quote two or more paragraphs, indent the first line of each paragraph an extra three spaces or a quarter-inch (see also page 000). Indent entries on the Works Cited page five spaces on the second and succeeding lines (also called a *hanging indent*). Indent the first line of content footnotes five spaces. Other styles (APA, CMS, and CSE) have different requirements (see Chapters 17-19).

Italics

If your word processing system and your printer can reproduce italic lettering, use it in place of *underscoring* if you prefer that style.

Length of the Research Paper

Try to generate a paper of 2,000 to 3,000 words or about ten pages, excluding the title page, outline, endnotes, and Works Cited pages. The length will depend on the assignment, nature of the topic, the reference material available, the time allotted to the project, and your initiative.

Margins

A one-inch margin on all sides of each page is recommended. Place your page number one-half inch down from the top edge of the paper and one inch from the right edge. Your software will provide a ruler, menu, or style palette that allows you to set the margins. *Tip:* If you develop a header, the running head may appear one inch from the top, in which case your first line of text will begin 1 1/2 inches from the top.

Monetary Units

Spell out monetary amounts only if you can do so in three words or fewer. Conform to the following:

$12 *or* twelve dollars
$14.25 *but not* fourteen dollars and twenty-five cents
$8 billion *or* eight billion dollars
$10.3 billion *or* $10,300,000,000
$63 *or* sixty-three dollars

The fee is one hundred dollars ($100) *or* The fee is one hundred (100) dollars
two thousand dollars *or* $2,000
thirty-four cents

Names of Persons

As a general rule, the first mention of a person requires the full name (e.g., Ernest Hemingway, Margaret Mead) and thereafter requires only usage of the surname (e.g., Hemingway, Mead). *Note:* APA style uses last name only in the text. Omit formal titles (Mr., Mrs., Dr., Hon.) in textual and note references to distinguished persons, living or dead. Convention suggests that certain prominent figures require the title (e.g., Lord Byron, Dr. Johnson, Dame Edith Sitwell) while others, for no apparent reason, do not (e.g., Tennyson, Browne, Hillary rather than Lord Tennyson, Sir Thomas Browne, Sir Edmund Hillary). Where custom dictates, you may employ simplified names of famous persons (e.g., Dante rather than the surname Alighieri and Michelangelo rather than Michelangelo Buonarroti). You may also use pseudonyms where custom dictates (e.g., George Eliot for Mary Ann Evans, Mark Twain for Samuel Clemens, Stendhal for Marie-Henri Beyle). Refer to fictional characters by the names used in the fictional work (e.g., Huck, Lord Jim, Santiago, Captain Ahab).

Numbering

Pagination

Use a header to number your pages in the upper right-hand corner of the page. Depending on the software, you can create the head with the Numbering or Header feature. It may appear one-half inch or a full inch down from the top edge of the paper and one inch from the right edge. Precede the number with your last name unless anonymity is required, in which case you may use a shortened version of your title rather than your name, as in APA style (see page 459). Otherwise, type the heading and then double-space to your text.

Use lowercase Roman numerals (ii, iii, iv) on any pages that precede the main portion of your text. If you have a separate title page, count it as page i, but do not type it on the page. You *should* put a page number on your opening page of text, even if you include course identification (see page 357).

Numbering a Series of Items

Within a sentence, incorporate a series of items into your text with parenthetical numbers or lowercase letters:

```
    College instructors are usually divided into four ranks:
(1) instructors, (2) assistant professors, (3) associate
professors, (4) full professors.
```

Present longer items in an enumerated list:

```
     College instructors are divided into four ranks:
  1. Full professors generally have 15 or more years of experience,
     have the Ph.D. or other terminal degree, and have achieved
     distinction in teaching and scholarly publications.
  2. Associate professors. . . .
```

Paper

Print on one side of white bond paper, sixteen- or twenty-pound weight, 8 1/2 by 11 inches. Use the best-quality paper available; avoid erasable paper. Staple the pages of your manuscript together with one staple in the top left corner. Do not enclose the manuscript within a cover or binder unless your instructor asks you to do so.

Percentages

Use numerals with appropriate symbols (3%, $5.60); otherwise, use numerals only when they cannot be spelled out in one or two words:

percent *not* per cent
one hundred percent *but* 150 percent
a two-point average *but* a 2.5 average
one metric ton *but* 0.907 metric ton *or* 3.150 metric tons
forty-five percent *but* 45 1/2 percent *or* 45 1/2%

In business, scientific, and technical writing that requires frequent use of percentages, write all percentages as numerals with appropriate symbols: 100%, 12%.

Proofreader Marks

Be familiar with the most common proofreading symbols so you can correct your own copy or mark your copy for a typist or keyboarder. Some of the most common proofreading symbols are shown on the following page.

Punctuation

Consistency is the key to punctuation. Careful proofreading of your paper for punctuation errors will generally improve the clarity and accuracy of your writing.

Apostrophe

To form the possessive of singular nouns, add an apostrophe and *s* (e.g., the typist's ledger). Add only the apostrophe with plural nouns ending in *s* (e.g., several typists' ledgers). Use the apostrophe and *s* with singular proper nouns of people and places even if the noun ends in an *s* (e.g., Rice's story, Rawlings's novel, Arkansas's mountains, *but* the Rawlingses' good fortune). To form the possessive of nouns in a series, add a single apostrophe and an *s* if the ownership is shared, (e.g., Lawson and Thompson's text on composition theory).

Exceptions are the names of Jesus and Moses (e.g. Jesus' scriptures, Moses' words) and hellenized names of more than one syllable ending in *es* (e.g., Euripides' dramas). Use apostrophes to form the plurals of letters (e.g., a's and b's) but not to form the plural of numbers or abbreviations (e.g., ACTs in the 18s and 19s, the 1980s, sevens, three MDs).

Brackets

Use brackets to enclose phonetic transcription, mathematical formulas, and interpolations into a quotation. An interpolation is the insertion of your words into the text of another person (see pages 333–334, for examples).

Use brackets to enclose parenthetical material inside parentheses:

> Consult the tables at the end of the report (i.e., the results for the experimental group [n = 5] are also listed in Figure 3, page 16.)

In addition, use brackets to present fractions:

$$\underline{a} = [(1 + \underline{b})/\underline{x}]^{1/2}$$

To present fractions in a line of text, use a slash mark (/) and parentheses first ( ), then brackets [( )], and finally braces {[( )]}.

Colon

Use colons to introduce a list of examples or an elaboration of what has been said in the first clause. (For proper use of colons and semicolons within quotations, see page 324, and for usage within documentation see Chapter 17, page 390.) Skip only one space after the colon.

Common Proofreading Symbols

i	error in spelling (mestake) with correction in margin
lc	lowercase (misTake)
⌒	close up (mis take)
	delete and close up (missstake)
	delete and close up more than one letter (the mistakes and errors continue)
^	insert (mitake)
∾ (tr)	transpose elements (thier)
◯	material to be corrected or moved, with instructions in the margin, or material to be spelled out, (corp.)
caps or ≡	capitalize (Huck finn and Tom Sawyer)
¶	begin a paragraph
No¶	do not begin a paragraph
^	insert
	delete (a mistakes)
#	add space
⊙	add a period
	add a comma
	add a semicolon
	add an apostrophe or single closing quotation mark
	add a single opening quotation mark
	add double quotation marks
(bf)	change to boldface
stet	let stand as it is; ignore marks

Weathers reminds us of crucial differences in rhetorical profiles that no writer should forget: colloquial wording differs radically from formal wording and a plain texture of writing differs greatly from a rich texture.

Comma

Use commas between items listed in a series of three or more, including before the *and* and *or* that precedes the last item. For example:

> Reader (34), Scott (61), and Wellman (615-17) agree with Steinbeck on this point.

Never use a comma and a dash together. The comma follows a parenthesis if your text requires the comma:

> How should we order our lives, asks Thompson (22-23), when we face "hostility from every quarter"?

The comma goes inside single quotation marks as well as double quotation marks:

> Such irony is discovered in Smith's article, "The Sources of Franklin's 'The Ephemera,'" but not in most textual discussions.

Dash

Use dashes to set off special parts of the text that require emphasis. On a computer, use the character set, which will give you an unbroken line. Otherwise, type two hyphens with no blank space before or after, as shown here:

> Two issues--slow economic growth and public debt--may prevent an early recovery for the banking industry.

Exclamation Mark

Exclamation marks make an emotional ending to a sentence. They should be avoided in research writing. A forceful declarative sentence is preferable.

Hyphen

Use hyphens to divide the syllables of words. Both MLA style and APA style discourage division of words at the end of a line, preferring instead that you leave the lines short, if necessary, rather than divide a word.

If you must use hyphenation for full justification of the text, always double-check word division by consulting a dictionary. Do not hyphenate proper names. Avoid separating two letters at the end or beginning of a line (for example, use "depend-able," not "de-pendable").

When using hyphenated words, follow a few general rules.

- Do not hyphenate unless the hyphen serves a purpose: a water treatment program *but* a water-powered turbine.
- Compound adjectives that *precede* a noun usually need a hyphen, but those that follow do not: same-age children *but* children of the same age.

- When a common base serves two or more compound modifiers, omit the base on all except the last modifier but retain the hyphens on every modifier: right- and left-hand margins *and* 5-, 10-, and 15-minute segments.
- Write most words with prefixes as one word: overaggressive, midterm, antisocial, postwar. But there are exceptions: self-occupied, self-paced, self-protection, post-1980. Consult a dictionary regularly to resolve doubts on such narrow problems as anti-Reagan *but* antisocial.
- Use a hyphen between pairs of coequal nouns: scholar-athlete, trainer-coach.

Parentheses

Use parentheses to enclose words and numbers in your text in the following situations:

- In-text citations:
  Larson (23-25) and Mitchell (344-45) report. . . .
- Independent matter:
  The more recent findings (see Figure 6) show. . . .
- Headings for a series:
  The tests were (1) . . . (2) . . . and (3). . . .
- First use of an abbreviation:
  The test proved reaction time (RT) to be. . . .

Period

Use a period to signal the end of complete sentences of the text, endnotes, footnotes, and all bibliography entries. Use one space after a period; however, when periods are used between numbers to indicate related parts (e.g., 2.4 for act 2, scene 4), use no space. The period normally follows the parenthesis. (The period is placed within the parenthesis only when the parenthetical statement is a complete sentence, as in this instance.) See also Chapter 16 for explanation of the period in conjunction with ellipsis points.

Quotation Marks

Use quotation marks to enclose all direct quotations used as part of your text (except for long indented quotations, where the indentation signals the quotation). Quotations require proper handling to maintain the style of the original; they also require precise documentation (see Chapter 16).

In addition, use quotation marks around titles of articles, essays, short stories, short poems, songs, chapters of books, unpublished works, and episodes of radio and television programs.

Use quotation marks for words and phrases you purposely misuse, misspell, or use in a special sense:

> The "patrons" turned out to be criminals searching for a way to launder their money.

However, a language study requires underscoring or italics for all linguistic forms (letters, words, and phrases) that are subjects of discussion (for example, "The word *patron*"). Use quotation marks around parenthetical translations of words or phrases from another language:

Jose Donoso's El jardin de al lado "The Garden Next Door" dramatizes an artistic crisis that has ethical and political implications.

Use single quotation marks for definitions that appear without intervening punctuation (for example, *nosu* 'nose'). In other cases, use quotation marks for foreign phrases and sentences and single quotation marks for your translation/definition.

It was important to Bacon that the 1625 collection appear in France as "un oeuvre nouveau" 'a new work' (14:536).

Semicolon

Use a semicolon to join two distinct independent clauses:

Weathers reminds us of crucial differences in rhetorical profiles that no writer should forget; the writer who does forget may substitute colloquial wording where formal is appropriate or may use a plain texture where rich texture is needed.

Compare this use of the semicolon with the use of the colon on the earlier pages.

Roman Numerals

Use capital Roman numerals in titles of persons as appropriate (Elizabeth II) and major sections of an outline. Use lowercase Roman numerals to number the preliminary pages of a text or paper, as for a preface or introduction (iii, iv, v). Otherwise, use Arabic numerals (e.g., Vol. 5, Act 2, Ch. 17, Plate 21, 2 Sam. 2.1–8, or *Iliad* 2.121–30), *except* when writing for some instructors in history, philosophy, religion, music, art, and theater, in which case you may need to use Roman numerals (e.g., III, Act II, I Sam. ii.1–8, *Hamlet* I.ii.5–6).

Running Heads

Repeat your last name in the upper right corner of every page just in front of the page number (see the sample paper, Chapter 16). APA style differs, see Chapter 18.

Short Titles in the Text

Use abbreviated titles of books and articles mentioned often in the text after a first full reference. For example, after initially citing *Backgrounds to English as Language,* shorten the title to *Backgrounds* in the text, notes, and in-text citations, but not in the bibliography entry. Mention *The Epic of Gilgamesh* and thereafter use *Gilgamesh* (*Note:* Be certain to italicize it when referring to the work).

Slang

Avoid the use of slang. When using it in a language study, enclose in double quotation marks any words to which you direct attention. Words used as words, however, require underlining (see the following page).

Spacing

As a general rule, double-space the body of the paper, all indented quotations, and all reference entries. Footnotes, if used, should be single-spaced, but endnotes should be double-spaced. APA style (see Chapter 18) requires doublespacing after all headings and before and after indented quotes and figures.

Space after punctuation according to these stipulations:

- Use one space after commas, semicolons, and colons (see also "Capitalize after a Colon," page A-10).
- Use one space after punctuation marks at the end of sentences.
- Use one space after periods that separate parts of a reference citation (see page 391).
- Do not space before or after periods within abbreviations (i.e., e.g., a.m.)
- Use one space between the initials of personal names (M. C. Bone).
- Do not use a space before of after a hyphen (a three-part test) *but* use one space before and after a hyphen used as a minus sign (e.g., a − b + c) and one space before but none after a hyphen for a negative value (e.g., −3.25)
- Do not use a space before or after a dash (e.g., The evidence—interviews and statistics—was published).
- Do not use a space before and after a virgale (e.g., and/or).

Spelling

Spell accurately. Always use the computer to check spelling if the software is available. When in doubt, consult a dictionary. If the dictionary says a word may be spelled two ways, employ one way consistently (e.g., theater *or* theatre), unless the variant form occurs in quoted materials. Use American (as opposed to English) spelling throughout.

Statistical and Mathematical Copy

Use the simplest form of equation that can be made by ordinary mathematical calculation. If an equation cannot be reproduced entirely by keyboard, type what you can and fill in the rest with ink on the printout. As a general rule, keep equations on one line rather than two:

$(a + b)/(x + y)$

APA style requires quadruple line spacing above and below an equation.

Table of Contents

A table of contents is unnecessary for undergraduate research papers, but *do* write a table of contents for a graduate thesis or dissertation (see "Theses and Dissertations", immediately below).

Theses and Dissertations

The author of a thesis or dissertation must satisfy the requirements of the college's graduate program. Therefore, even though you may use MLA style or APA style, you must abide by certain additional rules with regard to paper, typing, margins, and introductory matter such as title page, approval page, acknowledgment page, table of contents, abstract, and other matters. Use both the graduate school guidelines and this book to maintain the appropriate style and format.

Titles within Titles

For a book title that includes another title indicated by quotation marks, retain the quotation marks.

> <u>O. Henry's Irony in "The Gift of the Magi"</u>

For an article title within quotation marks that includes a book title, as indicated by underlining, retain the underlining or use italic lettering.

> "<u>Great Expectations</u> as a Novel of Initiation"

For an article title within quotation marks that includes another title indicated by quotation marks, enclose the internal title within single quotation marks.

> "A Reading of O. Henry's 'The Gift of the Magi' "

For an underscored book title that incorporates another title that is normally underscored, do not underscore or italicize the internal title nor place it within quotation marks.

> *Interpretations* of Great Expectations
> <u>Using Shakespeare's</u> Romeo and Juliet <u>in the Classroom</u>

Typing

Submit the paper in typed 12-point form, although some instructors will accept handwritten manuscripts if they are neat, legible, and written in blue or black ink on ruled paper. Print on only on one side of the page. In addition to the Courier font (traditional with typewriters), you may use clear, legible typefaces supported by computer software (Helvetica, Times Roman, Bodini, and others). Use no hyphens at the ends of lines. Avoid widows and orphans, which are single lines at the top of a page and single words at the bottom of a paragraph, respectively; some computers will help you correct this problem. Use special features—boldface, italics, graphs, color—with discretion. Your writing, not your graphics, will earn the credits and the better grades. You are ultimately responsible for correct pagination and accuracy of the manuscript. See also "Revising, Proofreading, and Formatting the Rough Draft," Chapter 16.

Underscoring (Italicizing)

Titles

Use italic type or underscoring for titles of the following types of works:

Type of work	Example
book	*A Quaker Book of Wisdom*
bulletin	*Production Memo 3*
drama	*Desire under the Elms*
film	*Treasure of the Sierra Madre*
journal	*Journal of Sociology*
magazine	*Newsweek*
newspaper	*Boston Globe*
novel	*Band of Angels*
poem (book-length)	*Idylls of the King*
short novel	*Billy Budd*
television program title	*Tonight Show*

If separately published, underline the titles of essays, lectures, poems, proceedings, reports, sermons, and stories.

Do not underscore sacred writings (Genesis, Old Testament); series (The New American Nation Series); editions (Variorum Edition of W. B. Yeats); societies (Victorian Society); courses (Greek Mythology); divisions of a work (preface, appendix, canto 3, scene 2); or descriptive phrases (Nixon's farewell address or Reagan's White House years).

Underscoring Individual Words for Emphasis

Italicizing words for emphasis is discouraged. A better alternative is to position the word in such a way as to accomplish the same purpose. For example:

Graphical emphasis: Perhaps an answer lies in preventing abuse, not in makeshift remedies after the fact.

Linguistic emphasis: Prevention of abuse is a better answer than makeshift remedies after the fact.

Some special words and symbols require underlining.

- Species, genera, and varieties:

  Penstemon caespitosus subsp. thompsoniae

- Letters, words, and phrases cited as a linguistic sample:

  the letter e in the word let

- Letters used as statistical symbols and algebraic variables:

  trial n of the t test or C(3, 14) = 9.432

Word Division

Avoid dividing any word at the end of a line. Leave the line short rather than divide a word (see "Hyphens").

APPENDIX B

Finding Reference Works for Your General Topic

We have tried to make this list as user-friendly as possible, which will enable you to select rather quickly a few basic references from one of nine general categories. Three of four items from a list will be more than sufficient to launch your investigation. Each category has two lists:

1. *Library reference books and electronic databases*. The books will require you to make a trip to the library, but the academic databases can be accessed anywhere by logging into your library's network—from your dorm room, computer lab, or at the library itself.
2. *Reputable Internet sources accessed by a browser,* such as Google, Lycos, AltaVista, and others—as listed on pages 167–168.

Remember, too, that the library gives you an electronic catalog to all books in the library as well as access to general-interest databases, such as:

InfoTrac
FirstSearch
NewsBank
Lexis-Nexis Academic
netLibrary
Online Books Page
Oxford Reference Online

Here are the nine sections and the page number that begins each:

1. Historic Issues of Events, People, and Artifacts, page B-28
2. Scientific Issues in Physics, Astronomy, and Engineering, page B-29
3. Issues of Health, Fitness, and Athletics, page B-30
4. Social and Political Issues, page B-32
5. Issues in the Arts, Literature, Music, and Language, page B-35
6. Environmental Issues, Genetics, and the Earth Sciences, page B-38
7. Issues in Communication and Information Technology, page B-39
8. Issues in Religion, Philosophy, Psychology, page B-41
9. Issues in Business and Economics, page B-43

By no means are the nine lists definitive, but one of them should serve as your launching pad at the beginning of the project. These works will carry you deeper and deeper toward specific material for collecting your summaries, paraphrases, and quotations.

Historic Issues of Events, People, and Artifacts

If you are interested in events of the past, classical architecture, famous people, and ancient artifacts, you need sources in history, biography, art history, architecture, anthropology, and similar sources. Listed below are important reference works in the library and on the Internet that can launch your investigation.

At the library, investigate these books and academic databases:

Abstracts in Anthropology. Farmingdale: Baywood, 1970–date. This reference book gives brief descriptions of thousands of articles on the cultural development of human history.

America: History and Life. This database gives you access to thousands of articles in history and the life of the nation.

American National Biography. 24 vols. New York: Oxford, 1999. This set of books is the place to start for a study of most historical figures in American history.

Anthropological Literature. Pleasantville: Redgrave, 1979–date. This reference book contains an excellent index to scholarly articles in all aspects of anthropological research.

Dictionary of American History. 3rd ed. 10 vols. New York: Scribner's, 2003. This set of books offers a well-documented, scholarly source on the people, places, and events in U.S. history and includes brief bibliographies to recommended sources.

Encyclopaedia Britannica. This database to the famous encyclopedia provides an ideal platform from which to launch your investigation.

Historical Abstracts. Santa Barbara, CA: ABC-CLIO, 1955–date. This set of printed abstracts provides a quick overview of historical issues and events worldwide.

Illustrated Encyclopedia of Mankind. 22 vols. Freeport, NY: Marshall Cavendish, 1989. This massive work has been a standard in the field for some time.

JSTOR. This database provides electronic images of historical documents and significant articles on a wide range of historical topics.

Lexis-Nexis Primary Sources in U.S. History. This academic database is wide-ranging and gives, for example, excellent sources on American women's studies.

Recently Published Articles. Washington: American Historical Association, 1976–date. These printed volumes provide an effective index to articles in *American Historical Review, Journal of American History, Journal of the West,* and many others.

World History FullTEXT. As the title indicates, this database provides full-text versions of documents and articles in world history.

On the Internet, investigate these sites:

Annual Reviews: Anthropology, at <http://anthro.AnnualReviews.org>This Web site provides a search engine for locating reviews of books and articles on hundreds of topics.

Anthropology Internet Resources, at <http://www.wcsu.edu/socialsci/antres.html> Western

Connecticut State University maintains this excellent academic site.

Archiving Early America, at <http://earlyamerica.com> This Internet site displays eighteenth-century documents in their original form for reading and downloading, such as the Bill of Rights and the speeches of Washington, Paine, Jefferson, and others.

History Best Information on the Net (BIOTN), at <http://library.sau.edu/bestinfo/Majors/History/hisindex.htm> This Internet site covers American history, ancient and medieval history, church and Christian history, and European history, and features sections devoted to historical documents, images, maps, and events.

Scientific Issues in Physics, Astronomy, and Engineering

If you are interested in the heavens (the stars, moon, and planets), the laws of supersonic flight, nuclear energy, plasma television screens, and similar topics, you need to begin your investigation with some of the reference works listed below, which you will find in the library and on the Internet.

At the library, investigate these books and academic databases:

American Chemical Society Publications (ACS). This database offers searchable access to online archives of chemistry journals dating back to 1879.

Astronomy Encyclopedia. Ed. Patrick Moore. New York: Oxford UP, 2002. This source suggests possible topic ideas for research in the field; good starting point for students.

Applied Science and Technology Index. New York: Wilson, 1958–date. This major reference work indexes recent articles in all areas of the applied sciences, engineering, and technology.

The Chronological Encyclopedia of Discoveries in Space. Ed. Robert Zimmerman. Westport, CT: Greenwood Press, 2000. This work gives an up-to-date guide to all of the important discoveries down through the ages.

Current Physics Index. New York: American Institute of Physics, 1975–date. This book indexes most articles in physics journals such as *Applied Physics, Journal of Chemical Physics, Nuclear Physics,* and *Physical Review*.

Encyclopedia of Technology and Applied Sciences. 11 vols. New York: Marshall Cavendish, 2000. This encyclopedia contains articles useful to the student new to technology.

Engineering Index. New York: Engineering Index Inc., 1884–date. This work is available in versions ranging from books to electronic databases; check the academic library to locate which version is available locally.

General Science Index. New York: Wilson, 1978–date. This index covers about 100 science periodicals, including many in the applied sciences.

Physics Abstracts. Surrey, England: Institute of Electrical Engineers, 1898-date. Using keywords, this reference helps you choose a topic and find abstracts to articles on that topic.

SPIN Web. SPIN (Searchable Physics Information Network), a database maintained by the American Institute of Physics, provides current indexing and abstracting of major American and Russian physics and astronomy journals.

On the Internet, investigate these sites:

American Astronomical Society, at <http://www.aas.org> The site presents the *Astrophysical Journal*, providing articles, reviews, educational information, and links to other astronomy Web sites.

Extrasolar Planets Encyclopaedia, at <http://cfa-www.harvard.edu/planets/> This site contains information on extrasolar planets and includes an overview of detection methods.

Hot Articles Directory, at <http://pubs.acs.org/hotartcl/index.html> Sponsored by the American Chemical Society, this source takes users to recent research of hot interest by reproducing articles from many chemical journals, such as *Chemical and Engineering News, Inorganic Chemistry*, and *Biochemistry*.

Internet Pilot to Physics, at <http://physics.hallym.ac.kr/education/TIPTOP/> This site maintains indexes and provides links to Internet articles listed by subject.

Mount Wilson Observatory, at <http://www.mtwilson.edu> This Web site takes users into the Mount Wilson Observatory for outstanding photography of the universe and for online journals, documents, agencies, and activities in astronomical science.

National Academy of Sciences, at <http://www.nas.edu> This site combines the resources of the National Academy of Engineering, the Institute of Medicine, and the National Research Council; it focuses on math and science education and has links to scientific societies.

PhysicsWeb, at <http://physicsweb.org/resources/search/phtml> This site provides an excellent search engine that links you to Internet sites in physics by organizations, country, and field of interest.

Issues of Health, Fitness, and Athletics

If you have an interest in sports medicine, jogging, dieting, good health, nutrition, and similar topics, you should begin your investigation with some of the reference works listed below, which you will find in the library and on the Internet.

At the library, investigate these books and academic databases:

Atlas of Human Anatomy. 3rd ed. Frank H. Netter. Teeterboro, NJ: ICON, 2003. This reference work contains wonderful illustrations of the human body, extensively labeled.

Black's Medical Dictionary. 39th ed. Lanham, MD: Barnes and Noble, 1999. This reference work is a standard resource in medicine.

Consumer Health and Nutrition Index. Phoenix: Oryx , 1985–date. This reference work contains an index, published quarterly, to sources for consumers and scholars.

Cumulated Index Medicus. Bethesda, MD: U.S. Department of Health and Human Services, 1959–date. This reference work is an essential starting point for most papers in medical science.

Cumulated Index to Nursing and Allied Health Literature. Glendale, CA: CINAHL, 1956–date. This reference work offers nursing students an index to *Cancer Nurse, Journal of Practical Nursing, Journal of Nursing Education*, and many more journals; may be listed as *CINAHL*.

Encyclopedia of the Human Body. Richard Walker. New York: DK, 2002. This reference work includes both bibliographical references and a useful index for students.

Encyclopedia of Human Nutrition. 3 vols. San Diego, CA: Academic, 1999. This reference work offers a good starting point for a paper on nutrition.

Health and Wellness. This health sciences and health care database lists citations and summaries of most articles and the entire text of some articles in journals, magazines, newspapers, pamphlets, and reference books.

Index Medicus. Bethesda, MD: U.S. National Library of Medicine, 1960–date. This reference work is a premier source of journal articles in the field of medicine; it is available as both book and electronic form.

Miller-Keane Encyclopedia and Dictionary of Medicine, Nursing, and Allied Health. 6th ed. Philadelphia: Saunders, 2003. This reference work offers practical applications as well as explanations of concepts and terminology. The reference is now offered in an electronic version also.

Physical Education Index. Cape Giradeau, MO: BenOak, 1978–date. This reference work indexes most topics in athletics, sports medicine, and athletics.

PubMed The public access gateway to MEDLINE, the National Library of Medicine's bibliographic database, which covers the fields of medicine, nursing, dentistry, veterinary medicine, the health care system, and the preclinical sciences.

On the Internet, investigate these sites:

Food Safety Web site, at <http://www.ces.ncsu.edu/depts/foodsci/agentinfo> Sponsored by the North Carolina Cooperative Extension Service, this site offers consumers and students information on food safety and links to other useful sites.

Global Health Network, at <http://www.pitt.edu/~super1/index.htm> This site gives users access to documents in public health as provided by scholars at the World Health Organization, NASA, the Pan-American Health Organization, and others; links to agencies, organizations, and health networks.

Healthfinder, at <http://www.healthfinder.gov> This site provides access to "reliable consumer health and human services information" online, including full-text publications, databases, Web sites, and libraries; contains links to over 550 other sites and some 500 full-text documents.

Medweb: Medical Libraries, at <http://www.medweb.emory.edu/MedWeb/> This site connects you with medical libraries and their storehouses of information. It also gives links to other health-related Web sites; sponsored by Emory University.

National Institutes of Health, at <http://www.nih.gov> This site leads the nation in medical research and provides substantive information on numerous topics from cancer and diabetes to malpractice and medical ethics as well as links to online journals for the most recent news in medical science.

PubMed, at <http://www.ncbi.nlm.nih.gov/PubMed> This site catalogs articles in journals and other periodicals, including many full-text articles.

SPORTQuest, at <http://www.sportquest.com> This site offers a searchable directory of links to thousands of selected sites dealing with eighty sports and related topics; some of the information is accessible only through paid subscriptions, but online offers links to free the site information about individual sports and their teams, history, rules, and events.

USDA Food and Nutrition Center, at <http://www.nal.usda.gov/fnic> This site connects readers to the vast nutrition-related resources of the National Agricultural Library.

Social and Political Issues

If you have an interest in social work at nursing homes, current events such as rap music or rave parties, congressional legislation on student loans, education, and the SAT examinations, gender issues, and similar topics, you should begin your investigation with some of the reference works listed below, which you will find in the library and on the Internet.

At the library, investigate these books and academic databases:

ABC: Pol Sci. Santa Barbara: ABC-CLIO, 1969–date. This reference work indexes the tables of contents of about 300 international journals in the original language.

CIAO (Columbia International Affairs Online). This database covers theory and research in international affairs from documents published from 1991 to the present.

CQ Researcher. This reference work provides access to a database containing documents covering hundreds of hot-topic issues such as abortion, child abuse, election reform, and civil liberties.

Education Abstracts. New York: Wilson, 1994. This reference work provides short descriptions of hundreds of articles.

Education Index. New York: Wilson, 1929–date. This reference work indexes articles in such journals as *Childhood Education, Comparative Education, Education Digest,* and *Journal of Educational Psychology.*

Encyclopedia of Sociology. Ed. Edgar F. Borgatta et al. 2nd ed. 5 vols. Detroit: Macmillan, 2000. This encyclopedia offers a starting point for research, giving you terms, issues, and theories to motivate your own ideas.

ERIC. ERIC (Educational Resources Information Center) is the premier national bibliographic database of education literature.

Facts on File World Political Almanac: From 1945 to the Present. Chris Cook and Whitney Walker. New York: Checkmark Books/Facts on File, 2001. This reference work examines current world political situations, issues, and statistics.

GPO. This reference work indexes the resources of the U.S. Government Printing Office; it corresponds to the print version, *Monthly Catalog of the Government Printing Office,* has a search engine, and provides links to more than 400,000 records.

Index to Legal Periodicals and Books. New York: Wilson, 1908–date. This reference work offers perspectives on laws that govern social and legal issues.

International Political Science Abstracts. Oslo: International Political Science Assn., 1951–date. This reference work provides comprehensive worldwide coverage of more than 600 periodicals, with abstracts in English.

JSTOR. This database provides electronic images of historical documents and significant articles on a wide range of historical topics.

NewsBank. NewsBank provides searchable full-text articles appearing in local publications.

Project MUSE. This database includes current issues of nearly 200 journals in the fields of literature and criticism, history, the visual and performing arts, cultural studies, education, political science, gender studies, economics, and others.

Public Affairs Information Service Bulletin (PAIS). New York: Public Affairs Information Service, 1915–date. This reference work provides an annual bulletin with bibliographies useful in all areas of the social sciences, including politics.

Social Sciences Index. New York: Wilson, 1974–date. This reference work provides a vital index to all aspects of topics in sociology, social work, education, political science, geography, and other fields.

Sociological Abstracts. San Diego: Sociological Abstracts, 1953–date. This reference work contains the key source for skimming sociology articles before going in search of the full article.

ViVa. This work provides a current bibliography of articles about women's and gender history, including related topics such as prostitution, witchcraft, housework, sexuality, birth control, infanticide, the family, gynecology, and masculinity.

Westlaw. This database contains federal and all state court cases and statutes (laws).

Women's Studies Index. Boston: Hall, 1989–date. This reference work offers an annual index considered by many librarians the best source for immediate information on women's issues.

Women's Studies Abstracts. Rush, NY: Rush, 1972–date. This reference work offers a quick overview of hundreds of articles and books on women's issues.

On the Internet, investigate these sites:

Bureau of the Census, at <http://www.census.gov> This site provides census data on geography, housing, and the population, and allows users to examine specific information about targeted counties.

Chronicle of Education, at <http://chronicle.merit.edu> This site contains "Academe This Week" from *The Chronicle of Education,* a weekly printed magazine about education on the undergraduate and graduate levels; a subscription is necessary to gain full access.

FedStats: One-Stop Shopping for Federal Statistics, at <http://www.fedstats.gov> This site provides access to official U.S. government statistical data and serves as a gateway to government agencies' Web pages where specific data can be found.

Feminist Theory Web site, at <http://www.cddc.vt.edu/feminism/> This site provides "research materials and information for students, activists, and scholars interested in women's conditions and struggles around the world."

Gallup Organization, at <http://www.gallup.com> One of the oldest, most trusted public opinion polling groups in the country provides data from opinion polls, indexed by subject, as well as information on polling methods.

Internet Legal Resources Guide, at <http://www.ilrg.com/> Designed for both legal professionals and laypersons, this site offers a categorized index of more than 4,000 select Web sites and thousands of locally stored Web pages, legal forms, and downloadable files.

Library of Congress, at <http://www.lcweb.loc.gov> This site provides the Library of Congress catalog online for books by author, subject, and title; also links to historical collections and research tools.

Online Educational Resources, at <http://quest.arc.nasa.gov/> This site provides an extensive list of educational articles and documents on everything from SAT scores to daycare programs.

Political Science Resources on the Web, at <http://www.lib.umich.edu/govdocs/polisci.html> This site contains a vast data file on government information—local, state, federal, foreign, and international; it is a good site for political theory and international relations, with links to dissertations, periodicals, reference sources, university courses, and other social science information.

Praxis, at <http://caster.ssw.upenn.edu/~restes/praxis.html> This site provides a massive collection of articles on socioeconomic topics, with links to other social science resources.

Thomas, at <http://thomas.loc.gov> This site gives access to congressional legislation and documents indexed by topic, by bill number, and by title. It also allows searches of the *Congressional Record*, the Constitution, and other government documents and links to the House, Senate, Government Printing Office, and General Accounting Office Sites.

United States Congress, at <http://www.congress.org> Designed to give citizens access to their elected officials through information bulletins and letters or e-mails, this site also has a section on the 2004 elections.

White House Web, at <http://www.whitehouse.gov> This site provides a graphical tour, messages from the president and vice president, and accounts of life at the White House. Visitors to this site can leave a message for the president in the guest book.

Issues in the Arts, Literature, Music, and Language

If you have an interest in Greek drama, the films of Mel Gibson, the postcolonial effects on languages in the Caribbean, the music of Andrew Lloyd Webber, the poetry of Dylan Thomas, and similar topics, you should begin your investigation with some of the reference works listed below, which you will find in the library and on the Internet.

At the library, investigate these books and academic databases:

Almanac of Architecture and Design. Ed. James P. Cramer. Norcross, GA: Greenway Group, 2001. This reference work provides a contemporary look at architectural and design issues.

Art Abstracts. New York: Wilson, 1994–date.This reference work provides brief summaries of thousands of articles by topic.

Art Index. New York: Wilson, 1929–date. This reference work indexes most art journals, including *American Art Journal, Art Bulletin*, and *Artforum*.

Avery Index to Architectural Periodicals. Boston: Hall, 1973–date. This reference work is a good source for periodical articles on ancient and modern edifices.

Bibliographic Guide to Art and Architecture. Boston: Hall, 1977–date. Published annually, this reference work provides bibliographies on most topics in art and architecture—an excellent place to begin research in this area.

Bibliographic Guide to Music. Boston: Hall, 1976–date. This reference work provides an excellent subject index to almost every topic in the field of music and gives the bibliographic data for several articles on most topics in the field.

Books in Print. This database includes current information on over 1.9 million books available for purchase from publishers, plus some out-of-print listings.

Contemporary Authors. Detroit: Gale, 1962–date. This reference work consists of excellent biographies and critical overviews on most major authors; updated articles on some authors provides currency.

Contemporary Literary Criticism (CLC). This database provides an extensive collection of full-text critical essays about novelists, poets, playwrights, short story writers, and other creative writers who are now living or who died after December 31, 1959.

Dictionary of Literary Biography. Detroit: Gale, 1978–date (in progress). Comprising more than 130 volumes, this excellent, well-documented encyclopedia is the best source for background information and selected bibliographies on individual authors.

Drama Criticism. 9 vols. Ed. Lawrence Trudeau. Detroit: Gale, 1991–date. This reference work provides a thorough and current look at criticism.

The Drama Handbook: A Guide to Reading Plays. John Lannard and Mary Luckhurst. New York: Oxford UP, 2002. With useful bibliographical references, this reference work provides help for student and professional scholar alike.

Essay and General Literature Index. New York: Wilson, 1900–date. This reference work is the best source for finding individual essays buried within a book's contents.

Grove Dictionary of Music. This reference work is a comprehensive online music encyclopedia that includes over 29,000 articles.

Humanities Index. New York: Wilson, 1974–date. This reference work indexes all of the major literary magazines and journals; it may be listed as *Wilson Humanities Index*.

LION. The LION database includes full-text poems and dramatic and prose works, literary encyclopedias and dictionaries, author biographies, and other sources related to literature and literary criticism.

LitFINDER. This database includes the full text of many poems and author biographies, thousands of full-text short stories plus explanations and biographies, and a database of full-text essays on the humanities and social sciences.

MLA International Bibliography of Books and Articles on the Modern Languages and Literatures. New York: MLA, 1921–date. This reference work indexes major literary figures, literary issues, and language topics; it may be listed on the library's network as *MLA Bibliography*.

Music Article Guide. Philadelphia: Information Services, 1966–date. This reference work indexes music education and instrumentation in such journals as *Brass and Wind News, Keyboard, Flute Journal,* and *Piano Quarterly*.

Music Index. Warren, MI: Information Coordinators, 1949–date. This reference work indexes music journals such as *American Music Teacher, Choral Journal, Journal of Band Research,* and *Journal of Music Therapy*.

Oxford Companion to Music. Ed. Alison Latham. Rev. ed. Oxford: Oxford UP, 2002. This reference work is a basic guide to the world of music and the topics and issues that provoke the greatest interest among scholars.

Oxford English Dictionary. 2nd ed. Ed. J. A. Simpson et al. 20 vols. New York: Oxford UP, 1989. This reference work is the definitive dictionary for language students.

Yale Dictionary of Art and Artists. Ed. E. Langmuir and N. Lynton. New Haven: Yale UP, 2000. This reference work provides a beginning point for research in art because it introduces the basic theories and key figures.

On the Internet, investigate these sites:

The Art History Research Centre, at <http://art-history.concordia.ca/AHRC/splash.htm> This site provides well-selected links to search engines, library catalogs, periodical indexes, online art collections, and other Web resources.

Brief Guide to Theatre and Performance Studies, Stetson University, at <http://www.stetson.edu/departments/csata/thr_guid.html> This site contains a useful collection of theater information for the scholar with many links to other such resources.

Electronic Literature Directory, at <http://directory.wordcircuits.com/browse.php?let=T&rectype=publishers> This site, sponsored by Syracuse University; provides a directory, with links, to specific pieces of literature, many of them new electronic examples.

Electronic Text Center, at <http://etext.lib.virginia.edu> Provides the full-text version of a vast collection of literature.

The English Server, at <http://eserver.org/> This site provides academic resources in the humanities, including rhetoric, drama, fiction, film, music, television, and history.

Great Books Online, at <http://www.bartleby.com/> This easily navigated site gives students and researchers access to books of literature, reference, and verse, such as Strunk's *Elements of Style*.

The Internet Movie Database, at <http://www. us.imdb.com> This is an especially useful searchable site with links to national and international film reviews as well as comprehensive information on thousands of films.

Musicals in the Ithaca College Library, at <http://www.ithaca.edu/library/music/music_bibliographies.html> This site provides links to bibliographies on scores and librettos.

Netlibrary, at <http://www.netlibrary.com> This site provides a vast collection of full-text stories, poems, novels, and dramas; search by title or author and then read the text online or print it out; one must create a membership account.

Project Gutenberg, at <http://promo.net/pg> This site provides literary texts in the public domain that can be downloaded via FTP and that are divided into three divisions: light literature such as fables, heavy literature such as *The Scarlet Letter*, and reference works.

Voice of the Shuttle: Art and Art History, at <http://vos.ucsb.edu/> This site offers hundreds of links to major online resources including artists, museums and their collections, and other art history Web sites.

World Wide Arts Resources, at <http:/wwar.world-arts-resources.com> This site provides an artist index as well as an index to exhibits, festivals, meetings, and performances.

Worldwide Internet Music Resources, at <http://theme.music.indiana.edu/music_resources/> Sponsored by the Indiana School of Music and Music Library, this site links you to musical concepts, composers, and groups.

Environmental Issues, Genetics, and the Earth Sciences

If you have an interest in cloning, abortion, the shrinking rain forest in Brazil, sinkholes in Florida, the Flint Hills grassland of Kansas, underground water tables in Texas, and similar topics, you should begin your investigation with some of the reference works listed below, which you will find in the library and on the Internet.

At the library, investigate these books and academic databases:

AGRICOLA. This database, produced by the National Agricultural Library, provides access to articles, books, and Web sites in agriculture, animal and plant sciences, forestry, and soil and water resources.

Bibliography and Index of Geology. Alexandria, VA: American Geological Institute, 1933–date. Organized monthly, with annual indexes, this reference work indexes excellent scholarly articles.

Biological and Agricultural Index. New York: H.W Wilson. 1916–date. This reference work is a standard index to periodicals in the field.

Biological Abstracts. Philadelphia: Biosis, 1926–date. This reference work contains abstracts useful to review before locating the full articles at the library's computer.

BioOne. This database provides access to scientific research focused on the biological, ecological, and environmental sciences.

Ecological Abstracts. Norwich, UK: Geo Abstracts, 1974–date. This reference work offers a chance to examine the brief abstract before finding and reading the complete article.

Environment Abstracts Annual. New York: Bowker, 1970–date. This reference work provides abstracts to major articles in the field.

The Environmental Index. Ann Arbor, MI: UMI, 1992–date. This reference work indexes numerous journals in the field, including *Environment, Environmental Ethics,* and *Journal of Applied Ecology*.

Geographical Abstracts. Norwich, UK: Geo Abstracts, 1972–date. This reference work provides a quick overview of articles that can be searched for full text later.

GeoRef. The GeoRef database includes the American Geological Institute's geoscience archive of over 1.9 million records of North American geology since 1785 and other areas of the world since 1933.

Grzimek's Animal Life Encyclopedia. 2nd ed. 17 vols. Bernhard Grzimek. Detroit: Thomson/Gale, 2003. This reference work provides extensive resources for the student plus bibliographies leading to additional resources.

Henderson's Dictionary of Biological Terms. Ed. Eleanor Lawrence. 12th ed. New York: Prentice Hall, 2000. This reference work provides terminology and precise meanings in the field.

Publications of the Geological Survey. Washington, DC: GPO, 1985–date. This reference work is kept up to date with regular supplements.

World Resources. Oxford: Oxford UP, 1986–date. This reference work contains chapters on conditions and trends in the environment worldwide. Also provides statistical tables.

On the Internet, investigate these sites:

The Academy of Natural Sciences, at <http://www.acnatsci.org/library/link.html> This site links the researcher to hundreds of articles and resource materials on issues and topics in the natural sciences.

Agricola, at <http://www.nalusda.gov/ag98> Created by the National Agricultural Library and including some links to full-text version of the materials, this site is a good starting point for the student researcher.

BioOnline, at <http://www.bio.com/os/start/home.html> This site features articles and research news; it is a good spot for searching out a research topic.

BIOSIS, at < http://www.biosis.org/> This site provides searchable databases in biology and life sciences, including *Biological Abstracts, Zoological Record,* and *Basic BIOSIS,* a life science database for students new to research.

The Core Historical Literature of Agriculture, at <http://chla.library.cornell.edu/frontpage.html> This site contains a collection of full-text nineteenth- and twentieth-century agricultural materials on agricultural economics, agricultural engineering, animal science, crops and their protection, food science, forestry, human nutrition, rural sociology, and soil science, selected by scholars in the field.

Discovery Channel Online, at <http://www.discovery.com> This site offers an online version of television's Discovery Channel and features a keyword search engine.

Envirolink, at <http://envirolink.org> This site offers a search engine that allows access to environmental articles, photographs, action alerts, organizations, and additional Web sources.

The Virtual Library of Ecology and Biodiversity, at <http://conbio.net/VL/welcome.cfm> Sponsored by the Center for Conservation Biology, this site consists primarily of an index of links to other Web sites in categories such as endangered species, global sustainability, and pollution.

West's Geology Directory, at <http://www.soton.ac.uk/~imw> This site provides an index to over 200 Web pages devoted to geology. Its massive directory has direct links to geological field guides and bibliographies.

Issues in Communication and Information Technology

If you have an interest in talk radio, television programming for children, bias in print journalism, developing computer software, the glut of cell phones, and similar topics, you should begin your investigation with some of the reference works listed below, which you will find in the library and on the Internet.

At the library, investigate these books and academic databases:

Computer Abstracts. London: Technical Information, 1957–date. This work provides short descriptions of important articles in the field.

Computer Literature Index. Phoenix: ACR, 1971–date. This index identifies articles on computer science in a timely fashion, with periodic updates.

Encyclopedia of Computer Science and Technology. Ed. J. Belzer. 22 vols. New York: Dekker, 1975–91. Supplement 1991–date. This reference work provides a comprehensive source for launching computer investigations.

Information Technology Research, Innovation, and E-Government. Washington, DC: National Press Academy, 2002. This site focuses on the use of the Internet in government administration.

The Elements of Style. William Strunk, Jr., and E. B. White. Boston: Allyn and Bacon, 1999. A classic book that teaches and exhorts writers to avoid needless words, urges them to use the active voice, and calls for simplicity in style.

On Writing Well. 25th anniversary ed. William K. Zinsser. New York: HarperResource, 2001. This book is a well-written text on the art of writing, especially on the best elements of nonfiction prose.

Style: Ten Lessons in Clarity and Grace. 7th ed. Joseph M. Williams. New York: Longman, 2003. This book provides an excellent discussion of writing style and the means to attain it.

On the Internet, investigate these sites:

AJR Newslink, at <http://newslink.org/menu.html> This site provides links to newspapers (including campus publications), television stations, and radio stations worldwide; not all links on the site are active, but it still merits attention by students.

American Communications Association: Communication Studies Center, at http://www.uark.edu/~aca/acastudiescenter.html> The parent site of the site listed next; it provides resources in business communication, communication education technologies, gender and communication, language and linguistics, and mass media and culture.

Communication Institute for Online Scholarship, at <http://www.cios.org/> Though the site requires either a library subscription or individual membership, it provides a good source for resources in the field of communications; check if your local library subscribes already.

Computer Science, at <http://library.albany.edu/subject/csci.htm> A good starting point for the student, this site provides numerous links to resources in the discipline.

The First Amendment Center, at <http://www.firstamendmentcenter.org/default.aspx> This site features comprehensive research coverage of key First Amendment issues and topics, a unique First Amendment Library, and guest analyses by respected legal specialists.

Information Technology Association of America, at <http://www.itaa.org/index.cfm> This site contains information and resources encompassing computers, software, telecommunications products and services, Internet and online services, systems integration, and professional services companies.

Internet Resources for Technical Communicators, at <http://www.soltys.ca/techcomm.html> This site offers links to Internet resources for technical writers and communicators.

Journalism and Mass Communication Resources on the Web, at <http:/www.lib.iastate.edu/collections/eresourc/journalism.html> This site takes users to resources and Web sites on associations, book reviews, bibliographies, libraries, media, information science programs, and departments of communication in various universities.

Newspapers.com, at <http://www.newspapers.com/> This site provides a comprehensive portal site for U.S. city and campus newspapers.

Technical Communication Online, at <http://www.techcommonline.org/> This site serves as the official Web site for the *Journal of the Society for Technical Communication,* with searchable articles and other information for researchers as well as links to related sites.

Virtual Computer Library, at <http://www.utexas.edu/computer/vcl/> This site gives access to academic computing centers at the major universities as well as an index of books, articles, and bibliographies.

Writing Research Papers, at <http://www.ablongman.com/lester> This site accompanies the eleventh edition of this textbook. Cross-reference icons throughout the text carry the user to the Web for a wealth of information on research and research writing.

Issues in Religion, Philosophy, Psychology

If you have an interest in human values, moral self-discipline, the ethics of religious wars, the power of religious cults, the behavior of children with single parents, the effect of the environment on personality, and similar topics, you should begin your investigation with some of the reference works listed below, which you will find in the library and on the Internet.

At the library, investigate these books and academic databases:

Cambridge Dictionary of Philosophy. 2nd ed. Ed. R. Audi. New York: Cambridge, 1999. This reference work provides an excellent base for launching your investigation into philosophical issues.

Encyclopedia of Psychology. Ed. Alan E. Kazdin. 8 vols. New York: Oxford, 2000. This reference work contains the most comprehensive basic reference work in the field; published under the auspices of the American Psychological Association.

Humanities Index. New York: Wilson, 1974–date. This reference work indexes religious journals such as *Church History, Harvard*

Theological Review, and *Muslim World.*

Mental Measurements Yearbook (MMY). This database contains information on all English-language standardized tests covering educational skills, personality, vocational aptitude, psychology, and related areas.

Philosopher's Index: A Retrospective Index. Bowling Green, OH: Bowling Green U, 1967-date. This reference work indexes philosophy articles in journals such as *American Philosophical Quarterly, Humanist, Journal of the History of Ideas, and Journal of Philosophy.*

Psychological Abstracts. Washington, DC: APA, 1927–date. This reference work provides brief abstracts to articles in such psychology journals as *American Journal of Psychology, Behavioral Science, and Psychological Review.* On the library's network, look for *PsycINFO.*

Religion: Index One: Periodicals, Religion and Theological Abstracts. Chicago: ATLA, 1949–date. This reference work indexes religious articles in such journals as *Biblical Research, Christian Scholar, Commonweal,* and *Harvard Theological Review.*

Routledge Encyclopedia of Philosophy. 10 vols. Ed. E. Craig. New York: Routledge, 1999. This work is the most comprehensive, authoritative, and up-to-date reference work in the field. A condensed version is available in some libraries.

Who's Who in Religion. Chicago: Marquis, 1975–date. This reference work provides a compendium of the most notable people in religious issues.

On the Internet, investigate these sites:

The American Philosophical Association, at <http://www.amphilsoc.org/> This site provides articles, bibliographies, software, a bulletin board, a gopher server, and links to other philosophical sites containing college courses, journals, texts, and newsletters.

Episteme Links: Philosophy Resources on the Internet, at <http://www.epistemelinks.com/> This site offers links to sites containing philosophical topics, traditions, and time periods as well as biographies, full-text works, individual philosophers, movements, and works.

Humanities: Religion Gateway, at <http://www.academicinfo.net/religindex.html> This site provides references and resources to all religions and religious studies.

PscyINFO. This database includes citations and summaries of journal articles, book chapters, and books covering psychological aspects in medicine, psychiatry, nursing, sociology, education, and related fields.

PscyREF: Resources in Psychologoy on the Internet, at <http://maple.lemonyne.edu/~hevern/psychref.html> This database is an index to research in psychology, academic skill development, and academic advisement issues such as graduate school and career planning.

Vanderbilt Divinity School, at <http://divinity.library.vanderbilt.edu/lib/> This site gives references to and interpretations of the Bible, links to other religious Web sites, and online journals, such as *Biblical Archaeologist.*

Issues in Business and Economics

If you wish to write about the impact of rising tuition costs, the effect of credit cards for college students, the marketing success of Wal-Mart stores, the economic impact of federal tax cuts, the stock market's effect on accounting practices, and similar topics, you should begin your investigation with some of the reference works listed below, which you will find in the library and on the Internet.

At the library, investigate these books and academic databases:

Business Abstracts. New York: Wilson, 1995–date. This reference work provides short descriptions of business, economic, and marketing articles.

Business Periodicals Index. New York: Wilson, 1958–date. This reference work indexes most journals in the field, such as *Business Quarterly, Business Week, Fortune,* and *Journal of Business*. See also on the library's network *Reference USA, Business Dateline,* and *Business and Company*.

Business Publications Index and Abstracts. Detroit: Gale, 1983–date. This reference work provides a place to launch searches on almost any topic related to business.

General Business File. This database lists citations and summaries of articles and the entire text of some articles in business, management, and economic periodicals.

Index of Economic Articles. Nashville: American Economic Association, 1886–date. This reference work, arranged as both a topic and an author index, provides a good start for the student and professional alike.

Journal of Economic Literature. Nashville: American Economic Association, 1886–date. This reference work offers articles followed by bibliographies for further research.

World Economic Survey. 1945–date. An annual publication originally from the League of Nations and currently from the United Nations, this reference work offers varying topics each year to researchers.

On the Internet, investigate these sites:

All Business Network, at <http://www.all-biz.com> This site provides a search engine to businesses with relevant information for newsletters, organizations, news groups, and magazines.

Finance: The World Wide Web Virtual Library, at <http://www.cob.ohiostate.edu/dept/fin/overview.html> This site links users to hundreds of articles and resource materials on banks, insurers, market news, jobs, and miscellaneous data.

FinWeb, at <http://www.finweb.com> This site provides substantive information concerning economics and finance topics.

International Resources in Business Economics, at <http://www.lib.berkeley.edu/BUSI/bbg18.html> This site contains a good selection of research guides and links to other useful sources of economic information. It serves primarily students and faculty at business schools, with a search engine that finds news, business journals, career opportunities in accounting, banking, finance, marketing, and other related fields.

Credits

Ch 3 pages 43–44 From "Drug Education," an article on the United States Olympic Committee Web site, http://www.usoc.org. Reprinted by permission. **Ch 3 Fig 3.5 page 47** Homepage of *Larchmont Chronicle*, www.larchmontchronicle.com. Used by permission. **Ch 3 Fig 3.6 page 52** Book search results for "Fad Dieting" from Barnes & Noble.com. Reprinted by permission of Barnes & Noble (www.bn.com). **Ch 3 Fig 3.7 page 54** Red Earth "homepage" from http://www.redearth.org/museum.htm. Copyright © Red Earth, Inc., 2000. Reprinted by permission. **Ch 4 Fig 4.1 page 61** Entry "Prehistoric War" from *Bibliographic Index, 2003*. Copyright © 2003 by H. W. Wilson Company. Reprinted by permission. **Ch 4 Fig 4.2 page 62** Entry "Heinrich, Richard" from *Subject Guide to Books In Print 2003–2004*, p. 4543. Copyright © 2003 by R. R. Bowker, LLC. Reprinted by permission. **Ch 4 Fig 4.3 page 63** Sample bibliography from the end of an article in *Encyclopedia of Psychology*, Second Edition, Vol. 1, p. 287, edited by Raymond J. Corsini. Reprinted by permission of John Wiley & Sons, Inc. **Ch 4 Fig 4.4 page 64** From *Out of the Storm: The End of the Civil War* by Noah Andre Trudeau. Copyright © 1994 by Noah Andre Trudeau. Reprinted by permission of Little, Brown, and Company. **Ch 4 Fig 4.5 page 65** From "Closing the School Gap" by William C. Symonds, *Business Week*, October 14, 2002. New York, New York: McGraw-Hill Companies, 2002. As seen on InfoTrac, college edition. Farmington Hills, Michigan: Gale Group, 2002. **Ch 4 Fig 4.6 page 68** From *PsycINFO*. Reprinted with permission of the American Psychological Association, publisher of the *PsycINFO Database*, all rights reserved. May not be reproduced without prior permission. **Ch 4 Fig 4.7 page 69** From *Dissertation Abstracts International,* Vol. 59, No. 12, June 1999. Reprinted by permission of ProQuest Digital Dissertations. **Ch 4 Fig 4.8 page 70** Abstract, "Constructions of Power in Thomas Hardy's Major Novels" by Kristin Johansen, from *Dissertation Abstracts International*, Vol. 59, No. 12, June 1999. Reprinted by permission of ProQuest Digital Dissertations. **Ch 4 Fig 4.9 page 71** From sample entry, "Clinton, Hillary Rodham," *Biography Index*, May 2000, p. 22. © 2000 by the H. W. Wilson Company. Reproduced by permission of the publisher. **Ch 4 Fig 4.10 page 73** From *CQ Researcher,* March 3, 2000, p. 181. Reprinted by permission of Congressional Quarterly, Inc. **Ch 5 Fig 5.1 page 82** From "Demographics & Statistics: Clarksville-Montgomery County, Tennessee" from Clarksville-Montgomery County Web site. Copyright © 2001. Used by permission. **Ch 7 pages 105–106** From "Writing the Autobiography of My Father," a review by Curdella Forbes in *Small Axe*, No. 13, Vol. 7, Issue 1, March 2003, pp. 172–176. Reprinted by permission of Indiana University Press. **Ch 7 Fig 7.1 pages 113–114** "Voice: The tide is rising and the world is coming to your front door," Ray Dasmann as interviewed by David Kupfer, from *Earth Island Journal,* 18, 2003. Used by permission of the author. **Ch 7 pages 114–115** Excerpts from *Oscar Wilde* by Richard Ellman. Vintage Books, 1988. Reprinted by permission of Alfred A. Knopf, a division of Random House, Inc. **Ch 7 Fig 7.2 page 116** Reprinted with permission from *Issues in Science and Technology*. Screen shot from Issues in Science and Technology Online, David Western, "Conservation in a Human-Dominated World." Copyright © 2000 by the University of Texas at Dallas, Richardson, TX. **Ch 9 page 151** From "The Love Song of J. Alfred Prufrock" in *Collected Poems 1909–1962* by T. S. Eliot. Reprinted by permission of the publisher, Faber and Faber Limited. **Ch 10 Figs 10.1, 10.2, 10.3 pages 172–174** Keats photo courtesy of Bettman/CORBIS. Grecian Urn photo courtesy of Scala/Art Resource, NY. **Ch 11 Fig 11.1 page 183** Sample pages from JSTOR database, "Shakespeare's Conception of Hamlet" from *PMLA*, Vol. 48, No. 3, pp. 777–8. Reprinted by permission of the Modern Language Association. **Ch 11 page 182–183** From "Parenthood" by Karen S. Peterson, *USA Today,* September 19, 1990. Copyright © 1990 USA Today. Reprinted with permission. **Ch 11 page 185** "The Red Wheelbarrow" by William Carlos Williams from *Collected Poems: 1909–1939, Volume 1.* Copyright 1938 by New Directions Publishing Corp. Reprinted by permission of New Directions Publishing Corp. **Ch 11 page 194** From "Morning Song" from *Ariel* by Sylvia Plath. Copyright © 1961 by Ted Hughes. Reprinted by permission of HarperCollins Publishers Inc. and by Faber and Faber Limited. **Ch 13 Fig 13.3 page 243** "The World's Renewable Water Supply" from *Atlas of World Water Balance.* Copyright © 1977 by UNESCO. Reproduced by permission of UNESCO. **Appendix Fig A-3** Line graph from "Cognitive Aspects of Psychomotor Performance" by Edwin A. Locke and Judith F. Bryan from *Journal of Applied Psychology*, Vol. 50, 1966. Copyright © 1966 by the American Psychological Association. Reprinted by permission of the author. **Appendix Fig A-4** Sample illustration: "Phonemes of Language" from "Pattern in English" by Anna H. Live from *The Journal of General Education,* Vol. 18, July 1996 by Penn State Press. Reprinted by permission. **Appendix Fig A-5** Chart from Carmen J. Finley, Jack M. Thompson, and Alberta Cognata, "Stability of the California Short Form Tests of Mental Maturity: Grades 3, 5, and 7," *California Journal of Educational Research* 17 (September 1966), 165. Reprinted by permission of the Educational Research Quarterly. **Appendix Fig A-6** Table: "Inhibitory Effects of Sugars . . . " from "Toxicity of Clostridium Histoylticum" by Nishida and Imaizumi, *Journal of Bacteriology*, Vol. 91, February 1966. Reprinted by permission of the American Society for Microbiology.

Index

Note: Page numbers followed by the letters *f* and *t* indicate figures and tables, respectively. **Bo** page numbers indicate main discussions.

Abbreviations
  of biblical works, A5–A6
  for literary works, A6
  numbers with, A8
  of publishers' names, A5
  for technical terms and institutions, A3
  use of, A3
Abstracts
  in APA style, **458–459**
  of articles, 246
  bibliographic entries for
    in APA style, 448–449, 452, 459
    in MLA style, 405-406, 415, 425
  definition of, 201
  to dissertations, 202–203
  indexes to, 201
  in long proposal, 161
  in MLA style, 358–359
  online, 167
  using précis notes for, 290–291
Academic citations, 226
Academic disciplines, providing questions, 150–151
Academic models. *See* Paradigms
Accent marks, A7
Acknowledgments, 484–485, A7
Address (speech), bibliographic entries for, 410
Addresses, Internet, 170–173
Advertisements, bibliographic entries for, 412, 415, 427
"Affirmative Action Is Driving Us Apart" (Chavez), 574
Afterword, in MLA bibliography, 398–399
Albacete, Lorenzo, 105
"All Go Down Together" (Traub), 28
Alphabetization, letter-by-letter, 384–385
Alphabetized works, bibliographic entries for, 393–394
American Psychological Association. *See* APA style
Ampersand, A7
"An Idea Whose Time Has Come" (Marable), 95
Analogy, 141, 345
Analysis
  in body of paper, 348
  of creative works, paradigm for, 270–271
  in research proposal, 164
Annotated bibliography, 252–254
  definition of, 384
  preparation of, A7–A8
  using précis notes for, 289–290
Anonymous authors
  in APA style, 441
  in MLA style, 313, 391, 406
Anthologies
  bibliographic entries for
    in CMS style, 477
    in MLA style, 320, 394–395
  citing
    in APA style, 440
    in MLA style, **319–320**
  cross-references to, 396–397
APA style, 137, **436–472**
  abstracts in, **458–459**
  empirical study reports in, 437, 457–458
  formatting in, **457–458**
  for in-text citations, 280, **438–444**
    of anthologies, 440
    authors in, 438–441
    of CD-ROMs, 444
    of classical works, 440–441
    of discussion groups, 444
    of e-mail interviews, **212**
    of e-mails, 444
    of government documents, 443
    of indirect sources, 440
    of Internet sources, 442–443
    page numbers in, 439
    of personal communication, 442
    of textbooks, 440
  for linguistic studies, 455–456
  for references list, **444–454**
    abstracts in, 448–449, 452, 454
    books in, 446–447
    e-mail interviews in, 212
    government documents in, 453
    index to, 445
    Internet sources in, 450–454
    journal articles in, 447
    magazine articles in, 448
    newspaper articles in, 448
    nonprint materials in, 449
    reports in, 449
    reviews in, 449
  review articles in, 437, 458
  sample paper in, **459–472**
  for sociological studies, 456–457
  tense in, 437–438
  theoretical articles in, 436, 457
"Apologia" (Lopez), 716
Apostrophe, A19
Appendix, in MLA style, 359
Applied sciences paper, CSE style for, 502–521
Arabic numerals, A7–A9
Archival research, on Internet, 185–188
Archives, bibliographic entries for, 415
Argument
  causal, 140–141
  components of, 137
  focusing, during draft stage, 293–294
Argument papers, paradigm for, 271
"Arranged Marriages: The Revival Is Online" (Nesbitt-Hall), 137, 459–472
Art, guide to sources in, **A35–A3**
Articles. *See also specific sources and types*
  reading key parts of, 246–247, 247*f*–248*f*
  using précis notes for brief review of, 289
Artwork, bibliographic entries fo 421, 427–428
Assumptions, challenging in introduction, 341
Asterisks, A9
Astronomy, guide to sources in, A29–A30
Athletics, guide to sources in, A30–A32
Audience
  engaging and challenging, 16
  identification of, 162
    in long proposal, 161–162
  meeting needs of, 162, 263
Audiovisual materials, **216–217,** 218
Author(s)
  anonymous
    in APA style, 441
    in MLA style, **313,** 391, 40
  in bibliographic entries
    in APA style, 446–448
    in CMS style, 476–477
    in CSE style, 504–505, 506
    in MLA style, 384–386, 390–393, 406
  corporate
    in APA style, 441, 447
    in MLA style, 313, 392
  credentials of, 246
  focus on, in conclusion, 350–351
  in-text citations of
    in APA style, 438–441
    in CSE style, 506–508
    in MLA style, 284, 311–31
  listed by initials with name supplied, 392
  multiple
    in APA style, 439–440
    in CMS style, 476–477
    in CSE style, 506–507
    in MLA style, 322, 392, 393
  with multiple works
    in APA style, 440
    in MLA style, 321–322, 3
  pseudonymous, in MLA style 391, 392

Background information, in introduction, 338–339, 340
Back-to-back modifiers, A9
"Bad Luck: Why Americans Exaggerate the Terrorist Threat" (Rosen), 775
Barry, Dave, 617
Berry, Wendell, 723
Bias, in questionnaire, 217
Biased language, in draft, **303–305**
Bible
  abbreviations for books of, A5–A6
  bibliographic entries for
    in CMS style, 480
    in MLA style, 395
  citing
    in APA style, 441
    in MLA style, A9
Bibliographic entries
  for abstracts
    in APA style, 448–449, 452, 454
    in MLA style, 405–406, 415, 425
  for advertisements, 412, 415, 427
  for afterword, 398–399
  for alphabetized works, 393–394
  for anthologies
    in CMS style, 477
    in MLA style, 320, 394–395
  for archives, 415
  for artwork, 421, 427–428
  for audiovisual materials, 217
  authors in
    in APA style, 446–448
    in CMS style, 476–477
    in CSE style, 506, 508
    in MLA style, 384–386, 390–393, 406
  for Bible
    in CMS style, 480
    in MLA style, 395
  for biographical dictionaries, 393–394
  for books
    in APA style, 446–447
    in CMS style, 476–477, 488
    in CSE style, 504, 508
    in MLA style, 192, **390–405,** 426
  for bulletin
    in APA style, 452–453
    in MLA style, 428
  for cartoons, 412, 416, 428–429
  for CD-ROMs
    in APA style, 454
    in CMS style, 479
    in MLA style, **424–426**
  for chapters of books
    in APA style, **447**
    in MLA style, 396, 416
  for classical works, 396
  for collection of works
    in CMS style, 477
    in MLA style, 396
  for comic strips, 412
  for comments, 408
  compilers in, 393, 398
  for computer software
    in APA style, 449
    in MLA style, 429
  for congressional papers, 413
  cross-references to, 396–397
  for dictionaries, 447
  for discussion groups
    in APA style, 453
    in MLA style, 420, 421
  for dissertation, 429
  editions in, 397–398
  for editorials, 408, 412, 421
  editors in, 393, 394–395, 397, 398
  for electronic articles
    in APA style, 450–451
    in CMS style, **478–480,** 489
    in CSE style, 505, 509
    in MLA style, 193, **414–423**
  for electronic databases
    in APA style, 454
    in CMS style, 479
    in MLA style, 192–193, 416–418
  for e-mail interviews, 212
  for e-mails, 214
    in CMS style, 480
    in MLA style, 418
  for encyclopedias
    in APA style, 447
    in CMS style, 479
    in MLA style, 393–394, 398, 418
  for executive branch documents, 413–414
  for films and videos
    in APA style, 449
    in CMS style, 480
    in MLA style, 418, 429–430
  for government documents, 216
    in APA style, 453
    in CMS style, 480
    in MLA style, **413–414**
  for home pages, 418–419
  for illustrations, 434
  illustrators in, 398
  for interviews
    in APA style, 449
    in MLA style, 406, 419
  for introduction of books, 398–399
  for journal articles
    in APA style, 447
    in CMS style, 447, 488
    in CSE style, 504, 508, 509
    in MLA style, 192–193, **405–411**
  for lectures, 215
  for legal citations, **414**
  for letters
    in APA style, 449
    in MLA style, 408, 419, 430
  for loose-leaf collections
    in CSE style, 505, 510
    in MLA style, 407, 431
  for magazine articles
    in APA style, 448
    in CMS style, 477
    in CSE style, 506, 509
    in MLA style, 193, 313, 405–411
  for manuscripts, 399, 420, 431
  for maps, 420, 431
  for memos, 449
  for microforms, 408, 431
  for musical composition, 432
  for newsgroups
    in APA style, 453
    in MLA style, 420
  for newsletters
    in APA style, 451
    in MLA style, 420
  for newspaper articles
    in APA style, 448
    in CMS style, 477, 489
    in CSE style, 505, 509
    in MLA style, **411–412,** 421
  for nonprint sources
    in APA style, 449
    in CMS style, 479
  for notes, 408
  page numbers in, 399, 411
  for paintings, 421
  for pamphlets, 432
  for performance, 432–433
  for personal papers, 214
  for photocopies, 434
  for photographs, 421, 434
  for plays, 399–400
  for poems, 400–401, 422
  for presentations, 505, 509
  for public addresses, 433
  publication information in, 401–402
  for public statutes, 414
  for queries, 408
  for reports
    in APA style, 449
    in MLA style, 408, 422, 434
  for republished books, 402
  for reviews
    in APA style, 449
    in CMS style, 477
    in MLA style, 409, 422
  for scholarly project
    in CMS style, 478
    in MLA style, 415
  for screenplays, 402
  for sculptures, 421
  for series, 402, 409–410
  for songs, 422
  for sourcebooks and casebooks, 403
  for speeches, 410
  for state government documents, 414
  for survey, 218
  for symposium, 453–454
  for tables, 434
  for television programs
    in CMS style, 480
    in MLA style, 423, 434–435
  titles in, in MLA style, 403–404, 410–411
  translators in, 393, 398, 404
  for transparencies, 434–435
  for virtual conferences, 453
  for voice mail, 434–435
  volumes in, 404–405, 411
Bibliography(ies)
  annotated. *See* Annotated bibliography
  in APA style. *See* References

in books, 197
in CMS style. *See* Footnote system
in CSE style. *See* Cited References
in encyclopedias, 197
general, 194–195
on Internet, **185**
in journal articles, 197
in MLA style. *See* Works Cited
selected, 384
in source evaluation, 170
trade, 195–196
working. *See* Working bibliography
Binders, A12
Biographical dictionaries, bibliographic entries for, 393–394
Biography
finding in electronic database, **203–205**
as source, 240–241
Blanket citation, 483
Block quotation, 328–329
Body of paper, **342–348**
for advancing ideas and theories, 270
for analysis of creative works, 271
for analysis of history, 272
for argument and persuasion, 271
cause and effect in, 345–346
classification and analysis in, 348
for comparative study, 272
comparison and contrast in, 345
criteria of judgment in, 348
critical views in, 348
defining key terms in, 346
evidence in, 347–348
generating dynamics of paper in, 263
location and setting in, 348
process explanation in, 346
questions and answers in, 347
revision of, 354–355
structure in, 348
time sequence in, 343–344
Book catalogs, electronic
guide to using, 193–194
for topic development, **155–156**
Book jacket, 248
Bookmarking files, 178
Books
bibliographic entries for
in APA style, 446–447
in CMS style, 476, 477, 488
in CSE style, 504, 508
in MLA style, 192, **390–405,** 425
bibliographies in, 197
chapters of, bibliographic entries for, 396, 416, 447
classical, 396, 440–441
index of, 156
in library, **193–197,** 238–240
online, 421
published before 1900, 395–396
reading key parts of, 248–249
republished, 402
scholarly, as source, 238–240
table of contents of, 156, 248
titles of, 156
in MLA bibliography, 403–404
trade, as source, 243
using précis notes for brief review of, 289
Bookstores, online, 185
Borders, A9
Botstein, Leon, 702
Brackets, A19–A20
in CSE citations, 503–504
in MLA citations, **333–334**
Brady, Judy, 55
Brooks, David, 638
Brophy, Beth, 622
Brown, Andrew, 628
Browsers, 154, 167–168. *See also* Search engines
Bulletin, bibliographic entries for
in APA style, 452–453
in MLA style, 428
Bullets, A9
Business
guide to sources in, A43
primary and secondary sources of, 246

Capitalization
after colon, A10
of compound words, A11
of departments and courses, A11
in MLA citations, **329–330**
of nouns used before numerals or letters, A11
of proper names, A11
of titles, A10
of trade names, A11
Carter, Jimmy, 735
Cartoon, bibliographic entry for, 412, 416, 428–429
"Case Against Chores, The" (Smiley), 633
Casebooks, bibliographic entries for, 403
Causal argument, 140–141
Causal hypothesis, 159–160
Cause and effect
arrangement by, 268
in body of paper, 345–346
CBE style. *See* CSE style
CD-ROMs
bibliographic entries for
in APA style, 454
in CMS style, 479
in MLA style, **424–426**
citing, in APA style, 444
Chapters of books, bibliographic entries for
in APA style, 447
in MLA style, 396, 416
Character set, A11
Charts, bibliographic entries for, 434
Chat groups
bibliographic entries for, 420
as sources, 184, 244
in topic selection, 152
Chaucer, Geoffrey, abbreviations for works of, A6
Chavez, Linda, 574
Chronology, in body of paper, 343–344
Citation(s). *See also* In-text citations
academic, 226
blanket, 483
in notetaking, 280–281
from primary and secondary sources, 245–246
required instances for, 233
Citation searching, 241–242
Cited References (CSE style)
Name-Year system of, **506–508**
number system of, 503–504
Cities, foreign, A15
"Clan of the One-Breasted Women, The" (Williams), 749
Classical works
bibliographic entries for, in MLA style, 396
citing, in APA style, 440–441
Classification, in body of paper, 348
Classroom e-mail groups, 152
Clip art, A11
Closing paragraph, of article, 246
Clustering, 149
CMS style, **473–501**
bibliography page in, **488–489**
content notes in, **482–485**
endnotes in, **481–482**
footnotes in, 280
for anthologies, 477
for books, 476–477
content, **482–485**
for electronic sources, **478–480**
for fine arts papers, 487–488
formatting, **475–477**
full or abbreviated, 475
for humanities papers, **485–487**
index to, 475
for journal articles, 477
for magazine articles, 477
for newspaper articles, 477
present tense for, 300
for review articles, 477
subsequent references in, **480–481**
superscript numerals for, **473–475**
sample paper in, **489–501**
Coherence, writing with, 299–300
Collaborative projects, sharing credit in, 233–234
Collection of works
bibliographic entries for
in CMS style, 477
in MLA style, 396
cross-references to, 396–397
Colons, A20
capitalization after, A10
in CMS footnote, 477
in MLA citations, 324
Comic strips, bibliographic entries for, 412

Commas, A21
in MLA citations, 322-324
in numbers, A8
Comments, bibliographic entries for, 408
Common knowledge exceptions, 226-228
Communication, guide to sources in, A39-A41
Comparative study, paradigm for, 272
Comparison, 141
arrangement by, 268-269
in body of paper, 345
narrowing topic by, 149-150
Compilers, bibliographic entries for, 393, 398
Compound words, capitalization of, A11
Computer
for editing, 361
notetaking with, 281
Computer software, bibliographic entries for
in APA style, 449
in MLA style, 429
Conclusion of paper, **349–352**
for advancing ideas and theories, 270
for analysis of creative works, 271
for analysis of history, 272
for argument and persuasion, 271
avoiding mistakes in, 352
for comparative study, 272
comparing past to present in, 351
directive or solution in, 351-352
effective quotation at end of, 350
focus on author in, 350-351
generating dynamics of paper in, 263
revision of, 355
test results in, 352
thesis statement in, 349-350
onditional hypothesis, 159
onference presentations, 505, 509
ongressional papers, bibliographic entries for, 413
onsistent design, 305-306, 306*f*
ontent notes
in CMS style, **482–485**
in MLA style, 359
ontext, for sources, **223–224**
ontrast, in body of paper, 345
opyright, 224-225, A11
rporate authors
in APA style, 441, 447
in MLA style, 313, 392
urses, capitalization of, A11
urthouse documents, 217
ver page, for long proposal, 161
vers, A12
eative works, paradigm for analysis of, 270-271
edentials of authors, 246
Credibility
enhancing with source materials, **222–223**
identifying, 314-315
Credit
sharing, in collaborative projects, 233-234
of sources, in online courses, 234
Criteria of judgment, in body of paper, 348
Critical thinking, 136, 170
Critical views
in body of paper, 348
in introduction, 340-341
Cross-references, in MLA bibliography, 396-397
CSE style, **502–503**
for Cited References
Name-Year system of, 506
number system of, 503-504
index to, 503
for in-text citations
Name-Year system of, 506-508
number system of, 218, **503–504**
sample paper in, 510-521
"Curtailing High School: A Radical Proposal" (Botstein), 702

"Dangerous Myth of Grade Inflation, The" (Kohn), 691
Dash, 21
Data, in introduction, 342
Databases. *See* Electronic databases
Data gathering. *See also* Source materials
field research for, **211–221**
on Internet, **166–189**
in libraries, **190–210,** 238
Date of source materials, 238
Dates, A8, A12
Deadlines. *See* Schedule
Decimal outline, 273
Declaration of Independence, The (Jefferson), 118
Decorative graphics, A16
Definitions
elements of, 139
examples of, 139
quotation marks around, A23
role of, 139
Departments, capitalization of, A11
Description of research methods, in long proposal, 163
Designing electronic research papers, 305-308
Development, modes of, in goal setting, 265-266
"Diabetes Management: A Delicate Balance" (Bentis), 138, 145, 510-521
Dictionaries, bibliographic entries for, in APA style, 447
"Did My Car Join Al Qaeda?" (Hochswender), 23
Didion, Joan, 89
Digital camera, A16
Direction charting, **262–269**
Directive, in conclusion, 351-352
Directories. *See also* Subject directories, online
for electronic articles, 179-180
in Internet addresses, 171
Direct quotation notes. *See* Quotation notes
Disability, nondiscriminatory references to, 305
Discipline(s). *See also specific disciplines*
for charting major ideas, 266-267
finding indexes by, 199-200
identification of, 162
indexes to, 177
language of, 301
Discussion, in report on experiment or observation, 220
Discussion groups, Internet, 183-189
for archival research, 187
bibliographic entries for
in APA style, 453
in MLA style, 420, 421
citing, in APA style, 444
evaluation of, 170
as sources, 244
for topic development, 152-153
Dissertation
abstracts to, 202-203
bibliographic entries for, 429
style for, A25
Documentation of sources, 226, 227. *See also* Bibliographic entries; Bibliography(ies); In-text citations
hypertext links for, 318
numbers in, A9
in online classrooms, 234
Domain, in Internet addresses, 171
Double-spacing, 359, 481, A24
Downloaded data, making notes for, 279
Draft, **292–310**
of electronic research paper, **305–309**
enthymeme in, 295, 296
focusing argument for, **293–294**
hypothesis in, 295, 296
of research proposal, **160–164**
in research schedule, 143
sexist/biased language in, **303–305**
thesis refinement for, **294–297**
title of, **297–298**
use of research journal and notes in, **298–303**
Dynamics of paper, 263

Earth sciences, guide to sources in, A38-A39
Easterbrook, Gregg, 664
E-books, **182–183**
Economics, guide to sources in, A43
Editing, **360–366,** 361*f*

Edition, in MLA bibliography, 397-398
Editorials, bibliographic entries for, 408, 412, 421
Editors, bibliographic entries for, 393, 394-395, 397, 398
Education, primary and secondary sources of, 246
Educational search engines, 177-178
Ehrenreich, Barbara, 18, 530
Electronic articles
  bibliographic entries for
    in APA style, 450-454
    in CMS style, **478–480,** 489
    in CSE style, 505, 509
    in MLA style, 193, **414–423**
  citing
    in APA style, 442-443
    in MLA style, **314–316**
  credentials of authors of, 246
  evaluation of, 153, 169-170
  in journals and magazines, **179–180**
  in newspapers, **180–182,** 188
  reading key parts of, 249, 250*f*
Electronic book catalogs
  guide to using, 193-194
  in topic selection, **155–156**
Electronic databases
  bibliographic entries for
    in APA style, 454
    in CMS style, 479
    in MLA style, 192-193, 416-418
  finding biographies in, **203–205**
  finding essays within books in, **208–209**
  finding government documents in, **207–208**
  finding magazine and journal articles in, **198–203**
  finding newspaper articles in, **205–206**
  reliable, 153, 155
  selecting, 155
  in topic selection, **154–155**
Electronic presentations, A12
Electronic research paper, **305–309**
  creating, 308-309
  delivering, 309
  designing, 305-308
  planning, 305
Ellipsis points, in MLA citations, **330–333**
E-mail interviews, bibliographic entry for, 212
E-mail news groups, 183
E-mails
  bibliographic entry for, 214
    in CMS style, 480
    in MLA style, 418
  citing, in APA style, 444
  data collection with, 213-214
  as sources, 244
Emphasis
  graphical, A26
  linguistic, A26
Empirical research, 218
Empirical study reports, in APA style, 432, 457-458
Encyclopedia
  bibliographic entries for, 418
    in APA style, 447
    in CMS style, 479
    in MLA style, 393-394, 397
  as source, 243
Encyclopedias, bibliographies in, 197
Endnotes
  in CMS style, **481–482**
  content, **482–485**
  in MLA style, 359, A13
Engineering, guide to sources in, A29-A30
Enthymeme
  definition of, 157
  in draft, 245, 296
  expressing, 158-159
  in introduction, 337-338
Environmental issues, guide to sources in, A38-A39
"Error Error Error" (Barry), 617
Essays, finding in electronic database, **208–209**
"Et al.", 392, 477
Ethical appeal, 294
Ethnic identity, nondiscriminatory references to, 304-305
Evaluation, 138
  arrangement by, 268
Evidence
  in body of paper, 347-348
  in content notes, 484-485
  in introduction, 342
Exclamation marks, A21
  in MLA citations, 324-325
Executive branch documents, bibliographic entries for, 413-414
Experiment
  data collection with, **218–220**
  and notetaking, 291
  as source, 243
Explanation
  in content notes, 484
  in research proposal, 164

Fabrication, 225
"Failed Mission, A" (Krugman), 32
Fair use, of copyrighted material, 224-225, 234, 235, A11
"False Gold" (Ng), 84
FAQs, 183
Federal government documents, 215-216
Field notes, 280, **291**
Field research, **211–221**
  conducting experiments, tests, and observation in, **218–220**
  conducting survey in, **217–218,** 219
  definition of, 211
  examining audiovisual materials in, **216–217,** 218
  investigating local sources in, **211–216**
Figures, A13-A15
  definition of, A13
  guidelines for, A13-A15
  sample, A13*f*, A14*f*
File(s)
  bookmarking, 178
  in Internet addresses, 171
  vertical, 206
Films, bibliographic entries for
  in APA style, 449
  in CMS style, 480
  in MLA style, **418, 429–430**
Fine arts, primary and secondary sources of, 245
Fine arts papers, in CMS style, **487–488**
Fitness, guide to sources in, A30-A32
"Fitting the Poor into the Economy" (Gans), 643
Fonts, A15
Footers, A16
Footnote system (CMS style), 280
  for anthologies, 477
  for books, 476-477
  content, **482–485**
  for electronic sources, **478–480**
  for fine arts papers, **487–488**
  formatting, **475–476**
  full or abbreviated, 475
  for humanities papers, **485–487**
  index to, 475
  for journal articles, 477
  for magazine articles, 477
  for newspaper articles, 477
  present tense for, 300
  for review articles, 477
  subsequent references in, **480–481**
  superscript numerals for, **473–475**
"For All the Good It Has Done, Title IX Is Still Plagued by Myths" (King), 538
Foreign cities, A15
Foreign languages, A15
Foreword, 249
  in MLA bibliography, 398-399
Formal outline, **273–277**
  sentence, 275-277
  topic, 274-275
Formatting
  in APA style, **457–458**
  in CMS style, **475–477**
  in MLA style, 356-360, 384-390, A1-A26
  in research schedule, 143
  variations in, **137**
Free writing, 147-148
Frequently asked questions, 183
Friedman, Thomas L., 760
"From Stone Age to Phone Age" (Ehrenreich), 18
FTP sites, 418, 444, 454

Gans, Herbert J., 643
Gelernter, David, 603
Gender, nondiscriminatory references to, 304

eral bibliographies, 194-195
eral paradigm, 269-270
eral questions, 150
etics, guide to sources in, A38-A39
er, Nathan, 583
oal revision, **354–356**
obalization, Alive and Well" (Friedman), 760
l setting, **262–269**
dall, Jane, 557
dman, Ellen, 681
PHER sites, 418
ernment documents
ibliographic entry for, 216
in APA style, 453
in CMS style, 480
in MLA style, **413–414**
iting, in APA style, 443
earching for, **207–208,** 215-216
ernment Printing Office (GPO), 215
mmar checker, 361
phical emphasis, A26
phics, 303, A16
phics program, A16
phs, bibliographic entries for, 434

V. Wilson indexes, 200-201
dwritten notes, 282
nging, A" (Orwell), 595
ging indent, A17
rmful Myth of Asian Superiority, The" (Takaki), 128
ders, A16
dings, A16-A17
lth, guide to sources in, A30-A31
lth & Wellness (database), 155
bert, Bob, 708
orical present tense, 300
ory
paradigm for analysis of, 271-272
rimary and secondary sources of, 245
eview of, in introduction, 340
ory paper
n CMS style, 486-487
uide to sources for, A28-A29
hswender, Woody, 23
ne pages
ibliographic entries for, 418-419
n source evaluation, 249
w to Duck Out of Teaching" (Stalker), 111
nanities papers, in CMS style, **485–487**
erNews posting, citing, 443
ertext links. *See* Link(s), hypertext
ertext markup language (HTML), 171, 308
hen, A21-A22
othesis
ausal, 159-160
onditional, 159
efinition of, 157, 219
n draft, 295, 296
xpressing, 159-160

in introduction, 338
in long proposal, 161-162
relational, 159
theoretical, 159

"I Surf, Therefore I Am" (Levine), 612-613
"I Want a Wife" (Brady), 55
"Ibid.", 477, 482
"Ice-T: The Issue Is Creative Freedom" (Ehrenreich), 530
Ideas
paradigm for advancing, 270
subjective, in draft, 294
Identity graphics, A16
Illustration graphics, A16
Illustrations, bibliographic entries for, 434
Illustrators, bibliographic entries for, 398
Implications, 142
"In Defense of Preference" (Glazer), 583
"In Distrust of Movements" (Berry), 723
Inclusive numbers, A7
Indentation, A17
in MLA citations, **325–326,** 327-328
Indented lists, A9
Index cards, 282
Indexes. *See also* Book catalogs; Electronic databases
to abstracts, 201
to bibliographic models
in APA style, 445
in CMS style, 475
in CSE style, 503
in MLA style, 386-390
to biographies, 204
of books, 156
for source evaluation, 249
discipline-specific, 199-200
H. W. Wilson, 200-201
to pamphlets, 206
to periodicals, 198-199
Indirect sources, citing
in APA style, 440
in MLA style, **316–318**
Information graphics, A16
Information technology, guide to sources in, A39-A41
Inquiry, in draft, 293
Instructors, as sources, 237
Intellectual property, 224-225
Internet, **166–189.** *See also* Electronic articles; Search engines; Web sites
accessing e-books on, **182–183**
addresses on, **170–173**
archival research on, **185–188**
beginning search on, **167–170**
bibliographies on, **185**
citation of sources on, 167
evaluating sources on, 153, 169-170
examining library holdings on, **184**
keyword search on, 154
vs. library sources, 190
and plagiarism, 166, 222

vs. print sources, 167
for topic development, **153–154**
Internet discussion groups. *See* Discussion groups, Internet
Internet service provider (ISP), 170
Internet subject directories. *See* Subject directories, online
Interpretation, 138-139, 268, 286
Interviews
bibliographic entries for
in APA style, 449
in MLA style, 406, 419
data collection with, 211-213
e-mail, bibliographic entry for, 212
example of, 212-213
guidelines of, 212, 217
notetaking during, 291
as sources, 242
for topic development, 151-152
In-text citations
in APA style, 280, **438–444**
of anthologies, 440
authors in, 438-441
of CD-ROMs, 444
of classical works, 440-441
of discussion groups, 444
of e-mail interviews, 212
of e-mails, 444
of government documents, 443
of indirect sources, 440
of Internet sources, 442-443
page numbers in, 439
of personal communication, 442
of textbooks, 440
in CMS style, 280
in CSE style, 281
Name-Year system of, 506-508
number system of, 281, 503-504
in MLA style, 146, 280, 311-335
altering quotations in, 329-334
of anthologies, **319–320**
authors in, 311-313
brackets in, **333–334**
capitalization in, **329–330**
ellipsis points in, 330-333
extra information in, **320–322**
of indirect sources, **316–318**
for Internet sources, **314–316**
of long quotations, **325–326**
with no authors, **313**
of nonprint sources, **314**
omissions in, **330–333**
page numbers in, 311-313, 318-319, 322
parentheses in, **333–334**
of plays, **329**
of poetry, **326–329**
present tense for, 300
punctuation of, **322–325**
of textbooks, **319–320**

Introduction
of books
in MLA bibliography, 398–399
for source evaluation, 249
of paper, **336–342**
for advancing ideas and theories, 270
for analysis of creative works, 270–271
for analysis of history, 272
for argument and persuasion, 271
avoiding mistakes in, 343
background information in, 338–339, 340
brief summary in, 341–342
challenging assumptions in, 341
for comparative study, 272
critical views in, 340–341
data in, **342**
defining key terms in, 342
enthymeme in, 337–338
evidence in, 342
generating dynamics of paper in, 263
hypothesis in, 338
relating to well known in, 338
review of history in, 340
review of literature in, 339
revision of, 354
statistics in, 342
thesis statement in, 336–337
of report on experiment or observation, 219–220
Irving, John, 543
"Is a Lab Rat's Fate More Poignant than a Child's?" (McCabe), 551
Issue identification, 265
Issues, arrangement by, 267
Italics, A17, A22

Jacket, book, 248
Jefferson, Thomas, 118
Jones, Greg, 525
Journal, research
drafting from, **298–299**
for enriching organizational plan, 277
Journal articles
bibliographic entries for
in APA style, 447
in CMS style, 477, 488
in CSE style, 192–193, 504, 508, 509
in MLA style, **405–411**
bibliographies in, 197
credentials of authors of, 246
finding in electronic database, **198–199**
online, 179
reading key parts of, 247*f*–248*f*
as sources, 241–242
Journalism questions, 151
Judgment, criteria of, in body of paper, 348

Kaminer, Wendy, 674
Kantrowitz, Barbara, 72–73
Key terms, defining
in body of paper, 346
in introduction, 342
Keywords
arranging into preliminary outline, 148–149
database searches with, 155
electronic book catalog searches with, 193
listing, 148
and notetaking, 264
online searches with, 154, 154*f*
for electronic articles, 179–182
for Internet bibliographies, 185
King, Billie Jean, 538
"Kissing Cousins" (Patchett), 64
Klinkenborg, Verlyn, 713
Kohn, Alfie, 691
Kristof, Nicholas, 60
Krugman, Paul, 32

Language
of disciplines, 301
foreign, A15
guide to sources in, A35–A37
Lectures, 214–215
Legal citations, bibliographic entries for, 414
Legal precedent, 141
Legibility, 307–308
"Let Gays Marry" (Sullivan), 68
"Let It Be" (Rauch), 740
Letter-by-letter alphabetization, 384–385
Letters (correspondence)
bibliographic entries for
in APA style, 449
in MLA style, 408, 419, 430
data collection with, 213–214, 217
Letters (of alphabet)
capitalization of nouns used before, A11
as outline symbols, 273
Levine, Judith, 612–613
Librarians, as sources, 238
Libraries
archival research in, 185–186
beginning search in, **190–191**
books in, **193–197,** 238–240
educational search engines maintained by, 178
electronic book catalogs of
guide to using, 193–194
in topic selection, **155–156**
electronic databases of. *See* Electronic databases
etiquette of, 191
Internet access to holdings of, **184**
microforms in, 191, **209**
as sources, **190–210,** 238
vs. Internet sources, **190**
Library of Congress Web site, 154*f*, 171–173, 171*f*–174*f*, 176, 184
"Limits of Freedom, The" (Brown), 628
Linguistic emphasis, A26
Linguistic studies, in APA style, 455–456
Link(s), hypertext
electronic research papers with, 309
source documentation with, 318
in source evaluation, 170, 249
List, A9, A18
"Listening to Hamlet: The Soliloquies" (Mosier), 144, 362–371
Listserv groups, 183, 187, 244
Literary study
example of, 362–371
focus on author in, 350–351
Literary works, abbreviations for, A6
Literature
in content notes, 483
guide to sources in, A35–A37
primary and secondary sources of, 245
Literature, review of. *See* Review of literature
Local government documents, 215
Local knowledge, 226–227
Logic, 136
Logical appeal, 294
Long research paper, 371–383
Long research proposals, 161–16
Loose-leaf collections, bibliographic entries for
in CSE style, 505, 510
in MLA style, 407, 431
Lopez, Barry, 716
"Love and Race" (Kristof), 60

Magazine articles
bibliographic entries for
in APA style, 448
in CMS style, 477
in CSE style, 505, 510
in MLA style, 193, 313, **405–411**
citations in, 226
citing, in MLA style, 313
credentials of authors of, 246
finding in electronic database **198–203**
online, 179–180
bibliographic entries for, 415–416
citing, 443
as sources, 243
Manuscript
bibliographic entries for, 399 420, 431
editing, **360–361,** 361*f*
preparing, rules and techniques for, A3–A26
proofreading, **361–362**
submitting, 143
Maps, bibliographic entries for, 420, 431
Marable, Manning, 95
Margins, A17
"Marrying Absurd" (Didion), 89
Materials, description of, in lon proposal, 163–164
Mathematical copy, A24
McCabe, Jane, 551
Media sources, 216–217, 318
Memos, bibliographic entries for, 449

Metasearch engines, 176, 187
Method, in report on experiment or observation, 220
Microfiche, 209, 431
Microfilm, 191, 209, 431
Microforms
bibliographic entries for, 408, 431
use of, **209**
MLA style, 137
formatting in, 356-360, 384-390, A3-A26
for in-text citations, 280, **311–335**
altering quotations in, **329–335**
of anthologies, **319–322**
authors in, 311-313
brackets in, **333–334**
capitalization in, **329–330**
ellipsis points in, **330–333**
extra information in, **320–322**
of indirect sources, **316–318**
for Internet sources, **314–316**
of long quotations, **325–326**
with no authors, **313**
of nonprint sources, **314**
omissions in, **330–333**
page numbers in, 284, 311-313, 318-319, 322
parentheses in, **333–334**
of plays, **329**
of poetry, **326–329**
present tense for, 300
punctuation of, **322–325**
of textbooks, **319–320**
tense in, 300
for works cited list, 360, **384–435**
articles from academic database in, 192-193
books in, 192, **390–405,** 425
CD-ROMs in, **424–426**
format of, **384–390**
government documents in, **413–414**
indention of, A17
index to, 386-390
Internet articles in, 193, **414–423**
journal articles in, 192
magazine articles in, 192, 193, 313, 405-411
newspapers in, **411–412**
›derated lists, 183
›des of development, in goal setting, 265-266
›netary units, A17-A18
›ney, A8
)O discussion groups, 152, 420
JD discussion groups, 152, 420
sic, guide to sources in, A35-A37
sical composition, bibliographic entries for, 432

nes
›f persons, A18
›roper, capitalization of, 10
›f publishers, abbreviations of, A5
rade, capitalization of, A11
Name-Year system, CSE
for Cited References, 508-510
for in-text citations, 506-508
Natural sciences paper, CSE style for, 502-521
Navigation tools, 307
Negotiation, in draft, 293
Newsgroups, bibliographic entries for
in APA style, 453
in MLA style, 420
Newsletters, bibliographic entries for
in APA style, 451
in MLA style, 420
Newspaper articles
bibliographic entries for
in APA style, 448
in CMS style, 477, 489
in CSE style, 505, 509
in MLA style, **411–412,** 421
citations in, 226
finding in electronic database, **205–206**
online, **180–182,** 188
as sources, 243-244
Ng, Fae Myenne, 84
"No Margin for Error" (Herbert), 708
Nondiscriminatory references, 303-305
Nonfiction trade books, as sources, 243
Nonprint sources
bibliographic entries for
in APA style, 449
in CMS style, 479
citing, in MLA style, **314**
Notes. *See also* Content notes; Endnotes; Footnote system
bibliographic entries for, 408
in MLA style, 359
Notetaking, **279–291**
citation style in, 280-281
with computer, 281
drafting from, **298–303**
effective, **280–282**
field notes, **280–291**
handwritten notes, **282**
high quality, 280
organization of
keyword/phase lists and, 264
research proposal and, 263-264
paraphrased notes, 280, **286–287**
personal notes, 280, **283**
précis notes, 280, **289–291**
in preliminary library search, 191
on printouts and photocopies, 279
quotation notes, 280, **283–286,** 287
in research schedule, 143
summary notes, 280, **288,** 290
writing from results of, 298-299
Number(s)
Arabic, A7-A9
capitalization of nouns used before, A11
for list, A9, A18
as outline symbols, 273
Roman, A18, A23
Number system, CSE
for Cited References, **504–505**
for in-text citations, 281, **503**

Oates, Joyce Carol, 769
Objective facts, in draft, 294
Observation
data collection with, **218–219**
and notetaking, 291
as source, 243
Omissions, in MLA citations, **330–333**
"One Nation, Indivisible? Wanna Bet?" (Quindlen), 36-37
Online bookstores, 185
Online courses, 152, 183, 234
Opening page, in MLA style, 357
Opening paragraph, of article, 246
Orwell, George, 595
"Our Rainbow Underclass" (Zuckerman), 568
"Out of the Wild" (Klinkenborg), 713
Outline
arranging keywords into preliminary, 148-149
drafting from, **298–303**
formal, **273–277**
sentence, 275-277
topic, 274-275
in MLA style, 358
rough, 264-265
of sources, **251**
standard symbols for, 273
Oz, Amos, 745

Page numbers, A18
in APA citations, 439
in MLA bibliography, 399, 411
in MLA citations, 284, 311-313, 318-319, 322
Paintings, bibliographic entries for, 421
Pamphlets
bibliographic entries for, 432
indexes to, 206
Paper, A19
Paradigms, **269–272**
for advancing ideas and theories, 270
for analysis of creative works, 270-271
for analysis of history, 271-272
for argument and persuasion papers, 271
for comparative study, 272
general, 269-270
Paragraphs
developing, 348
indention of, A17
online, in MLA citations, 315-316
quotation of, omissions in, 331-332
Paraphrased notes, 280, 286-287
Parentheses, A22
in CSE citations, 503-504
in MLA citations, **333–334**
Passive voice, 302-303, 361
Past, comparing to present, in conclusion, 351

Past tense, 300
Patchett, Ann, 64
Peer review, in revision, 355–356
Pentad questions, 151
Percentages, A9, A19
Performance, bibliographic entries for, 432–433
Period, A22
Periodicals. *See also* Journal articles; Magazine articles
bibliographic entries for
in APA style, 447–448
in MLA style, **405–411**
indexes to, 198–199
Periods, in MLA citations, 322–324
Personal communication, citing, in APA style, 442
Personal essay, *vs.* research paper, 135
Personal ideas, relating to scholarly problem, **146–151**
Personal notes, 280, **283**
Personal papers, 214, 217
Persons, names of, A18
Persuasion
in draft, 293
in research proposal, 164
Persuasion papers, paradigm for, 271
Philosophy, guide to sources in, A41–A42
Photocopied materials
bibliographic entries for, 434
making notes on, 279
Photographs
bibliographic entries for, 421, 434
created by digital camera, A16
Phrases, listing, and notetaking, 264
Physics, guide to sources in, A29–A30
Plagiarism, **222–236**
avoiding, **225–233**
definition of, 225
examples of, 225, 229–230
Internet and, 166, 222
Plays
bibliographic entries for, in MLA style, 399–400
citing, in MLA style, **329**
Plot summary, in body of paper, 343–344
Plot summary note, 290
Poetry
bibliographic entries for, 400–401, 422
citing
in MLA style, **326–329**
omissions in, 332
Political issues, guide to sources in, A32–A35
Political science, primary and secondary sources of, 245
Precedence, 141–142
Précis notes, 280, **289–291**
Preface, 249
in MLA bibliography, 398–399
"Prehistoric Wars: We Have Always Hated Each Other" (Johnston), 137, 489–501
Present, comparing past to, in conclusion, 351
Presentations
bibliographic entry for, 505, 509
electronic, A12
research paper, 305–306, 306*f*
Present tense, 300–301
Primary sources, **244–246**
citation from, 245–246
definition of, 244
examples of, 244
quoting, 284–285
Printouts, making notes on, 279
Print sources, *vs.* online sources, 167
Proceedings, 505, 509
Process explanation, in body of paper, 346
Professional affiliation of writer, 170
Prologue, in MLA bibliography, 399
Proofreader marks, A19, A20
Proofreading, **361–362**
in research schedule, 143
Proper names, capitalization of, A11
Property rights, honoring, 224–225
Proposal
in paper, 140
research
drafting, **160–164**
explaining purpose in, 164
and notetaking, 263–264
thesis in, 157
Protocol, in Internet addresses, 171
Pseudonymous authors, in MLA style, 391, 392
Psychology, guide to sources in, A41–A42
Public addresses, 214
bibliographic entries for, 433
Publication information, in bibliographic entries, 401–402
Public domain, 235
Public statutes, bibliographic entries for, 414
Publishers, names of
abbreviations of, A5
citing, 313
Punctuation, A19–23
of MLA citations, **322–325**
Purpose statement, in long proposal, 161–162
Pyramid of source materials, 238

Quadruple spacing, 358
Qualification, statement of, in long proposal, 162
Queries, bibliographic entries for, 408
"Question of Ethics, A" (Goodall), 557
Question marks, in MLA citations, 324–325
Questionnaires, **217–218,** 219, 291
Questions
academic disciplines providing, 150–151
in body of paper, 347
general, 150
for interviews, 212
in issue identification, 265
journalism, 151
pentad, 151
rhetorical, 150
in thesis refinement, 295–296
in topic selection, 150–151
Quindlen, Anna, 36–37
Quotation(s)
in conclusion, 350
indented, A17
Quotation marks, 284, A22–A23
around definitions, A12
comma inside, A21
in keyword searches, 154, 155
in MLA citations, 322–325
single, 325, A23
Quotation notes, 280, **283–286,** 287

Racial identity, nondiscriminatory references to, 304–305
Radio, as source, **216–217**
Random sample, 217
"Rap Fans Desire a More Positive Product" (Jones), 525
"Rarely the Twain Shall Meet, And" (Tannen), 99
Raspberry, William, 687
Rationale, in long proposal, 161–162
Rauch, Jonathan, 740,
Reading source materials, **246–24**
Reference books, bibliographic entries for, 398
References (APA style), **444–454**
abstracts in, 448–449, 452, 45
books in, 446–447
e-mail interviews in, 212
government documents in, 45
index to, 445
Internet sources in, 450–452
journal articles in, 447
magazine articles in, 448
newspaper articles in, 448
nonprint materials in, 449
reports in, 449
reviews in, 449
Related numbers, A8
Relational hypothesis, 159
"Religion in the Textbooks" (Goodman), 681
Religious paper
in CMS style, 485–486
guide to sources for, A41–A4
Reports
bibliographic entries for
in APA style, 449
in MLA style, 408, 422, 43
citing, in MLA style, 313
empirical study, in APA style, 4
Republished books, bibliograph entries for, 402
Research. *See also* Data gatheri Field research
archival, on Internet, **185–1**
empirical, 218
purposes of, **136–137**
Researched writing, as alternati term, 136
Research journal
drafting from, **298–303**
for enriching organizational plan, 277

Research methods, description of, in long proposal, 163-164
Research paper. *See also* Sample papers
electronic. *See* Electronic research paper
length of, A17
vs. personal essay, 135
Research proposal
drafting, 160-164
explaining purpose in, 164
and notetaking, 263-264
thesis in, 157
Restrictive clauses, 329-330
Results, in report on experiment or observation, 220
Review articles
in APA style, 437, 458
bibliographic entries for, in CMS style, 477
Review of history, in introduction, 340
Review of literature, **254–260**
example of, 255-260
in introduction, 339
in long proposal, 162-163
purposes of, 254
Reviews, bibliographic entries for
in APA style, 449
in CMS style, 477
in MLA style, 409, 422
Revision, **354–356**
of body of paper, 354-355
of conclusion, 335
global, **354–356**
of introduction, 354
peer review in, 355-356
in research schedule, 143
Rifkin, Jeremy, 648
Rhetorical questions, 150
Robot-driven search engines, 176
Rodriguez, Richard, 563
Roman numerals, A18, A23
Rosen, Jeffrey, 175
Rough outline, 264-265
Running heads, A23

Sample, random, 217
Sample papers
in APA style, **459–472**
in CMS style, **489–501**
in CSE style, **510–521**
long, 371-383
short literary, 362-371
"Saturday Night and You're All Alone? Maybe You Need a Cyberdate" (Brophy), 622
Scanned images, making notes on, 279
Scanner, A16
Schedule
description of, in long proposal, 163-164
establishing, **142–143**
Scholarly articles. *See* Journal articles
Scholarly book, as source, 238-240
Scholarly documentation, 226
Scholarly problem, relating personal ideas to, **146–151**
Scholarly project, bibliographic entries for
in CMS style, 478
in MLA style, 415
Scholarly topic, narrowing general subject into, 144-145, 146
Sciences
guide to sources in, A29-A30
primary and secondary sources of, 245
Screenplays, bibliographic entries for, 402
Sculptures, bibliographic entries for, 421
Search engines
archival research with, 186-187
educational, 177-178
keyword search with, 154
for electronic articles, 179-182
for Internet bibliographies, 185
list of, 167-168, 175, 176, 177, 178
metasearch, 176, 187
robot-driven, 176
in source evaluation, 170
specialized, 176-177
subject directories of, 153, 174-175, 179
for archival research, 187
using, **174–178**
Secondary sources, **244–246**
citation from, 245-246
definition of, 244
examples of, 244-245
quoting, 285-286
Selected bibliography, 384
Semicolons, A23
in MLA citations, 324
Sen, Amartya, 123
Sentence outline, 275-277
Sentences
numbers at beginning of, A8
quotation of, omissions in, 330-332
Series, bibliographic entries for, 402, 409-410
Series comma, A21
Server, in Internet addresses, 171
Setting, in body of paper, 348
Sexist language, in draft, **303–305**
Sexual orientation, nondiscriminatory references to, 304
Shakespeare, William, abbreviations for works of, A6
Shared experiences, 227
Short research proposals, 160-161
Single quotation marks, 325, A23
Single spacing, A24
Slang, A24
Slide presentation, 305-306, 306*f*
Smiley, Jane, 633
Social issues, guide to sources in, A32-A35
Social science, primary and secondary sources of, 245
Social Sciences Index, 200-201
Sociological studies, in APA style, 456-457
Solution, in conclusion, 351-352
Songs, bibliographic entries for, 422
Sourcebooks, bibliographic entries for, 403
Source materials, **237–261**
citing evidence from, 347-348
context for, **223–224**
correctly borrowing from, 228-232
date of, 238
documentation of. *See* Documentation of sources
enhancing credibility with, **222–223**
enhancing writing with, 301-302
evaluation of, 190-191, 246-249
finding, **237–244.** *See also* Data gathering
outlining, **251**
primary. *See* Primary sources
publishing on Web site, seeking permission for, 235
pyramid of, 238
reading, **246–249**
secondary. *See* Secondary sources
summarizing, **251–252**
Spacing, A24
Specialized search engines, 176-177
Speeches, bibliographic entries for, 410
Spelling, A24
Spelling checker, 361
Spelling out numbers, A7
Springen, Karen, 659
Stalker, Douglas, 111
State government documents, 215
bibliographic entries for, 415
Statement of qualification, in long proposal, 162
Statistical copy, A24
Statistics
in content notes, 484
in introduction, 342
Structure, in body of paper, 348
"Struggle with Celibacy, The" (Albacete), 105
Subject directories, online
of search engines, 153, 174-175, 179
for archival research, 187
for topic development, 153
Subjective ideas, in draft, 294
Subjective terminology, 139
Subscription, to Web sites, 167, 180
Subtle design, 306, 307*f*
Suffix, in Internet addresses, 171
Sullivan, Andrew, 68
Summarizing sources, **251–252**
Summary, in introduction, 341-342
Summary notes, 280, **288,** 290
Superscript numerals, for CMS footnotes, **473–475**
Survey, conducting, **217–218,** 219
Symbols, numbers with, A8
Symposium, bibliographic entry for, 453-454

Table of contents
of books, 156, 248
of thesis or dissertation, A24
Tables, A13–A15
bibliographic entries for, 434
definition of, A13
guidelines for, A9–A15
sample, A13*f*–A14*f*
Takaki, Ronald, 128
Tannen, Deborah, 99
Technical terms and institutions, abbreviations for, A4–A5
Television, as source, 216–217
Television program, bibliographic entries for
in CMS style, 480
in MLA style, 423, 434–435
Tense, writing in proper, 300–301, **437–438**
Terminology
of assignments, **138–42**
subjective, 139
Test results, in conclusion, 352
Tests
data collection with, **218–220**
and notetaking, 291
as sources, 243
Textbooks, citing
in APA style, 440
in MLA style, **319–320**
Text of paper, in MLA style, 359
"Their Cheating Hearts" (Raspberry), 687
Theoretical articles, in APA style, 436, 457
Theoretical hypothesis, 159
Theories, paradigm for advancing, 270
Theses, style for, A25
Thesis statement
built on precedence, 141
changes to, 296–297
in conclusion, 349–350
definition of, 157
in direction charting, 267–269
in draft stage, **294–297**
expressing, 157–158
final, checklist for, 297
in introduction, 236–237
in long proposal, 161–162
Thinking, critical, 136, 170
Third person, writing in, 302
Time sequence, in body of paper, 343–344
Times of day, A8
Timetable. *See* Schedule
Title(s)
of articles, 246
in MLA bibliography, 410–411
of books, 156
in MLA bibliography, 403–404
capitalization of, A10
citing, in MLA style, 313, 314
of drafts, **297–298**
in italics, A25
personal, use of, 391
short, in text, A23
within title, 410, A25
Title page, in MLA style, 357
Topic approval, 142
Topic outline, 274–275
Topic selection, **144–156**
electronic book catalogs in, **155–156**
electronic databases in, 154–155
Internet sources in, **153–154**
narrowing general subject into scholarly topic in, 144–145, 146
personal ideas in, **146–151**
and source evaluation, 190–191
talking with others in, 151–153
Topic sentence, of article, 246
"Toxic Media" (Kaminer), 674
Trade bibliographies, 195–196
Trade books, as sources, 243
Trademark, 224
Trade names, capitalization of, A11
Translations, in MLA citations, 328–329
Translators, bibliographic entries for, 393, 398, 404
Transparencies, bibliographic entries for, 434–435
Traub, James, 28
"Triumph of Hope Over Self-Interest, The" (Brooks), 638
"Trouble Is, Native-Born Just Don't Measure Up" (Rodriguez), 563
"Two Stubborn Men, Many Dead" (Oz), 745
Typescript, bibliographic entries for, 399, 431
Typing, A25

Underscoring, A26
Uniform Resource Locator (URL), 171, 178, 416, 417
Unity, writing with, 299–300
"Unmarried, with Children" (Kantrowitz), 72–73
Unmoderated lists, 183
Usenet discussion groups
bibliographic entries for, 420, 454
as sources, 170, 183, 184, 187, 244

"Vanishing Jobs" (Rifkin), 648
Verb tense, writing in proper, 300–301
Videos, bibliographic entries for
in APA style, 449
in CMS style, 480
in MLA style, 418, 429–430
Virtual conference, bibliographic entry for, 453
Voice mail, bibliographic entries for, 434–435
Volumes
in bibliographic entries, 404–405, 411
in MLA citations, 321

"Watch and Learn" (Easterbrook), 664
Web sites. *See also* Electronic articles; Internet
bibliographic entries for, 423
for electronic research papers, 306, 307*f*, 308–309, 308*f*
evaluation of, 169–170
individual, as sources, 244
seeking permission to publish materials on, 235
sponsored, as sources, 242
subscription to, 167, 180
"What Do Murderers Deserve?" (Gelernter), 603
"Why We Tuned Out" (Springen), 659
Williams, Terry Tempest, 749
Wilson indexes, 200–201
Word division, A21, A26
"Words Fail, Memory Blurs, Life Wins" (Oates), 769
Working bibliography
creating, 142, **191–193**
information in, 192
purposes of, 192
reading, 142
Works Cited (MLA style), 360, **384–435**
articles from academic database in, 192–193
books in, 192, **390–405,** 425
CD-ROMs in, **424–426**
format of, **384–390**
government documents in, **413–414**
indention of, A17
index to, 386–390
Internet articles in, 193, **414–423**
journal articles in, 192
magazine articles in, 193, 313, **405–411**
newspapers in, **411–412**
Works Consulted, 384
"World Criminal Court Is Urgently Needed, A" (Carter), 735
"The World's Water Supply: The Ethics of Distribution" (Berkowitz), 141, 371–383
"Wrestling with Title IX" (Irving), 543
Writer, professional affiliation of, 170
Writing
body of paper, **342–348**
conclusion of paper, **349–352**
draft, **298–303**
enhancing with source materials, 301–302
free, 147–148
introduction of paper, **336–342**
with language of disciplines, 301
from notes, 298–299
with passive voice, 302–303
in proper tense, 300–301
in third person, 302
with unity and coherence, 299–300

Yaqub, Reshma Memon, 765
"You People Did This" (Yaqub), 765

Zero, A8
Zuckerman, Mortimer B., 568

We fit *your* life

1-888-4-STRAYER
www.strayer.edu

PEARSON
Custom Publishing